★ ★

CONTEMPORARY AMERICAN VOICES

Developed under the advisory editorship of
Beverly Long, University of North Carolina at Chapel Hill

CONTEMPORARY AMERICAN VOICES

SIGNIFICANT SPEECHES IN AMERICAN HISTORY, 1945-PRESENT

JAMES R. ANDREWS
Indiana University

DAVID ZAREFSKY
Northwestern University

Longman
New York & London

CONTEMPORARY AMERICAN VOICES:
Significant Speeches in American History, 1945–Present

Longman, 95 Church Street, White Plains, N.Y. 10601

Associated companies:
Longman Group Ltd., London
Longman Cheshire Pty., Melbourne
Longman Paul Pty., Auckland
Copp Clark Pitman, Toronto

Executive editor: Gordon T.R. Anderson
Production editor: Dee Amir Josephson
Text design adaption: Kevin Kall
Cover design: Susan J. Moore
Production supervisor: Richard Bretan
Credits appear on p. xxviii

Library of Congress Cataloging-in-Publication Data

Andrews, James Robertson, 1936-
   Contemporary American Voices : significant speeches in American
history, 1945-present / James Andrews, David Zarefsky.
      p. cm.
   Includes bibliographical references.
   ISBN 0-8013-0218-8   ·
   1. United States—History—Sources. 2. Speeches, addresses, etc.,
American. I. Zarefsky, David. II. Title.
E173.A786   1991
973.92—dc20
                                                    90-47685
                                                    CIP

1 2 3 4 5 6 7 8 9 10-AL-9594939291

Contents

SOCIAL PROTEST AND TURMOIL

THE POLITICS OF THE EIGHTIES

CHALLENGES FOR AMERICANS

Alternate Tables of Contents

The principal Table of Contents lists most speeches in an approximate chronological order within topic headings. Speeches also may be read and studied according to their primary purposes—the responses desired from the audience. The first alternate Table of Contents, "Speeches Listed According to Purpose," identifies three primary purposes: speeches that attempt to influence beliefs and attitudes, speeches that are meant to inspire or to reinforce existing beliefs held by the audience, and speeches that are directly related to a specific issue or campaign and, therefore, are designed to produce specific action. The purposes of these speeches will overlap to some extent, and some speeches may incorporate elements of all these purposes. We have tried to group the speeches according to what would seem to be the principal goal of the speaker, given the audience and context.

Speeches could also be arranged from the perspective of the setting or circumstances that brought them about. The second alternate Table of Contents, "Speeches Listed According to Settings and Circumstances," lists inaugural addresses, commencement addresses, other ceremonial addresses, addresses to Congress, legislative speeches, political campaign speeches, lectures and invited addresses, speeches at public meetings and rallies, speeches on public policy and values addressed to a wide audience, and speeches of self-defense.

Speeches Listed According to Purpose

SPEECHES TO INFLUENCE BELIEFS AND ATTITUDES

SPEECHES TO INSPIRE OR REINFORCE AUDIENCE VALUES

SPEECHES TO PRODUCE SPECIFIC ACTION

Speeches Listed According to Settings and Circumstances

INAUGURAL ADDRESSES

COMMENCEMENT ADDRESSES

OTHER CEREMONIAL SPEECHES

ADDRESSES TO CONGRESS

LEGISLATIVE SPEECHES

POLITICAL CAMPAIGN SPEECHES

LECTURES AND INVITED ADDRESSES

SPEECHES AT PUBLIC MEETINGS AND RALLIES

SPEECHES ON PUBLIC POLICY AND VALUES
ADDRESSED TO A WIDE AUDIENCE

SPEECHES OF SELF-DEFENSE

Preface

Contemporary American Voices is the sequel to *American Voices,* which contained texts of significant speeches delivered between 1640 and 1945. This time the chronological span is far more limited, confined to the years since World War II. As a result, it is possible to provide a richer sample of the discourse of the period.

The goal of this book, like its predecessor volume, is to make easily available to students of public address and public speaking, as well as students of American history and culture, a significant sample of speeches that illustrate how people have attempted to deal with important public issues and to influence the belief and action of others. Public issues by their nature affect the society at large and do not yield clear-cut or certain answers. Deliberation is the means by which a nation or society chooses its course, and in the contemporary period no less than in earlier ages, speeches are among the principal instruments of public deliberation.

There are significant differences, however, between postwar American speeches and those of earlier ages. The contemporary speeches tend to be shorter, so we have included only complete texts and a larger number of them. A wider range of speakers have been prominent. Women and minorities have increasingly occupied a forum once thought reserved for white males. A larger number of topics is addressed than the traditional concerns of religion and politics, although these continue to be important matters of concern as well. Perhaps most significantly, public speaking has been powerfully affected by television, which has broadened the audience, emphasized the visual, shortened the message, and sometimes contextualized public discourse as entertainment.

With the rich resources of contemporary American speaking, selection of speeches for this volume posed a special problem. We have tried to include both a sample of speeches whose significance outlasts the situation in which they were first delivered and a sample of those that primarily represent a specific issue or context. We have tried to include speakers in powerful institutional roles as well as speakers previously unfamiliar to the public forum. And we often have included multiple speeches by the same person, in order to illustrate changes and continuities in a speaker's rhetorical practice. We hope that our selection will give students a fair and broad sample of significant discourse on important issues by articulate speakers.

Within broad categories, we generally have arranged speeches in chronological order. There is some overlapping of chronology among the sections of the book, and the final section includes speeches that pose challenges that apply to the entire postwar period. For those who would prefer not to approach the study of speeches chronologically, we have included alternate tables of contents that organize by purpose or by setting.

We do not prescribe any particular method of analysis or criticism, believing instead that the texts should encourage many approaches. The introduction describes the nature of rhetorical analysis and criticism and alludes to different methods by which these tasks can be done. Essays introducing the individual speeches attempt to explicate the specific rhetorical context or situation in which the speaker sought to deal. The Appendix provides specific biographical information about each speaker and directs the reader to other useful sources.

We wish to acknowledge our debts to those who helped in the preparation of this volume. Isolde Anderson, Nicol C. Brock, Ann Burnette, and Trevor Parry-Giles were especially helpful in the difficult tasks of selecting the speeches for inclusion and locating authoritative manuscripts. Esther Langer provided valuable assistance in typing and manuscript preparation.

We have enjoyed our collaboration in the editing of this and its predecessor volume, and we hope that they will be useful in helping students to understand and appreciate the richness of American public discourse.

James R. Andrews

David Zarefsky

Introduction: The Study of Contemporary Speeches

RHETORIC AND PUBLIC DISCOURSE

When people interact with one another, they produce and exchange symbols. Since no one can know another's mind, we make inferences about other people's mental states from the symbols they produce. Our symbolic exchanges thereby enable us to develop shared meanings and understandings, to relate to one another.

A symbol is anything that stands for something else. In human interaction, words are our most common symbols. Language becomes a way to represent thought and feeling so as to make them accessible to others. Of course, not all symbols are verbal. Gesture, tone of voice, and facial response may all be symbols that convey ideas and meanings. The same may be said of pictures, musical rhythm, color, and even such physical actions as the massing of bodies or the dispatching of armies in order to convey a message.

Rhetoric is the study of how symbols influence people. Although the term *rhetoric* is sometimes used negatively, to refer to ornate and flowery language or to bombast and invective, it has a much richer heritage going all the way back to classical times. Aristotle regarded it as the faculty of discovering the available means of persuasion in any given case. He saw it, in other words, as the selection and arrangement of symbols and as the understanding of what made symbols persuasive in specific situations. The Romans regarded this study as one of the seven liberal arts. With differing emphases and sometimes under different names, the study of rhetoric has remained of central importance down to the present day.

To talk about symbols "influencing" people is to acknowledge that they are not neutral. Language is not just a vehicle to convey thought. Rather, it is fundamentally tied together with thought. The selection of symbols involves choices—conscious or otherwise—about how thoughts should be interpreted and consequently what they mean. Symbols suggest both context and attitude. When President Kennedy used the term *quarantine* rather than *blockade* to describe his policy in the Cuban missile crisis, for example, he sought to frame his action in a medical context, as the isolation of disease, rather than as an aggressive act of war. Through his choice of symbols he was trying to define a potentially ambiguous action in a certain way. What was actually happening in Vietnam was likewise ambiguous. If President Johnson succeeded in arguing that the United States was making progress toward its objectives in Vietnam, he would be more likely to evoke a positive attitude toward American policy than would be the case if Sen. Eugene McCarthy prevailed in his claims that we were destined for a stalemate.

Two implications of the preceding paragraph require elaboration. First, reality is not a given. This is not to say that there is no definite, certain "real world" but rather that we cannot have definite, certain knowledge of it because our knowledge is mediated by symbols. When advocates select particular symbols, they are implicitly pleading for a way of viewing reality—for a specific definition of the situation. Common bonds are established among people as they come to view the world in the same way. These common bonds, in turn, can become the stated or unstated premises of arguments that appeal for a specific course of action. The motivations of the Soviet Union in international politics are not directly knowable. For most of the years between 1945 and 1990, however, Americans shared a common belief represented in symbols suggesting aggressiveness, deceit, and threat. These common beliefs provided the grounds for Americans to endorse specific policies ranging from enhancement of our own defense to military intervention in other nations.

Second, it is worth highlighting that the selection of symbols is a matter of choice. There is no one-to-one correspondence between a thing and the symbol that represents it. A given idea or thought can be symbolized in many different ways. During the 1960's, moderate leaders saw the state of race relations in America as progress while more militant blacks viewed the same conditions as intransigent white racism. During most of the political campaigns represented here, one party viewed events as triumphs and the other saw the same events as disasters. The point is simply that, even if they are not aware of it, people make choices when they develop symbols. Those choices are important and certainly worthy of our attention.

The process of influencing people through symbols can occur in any context, from the casual meeting of two friends to a television program watched by millions. Historically, however, the study of rhetoric has been centrally concerned with *public* affairs. Public deliberation occurs when a collective, rather than an individual, decision must be made and when the results of the decision will affect people in general rather than identifiable individuals. President Reagan proposed a specific defense policy, the Strategic Defense Initiative. No one person or group can decide matters of national defense for themselves; nor can anyone formulate a defense policy that does not affect all Americans. National defense is an obvious example of a public issue, but so too are matters of the public good, justice and equal opportunity, foreign policy, general welfare, and so on.

When public deliberation is involved, the symbols used are intended to appeal to a broader audience than just those people who might be directly affected in the case of a private matter. It is also more likely that the discourse will be preserved and that it will be of interest to others. The speeches in this book are examples of rhetorical public discourse. They are rhetorical, since they are attempts to influence people through the use of symbols. They are public, since they are attempts to influence the course of public discussion and collective decision making. And they are discourses, since they are cast in language. They provide us with valuable resources for studying the process of persuasion about important issues during the period since the end of World War II.

THE NATURE OF RHETORICAL ANALYSIS

One could, of course, read speech texts in the same way as any other literature, for enjoyment and appreciation alone. But speeches are delivered for instrumental reasons; they are means to ends rather than ends in themselves. Particularly since they seek persuasive effects, therefore, speeches more commonly are treated as functional rather than literary, and their effectiveness becomes a matter for analysis. To undertake rhe-

torical analysis requires reading the texts critically. A critical reading is not necessarily negative, but rather is a reading with the aim of understanding and informed judgment.

In analyzing a rhetorical document, one attempts to answer two basic questions: What is going on in the text? And what insight can be gained from it? The first question involves *identifying* the underlying dynamics of the text, its implicit processes of symbolic influence. It is a matter of making clear what makes the speech work or why it fails. The second question involves *making a statement about* the text and its underlying dynamics. The statement might relate to their meaning, meaningfulness, value, historical significance, artistry, and so on.

What these two questions have in common is that they go beyond the speech text itself. For any of the speeches in this book, merely reading the text would not be sufficient to answer the questions. As a result, there is no one ultimately "right" answer to the questions. Instead, both questions require that one make and defend inferences. Study of the speech will suggest answers to the questions, and then the analyst will search for reasons to justify those answers.

The supporting reasons could be found in any of several sources. Perhaps the most obvious is a close reading of the text itself and an awareness of its structure, organization, style, and argument. The judgment of other critics about the speech is another source of good reasons. Yet another is the consistency of the reason with known background conditions surrounding the speech. Theoretical and ethical precepts furnish another source of reasons. The strength of the inference is always dependent on the strength of the reasons adduced for it. To engage in analysis of a speech text, then, is to make arguments about it. Like any other argument, the acceptability of the claim will be a function of the acceptability of the reasons for it. Since no analysis will be absolutely and necessarily true, the test for any analytical statement about a speech is whether there is an alternative inference that can account for the speech more plausibly.

This explanation of analysis should make clear that simply summarizing what is said in the speech does not constitute analysis; neither does an impressionistic judgment that the speech is "good" or "bad," unsupported by reasons. The goal of analysis is to illumine the speech through an explication of the processes of symbolic influence on which it depends.

An example may help to make clearer what is at

issue. Among the significant speeches in this book is the inaugural address of President John F. Kennedy. In trying to discern the underlying dynamics of this speech, one instantly would note several of its aspects. It is almost totally concerned with foreign affairs. It is very general. Its structure reveals both parallelism and antithesis. It includes reference to God and quotation from Scripture. It adopts the tone of a summons and makes an explicit request for participation of the audience.

Having identified "what is going on" in the inaugural address, the analyst's next task would be to account for the phenomena. So, for example, the almost exclusive emphasis on foreign affairs might be explained by reference to the circumstances of the 1960 election. Kennedy's margin of victory had been very narrow, so there was no clear mandate for Presidential action on matters that might be controversial. It would make sense, therefore, for Kennedy to emphasize those things on which most Americans agreed, particularly the strong consensus that communism must be resisted. This choice on the President's part, then, might be an appropriate response to the situation. The use of parallelism and antithesis reflected not only the President's habitual ways of thinking but also a familiar pattern that enabled listeners to follow what was being said and to anticipate what would come next. The general nature of the discourse, the reference to God, and the quotation from Scripture are aspects of virtually every Presidential inaugural address and suggest that Kennedy was conforming to the expectations of the genre. The explicit call for audience commitment may have served to strengthen the listeners' adherence to the speech by placing them "on the record" in response to Kennedy's call for volunteers.

This example illustrates how analysis goes beyond the text of the speech to explicate what is happening in the speech and to comment about it. The reader of the text has achieved a deeper level of understanding of the speech as a public rhetorical discourse. Although this example involves rather small, individual components of the speech, the same process could be undertaken for the speech as a whole. One might, for instance, conclude that the overarching motif of the speech is its call for sacrifice and explain how the individual choices help to advance that goal.

For that matter, the analyst need not restrict himself or herself to a single text. One could undertake a comparative analysis of speeches whose rhetorical dynamics are similar. For example, President Kennedy's commencement address at Yale University and Senator Fulbright's "Old Myths and New Realities" involve challenges to conventional wisdom. It would be interesting to discover if there are common ways that speeches on different subjects approach a similar rhetorical problem. Or one might undertake a biographical analysis, looking for patterns or changes across multiple speeches delivered by the same person. A comparison of the rhetorical method of Richard Nixon in the 1950's and the 1970's would illustrate the creation of rhetorical biography. Another possibility is to undertake a generic analysis, looking at different speeches of the same basic type. Such a study might examine the Presidential nomination acceptance addresses of Adlai Stevenson, Barry Goldwater, Richard Nixon, Ronald Reagan, Michael Dukakis, and George Bush in an attempt to identify and explain recurrent features of this particular type of speech. Finally, one might undertake a topical analysis tracing the development of ideas through public discourse over time. An examination of changes in the treatment of African-Americans in speeches since World War II, or a study of the evolution of defenses of American policy in Vietnam, would illustrate topical rhetorical analyses.

Although it is beyond the scope of this volume, rhetorical analysis also could be performed on nonverbal texts such as popular music and art, or on actions that serve to relate symbols to people, such as the 1963 March on Washington or the "signaling" strategy behind the bombing of North Vietnam.

In summary, then, rhetorical analysis probes the underlying dynamics of a text to explain what principles and strategies of symbolic influence are reflected in it, and assesses those principles and strategies according to some criterion. Its goal is a deeper understanding and appreciation of the text.

PURPOSES OF RHETORICAL ANALYSIS

Analysis of the sort described here is undertaken for two different, but mutually reinforcing, purposes: to enhance our understanding of the historical past and to enhance our understanding of how symbols influence people.

Speeches are one type of primary source available to the historian. When studied by people not trained in rhetoric, however, they often are treated simply as events rather than as texts. Historians will note that a major speech was delivered but will not concern themselves either with how it worked or with what it reflects about a culture. Rhetorical analysis will fill in these missing pieces.

In composing a speech, a person tries to influence others by selecting and arranging symbols that will incline them positively toward the speaker's ideas or proposals. In order to accomplish this task, the speaker—whether consciously or not—examines the beliefs and values of the audience in order to determine those points at which the "common knowledge" of the audience might mesh with his or her ideas, and then frames those ideas in a way that will best facilitate these connections. This complex process is called identification. The speaker seeks to identify with his or her audience through the establishment and evocation of common bonds. Although identification has been described here as a positive force (inclining the audience favorably toward the speaker's goals), it can also be negative if the speaker identifies with the audience against a common enemy.

Identification is the process through which people transcend their individual selves and become part of a community, society, or culture. They subsume their individual needs and desires within a larger, shared vision and on occasion will even sacrifice their individual needs for the sake of that vision. The overriding power of such shared visions is most evident in the rhetoric of war, but other examples can be found as well. During the 1960's, by evoking a vision of the "Great Society," President Lyndon Johnson successfully appealed to the economically prosperous to support programs intended to aid the unfortunate. During the 1980's, by evoking a vision of government as enemy of the people, President Ronald Reagan successfully appealed to many who stood to lose from his economic policies to support them anyway. At other times, however, the attempt at identification fails, as when President Jimmy Carter tried unsuccessfully to evoke a vision of the energy problem as a moral failure shared by all Americans.

Identification, in short, is both the glue that holds society together and the force that moves people toward goals. Rhetorical documents are the primary sources that illustrate attempts at identification. So a study of speeches in the years since 1945 will enable us to discern how community and culture were strengthened or weakened, maintained or transformed, during those years by examining how the process of identification succeeded and failed. This is a special contribution that the study of rhetorical texts can make to historical

understanding. Along the way, such study also can provide a good index of the value hierarchies of a society. By learning how speakers sought to identify with audiences, one can determine what they thought was especially prized or loathed by those to whom they wished to appeal. Consistency in such choices over a number of speakers and occasions will yield an increasingly reliable map of society's values and preferences.

There is yet another contribution that rhetorical analysis can make to historical study. Like it or not, the present inevitably influences our understanding of the past. We know how the story came out. This knowledge affects the way we interpret the statements and actions of people who, of course, did *not* know the ending of the story. There is a strong temptation to assume that things had to happen in the way that they did and to view historical struggles from the perspective of the winners. This tendency is called presentism.

Rhetorical analysis offers a powerful antidote to presentism. A key assumption of symbolic influence processes is choice. Knowingly or not, people decide how to frame reality in the way they select and arrange symbols in order to appeal to others. To insist that choices are made is to acknowledge that there are alternatives; to identify the choices one must be conscious of the alternatives. The proverbial road not taken is brought back into view, and what happened is interpreted in light of what might have happened instead. Recognizing that choices are made as people influence others, build societies, and move toward goals enhances understanding of how things developed in the way they did.

In addition to its contribution to history, rhetorical analysis also makes a powerful contribution to rhetorical theory. Indeed, theory and analysis have a reciprocal relationship. The study of particular cases enables us to test more general theories, and the circumstances of a particular case may suggest explanations that have broader theoretical power. Specific rhetorical texts, then, are crucial to the "data base" for more general theories.

In the physical and life sciences, controlled observation in a laboratory setting is often the means for testing or validating theories. A test situation is contrived and the relevant variables are either controlled or manipulated. In those fields that study human action, however, there is a long-standing dispute about the relative merits of experimental and natural conditions for determining theory. The former increase the degree of control, and hence the likelihood that the results are reliable and valid, but raise the risk that the results may not be generalizable beyond the particular experimental situation itself. The latter increase the potency and generalizability of the findings, but raise the risk that they are contaminated by factors external to the study. Some fields, such as psychology and communication, make use of both approaches. The speeches in this book are naturalistic data. They are actual attempts at symbolic influence; their contexts are real and not contrived. From these data more general theories can be derived; against them more general theories can be tested.

Rhetorical theories are of many types. Some are simple propositions, such as the claim that people are influenced more powerfully by appeals to fear than by appeals to justice. This premise was the operative rhetorical theory for some of the more militant and radical protesters during the 1960's. The theoretical proposition can be derived from the choices they made, and the soundness of the principle can be assessed in part by examining the available options and where they might have led.

Another sort of rhetorical theory posits continuity or evolution in the power of appeals. Study of a large body of texts, for example, might support the claim that "family" is a persistent metaphor to characterize the American people, or that conspiracy arguments usually surface in times of rapid social change. Such a study might also indicate that, while religious references frequently can be found in political discourse,there has been a shift away from the tendency to view political affairs in religious terms and toward the tendency for speakers to make brief general references to the existence of God. This theory might be suggested, for instance, by comparing reactions to the political evangelists of the 1980's with those of eighteenth- and nineteenth-century speakers who regarded human misfortune as divine punishment.

Yet another kind of rhetorical theory is a theory about form. Genre theorists, for instance, maintain that there are recurrent patterns in rhetorical situations and in the features of the discourse that creates or responds to these situations. The Presidential inaugural address and the apologia, or speech of self-defense, are examples of these recurrent situational forms. Study of the particular texts should facilitate identifying the features of the genre and accounting for them.

Finally, there are overarching theories of communication, such as the theory that human interaction is ritual drama or that it is storytelling, or that rhetoric is

a way of knowing, or that symbols encapsulate ideological commitments. Individual rhetorical texts might provide examples to support these overarching theories, or to provide the grounds for testing one such theory against another.

In summary, then, critical analysis of rhetoric is an instrument for enhancing knowledge of both history and rhetorical theory. Careful study of rhetorical texts should offer both the historian and the theorist rich rewards.

METHODS OF RHETORICAL ANALYSIS

If one is convinced of the value of undertaking rhetorical analysis, the next obvious question is how to do it. Broadly speaking, there are two general approaches. One is *formulary*, meaning that it involves the application of formulas or guidelines. The other is *organic*, meaning that the method is derived from the particular questions that prompt interest in a specific text.

Theorists of rhetorical analysis have offered several general or formulary approaches. These are like templates in that they can be applied to any specific text. Probably the most widespread of these approaches is neo-Aristotelianism, which attempts to use principles derived from Aristotle's *Rhetoric* in order to examine a text. Studies relying on neo-Aristotelian methods examine the speaker's background and training, the nature of the audience and occasion, and the selection of logical, emotional, and ethical proofs. Ultimately the analysis judges the effectiveness of the speaker at the task. These same topics can be used to explore virtually any text.

A contemporary approach that has received widespread use is dramatism, heavily influenced by the writing of Kenneth Burke. Beginning with the assumption that human action is drama, dramatistic studies find in rhetorical texts the re-enactment of the symbolic drama of order, guilt, sacrifice or mortification, and redemption. Analytical tools such as cluster and agon analysis, key term analysis, and the pentad of act, scene, agent, agency, and purpose become ways to find and explicate the underlying dramatic structure of human interaction.

Another contemporary approach to rhetorical analysis is genre criticism. It begins with the premise that rhetorical situations recur and that similar situations will call forth similar rhetorical responses. According to this approach, the task is to identify the underlying patterns and to evaluate any given rhetorical text by reference to the possibilities of the pattern. So, for example, the fact that President Kennedy's inaugural address is remembered, whereas President Eisenhower's is not, suggests that Kennedy's speech better achieved the potential that inheres in the inaugural address as a type of situation. The analyst would then proceed to a fairly close reading of Kennedy's text to try to determine how and why the speech achieved the potential of the genre.

Theories of narrative have enjoyed resurgent interest in recent years, and the narrative paradigm represents another example of a popular contemporary approach. It assumes that people are basically storytellers and examines the text for evidence of how speaker and audience organize their experience into stories characterized by coherence and narrative fidelity. The analysis often will suggest a narrative logic that is far more influential than traditional patterns of reasoning.

Fantasy theme analysis is an analytical approach that focuses on the images and visions of the world that appear to be shared by speakers and audiences and are elaborated through discourse. Mythic analysis examines the "deep structure" of messages to discern the underlying myths, the beliefs that are taken on faith and that serve as a starting point for inference and appeal. Argumentative analysis examines the soundness of the arguments and appeals in a text, whether according to formal or informal means of reasoning. Ideological analysis frequently involves "reading against" the text as the analyst tries to bring to the surface the assumptions about the world that are taken for granted in the discourse, in order to suggest that these underlying assumptions are not neutral.

In theory, there is no end to the number of analytical or critical approaches one might examine. Classes in rhetorical criticism often survey and practice using each of the major approaches. There is value in doing so, in order to become familiar with the questions that concern each approach and to see how each approach can illumine a text. It is especially valuable to examine the same text from different critical vantage points.

There is a potential danger, however, in the use of formulary approaches. Precisely because they are templates, they can be used to fit virtually any text. The application of neo-Aristotelian, or dramatistic, or other categories may become a mechanical exercise in which one basically finds what one seeks. The approach ends up not so much shedding light on the text as establish-

ing that the text can be made to fit the particular analytical method. Since we are virtually certain of that in the first place, the analytical project has become circular. To say that a text can fit the form of dramatism, for example, is not to say anything profound, since we already know that virtually any text can. Moreover, in saying that the template fits the text, the analyst can easily forget to say anything that helps to explain the special dynamics of the particular text.

Organic analysis attempts to avoid these problems by bringing no preconceived analytical pattern to the text. Rather, a reading or hearing of the text suggests one or more questions about what is going on, and the analyst devises a method that is particularly suited to those questions. Typically, the question will be prompted by a puzzle or anomaly in the text that will pose a problem. Reading the speeches of Stokely Carmichael, for example, might prompt one to inquire why Carmichael seemingly went out of his way to antagonize white audiences. This puzzle—flying as it does in the face of the theory that rhetoric involves identification—naturally prompts assessment of what is happening in the speech and how it might be explained. A particular analytical method is then devised that will permit answering that question.

Of course, the distinction between formulary and organic approaches has been overstated for purposes of explanation. Organic critics do not approach a text with an altogether blank slate. Instead of a particular analytical method they bring a frame of mind that is broadly oriented toward problems and solutions. Even organic critics start with several basic assumptions.

First, a speech is given within a specific context. To be sure, speeches are judged great because they remain meaningful even outside the context in which they were given. But the first test of a speech is its suitability to the context. Only when one understands the specific context can one fairly assess the choices reflected in the speech. These choices are not made in the abstract but according to the requirements of particular situations.

Second, the speaker's persuasiveness is not entirely a function of the verbal content of the message. The speaker's prior reputation and credibility and the image of character portrayed through the speech itself also are important considerations.

Third, the audience presents a speaker with both challenges and opportunities. To understand the rhetorical possibilities in the situation and to assess the choices made by the speaker, one must understand the audience. Of course, the audience for most contemporary speeches is far larger than the number of those physically present when the speech was first delivered.

Finally, the interaction between speaker and audience focuses on a specific message. The text is not incidental to the analysis but central to it. Analysts should be aware of how such factors as argument, organization, and style work together to promote or hinder the speaker's purpose within a given situation.

If the organic approach to analysis does not require the same detailed knowledge of critical methods as does the formulary approach, it nevertheless requires a certain cast of mind. An alert and inquisitive mind, an able imagination that is capable of recognizing what is not obvious, the ability to detect similarities and differences that are not immediately evident, and time to sort through ideas are the habits and attitudes especially required for criticism of this type. The reward comes in insight that deepens understanding and appreciation of the particular text under scrutiny.

THE CONTEMPORARY WORLD

The speeches in this book were delivered between 1945 and 1990. During those years, both American and world society underwent significant transformations affecting the nature of public discourse. Changes in the technology of communication also shaped the character of speeches and their prominence in American society, even while making traditional notions of eloquence harder to attain.

At the end of World War II the United States found itself, for the first time in its history, one of the world's two superpowers. This role imposed new burdens and responsibilities for a nation traditionally uninvolved in foreign affairs, and speakers needed to convince audiences who wanted a rest from world problems that it was necessary to continue to play an active leadership role. Moreover, the wartime alliance with the Soviet Union quickly gave way to a new phenomenon—cold war. In place of overt hostilities between the two powers, verbal and symbolic confrontations marked the years from the late 1940's until the late 1980's. The advent of the atomic age and the dangers of nuclear war constrained both nations from becoming belligerents in the traditional sense, and instead inspired wars of words and nerves. At the same time, the opportunity to control and limit the dangers of nuclear

weapons became an incentive for speakers and policymakers to think in new ways about armament and disarmament.

Domestically, the most significant development of the postwar years was the emergence of the civil rights movement during the 1950's. The call for justice and equal opportunity reverberated across the country in landmark demonstrations and speeches that finally lay to rest the notion that officially sanctioned racial discrimination had a place in American life. Early civil rights advocates assumed that the solution was integration of blacks into a presumably good American society. By the 1960's, however, that assumption was called into question, as growing numbers of younger and more militant blacks explicitly rejected integration as a goal and demanded a much more radical cultural transformation.

One curve of development that began with the New Deal, another that began with the cold war, and another that began with the civil rights movement all reached moments of climax during the turbulent 1960's. The Great Society of President Lyndon Johnson represented the natural culmination of the New Deal, but was achieved at just the time when growing numbers of Americans came to doubt the validity of large-scale social programs. The belief that America must resist communism everywhere received its most severe test in Vietnam. Controversy surrounding that war lasted for many years. Increasingly strident calls for withdrawal were met with increasingly shrill defenses of the government's policy. The impasse was broken, if only momentarily, by Lyndon Johnson's surprise announcement that he would not be a candidate for re-election in 1968. But both the war and the controversy persisted into the administration of President Nixon. The civil rights movement achieved its greatest successes during the mid-1960's, but at the same time some black leaders began to question the goal of integration into white society. Controversy developed among blacks as Stokely Carmichael and Eldridge Cleaver, among others, challenged what they viewed as the overly moderate approach of Martin Luther King.

The turmoil and creative energy unleashed by the civil rights movement found echoes in many other protest movements during the 1960's and 1970's. The student protest movement, the contemporary women's movement, the cause of native Americans, and the growing political influence of Hispanics are a few examples. Often these movements followed the rhetorical example of the civil rights movement. Almost invariably, their cause was espoused by speakers previously unfamiliar to a national audience. The growing diversity of speakers is one of the striking characteristics of postwar American public discourse and is reflected in the selections in this book.

Movements beget countermovements, among those who feel threatened by the pace of change or who wish to restore a presumably happier past. The countermovements achieved their greatest strength in the late 1970's and 1980's and coincided with the prominence of television evangelists. Religion fueled many of the right-wing movements, culminating perhaps in the candidacy of Marion G. (Pat) Robertson for President in 1988. No issue more galvanized the right, or evoked a more strident defense from the left, than the question of abortion, which remains a crucial unresolved issue of public policy as these words are written.

If society was beset by turmoil and change, politics by the 1970's reflected the desire for calm. The Nixon administration began with the hope of recreating a national consensus but came apart under the impact of Vietnam, the energy crisis, and especially the Watergate scandal. The Ford Presidency seemed to many to be tainted by Ford's pardon of Nixon a month after taking office. Jimmy Carter narrowly won the 1976 election but soon was perceived as unable to govern effectively, partly because of his response to the energy crisis of 1979 but particularly because of his failure to extricate fifty-two American diplomats held hostage in Iran for over a year.

The conservative turn that many expected of Nixon was achieved in the early 1980's following the election of Ronald Reagan. Reagan, who quickly became known as the "great communicator," set out to reverse the course of the past five decades of history by reducing the size and scale of the federal government in Americans' lives. A controversial economic policy proposed to reduce taxes, increase defense spending, and balance the budget, all at the same time. The resulting federal deficit both thwarted new domestic initiatives and became the centerpiece of debate for much of the decade. Reagan's military policy was highlighted by his call for a new strategic defense initiative that would use laser technology to intercept and destroy attacking missiles, a policy that critics labeled "Star Wars." Although many of Reagan's specific policies were unpopular, the President himself enjoyed very high approval ratings and easily won re-election in 1984, particularly when he was able to characterize the Democrats as the party of special interests. The Demo-

crats engaged in several efforts to redefine themselves, but these proved to be unsuccessful.

In late 1986, Reagan's popularity began to drop, with the discovery that the United States had secretly sold arms to Iran, in the face of Reagan's pledge never to negotiate with terrorists, and then diverted some of the profits to support Nicaraguan rebels to circumvent a congressional prohibition on aid. The Iran-Contra scandal consumed much of his last two years in office but never reached the proportions of Watergate. It did not immobilize the President and did not prevent his successor, George Bush, from running successfully on the Reagan record.

The quickening pace of change during the postwar period has made events seem even more ephemeral than in the past. Some of the contemporary American voices, however, summoned the nation to enduring problems and issues. These included the place of the arts and culture in American society, the social roles of labor and capital, the challenges of new discovery and exploration, the nature of American law and justice, and the meaning of peace in the nuclear age. A sample of these voices appears in this book as well.

The communication environment of postwar America also reflected many changes from earlier years, and some of these are worthy of brief note. The most significant has been the penetration of American society by television, which has made both verbal and visual communication instantly accessible but also has placed a premium on brief messages and has sometimes framed public affairs within the context of mass entertainment. It also has affected the economics of communication and raised issues about whether diverse viewpoints indeed do enjoy access to the public forum.

Another notable change is the diversity of the speakers and topics. Increasingly, women and minorities are found among the ranks of leading advocates, and topics extend beyond the traditional issues of politics and religion to encompass social and cultural questions and matters of personal life-style.

The prevalence of mass media also has knit the American people together as an audience. Speakers increasingly find their audience—those who hear their words directly and those who ultimately attend to them—to be large and heterogeneous. It is far more likely than it used to be that a message intended for one segment of the audience will be "overheard" by others. A premium has been placed on general and ambiguous appeals, icons, and "sound bites" in order to enable diverse members of the audience to identify with the message. Scholars have questioned whether these trends enrich or impoverish public discourse, but they appear to be irreversible. They certainly have transformed our conception of eloquence and suggest the need for analysts to be thoroughly familiar with the contemporary communication environment.

The visual bias of television, among other factors, has also placed a premium on symbolic action even more than talk. Protest movements and campaigns have recognized that the surest way to attract national attention is to disrupt the smooth and orderly conduct of affairs. It is the dramatic, the unexpected, that is newsworthy and attracts attention. Widespread attention is needed if any movement or campaign is to move beyond its early followers and broaden its base in the hope of having a major impact.

Other changes have marked the communication environment as well, but those discussed here should suggest that the postwar world marked a new era in American public discourse. The contemporary voices that shaped and engaged in that discourse are represented in the pages that follow.

Credits

Cold War, Domestic Politics, and the Nuclear Age

———Henry Wallace———

The Way to Peace
(September 12, 1946)

With the final defeat of Germany and Japan in 1945, the "Grand Alliance" of nations opposing the Axis powers began to come apart. World War II had thrown the United States and the Soviet Union together against the common Nazi foe, but only after decades of suspicion and hostility. The Bolshevik Revolution of 1917, in the midst of World War I, was followed by the conclusion of a separate peace treaty between Germany and Russia, freeing the German military to concentrate its resources in the fight against the Allies, including the United States, on the Western front. In return, the Allies occupied Russian ports, leading the new Soviet government to conclude that the Western powers were doing their utmost to support the anti-Communists in the fierce civil war raging in Russia.

In the years following the end of the war, Americans continued to view the "Reds" with suspicion, but some commercial ties were established and the United States finally recognized the Soviet government in 1933. From 1936 to 1938, however, the Soviet leader Joseph Stalin carried out a brutal and bloody purge of all opposition. The Moscow Trials, through which Stalin eliminated all of his real or imagined enemies, including many of the old revolutionary leaders, shocked American opinion. Then, in August of 1939, Russia entered into a nonaggression pact with Germany, allowing Hitler to invade Poland without the threat of Soviet intervention. This cynical diplomatic maneuver undermined supporters of the Soviet Union who argued that Russian power was a counterweight to Nazism.

Once the Soviet Union had been attacked by Germany in defiance of the nonaggression pact and America had entered the war, Russia and the United States found themselves allies against Hitler. The Russians came to be seen in America as guardians of their country, patriots resisting the Nazi hordes in defense of "Mother Russia." The alliance was, in reality, a military necessity, and the political, ideological, and economic differences between the two countries were in no way mitigated by wartime cooperation. Once the war was over, it became apparent that the United States and the Soviet Union had emerged as "superpowers," suspicious of each other's goals and intentions and clearly in competition for world leadership.

In 1945, after meeting with Stalin at Potsdam, the new President, Harry S Truman, returned with the conviction that the Russian aims could be countered only with force and that the Soviets were "planning world conquest." As it became clear to the Truman administration that no previous agreements would deter Soviet efforts to dominate Eastern Europe and fears of Russian expansionism and subversion grew, the American position toward the Soviets hardened.

One member of the President's cabinet viewed the direction of American foreign policy with growing alarm. Henry Wallace, secretary of commerce, had been Franklin D. Roosevelt's secretary of agriculture and then, during FDR's third term, from 1941 to 1945, Vice President of the United States. Yielding to conservative Democratic pressure, Roosevelt allowed the 1944 Democratic convention to drop Wallace and nominate instead a border state senator on whom the various factions could agree: Harry S Truman of Missouri. When Franklin Roosevelt died suddenly on April 12, 1945, Truman became President of the United States. Within weeks Germany surrendered; in early August, Americans dropped atomic bombs on Hiroshima and Nagasaki and Japan quickly surrendered. World War II was over; the "cold war" was about to begin.

Henry Wallace and his supporters were of the opinion—which was decidedly a minority opinion at the time—that Soviet control of Eastern Europe was not only inevitable but had the positive virtue of ensuring against another rise of a powerful Germany. He saw Eastern Europe as falling legitimately into the Soviet sphere of interest, and he feared that the peace of the world was threatened by those who advocated that the United States should "get tough with Russia." Such was clearly not the view of the Truman administration and its chief foreign policy spokesman, Secretary of State James Byrnes. The rift within the President's cabinet became apparent when Secretary Wallace addressed a rally in support of New York Democratic candidates on September 12, 1946, in Madison Square Garden.

In the speech, Wallace lambasted British imperialism, advocated free trade with and the resumption of aid to the Russians, and called for American disarmament. He suggested that the United States "should recognize that we have no more business in the *political* affairs of Eastern Europe than Russia has in the *political* affairs of Latin America," and, reminding his audience that "the Balkans are closer to Russia than to us," asserted that Russia could not allow English or American domination in that area.

In recent years, revisionist historians have been sympathetic to Wallace's view that American policy was a determining factor in bringing about the cold war, but their interpretations have been hotly contested by other historians. In any case, most Americans in the postwar period found little evidence in Russian actions to suggest that trusting the Russians would be an effective strategy to ensure world peace, and Wallace's sentiments were not widely shared. Furthermore, Wallace's assertion that he spoke for the Truman administration was soon repudiated. After a fumbling press conference in which the President claimed that the views of the secretary of commerce were consistent with administration policy, and after Secretary of State Byrnes made it clear that he would resign unless Wallace ceased making foreign policy statements—a pledge Wallace publicly declined to make—President Truman demanded Wallace's resignation.

Henry Wallace was ultimately to take his case to the people as the Presidential candidate of the newly formed and short-lived Progressive Party in 1948. By then, however, the cold war was being fought in earnest, both American political parties were clearly and vociferously anti-Communist, and Wallace, his new party, and his policy were roundly rejected.

First off, I want to give my own personal endorsement to the candidates chosen by the Democratic Party and the American Labor Party in New York. James Mead long has been one of the ablest public servants in Washington—a constant, faithful and intelligent proponent of the New Deal of Franklin Roosevelt. The Senate will miss him—but Albany needs him. He will make a great governor—worthy of the tradition of Smith and Roosevelt and Lehman.

Herbert Lehman knows full well the problems and the opportunities facing the State of New York, the United States, and the United Nations. His great heart and great mind will be increasingly useful when he is a member of the United States Senate.

Victory for Mead and Lehman in November will mean a long stride in the people's progress.

Tonight I want to talk about peace—and how to get peace. Never have the common people of all lands so longed for peace. Yet, never in a time of comparative peace have they feared war so much.

Up till now peace has been negative and unexciting. War has been positive and exciting. Far too often, hatred and fear, intolerance and deceit have had the upper hand over love and confidence, trust and joy. Far too often, the law of nations has been the law of the jungle; and the constructive spiritual forces of the Lord have bowed to the destructive forces of Satan.

During the past year or so, the significance of peace has been increased immeasurably by the atom bomb, guided missiles and airplanes which soon will travel as fast as sound. Make no mistake about it—another war would hurt the United States many times as much as the last war. We cannot rest in the assurance that we invented the atom bomb—and therefore that this agent of destruction will work best for us. He who trusts in the atom bomb will sooner or later perish by the atom bomb—or something worse.

I say this as one who steadfastly backed preparedness throughout the Thirties. We have no use for namby-pamby pacifism. But we must realize that modern inventions have now made peace the most exciting thing in the world—and we should be willing to pay a just price for peace. If modern war can cost us $400 billion, we should be willing and happy to pay much more for peace. But certainly, the cost of peace is to be measured not in dollars but in the hearts and minds of men.

The price of peace—for us and for every nation in the world—is the price of giving up prejudice, hatred, fear, and ignorance.

Let's get down to cases here at home.

First we have prejudice, hatred, fear and ignorance of certain races. The recent mass lynching in Georgia was not merely the most unwarranted, brutal act of mob violence in the United States in recent years; it was also an illustration of the kind of prejudice that makes war inevitable.

Hatred breeds hatred. The doctrine of racial superiority produces a desire to get even on the part of its victims. If we are to work for peace in the rest of the world, we here in the United States must eliminate racism from our unions, our business organizations, our educational institutions, and our employment practices. Merit alone must be the measure of man.

Second, in payment for peace, we must give up prejudice, hatred, fear and ignorance in the economic world. This means working earnestly, day after day, for a larger volume of world trade. It means helping undeveloped areas of the world to industrialize themselves with the help of American technical assistance and loans.

We should welcome the opportunity to help along the most rapid possible industrialization in Latin America, China, India, and the Near East. For as the productivity of these people increases, our exports will increase.

We all remember the time, not so long ago, when the high tariff protectionists blindly opposed any aid to the industrialization of Canada. But look at our exports to Canada today. On a per capita basis our Canadian exports are seven times greater than our exports to Mexico.

I supported the British loan of almost four billion dollars because I knew that without this aid in the rehabilitation of its economy, the British government would have been forced to adopt totalitarian trade methods and economic warfare of a sort which would have closed the markets of much of the world to American exports.

For the welfare of the American people and the world it is even more important to invest $4 billion in the industrialization of undeveloped areas in the so-called backward nations, thereby promoting the long-term stability that comes from an ever-increasing standard of living. This would not only be good politics and good morals, it would be good business.

The United States is the world's great creditor nation. And low tariffs by creditor nations are a part of the price of peace. For when a great creditor demands payment, and at the same time, adopts policies which make it impossible for the debtors to pay in goods—the first result is the intensification of depression over large ares of the world; and the final result is the triumph of demagogues who speak only the language of violence and hate.

Individual Republicans may hold enlightened views—but the Republican party as a whole is irrevocably committed to tariff and trade policies which can only mean world-wide depression, ruthless economic warfare and eventual war. And if the Republicans were in power in the United States today, intelligent people all over the world would fear that once more we would be headed straight for boom, bust and world-wide chaos.

I noticed in the papers recently that Governor Dewey doesn't like my prophecies. I said weeks before the last election—and said it repeatedly—that Franklin Roosevelt would carry 36 states and have a popular majority of three million. Of course, Mr. Dewey didn't like that one. I say now—as I have said repeatedly—that Republican foreign economic policies carried into action would mean disaster for the nation and the world. Mr. Dewey won't like that one either.

The Republican party is the party of economic nationalism and political isolation—and as such is as anachronistic as the dodo and as certain to disappear. The danger is that before it disappears it may enjoy a brief period of power during which it can do irreparable damage to the United States and the cause of world peace.

Governor Dewey has expressed himself as favoring an alliance of mutual defense with Great Britain as the key to our foreign policy. This may sound attractive because we both speak the same language and many of our customs and traditions have the same historical

background. Moreover, to the military men, the British Isles are our advanced air base against Europe.

Certainly we like the British people as individuals. But to make Britain the key to our foreign policy would be, in my opinion, the height of folly. We must not let the reactionary leadership of the Republican party force us into that position. We must not let British balance-of-power manipulations determine whether and when the United States gets into war.

Make no mistake about it—the British imperialistic policy in the Near East alone, combined with Russian retaliation, would lead the United States straight to war unless we have a clearly-defined and realistic policy of our own.

Neither of these two great powers wants war now, but the danger is that whatever their intentions may be, their current policies may eventually lead to war. To prevent war and insure our survival in a stable world, it is essential that we look abroad through our own American eyes and not through the eyes of either the British Foreign Office or a pro-British or anti-Russian press.

In this connection, I want one thing clearly understood. I am neither anti-British nor pro-British—neither anti-Russian nor pro-Russian. And just two days ago, when President Truman read these words, he said that they represented the policy of his administration.

I plead for an America vigorously dedicated to peace—just as I plead for opportunities for the next generation throughout the world to enjoy the abundance which now, more than ever before, is the birthright of man.

To achieve lasting peace, we must study in detail just how the Russian character was formed—by invasions of Tartars, Mongols, Germans, Poles, Swedes, and French; by the czarist rule based on ignorance, fear and force; by the intervention of the British, French and Americans in Russian affairs from 1919 to 1921; by the geography of the huge Russian land mass situated strategically between Europe and Asia; and by the vitality derived from the rich Russian soil and the strenuous Russian climate. Add to all this the tremendous emotional power which Marxism and Leninism gives to the Russian leaders—and then we can realize that we are reckoning with a force which cannot be handled successfully by a "Get tough with Russia" policy. "Getting tough" never bought anything real and lasting—whether for schoolyard bullies or businessmen or world powers. The tougher we get, the tougher the Russians will get.

Throughout the world there are numerous reactionary elements which had hoped for Axis victory—and now profess great friendship for the United States. Yet, these enemies of yesterday and false friends of today continually try to provoke war between the United States and Russia. They have no real love of the United States. They only long for the day when the United States and Russia will destroy each other.

We must not let our Russian policy be guided or influenced by those inside or outside the United States who want war with Russia. This does not mean appeasement.

We most earnestly want peace with Russia—but we want to be met half way. We want cooperation. And I believe that we can get cooperation once Russia understands that our primary objective is neither saving the British Empire nor purchasing oil in the Near East with the lives of American soldiers. We cannot allow national oil rivalries to force us into war. All of the nations producing oil, whether inside or outside of their own boundaries, must fulfill the provisions of the United Nations Charter and encourage the development of world petroleum reserves so as to make the maximum amount of oil available to all nations of the world on an equitable peaceful basis—and not on the basis of fighting the next war.

For her part, Russia can retain our respect by cooperating with the United Nations in a spirit of open-minded and flexible give-and-take.

The real peace treaty we now need is between the United States and Russia. On our part, we should recognize that we have no more business in the *political* affairs of Eastern Europe than Russia has in the *political* affairs of Latin America, Western Europe and the United States. We may not like what Russia does in Eastern Europe. Her type of land reform, industrial expropriation, and suppression of basic liberties offends the great majority of the people of the United States. But whether we like it or not the Russians will try to socialize their sphere of influence just as we try to democratize our sphere of influence. This applies also to Germany and Japan. We are striving to democratize Japan and our area of control in Germany, while Russia strives to socialize eastern Germany.

As for Germany, we all must recognize that an equitable settlement, based on a unified German nation, is absolutely essential to any lasting European settlement. This means that Russia must be assured that never again can German industry be converted into military might to be used against her—and Britain, Western Europe and the United States must be certain that Russia's Germany policy will not become a tool of Russian design against Western Europe.

The Russians have no more business in stirring up native communists to political activity in Western Europe, Latin America and the United States than we have in interfering in the politics of Eastern Europe and Russia. We know what Russia is up to in Eastern Europe, for example, and Russia knows what we are up to. We cannot permit the door to be closed against our trade in Eastern Europe any more than we can in China. But at the same time we have to recognize that the Balkans are closer to Russia than to us—and that Russia cannot permit either England or the United States to dominate the politics of that area.

China is a special case and although she holds the longest frontier in the world with Russia, the interests of world peace demand that China remain free from any sphere of influence, either politically or economically. We insist that the door to trade and economic development opportunities be left wide open in China as in all the world. However, the open door to trade and opportunities for economic development in China are meaningless unless there is a unified and peaceful China—built on the cooperation of the various groups in that country and based on a hands-off policy of the outside powers.

We are still arming to the hilt. Our excessive expenses for military purposes are the chief cause for our unbalanced budget. If taxes are to be lightened we must have the basis of a real peace with Russia—a peace that cannot be broken by extremist propagandists. We do not want our course determined for us by master minds operating out of London, Moscow or Nanking.

Russian ideas of social-economic justice are going to govern nearly a third of the world. Our ideas of free enterprise democracy will govern much of the rest. The two ideas will endeavor to prove which can deliver the most satisfaction to the common man in their respective areas of political dominance. But by mutual agreement, this competition should be put on a friendly basis and the Russians should stop conniving against us in certain areas of the world just as we should stop scheming against them in other parts of the world. Let the results of the two systems speak for themselves.

Meanwhile, the Russians should stop teaching that their form of communism must, by force if necessary, ultimately triumph over democratic capitalism—while we should close our ears to those among us who would have us believe that Russian communism and our free enterprise system cannot live, one with another, in a profitable and productive peace.

Under friendly peaceful competition the Russian world and the American world will gradually become more alike. The Russians will be forced to grant more and more of the personal freedoms; and we shall become more and more absorbed with the problems of social-economic justice.

Russia must be convinced that we are not planning for war against her and we must be certain that Russia is not carrying on territorial expansion or world domination through native communists faithfully following every twist and turn in the Moscow party line. But in this competition, we must insist on an open door for trade throughout the world. There will always be an ideological conflict—but that is no reason why diplomats cannot work out a basis for both systems to live safely in the world side by side.

Once the fears of Russia and the United States Senate have been allayed by practical regional political reservations, I am sure that concern over the veto power would be greatly diminished. Then the United Nations would have a really great power in those areas which are truly international and not regional. In the world-wide, as distinguished from the regional field, the armed might of the United Nations should be so great as to make opposition useless. Only the United Nations should have atomic bombs and its military establishment should give special emphasis to air power. It should have control of the strategically located air bases with which the United States and Britain have encircled the world. And not only should individual nations be prohibited from manufacturing atomic bombs, guided missiles, and military aircraft for bombing purposes, but no nation should be allowed to spend on its military establishment more than perhaps 15 per cent of its budget.

Practically and immediately, we must recognize that we are not yet ready for World Federation. Realistically, the most we can hope for now is a safe reduction in military expense and a long period of peace based on mutual trust between the Big Three.

During this period, every effort should be made to develop as rapidly as possible a body of international law based on moral principles and not on the Machiavellian principles of deceit, force and distrust—which, if continued, will lead the modern world to rapid disintegration.

In brief, as I see it today, the World Order is bankrupt—and the United States, Russia and England are the receivers. These are the hard facts of power politics on which we have to build a functioning, powerful United Nations and a body of international law. And as we build, we must develop fully the doctrine of the rights of small peoples as contained in the United Nations Charter. This law should ideally apply as much to Indonesians and Greeks as to Bulgarians and Poles—but practically, the application may be delayed until both British and Russians discover the futility of their methods.

In the full development of the rights of small nations, the British and Russians can learn a lesson from the Good Neighbor policy of Franklin Roosevelt. For under Roosevelt, we in the Western Hemisphere built a workable system of regional internationalism that fully protected the sovereign rights of every nation—a system of multilateral action that immeasurably strengthened the whole of world order.

In the United States an informed public opinion will be all-powerful. Our people are peace-minded. But they often express themselves too late—for events today move much faster than public opinion. The people here, as everywhere in the world, must be convinced that another war is not inevitable. And through mass meetings such as this, and through persistent pamphleteering, the people can be organized for peace—even though a large segment of our press is propagandizing our people for war in the hope of scaring Russia. And we who look on this war-with-Russia talk as criminal foolishness must carry our message direct to the people—even though we may be called communists because we dare to speak out.

I believe that peace—the kind of peace I have outlined tonight—is the basic issue, both in the Congressional campaign this fall and right on through the Presidential election in 1948. How we meet this issue will determine whether we live not in "one world" or "two worlds"—but whether we live at all.

————Harry S Truman————

Aid to Greece and Turkey: The Truman Doctrine
(March 12, 1947)

World War II had been over for less than a year when the great British war leader, Winston Churchill, traveled with President Truman to a small college in the President's home state to deliver an address. On March 5, 1946, with the President of the United States on the platform, Churchill told the assembled audience at Westminster College in Fulton, Missouri, that "from Stettin in the Baltic to Trieste in the Adriatic, an iron curtain has descended across the continent." While it was apparent that the Soviet Union was tightening its grip on Eastern Europe, public opinion in America was not yet ready to accept the inevitable conflict between East and West implied by Churchill's stark statement. Americans were clamoring for the return of soldiers from Europe; they were preoccupied with labor struggles, housing shortages, and inflation. The newly established United Nations was supposed to encourage international cooperation, and many took comfort in the fact that the United States had the ultimate weapon—the atomic bomb—as a deterrent to future aggression by any hostile power.

As events unfolded over the next year, however, the lines of confrontation cleared. The exploitation of Europe's economic distress by Communist parties in Western Europe was viewed increasingly as a threat to democratic government. Russian control of East Germany, Poland, and Rumania was virtually absolute and was tightening in Hungary and Czechoslovakia. The Soviets exerted pressure on Iran and Turkey, and Communist guerrillas, abetted by the Communist Balkan states, Albania and Bulgaria, launched a civil war against the British-supported Greek government. Through all this, the Truman administration became convinced that the Soviet Union was impervious to diplomatic pressure and came to believe that Communist expansionism was a threat to the vital interests of the United States and its democratic allies.

In February of 1947 a crisis developed. Great Britain, exhausted by the monumental effort required to sustain six years of war, hard pressed financially, and facing problems throughout its disintegrating empire, informed the American government that it could no longer provide Greece with the economic and military assistance needed to continue the fight against Communist insurgents. The possibility of a Communist-controlled Greece that would, in turn, threaten the independence of Turkey raised the specter of the iron curtain extending across the entire eastern Mediterranean. President Truman and his advisers, now convinced that little could be done to extract those countries already held firmly in the Russian orbit, opted for a strategy designed to contain Soviet expansion. They resolved to fill the vacuum left by British withdrawal by providing $400 million in military and economic assistance to Greece. In a White House conference, the President, Secretary of State George C. Marshall, and Undersecretary Dean Acheson explained the Greek situation and won support for action from congressional leaders. Sen. Arthur Vandenberg, chairman of the Foreign Relations Committee in the Republican-controlled Senate, concurred with the President's plan to go before Congress and personally describe the gravity of the situation; he suggested that Truman give a speech that would "scare hell out of the country."

President Truman was determined that in the address he was to give there would be "no hedging," that it would be "clear and free of hesitation or double talk." Indeed, in the sentence that stated what was to become known as the Truman Doctrine—"I believe that it must be the policy of the United States to support free peoples who are resisting attempted subjugation by armed minorities or by outside pressures"—Truman had crossed out *should* and substituted *must* in the draft submitted to him by the State Department. For the President, the speech represented "America's answer to the surge of expansion of Communist tyranny," and he tried to make as tough, compelling, and lean a case as possible. He cut from the State Department draft, for example, statistical data and background information that made the speech, Truman later wrote, "sound like an investment prospectus." Instead, the speech was a blunt warning that Communist actions endangered America's security.

This speech was doubtless influential in galvanizing public opinion and prompting congressional action in favor of support for Greece and Turkey. Furthermore, it defined in stark terms the nature of the cold war struggle as it was to be viewed for years to come: a struggle between "the free peoples of the world who look to us for support in maintaining their freedoms" and the "totalitarian regimes" fostered by Communism, a desperate struggle between two ways of life, and a struggle in which the United States was clearly to be seen as the champion of the free world.

The gravity of the situation which confronts the world today necessitates my appearance before a joint session of the Congress. The foreign policy and the national security of this country are involved.

One aspect of the present situation, which I wish to present to you at this time for your consideration and decision, concerns Greece and Turkey.

The United States has received from the Greek Government an urgent appeal for financial and economic assistance. Preliminary reports from the Ameri-can Economic Mission now in Greece and reports from the American Ambassador in Greece corroborate the statement of the Greek Government that assistance is imperative if Greece is to survive as a free nation.

I do not believe that the American people and the Congress wish to turn a deaf ear to the appeal of the Greek Government.

Greece is not a rich country. Lack of sufficient natural resources has always forced the Greek people to work hard to make both ends meet. Since 1940, this industrious and peace-loving country has suffered invasion, four years of cruel enemy occupation, and bitter internal strife.

When forces of liberation entered Greece they found that the retreating Germans had destroyed virtually all the railways, roads, port facilities, communications and merchant marine. More than a thousand villages had been burned. Eighty-five per cent of the children were tubercular. Livestock, poultry and draft animals had almost disappeared. Inflation had wiped out practically all savings.

"MILITANT MINORITY" BLAMED

As a result of these tragic conditions, a military minority, exploiting human want and misery, was able to create political chaos which, until now, has made economic recovery impossible.

Greece is today without funds to finance the importation of those goods which are essential to bare subsistence. Under these circumstances the people of Greece cannot make progress in solving their problems of reconstruction. Greece is in desperate need of financial and economic assistance to enable it to resume purchases of food, clothing, fuel and seeds. These are indispensable for the subsistence of its people and are obtainable only from abroad. Greece must have help to import the goods necessary to restore internal order and security so essential for economic and political recovery.

The Greek Government has also asked for the assistance of experienced American administrators, economists and technicians to insure that the financial and other aid given to Greece shall be used effectively in creating a stable and self-sustaining economy and in improving its public administration.

The very existence of the Greek state is today threatened by the terrorist activities of several thousand armed men, led by Communists, who defy the Government's authority at a number of points, particularly along the northern boundaries. A commission appointed by the United Nations Security Council is at present investigating disturbed conditions in northern Greece and alleged border violations along the frontier between Greece on the one hand and Albania, Bulgaria and Yugoslavia on the other.

Meanwhile, the Greek Government is unable to cope with the situation. The Greek Army is small and poorly equipped. It needs supplies and equipment if it is to restore the authority of the Government throughout Greek territory.

U. S. ALONE CAN HELP

Greece must have assistance if it is to become a self-supporting and self-respecting democracy.

The United States must supply that assistance. We have already extended to Greece certain types of relief and economic aid but these are inadequate.

There is no other country to which democratic Greece can turn.

No other nation is willing and able to provide the necessary support for a democratic Greek Government.

The British Government, which has been helping Greece, can give no further financial or economic aid after March. Great Britain finds itself under the necessity of reducing or liquidating its commitments in several parts of the world, including Greece.

We have considered how the United Nations might assist in this crisis. But the situation is an urgent one requiring immediate action, and the United Nations and its related organizations are not in a position to extend help of the kind that is required.

It is important to note that the Greek Government has asked for our aid in utilizing effectively the financial and other assistance we may give to Greece, and in improving public administration. It is of the utmost importance that we supervise the use of any funds made available to Greece, in such a manner that each dollar spent will count toward making Greece self-supporting, and will help to build an economy in which a healthy democracy can flourish.

GREEK ELECTION CITED

No government is perfect. One of the chief virtues of a democracy, however, is that its defects are always visible and under democratic processes can be pointed out and corrected. The Government of Greece is not perfect. Nevertheless it represents 85 per cent of the members of the Greek parliament who were chosen in an election last year. Foreign observers, including 692 Americans, considered this election to be a fair expression of the views of the Greek people.

The Greek Government has been operating in an atmosphere of chaos and extremism. It has made mistakes. The extension of aid by this country does not mean that the United States condones everything that the Greek Government has done or will do. We have condemned in the past, and we condemn now, extremist measures of the Right or the Left. We have in the past advised tolerance, and we advise tolerance now.

TURKEY NEEDS AID

Greece's neighbor, Turkey, also deserves our attention.

The future of Turkey as an independent and economically sound State is clearly no less important to the freedom-loving peoples of the world than the future of Greece. The circumstances in which Turkey finds itself today are considerably different from those of Greece. Turkey has been spared the disasters that have beset Greece. And during the war, the United States and Great Britain furnished Turkey with material aid.

Nevertheless, Turkey now needs our support.

Since the war Turkey has sought financial assistance from Great Britain and the United States for the purpose of effecting that modernization necessary for the maintenance of its national integrity.

That integrity is essential to the preservation of order in the Middle East.

The British Government has informed us that, owing to its own difficulties, it can no longer extend financial or economic aid to Turkey.

As in the case of Greece, if Turkey is to have the assistance it needs, the United States must supply it. We are the only country able to provide that help.

I am fully aware of the broad implications involved if the United States extends assistance to Greece and Turkey, and I shall discuss these implications with you at this time.

FOREIGN POLICY OBJECTIVES

One of the primary objectives of the foreign policy of the United States is the creation of conditions in which we and other nations will be able to work out a way of life free from coercion. This was a fundamental issue in the war with Germany and Japan. Our victory was won over countries which sought to impose their will, and their way of life, upon other nations.

To ensure the peaceful development of nations, free from coercion, the United States has taken a lead-

ing part in establishing the United Nations. The United Nations is designed to make possible lasting freedom and independence for all its members. We shall not realize our objectives, however, unless we are willing to help free people to maintain their free institutions and their national integrity against aggressive movements that seek to impose upon them totalitarian regimes. This is no more than a frank recognition that totalitarian regimes imposed on free peoples, by direct or indirect aggression, undermine the foundations of international peace and hence the security of the United States.

The peoples of a number of countries of the world have recently had totalitarian regimes forced upon them against their will. The Government of the United States has made frequent protests against coercion and intimidation in violation of the Yalta agreement, in Poland, Rumania, and Bulgaria. I must also state that in a number of other countries there have been similar developments.

At the present moment in world history nearly every nation must choose between alternative ways of life. The choice is too often not a free one.

WAYS OF LIFE CONTRASTED

One way of life is based upon the will of the majority, and is distinguished by free institutions, representative government, free elections, guaranties of individual liberty, freedom of speech and religion, and freedom from political oppression.

The second way of life is based upon the will of a minority forcibly imposed upon the majority. It relies upon terror and oppression, a controlled press and radio, fixed elections, and the suppression of personal freedoms.

I believe that it must be the policy of the United States to support free peoples who are resisting attempted subjugation by armed minorities or by outside pressures. I believe that we must assist free peoples to work out their own destinies in their own way. I believe that our help should be primarily through economic and financial aid which is essential to economic stability and orderly political processes.

The world is not static, and the status quo is not sacred. But we cannot allow changes in the status quo in violation of the Charter of the United Nations by such methods as coercion, or by such subterfuges as political infiltration. In helping free and independent nations to maintain their freedom, the United States will be giving effect to the principles of the Charter of the United Nations.

It is necessary only to glance at a map to realize that the survival and integrity of the Greek nation are of grave importance in a much wider situation. If Greece should fall under the control of an armed minority, the effect upon its neighbor, Turkey, would be immediate and serious. Confusion and disorder might well spread throughout the entire Middle East.

Moreover, the disappearance of Greece as an independent State would have a profound effect upon those countries in Europe whose peoples are struggling against great difficulties to maintain their freedoms and their independence while they repair the damages of war. It would be an unspeakable tragedy if these countries, which have struggled so long against overwhelming odds, should lose that victory for which they sacrificed so much. Collapse of free institutions and loss of independence would be disastrous not only for them but for the world. Discouragement and possibly failure would quickly be the lot of neighboring peoples striving to maintain their freedom and independence.

Should we fail to aid Greece and Turkey in this fateful hour, the effect will be far-reaching to the West as well as to the East. We must take immediate and resolute action.

I therefore ask the Congress to provide authority for assistance to Greece and Turkey in the amount of $400,000,000 for the period ending June 30, 1948. In requesting these funds, I have taken into consideration the maximum amount of relief assistance which would be furnished to Greece out of the $350,000,000 which I recently requested that the Congress authorize for the prevention of starvation and suffering in countries devastated by the war.

In addition to funds, I ask the Congress to authorize the detail of American civilian and military personnel to Greece and Turkey, at the request of those countries, to assist in the tasks of reconstruction, and for the purpose of supervising the use of such financial and material assistance as may be furnished. I recommend that authority also be provided for the instruction and training of selected Greek and Turkish personnel.

Finally, I ask that the Congress provide authority which will permit the speediest and most effective use, in terms of needed commodities, supplies and equipment, of such funds as may be authorized.

INVESTMENT IN PEACE

If further funds, or further authority, should be needed for purposes indicated in this message, I shall not hesitate to bring the situation before the Congress. On this subject the executive and legislative branches of the Government must work together.

This is a serious course upon which we embark. I would not recommend it except that the alternative is much more serious.

The United States contributed $341,000,000,000 toward winning world war II. This is an investment in world freedom and world peace. The assistance that I am recommending for Greece and Turkey amounts to little more than one-tenth of 1 per cent of this investment. It is only common sense that we should safeguard this investment and make sure that it was not in vain.

The seeds of totalitarian regimes are nurtured by misery and want. They spread and grow in the evil soil of poverty and strife. They reach their full growth when the hope of a people for a better life has died. We must keep that hope alive.

The free peoples of the world look to us for support in maintaining their freedoms. If we falter in our leadership, we may endanger the peace of the world— and we shall surely endanger the welfare of our own nation.

Great responsibilities have been placed upon us by the swift movement of events. I am confident that the Congress will face these responsibilities squarely.

George C. Marshall

European Unity: The Marshall Plan
(June 5, 1947)

At the close of World War II, Europe was in shambles not only physically but economically. The war had virtually destroyed the industrial capacity of many European countries; normal financial processes were woefully disrupted; food shortages were widespread and devastating; tuberculosis was fast becoming the leading cause of death in Europe. The legacy of the Nazi occupation and the colossal effort to overthrow it was economic and social chaos. As Winston Churchill mournfully observed in the spring of 1947, Europe was "a rubble-heap, a charnel house, a breeding ground of pestilence and hate."

In his "Truman Doctrine" speech, the President had asserted that "the seeds of totalitarian regimes are nurtured by misery and want. They spread and grow in the evil soil of poverty and strife." The Truman Doctrine itself, pledging American assistance in the fight against the spread of communism, did not aim at the total reconstruction of the European economy even though American policymakers were generally agreed that the unstable conditions in Europe made it ripe for Communist exploitation. If the worsening situation in Europe was to be radically altered, some scheme for European cooperation and development had to be devised.

Immediately following the war, the United States had made loans to Britain and other European countries and had shipped large quantities of food. These piecemeal efforts, however, had failed to bring about any significant and lasting solutions to economic problems. Secretary of State George Marshall directed the efforts of State Department policymakers, most notably Undersecretary Dean Acheson and George Kennan and his Policy Planning Staff, toward finding a workable and permanent solution to the problem.

General George C. Marshall, as chief of staff during the war, had proven himself capable not only as a military leader but as a diplomat and politician as well. He was highly respected both in America and abroad. President Truman thought Marshall "one of the most astute and profound men I have ever known," and summed up the "European Unity" speech and Marshall himself when he wrote, "This was a speech that was typical of the man. It was matter-of-fact and without oratorical flourishes, compact and to the point...."

What Marshall finally recommended to the President was that the nations of Europe themselves be encouraged to develop, with the aid of the United States, but primarily on their own initiative, a far-reaching plan that would benefit all of Europe and not just individual nations; and that the United States stand prepared to devote massive resources to implementing the plan. Marshall, although he and his advisers did see the desperate European situation as one offering opportunities for Communist exploitation and wished to forestall potential Communist gains, agreed that the American commitment to European revival should not be ideological; it was not to be promoted as an anti-Communist measure and the Communist countries themselves would be invited to participate. "Our policy," as Marshall stated in his speech outlining the proposal, "is directed not against any country or doctrine but against hunger, poverty, desperation, and chaos." In the event, the Soviet Union refused to participate or to allow its satellites to do so; but the offer made was generally seen as humanitarian and far-sighted (in contrast with the more clearly politically motivated Truman Doctrine). The offer was quickly seized upon by the British and French governments and in just over three weeks representatives from sixteen nations met in Paris (exclusive of the Soviet Union, whose foreign minister had come to Paris and then withdrawn from the conference), and the first step toward making the Marshall Plan a reality was taken.

I need not tell you gentlemen that the world situation is very serious. That must be apparent to all intelligent people. I think one difficulty is that the problem is one of such enormous complexity that the very mass of facts presented to the public by press and radio make it exceedingly difficult for the man in the street to reach a clear appraisement of the situation. Furthermore, the people of this country are distant from the troubled areas of the earth and it is hard for them to comprehend the plight and consequent reactions of the long-suffering peoples, and the effect of those reactions on their governments in connection with our efforts to promote peace in the world.

In considering the requirements for the rehabilitation of Europe the physical loss of life, the visible destruction of cities, factories, mines and railroads was correctly estimated, but it has become obvious during recent months that this visible destruction was probably less serious than the dislocation of the entire fabric of European economy. For the past ten years conditions have been highly abnormal. The feverish preparation for war and the more feverish maintenance of the war effort engulfed all aspects of national economics. Machinery has fallen into disrepair or is entirely obsolete. Under the arbitrary and destructive Nazi rule, virtually every possible enterprise was geared into the German war machine. Long-standing commercial ties, private institutions, banks, insurance companies and shipping companies disappeared, through loss of capital, absorption through nationalization or by simple destruction. In many countries, confidence in the local currency has been severely shaken. The breakdown of the business structure of Europe during the war was complete. Recovery has been seriously retarded by the fact that two years after the close of hostilities a peace settlement with Germany and Austria has not been agreed upon. But even given a more prompt solution of these difficult problems, the rehabilitation of the economic structure of Europe quite evidently will require a much longer time and greater effort than had been foreseen.

There is a phase of this matter which is both interesting and serious. The farmer has always produced the foodstuffs to exchange with the city dweller for the other necessities of life. This division of labor is the basis of modern civilization. At the present time it is threatened with breakdown. The town and city industries are not producing adequate goods to exchange with the food-producing farmer. Raw materials and fuel are in short supply. Machinery is lacking or worn out. The farmer or the peasant cannot find the goods for sale which he desires to purchase. So the sale of his farm produce for money which he cannot use seems to him an unprofitable transaction. He, therefore, has withdrawn many fields from crop cultivation and is using them for grazing. He feeds more grain to stock and finds for himself and his family an ample supply of food, however short he may be on clothing and the other ordinary gadgets of civilization. Meanwhile people in the cities are short of food and fuel. So the governments are forced to use their foreign money and credits to procure these necessities abroad. This process exhausts funds which are urgently needed for reconstruction. Thus a very serious situation is rapidly developing which bodes no good for the world. The modern system of the division of labor upon which the exchange of products is based is in danger of breaking down.

The truth of the matter is that Europe's requirements for the next three or four years of foreign food and other essential products—principally from America—are so much greater than her present ability to pay that she must have substantial additional help, or face economic, social and political deterioration of a very grave character.

The remedy lies in breaking the vicious circle and restoring the confidence of the European people in the economic future of their own countries and of Europe as a whole. The manufacturer and the farmer throughout wide areas must be able and willing to exchange their products for currencies the continuing value of which is not open to question.

Aside from the demoralizing effect on the world at large and the possibilities of disturbances arising as a result of the desperation of the people concerned, the consequences to the economy of the United States should be apparent to all. It is logical that the United States should do whatever it is able to do to assist in the return of normal economic health in the world, without which there can be no political stability and no assured peace. Our policy is directed not against any country or doctrine but against hunger, poverty, desperation and chaos. Its purpose should be the revival of a working economy in the world so as to permit the emergence of political and social conditions in which free institutions can exist. Such assistance, I am convinced, must not be on a piece-meal basis as various crises develop. Any assistance that this Government may render in the future should provide a cure rather than a mere palliative. Any government that is willing to assist in the task of recovery will find full cooperation, I am sure, on the part of the United States Government. Any government which maneuvers to block the recovery of other countries cannot expect help from us. Furthermore, governments, political parties or groups which seek to perpetuate human misery in order to profit therefrom politically or otherwise will encounter the opposition of the United States.

It is already evident that, before the United States Government can proceed much further in its efforts to alleviate the situation and help start the European world on its way to recovery, there must be some agreement among the countries of Europe as to the requirements of the situation and the part those countries themselves will take in order to give proper effect to whatever action might be undertaken by this Government. It would be neither fitting nor efficacious for this Government to undertake to draw up unilaterally a program designed to place Europe on its feet economically. This is the business of the Europeans. The initiative, I think, must come from Europe. The role of this country should consist of friendly aid in the drafting of a European program and of later support of such a program so far as it may be practical for us to do so. The program should be a joint one, agreed to by a number, if not all European nations.

An essential part of any successful action on the part of the United States is an understanding on the part of the people of America of the character of the problem and the remedies to be applied. Political passion and prejudice should have no part. With foresight, and a willingness on the part of our people to face up to the vast responsibility which history has clearly placed upon our country, the difficulties I have outlined can and will be overcome.

─────Ralph Bunche─────

The Road to Peace: The United Nations Way
(June 19, 1949)

The idea for an international organization to preserve world peace was conceived while World War II was still raging. In January of 1942, the twenty-six countries then allied against the Axis powers met in Washington, where they voiced their intention to work together to combat future aggression and ensure economic and social rights for all peoples. This "United Nations Declaration" was followed by a meeting of the major powers later that year in Moscow in which Great Britain, the United States, China, and the Soviet Union announced their intention to work toward the establishment of an organization to maintain international peace and security. As the war came nearer to its conclusion, the major powers met once again—in August 1944 at Dumbarton Oaks, Washington, D.C.—and agreed generally on the structure of the new organization. The 1945 Yalta conference between the principal allies further refined details, and, with the war in Europe virtually over and the conflict in Asia nearing an end, the United Nations Conference on International Organization opened in San Francisco on April 25, 1945. On June 26 the United Nations Charter was signed. The United States Senate ratified the charter a month later, and by October 24, 1945, enough countries had followed suit to bring the UN officially into being.

East-West tensions following the war inevitably weakened the power of the United Nations to act decisively in resolving conflicts. The Security Council, charged with keeping and enforcing the peace, had as permanent members the great powers, each with a right of veto. As the cold war intensified, the council increasingly became a forum in which bitter disputes between the United States and the Soviet Union thwarted concerted UN action. In America, there were some calls, notably by former president Herbert Hoover, for the formation of a new world organization that excluded the Soviets.

The UN, however, as imperfect as it might be, was still seen by many as the world's best hope for preserving peace. A strong advocate for the UN was Dr. Ralph Bunche, a black American educator and diplomat, who, in 1949, was director of the United Nations Department of Trusteeships. This organization had been set up by the UN to deal with certain colonial territories that included those set up by the old League of Nations (the "mandates"), former Italian and Japanese colonies, and some territories voluntarily placed in the trusteeship system by powers administering them. The goal of the Trusteeship Council was to work toward independence for the territories administered by an outside power.

Bunche, the grandson of a former slave, earned a Ph.D. from Harvard and was chairman of the political science department at Howard University before World War II. As an expert on African affairs, he worked in several government posts during the war. After entering the State Department in 1944, he worked intensively on plans to form the United Nations and was the principal author of the section dealing with trust territories that was incorporated in the UN Charter. In 1946 he left the State Department to join the UN Secretariat, heading the Trusteeship Council.

In June of 1949 Bunche traveled to Waltham, Massachusetts, to deliver an address at Brandeis University. In the speech, Bunche answered critics and made a strong appeal to Americans to continue their support for the United Nations "as the one great hope for all of us that the world will not be consumed by atomic warfare." Bunche referred specifically to recent events in the Middle East in which the United Nations, and Bunche himself, were deeply involved. The British government decided to give up its old League mandate for Palestine, leaving to the United Nations the problem of setting up an independent Jewish state. While debate on partitioning Palestine was going on at the General Assembly, the State of Israel was proclaimed (May 1948) and was recognized by the United States. Jewish-Arab fighting broke out in earnest, and the UN attempted to mediate. The chief mediator, Count Bernadotte of Sweden, secured a temporary cease-fire, but this broke down when Bernadotte was assassinated in Jerusalem. Bunche took Bernadotte's place and worked out a series of settlements between Israel and Arab states that led to a cease-fire and finally an armistice. For this achievement, Bunche was awarded the Nobel Peace Prize in 1950.

Ralph Bunche, of course, did not solve the Israeli-Arab problem in the Middle East, a problem that still exists forty years later. But, for Bunche, he had begun the "slow and tedious" mediation process. Bunche argued that the UN role in Palestine showed that "although the United Nations is not a world government, that although lacking in enforcement machinery, its voice can be an instrument of tremendous influence and great good."

There is no road in the world today more important than the road to peace. It is, to date, insufficiently traveled, and indeed, not at all clearly charted. The United Nations is attempting both to chart it and to guide the nations and peoples of the world along it. For peace is the business of the United Nations. At times it is a pretty grim business.

The United Nations was conceived in the throes of war. When the United Nations Conference on International Organization convened at San Francisco in the spring of 1945 for the purpose of drafting the United Nations Charter neither Germany nor Japan had yet capitulated. The war in both east and west was in its final, decisive phase.

It was inevitable, therefore, that peace should be the overriding concern of the delegates to that historic Conference. They sought to devise an international organization to succeed the League of Nations which would have the achievement of a peaceful world as its most fundamental objective, and which would possess the means to give maximum assurance against war or the threat of war. They spoke of peace-loving peoples. They made the desire to maintain peace the basic qualification for membership in the Organization.

They strove to avoid the weaknesses of the League of Nations. They were sick unto death of war. They did not seek peace at any price, but they were eager to go very far to insure it.

Thus the United Nations was designed to prevent wars and to stop them if unhappily they should break out. Elaborate machinery for this purpose was created. To this end the United Nations was endowed with certain enforcement powers and was to have an international security force.

It was recognized also that to insure a peaceful world solid foundations for peace must be laid. Therefore, great stress was put on human rights and fundamental freedoms, on the equality of peoples irrespective of race or creed, on economic collaboration and advancement, on the rights of colonial peoples to aspire to and move toward freedom and the control of their own destinies. The intent was to eliminate the irritants, the foci of unrest and rivalry, the inexorable pressures, which in the past had twice set the world on fire.

For many reasons, not the least of which is the unfortunate conflict between East and West, the enforcement machinery of the United Nations has never become operative; the international security force has not yet materialized. Does this mean that the effectiveness of the United Nations as an instrument for the cultivation and preservation of a peaceful world has been destroyed?

I believe that the answer is emphatically no. The United Nations today has no military force with which to impose its decisions. It does not presume to be a world government. It has obvious imperfections and weaknesses. It suffers from that dread virus, veto. It often appears that the great powers have it at their mercy. Yet the voice of the United Nations has become an instrument of tremendous and increasing influence in our world. That voice is the one great hope for all of us that the world will not be consumed by atomic warfare.

There is a popular tendency to take a somewhat cynical attitude toward the United Nations. This is because, in the turbulent postwar period, the United Nations has been seized with so many delicate, complex, and explosive problems and has not produced definitive solutions for most of them. But if United Nations action has not often produced definitive results and tidy decisions, it has nevertheless always dulled the dangerous edges of the problems and has at least eliminated them as frightening threats to the peace of the world. This has been the case in an impressive array of situations, including such disputes as those in Iran, Indonesia, Korea, Kashmir, Palestine and even Berlin, where United Nations intervention has been an important catalytic agent. Each of these situations has been heavily charged; each posed a potential and frightening threat to the peace of the world. In each the tension has been greatly eased as a consequence of United Nations intervention, and the threat to the peace has been either eliminated or greatly lessened.

Because the United Nations is functioning in this way, I am optimistic about the prospects for peace in the future. War, in our day and age, is a product of the state of mind of peoples. If the generality of peoples are peace-loving and are determined to live in peace—and I firmly believe that throughout the world they are—the prospects of war are remote. But it is not necessary for people to be warlike, to be wishing for war, to demand it, in order that war will come to their doorsteps. It is fatefully ironic that essentially peaceful peoples may have war thrust upon them only because they have fallen into a fatalistic state of mind which persuades them that for one or another reason, war is inevitable.

There is too much of that kind of dangerously loose thinking in the contemporary world. There are too many people who are prepared to draw the fatal conclusion that war is inevitable, or virtually so, because of the apparent inability of the United Nations thus far to repair the breach between East and West. That is reckless and irresponsible reasoning in an atomic age. In the final analysis, the United Nations can be an instrument for peace no stronger and no more effective than the peoples of the world make it, by their confidence and support.

Many, perhaps most, of the problems which beset the contemporary world are due in large measure to a lack of understanding among peoples, and to the suspicions and recriminations which are the inevitable by-product of misunderstanding. Despite the great technical advances in transportation and communication, which in fact, make the world physically "one world," there is as yet no deep sense of world brotherhood among peoples. That which is strange and foreign is still looked at askance by most of us. Barriers of language, religion, modes, and ideology continue to be formidable, and these barriers become even more formidable by political curtains and the instruments of propaganda.

The United Nations ideal whereby peoples would "practice tolerance and live together in peace with one another as good neighbors" is still far from realization. But no ideal has ever been more worthy.

The vital role of the United Nations in the settlement of disputes is to bring representatives of peoples together in order that they may apply reason to their problems, that they may argue out their differences in the full glare of international public opinion—to give them every possible assistance in finding means of peaceful settlement.

That the role of the United Nations in this regard may be decisive is perhaps no better illustrated than in the experience of the United Nations with the Palestine problem.

The encouraging results thus far achieved in Palestine are the product of a prolonged and intensive United Nations effort to restore and secure peace. But they have not been achieved without great cost. Ten members of the United Nations staff in Palestine, including Count Bernadotte himself, have sacrificed their lives in this peace expedition and twice that many have been wounded.

Because there is a readiness on the part of Arabs and Jews to heed the insistence of the United Nations that peace shall reign in Palestine; because a great number of men and women have been willing to risk their lives in serving the United Nations ideal; because Arabs and Jews have been sensible enough to sit down together and negotiate their differences; because of these factors big steps toward permanent peace have been taken in Palestine. The truce checked the fighting. The armistice agreements have taken the warring parties much further along the road to peace. They define armistice demarcation lines. They provide for substantial reduction and withdrawal of armed forces on both sides, with a view toward eliminating any possibility of offensive military action by either side. Each agreement incorporates an article which, in substance, is a nonaggression pact. In each instance, mixed armistice commissions are established whereby, through joint and cooperative effort, assisted by United Nations observers, the parties themselves supervise the application of the armistice terms. The agreements were signed at the governmental level and firmly bind the governments. Any violations of their terms would be an act of bad faith by the responsible government.

But undoubtedly the greatest significance of the agreements is to be found in the fact that they are voluntary agreements, that the representatives of the Arab and Israeli Governments have now, for the first time, sat down together as equal parties in earnest consultation, and have learned that it is possible for them to resolve vital differences by statesmanship and a mutual spirit of conciliation. This is the United Nations way. This is a vital lesson not only for Arabs and Israelis but for a troubled world at large.

It would be a serious mistake, however, to exaggerate the significance of the Palestine armistice agreements. Serious problems of a nonmilitary character await solution. These include the repatriation and resettlement of the Arab refugees, those tragic and innocent victims of the conflict of whom there are now estimated at some 900,000; the status of Jerusalem and the holy places; and the definition of permanent frontiers. The United Nations Palestine Conciliation Commission, now meeting at Lausanne with Arab and Jewish delegations, is engaged in assisting the parties to find amicable and just solutions for all of their outstanding differences. The settlement of these differences poses a strong challenge for both Arab and Jewish statesmanship. Their settlement will require important concessions from both sides.

The burden of finding agreement rests upon the parties themselves, but it has been abundantly demonstrated that the United Nations is the indispensable catalytic agent in the process. I am quite convinced that the Palestine experience has amply demonstrated that the United Nations has a vital role to play in world disputes as mediator and conciliator, quite apart from any enforcement action, and that it can play this role effectively. It has shown that by persistence and by firm resolve to maintain the peace the United Nations can assist the opposing parties, bitterly antagonistic though they may be, along the road to peaceful settlement of their differences, however serious, and thus avert a dangerous threat to the peace.

The processes of conciliation and mediation are slow and tedious, but they can pay handsome dividends. In the long run it may well be that they will provide the most firm procedural foundations for a peaceful world. It is very doubtful, in my view, that a peace founded upon force alone could long endure. In the final analysis, lasting peace must be founded upon consent freely given and agreement voluntarily achieved.

In Palestine, as in many other troubled areas of the world, the United Nations has been pursuing vigorously its vital role of insuring a world at peace, a secure world in which men will walk together as brothers. When men think and act as brothers, the world is big enough for all of us. It is only when, in their perversity, they govern their conduct by the law of the jungle that the world becomes too small.

The problems of the world are problems of the relations among its people. They are human problems, and therefore they should be and are susceptible to man's reason and conscience and elemental decency. I believe that the world has a rich supply of men and women of good will and vision, of peace-loving individuals, and that these men and women, working through the channels offered by the United Nations, can light the way to universal peace and justice in our time.

The United Nations' experience in Palestine is demonstrating cogently that although the United Nations is not a world government, that although lacking in enforcement machinery, its voice can be an instrument of tremendous influence and great good. This is a voice which must be forcefully and increasingly heard and heeded in all the troubled areas of the world. It is, perhaps, more difficult to wage peace than war. There is certainly no magic means of achieving peace once war has begun. Nor is there any easy way to give expression to the will of the overwhelming majority of the people throughout the world that peace shall reign. It is only by tireless, persevering, and courageous action of the United Nations that peace can be secured, whether in Palestine or elsewhere in the present-day world.

But it is not only on behalf of a world at peace that the voice of the United Nations is raised. That voice is also being increasingly heard and felt for a just world, a good world, a world fit to live in for all the people. A just world, in the eyes of the United Nations, and, I submit, in the eyes of all honest and fair-minded people, is a world in which racial and religious bigotries are universally outlawed, a world in which all peoples, irrespective of race or creed, are accepted as equals in a fraternal bond of human kinship; a world in which the right of a people to self-determination is unchallenged; a world in which discrimination, segregation, underprivilege, imperialism and colonialism will have become the unsavory relics of a dark age happily past. To insure peace in the world it is not enough to stop wars once they are started or are threatened. It is indispensable that secure foundations for peace be laid. The foundations for peace will be insecure and uneasy so long as hundreds of millions of non-self-governing peoples throughout the world are denied the elemental right to control their own destinies, to govern themselves, and a reasonable hope for the realization of their aspirations. The Charter of the United Nations has recognized this and holds forth the promise of a new day and a new way of life for the colonial peoples. That promise remains a long way from fulfillment.

The Charter also reinforces and gives new inspiration to the heroic struggles of racial and religious minorities as, for example, the Negroes and Jews of America, to free themselves of unjust disabilities which they suffer only because of race or creed.

There is much to be done in our world. But in a democracy what needs to be done can be done if the people are alert and determined. I have great faith in democracy because I have great faith in the basic goodness, in the conscience and instincts of mankind. I am convinced that the common people everywhere long for a world in which peace and justice shall reign. That kind of world is the world which the United Nations seeks to achieve. It is lighting the way that man may live in peace, happiness, and security. It is still a dim and flickering light, but it grows stronger and surer each day. Can there be any who doubt that better this light than the oppressive darkness of a modern dark age?

Better it is to make sacrifices and to strive mightily now for a world of peace and justice than later to fight an unwelcome war for mere survival only because we lacked both realism and vision.

Albert Einstein

Peace in the Atomic Era
(February 19, 1950)

In the late summer of 1939 Franklin D. Roosevelt received a letter prepared by scientist Leo Szilard and signed by the distinguished physicist Albert Einstein, bringing to the President's attention the possible military significance of atomic energy. It was ironic that Einstein, an admirer of Gandhi and personally inclined toward pacifism, should have been associated with the historic suggestion that initiated a series of events leading to the development and eventual use of atomic weapons. There is no doubt that, in the years following World War II, Einstein was alarmed by the destructive potential of atomic warfare and was to become an outspoken proponent of world peace.

Einstein achieved worldwide recognition in the scientific community with the publication of three papers in 1905, one of which dealt with the special theory of relativity that was to have a profound effect on modern physics. His challenge to Newtonian physics published in 1916 was confirmed by British scientists in 1919 and Einstein became an internationally known figure. For his work in theoretical physics he was awarded the Nobel Prize for 1921.

Einstein also asserted his political beliefs by joining an antiwar political party that was banned in Germany in 1916, by signing an appeal to the great powers to conclude a just peace, and by supporting the Zionist movement. His pacifist and internationalist sentiments, coupled with the fact that he was a Jew, made him an obvious enemy of the rising Nazi party in Germany. When Hitler came to power in 1933 Einstein was on a visiting appointment at Princeton's Institute for Advanced Study. He elected to stay in the United States and remained at the institute for the rest of his life. He became an American citizen in 1940.

Following the war, Einstein became increasingly concerned about the nuclear arms race and the growing potential for human destruction. The cold war, Einstein believed, had led to a "mechanistic, technical-military psychological attitude" that supported the belief that only through military strength could security be achieved. Instead, Einstein argued in 1950, "peaceful coexistence" and "loyal cooperation" among nations could be brought about only by renouncing violence and acting on the basis of "mutual trust." In the last years of his life, Einstein was to speak out against the Red scare of the 1950s, deploring the pressure put on intellectuals by congressional investigating committees; he also served as chairman of the Emergency Committee of Atomic Scientists formed to lobby for control of nuclear weapons. In the climate of the cold war years, such activities made him politically suspect and the target of an FBI investigation.

In the short speech that follows, given five years before his death in 1955, Einstein decried the arms race and warned against the growing political intimidation that he saw as a threat to "people of independent political thinking." The speech is a plea to turn from the path of "general annihilation" by putting an end to "mutual fear and distrust" that characterized, for Einstein, Soviet-American relations in the postwar years.

I am grateful to you for the opportunity to express my conviction in this most important political question.

The idea of achieving security through national armament is, at the present state of military technique, a disastrous illusion. On the part of the United States this illusion has been particularly fostered by the fact that this country succeeded first in producing an atomic bomb. The belief seemed to prevail that in the end it were possible to achieve decisive military superiority.

In this way, any potential opponent would be intimidated, and security, so ardently desired by all of us, brought to us and all of humanity. The maxim which we have been following during these last five years has been, in short: security through superior military power, whatever the cost.

This mechanistic, technical-military psychological attitude had inevitable consequences. Every single act in foreign policy is governed exclusively by one viewpoint.

How do we have to act in order to achieve utmost superiority over the opponent in case of war? Establishing military bases at all possible strategically important points on the globe. Arming and economic strengthening of potential allies.

Within the country—concentration of tremendous financial power in the hands of the military, militarization of the youth, close supervision of the loyalty of the citizens, in particular, of the civil servants by a police force growing more conspicuous every day. Intimidation of people of independent political thinking. Indoctrination of the public by radio, press, school. Growing restriction of the range of public information under the pressure of military secrecy.

The armament race between the U.S.A. and the U.S.S.R., originally supposed to be a preventive measure, assumes hysterical character. On both sides, the means to mass destruction are perfected with feverish haste—behind the respective walls of secrecy. The H-bomb appears on the public horizon as a probably attainable goal. Its accelerated development has been solemnly proclaimed by the President.

If successful, radioactive poisoning of the atmosphere and hence annihilation of any life on earth has been brought within the range of technical possibilities. The ghostlike character of this development lies in its apparently compulsory trend. Every step appears as the unavoidable consequence of the preceding one. In the end, there beckons more and more clearly general annihilation.

Is there any way out of this impasse created by man himself? All of us, and particularly those who are responsible for the attitude of the U.S. and the U.S.S.R., should realize that we may have vanquished an external enemy, but have been incapable of getting rid of the mentality created by the war.

It is impossible to achieve peace as long as every single action is taken with a possible future conflict in view. The leading point of view of all political action should therefore be: What can we do to bring about a peaceful co-existence and even loyal cooperation of the nations?

The first problem is to do away with mutual fear

and distrust. Solemn renunciation of violence (not only with respect to means of mass destruction) is undoubtedly necessary.

Such renunciation, however, can only be effective if at the same time a supra-national judicial and executive body is set up empowered to decide questions of immediate concern to the security of the nations. Even a declaration of the nations to collaborate loyally in the realization of such a "restricted world government" would considerably reduce the imminent danger of war.

In the last analysis, every kind of peaceful cooperation among men is primarily based on mutual trust and only secondly on institutions such as courts of justice and police. This holds for nations as well as for individuals. And the basis of trust is loyal give and take.

What about international control? Well, it may be of secondary use as a police measure. But it may be unwise to overestimate its importance. The times of prohibition come to mind and give one pause.

Eleanor Roosevelt

Address to the Americans for Democratic Action
(April 1, 1950)

Following the conclusion of World War II, as Soviet-American relations deteriorated into the cold war, the role of American Communists in domestic politics raised concerns all along the political spectrum. The Progressive Citizens of America, which included Communists in prominent roles, was endorsed by Franklin Roosevelt's former Vice President, Henry Wallace. Many liberals were fearful that the progressive policies of the New Deal would be discarded or destroyed in the postwar years and adamantly opposed Communist preemption of liberal issues.

In January of 1947 a group of intellectuals, labor leaders, and political figures—the columnist Drew Pearson called them the "New Deal in Exile"—gathered in Washington to form an organization to "formulate liberal domestic and foreign policies based on the realities and changing needs of American democracy." The group was explicitly anti-Communist, and no Communists were to have positions of leadership in the new organization. "The American Communists," Eleanor Roosevelt observed, "seem to have succeeded very well in jeopardizing whatever the liberals work for. Therefore, to keep them out of policy-making and staff positions seems to be very essential even at the price of being called red-baiters...."

Eleanor Roosevelt's support for the new organization, the Americans for Democratic Action, was critical to its success. The widow of the late President had become, in her own right, a formidable political figure, one around whom liberals could rally.

Eleanor Roosevelt had always taken an active role in her husband's political career; after the election of Franklin Roosevelt to the White House, Mrs. Roosevelt became the acknowledged advocate for liberal social policy among those close to the President. The President's close adviser Harry Hopkins observed, "She is forever finding someone underprivileged and unbefriended in whose behalf she takes up the cudgels....I never cease to admire her burning determination to see that justice is done, not only to individuals, but to underprivileged groups." She embraced a variety of causes—economic reform, education, minority rights—and argued her position forcefully, if not always successfully, to the President. As First Lady, she also created a public personality. She had her own radio program, and was so successful that WNBC dubbed her the "First Lady of Radio" in 1939. She wrote magazine articles and traveled back and forth across the country speaking and meeting with a variety of groups. During World War II her travels extended throughout the world from meeting with the Royal family in war-torn London to visiting wounded GIs in the South Pacific.

On April 12, 1945, Eleanor Roosevelt held a press conference in which she stressed the need for thinking in international terms in the future and supported the just-forming United Nations organization that would exist "for the very purpose of making it possible that all the world's opinion will have a clearing place." Later that same day, the President died suddenly at his Warm Springs, Georgia, retreat.

Mrs. Roosevelt believed that the United Nations was one of the great legacies of her husband's policy and, in December of 1945, accepted President Truman's strongly urged offer to join the American delegation for the first meeting of the United Nations Assembly in London. She was to serve as a delegate to the assembly until August of 1953. In 1946 she became a member of the Commission on Human Rights and was chosen to chair it. In this position, she was instrumental in drafting the Universal Declaration of Human Rights, a document she referred to as "a Magna Charta for mankind."

When Mrs. Roosevelt addressed the Americans for Democratic Action in April of 1950 she made clear her belief that domestic and international affairs were related. In the struggle to determine "whether democracy or communism wins out in the world," Mrs. Roosevelt argued that domestic problems such as unemployment and racial discrimination had to be addressed if America was to "prove to the world that democracy has more to offer than communism."

Her conviction of the superiority of democracy over communism, however, did not incline her toward accepting the growing fear of communism in America, a fear leading some politicians into virulent attacks on anyone suspected of having Communist connections and beginning to take on the characteristics of a hunt for Red witches. Her speech to the ADA vigorously defends "the right to think and to differ in the United States." When people were afraid to talk with others who might someday be exposed as Communists, when guilt by such association threatened the free exchange of ideas, "that," the former First Lady declared, "would be a bad day for democracy." Her plea for human rights in this speech is a plea for "the value of human personality and freedom" both at home and throughout the world.

Mr. Chairman, ladies and gentlemen,—It's a very inspiring thing these days to come to a meeting such as this and find so many people coming together to discuss and make plans for an organization devoted to obtaining in our country as good a government as we can have. This organization is made up of both Democrats and Republicans.

I was amused the other night to have a young boy at a meeting where we were discussing good government say, "Mrs. Roosevelt, you've talked about the liberals, but if you really have conservative convictions, what should you do?" I think the thing that makes one happy about ADA is that it really has convictions. And the people who belong, belong because they want to find a way to put those convictions to work. They recognize—everyone in this room at this meeting knows—

that our democracy is not perfect. But they also know that it's working to improve democracy. That is the important thing. Those who are satisfied—those who feel that there is nothing they can do—they are the people who will do harm to the Government and the citizenship in the United States.

We live in a time when every single one of us must realize that what actually is important in a democracy is that sense of individual responsibility. And there are certain things here in our country that I think we must watch very carefully. It is true, as has been said, that there is a sense of insecurity—I might almost say a sense of fear—among many people in this country of ours. With some people it's a fear of the possibility of war; with others it's a fear of what the new weapons of war may mean if we should come to war; with others it's a fear of what may happen to them personally if by chance they offend in any way. That is the fear that bothers me most—the fear of people who are afraid to be themselves, to hold convictions, to stand up for them—because that fear, I think, is the fear which can really hurt our democracy more than any other.

This is a time when it takes courage to live. It takes the kind of courage that it took in the earliest days of our history. I'm quite sure that George Washington and his men must have had moments when they wondered how on earth the United States was ever going to exist. And I'm sure that there have been other times in our history which have looked black indeed to the citizens of the country and its leaders. But at present we need all the courage that our forefathers had and perhaps a little more, because we have a job to do at home and a job to do in the world.

The job at home has to be done, and has to be done first. We have to be unafraid. And we have to realize that here is where we as individuals have to fulfill our belief in democracy. If we cannot prove here that we believe in freedom, in the ability of people to govern themselves, if we cannot have confidence in each other, if we cannot feel that fundamentally we are all trying to retain the best in our democracy and improve it, if we cannot find some basic unity even in peace, then we are never going to be able to lead the world. This is the problem that is before us today. If we do not lead the world, who is going to lead it? We have to accept the fact that it's what we do here that makes us fit to lead the world. So every day in our daily lives as citizens we are building our world leadership.

Our great struggle today is to prove to the world that democracy has more to offer than communism.

You can't just say that anyone who understands communism must be against it. You have to face the fact that this is a struggle, and a very great struggle. If we want to win the cold war, if we want to reach a greater security—I think it's going to take us a long time, and I think we have to develop a courage and a staunchness that perhaps we have never had. If we want to achieve it, then we must prove to the world what we can offer. That means we have to take certain definite steps. We have, for instance, to make sure that we have civil rights in this country. There was time when we could look on that question as a purely domestic one—that we could take all the time we wanted to educate ourselves to solve the problem. It isn't any longer a domestic question—it's an international question. It is perhaps the question which may decide whether democracy or communism wins out in the world.

I sit in the United Nations; have sat in the General Assembly since 1946, and I sit in the Human Rights Commission. Over and over again the failures of democracy are pointed out to me in terms of specific instances of things that have happened in our country. I don't try to say they didn't happen, because usually I know that they did. All I can say is that we know about them, and those of us who really care, work to improve our democracy. Therefore, we must actually look at ourselves with more critical eyes than we have in the past.

Where do we fail, and how hard do we try to live up to the things we've given lip service to? It's not a domestic question; it's a question that perhaps is one of the most important factors in the winning of the struggle. Of course, economic questions enter into this struggle, too. We cannot be complacent about unemployment in our country—about injustices. Not long ago I remember hearing in a certain city that the papers actually printed what certain rather well-paid officials would have as pensions in an industry, and yet when it came to the point of pensions to the workers, that was too heavy a burden for the industry. Well now, I'm not a Socialist. I'm a very practical capitalist, I'm sure. But if we want to keep capitalism, we in this country have got to learn that there must be a real sharing, a real understanding, between management and labor. They must plan together because their interests are really identical. But both sides must realize it.

Now, the answer to unemployment, I didn't get an answer when I asked some of our Democratic Senators the other day, "What is the answer to unemployment?" I doubt if many people know. I think it's one of the things that perhaps we need to experiment, and perhaps it may be tied up, too, with some of our decisions in the realm of foreign affairs. Perhaps backing the United Nations with our own four-point program, seeing what can be done through them, to work with other nations in the world, that may have some tie with unemployment. There may be other things that I know nothing about, but I never like to feel that we don't face problems and that we don't set people to work on finding the answers. There's no reason why we shouldn't say we don't know the answer now; there's every reason why we shouldn't say we're not trying to find out. It is essential, I think, to our winning this struggle that we actually find answers, because in this economic area communism has a program. And democracy has to have a better one. If it doesn't, we're being judged before the bar of the world, and we have to win. We have to win because we have a conviction that democracy does offer people something that no other form of government and no other way of life can offer.

There's one thing that always strikes me, and that is that the Communist representatives in the United Nations never talk about liberty; they never mention it. On one occasion when Mr. Vishinsky was forced to do so, he said that was a foolish thing to talk about because no one could have liberty. Well, you and I know quite well that everyone's liberty is conditioned by the rights of other people. But we must think about liberty, because that is really one of the basic reasons why we prefer democracy to communism. And somehow we must keep ourselves free from fear and suspicion of each other. I sit with people who are representatives of Communist countries, and to sit with them is a lesson in what fear can do. Fear can take away from you all the courage to be an individual. You become a mouthpiece for the ideas which you have been told you must give forth. I have no feeling of real antagonism toward these representatives because, poor things, they can do no other. They must do that; their lives depend on it.

Now, it seems to me that the ADA is an organization that has thinking people in it, and we must preserve the right to think and to differ in the United States. We must be able to disagree with people, and to consider new ideas, and not to be afraid. The day that I am afraid to sit down in a room with people that I do not know because perhaps 5 years from now, someone will say, "You sat in the room and five people were Communists, and so you are a Communist," that day will be a bad day for democracy. We must be sure enough of ourselves, of our own convictions, to sit down with anyone and not be afraid of listening to what they have to say, and not be afraid of contamination by association. It's true that the company you keep may say something about what you are. But to be able to meet with people and argue your own point of view, and to meet with people whom you do not have screened beforehand to be sure they are safe to meet with—that must be a part of the freedom of every citizen in the United States.

So I'm grateful that ADA prods us to think, that it has an opportunity to bring before us the ideas that seem important, that it also has the opportunity of backing people in elections who promise to be good public servants. I'm grateful that it is representative of people in both political parties, and I'm grateful for the numbers that have come today. I think it shows that we as a Nation are waking up to the need to preserve our basic ideals in our Republic, that we are waking up to the fact that we have to live those ideals, and that we have to improve our democracy by the way we live. To do that we must come together, and consult together, and get other people to help us where we need help. There must be no one who fights the battle of good government, of freedom of thought, of real democracy, with a sense of doing it alone. That is the value of ADA—you do not have to be alone.

I was speaking to a little group of college students the other day who had started an organization where they tried to live the ideals of democracy, and one of them said to me, "I graduate this year. What do I do when I go home?" And I said, "You find people who feel as you do." He said, "I don't know any, where I live." Now, that shouldn't happen to any young person, because they should be sure that if they were really trying to live their convictions they would find support in their community. That's why I stress that it is in our own communities that we must fight this struggle, not only the struggle against communism but the struggle for peace.

We will have on a world-wide scale, a human rights convention, probably before the General Assembly next autumn at the United Nations, and then before our Senate, a ratification. That's part of our struggle. If we don't ratify, who else will ratify in the world? And yet human rights are basic to establishing peace. A common understanding throughout the world of human rights—of the value of human personality and freedom—that understanding, spread throughout the world, is one of the cornerstones on which we must build for peace.

Douglas MacArthur

Address to Congress
(April 19, 1951)

Korea, formally annexed to Japan since 1910, was freed of Japanese dominance at the end of World War II. By an agreement between the two Allied powers, the United States accepted the surrender of Japanese forces in Korea below the 38th parallel while the Soviet Union occupied Korean territory north of the demarcation line. Even though the Allies had agreed to the establishment of a unified Korea and the Soviet Union had affirmed its pledge to help set up an independent Korea at the time the Russians declared war on Japan, efforts to bring about national elections failed. In an attempt to solve the Korean problem, the United States referred the issue to the UN, where the General Assembly called for national elections under UN supervision. When the USSR refused to cooperate, elections were held in the south only in May of 1948. In August, after the drafting of a constitution, the Republic of Korea was proclaimed with Syngman Rhee as president. The Communist provisional government in the north held its own elections and established the Democratic People's Republic of Korea.

By June of 1949, American troops in the south and Soviet soldiers in the north were withdrawn. Both Korean governments considered themselves the only legitimate rulers of Korea, and both desired reunification of the country under their control. The peace between them was uneasy, and skirmishes along the 38th parallel were frequent. Then, on June 25, 1950, North Korean forces launched a full-scale attack across the 38th parallel. With the South Korean forces dispersed, the better-armed and concentrated North Koreans moved quickly to capture Seoul, the South Korean capital.

While the North Koreans moved relentlessly south, the United Nations acted quickly. With the Soviets boycotting the Security Council, that body passed a resolution sponsored by the United States calling on member states to go to the aid of Korea. On the same day, June 27, President Truman authorized the use of American military forces. General of the Army Douglas MacArthur was quickly appointed to head the United Nations Command.

Initial attempts by the first American troops to halt the North Koreans failed, and by August the UN forces, principally the American Eighth Army, held only a small perimeter near the southern port city of Pusan. Then, in September, MacArthur carried off a brilliant military maneuver by landing troops at Inchon, near Seoul, and attacking the North Koreans from the rear as the Eighth Army launched a frontal assault. So successful was MacArthur that the North Koreans not only were driven from the south, but, by November, United Nations forces had overrun North Korea, advancing almost to the banks of the Yalu River that separated the Korean peninsula from China. At this point, contrary to the expectation that General MacArthur had expressed to President Truman, the Chinese intervened in force, pushing the American and South Korean units back to a position roughly equivalent to the 38th parallel. At this point there erupted the controversy that led to the recall of General MacArthur and his triumphal return to America amid ticker tape parades and an invitation to address a joint session of the Congress of the United States.

Douglas MacArthur had had a distinguished military and administrative career when he was called to command the UN forces in Korea. The son of a career officer, Arthur MacArthur, Douglas graduated first in his class from West Point, earned recognition as the organizer of the Rainbow Division in World War I, was wounded twice in that conflict, and returned home a much-decorated and respected officer. After the war, he served as superintendent of West Point and held many posts in the United States and the Philippines before becoming, in 1930, at age 50, the youngest man to be appointed chief of staff of the United States Army. After his term ended, MacArthur was posted to Manila as military adviser to the newly formed Commonwealth of the Philippines. Two years later he retired from the United States Army, but remained in the Philippines as military adviser with the rank of field marshal.

In July of 1941, with the European powers at war and American relations in the Pacific with the Japanese Empire deteriorating, MacArthur was recalled to active duty and placed in command of the U.S. Army forces in the Far East. In less than five months, Japan attacked the American naval forces in Pearl Harbor. On the same day, Japanese planes raided Clark Field in the Philippines and destroyed almost half of the bombers of the American Far East air force. A few weeks later Japanese forces landed north and south of Manila, forcing American and Philippine troops to retreat to the fortress of Corregidor. With the situation hopeless, President Roosevelt ordered MacArthur to leave for Australia, where he was to take command of Allied forces as supreme commander of the Southwest Pacific area. As he left the Philippines, MacArthur made his famous pledge, "I shall return." And, after a grueling campaign in the Pacific, MacArthur did return, landing at Leyte with the invasion force in 1944. Less than a year later, after atomic bombs had been dropped on Hiroshima and Nagasaki, the Japanese accepted Allied surrender terms, and General MacArthur, now supreme commander in Japan for the Allied powers, formally accepted the Japanese surrender aboard the battleship *Missouri* in Tokyo Bay.

MacArthur then set to the task of rebuilding the Japanese economy and transforming that country into a democratic state, a task that all agree he carried out with stunning success. By the time the Japanese peace treaty was signed in September of 1951, MacArthur had begun the process that ultimately restored Japan as a world power, firmly allied to the United States.

MacArthur was clearly a distinguished military strategist and a superb administrator;

yet, although he was a popular war hero, he never received the warm admiration that was accorded to his one-time aide, Dwight Eisenhower. MacArthur was fully aware of his own brilliance and seemed simply incapable of modesty; indeed, many deprecated his obvious efforts to remain in the spotlight and his inability to share the stage with his subordinates. MacArthur rarely doubted his abilities and his own judgment. In Korea his prediction that the Chinese would not intervene proved wrong, and his advice to send bombers across the Yalu River to bomb China itself alarmed President Truman and American allies. The threat of a world war precluded that strategy, but MacArthur was convinced of the rightness of his proposed course of action and openly contemptuous of some UN diplomats.

MacArthur, his advice rejected, violated the long tradition of military subordination to civilian control of policy by making the matter a public controversy and by airing his views in communications with Republican leaders of Congress. On April 11, 1951, Truman announced that, since MacArthur was "unable to give his wholehearted support to the policies of the United States," the President had decided to relieve the general of his duties.

Reactions to MacArthur's recall varied: many newspapers supported the President's decision while some called for his impeachment. Congressmen reacted in predictably partisan ways: Republicans were outraged while Democrats defended the chief executive. But there was no doubt about the immediate outpouring of public acclaim for the general. His return was triumphal. He was greeted upon his arrival in San Francisco by a cheering crowd of 500,000, and over seven million turned out for a ticker tape parade in New York City. Invited to address a joint session, MacArthur appeared before Congress on April 19, 1951, and presented his case for the direction of American policy in the Far East, and in Korea in particular, arguing that "in war there can be no substitute for victory." His emotional reference to "old soldiers" who "never die" but just "fade away" was considered by some to be a maudlin appeal to pity, while others were moved by this climactic moment of a long military career. Republican minority leader Joseph Martin thought MacArthur's speech "the great address of our time," while the speech appeared to journalist Richard Rovere to be a " weak" one that "never came to grips with the issues."

Mr. President, Mr. Speaker, and distinguished Members of the Congress,—I stand on this rostrum with a sense of deep humility and great pride—humility in the wake of those great American architects of our history who have stood here before me, pride in the reflection that this forum of legislative debate represents human liberty in the purest form yet devised. [*Applause.*] Here are centered the hopes, and aspirations, and faith of the entire human race.

I do not stand here as advocate for any partisan cause, for the issues are fundamental and reach quite beyond the realm of partisan consideration. They must be resolved on the highest plane of national interest if our course is to prove sound and our future protected. I trust, therefore, that you will do me the justice of re-

ceiving that which I have to say as solely expressing the considered viewpoint of a fellow American. I address you with neither rancor nor bitterness in the fading twilight of life with but one purpose in mind—to serve my country. [*Applause.*]

The issues are global and so interlocked that to consider the problems of one sector, oblivious to those of another, is but to court disaster for the whole.

While Asia is commonly referred to as the gateway to Europe, it is no less true that Europe is the gateway to Asia, and the broad influence of the one cannot fail to have its impact upon the other.

There are those who claim our strength is inadequate to protect on both fronts—that we cannot divide our effort. I can think of no greater expression of defeatism. [*Applause.*] If a potential enemy can divide his strength on two fronts, it is for us to counter his effort.

The Communist threat is a global one. Its successful advance in one sector threatens the destruction of every other sector. You cannot appease or otherwise surrender to communism in Asia without simultaneously undermining our efforts to halt its advance in Europe. [*Applause.*]

Beyond pointing out these general truisms, I shall confine my discussion to the general areas of Asia. Before one may objectively assess the situation now existing there, he must comprehend something of Asia's past and the revolutionary changes which have marked her course up to the present. Long exploited by the so-called colonial powers, with little opportunity to achieve any degree of social justice, individual dignity, or a higher standard of life such as guided our own noble administration of the Philippines, the peoples of Asia found their opportunity in the war just past to throw off the shackles of colonialism, and now see the dawn of new opportunity, a heretofore unfelt dignity and the self-respect of political freedom.

Mustering half of the earth's population and 60 percent of its natural resources, these peoples are rapidly consolidating a new force, both moral and material, with which to raise the living standard and erect adaptations of the design of modern progress to their own distinct cultural environments. Whether one adheres to the concept of colonization or not, this is the direction of Asian progress and it may not be stopped. It is a corollary to the shift of the world economic frontiers, as the whole epicenter of world affairs rotates back toward the area whence it started. In this situation it becomes vital that our own country orient its policies in consonance with this basic evolutionary condition rather than pursue a course blind to the reality that the colonial era is now past and the Asian peoples covet the right to shape their own free destiny. What they seek now is friendly guidance, understanding, and support, not imperious direction [*applause*]; the dignity of equality, not the shame of subjugation. Their prewar standard of life, pitifully low, is infinitely lower now in the devastation left in war's wake. World ideologies play little part in Asian thinking and are little understood. What the peoples strive for is the opportunity for a little more food in their stomachs, a little better clothing on their backs, a little firmer roof over their heads, and the realization of the normal nationalist urge for political freedom. These political-social conditions have but an indirect bearing upon our own national security, but do form a backdrop to contemporary planning which must be thoughtfully considered if we are to avoid the pitfalls of unrealism.

Of more direct and immediate bearing upon our national security are the changes wrought in the strategic potential of the Pacific Ocean in the course of the past war. Prior thereto, the western strategic frontier of the United States lay on the littoral line of the Americas with an exposed island salient extending out through Hawaii, Midway, and Guam to the Philippines. That salient proved not an outpost of strength but an avenue of weakness along which the enemy could and did attack. The Pacific was a potential area of advance for any predatory force intent upon striking at the bordering land areas.

All this was changed by our Pacific victory. Our strategic frontier then shifted to embrace the entire Pacific Ocean which became a vast moat to protect us as long as we hold it. Indeed, it acts as a protective shield for all of the Americas and all free lands of the Pacific Ocean area. We control it to the shores of Asia by a chain of islands extending in an arc from the Aleutians to the Mariannas held by us and our free allies.

From this island chain we can dominate with sea and air power every Asiatic port from Vladivostok to Singapore and prevent any hostile movement into the Pacific. Any predatory attack from Asia must be an amphibious effort. No amphibious force can be successful without control of the sea lanes and the air over those lanes in its avenue of advance. With naval and air supremacy and modest ground elements to defend bases, any major attack from continental Asia toward us or our friends of the Pacific would be doomed to failure. Under such conditions the Pacific no longer represents menacing avenues of approach for a prospective invader—it assumes instead the friendly aspect of a peaceful lake. Our line of defense is a natural one and can be maintained with a minimum of military effort and expense. It envisions no attack against anyone nor does it provide the bastions essential for offensive operations, but properly maintained would be an invincible defense against aggression.

The holding of this littoral defense line in the western Pacific is entirely dependent upon holding all segments thereof, for any major breach of that line by an unfriendly power would render vulnerable to determined attack every other major segment. This is a military estimate as to which I have yet to find a military leader who will take exception. [*Applause.*]

For that reason I have strongly recommended in

the past as a matter of military urgency that under no circumstances must Formosa fall under Communist control. [*Applause.*] Such an eventuality would at once threaten the freedom of the Philippines and the loss of Japan, and might well force our western frontier back to the coasts of California, Oregon, and Washington.

To understand the changes which now appear upon the Chinese mainland, one must understand the changes in Chinese character and culture over the past 50 years. China up to 50 years ago was completely non-homogeneous, being compartmented into groups divided against each other. The war-making tendency was almost nonexistent, as they still followed the tenets of the Confucian ideal of pacifist culture. At the turn of the century, under the regime of Chan So Lin, efforts toward greater homogeneity produced the start of a nationalist urge. This was further and more successfully developed under the leadership of Chiang Kai-shek, but has been brought to its greatest fruition under the present regime, to the point that it has now taken on the character of a united nationalism of increasingly dominant aggressive tendencies. Through these past 50 years, the Chinese people have thus become militarized in their concepts and in their ideals. They now constitute excellent soldiers with competent staffs and commanders. This has produced a new and dominant power in Asia which for its own purposes is allied with Soviet Russia, but which in its own concepts and methods has become aggressively imperialistic with a lust for expansion and increased power normal to this type of imperialism. There is little of the ideological concept either one way or another in the Chinese make-up. The standard of living is so low and the capital accumulation has been so thoroughly dissipated by war that the masses are desperate and avid to follow any leadership which seems to promise the alleviation of local stringencies. I have from the beginning believed that the Chinese Communists' support of the North Koreans was the dominant one. Their interests are at present parallel to those of the Soviet, but I believe that the aggressiveness recently displayed not only in Korea, but also in Indochina and Tibet and pointing potentially toward the south, reflects predominantly the same lust for the expansion of power which has animated every would-be conqueror since the beginning of time. [*Applause.*]

The Japanese people since the war have undergone the greatest reformation recorded in modern history. With a commendable will, eagerness to learn, and marked capacity to understand, they have, from the ashes left in war's wake, erected in Japan an edifice dedicated to the primacy of individual liberty and personal dignity, and in the ensuing process there has been created a truly representative government committed to the advance of political morality, freedom of economic enterprise and social justice. [*Applause.*] Politically, economically and socially Japan is now abreast of many free nations of the earth and will not again fail the universal trust. That it may be counted upon to wield a profoundly beneficial influence over the course of events in Asia is attested by the magnificent manner in which the Japanese people have met the recent challenge of war, unrest, and confusion surrounding them from the outside, and checked communism within their own frontiers without the slightest slackening in their forward progress. I sent all four of our occupation divisions to the Korean battle front without the slightest qualms as to the effect of the resulting power vacuum upon Japan. The results fully justified my faith. [*Applause.*] I know of no nation more serene, orderly, and industrious—nor in which higher hopes can be entertained for future constructive service in the advance of the human race. [*Applause.*]

Of our former wards, the Philippines, we can look forward in confidence that the existing unrest will be corrected and a strong and healthy nation will grow in the longer aftermath of war's terrible destructiveness. We must be patient and understanding and never fail them, as in our hour of need they did not fail us. [*Applause.*] A Christian nation, the Philippines stand as a mighty bulwark of Christianity in the Far East, and its capacity for high moral leadership in Asia is unlimited.

On Formosa, the Government of the Republic of China has had the opportunity to refute by action much of the malicious gossip which so undermined the strength of its leadership on the Chinese mainland. [*Applause.*] The Formosan people are receiving a just and enlightened administration with majority representation on the organs of government; and politically, economically and socially they appear to be advancing along sound and constructive lines.

With this brief insight into the surrounding areas I now turn to the Korean conflict. While I was not consulted prior to the President's decision to intervene in support of the Republic of Korea, that decision, from a military standpoint, proved a sound one [applause] as we hurled back the invaders and decimated his forces. Our victory was complete and our objectives within reach when Red China intervened with numerically superior ground forces. This created a new war and an entirely new situation—a situation not contemplated when our forces were committed against the North Korean invaders—a situation which called for new decisions in the diplomatic sphere to permit the realistic adjustment of military strategy. Such decisions have not been forthcoming. *[Applause.]*

While no man in his right mind would advocate sending our ground forces into continental China and such was never given a thought, the new situation did urgently demand a drastic revision of strategic planning if our political aim was to defeat this new enemy as we had defeated the old. *[Applause.]*

Apart from the military need as I saw it to neutralize the sanctuary protection given the enemy north of the Yalu, I felt that military necessity in the conduct of the war made mandatory:

1   The intensification of our economic blockade against China;

2   The imposition of a naval blockade against the China coast;

3   Removal of restrictions on air reconnaissance of China's coast areas and of Manchuria [applause];

4   Removal of restrictions on the forces of the Republic of China on Formosa with logistical support to contribute to their effective operations against the common enemy. *[Applause.]*

For entertaining these views, all professionally designed to support our forces committed to Korea and bring hostilities to an end with the least possible delay and at a saving of countless American and Allied lives, I have been severely criticized in lay circles, principally abroad, despite my understanding that from a military standpoint the above views have been fully shared in the past by practically every military leader concerned with the Korean campaign, including our own Joint Chiefs of Staff. *[Applause, the Members rising.]*

I called for reinforcements, but was informed that reinforcements were not available. I made clear that if not permitted to destroy the build-up bases north of the Yalu; if not permitted to utilize the friendly Chinese force of some 600,000 men on Formosa; if not permitted to blockade the China coast to prevent the Chinese Reds from getting succor from without; and if there were to be no hope of major reinforcements, the position of the command from the military standpoint forbade victory. We could hold in Korea by constant maneuver and at an approximate area where our supply line advantages were in balance with the supply line disadvantages of the enemy, but we could hope at best for only an indecisive campaign, with its terrible and constant attrition upon our forces if the enemy utilized his full military potential. I have constantly called for the new political decisions essential to a solution. Efforts have been made to distort my position. It has been said, in effect, that I am a warmonger. Nothing could be further from the truth. I know war as few other men now living know it, and nothing to me is more revolting. I have long advocated its complete abolition as its very destructiveness on both friend and foe has rendered it useless as a means of settling international disputes. Indeed, on the 2d of September 1945, just following the surrender of the Japanese Nation on the battleship *Missouri*, I formally cautioned as follows:

> Men since the beginning of time have sought peace. Various methods through the ages have been attempted to devise an international process to prevent or settle disputes between nations. From the very start, workable methods were found insofar as individual citizens were concerned, but the mechanics of an instrumentality of larger international scope have never been successful. Military alliances, balances of power, leagues of nations, all in turn failed, leaving the only path to be by way of the crucible of war. The utter destructiveness of war now blots out this alternative. We have had our last chance. If we will not devise some greater and more equitable system, Armageddon will be at our door. The problem basically is theological and involves a spiritual recrudescence and improvement of human character that will synchronize with our almost matchless advances in science, art, literature, and all material and cultural developments of the past 2,000 years. It must be of the spirit if we are to save the flesh. *[Applause.]*

But once war is forced upon us, there is no other alternative than to apply every available means to bring it to a swift end. War's very object is victory—not prolonged indecision. *[Applause.]* In war, indeed, there can be no substitute for victory. *[Applause.]*

There are some who for varying reasons would appease Red China. They are blind to history's clear lesson. For history teaches with unmistakable emphasis that appeasement but begets new and bloodier war. It points to no single instance where the end has justified that means—where appeasement has led to more than a sham peace. Like blackmail, it lays the basis for new and successively greater demands, until, as in blackmail, violence becomes the only other alternative. Why, my soldiers asked of me, surrender military advantages to an enemy in the field? I could not answer. [*Applause.*] Some may say to avoid spread of the conflict into an all-out war with China; others, to avoid Soviet intervention. Neither explanation seems valid. For China is already engaging with the maximum power it can commit and the Soviet will not necessarily mesh its actions with our moves. Like a cobra, any new enemy will more likely strike whenever it feels that the relativity in military or other potential is in its favor on a world-wide basis.

The tragedy of Korea is further heightened by the fact that as military action is confined to its territorial limits, it condemns that nation, which it is our purpose to save, to suffer the devastating impact of full naval and air bombardment, while the enemy's sanctuaries are fully protected from such attack and devastation. Of the nations of the world, Korea alone, up to now, is the sole one which has risked its all against communism. The magnificence of the courage and fortitude of the Korean people defies description. [*Applause.*] They have chosen to risk death rather than slavery. Their last words to me were "Don't scuttle the Pacific." [*Applause.*]

I have just left your fighting sons in Korea. They have met all tests there and I can report to you without reservation they are splendid in every way. [*Applause.*] It was my constant effort to preserve them and end this savage conflict honorably and with the least loss of time and a minimum sacrifice of life. Its growing bloodshed has caused me the deepest anguish and anxiety. Those gallant men will remain often in my thoughts and in my prayers always. [*Applause.*]

I am closing my 52 years of military service. [*Applause.*] When I joined the Army even before the turn of the century, it was the fulfillment of all my boyish hopes and dreams. The world has turned over many times since I took the oath on the plain at West Point, and the hopes and dreams have long since vanished. But I still remember the refrain of one of the most popular barrack ballads of that day which proclaimed most proudly that—

"Old soldiers never die; they just fade away."

And like the old soldier of that ballad, I now close my military career and just fade away—an old soldier who tried to do his duty as God gave him the light to see that duty.

Good-by.

Adlai E. Stevenson

WELCOMING SPEECH TO THE DEMOCRATIC NATIONAL CONVENTION
(July 16, 1952)

ACCEPTANCE OF THE DEMOCRATIC NOMINATION FOR PRESIDENT
(July 21, 1952)

In 1948, in an election whose results surprised virtually everyone, Harry S Truman defeated his Republican opponent, Gov. Thomas Dewey of New York. Truman, who had succeeded to the office on the death of Franklin Roosevelt in 1945, became President in his own right. The next few years, however, were difficult ones for the President and for the Democratic party he led. The fall of mainland China to the Communists, the war in Korea, and the controversial recall of General MacArthur fueled attacks on the Democratic party as "soft" on communism and encouraged the growing anticommunism of the far right, who began to see the treacherous machinations of internal subversives behind every foreign policy setback.

At home, Truman's administration was plagued with charges of corruption, and the President finally fired Attorney General McGrath for his inefficiency in investigating these charges. Labor difficulties also beset the President. Truman was firmly committed to checking inflation and, in the case of the steel industry, believed that both labor and management were being unreasonable. He placed the steel mills under federal control, but was forced by the Supreme Court's *Youngstown v. Sawyer* decision to return the mills to the owners' control. By late in 1951, public opinion polls were reporting the President's approval rate at only 23 percent, lower than any President's rating had, or has since, ever sunk. Few were surprised when Harry Truman announced that he would not seek re-election in 1952.

In 1948, when Democratic Presidential candidate Truman carried Illinois by 33,612 votes, that state elected Adlai Stevenson as its Democratic governor with a plurality of 572,067 votes. This led Arthur Krock to observe in his column in the *New York Times* that "after such a triumph in the vital state of Illinois, Mr. Stevenson is being surveyed as a possible Presidential candidate of the Democrats in 1952." Stevenson, the grandson of a Vice President of the United States, came from a wealthy and politically aware Illinois family. After earning a B.A. from Princeton and a law degree from Northwestern, Adlai began his career in government, working for various New Deal agencies in the 1930's. His major interest, however, was in foreign affairs. He took an active part in battling isolationism before World War II, served as assistant secretary of the navy during the war, and, when transferred to the State Department in 1945, was a participant in the conferences that led to the establishment of the United Nations; in 1946 and 1947 he served as a UN delegate.

The new governor concentrated on his role in Illinois and discouraged efforts to promote him as a Presidential candidate. He irritated President Truman, who urged him to make the race, by his obvious reluctance to become a candidate. Stevenson did not believe that he should run in 1952. He preferred to attempt re-election to the governorship and keep his options open for 1956. In private, he confided that it might be time for a change in the White House, dominated for twenty years by the Democrats, and did not believe that Eisenhower, with his internationalist outlook, would be a bad President.

Right up to the convention in July of 1952, Stevenson remained unwilling to seek the nomination. Democratic leaders, however, saw him as a proven vote-getter who could appeal to the liberal centers of Democratic power in the North and who was also acceptable to the Southern wing of the party. Few other Democrats had widespread party support, and Stevenson was drafted by the convention, a much talked about but actually very rare political occurrence.

As governor of Illinois, Stevenson was slated to make the usually ritualistic and generally unmemorable address of welcome to the delegates gathered in Chicago. One of the most articulate and eloquent speakers of the twentieth century, Stevenson gave a speech of welcome that singularly impressed the delegates and virtually locked up the nomination. His fourteen-minute speech had delegates on their feet, constantly interrupting with applause and chanting, "We want Stevenson." The governor's stirring account of "the American story written by the Democratic party here on the prairies of Illinois" carried the message that "*who* leads us is less important than *what* leads us—what convictions, what courage, what faith—win or lose. A man does not save a century, or a civilization, but a militant party wedded to a principle can."

Four days later, Adlai Stevenson was nominated by his party to run for President of the United States. Given the difficulties of the Truman administration and the fact that the Republicans had just nominated an enormously popular war hero, Dwight Eisenhower, Stevenson knew that the campaign would be a hard one. He also knew that the real issues were complex and would not simply yield to political slogans. "The ordeal of the twentieth century," Stevenson proclaimed, "is far from over." He implored his fellow Democrats to "talk sense to the American people." Stevenson urged them to tell the American people the truth "that there are no gains without pains, that we are now on the eve of great decisions, not easy decisions, like resistance when you are attacked, but a long, patient, costly struggle which alone can assure triumph over the great enemies of man—war, poverty and tyranny—and the assaults upon human dignity which are the most grievous consequences of each."

Adlai Stevenson was soundly defeated by Dwight Eisenhower in the election of 1952 and again by Eisenhower in 1956. The 1960 Democratic convention denied Stevenson a third try and nominated instead John Kennedy, who subsequently appointed Stevenson ambassador to the United Nations. Stevenson had brought to politics a strong sense of moral conviction and a deep, if not always popularly appreciated, understanding of the intricacies of the political affairs. But, as his campaign manager sadly observed, "what earned him admiration often did not gather him support." Recognized as one of the great minds and most eloquent speakers of contemporary American politics, Adlai Stevenson's candor and astuteness contributed much to the continuing modern American dialogue.

Adlai E. Stevenson

Welcoming Speech to the Democratic National Convention (July 16, 1952)

Mr. Chairman, Delegates and Guests of the Convention:—I thought I came here to greet you, not you to greet me. I am grateful for your courtesy, but I have an assignment here this morning as Governor of the host state to welcome the 1952 Democratic convention. And, in the name of 9,000,000 people of Illinois, I extend to you the heartiest of greetings.

Chicago and Illinois are proud that once again the party conventions by which we restate our principles and choose our candidates for the greatest temporal office on earth are held here at Chicago at the crossroads of the continent.

Here, my friends, on the prairies of Illinois and of the Middle West we can see a long way in all directions. We look to East, to West, to North and South. Our commerce, our ideas, come and go in all directions.

Here there are no barriers, no defenses, to ideas and to aspirations. We want none; we want no shackles on the mind or the spirit, no rigid patterns of thought, and no iron conformity. We want only the faith and the conviction that triumph in free and fair contest.

As a Democrat perhaps you will permit me to remind you that until four years ago the people of Illinois had chosen but three Democratic Governors in a hundred years. One was John Peter Altgeld, whom the great Illinois poet, Vachel Lindsay, called the Eagle Forgotten. He was an immigrant. One was Edward F. Dunne, whose parents came from the old sod of Ireland, and the last was Henry Horner, but one generation removed from Germany. John Peter Altgeld, my friends, was a Protestant, Governor Dunne was a Catholic, Henry Horner was a Jew.

And that, my friends, is the American story, written by the Democratic party here on the prairies of Illinois.

You are very welcome here in the heartland of the nation. Indeed, we think that you were wise to come here for your deliberations in this fateful year of grace. For it was in Chicago that the modern Democratic story began. It was here just twenty years ago this month in the depths of shattering national misery at the end of a dizzy decade of Republican rule that you commenced the greatest era of economic and social progress in our history.

It was here, my friends, in Chicago just twenty years ago this month that you nominated Franklin Roosevelt; twenty years during which we have fought total depression to victory and have never been more prosperous; twenty years during which we have fought total war to victory, both East and West, and have launched the United Nations—history's most ambitious experiment in international security; twenty years, my friends, that close now in the grim contest with the Communist conspiracy on every continent.

But our Republican friends have said that it was all a miserable failure. For almost a week pompous phrases marched over this landscape in search of an idea, and the only idea they found was that the two great decades of progress in peace, and of victory in war, and of bold leadership in this anxious hour, were the misbegotten spawn of bungling, of corruption, of socialism, of mismanagement, of waste and of worse. They captured, they tied and they dragged that ragged idea here into this hall and they furiously beat it to death for a solid week.

After listening to this everlasting procession of epithets about our misdeeds I was even surprised the next morning when the mail was delivered on time. I guess our Republican friends were out of patience, out of sorts, and need I add, out of office.

But we Democrats were by no means the only victims here. First, they slaughtered each other and then they went after us. And the same vocabulary was good for both exercises. Perhaps the proximity of the stockyards accounts for the carnage.

My friends, the constructive spirit of the two great Democratic decades must not die here on its twentieth anniversary; they must not die here in destructive indignity and disorder. And I hope and pray, as you all do, that we can conduct our deliberations with a businesslike precision and a dignity befitting our responsibility and the solemnity of the hour in history in which we meet.

For it is a very solemn hour indeed, freighted with the hopes and the fears of millions of mankind who seek in us, the Democratic party, sober understanding of the breadth and depth of the revolutionary currents in the world. Here and abroad they see in us awareness that there is no turning back, and that, as Justice Holmes said, "We must sail sometimes with the wind, sometimes against it; but we must sail and not drift or lie at anchor." They see in us, the Democratic party that has steered this country through a storm of spears for twenty years, an understanding of a world in the torment of transition from an age that has died in an age of struggling to be born. They see in us relentless determination to stand fast against the barbarian at the gate, to cultivate allies with a decent respect for the opinion of others, to patiently explore every misty path to peace and security which is the only certainty of lower taxes and a better life.

This is not the time for superficial solutions and for endless elocution, this is not the time for frantic boasts and foolish words. For words are not deeds and there are no cheap and painless solutions to war, to hunger, to ignorance, to fear and to the new imperialism of the Soviet Union. My friends, you know full well that intemperate criticism is not a policy for the nation; and denunciation is not a program for our salvation. Words that are calculated to catch everyone may catch no one. And I hope that we can profit from their mistakes not just for our partisan benefit but for the benefit of all of us, Republicans and Democrats alike.

Where we have erred, let there be no denial, and where we have wronged the public trust, let there be no excuses. Self-criticism is the secret weapon of democracy, and candor and confession are good for the political soul. But we will never appease, we will never apologize for our leadership of the great events of this critical century all the way from Woodrow Wilson to Harry Truman.

We glory rather in these imperishable pages of our country's chronicle. But a great record of past achievement is not good enough. There can be no complacency perhaps for years to come. We dare not just look back to great yesterdays. We must look forward to great tomorrows.

What counts now is not just what we are against, but what we are for. And who leads us is less important than what leads us—what convictions, what courage, what faith—win or lose. A man does not save a century or a civilization, but a militant party wedded to a principle can.

So I hope that our preoccupation here is not just with personalities but with objectives. And I hope that the spirit of this convention is a confident reaffirmation that the United States is strong, resolved, resourceful and rich; that we know our duty and the destiny of this Heaven-rescued land; that we can and we will pursue a strong, consistent, honorable policy abroad, and meanwhile preserve the free institutions of life and of commerce at home.

What America needs and what the world wants is not bombast, abuse and double talk, but a sober message of firm faith and of confidence. St. Francis said: "Where there is patience and humility there is neither anger nor worry." And that might well be our text.

And let us remember that we are not meeting here

alone. All the world is watching and listening to what we say, what we do and how we behave. So let us give them a demonstration of democracy in action at its best—our manners good, our proceedings orderly and dignified—and, above all, let us make our decisions openly, fairly, not by the processes of synthetic excite-ment or mass hysteria. Let us make them as these solemn times demand, by earnest thought and by prayerful consideration.

And thus can the people's party reassure the people and vindicate and strengthen the forces of democracy throughout the world. Thank you.

Adlai E. Stevenson

Acceptance of the Democratic Nomination for President (July 21, 1952)

First let me say how much I regret the inconvenience that all of you news men have suffered. I'm sorry that you've had to maintain your vigil here for several days.

I'm deeply moved by what has taken place tonight and I have never been more conscious of the appalling responsibilities of the office. I did not seek it. I did not want it.

I am, however, persuaded that to shirk it, to evade, to decline, would be to repay honor with dishonor.

I shall go now to the convention hall and accept the nomination of the Democratic party.

My party reached its decision openly and fairly. It has asked of me nothing except that I give such poor talents as I have to the service of my country. That I will do and gladly on behalf of the millions for whom my party speaks; and I hope on behalf of millions more. I feel no exultation and no sense of triumph whatever; nothing but humbleness and humility.

And like all of us in need, I shall ask my God to nourish my spirit and to give me the strength and the courage for this great undertaking in the great hour of history.

Thank you.

FORMAL ACCEPTANCE

I accept your nomination—and your program.

I should have preferred to hear those words uttered by a stronger, wiser, better man than myself.

None of you can wholly appreciate what is in my heart. I can only hope that you may understand my words. They will be few.

I have not sought the honor you have done me. I would not seek it because I aspired to another office, which was the full measure of my ambition. One does not treat the highest office within the gift of the people of Illinois as an alternative or a consolation prize.

I would not seek your nomination for the Presidency because the burdens of that office stagger the imagination. Its potential for good or evil now and in the years of our lives smothers exultation and converts vanity to prayer.

I have asked the merciful Father of us all to let this cup pass from me. But from such dread responsibility one does not shrink in fear, in self-interest, or in false humility.

So, "If this cup may not pass away from me, except I drink it, Thy will be done."

That my heart has been troubled, that I have not sought this nomination, that I could not seek it in good conscience, that I would not seek it in honest self-appraisal, it is not to say that I value it the less. Rather it is that I revere the office of President of the United States.

NO DOUBT OF VICTORY

And now that you have made your decision I will fight to win that office with all my heart and soul. With your help, I have no doubt that we will win.

You have summoned me to the highest mission within the gift of any people. I could not be more proud. Better men than I were at hand for this mighty task, and I owe to you and to them every resource of mind and strength that I possess to make your deed of today a good one for our country and our party. I am confident, too, that your selection of a candidate for Vice President will strengthen me and our party immeasurably in the hard, implacable work that lies ahead for all of us.

I know you join with me in gratitude and respect for the great Democrats and leaders of our generation whose names you have considered here in this convention, whose vigor, character and devotion to the Republic have won the respect of countless Americans and enriched our party.

I shall need them, we shall need them, because I have not changed in any respect since yesterday. Your nomination, awesome as I find it, has not enlarged my own capacities. So I shall be profoundly grateful and emboldened by their comradeship and fealty.

Let me say, too, that I have been heartened by the conduct of this convention. You have argued and disagreed because as Democrats you care and care deeply. But you have disagreed and argued without calling each other liars and thieves, without despoiling our best traditions in naked, shameless struggles for power.

And you have written a platform that neither equivocates, contradicts nor evades.

You have restated our party's record, its principles and its purposes, in language that none can mistake, and with a firm confidence in justice, freedom and peace on earth that will raise the hearts and hopes of mankind for the day when no one rattles a saber and no one drags a chain.

TROUBLES ALL AHEAD

For all these things, for unity, vigor and vision, I am grateful to you. But I feel no exultation, no sense of triumph. Our troubles are all ahead of us.

Some will call us appeasers; others will say we are the war party.

Some will say we are reactionary.

Others will say we stand for socialism.

There will be the inevitable cries of "throw the rascals out"; "it's time for a change"; and so on and on.

We'll hear all those things and many more besides. But we will hear nothing that we have not heard before. I am not too much concerned with partisan denunciation, epithets and abuse, because the working man, the farmer, the thoughtful business man, all know that they are better off than ever before and that the greatest danger to free enterprise in this country died with the great depression under Democratic blows.

Nor am I afraid that the two-party system is in danger. Certainly the Republican party looked brutally alive here a couple of weeks ago, and I mean both Republican parties! Nor am I afraid that the Democratic party is old and fat and indolent.

After 150 years it has been old for a long time; and it will never be indolent as long as it looks forward and not back, as long as it commands the allegiance of the young and hopeful who dream the dreams and see the visions of a better America and a better world.

NO CHANGE FOR OWN SAKE

You will hear many sincere and thoughtful people express concern about the continuation of one party in power for twenty years. I do not belittle this attitude. But change for the sake of change has no merit.

If our greatest hazard is preservation of the values of Western civilization, in our self-interest alone, if you please, is it the part of wisdom to change for the sake of change to a party with a split personality; to a leader, whom we all respect, but who has been called upon to minister to a hopeless case of political schizophrenia?

If the fear is corruption in official position, do you believe with Charles Evans Hughes that guilt is personal and knows no party? Do you doubt the power of any political leader, if he has the will to do so, to set his own house in order without his neighbors' burning it down?

What does concern me, in common with thinking partisans of both parties, is not just winning the election, but how it is won, how well we can take advantage of this great quadrennial opportunity to debate issues sensibly and soberly. I hope and pray that we Democrats, win or lose, can campaign not as a crusade to exterminate the opposing party, as our opponents seem to prefer, but as a great opportunity to educate and elevate a people whose destiny is leadership, not alone of a rich, prosperous, contented country as in the past, but of a world in ferment.

And more important than winning the election is governing the nation. That is the test of a political party—the acid, final test. When the tumult and the shouting die, when the bands are gone and the lights are dimmed, there is the stark reality of responsibility in an hour of history haunted with those gaunt, grim specters of strife, dissension and materialism at home, and ruthless, inscrutable and hostile power abroad.

The ordeal of the twentieth century—the bloodiest, most turbulent age of the Christian era—is far from over. Sacrifice, patience, understanding and implacable purpose may be our lot for years to come.

Let's face it. Let's talk sense to the American people. Let's tell them the truth, that there are no gains without pains, that this is the eve of great decisions, not easy decisions, like resistance when you're attacked, but a long, patient, costly struggle which alone can assure triumph over the great enemies of men—war and poverty and tyranny—and the assaults upon human dignity which are the most grievous consequences of each.

Let's tell them that the victory to be won in the twentieth century, this portal to the golden age of man, mocks the pretensions of individual acumen and ingenuity. For it is a citadel guarded by thick walls of ignorance and mistrust which do not fall before the trumpets' blast or the politicians' imprecations. They must be directly stormed by the hosts of courage, morality and wisdom, standing shoulder to shoulder, unafraid of ugly truth, contemptuous of lies, half truths, circuses and demagoguery.

THE PARTY OF EVERYONE

The people are wise—wiser than the Republicans think. And the Democratic party is the people's party, not the labor party, not the farmers' party, not the employers' party—it is the party of no one because it is the party of everyone.

That is our ancient mission. Where we have deserted it we have failed. With your help there will be no desertion now. Better we lose the election than mislead the people; better we lose than misgovern the people.

Help us to do the job in this autumn of campaign and conflict; help me to do the job in these years of darkness, doubt and crisis that stretch beyond the horizon of tonight's happy vision, and we will justify our glorious past and the loyalty of silent millions who look to us for compassion, understanding and honest purpose. Thus we will serve our great tradition greatly.

I ask of you all you have; I will give to you all I have, even as he who came here tonight and honored me, as he has honored you—the Democratic party—by a lifetime of service and bravery that will find him an imperishable page in the history of the republic and of the Democratic party—President Harry S. Truman.

And finally, in the staggering task you have assigned me, I shall always try "to do justly and to love mercy and to walk humbly with my God."

Richard M. Nixon

The "Checkers" Speech
(September 23, 1952)

General Dwight Eisenhower, nominated by the Republicans in the summer of 1952, chose as his running mate the young senator from California, Richard M. Nixon. Returning from active service in the navy at the end of World War II, Richard Nixon was elected to Congress in 1946. Once in the House of Representatives, the young congressman earned a national reputation: as a member of the House Un-American Activities Committee, he led the attack on State Department employee Alger Hiss, exposing Hiss's Communist ties. In 1950, the 37-year-old Nixon gained national attention in the California senatorial campaign in which he savaged the liberal Democratic candidate, Helen Gahagan Douglas, for her left-wing political views. By the time he was chosen as the Vice Presidential candidate in 1952, Senator Nixon had established his credentials as a tough campaigner and a strident anti-Communist. Since Nixon's links with the conservative wing of the Republican party were strongly forged, his nomination was seen as a way of unifying the party after the bruising battle between the liberal Eisenhower and conservative Taft wings at the convention.

With a popular war hero at their head, with examples of corruption in government well publicized, with the Korean War dragging on, and with the fears of Communist subversion roused almost to hysteria by Sen. Joe McCarthy and his ilk, the Republicans looked forward to a triumphant campaign; certainly it proved to be a bitter one. Nixon waded into the campaign with characteristic venom, calling the Democratic nominee "Adlai the appeaser," while Senator McCarthy denounced the long period of Democratic control as "twenty years of treason." The Vice Presidential candidate charged that Stevenson had been elected governor of Illinois through the auspices of a political organization backed by "mobsters, gangsters, and the remnants of the Capone gang." If anyone suggested that Nixon had become a hatchet man carrying out a smear campaign, the candidate had an answer: "If the record itself smears, let it smear," he told a Maine audience early in September. "If the dry rot of corruption and communism which has eaten deep into our body politic during the past seven years, can only be chopped out with a hatchet—then let's call for a hatchet." Republican campaigners generally, hitting hard at Democratic scandals, hammered away at "the mess in Washington" and spoke derisively of the "Mink Dynasty."

With the campaign in high gear, on September 18, 1952, the *New York Post* reported that there were allegations that Senator Nixon had a "secret fund," collected by a group of California millionaires, from which Nixon had paid personal and campaign expenses. In fact, the $18,000 fund was not exceptional; other politicians had set up similar funds in the past, nor had Nixon used the fund for personal gain. But, given the tenor of the Republican campaign, its disclosure was embarrassing. Eisenhower himself expressed his conviction in a discussion with reporters on his campaign train that, given the party's denunciation of Democratic malfeasance, "we ourselves" have to be "as clean as a hound's tooth."

Nixon fought back, charging that he was being smeared by "Communists and crooks in the Government." Many Republican leaders, however, were dubious and urged the general to drop Nixon from the ticket; even the *New York Herald Tribune*, a firm supporter of Eisenhower, called on Nixon to resign from the ticket. Eisenhower wavered, finally deciding to reserve his decision until after Nixon had the opportunity to take his case directly to the people via a national radio and television address. It was clear that Nixon's place on the national ticket, perhaps his entire political future, rode on the outcome of the speech he was about to give.

In the speech, Nixon not only defended himself from the charge of misuse of campaign funds, but he laid bare his personal life in a way candidates had not done. With his wife Pat sitting quietly supportive at his side, seated at a desk beneath a portrait of Lincoln, Nixon discussed the fund and the independent audit that he claimed had cleared him. He went on to disclose his own financial affairs, adding the story of the present his daughter had received, the black and white dog Checkers. In contrast with Governor Stevenson, "who inherited a fortune from his father," Nixon depicted himself as one of the "common people," a theme that permeates the speech. In addition, the speech was a clear attack on the Democrats: Stevenson and his Vice Presidential running mate, Senator Sparkman of Alabama, were challenged to make financial disclosures on the basis of the innuendo that they had something to hide; Pat's "Republican cloth coat" was mentioned in a reference meant to remind the audience of the "mink coat" scandals associated with the Democrats; the "smear" against him, Nixon suggested, was because of his tough anti-Communist stand. Finally, Nixon called upon his audience to show their support for him by contacting the Republican National Committee directly, an astute political move to put pressure on Eisenhower to keep his young running mate.

Whether or not, in the long run, the speech helped Nixon and his party is a matter of some dispute among historians, but it was clear from the volume of telegrams and letters that poured in that the speech was an immediate success; certainly Eisenhower was persuaded to keep Nixon on the ticket and greeted Nixon the next day in Wheeling, West Virginia, with the words, "You're my boy."

Besides saving Nixon's political career, the speech demonstrated the potential power of the new television medium. Furthermore, it set a standard for personal disclosure that influenced both the political behavior of future candidates and the kind of public scrutiny of their private lives to which they would be subjected.

My Fellow Americans:—I come before you tonight as a candidate for the Vice Presidency and as a man whose honesty and integrity have been questioned.

The usual political thing to do when charges are made against you is to either ignore them or to deny them without giving details.

I believe we've had enough of that in the United States, particularly with the present Administration in Washington, D.C. To me the office of the Vice Presidency of the United States is a great office, and I feel that the people have got to have confidence in the integrity of the men who run for that office and who might obtain it.

I have a theory, too, that the best and only answer to a smear or to an honest misunderstanding of the facts is to tell the truth. And that's why I'm here tonight. I want to tell you my side of the case.

I am sure that you have read the charge and you've heard that I, Senator Nixon, took $18,000 from a group of my supporters.

WAS IT WRONG?

Now, was that wrong? And let me say that it was wrong—I'm saying, incidentally, that it was wrong and not just illegal. Because it isn't a question of whether it was legal or illegal, that isn't enough. The question is, was it morally wrong?

I say that it was morally wrong if any of the $18,000 went to Senator Nixon for my personal use. I say that it was morally wrong if it was secretly given and secretly handled. And I say that it was morally wrong if any of the contributors got special favors for the contributions that they made.

And now to answer those questions let me say this:

Not one cent of the $18,000 or any other money of that type ever went to me for my personal use. Every penny of it was used to pay for political expenses that I did not think should be charged to the taxpayers of the United States.

It was not a secret fund. As a matter of fact, when I was on "Meet the Press," some of you may have seen it last Sunday—Peter Edson came up to me after the program and he said, "Dick, what about this fund we hear about?" And I said, Well, there's no secret about it. Go out and see Dana Smith, who was the administrator of the fund. And I gave him his address, and I said that you will find that the purpose of the fund simply was to defray political expenses that I did not feel should be charged to the Government.

And third, let me point out, and I want to make this particularly clear, that no contributor to this fund, no contributor to any of my campaign, has ever received any consideration that he would not have received as an ordinary constituent.

I just don't believe in that and I can say that never, while I have been in the Senate of the United States, as far as the people that contributed to this fund are concerned, have I made a telephone call for them to an agency, or have I gone down to an agency in their behalf. And the record will show that, the records which are in the hands of the Administration.

WHAT FOR AND WHY?

But then some of you will say and rightly, "Well, what did you use the fund for, Senator? Why did you have to have it?"

Let me tell you in just a word how a Senate office operates. First of all, a Senator gets $15,000 a year in salary. He gets enough money to pay for one trip a year, a round trip that is, for himself and his family between his home and Washington, D.C.

And then he gets an allowance to handle the people that work in his office, to handle his mail. And the allowance for my State of California is enough to hire thirteen people.

And let me say, incidentally, that that allowance is not paid to the Senator—it's paid directly to the individuals that the Senator puts on his payroll, that all of these people and all of these allowances are for strictly official business. Business, for example, when a constituent writes in and wants you to go down to the Veterans Administration and get some information about his GI policy. Items of that type for example.

But there are other expenses which are not covered by the Government. And I think I can best discuss those expenses by asking you some questions. Do you think that when I or any other Senator makes a political speech, has it printed, should charge the printing of that speech and the mailing of that speech to the taxpayers?

Do you think, for example, when I or any other Senator makes a trip to his home state to make a purely political speech that the cost of that trip should be charged to the taxpayers?

Do you think when a Senator makes political

broadcasts or political television broadcasts, radio or television, that the expense of those broadcasts should be charged to the taxpayers?

Well, I know what your answer is. The same answer that audiences give me whenever I discuss this particular problem. The answer is, "no." The taxpayers shouldn't be required to finance items which are not official business but which are primarily political business.

But then the question arises, you say, "Well, how do you pay for these and how can you do it legally?"

And there are several ways that it can be done, incidentally, and that it is done legally in the United States Senate and in the Congress.

The first way is to be a rich man. I don't happen to be a rich man so I couldn't use that.

Another way that is used is to put your wife on the payroll. Let me say, incidentally, my opponent, my opposite number for the Vice Presidency on the Democratic ticket, does have his wife on the payroll. And has had her on his payroll for the ten years—the past ten years.

Now just let me say this. That's his business and I'm not critical of him for doing that. You will have to pass judgment on that particular point. But I have never done that for this reason. I have found that there are so many deserving stenographers and secretaries in Washington that needed the work that I just didn't feel it was right to put my wife on the payroll.

My wife's sitting over here. She's a wonderful stenographer. She used to teach stenography and she used to teach shorthand in high school. That was when I met her. And I can tell you folks that she's worked many hours at night and many hours on Saturdays and Sundays in my office and she's done a fine job. And I'm proud to say tonight that in the six years I've been in the House and the Senate of the United States, Pat Nixon has never been on the Government payroll.

There are other ways that these finances can be taken care of. Some who are lawyers, and I happen to be a lawyer, continue to practice law. But I haven't been able to do that. I'm so far away from California that I've been so busy with my Senatorial work that I have not engaged in any legal practice.

And also as far as law practice is concerned, it seemed to me that the relationship between an attorney and the client was so personal that you couldn't possibly represent a man as an attorney and then have an unbiased view when he presented his case to you in the event that he had one before the Government.

And so I felt that the best way to handle these necessary political expenses of getting my message to the American people and the speeches I made, the speeches that I had printed, for the most part, concerned this one message—of exposing this Administration, the communism in it, the corruption in it—the only way that I could do that was to accept the aid which people in my home state of California who contributed to my campaign and who continued to make these contributions after I was elected were glad to make.

NO SPECIAL FAVORS

And let me say I am proud of the fact that not one of them has ever asked me for a special favor. I'm proud of the fact that not one of them has ever asked me to vote on a bill other than as my own conscience would dictate. And I am proud of the fact that the taxpayers by subterfuge or otherwise have never paid one dime for expenses which I thought were political and shouldn't be charged to the taxpayers.

Let me say, incidentally, that some of you may say, "Well, that's all right, Senator; that's your explanation, but have you got any proof?"

And I'd like to tell you this evening that just about an hour ago we received an independent audit of this entire fund.

I suggested to Gov. Sherman Adams, who is the chief of staff of the Dwight Eisenhower campaign, that an independent audit and legal report be obtained. And I have that audit here in my hand.

It's an audit made by the Price, Waterhouse & Co. firm, and the legal opinion by Gibson, Dunn & Crutcher, lawyers in Los Angeles, the biggest law firm and incidentally one of the best ones in Los Angeles.

I'm proud to be able to report to you tonight that this audit and this legal opinion is being forwarded to General Eisenhower. And I'd like to read to you the opinion that was prepared by Gibson, Dunn & Crutcher and based on all the pertinent laws and statutes, together with the audit report prepared by the certified public accountants.

"It is our conclusion that Senator Nixon did not obtain any financial gain from the collection and disbursement of the fund by Dana Smith; that Senator Nixon did not violate any Federal or state law by reason of the operation of the fund, and that neither the portion of the fund paid by Dana Smith directly to third persons nor the portion paid to Senator Nixon to reimburse him for designated office expenses constituted income to the Senator which was either reportable or taxable as income under applicable tax laws. (signed) Gibson, Dunn & Crutcher by Alma H. Conway."

Now that, my friends, is not Nixon speaking, but that's an independent audit which was requested because I want the American people to know all the facts and I'm not afraid of having independent people go in and check the facts, and that is exactly what they did.

But then I realize that there are still some who may say, and rightly so, and let me say that I recognize that some will continue to smear regardless of what the truth may be, but that there has been understandably some honest misunderstanding on this matter, and there's some that will say:

"Well, maybe you were able, Senator, to fake this thing. How can we believe what you say? After all, is there a possibility that maybe you got some sums in cash? Is there a possibility that you may have feathered your own nest?"

FINANCIAL HISTORY

And so now what I am going to do—and incidentally this is unprecedented in the history of American politics—I am going at this time to give to this television and radio audience a complete financial history; everything I've earned; everything I've spent; everything I owe. And I want you to know the facts. I'll have to start early.

I was born in 1913. Our family was one of modest circumstances and most of my early life was spent in a store out in East Whittier. It was a grocery store—one of those family enterprises. The only reason we were able to make it go was because my mother and dad had five boys and we all worked in the store.

I worked my way through college and to a great extent through law school. And then, in 1940, probably the best thing that ever happened to me happened, I married Pat—sitting over here. We had a rather difficult time after we were married, like so many of the young couples who may be listening to us. I practiced law; she continued to teach school. I went into the service.

Let me say that my service record was not a particularly unusual one. I went to the South Pacific. I guess I'm entitled to a couple of battle stars. I got a couple of letters of commendation but I was just there when the bombs were falling and then I returned. I returned to the United States and in 1946 I ran for the Congress.

When we came out of the war, Pat and I—Pat during the war had worked as a stenographer and in a bank and as an economist for a Government agency—and when we came out the total of our savings from both my law practice, her teaching and all the time that I was in the war—the total for that entire period was just a little less than $10,000. Every cent of that, incidentally, was in Government bonds.

Well, that's where we start when I go into politics. Now what have I earned since I went into politics? Well, here it is—I jotted it down, let me read the notes. First of all I've had my salary as a Congressman and as a Senator. Second, I have received a total in this past six years of $1,600 from estates which were in my law firm at the time that I severed my connection with it.

And, incidentally, as I said before, I have not engaged in any legal practice and have not accepted any fees from business that came into the firm after I went into politics. I have made an average of approximately $1,500 a year from nonpolitical speaking engagements and lectures. And then, fortunately, we've inherited a little money. Pat sold her interest in her father's estate for $3,000 and I inherited $1,500 from my grandfather.

We live rather modestly. For four years we lived in an apartment in Park Fairfax, in Alexandria, Va. The rent was $80 a month. And we saved for the time that we could buy a house.

Now, that was what we took in. What did we do with this money? What do we have today to show for it? This will surprise you, because it is so little, I suppose, as standards generally go, of people in public life. First of all, we've got a house in Washington which cost $41,000 and on which we owe $20,000.

We have a house in Whittier, Calif., which cost $13,000 and on which we owe $10,000. My folks are living there at the present time.

I have just $4,000 in life insurance, plus my G.I. policy which I've never been able to convert and which will run out in two years. I have no life insurance whatever on Pat. I have no life insurance on our two youngsters, Patricia and Julie. I own a 1950 Oldsmobile car. We have our furniture. We have no stocks and bonds of any type. We have no interest of any kind, direct or indirect, in any business.

WHAT DO WE OWE?

Now, that's what we have. What do we owe? Well, in addition to the mortgage, the $20,000 mortgage on the house in Washington, the $10,000 one on the house in Whittier, I owe $4,500 to the Riggs Bank in Washington, D.C. with interest 4 1/2 per cent.

I owe $3,500 to my parents and the interest on that loan which I pay regularly, because it's the part of the savings they made through the years they were working so hard, I pay regularly 4 per cent interest. And then I have a $500 loan which I have on my life insurance.

Well, that's about it. That's what we have and that's what we owe. It isn't very much but Pat and I have the satisfaction that every dime that we've got is honestly ours. I should say this—that Pat doesn't have a mink coat. But she does have a respectable Republican cloth coat. And I always tell her that she'd look good in anything.

One other thing I probably should tell you because if I don't they'll probably be saying this about me too, we did get something—a gift—after the election. A man down in Texas heard Pat on the radio mention the fact that our two youngsters would like to have a dog. And, believe it or not, the day before we left on this campaign trip we got a message from Union Station in Baltimore saying they had a package for us. We went down to get it. You know what it was.

It was a little cocker spaniel dog in a crate that he sent all the way from Texas. Black and white spotted. And our little girl—Trisha, the 6-year-old—named it Checkers. And you know, the kids love the dog and I just want to say this right now, that regardless of what they say about it, we're gonna keep it.

It isn't easy to come before a nation-wide audience and air your life as I've done. But I want to say some things before I conclude that I think most of you will agree on. Mr. Mitchell, the chairman of the Democratic National Committee, made the statement that if a man couldn't afford to be in the United States Senate he shouldn't run for the Senate.

And I just want to make my position clear. I don't agree with Mr. Mitchell when he says that only a rich man should serve his Government in the United States Senate or in the Congress.

I don't believe that represents the thinking of the Democratic party, and I know that it doesn't represent the thinking of the Republican Party.

I believe that it's fine that a man like Governor Stevenson who inherited a fortune from his father can run for President. But I also feel that it's essential in this country of ours that a man of modest means can also run for President. Because, you know, remember

Abraham Lincoln, you remember what he said: 'God must have loved the common people—he made so many of them.'

COURSES OF CONDUCT

And now I'm going to suggest some courses of conduct.

First of all, you have read in the papers about other funds now. Mr. Stevenson, apparently, had a couple. One of them in which a group of business people paid and helped to supplement the salaries of state employees. Here is where the money went directly into their pockets.

And I think that what Mr. Stevenson should do should be to come before the American people as I have, give the names of the people that have contributed to that fund; give the names of the people who put this money into their pockets at the same time that they were receiving money from their state government, and see what favors, if any, they gave out for that.

I don't condemn Mr. Stevenson for what he did. But until the facts are in there there is a doubt that will be raised.

And as far as Mr. Sparkman is concerned, I would suggest the same thing. He's had his wife on the payroll. I don't condemn him for that. But I think that he should come before the American people and indicate what outside sources of income he has had.

I would suggest that under the circumstances both Mr. Sparkman and Mr. Stevenson should come before the American people as I have and make a complete financial statement as to their financial history. And if they don't it will be an admission that they have something to hide. And I think that you will agree with me.

Because, folks, remember, a man that's to be President of the United States, a man that's to be Vice President of the United States must have the confidence of all the people. And that's why I'm doing what I'm doing, and that's why I suggest that Mr. Stevenson and Mr. Sparkman since they are under attack should do what I am doing.

Now, let me say this: I know that this is not the last of the smears. In spite of my explanation tonight other smears will be made; others have been made in the past. And the purpose of the smears, I know, is this—to silence me, to make me let up.

Well, they just don't know who they're dealing with. I'm going to tell you this: I remember in the dark days of the Hiss case some of the same columnists, some of the same radio commentators who are attacking me now and misrepresenting my position were violently opposing me at the time I was after Alger Hiss.

TO CONTINUE THE FIGHT

But I continued the fight because I knew I was right. And I can say to this great television and radio audience that I have no apologies to the American people for my part in putting Alger Hiss where he is today.

And as far as this is concerned, I intend to continue the fight.

Why do I feel so deeply? Why do I feel that in spite of the smears, the misunderstandings, the necessities for a man to come up here and bare his soul as I have? Why is it necessary for me to continue this fight?

And I want to tell you why. Because, you see, I love my country. And I think my country is in danger. And I think that the only man that can save America at this time is the man that's running for President on my ticket—Dwight Eisenhower.

You say, "Why do I think it's in danger?" and I say look at the record. Seven years of the Truman-Acheson Administration and what's happened? Six hundred million people lost to the Communists, and a war in Korea in which we have lost 117,000 American casualties.

And I say to all of you that a policy that results in a loss of 600,000,000 to the Communists and a war which costs us 117,000 American casualties isn't good enough for America.

And I say that those in the State Department that made the mistakes which caused that war and which resulted in those losses should be kicked out of the State Department just as fast as we can get 'em out of there.

And let me say that I know Mr. Stevenson won't do that. Because he defends the Truman policy and I know that Dwight Eisenhower will do that, and that he will give America the leadership that it needs.

Take the problem of corruption. You've read about the mess in Washington. Mr. Stevenson can't clean it up because he was picked by the man, Truman, under whose Administration the mess was made. You wouldn't trust a man who made the mess to clean it up—that's Truman. And by the same token you can't

trust the man who was picked by the man that made the mess to clean it up—and that's Stevenson.

And so I say, Eisenhower, who owes nothing to Truman, nothing to the big city bosses, he is the man that can clean up the mess in Washington.

Take Communism. I say that as far as that subject is concerned, the danger is great to America. In the Hiss case they got the secrets which enabled them to break the American secret State Department code. They got secrets in the atomic bomb case which enabled 'em to get the secret of the atomic bomb, five years before they would have gotten it by their own devices.

And I say that any man who called the Alger Hiss case a "red herring" isn't fit to be President of the United States. I say that a man who like Mr. Stevenson has pooh-poohed and ridiculed the Communist threat in the United States—he said that they are phantoms among ourselves; he's accused us that have attempted to expose the Communists of looking for Communists in the Bureau of Fisheries and Wildlife—I say that a man who says that isn't qualified to be President of the United States.

And I say that the only man who can lead us in this fight to rid the Government of both those who are Communists and those who have corrupted this Government is Eisenhower, because Eisenhower, you can be sure, recognizes the problem and he knows how to deal with it.

Now let me say that, finally, this evening I want to read to you just briefly excerpts from a letter which I received, a letter which, after all this is over, no one can take away from me. It reads as follows:

"Dear Senator Nixon,

"Since I'm only 19 years of age I can't vote in this Presidential election but believe me if I could you and General Eisenhower would certainly get my vote. My husband is in the Fleet Marines in Korea. He's a corpsman on the front lines and we have a two-month-old son he's never seen. And I feel confident that with great Americans like you and General Eisenhower in the White House, lonely Americans like myself will be united with their loved ones now in Korea.

"I only pray to God that you won't be too late. Enclosed is a small check to help you in your campaign. Living on $85 a month it is all I can afford at present. But let me know what else I can do."

Folks, it's a check for $10, and it's one that I will never cash.

And just let me say this. We hear a lot about prosperity these days but I say, why can't we have prosperity built on peace rather than prosperity built on war? Why can't we have prosperity and an honest government in Washington, D.C., at the same time. Believe me, we can. And Eisenhower is the man that can lead this crusade to bring us that kind of prosperity.

And now, finally, I know that you wonder whether or not I am going to stay on the Republican ticket or resign.

Let me say this: I don't believe that I ought to quit because I'm not a quitter. And, incidentally, Pat's not a quitter. After all, her name was Patricia Ryan and she was born on St. Patrick's Day, and you know the Irish never quit.

But the decision, my friends, is not mine. I would do nothing that would harm the possibilities of Dwight Eisenhower to become President of the United States.

And for that reason I am submitting to the Republican National Committee tonight through this television broadcast the decision which it is theirs to make.

Let them decide whether my position on the ticket will help or hurt. And I am going to ask you to help them decide. Wire and write the Republican National Committee whether you think I should stay on or whether I should get off. And whatever their decision is, I will abide by it.

But just let me say this last word. Regardless of what happens I'm going to continue this fight. I'm going to campaign up and down America until we drive the crooks and the Communists and those that defend them out of Washington. And remember, folks, Eisenhower is a great man. Believe me. He's a great man. And a vote for Eisenhower is a vote for what's good for America.

Dwight D. Eisenhower

Atoms for Peace
(December 8, 1953)

In the closing days of the 1952 Presidential campaign, the United States conducted a test of a new weapon, a thousand times more powerful than the atomic device that had leveled Hiroshima seven years earlier. The awesome fireball that completely devoured a Pacific island a mile wide signaled the birth of the hydrogen bomb. The almost unimaginable destructive power of this weapon added a new, more terrifying, dimension to the arms race between the superpowers.

The threat to human civilization posed by the intensified and deadly arms race prompted the new President, Dwight David Eisenhower, to ask in his inaugural address: "How far have we come in man's long pilgrimage from darkness toward light? Are we nearing the light—a day of freedom and of peace for all mankind? Or are the shadows of another night closing in upon us?" Peace was very much on the President's mind. Six weeks after the inauguration, Joseph Stalin died of a heart attack, and Eisenhower hoped to take the opportunity to change the direction of cold war rhetoric. Discussing with Emmet Hughes a speech he was to give before the American Society of Newspaper Editors, Eisenhower told his speechwriter that he wanted to "talk straight; no double-talk, no sophisticated political formulas, no slick propaganda devices." He was tired of simply indicting the Russians for their past sins; the President wanted to say that he was "interested in the future." With new leadership in both Russia and America, the President was ready to announce that the "slate was clean" and to propose that both sides "begin talking to each other."

In the speech that resulted from this conversation, "The Chance for Peace," given on April 16, 1953, Eisenhower denounced the cost of the arms race, not only in terms of wealth—"This world in arms is not spending money alone"—but also in human terms: "It is

spending the sweat of its laborers, the genius of its scientists, the hopes of its children."
And the President declared his readiness to come to an agreement with the Soviets that
would establish international arms control under the auspices of the United Nations. Four
months later, however, the Russians successfully tested a hydrogen bomb of their own
and showed little sign of entering into any accord with the United States that would limit
their ability to counter American nuclear superiority.

Eisenhower and his advisers were faced with a set of problems that the "Atoms for
Peace" speech was designed to overcome. The American people had to be told of the risks
involved in the struggle with a Russia now armed with atomic weapons as sophisticated
as those of the United States, the Russians had to be warned against nuclear
adventurism, and the United States needed to capitalize on the confusion and uncertainty
created within the Soviet hierarchy by the death of Stalin and the transfer of power.
Months before the "Atoms for Peace" speech was given, the President's advisers had been
struggling with a way to do this, and in November the speech, which eventually went
through eleven major revisions, was first drafted.

The address, delivered before the United Nations General Assembly on December 8,
1953, was a complex one with a variety of purposes to serve—some explicit and some
implicit. As Professor Martin Medhurst has observed, the speech was "conceived in
pragmatism, dedicated in realism, and promoted in the spirit of idealism." It was a speech
that clearly fit into the pattern of psychological warfare of the cold war in its bid for
favorable world public opinion, it both warned and challenged the Soviet Union, and it
purported to be a commitment to nuclear arms control and ultimate nuclear disarmament.
The speech, as Professor Medhurst has argued, may not have been as straightforward as
it was alleged to be, but it did bring the UN delegates to their feet and did become a
significant part of the ongoing debate over both the peaceful uses of atomic energy and
nuclear disarmament.

Madame President, Members of the General Assembly:—When Secretary General Hammarskjold's invitation to address this General Assembly reached me in Bermuda, I was just beginning a series of conferences with the Prime Ministers and Foreign Ministers of Great Britain and of France. Our subject was some of the problems that beset our world.

During the remainder of the Bermuda Conference, I had constantly in mind that ahead of me lay a great honor. That honor is mine today as I stand here, privileged to address the General Assembly of the United Nations.

At the same time that I appreciate the distinction of addressing you, I have a sense of exhilaration as I look upon this assembly.

Never before in history has so much hope for so many people been gathered together in a single organization. Your deliberations and decisions during these somber years have already realized part of those hopes.

But the great tests and the great accomplishments still lie ahead. And in the confident expectation of those accomplishments, I would use the office which, for the time being, I hold, to assure you that the Government of the United States will remain steadfast in its support of this body. This we shall do in the conviction that you will provide a great share of the wisdom, of the courage and the faith which can bring to this world lasting peace for all nations and happiness and well-being for all men.

Clearly, it would not be fitting for me to take this occasion to present to you a unilateral American report on Bermuda. Nevertheless, I assure you that in our deliberations on that lovely island we sought to invoke those same great concepts of universal peace and human dignity which are so cleanly etched in your Charter.

Neither would it be a measure of this great opportunity merely to recite, however hopefully, pious platitudes.

I therefore decided that this occasion warranted

my saying to you some of the things that have been on the minds and hearts of my legislative and executive associates and on mine for a great many months—thoughts I had originally planned to say primarily to the American people.

I know that the American people share my deep belief that if a danger exists in the world, it is a danger shared by all—and equally, that if hope exists in the mind of one nation, that hope should be shared by all.

Finally, if there is to be advanced any proposal designed to ease, even by the smallest measure, the tensions of today's world, what more appropriate audience could there be than the members of the General Assembly of the United Nations.

LANGUAGE OF ATOMIC WARFARE

I feel impelled to speak today in a language that, in a sense, is new—one, which I, who have spent so much of my life in the military profession, would have preferred never to use.

That new language is the language of atomic warfare.

The atomic age has moved forward at such a pace that every citizen of the world should have some comprehension, at least in comparative terms, of the extent of this development, of the utmost significance to every one of us. Clearly if the peoples of the world are to conduct an intelligent search for peace, they must be armed with the significant facts of today's existence.

My recital of atomic danger and power is necessarily stated in United States terms, for these are the only incontrovertible facts that I know. I need hardly point out to this assembly, however, that this subject is global, not merely national in character.

On July 16, 1945, the United States set off the world's first atomic test explosion. Since that date in 1945, the United States has conducted forty-two test explosions.

Atomic bombs today are more than twenty five times as powerful as the weapons with which the atomic age dawned, while hydrogen weapons are in the ranges of millions of tons of TNT equivalent.

Today the United States' stockpile of atomic weapons, which, of course, increase daily, exceeds by many times the explosive equivalent of the total of all bombs and all shells that came from every plane and every gun in every theatre of war through all the years of World War II.

A single air group, whether afloat or land based, can now deliver to any reachable target a destructive cargo exceeding in power all the bombs that fell on Britain in all of World War II.

In size and variety the development of atomic weapons has been no less remarkable. This development has been such that atomic weapons have virtually achieved conventional status within our armed services. In the United States services, the Army, the Navy, the Air Force and the Marine Corps are all capable of putting this weapon to military use.

But the dread secret and the fearful engines of atomic might are not ours alone.

In the first place, the secret is possessed by our friends and Allies, Great Britain and Canada, whose scientific genius made a tremendous contribution to our original discoveries and the designs of atomic bombs.

The secret is also known by the Soviet Union.

The Soviet Union has informed us that, over recent years, it has devoted extensive resources to atomic weapons. During this period, the Soviet Union has exploded a series of atomic devices, including at least one involving thermonuclear reactions.

MONOPOLY ENDED

If at one time the United States possessed what might have been called a monopoly of atomic power, that monopoly ceased to exist several years ago. Therefore, although our earlier start has permitted us to accumulate what is today a great quantitative advantage, the atomic realities of today comprehend two facts of even greater significance.

First, the knowledge now possessed by several nations will eventually be shared by others, possibly all others.

Second, even a vast superiority in numbers of weapons, and a consequent capability of devastating retaliation, is no preventive, of itself, against the fearful material damage and toll of human lives that would be inflicted by surprise aggression.

The free world, at least dimly aware of these facts, has naturally embarked on a large program of warning and defense systems. That program will be accelerated and expanded.

But let no one think that the expenditure of vast sums for weapons and systems of defense can guarantee absolute safety for the cities and the citizens of any nation. The awful arithmetic of the atomic bomb does not permit of such an easy solution. Even against the most powerful defense, an aggressor in possession of the effective minimum number of atomic bombs for a surprise attack could probably place a sufficient number of his bombs on the chosen targets to cause hideous damage.

Should such an atomic attack be launched against the United States, our reaction would be swift and resolute. But for me to say that the defense capabilities of the United States are such that they could inflict terrible losses upon an aggressor—for me to say that the retaliation capabilities of the United States are so great that such an aggressor's land would be laid waste—all this, while fact, is not the true expression of the purpose and the hope of the United States.

To pause there would be to confirm the hopeless finality of a belief that two atomic colossi are doomed malevolently to eye each other indefinitely across a trembling world. To stop there would be to accept helplessly the probability of civilization destroyed—the annihilation of the irreplaceable heritage of mankind handed down to us generation from generation—and the condemnation of mankind to begin all over again the age-old struggle upward from savagery toward decency and right and justice.

NO VICTORY IN DESOLATION

Surely no sane member of the human race could discover victory in such desolation. Could anyone wish his name to be coupled by history with such human degradation and destruction?

Occasional pages of history do record the faces of the "Great Destroyers" but the whole book of history reveals mankind's never-ending quest for peace and mankind's God-given capacity to build.

It is with the book of history, and not with isolated pages, that the United States will ever wish to be identified. My country wants to be constructive, not destructive. It wants agreements, not wars, among nations. It wants, itself, to live in freedom and in the confidence that the people of every other nation enjoy equally the right of choosing their own way of life.

So my country's purpose is to help us move out of the dark chamber of horrors into the light, to find a way by which the minds of men, the hopes of men, the souls of men everywhere, can move forward toward peace and happiness and well-being.

In this quest, I know that we must not lack patience.

I know that in a world divided, such as ours today, salvation cannot be attained by one dramatic act.

I know that many steps will have to be taken over many months before the world can look at itself one day and truly realize that a new climate of mutually peaceful confidence is abroad in the world.

But I know, above all else, that we must start to take these steps—now.

The United States and its Allies, Great Britain and France, have, over the past months, tried to take some of these steps. Let no one say that we shun the conference table.

On the record has long stood the request of the United States, Great Britain and France, to negotiate with the Soviet Union the problems of a divided Germany.

On that record has long stood the request of the same three nations to negotiate an Austrian peace treaty.

On the same record still stands the request of the United Nations to negotiate the problems of Korea.

CONFERENCE WITH THE RUSSIANS

Most recently, we have received from the Soviet Union what is in effect an expression of willingness to hold a four-power meeting. Along with our Allies, Great Britain and France, we were pleased to see that this note did not contain the unacceptable preconditions previously put forward.

As you already know from our joint Bermuda communique, the United States, Great Britain and France have agreed promptly to meet with the Soviet Union.

The Government of the United States approaches this conference with hopeful sincerity. We will bend every effort of our minds to the single purpose of emerging from that conference with tangible results toward peace—the only true way of lessening international tension.

We never have, we never will, propose or suggest that the Soviet Union surrender what is rightfully theirs.

We will never say that the peoples of Russia are an enemy with whom we have no desire ever to deal or mingle in friendly and fruitful relationship.

On the contrary, we hope that this coming conference may initiate a relationship with the Soviet Union which will eventually bring about a free intermingling of the peoples of the East and of the West—the one sure, human way of developing the understanding required for confident and peaceful relations.

Instead of the discontent which is now setting upon Eastern Germany, occupied Austria and the countries of Eastern Europe, we seek a harmonious family of free European nations, with none a threat to the other, and least of all a threat to the peoples of Russia.

Beyond the turmoil and strife and misery of Asia, we seek peaceful opportunity for these peoples to develop their natural resources and to elevate their lot.

These are not idle words of shallow vision. Behind them lies a story of nations lately come to independence, not as a result of war but through free grant or peaceful negotiation. There is a record already written of assistance gladly given by nations of the West to needy peoples and to those suffering the temporary effects of famine, drought and natural disaster.

These are deeds of peace. They speak more loudly than promises or protestations of peaceful intent.

But I do not wish to rest either upon the reiteration of past proposals or the restatement of past deeds. The gravity of the time is such that every new avenue of peace, no matter how dimly discernible, should be explored.

There is at least one new avenue of peace which has not yet been well explored—an avenue now laid out by the General Assembly of the United Nations.

In its resolution of Nov. 18, 1953, this General Assembly suggested—and I quote—"that the Disarmament Commission study the desirability of establishing a sub-committee consisting of representatives of the powers principally involved, which should seek, in private, an acceptable solution—and report such a solution to the General Assembly and to the Security Council not later than 1 September, 1954."

The United States, heeding the suggestion of the General Assembly of the United Nations, is instantly prepared to meet privately with such other countries as may be "principally involved," to seek "an acceptable solution" to the atomic armaments race which overshadows not only the peace but the very life of the world.

We shall carry into these private or diplomatic talks a new conception.

The United States would seek more than the mere reduction or elimination of atomic materials for military purposes.

It is not enough to take this weapon out of the hands of the soldiers. It must be put into the hands of those who will know how to strip its military casing and adapt it to the arts of peace.

The United States knows that if the fearful trend of atomic military build-up can be reversed, this greatest of destructive forces can be developed into a great boon for the benefit of all mankind.

The United States knows that peaceful power from atomic energy is no dream of the future. That capability, already proved, is here now—today. Who can doubt, if the entire body of the world's scientists and engineers had adequate amounts of fissionable material with which to test and develop their ideas, that this capability would rapidly be transformed into universal, efficient and economic usage?

To hasten the day when fear of the atom will begin to disappear from the minds of people and the governments of the East and West there are certain steps that can be taken now.

I therefore make the following proposals:

The governments principally involved to the extent permitted by elementary prudence, to begin now and continue to make joint contributions from their stockpiles of normal uranium and fissionable materials to an international atomic energy agency. We would expect that such an agency would be set up under the aegis of the United Nations.

The ratios of contributions, the procedures and other details would properly be within the scope of the "private conversations" I have referred to earlier.

The United States is prepared to undertake these explorations in good faith. Any partner of the United States acting in the same good faith will find the United States a not unreasonable or ungenerous associate.

Undoubtedly initial and early contributions to this plan would be small in quantity. However, the proposal has the great virtue that it can be undertaken without irritations and mutual suspicions incident to any attempt to set up a completely acceptable system of world-wide inspection and control.

The Atomic Energy Agency could be made responsible for the impounding, storage and protection of the contributed fissionable and other materials. The ingenuity of our scientists will provide special, safe conditions under which such a bank of fissionable material can be made essentially immune to surprise seizure.

The more important responsibility of this atomic energy agency would be to devise methods whereby this fissionable material would be allocated to serve the peaceful pursuits of mankind. Experts would be mobilized to apply atomic energy to the needs of agriculture, medicine and other peaceful activities. A special purpose would be to provide abundant electrical energy in the power-starved areas of the world. Thus the contributing powers would be dedicating some of their strength to serve the needs rather than the fears of mankind.

EXPEDITE PEACEFUL USE

The United States would be more than willing—it would be proud—to take up with others "principally involved" the development of plans whereby such peaceful use of atomic energy would be expedited.

Of those "principally involved" the Soviet Union must of course, be one.

I would be prepared to submit to the Congress of the United States, and with every expectation of approval, any such plan that would:

First, encourage world-wide investigation into the most effective peacetime uses of fissionable material; and with the certainty that they had all the material needed for the conduct of all experiments that were appropriate;

Second, begin to diminish the potential destructive power of the world's atomic stockpiles;

Third, allow all peoples of all nations to see that, in this enlightened age, the great powers of the earth, both of the East and of the West, are interested in human aspirations first rather than in building up the armaments of war.

Fourth, open up a new channel for peaceful discussion and initiate at least a new approach to the many difficult problems that must be solved in both private and public conversations if the world is to shake off the inertia imposed by fear and is to make positive progress toward peace.

Against the dark background of the atomic bomb, the United States does not wish merely to present strength, but also the desire and the hope for peace.

The coming months will be fraught with fateful decisions. In this Assembly, in the capitals and military headquarters of the world; in the hearts of men everywhere, be they governed or governors, may they be the decisions which will lead this world out of fear and into peace.

To the making of these fateful decisions, the United States pledges before you—and therefore before the world—its determination to help solve the fearful atomic dilemma—to devote its entire heart and mind to find the way by which the miraculous inventiveness of man shall not be dedicated to his death, but consecrated to his life.

I again thank the delegates for the great honor they have done me in inviting me to appear before them and in listening to me so courteously.

Thank you.

Clare Boothe Luce

American Morality and Nuclear Diplomacy
(October 27, 1961)

The decade of the 1950's ended with the United States and the Soviet Union still locked in the cold war struggle. The war in Korea had been brought to an end with the country divided between North and South Korea. In Vietnam, French power had been broken, and by 1955 the French were forced to abandon their former colony. Partitioned into North and South Vietnam, the country was to have had free elections in 1956, but these were forestalled by the South Vietnamese government with the support of the United States, which now virtually replaced France as the mainstay of the anti-Communist South. Also in Asia, the Chinese provoked a crisis by shelling the islands held by the Nationalist Chinese off the mainland, Quemoy and Matsu. The Nationalists had been driven out of China by Communist armies and sought refuge on the island of Taiwan. President Eisenhower pledged to defend the islands, but few Americans believed they were worth fighting a war over, and under pressure from the United States the Nationalist leader Chiang Kai-shek publicly renounced the use of force to regain control of mainland China; for its part, the Communist government of China agreed to a cease-fire.

Other problems erupted in various parts of the globe. In 1956 Hungarians rose against their Communist government, undoubtedly with the hope that the United States would aid them. The use of American military power in Eastern Europe was, however, in no way practical, and the uprising was crushed by Russian tanks. In Latin America, the Cuban revolution established a Communist government in the Western Hemisphere.

In 1960, the torch was passed, as John Kennedy said in his inaugural, to a new generation. Eisenhower, then the oldest President to serve in that office, was succeeded by the youngest man ever elected to the Presidency. Communism, however, was still seen as a threat to America, indeed, to the entire "free world." And there were still those, looking back over the post–World War II years, who believed that America had failed to properly use its enormous power to thwart Communist designs.

Clare Boothe Luce, former member of Congress and ambassador to Italy under the Eisenhower administration, wife of the influential publisher of *Time*, Henry Luce, was one of those calling on Americans to be prepared to risk war in order to prevent the Russians from achieving their "goal of world conquest." In her Given Foundation Lecture at Wilson College, Luce deprecated what she saw as the historical conviction that guided United States foreign policy: America should never strike the first military blow.

Seeing such a belief as the outgrowth of a fuzzy or false morality, Luce argued that our failure to threaten, and if need be to use, military force—even atomic weapons—to curb Communist aggression after the end of World War II had given the Soviets an enormous advantage in the cold war years. While most Americans hoped for some solution that would reduce the terrible possibility of nuclear warfare, Luce spoke for the hard-line anti-Communists who advocated a diplomatic and economic assault on Communism backed by a "Public Will" determined to risk war rather than suffer a slow defeat. "Our moral attitude toward nuclear war," she maintained, "must be that there *are* moral values worth dying for."

Today the two strongest nations in the world are drawn up in full battle array, facing one another across half the world. Their bombs testing in air, their rockets' red glare, seem proof to the world that war may be near.

Wrote Churchill in *The Gathering Storm*, "Statesmen are not called upon to settle easy questions ... it is when the balance quivers, and the proportions are veiled in mist that the opportunity for world-saving decisions presents itself."

The same opportunity presents itself to the American people.

In a democracy, the vital decisions of statesmen are seldom taken in defiance of the Public Will. Whoever changes his own opinion in a national crisis, by just so much changes the Public Will and, by just so much, influences the decisions of statesmen.

The purpose of this paper is to raise the question of the *morality* of America's attitude in this century toward the *uses* of force, in international affairs, to submit that our morality has been a fuzzy if not false one, and to suggest that unless [sic] that attitude does not soon change, we dare not hope that American diplomacy can win the cold war.

What *is* the historic American attitude toward force, toward the purpose of force, the possession of force, and the use of force? In speaking of force, I am speaking not only of America's armies-in-being at any given moment since the turn of the century, but of America's war-making *capacity*, its total realizable military potential.

Until most recent times America's attitude was that the sole purpose of American force was the military self-defense—of America; that the possession of force was solely for a deterrent to military aggression—against America; and that the only use to which American force could ever *morally* be put was retaliation against military aggression—*on* America.

Morality in respect of force consisted in *not striking the first military blow*. Conversely, any nation who struck the first military blow against America, *ipso facto* established its own immorality.

Consequently, the only moral *casus bellum*, or cause of war, which the Public Will has fully supported is the initiation of war on the United States. For almost a century, statesmanship has been constrained, diplomacy has been confined, and patriotism itself has been defined, by the moral necessity of waiting for Pearl Harbors.

There are, of course, many explanations of this attitude. Even if there were time I could not do justice to the whole of this complex problem. A review of it would begin with General George Washington's unique role in insuring that the military forces should be absolutely subject to the civil government; that of the two hats the President wears, his commander-in-chief hat should be kept in the closet of Congress. The scholar could then go on to show that one of the strongest of American feelings was always its antipathy toward the militaristic traditions of Europe. Indeed, throughout most of history, the flaunting of military power was closely tied to old world dynastic, monarchical and feudal institutions and rivalries. From the beginning, the United States sought to set a new example to the world, an example not only of democracy but also of repudiation of war as the normal more or less continuous, instrument of government policy. To all such considerations as these, most historians would add the fact of America's geographical isolation. During the first century and a half of our history as a nation, the United States was perhaps not so isolated as historical generalizations make out, but it can certainly be agreed that from President Washington's time to President Wilson's there was a firm determination not to involve ourselves in what is called the "power politics" of Europe. This led in turn to a diplomatic isolation from Europe's political problems, and this aloofness from European power politics—which meant world power politics—resulted, it could be said, in a national ignorance of how the world is run and of how, *mutatis mutandis*, it must be run.

Consequently America in this century has twice failed, with a third time threatening, to prevent the outbreak of world war. And to prevent the outbreak of world war was our moral duty and our prime task as the world's strongest nation. America failed because the Public Will would seldom support a foreign policy or a diplomacy which would permit our statesmen to introduce the subject of the war-making capacity of the United States into the normal conduct of international negotiations. We would not allow—we positively forbade—our diplomats to convert our tremendous physical power into diplomatic or political victories for peace.

Have we always been blind to this necessity? No, we have not.

Let me give you an elegant historical example of wise American statesmanship: the proclamation of the Monroe Doctrine, on December 2nd, 1823. This was a clearly stated political and diplomatic warning to all the nations of the world that the United States would rapidly raise armies to fight any nation which, for any reason good or bad, sought any conquest in this hemisphere. We said, in effect, that we would not wait until a conflict situation, involving a European power, developed in South America to determine whether our interests were affected. And we certainly would not wait until we ourselves were hit. We would, on the contrary,

act at the first sign of European aggression in our hemisphere. This positive warning, because it was believed in all the chanceries of Europe, discouraged even the smallest military adventure in our part of the world. No armies were raised in the Untied states, no taxes were paid to support vast flexible defense systems designed not only to repulse massive attacks on the U. S. A., but to participate in far away "brush-fire" wars in South America. None were needed. The clear unambiguous political warning to Europe that America stood ready to convert its potential power into actual firing power if the general peace of our hemisphere were threatened helped to keep our country at peace for almost a hundred years. In fact, so well did that political warning preserve peace in this hemisphere, that over the long years we quite forgot to what we owed our security. We forgot that the best deterrent to aggression of any serious nature is a firm political warning, uttered well in advance, that a nation stands ready to go to war to protect not only its own shores, but the general peace in a whole area where its interests are involved.

A vast, rich, self-contained, self-sufficient, and ever-growing country, we ourselves did not need to use force against other nations to acquire territory, trade, or raw materials. To be sure, when there was anything America wanted that lay conveniently near, we did not hesitate to use force to get it. Our second-class citizens, the Indians, still living on reservations, and the Mexicans from whom we wrested New Mexico can testify to that. But gradually, despite these lapses on the score of force, we began to make a virtue, not of our necessity but of our *lack* of necessity for using force in the world. *We* did not fight or threaten to fight anyone in Europe or Asia. *We* were a non-aggressive, non-military, thoroughly moral nation. Morality consisted, therefore, in not going to war or threatening war. It also consisted in not "getting mixed up" in the wars of "warlike" nations, which by historic definition included every nation in the old world. We began to pride ourselves on our superior moral attitude toward the rest of the world. Force was something decent nations never used except in the case of overt attack. And America, the most decent nation in the world, would never use force until America herself was attacked.

"There is such a thing as a man being too proud to fight," said Woodrow Wilson in the spring of 1915. This was certainly a statement which the embattled French and British heard with dismay and contempt and bitterness. How can a man be proud *not* to fight while his friends are being killed and even conquered in a war *they* did not start? America was not too proud to sell guns, make loans, ship supplies to the Allied side, and to heap abuse on Kaiser Bill—a procedure which American morality permitted us nevertheless to call "neutrality," since neutrality also consisted entirely in *not* joining the fighting until "war came."

Even after World War I, America clung to the idea that the unilateral renunciation—America's renunciation of the First Use of Force—would preserve peace in the world.

But by 1937, World War II was plainly in the making. Once again American statesmanship and diplomacy were confronted with the stern necessity of taking a firm stand against the outbreak of hostilities in Europe. What stand did we take? I do not know how clearly you remember Franklin Roosevelt's famous "quarantine" speech in that year. But let me read a sentence to you: (Said President Roosevelt) "... the mere fact that we *rightly* decline to intervene with arms to prevent acts of aggression does not mean that we must act as if there were no aggression at all.... There are many methods short of war, but *stronger and more effective* than mere words, of bringing home to aggressor governments the aggregate sentiments of our people."

The record, which includes Pearl Harbor, shows that the "many methods short of war," which the United States used between 1938-1941, did not bring home "the aggregate sentiments of our people." Does this mean that war was inevitable? No. Because the "mere words" to which President Roosevelt referred were never tried. These words would have been exactly the strongest and most effective thing to have prevented World War II. What words? Why, the very opposite words from the ones Mr. Roosevelt used when he said, "we rightly decline to intervene with arms...." The quietly spoken words of American diplomats in Rome and Berlin and Tokyo and Moscow—that *if* Hitler plunged Europe into war, Germany would have to reckon with American military power because America *would rightly decide to intervene on the side of the Allies*. This warning never came.

As late as 1939, Mr. Roosevelt said, "At this moment there is being prepared a proclamation of American neutrality...." And in October 1940, after France had fallen, and when Great Britain alone held the fortress of the West against Hitler's Germany, our President said, "I have said this before, but I shall say it again and again: Your boys are not going to be sent into any foreign wars."

But just as we had in World War I, we again sent guns, supplies, money to the Allies. We opened the Burma Road, embargoed aviation fuel to the Japanese, thus stalling their war machine in China. Again, the American press and the American people heaped words of scorn and hatred on the Germans and Japanese.

The whole world pondered all over again America's strange definition of a "foreign war" and "neutrality." Except in respect of shedding her blood, America had plainly taken the sides of the Allies.

What Europe did not understand, what the world did not understand was that when it came to war—the use of military force—the American people sincerely felt that while it was not immoral to fight a war, it *was* immoral to start one. The Public will would not support diplomatic efforts to prevent war, and would not fight it until America was first attacked.

We must note here that the American idea that, however well prepared, a country is not justified in going to war against another country who is preparing to fight it until that country has first rammed our front teeth down our bloodied throat, has never before been known in history. Other nations have consistently viewed this attitude as cowardice or selfishness—or worst of all, stupidity on America's part. Most of the nations of the world consequently regarded Pearl Harbor, not as "a day of infamy," but as a day of awakening for America.

Isolation and its resulting ignorance or naivete about the political and diplomatic uses of power do explain much about the ambiguity of the American attitude toward force in both pre-World War I and II days. But equally certain by 1945, a thorough re-examination of the morality of our position was in order. All the historical evidence showed that neither the Kaiser nor Hitler nor Mussolini would have started World War I and II in the first place, if American diplomacy had been permitted by the Public Will to warn them that America's war-making potential would be mobilized on the Allied side if they did so. A stern warning from American diplomats might have prevented even the war in Ethiopia, the taking of the Rhineland, and the Anschluss. I have spent many years in Italy. I never knew an Italian who did not insist that if the United States had given Mussolini a firm warning that the U.S. would, sooner or later, stand against Hitler, Italy would have stayed out of the war.

A good deal of the blood that was spilled in World Wars I and II must be laid, and is laid by responsible historians, at the door of America's strange morality about force.

Unhappily, America did not learn from the terrible lessons of these two wars. The *proof* we gave ourselves that our *morality* "paid off" laid in the fact that we not only won both wars but emerged from them stronger and richer and more powerful than ever.

Despite the warnings of history, we have held to our morality, and we have done so until this present hour. The Kaiser and Hitler began our education in the political uses of military power. They were not tough enough to finish it. It is now being finished by Mr. Khrushchev and Mao Tse-tung.

Like the immortal Killeeloo bird that always flies backward because it can't tell where it is until it sees where it has been, let us go back to the year 1945.

That year the United States emerged from the war as the first atomic power in history. One American A-bomb was one thousand times more destructive than any "block buster" dropped in World War II. Never before in the story of mankind had one nation possessed such a monopoly of decisive military power, and the means of delivering it anywhere on the globe.

How did we view the *purpose* of this power? As self-defense, quite proper. How did we view the *possession* of this power? As a deterrent to the use of force against ourselves and our allies by others. So far, excellent. But what political or diplomatic use did we make of this power? Very little. Let us review the record.

The war had no sooner ended in 1945 than it became plain to many students of the international scene that Soviet Russia—in spite of the grievous wounds she had sustained (ten per cent of her population had been killed in the war)—had *not* abandoned her dream of the ideological conquest of the world. The world balance of power was again being threatened. World War III was in the making. The warnings came early. First, United States armies executed their habitual retreat to the homeland. This fact destroyed the credibility of America's intention to remain in Europe until Russia ceased to be a threat. Russia did not disband her armies. The Russian divisions which were affronting Germany at war's end were maintained, still facing west, against her recent allies. No doubt our atomic power in the immediate post-war period did deter Red armies of "liberation" from an easy march to the Channel. But it did not automatically disband, no less roll back those armies. Why not?

Said Harry Truman in 1945, "In our possession of this (atomic) weapon, there is no threat to any nation ... we regard (it) as a sacred trust ... the thoughtful people of the world know that trust will not be violated."

The Russians, being a thoughtful people, wondered if this meant that America, even after Pearl Harbor, intended to cling to her moral view that she would wait patiently, permitting all forms of political aggression in Europe and elsewhere, until Russia was ready to strike the first atomic blow. It seemed too good to be true. But that was exactly what it *did* mean.

In 1946, troubled about her monopoly of so much destructive power, the United States offered the world the Baruch Plan—a plan to share our atomic secrets with the whole world, for peaceful purposes. This wonderfully generous plan contained one very logical feature: It was, in Mr. Baruch's words, "an international law with teeth in it." Like all laws, it proposed punishment for those who used atomic energy for making weapons. The Russians turned it down. That was our second warning. The Plan went into the wastebasket; the teeth, the United States threw in right after it.

By 1947, any doubt that the American people may have had on the score of Russia's ultimate, not to say ulterior, political intentions had been largely dispelled. It was clear to the majority of Americans that Russia was determined, if not destined, to be America's No. 1 political and military enemy. Every passing day gave its own savage proof that bomb or no bomb, Russia intended to pursue her goal of world conquest by every means her sovereign will could command. Lacking atomic capacity herself that meant by subversion, infiltration, propaganda, and a diplomacy based on ruthless deceit. The mere possession by America of atomic supremacy may have deterred an all-out Russian hot-war on land against our European allies, but it did not halt Russia's cold-war anywhere in the world, nor her agitation of lukewarm wars and Red revolutions in Asia.

How did the United States react to this situation in which Russia was clearly rearming for a hot war against America, while fiercely pursuing the cold war? Able to reduce Russia to rubble in hours, did we permit our diplomats quietly to warn Russia to halt and desist lest she risk bringing down destruction upon herself? No, we did not.

American foreign policy promptly geared itself to fight the war Russia chose to fight—the cold war. For every cold war tit of the Russians there would come a cold war tat from America. We went into "partnership" with the nations of the "free" world against communism. They provided the ocean of economic demands. We provided the ships full of supplies.

By 1948, the Marshall Plan, originally conceived as an economic rehabilitation measure for the destroyed economies of both European friend and foe, was being primarily used as a political tool to thwart Russia's effort to communize countries outside the Iron Curtain. Beefed up with billions and changed into the MSA (Mutual Security Administration) it was used lavishly in an effort to bolster up weak governments and calm down revolutionary ferment among needy peoples by raising their living standards.

Nor was the United States laggard in responding to Soviet world propaganda. Tooling up the most formidable propaganda machinery that the U.S. Congress would buy, the United States struggled valiantly to save the ears of the world from Red contamination. USIS, the Voice of America, Radio Free Europe, the Voice of Liberty, delivered a tittle for every Russian tattle.

The bill for America's political efforts in this cold war has so far run into 85 billions of dollars.

Nevertheless, despite our prodigious cold war efforts during the years 1945 to 1950, the years of U.S. atomic supremacy and superiority, Russia not only maintained the Iron Curtain around Eastern Europe and China, but also launched subversive attacks on a dozen countries such as Indo China, Malaya, and even France and Italy. Soviet Russia and Red China also supported the Red invasion of South Korea.

Our overwhelming military power here and there translated itself into regional military power: in Greece, in Turkey, and of course into the formation of NATO. Where military aggression threatened or military initiatives were taken we responded in kind, or reacted. But our prodigious war capacity simply did not translate itself into political cold war victories. Indeed, in the very shadow of the mushroom cloud, Soviet Russia proceeded to her political goals with a confidence that became with every passing year more arrogant.

On what was Russia's confidence based? It was certainly not based on ignorance of what the A-bomb could do and would do to Russia if war came. Americans, on the record, had had little compunction about slaughtering millions of defenseless men and women in order to achieve a war objective, even if that objective might have been won by less frightful means.

Russia knew (and had not forgotten) what all the world knew (and has not forgotten) that the A-bomb was a proven weapon. We had already used it to slaughter and maim over 300,000 defenseless non-combatants in Hiroshima and Nagasaki, and when the war was all but won—when General MacArthur's huge armada was almost ready to strike at the Japanese heartland.

Russia's brash and increasing confidence in pursuing her cold war goals was based largely on one thing: *her shrewd understanding of U.S. morality—or the American Public Will—in respect of the initiation of war.*

When we look back now on the past 15 years, we can see that the prime goal of Russian psychological warfare at any given time was to encourage this simple bit of "morality." So long as Americans held to it firmly, Russia had only to refrain from a direct attack on the United States—on United States military personnel abroad—or on formal U.S. allies. And she need fear America's A-bombs, bombers, or navies less than the rotten eggs which a frustrated American or two had sometimes thrown at Russian envoys.

We American citizens will never understand the failure of our cold war diplomacy to "stop Russia," until we are willing to recognize that our own morality in respect of force *politically* castrated our colossal atomic power. We ourselves subtracted our overwhelming power to warn the wrongdoer that he would be punished from the international political and diplomatic equation. We refused to convert it into diplomatic and political terms. We renounced *a priori* our responsibility as the world's greatest power to restore order and stability to a suffering world. Just as we had done in the days when Hitler was rising, once again we talked of "quarantining aggressors" and "containment of aggressors" but what we really did was to quarantine the only strong police force in a lawless world: American power. In short, we proclaimed, in 1945, a *de jure* atomic stalemate.

To this point of view, it will be objected that our own allies approved—at least partially—this *de jure* stalemate. Publicly, no nation, including Soviet Russia, will ever admit that it *intends* to initiate war. And, indeed, *no* nation wants to fight a war if the advantages it hopes to achieve *can* be had by negotiation. All statesmanship consists in seeking advantages, short of war, if possible. But—and do let's try to get this clearly in mind—the clear diplomatic warning that force will be used if all the processes of diplomacy, negotiation and reason fail, the Monroe Doctrine type diplomacy, is the only thing which can *hope* to discourage the inordinate ambitions of other nations. After 1945, only one nation in the world was strong enough to utter the warning to Russia that she must abandon her desire for world conquest. It was never uttered. On the contrary, not only did we not warn, we reassured her that we would never fight until (a) Russia became as strong as ourselves and (b) we, or our Allies, were first struck!

The diplomatic consequences of renouncing force, and setting ourselves goals which only the discreet backing of force made realizable, were dismal indeed. American diplomats were often as ineffective as the diplomats of the smallest and weakest nation in pursuing their goal of making friends and influencing peoples. They sometimes found that they could not achieve the simplest political objective, even in respect of an ally, unless they were willing to pay dollars for it through the nose. The result was economic blackmail.

There were other consequences. Our deterrent concept which logically led to the concept of an unlimited war of *retaliation* against Russia, left us with vague military policies, confused tactics and inadequate weapons to fight the limited or brush-fire wars which Russia (to whom our morality granted everywhere the military right of way), instigated against her world neighbors and ours. We had no clear military design to stop the small Russian gobbling of bits of the earth, except to gobble up Russia herself—a thing which morality forbade us to do until Russia took her first big bite from our hide. And even then, our morality held that "we won't use anything on you you don't use on us." We responded to the war initiative of the Red Koreans by letting them choose the caliber of weapons, determine the battle area, and blow the cease-fire whistle when they began to fall behind.

In 1949 Russia detonated her first atomic bomb and ended our atomic monopoly. There was no question in any American's mind what target her bombs, when they came in sufficient numbers, were designed to find. This must have been a bad moment for Russia. Would America, Russia must have wondered uneasily, snap out of her strange moral attitude? Would America see at last that Russia was at war with her, even though Russia had fired no shot at us? (If we didn't see that in '49 we see it now: The fallout of 30- and 50- megaton bombs exploded by Russia, *inside* Russia, is headed our way now. Our frontiers have been militarily crossed, have they not, by death-dealing Russian fallout?) Would America see that in this war, nuclear time must soon run out? Would she come to her military, if not moral, senses? Would America permit her diplomats to warn Russia that she still possesses superior strength, and that unless Russia halted and desisted her bomb testing, unless she signed an atomic agree-

ment with adequate safeguards, the American people might see the necessity of this force? Would America take *any* diplomatic action to prevent Russia from arming for America's destruction? Another very bad moment, indeed, for the Russians. But all went well. President Truman had said in October 1948, "We hunger for peace. The world knows that the United States will never use the atom bomb to wage aggressive war...." In 1949 he said, "The purpose of what we are doing is to prevent World War III. Starting a war is no way to make peace." American morality prevailed. Our diplomats were hamstrung. They could not warn Russia. Aggression, even atomic aggression, the most fearsome form of aggression which ever threatened America, was again, by definition, dropping the *first* atomic bomb. The President was, of course, supported again by the public will. Americans were quite ready, indeed eager, to wait patiently until Russia was in a better position to knock out all America. Well, Russia is now in that position. We now have the very situation we encouraged.

As a proof of the sincerity of our position and the purity of our intentions, we pursued that long series of disarmament negotiations which began with the Baruch plan, but which have today ended in utter nothingness.

When the policy of general atomic disarmament failed, we began at last to threaten Russia. But again, not diplomatically with the prospect of a war which even as late as 1952 we might still have won without too much damage to America. We threatened Russia with military *reprisals*. We swore a mighty oath: Our *retaliation* would be supercolossal, stupendously massive. We would make bigger and more terrible bombs. And if war *came* we would give two nuclear tits for every Russian nuclear tat. A bigger bang for a billion bucks. By 1953 Russia had made our *de jure* stalemate of 1945 the nuclear stalemate *de facto*.

In Eisenhower's regime the nuclear armament race began in earnest. As Professor Henry Kissinger pointed out at the time, our failure to incorporate our atomic power into *military, political, and diplomatic* thinking led to a ghastly paradox: Having refused to warn Russia that if pressed too far, we might have to fight a war, which we could certainly have won, we began to arm for a 10 million ton nuclear bomb war which *nobody* could win.

During his 8 years in office, time and time again President Eisenhower reiterated America's moral position on war. "There is no alternative to peace," said the President in 1956. Commenting dryly on this, Professor Kissinger wrote, "to the extent that this is taken seriously by the Soviets as a statement of American intentions, it will remove a powerful brake on Soviet probing actions, and any incentive for the Soviet to make concessions." We meant it seriously. The Russians made no concessions. Summitry had to fail.

Our attitude in 1945 that it was immoral to alert the Russians to the fact that *we* might strike first unless a real peace could be negotiated, our long refusal even to warn an avowed enemy, an enemy whose intention to bury us and the free world had been clear from the beginning, had paralyzed our diplomacy, saw 600 millions of peoples dragged into slavery behind the Iron Curtain, intensified the cold war throughout the world, neutralized many countries, brought Russian power to our very own shores in Cuba, left us inert and humiliated before Castro—and now has at long last carried the whole suffering world to Armageddon.

Was, then, this moral attitude just?

Our allies in pre-World War I and II days did not think so. Fortunately they survived it ... because we got hit. But after 1945 many other nations, in Robert Tucker's words, saw "no moral virtue" in a foreign policy which renounced the diplomatic uses of force and thus jeopardized what little security for them had existed.

If we wish to find one big cause for America's unpopularity around the world today, especially in the captive nations, we can find it in the image of the really Ugly American: the great big man with the great big gun in his hand, who watched for a decade while a hoodlum raped the children in the neighborhood. And then passed out lollipops to the next victims on the list to comfort them, and sling shots to ward off the hoodlum when he showed up again. Ask any Hungarian, any citizen of the captive countries, any free Cuban, if this is not *their* image of the Ugly American.

The idea that a nation, although the mightiest power on earth, has no moral obligation to warn, no less to punish the international hoodlum who is raping the independence of nations whose interests are closely tied to its own, until shores are bombarded, it then gains a moral advantage which gives it the right to plunge everyone into all-out war, *guerre aà l'outrance*—all this is so far from being moral, that it has long been viewed in the chanceries of the world as a moral aberration, of a peculiarly stupid—and dangerous—sort. And indeed, some *hubris*, or pride, ignorance and selfishness do lie close to the root of it.

As to whether or not this attitude has "paid off"

since the end of World War II, we have only to remind ourselves that all Americans are being urged today to build fallout shelters. Moral or not, sheer common sense must tell us that our attitude was imprudent.

And now, before we come to the future consequences of holding to it, let us consider what a *moral* idea of force should be.

A correct *moral* attitude toward force must begin by the clear and never-to-be-forgotten truth that force is itself neutral. The fact that men can now make use of nuclear energy does not alter this truth by one jot. Nuclear energy is *force*. Force is neutral. It is not something that uses man. Man uses it. In international questions force can be used to exert *diplomatic* pressures which can, and often have prevented wars.

Every nation claiming to be in any serious or responsible sense sovereign organizes military force in time of crisis. But again, the organized military force is itself neutral. It is probably true that the existence of military force sets up a bias for its own use—that is for war. But if anything is clear historically, it is that in America the influence of the military establishment upon national policy is minimal.

Our military establishment, huge though it is, will not move, would not know how to move, except at the direction of the civil power—and that means you and me—the Public Will.

We are faced then with ourselves—with our share in forming the Public Will on the use of force.

Today, our diplomats and statesmen can no longer warn Russia that if she persists in her plan for world conquest we may wage a war on her which she would lose and we would win. They know, and we know, the threat would be empty. The use of nuclear force would result in the destruction of America as well as Russia. All our statesmanship and diplomacy today must be directed toward preventing nuclear war. Whether we wait to be struck, or strike first now, it will come in the end to the same thing—the end of our way of life—the death of America, possibly the end of *Western* civilization.

What is the Public Will now? The Public Will, or so it seems to me, is to prevent the nuclear war, *and at the same time win the cold war*. How good are our chances of doing so?

Let us take the most recent dramatic incident in the US-USSR conflict: the building of the Berlin wall.

Symbols are more mighty than words. They are a universal language. They are the quintessence of human communication. The Berlin wall is far more than a wall. It is a symbol. Everyone knows what it stands for today. It stands for the permanent division of Germany, a thing we have vowed to prevent, not only for all Germany's sake, but for our own sake. West Germany, offered unity by the Russians in 1952, freely chose our side, on one condition—that the United States would never recognize the division of Germany. The wall is the symbol to them and the world that we view West Berlin as a ghetto of freedom, and that we have accepted the slavery of East Berlin. Above all, it is the symbol that the Iron Curtain cannot be raised by an American diplomacy that does not dare even to destroy one small brick wall, for fear now of risking a nuclear war.

The wall was built brick by brick—one brick at a time. And American diplomats, American soldiers, American statesmen stood by, paralyzed watching it go up.

What is the *official* U.S. explanation of this incident that has now become a symbol to the world? That Russian tanks were in the background; that the USA feared to create a disturbance lest any disturbance in West Berlin might.... Might what? Trigger World War III and *never* forget, Americans that one 10-million ton Russian bomb would certainly destroy any American city. And, fellow Americans, was the wall worth that?

Let us be brutally honest with ourselves. Until the nuclear stalemate is ended, the United States and the USSR will remain in conflict over many issues, at many points, in many situations around the world. No particular brick, no particular wall, no particular group of people, indeed no particular nation, not West Germany, not France, not Great Britain, certainly not Laos or Viet Nam, or Quemoy or Matsu, or Cuba, if thrown by Russia into the balance, *one at a time*, will seem to be "worth" the destruction of Washington, New York, Los Angeles, or for that matter, Chambersburg.

If you have followed my argument so far, you will *not* misunderstand me. I am not saying that in the future we must risk nuclear war *everywhere*, or that we must yield *nowhere*. Each risk must prudentially be calculated. And the more desperate the cold war, the more difficult the lukewarm wars that are proceeding in Asia, the more tactical retreats may have to be made. What I *am* saying is that an unbroken string of tactical retreats must add up, in the end, to a strategic defeat.

The chain of destiny is forged link by link. And so is the chain of captivity.

Surely we see now, at long last, that for fifteen years we have been locked in a life or death struggle with Soviet Russia. Surely we see now that we have imprudently sacrificed, in the name of a fuzzy and egocentric morality, all the political and diplomatic advantages that our monopoly of power once gave us. We have long since passed the point of no return.

Nevertheless our great task remains. It is to take down the Russian wall around the world in the same way that Russia built it. Not overnight, but brick by brick. And, of course, first the loose bricks. Far from abandoning our non-military tools—economic, political, and cultural—we must increase them in size. But what I am saying is that we must be prepared ourselves as a people to risk war at every hour while we use these tools for all *they* are worth.

The President has said that we must win the cold war with the nuclear Sword of Damocles hanging over us. Let us remember that Russia built the wall we must now breach with the Sword of Damocles hanging over *her* head *only*. Shall we be less courageous now that it also hangs over ours?

The greatest virtue we can bring to the struggle now is courage. That side will win who least fears to be threatened, who most fearlessly takes the initiative in every cold war effort. That side will win who turns not a profile but a full face in courage to the struggle. American diplomacy can win the cold war if the Public Will now supports its President and its diplomats in showing our determination to win, in spite of the nuclear risks. Armed with this courage—which only we can give them, they will make the right decisions. We may safely leave the details of carrying out these decisions to them and to our diplomats. It will take time, so we must also have the virtue of patience.

Our moral attitude toward nuclear war must be that there *are* moral values worth dying for. Our moral attitude toward the cold war must be that there are moral values worth great economic sacrifices. For if this be not true, then morality itself will die at our own hands.

Said Abraham Lincoln, 100 years ago, America is "the last best hope of earth...." It still is.

The one great and decisive force which we must now translate into political and diplomatic action is the force of our free spirits.

Equal Rights and Equal Opportunities

———Dwight D. Eisenhower———

Federal Court Orders Must Be Upheld
(September 24, 1957)

The modern era in race relations began on May 17, 1954, when the Supreme Court, in *Brown v. Board of Education*, ruled that segregated public school facilities were inherently unequal and therefore unconstitutional. A second decision the following year directed school districts to eliminate segregation with "all deliberate speed." Some districts moved quickly and uneventfully to comply with the order of the Supreme Court. In many parts of the South, however, "all deliberate speed" was understood to mean "all possible delay." Legal and extralegal means were employed to forestall enforcement, so that case-by-case litigation was needed to bring about any measure of enforcement. There were cases of violence and intimidation in defiance of court rulings. Across the South, the pace of integration was very slow. Extremist opponents of the *Brown* decision wished to establish that there were alternatives to compliance, and they viewed Little Rock, Arkansas, as a promising test case.

Little Rock was a moderate city in which progress had been made in desegregating public facilities during the early 1950's, but it lay in the middle of a segregationist state. Three proposals to circumvent or nullify the Supreme Court's decision had been approved in statewide referenda in November 1956. Governor Faubus, sensitive to the political realities, had moved closer to the segregationist position, although he was subjected to criticism for not going far enough. The school board adopted a plan for school integration in 1954. It would not begin until the fall of 1957, it would start at the high school level only, and it would focus on Central High, the only school with a racially diverse attendance area. Although challenged by black leaders as insufficient, the plan was upheld as constitutional by the Eighth Circuit Court of Appeals. Many whites reconciled themselves to the plan as the least possible integration that would comply with the Supreme Court order. But opponents came to Little Rock to force a confrontation that, they hoped, would inspire resistance elsewhere in the Deep South.

School was set to open on September 3. The night before, Faubus called out the militia to maintain order, but expressed his opinion that order could not be kept if "forcible integration" were carried out. Grounding his argument for delay in the expectation of violence, Faubus virtually assured that mobs would be present at Central High. On the first day of school, black students were refused entrance by the militia commander, who said he was acting on orders of Governor Faubus. The National Association for the Advancement of Colored People filed suit to have the desegregation plans implemented without delay. President Eisenhower conferred with Faubus and assured him that the Constitution would be upheld, but did not explicitly counter the governor's assertion that the *Brown* decision left room for delay.

On September 20 the court enjoined Faubus from interfering with the desegregation plan, so he withdrew the National Guard altogether. As a consequence the eight black students who entered Central High had no protection from the mob that gathered outside. The mood became more violent, and school officials decided to remove the black students—for their own safety—less than half a day after they had been admitted. This action by local officials created the impression of mob rule in Little Rock. President Eisenhower, sharing this view of the situation, ordered federal troops to Little Rock, and explained his action in a nationally televised address.

This speech is one of the first Presidential pronouncements on civil rights, but it is strikingly narrow in its approach. The President did not speak to the moral imperative of school desegregation, about which he was thought to have misgivings, but focused on the sanctity of the federal courts. The speech exhibits a familiar pattern of using procedural issues to pre-empt consideration of substantive questions. The President also described his action as reluctant but mandatory, suggesting that it was not a matter over which he had any discretion. And he was sensitive to the concerns about states' rights being raised in the South. He perceived the desegregation crisis as a legal rather than a moral concern.

Eisenhower's speech is not a milestone in presidential leadership on civil rights, but it does illustrate the intensity of resistance and the concern for limited, gradual action. The President made no further statements on integration for the remainder of his term. Desegregation was implemented in Little Rock, owing to the presence of federal troops. Soon, however, the specific controversy in Little Rock would be eclipsed by a new wave of civil rights protest, across the South and in the North as well.

Good Evening, My Fellow Citizens:—For a few minutes this evening I want to speak to you about the serious situation that has arisen in Little Rock. To make this talk I have come to the President's office in the White House. I could have spoken from Rhode Island, where I have been staying recently, but I felt that, in speaking from the house of Lincoln, of Jackson and of Wilson, my words would better convey both the sadness I feel in the action I was compelled today to take and the firmness with which I intend to pursue this course until the orders of the Federal Court at Little Rock can be executed without unlawful interference.

In that city, under the leadership of demagogic extremists, disorderly mobs have deliberately prevented the carrying out of proper orders from a Federal Court. Local authorities have not eliminated that violent opposition and, under the law, I yesterday issued a Proclamation calling upon the mob to disperse.

This morning the mob again gathered in front of the Central High School of Little Rock, obviously for the purpose of again preventing the carrying out of the Court's order relating to the admission of Negro children to that school.

Whenever normal agencies prove inadequate to

the task and it becomes necessary for the Executive Branch of the Federal Government to use its powers and authority to uphold Federal Courts, the President's responsibility is inescapable.

In accordance with that responsibility, I have today issued an Executive Order directing the use of troops under Federal authority to aid in the execution of Federal law at Little Rock, Arkansas. This became necessary when my Proclamation of yesterday was not observed, and the obstruction of justice still continues.

It is important that the reasons for my action be understood by all our citizens.

As you know, the Supreme Court of the United States has decided that separate public educational facilities for the races are inherently unequal and therefore compulsory school segregation laws are unconstitutional.

Our personal opinions about the decision have no bearing on the matter of enforcement; the responsibility and authority of the Supreme Court to interpret the Constitution are very clear. Local Federal Courts were instructed by the Supreme Court to issue such orders and decrees as might be necessary to achieve admission to public schools without regard to race—and with all deliberate speed.

During the past several years, many communities in our Southern States have instituted public school plans for gradual progress in the enrollment and attendance of school children of all races in order to bring themselves into compliance with the law of the land.

They thus demonstrated to the world that we are a nation in which laws, not men, are supreme.

I regret to say that this truth—the cornerstone of our liberties—was not observed in this instance.

It was my hope that this localized situation would be brought under control by city and State authorities. If the use of local police powers had been sufficient, our traditional method of leaving the problems in those hands would have been pursued. But when large gatherings of obstructionists made it impossible for the decrees of the Court to be carried out, both the law and the national interest demanded that the President take action.

Here is the sequence of events in the development of the Little Rock school case.

In May of 1955, the Little Rock School Board approved a moderate plan for the gradual desegregation of the public schools in that city. It provided that a start toward integration would be made at the present term in the high school, and that the plan would be in full operation by 1963. Here I might say that in a number of communities in Arkansas integration in the schools has already started and without violence of any kind. Now this Little Rock plan was challenged in the courts by some who believed that the period of time as proposed in the plan was too long.

The United States Court at Little Rock, which has supervisory responsibility under the law for the plan of desegregation in the public schools, dismissed the challenge, thus approving a gradual rather than an abrupt change from the existing system. The court found that the school board had acted in good faith in planning for a public school system free from racial discrimination.

Since that time, the court has on three separate occasions issued orders directing that the plan be carried out. All persons were instructed to refrain from interfering with the efforts of the school board to comply with the law.

Proper and sensible observance of the law then demanded the respectful obedience which the nation has a right to expect from all its people. This, unfortunately, has not been the case at Little Rock. Certain misguided persons, many of them imported into Little Rock by agitators, have insisted upon defying the law and have sought to bring it into disrepute. The orders of the court have thus been frustrated.

The very basis of our individual rights and freedoms rests upon the certainty that the President and the Executive Branch of Government will support and insure the carrying out of the decisions of the Federal Courts, even, when necessary with all the means at the President's command.

Unless the President did so, anarchy would result.

There would be no security for any except that which each one of us could provide for himself.

The interest of the nation in the proper fulfillment of the law's requirements cannot yield to opposition and demonstrations by some few persons.

Mob rule cannot be allowed to override the decisions of our courts.

Now, let me make it very clear that Federal troops are not being used to relieve local and state authorities of their primary duty to preserve the peace and order of the community. Nor are the troops there for the purpose of taking over the responsibility of the School Board and the other responsible local officials in running Central High School. The running of our school system and the maintenance of peace and order in each of our States are strictly local affairs and the Federal

Government does not interfere except in a very few special cases and when requested by one of the several States. In the present case the troops are there, pursuant to law, solely for the purpose of preventing interference with the orders of the Court.

The proper use of the powers of the Executive Branch to enforce the orders of a Federal Court is limited to extraordinary and compelling circumstances. Manifestly, such an extreme situation has been created in Little Rock. This challenge must be met and with such measures as will preserve to the people as a whole their lawfully-protected rights in a climate permitting their free and fair exercise.

The overwhelming majority of our people in every section of the country are united in their respect for observance of the law—even in those cases where they may disagree with that law.

They deplore the call of extremists to violence.

The decision of the Supreme Court concerning school integration, of course, affects the South more seriously than it does other sections of the country. In that region I have many warm friends, some of them in the city of Little Rock. I have deemed it a great personal privilege to spend in our Southland tours of duty while in the military service and enjoyable recreational periods since that time.

So from intimate personal knowledge, I know that the overwhelming majority of the people in the South—including those of Arkansas and of Little Rock—are of good will, united in their efforts to preserve and respect the law even when they disagree with it.

They do not sympathize with mob rule. They, like the rest of our nation, have proved in two great wars their readiness to sacrifice for America.

A foundation of our American way of life is our national respect for law.

In the South, as elsewhere, citizens are keenly aware of the tremendous disservice that has been done to the people of Arkansas in the eyes of the nation, and that has been done to the nation in the eyes of the world.

At a time when we face grave situations abroad because of the hatred that Communism bears toward a system of government based on human rights, it would be difficult to exaggerate the harm that is being done to the prestige and influence, and indeed to the safety, of our nation and the world.

Our enemies are gloating over this incident and using it everywhere to misrepresent our whole nation. We are portrayed as a violator of those standards of conduct which the peoples of the world united to proclaim in the Charter of the United Nations. There they affirmed "faith in fundamental human rights" and "in dignity and worth of the human person" and they did so "without distinction as to race, sex, language or religion."

And so, with deep confidence, I call upon the citizens of the State of Arkansas to assist in bringing to an immediate end all interference with the law and its processes. If resistance to the Federal Court orders ceases at once, the further presence of Federal troops will be unnecessary and the City of Little Rock will return to its normal habits of peace and order and a blot upon the fair name and high honor of our nation in the world will be removed.

Thus will be restored the image of America and of all its parts as one nation, indivisible, with liberty and justice for all.

Good night, and thank you very much.

George C. Wallace

Proclamation at the University of Alabama
(June 11, 1963)

The Supreme Court's 1954 decision was confined to school desegregation, but it spurred calls for racial integration in virtually all aspects of American public life. Galvanized by the Court's decision and by rising expectations, the civil rights movement by the early 1960's focused on a variety of direct-action protests as well as the more traditional litigation. Sit-ins at public facilities, picketing and boycotts of stores and restaurants denying service to blacks on an integrated basis, and marches and rallies became increasingly common. Sometimes they produced results, when they aroused the conscience of a community and led to local negotiations. Sometimes they produced a federal response through executive action, such as the order by the Interstate Commerce Commission to desegregate interstate bus terminal facilities. But where new laws were needed, the federal government was slow to act, fearful of antagonizing powerful Southerners in Congress. Meanwhile, federal courts consistently ruled that school segregation was unconstitutional and oversaw orders for its abolition.

Resistance to integration also took many forms. In addition to the mobs and vigilantes characterizing Little Rock, there were legal challenges as well. These usually revived the century-old doctrines of interposition and nullification developed by John C. Calhoun in an attempt to forestall congressional action against slavery. According to these theories, the United States Constitution was the creature of sovereign states. The states, having made the federal government, were sovereign over it. Consequently, when the federal government embarked on an unjust or unconstitutional course, it was the duty of the states to call it to account. They did so either by interposition—placing themselves between the central government and the people, appealing to the national government to reconsider or rescind its illegal act—or by nullification, a declaration that the offensive act was null and void within the state. Many thought these doctrines were discredited by the Civil War, but articulate Southerners maintained that the Civil War was only a test of the might of armies, not of the right of constitutional principles. Several Southern states, resisting the Supreme Court decision, invoked the theory in some form.

Resistance to integration had polarized Southern politics. George C. Wallace had lost a gubernatorial primary in 1958 because, he thought, he was seen as too moderate on racial issues. He hardened his own views and was elected to the governor's chair in 1962. His inaugural address threw down the gauntlet and proclaimed, "Segregation now, segregation tomorrow, segregation forever." Particularly since blacks did not yet vote in large numbers, it is fair to say that Wallace generally reflected the voting public's opinion in Alabama. Meanwhile, a lawsuit to compel desegregation at the University of Alabama was working its way through the courts in the spring of 1963. The stage seemed set for a confrontation, since Wallace vowed to "stand in the schoolhouse door" physically to prevent integration.

The university trustees would have preferred to be conciliatory, and several federal officials tried to bring economic pressure or directly urged Wallace to withdraw his threat, but the governor was adamant. He had no illusions that he would be able to prevail, but he insisted on making the stand, in order to show symbolically that only superior federal force had prevented him—just as Alabamians a century before had conceded no principle but only the superior might of the federal government.

Wallace, however, was also eager to avoid the economic and political damage Mississippi had suffered the year before when riots broke out over the integration of Ole Miss. Accordingly, without confiding in the federal government, he determined that he would perform a symbolic act of protest—standing in the schoolhouse door and issuing his proclamation, but then withdrawing from the scene and not blocking the registration of two black students. In this way Wallace could remain true to his principles and also recognize the reality of superior force.

The door in which Wallace stood was actually a side entrance to the building in which students registered. Television cameras recorded his proclamation in which he forbade the federal government to unconstitutionally intrude into state affairs. He did not act on his proclamation, however, and later on the same day he stepped aside when asked to do so by the National Guard. The students were taken to their dormitories and then registered without incident. By this time Wallace was en route back to the state capital at Montgomery, after thanking the citizens of Alabama for their great restraint and predicting ultimate victory for the states' rights cause.

As Governor and Chief Magistrate of the State of Alabama, I deem it to be my solemn obligation and duty to stand before you representing the rights and sovereignty of this state and its peoples.

The unwelcomed, unwanted, unwarranted and force-induced intrusion upon the campus of the University of Alabama today of the might of the Central Government offers frightful example of oppression of the rights, privileges and sovereignty of this state by officers of the Federal Government. This intrusion results solely from force, or threat of force, undignified by any reasonable application of the principle of law, reason and justice. It is important that the people of this state and nation understand that this action is in violation of rights reserved to the state by the Constitution of the United States and the Constitution of the State of Alabama. While some few may applaud these acts, millions of Americans will gaze in sorrow upon the situation existing at this great institution of learning.

Only the Congress makes the law of the United States. To this date, no statutory authority can be cited to the people of this country which authorizes the Central Government to ignore the sovereignty of this state and attempt to subordinate the rights of Alabama and millions of Americans. There has been no legislative action by Congress justifying this intrusion.

When the Constitution of the United States was enacted, a Government was formed upon the premise that people, as individuals, are endowed with the rights of life, liberty, and property, and with the rights of local self-government. The people and their local self-governments formed a Central Government and conferred upon it certain stated and limited powers. All other powers were reserved to the states and to the people.

Strong local government is the foundation of our system and must be continually guarded and maintained. The 10th Amendment to the Constitution of the United States reads as follows: "The powers not delegated to the United States by the Constitution, nor prohibited by it to the states, are reserved to the states respectively, or to the people." This amendment sustains the right of self-determination and grants the state of Alabama the right to enforce its laws and regulate its internal affairs.

This nation was never meant to be a unit of one but a united of the many—that is the exact reason our freedom-loving forefathers established the states, so as to divide the rights and powers among the many states, insuring that no central power could gain massive government control.

There can be no submission to the theory that the Central Government is anything but a servant of the people. We are God-fearing people, not government-fearing people. We practice today the free heritage bequeathed to us by the founding fathers.

I stand here today, as Governor of this sovereign state, and refuse to willingly submit to illegal usurpation of power by the Central Government. I claim today for all the people of the state of Alabama those rights reserved to them under the Constitution of the United States. Among those powers so reserved and claimed is the right of state authority in the operation of the public schools, colleges and universities. My action does not constitute disobedience to legislative and constitutional provisions. It is not defiance for defiance sake, but for the purpose of raising basic and fundamental constitutional questions. My action is a call for strict adherence to the Constitution of the United States as it was written—for a cessation of usurpation and abuses. My action seeks to avoid having state sovereignty sacrificed on the altar of political expediency.

Further, as the Governor of the State of Alabama,

I hold the supreme executive power of this state, and it is my duty to see that the laws are faithfully executed. The illegal and unwarranted actions of the Central Government on this day, contrary to the laws, customs and traditions of this state, is calculated to disturb the peace.

I stand before you today in place of thousands of other Alabamians whose presence would have confronted you had I been derelict and neglected to fulfill the responsibilities of my office. It is the right of every citizen, however humble he may be, through his chosen officials of representative government to stand courageously against whatever he believes to be the exercise of power beyond the constitutional rights conferred upon our Federal Government. It is this right which I assert for the people of Alabama by my presence here today.

Again I state this is the exercise of the heritage of freedom and liberty under the law—coupled with responsible government.

Now, therefore, in consideration of the premises, and in my official capacity as Governor of the State of Alabama, I do hereby make the following solemn proclamation:

Whereas, the Constitution of Alabama vests the supreme executive powers of the state in the Governor as the chief magistrate, and said Constitution requires of the Governor that he take care that the laws be faithfully executed; and

Whereas, the Constitution of the United States, Amendment 10, reserves to the states respectively or to the people, those powers not delegated to the United States, nor prohibited to the states; and

Whereas, the operation of the public school system is a power reserved to the State of Alabama under the Constitution of the United States and Amendment 10 thereof; and

Whereas, it is the duty of the Governor of the State of Alabama to preserve the peace under the circumstances now existing, which power is one reserved to the State of Alabama and the people thereof under the Constitution of the United States and Amendment 10 thereof:

Now, therefore, I, George C. Wallace, as Governor of the State of Alabama, have by my action raised issues between the Central Government and the sovereign State of Alabama, which said issues should be adjudicated in the manner prescribed by the Constitution of the United States; and now being mindful of my duties and responsibilities under the Constitution of the

United States, the Constitution of the State of Alabama, and seeking to preserve and maintain the peace and dignity of this state, and the individual freedoms of the citizens thereof, do hereby denounce and forbid this illegal and unwarranted action by the Central Government.

John F. Kennedy

Civil Rights Message
(June 11, 1963)

The 1960 Presidential election had been extremely close, and the black vote for John F. Kennedy was probably critical to his success. Although his previous record on civil rights had been lackluster, he had campaigned on the strong plank in the Democratic platform and achieved a political triumph in the black community with his telephone call to Mrs. King upon Martin Luther King, Jr.'s arrest. Understandably, those committed to faster progress in race relations looked expectantly to the new administration.

But the closeness of the vote left Kennedy few coattails. Though nominally Democratic, the Congress was effectively controlled by a coalition of Republicans and Southern Democrats. The Congress elected in 1960 was, if anything, more conservative than the one it replaced. It was unlikely to respond favorably to any request for civil rights legislation. And the political capital expended in an unsuccessful quest for civil rights laws might doom other aspects of the Kennedy program as well.

The President tried to resolve this dilemma by relying on executive action, stressing measures that could be taken without congressional approval. Prodded by the "Freedom Rides" of 1961, for example, the Interstate Commerce Commission issued rules requiring desegregation of public facilities in most bus terminals. Yet even with this approach there were problems. Throughout the campaign Kennedy had chided President Eisenhower for not issuing an executive order to combat discrimination in housing; it could be done, the candidate said, by the stroke of a pen. Two years into his own Presidency he still had not signed it, fearful that to do so would cost the Southern votes in Congress that he needed for the creation of a Department of Urban Affairs.

Meanwhile, the pressure for change grew. The Freedom Rides were followed by sit-ins in places of public accommodation. In the fall of 1962, Kennedy had sent troops to the University of Mississippi to ensure the enrollment and safety of James Meredith. On that occasion Kennedy made his first Presidential speech devoted to civil rights, but the tone suggested his reluctance to confront the issue and his emphasis on his responsibility to enforce the laws rather than on recognition of a moral crisis. Then, in the spring of 1963, the focus of attention was on Birmingham. There peaceful sit-ins had escalated into violent response from the authorities, captured most notably in photographs of Police Commissioner Eugene "Bull" Connor unleashing police dogs and opening fire hydrants on children. Kennedy, who recognized that the grievances of the civil rights movement lay largely outside the scope of federal law, concluded that he could wait no longer. In February he sent Congress the first proposal for comprehensive civil rights legislation since Reconstruction.

In June, two qualified black students sought to enroll at the University of Alabama. Gov. George Wallace, who had proclaimed "segregation forever!" in his inaugural address, symbolically acted to block their admission by "standing in the schoolhouse door" to interpose the authority of the state between the people and the power of the federal government. He stepped aside when ordered to do so by federal marshals and the two students successfully registered. Kennedy, affected by the quickened pace of the movement, concerned that Wallace had been permitted to make his case on national television, was pressured by Martin Luther King to speak to the moral issues. On Tuesday, June 11, Kennedy decided to speak to the nation that very night, to explain the strengthened civil rights bill he would send to Congress the following week. His advisers were not enthusiastic and it was not possible to have a complete draft ready on time. But Kennedy was insistent. He took the text he was given, made frequent interpolations while speaking, and went on extemporaneously when the manuscript ran out.

The speech is remarkable for its explicit delineation of civil rights as a moral issue, "as old as the scriptures and as clear as the American Constitution." Kennedy explained his position by reference to the concept of justice, "whether we are going to treat our fellow Americans as we want to be treated." As he had done in earlier speeches, he also stressed how failure to act on civil rights diminished America in the eyes of the world.

This speech launched the campaign that would culminate in the passage, almost exactly a year later, of the Civil Rights Act of 1964. Kennedy would not live to see that day. Neither would the Mississippi field secretary for the National Association for the Advancement of Colored People. Medgar Evers was killed as he stepped from his car at home after a meeting on the night of June 11, 1963, the very night that Kennedy spoke. It was a vivid reminder of how far the country still had to go.

Good evening, my fellow citizens:—This afternoon, following a series of threats and defiant statements, the presence of Alabama National Guardsmen was required on the University of Alabama to carry out the final and unequivocal order of the United States District Court of the Northern District of Alabama. That order called for the admission of two clearly qualified young Alabama residents who happened to have been born Negro.

That they were admitted peacefully on the campus is due in good measure to the conduct of the students of the University of Alabama, who met their responsibilities in a constructive way.

I hope that every American, regardless of where he lives, will stop and examine his conscience about this and other related incidents. This Nation was founded by men of many nations and backgrounds. It was founded on the principle that all men are created equal, and that the rights of every man are diminished when the rights of one man are threatened.

Today we are committed to a worldwide struggle to promote and protect the rights of all who wish to be free. And when Americans are sent to Viet-Nam or West Berlin, we do not ask for whites only. It ought to be possible, therefore, for American students of any color to attend any public institution they select without having to be backed up by troops.

It ought to be possible for American consumers of any color to receive equal service in places of public accommodation, such as hotels and restaurants and theaters and retail stores, without being forced to resort to demonstrations in the street, and it ought to be possible for American citizens of any color to register and to vote in a free election without interference or fear of reprisal.

It ought to be possible, in short, for every American to enjoy the privileges of being American without regard to his race or his color. In short, every American ought to have the right to be treated as he would wish to be treated, as one would wish his children to be treated. But this is not the case.

The Negro baby born in America today, regardless of the section of the Nation in which he is born, has about one-half as much chance of completing a high school as a white baby born in the same place on the same day, one-third as much chance of completing college, one-third as much chance of becoming a professional man, twice as much chance of becoming unemployed, about one-seventh as much chance of earning $10,000 a year, a life expectancy which is 7 years shorter, and the prospects of earning only half as much.

This is not a sectional issue. Difficulties over segregation and discrimination exist in every city, in every State of the Union, producing in many cities a rising tide of discontent that threatens the public safety. Nor is this a partisan issue. In a time of domestic crisis men of good will and generosity should be able to unite regardless of party or politics. This is not even a legal or legislative issue alone. It is better to settle these matters in the courts than on the streets, and new laws are needed at every level, but law alone cannot make men see right.

We are confronted primarily with a moral issue. It is as old as the scriptures and is as clear as the American Constitution.

The heart of the question is whether all Americans are to be afforded equal rights and equal opportunities, whether we are going to treat our fellow Americans as we want to be treated. If an American, because his skin is dark, cannot eat lunch in a restaurant open to the public, if he cannot send his children to the best public school available, if he cannot vote for the public officials who represent him, if, in short, he cannot enjoy the full and free life which all of us want, then who among us would be content to have the color of his skin changed and stand in his place? Who among us would then be content with the counsels of patience and delay?

One hundred years of delay have passed since President Lincoln freed the slaves, yet their heirs, their grandsons, are not fully free. They are not yet freed from the bonds of injustice. They are not yet freed from social and economic oppression. And this Nation, for all its hopes and all its boasts, will not be fully free until all its citizens are free.

We preach freedom around the world, and we mean it, and we cherish our freedom here at home, but are we to say to the world, and much more importantly, to each other that this is a land of the free except for the Negroes; that we have no second-class citizens except Negroes; that we have no class or caste system, no ghettoes, no master race except with respect to Negroes?

Now the time has come for this Nation to fulfill its promise. The events in Birmingham and elsewhere have so increased the cries for equality that no city or State or legislative body can prudently choose to ignore them.

The fires of frustration and discord are burning in every city, North and South, where legal remedies are not at hand. Redress is sought in the streets, in demonstrations, parades, and protests which create tensions and threaten violence and threaten lives.

We face, therefore, a moral crisis as a country and as a people. It cannot be met by repressive police action. It cannot be left to increased demonstrations in the streets. It cannot be quieted by token moves or talk. It is a time to act in the Congress, in your State and local legislative body and, above all, in all of our daily lives.

It is not enough to pin the blame on others, to say this is a problem of one section of the country or another, or deplore the fact that we face. A great change is at hand, and our task, our obligation, is to make that revolution, that change, peaceful and constructive for all.

Those who do nothing are inviting shame as well as violence. Those who act boldly are recognizing right as well as reality.

Next week I shall ask the Congress of the United States to act, to make a commitment it has not fully made in this century to the proposition that race has no place in American life or law. The Federal judiciary has upheld that proposition in a series of forthright cases. The executive branch has adopted that proposition in the conduct of its affairs, including the employment of Federal personnel, the use of Federal facilities, and the sale of federally financed housing.

But there are other necessary measures which only the Congress can provide, and they must be provided at this session. The old code of equity law under which we live commands for every wrong a remedy, but in too many communities, in too many parts of the country, wrongs are inflicted on Negro citizens and there are no remedies at law. Unless the Congress acts, their only remedy is in the street.

I am, therefore, asking the Congress to enact legislation giving all Americans the right to be served in facilities which are open to the public—hotels, restaurants, theaters, retail stores, and similar establishments.

This seems to me to be an elementary right. Its denial is an arbitrary indignity that no American in 1963 should have to endure, but many do.

I have recently met with scores of business leaders urging them to take voluntary action to end this discrimination and I have been encouraged by their response, and in the last 2 weeks over 75 cities have seen progress made in desegregating these kinds of facilities. But many are unwilling to act alone, and for this reason, nationwide legislation is needed if we are to move this problem from the streets to the courts.

I am also asking Congress to authorize the Federal Government to participate more fully in lawsuits designed to end segregation in public education. We have succeeded in persuading many districts to desegregate voluntarily. Dozens have admitted Negroes without violence. Today a Negro is attending a State-supported institution in every one of our 50 States, but the pace is very slow.

Too many Negro children entering segregated grade schools at the time of the Supreme Court's decision 9 years ago will enter segregated high schools this fall, having suffered a loss which can never be restored. The lack of an adequate education denies the Negro a chance to get a decent job.

The orderly implementation of the Supreme Court decision, therefore, cannot be left solely to those who may not have the economic resources to carry the legal action or who may be subject to harassment.

Other features will be also requested, including greater protection for the right to vote. But legislation, I repeat, cannot solve this problem alone. It must be solved in the homes of every American in every community across our country.

In this respect, I want to pay tribute to those citizens North and South who have been working in their communities to make life better for all. They are acting not out of a sense of legal duty but out of a sense of human decency.

Like our soldiers and sailors in all parts of the world they are meeting freedom's challenge on the firing line, and I salute them for their honor and their courage.

My fellow Americans, this is a problem which faces us all—in every city of the North as well as the South. Today there are Negroes unemployed, two or three times as many compared to whites, inadequate in education, moving into the large cities, unable to find work, young people particularly out of work without hope, denied equal rights, denied the opportunity to eat at a restaurant or lunch counter or go to a movie theater, denied the right to a decent education, denied almost today the right to attend a State university even though qualified. It seems to me that these are matters which concern us all, not merely Presidents or Congressmen or Governors, but every citizen of the United States.

This is one country. It has become one country because all of us and all the people who came here had an equal chance to develop their talents.

We cannot say to 10 percent of the population that you can't have that right; that your children can't have the chance to develop whatever talents they have; that the only way that they are going to get their rights is to go into the streets and demonstrate. I think we owe them and we owe ourselves a better country than that.

Therefore, I am asking for your help in making it easier for us to move ahead and to provide the kind of equality of treatment which we would want ourselves; to give a chance for every child to be educated to the limit of his talents.

As I have said before, not every child has an equal talent or an equal ability or an equal motivation, but they should have the equal right to develop their talent and their ability and their motivation, to make something of themselves.

We have a right to expect that the Negro community will be responsible, will uphold the law, but they have a right to expect that the law will be fair, that the

Constitution will be color blind, as Justice Harlan said at the turn of the century.

This is what we are talking about and this is a matter which concerns this country and what it stands for, and in meeting it I ask the support of all our citizens.

Thank you very much.

Martin Luther King, Jr.

I Have a Dream
(August 28, 1963)

The idea for a civil rights march on Washington had been nurtured by A. Philip Randolph, of the Brotherhood of Sleeping Car Porters, for over twenty years. In 1963 Bayard Rustin took up the call, in the belief that the march would dramatize the cause, attract widespread national attention, and pressure the administration and Congress to approve the civil rights bill. Some leaders were opposed, either because of internecine quarrels over which organizations would get credit or because the march might undermine the political stature of the five black congressmen. In late June, however, agreement was reached for a March on Washington for Jobs and Freedom, to be held on August 28.

President Kennedy was less than enthusiastic about the march. He feared that it might degenerate into violence or that it might be construed as an attempt to intimidate Congress—either result being counterproductive to the cause of the civil rights bill. Seeing that the march could not be prevented, however, he embraced it as being in the tradition of peaceful assembly for redress of grievances. Government agencies developed plans to assure order and safety, including portable toilets and plastic drinking cups. In the event, these concerns proved to be unnecessary. Two hundred thousand people, both black and white, gathered without incident in Washington and, at the end of the march, lined both sides of the Reflecting Pool facing the Lincoln Memorial to hear a series of speakers.

These, too, had been controversial. Some civil rights groups, believing the pace of change to be glacial, wanted to excoriate the leaders of white society, the very people whom others regarded as their allies in the civil rights struggle. The fact that the march was sponsored by a coalition of groups toned down the more radical, and personal pressure caused John Lewis of the Student Nonviolent Coordinating Committee to delete strong criticism of the administration from his remarks. The final speaker was Martin Luther King, Jr., who had achieved a leadership role in the movement but who had been criticized by more militant figures for the ineffectuality of his methods of civil disobedience and nonviolent resistance.

The speech King delivered has become one of the classics of modern American public discourse. It effectively balanced militancy and moderation, stressing the urgency of the moment but denouncing violence and repudiating attacks on white liberals. The prosaic metaphor of "cashing a check" was appropriate to this goal, since a check is a demand instrument that is presented in civil fashion. The speech also subsumed the tactical disputes among civil rights leaders with a vision of the ideal to be achieved, yet reassuringly rooted this ideal in "the American dream." The demand was for inclusion within society, not a challenge to it. And the speech merged the appeal of political oratory with the cadence, crescendo, and emotional intensity of the Southern black church. Most of the speech was not new; parts of it can be found in other King speeches during the preceding years. But the combination of elements so fused speaker and situation that it is this speech for which both King and the March on Washington are known.

President Kennedy met the leaders of the march afterward at the White House, greeting them with the words, "I have a dream." Originally intended to stress jobs and economic issues, the march was used in support of the civil rights bill. That measure was still working its way through the Congress at the time of Kennedy's death; eventual passage seemed likely but difficult days lay ahead. Lyndon Johnson championed the bill as a memorial to his slain predecessor. After a lengthy filibuster in the Senate, it passed the Congress in June 1964, and was signed into law on July 2. Although much remains to be done, the act has played a major role in the transformation of race relations in America during the past quarter century.

Five score years ago, a great American, in whose symbolic shadow we stand, signed the Emancipation Proclamation. This momentous decree came as a great beacon light of hope to millions of Negro slaves who had been seared in the flames of withering injustice. It came as a joyous daybreak to end the long night of captivity.

But one hundred years later, we must face the tragic fact that the Negro is still not free. One hundred years later, the life of the Negro is still sadly crippled by the manacles of segregation and the chains of discrimination. One hundred years later, the Negro lives on a lonely island of poverty in the midst of a vast ocean of material prosperity. One hundred years later, the Negro is still languished in the corners of American society and finds himself an exile in his own land. So we have come here today to dramatize an appalling condition.

In a sense we have come to our nation's Capital to cash a check. When the architects of our republic wrote the magnificent words of the Constitution and the Declaration of Independence, they were signing a promissory note to which every American was to fall heir. This note was a promise that all men would be guaranteed the unalienable rights of life, liberty, and the pursuit of happiness.

It is obvious today that America has defaulted on this promissory note insofar as her citizens of color are concerned. Instead of honoring this sacred obligation, America has given the Negro people a bad check; a check which has come back marked "insufficient funds." But we refuse to believe that the bank of justice is bankrupt. We refuse to believe that there are insufficient funds in the great vaults of opportunity of this nation. So we have come to cash this check—a check that will give us upon demand the riches of freedom and the security of justice. We have also come to this hallowed spot to remind America of the fierce urgency of *now*. This is no time to engage in the luxury of cooling off or to take the tranquilizing drug of gradualism. *Now* is the time to make real the promises of Democracy. *Now* is the time to rise from the dark and desolate valley of segregation to the sunlit path of racial justice. *Now* is the time to open the doors of opportunity to all of God's children. *Now* is the time to lift our nation from the quicksands of racial injustice to the solid rock of brotherhood.

It would be fatal for the nation to overlook the urgency of the moment and to underestimate the determination of the Negro. This sweltering summer of the Negro's legitimate discontent will not pass until there is an invigorating autumn of freedom and equality. 1963 is not an end, but a beginning. Those who hope that the Negro needed to blow off steam and will now be content will have a rude awakening if the nation returns to business as usual. There will be neither rest nor tranquillity in America until the Negro is granted his citizenship rights. The whirlwinds of revolt will continue to shake the foundations of our nation until the bright day of justice emerges.

But there is something that I must say to my people who stand on the warm threshold which leads into the palace of justice. In the process of gaining our rightful place we must not be guilty of wrongful deeds. Let us not seek to satisfy our thirst for freedom by drinking from the cup of bitterness and hatred. We must forever conduct our struggle on the high plane of dignity and discipline. We must not allow our creative protest to degenerate into physical violence. Again and again we must rise to the majestic heights of meeting physical force with soul force. The marvelous new militancy which has engulfed the Negro community must not lead us to a distrust of all white people, for many of our white brothers, as evidenced by their presence here today, have come to realize that their destiny is tied up with our destiny and their freedom is inextricably bound to our freedom. We cannot walk alone.

And as we walk, we must make the pledge that we shall march ahead. We cannot turn back. There are those who are asking the devotees of civil rights, "When will you be satisfied?" We can never be satisfied as long as the Negro is the victim of the unspeakable horrors of police brutality. We can never be satisfied as long as our bodies, heavy with the fatigue of travel, cannot gain lodging in the motels of the highways and the hotels of the cities. We cannot be satisfied as long as the Negro's basic mobility is from a smaller ghetto to a larger one. We can never be satisfied as long as a Negro in Mississippi cannot vote and a Negro in New

York believes he has nothing for which to vote. No, no, we are not satisfied, and we will not be satisfied until justice rolls down like waters and righteousness like a mighty stream.

I am not unmindful that some of you have come here out of great trials and tribulations. Some of you have come fresh from narrow jail cells. Some of you have come from areas where your quest for freedom left you battered by the storms of persecution and staggered by the winds of police brutality. You have been the veterans of creative suffering. Continue to work with the faith that unearned suffering is redemptive.

Go back to Mississippi, go back to Alabama, go back to South Carolina, go back to Georgia, go back to Louisiana, go back to the slums and ghettos of our northern cities, knowing that somehow this situation can and will be changed. Let us not wallow in the valley of despair.

I say to you today, my friends, that in spite of the difficulties and frustrations of the moment I still have a dream. It is a dream deeply rooted in the American dream.

I have a dream that one day this nation will rise up and live out the true meaning of its creed: "We hold these truths to be self-evident; that all men are created equal."

I have a dream that one day on the red hills of Georgia the sons of former slaves and the sons of former slaveowners will be able to sit down together at the table of brotherhood.

I have a dream that one day even the state of Mississippi, a desert state sweltering with the heat of injustice and oppression, will be transformed into an oasis of freedom and justice.

I have a dream that my four little children will one day live in a nation where they will not be judged by the color of their skin but by the content of their character.

I have a dream today.

I have a dream that one day the state of Alabama, whose governor's lips are presently dripping with the words of interposition and nullification, will be transformed into a situation where little black boys and black girls will be able to join hands with little white boys and white girls and walk together as sisters and brothers.

I have a dream today.

I have a dream that one day every valley shall be exalted, every hill and mountain shall be made low, the rough places will be made plain, and the crooked places will be made straight, and the glory of the Lord shall be revealed, and all flesh shall see it together.

This is our hope. This is the faith with which I return to the South. With this faith we will be able to hew out of the mountain of despair a stone of hope. With this faith we will be able to transform the jangling discords of our nation into a beautiful symphony of brotherhood. With this faith we will be able to work together, to pray together, to struggle together, to go to jail together, to stand up for freedom together, knowing that we will be free one day.

This will be the day when all of God's children will be able to sing with new meaning

My country, 'tis of thee,
Sweet land of liberty,
  Of thee I sing:
Land where my fathers died,
Land of the pilgrims' pride,
From every mountain-side
  Let freedom ring.

And if America is to be a great nation this must become true. So let freedom ring from the prodigious hilltops of New Hampshire. Let freedom ring from the mighty mountains of New York. Let freedom ring from the heightening Alleghenies of Pennsylvania!

Let freedom ring from the snowcapped Rockies of Colorado!

Let freedom ring from the curvacious peaks of California!

But not only that; let freedom ring from Stone Mountain of Georgia!

Let freedom ring from Lookout Mountain of Tennessee!

Let freedom ring from every hill and molehill of Mississippi. From every mountainside, let freedom ring.

When we let freedom ring, when we let it ring from every village and every hamlet, from every state and every city, we will be able to speed up that day when all of God's children, black men and white men, Jews and Gentiles, Protestants and Catholics, will be able to join hands and sing in the words of the old Negro spiritual, "Free at last! free at last! thank God almighty, we are free at last!"

Malcolm X

The Ballot or the Bullet
(April 3, 1964)

For most thoughtful observers during the early 1960's, the solution to America's race relations problem was the full integration of blacks into every segment of American life. Few knew of the Black Muslims or their proposals for separate black states; most who did believed that black separatism was retrogressive and antithetical to the goals of civil rights.

One of the few Black Muslims who was reasonably well known was Malcolm X. Born Malcolm Little and having had a difficult childhood, he converted to Islam while in prison. He became a disciple of Elijah Muhammed and believed that the separation of the races had been ordained by God. He was but an agent for God's divine plan. Malcolm was regarded by many as a rabble-rouser because he did not explicitly reject violence as a tactical method. He had no clear political program and there was little connection between his theology and his advocacy.

Malcolm X attracted increasing support among younger blacks in northern ghettoes, for whom the Southern approach of nonviolent protest, seeking equal admission into a good society, was not relevant. To Malcolm, an a priori commitment to nonviolence put blacks in the position of supplicants. He urged that they demand what was rightfully theirs and then act to satisfy their demands by whatever means were necessary. He did not advocate violence, but he certainly did not preclude it as a means of self-defense.

Malcolm X bespoke the rage and impotence of the ghetto. He sought to instill race pride in black audiences and to accuse white America of crimes against blacks. He believed that American society was inherently racist, and therefore that no good could come of racial integration. He dismissed the 1963 March on Washington as a "farce on Washington" and bitterly opposed the leadership of Martin Luther King. The only remedy he could envision was separation from white America, either by returning to Africa (thus ending exile) or by establishing separate black states. "Separation," indeed, is the key term of Malcolm's rhetoric. In speaking on topics such as "the Negro's position in contemporary American society," he argued that the title was self-contradictory.

The speech for which Malcolm is best known is "The Ballot or the Bullet," portions of which are reproduced here. In this speech, instead of petitioning or requesting the right to vote, Malcolm demands it by clearly implying that the bullet was the alternative. Blacks would assert themselves and would obtain their rights, through ballots if possible but with bullets if necessary.

Malcolm's growing popularity in the ghetto made him a threat to Black Muslim leaders. Elijah Muhammed silenced Malcolm in late 1963 and, the following spring, moved him out of the organization. This move left Malcolm without a theological anchor but also left him freer to espouse his black nationalism. He aroused enmity among Black Muslims, though, and in early 1965 he was assassinated by his Muslim enemies.

The program of black nationalism has never proved to be persuasive. But in questioning the value of integration, Malcolm X was ahead of his time. Within a year of his death, both white and black leaders were having second thoughts. Integration wrenched blacks from their culture and in its own way implied that the values of white society were superior to their own. While they did not specifically reject integration, civil rights leaders increasingly argued that fundamental changes in white society were preconditions for success. From the unquestioned assumption that America was a good society, advocates moved closer to embracing cultural pluralism and seeking a new synthesis. The eloquence of Malcolm X helped to contribute to this result.

Mr. Moderator, Brother Lomax, brothers and sisters, friends and enemies:—I just can't believe everyone in here is a friend and I don't want to leave anybody out. The question tonight, as I understand it, is "The Negro Revolt, and Where Do We Go From Here?" or "What's Next?" In my little humble way of understanding it, it points toward either the ballot or the bullet.

Before we try and explain what is meant by the ballot or the bullet, I would like to clarify something concerning myself. I'm still a Muslim, my religion is still Islam. That's my personal belief. Just as Adam Clayton Powell is a Christian minister who heads the Abyssinian Baptist Church in New York, but at the same time takes part in the political struggles to try and bring about rights to the black people in this country; and Dr. Martin Luther King is a Christian minister down in Atlanta, Georgia, who heads another organization fighting for the civil rights of black people in this country; and Rev. Galamison, I guess you've heard of him, is another Christian minister in New York who has been deeply involved in the school boycotts to eliminate segregated education; well, I myself am a minister, not a Christian minister, but a Muslim minister; and I believe in action on all fronts by whatever means necessary.

Although I'm still a Muslim, I'm not here tonight to discuss my religion. I'm not here to try and change your religion. I'm not here to argue or discuss anything that we differ about, because it's time for us to submerge our differences and realize that it is best for us to first see that we have the same problem, a common problem—a problem that will make you catch hell whether you're a Baptist, or a Methodist, or a Muslim, or a nationalist. Whether you're educated or illiterate, whether you live on the boulevard or in the alley, you're going to catch hell just like I am. We're all in the same boat and we all are going to catch the same hell from the same man. He just happens to be a white man. All of us have suffered here, in this country, political oppression at the hands of the white man, economic exploitation at the hands of the white man, and social degradation at the hands of the white man.

Now in speaking like this, it doesn't mean that we're anti-white, but it does mean we're anti-exploitation, we're anti-degradation, we're anti-oppression. And if the white man doesn't want us to be anti-him, let him stop oppressing and exploiting and degrading us. Whether we are Christians or Muslims or nationalists or agnostics or atheists, we must first learn to forget our differences. If we have differences, let us differ in the closet; when we come out in front, let us not have anything to argue about until we get finished arguing with the man. If the late President Kennedy could get together with Khrushchev and exchange some wheat, we certainly have more in common with each other than Kennedy and Khrushchev had with each other.

If we don't do something real soon, I think you'll have to agree that we're going to be forced either to use the ballot or the bullet. It's one or the other in 1964. It isn't that time is running out—time has run out! 1964 threatens to be the most explosive year America has ever witnessed. The most explosive year. Why? It's also a political year. It's the year when all of the white politicians will be back in the so-called Negro community jiving you and me for some votes. The year when all of the white political crooks will be right back in your and my community with their false promises, building up our hopes for a letdown, with their trickery and their treachery, with their false promises which they don't intend to keep. As they nourish these dissatisfactions, it can only lead to one thing, an explosion; and now we have the type of black man on the scene in America today—I'm sorry, Brother Lomax—who just doesn't intend to turn the other cheek any longer.

Don't let anybody tell you anything about the odds are against you. If they draft you, they send you to Korea and make you face 800 million Chinese. If you can be brave over there, you can be brave right here. These odds aren't as great as those odds. And if you fight here, you will at least know what you're fighting for.

I'm not a politician, not even a student of politics; in fact, I'm not a student of much of anything. I'm not a Democrat, I'm not a Republican, and I don't even consider myself an American. If you and I were Americans, there'd be no problem. Those Hunkies that just got off the boat, they're already Americans; Polacks are already Americans; the Italian refugees are already Americans. Everything that came out of Europe, every blue-eyed thing, is already an American. And as long as you and I have been over here, we aren't Americans yet.

Well, I am one who doesn't believe in deluding myself. I'm not going to sit at your table and watch you eat, with nothing on my plate, and call myself a diner. Sitting at the table doesn't make you a diner, unless you eat some of what's on that plate. Being here in America doesn't make you an American. Being born here in America doesn't make you an American. Why, if birth made you American, you wouldn't need any legislation, you wouldn't need any amendments to the Constitution, you wouldn't be faced with civil-rights filibustering in Washington, D.C., right now. They don't have to pass civil-rights legislation to make a Polack an American.

No, I'm not an American. I'm one of the 22 million black people who are the victims of Americanism. One of the 22 million black people who are the victims of democracy, nothing but disguised hypocrisy. So, I'm not standing here speaking to you as an American, or a patriot, or a flag-saluter, or a flag-waver—no, not I. I'm speaking as a victim of this American system. And I see America through the eyes of the victim. I don't see any American dream; I see an American nightmare.

These 22 million victims are waking up. Their eyes are coming open. They're beginning to see what they used to only look at. They're becoming politically mature. They are realizing that there are new political trends from coast to coast. As they see these new political trends, it's possible for them to see that every time there's an election the races are so close that they have to have a recount. They had to recount in Massachusetts to see who was going to be governor, it was so close. It was the same way in Rhode Island, in Minnesota, and in many other parts of the country. And the same with Kennedy and Nixon when they ran for president. It was so close they had to count all over again. Well, what does this mean? It means that when white people are evenly divided, and black people have a bloc of votes of their own, it is left up to them to determine who's going to sit in the White House and who's going to be in the dog house.

It was the black man's vote that put the present administration in Washington, D.C. Your vote, your dumb vote, your ignorant vote, your wasted vote put in an administration in Washington, D.C., that has seen fit to pass every kind of legislation imaginable, saving you until last, then filibustering on top of that. And your and my leaders have the audacity to run around clapping their hands and talk about how much progress we're making. And what a good president we have. If he wasn't good in Texas, he sure can't be good in Washington, D.C. Because Texas is a lynch state. It is in the same breath as Mississippi, no different; only they lynch you in Texas with a Texas accent and lynch you in Mississippi with a Mississippi accent. And these

Negro leaders have the audacity to go and have some coffee in the White House with a Texan, a Southern cracker—that's all he is—and then come out and tell you and me that he's going to be better for us because, since he's from the South, he knows how to deal with the Southerners. What kind of logic is that? Let Eastland be president, he's from the South too. He should be better able to deal with them than Johnson.

In this present administration they have in the House of Representatives 257 Democrats to only 177 Republicans. They control two-thirds of the House vote. Why can't they pass something that will help you and me? In the Senate, there are 67 senators who are of the Democratic Party. Only 33 of them are Republicans. Why, the Democrats have got the government sewed up, and you're the one who sewed it up for them. And what have they given you for it? Four years in office, and just now getting around to some civil-rights legislation. Just now, after everything else is gone, out of the way, they're going to sit down now and play with you all summer long—the same old giant con game that they call filibuster. All those are in cahoots together. Don't you ever think they're not in cahoots together, for the man that is heading the civil-rights filibuster is a man from Georgia named Richard Russell. When Johnson became president, the first man he asked for when he got back to Washington, D.C., was "Dicky"—that's how tight they are. That's his boy, that's his pal, that's his buddy. But they're playing that old con game. One of them makes believe he's for you, and he's got it fixed where the other one is so tight against you, he never has to keep his promise.

So it's time in 1964 to wake up. And when you see them coming up with that kind of conspiracy, let them know your eyes are open. And let them know you got something else that's wide open too. It's got to be the ballot or the bullet. The ballot or the bullet. If you're afraid to use an expression like that, you should get on out of the country, you should get back in the cotton patch, you should get back in the alley. They get all the Negro vote, and after they get it, the Negro gets nothing in return. All they did when they got to Washington was give a few big Negroes big jobs. Those big Negroes didn't need big jobs, they already had jobs. That's camouflage, that's trickery, that's treachery, window-dressing. I'm not trying to knock out the Democrats for the Republicans, we'll get to them in a minute. But it is true—you put the Democrats first and the Democrats put you last.

Look at it the way it is. What alibis do they use,

since they control Congress and the Senate? What alibi do they use when you and I ask, "Well, when are you going to keep your promise?" They blame the Dixiecrats. What is a Dixiecrat? A Democrat. A Dixiecrat is nothing but a Democrat in disguise. The titular head of the Democrats is also the head of the Dixiecrats, because the Dixiecrats are a part of the Democratic Party. The Democrats have never kicked the Dixiecrats out of the party. The Dixiecrats bolted themselves once, but the Democrats didn't put them out. Imagine, these lowdown Southern segregationists put the Northern Democrats down. But the Northern Democrats have never put the Dixiecrats down. No, look at that thing the way it is. They have got a con game going on, a political con game, and you and I are in the middle. It's time for you and me to wake up and start looking at it like it is, and trying to understand it like it is; and then we can deal with it like it is.

The Dixiecrats in Washington, D.C., control the key committees that run the government. The only reason the Dixiecrats control these committees is because they have seniority. The only reason they have seniority is because they come from states where Negroes can't vote. This is not even a government that's based on democracy. It is not a government that is made up of representatives of the people. Half of the people in the South can't even vote. Eastland is not even supposed to be in Washington. Half of the senators and congressmen who occupy these key positions in Washington, D.C., are there illegally, are there unconstitutionally.

I was in Washington, D.C., a week ago Thursday, when they were debating whether or not they should let the bill come onto the floor. And in the back of the room where the Senate meets, there's a huge map of the United States, and on that map it shows the location of Negroes throughout the country. And it shows that the Southern section of the country, the states that are most heavily concentrated with Negroes, are the ones that have senators and congressmen standing up filibustering and doing all other kinds of trickery to keep the Negro from being able to vote. This is pitiful. But it's not pitiful for us any longer; it's actually pitiful for the white man, because soon now, as the Negro awakens a little more and sees the vise that he's in, sees the bag that he's in, sees the real game that he's in, then the Negro's going to develop a new tactic.

These senators and congressmen actually violate the constitutional amendments that guarantee the people of that particular state or county the right to vote.

And the Constitution itself has within it the machinery to expel any representative from a state where the voting rights of the people are violated. You don't even need new legislation. Any person in Congress right now, who is there from a state or a district where the voting rights of the people are violated, that particular person should be expelled from Congress. And when you expel him, you've removed one of the obstacles in the path of any real meaningful legislation in this country. In fact, when you expel them, you don't need new legislation, because they will be replaced by black representatives from counties and districts where the black man is in the majority, not in the minority.

If the black man in these Southern states had his full voting rights, the key Dixiecrats in Washington, D.C., which means the key Democrats in Washington, D.C., would lose their seats. The Democratic Party itself would lose its power. It would cease to be powerful as a party. When you see the amount of power that would be lost by the Democratic Party if it were to lose the Dixiecrat wing, or branch, or element, you can see where it's against the interests of the Democrats to give voting rights to Negroes in states where the Democrats have been in complete power and authority ever since the Civil War. You just can't belong to that party without analyzing it.

I say again, I'm not anti-Democrat, I'm not anti-Republican, I'm not anti-anything. I'm just questioning their sincerity, and some of the strategy that they've been using on our people by promising them promises that they don't intend to keep. When you keep the Democrats in power, you're keeping the Dixiecrats in power. I doubt that my good Brother Lomax will deny that. A vote for a Democrat is a vote for a Dixiecrat. That's why, in 1964, it's time now for you and me to become more politically mature and realize what the ballot; and that if we don't cast a ballot, it's going to end up in a situation where we're going to have to cast a bullet. It's either a ballot or a bullet.

In the North, they do it a different way. They have a system that's known as gerrymandering, whatever that means. It means when Negroes become too heavily concentrated in a certain area, and begin to gain too much political power, the white man comes along and changes the district lines. You may say, "Why do you keep saying white man?" Because it's the white man who does it. I haven't ever seen any Negro changing any lines. They don't let him get near the line. It's the white man who does this. And usually, it's the white man who grins at you the most, and pats you on the

back, and is supposed to be your friend. He may be friendly, but he's not your friend.

So, what I'm trying to impress upon you, in essence, is this: You and I in America are faced not with a segregationist conspiracy, we're faced with a government conspiracy. Everyone who's filibustering is a senator—that's the government. Everyone who's finagling in Washington, D.C., is a congressman—that's the government. You don't have anybody putting blocks in your path but people who are a part of the government. The same government that you go abroad to fight for and die for is the government that is in a conspiracy to deprive you of your voting rights, deprive you of your economic opportunities, deprive you of decent housing, deprive you of decent education. You don't need to go to the employer alone, it is the government itself, the government of America, that is responsible for the oppression and exploitation and degradation of black people in this country. And you should drop it in their lap. This government has failed the Negro. This so-called democracy has failed the Negro. And all these white liberals have definitely failed the Negro.

So, where do we go from here? First, we need some friends. We need some new allies. The entire civil-rights struggle needs a new interpretation, a broader interpretation. We need to look at this civil-rights thing from another angle—from the inside as well as from the outside. To those of us whose philosophy is black nationalism, the only way you can get involved in the civil-rights struggle is give it a new interpretation. That old interpretation excluded us. It kept us out. So, we're giving a new interpretation to the civil-rights struggle, an interpretation that will enable us to come into it, take part in it. And these handkerchief-heads who have been dillydallying and pussyfooting and compromising—we don't intend to let them pussyfoot and dillydally and compromise any longer.

How can you thank a man for giving you what's already yours? How then can you thank him for giving you only part of what's already yours? You haven't even made progress, if what's being given to you, you should have had already. That's not progress. And I love my Brother Lomax, the way he pointed out we're right back where we were in 1954. We're not even as far up as we were in 1954. We're behind where we were in 1954. There's more segregation now than there was in 1954. There's more racial animosity, more racial hatred, more racial violence today in 1964, than there was in 1954. Where is the progress?

And now you're facing a situation where the

young Negro's coming up. They don't want to hear that "turn-the-other-cheek" stuff, no. In Jacksonville, those were teenagers, they were throwing Molotov cocktails. Negroes have never done that before. But it shows you there's a new deal coming in. There's new thinking coming in. There's new strategy coming in. It'll be Molotov cocktails this month, hand grenades next month, and something else next month. It'll be ballots, or it'll be bullets. It'll be liberty, or it will be death. The only difference about this kind of death—it'll be reciprocal. You know what is meant by "reciprocal"? That's one of Brother Lomax's words, I stole it from him. I don't ususally deal with those big words because I don't usually deal with big people. I deal with small people. I find you can get a whole lot of small people and whip hell out of a whole lot of big people. They haven't got anything to lose, and they've got everything to gain. And they'll let you know in a minute: "It takes two to tango; when I go, you go."

The black nationalists, those whose philosophy is black nationalism, in bringing about this new interpretation of the entire meaning of civil rights, look upon it as meaning, as Brother Lomax has pointed out, equality of opportunity. Well, we're justified in seeking civil rights, if it means equality of opportunity, because all we're doing there is trying to collect for our investment. Our mothers and fathers invested sweat and blood. Three hundred and ten years we worked in this country without a dime in return—I mean without a *dime* in return. You let the white man walk around here talking about how rich this country is, but you never stop to think how it got rich so quick. It got rich because you made it rich.

You take the people who are in this audience right now. They're poor, we're all poor as individuals. Our weekly salary individually amounts to hardly anything. But if you take the salary of everyone in here collectively it'll fill up a whole lot of baskets. It's a lot of wealth. If you can collect the wages of just these people right here for a year, you'll be rich—richer than rich. When you look at it like that, think how rich Uncle Sam had to become, not with this handful, but millions of black people. Your and my mother and father, who didn't work an eight-hour shift, but worked from "can't see" in the morning until "can't see" at night, and worked for nothing, making the white man rich, making Uncle Sam rich.

This is our investment. This is our contribution—our blood. Not only did we give of our free labor, we gave of our blood. Every time he had a call to arms, we were the first ones in uniform. We died on every battlefield the white man had. We have made a greater sacrifice than anybody who's standing up in America today. We have made a greater contribution and have collected less. Civil rights, for those of us whose philosophy is black nationalism, means: "Give it to us now. Don't wait for next year. Give it to us yesterday, and that's not fast enough."

I might stop right here to point out one thing. Whenever you're going after something that belongs to you, anyone who's depriving you of the right to have it is a criminal. Understand that. Whenever you are going after something that is yours, you are within your legal rights to lay claim to it. And anyone who puts forth any effort to deprive you of that which is yours, is breaking the law, is a criminal. And this was pointed out by the Supreme Court decision. It outlawed segregation. Which means segregation is against the law. Which means a segregationist is breaking the law. A segregationist is a criminal. You can't label him as anything other than that. And when you demonstrate against segregation, the law is on your side. The Supreme Court is on your side.

Now, who is it that opposes you in carrying out the law? The police department itself. With police dogs and clubs. Whenever you demonstrate against segregation, whether it is segregated education, segregated housing, or anything else, the law is on your side, and anyone who stands in the way is not the law any longer. They are breaking the law, they are not representatives of the law. Any time you demonstrate against segregation and a man has the audacity to put a police dog on you, kill that dog, kill him, I'm telling you, kill that dog. I say it, if they put me in jail tomorrow, kill—that—dog. Then you'll put a stop to it. Now, if these white people in here don't want to see that kind of action, get down and tell the mayor to tell the police department to pull the dogs in. That's all you have to do. If you don't do it, someone else will.

If you don't take this kind of stand, your little children will grow up and look at you and think "shame." If you don't take an uncompromising stand—I don't mean go out and get violent; but at the same time you should never be nonviolent unless you run into some nonviolence. I'm nonviolent with those who are nonviolent with me. But when you drop that violence on me, then you've made me go insane, and I'm not responsible for what I do. And that's the way every Negro should get. Any time you know you're within the law, within your legal rights, within your moral rights, in accord with justice, then die for what you believe in. But don't die alone. Let your dying be reciprocal. This is what is meant by equality. What's good for the goose is good for the gander.

When we begin to get in this area, we need new friends, we need new allies. We need to expand the civil-rights struggle to a higher level—to the level of human rights. Whenever you are in a civil-rights struggle, whether you know it or not, you are confining yourself to the jurisdiction of Uncle Sam. No one from the outside world can speak out in your behalf as long as your struggle is a civil-rights struggle. Civil rights comes within the domestic affairs of this country. All of our African brothers and our Asian brothers and our Latin-American brothers cannot open their mouths and interfere in the domestic affairs of the United States. And as long as it's civil rights, this comes under the jurisdiction of Uncle Sam.

But the United Nations has what's known as the charter of human rights, it has a committee that deals in human rights. You may wonder why all of the atrocities that have been committed in Africa and in Hungary and in Asia and in Latin America are brought before the UN, and the Negro problem is never brought before the UN. This is part of the conspiracy. This old, tricky, blue-eyed liberal who is supposed to be your and my friend, supposed to be in our corner, supposed to be subsidizing our struggle, and supposed to be acting in the capacity of an adviser, never tells you anything about human rights. They keep you wrapped up in civil rights. And you spend so much time barking up the civil-rights tree, you don't even know there's a human-rights tree on the same floor.

When you expand the civil-rights struggle to the level of human rights, you can then take the case of the black man in this country before the nations in the UN. You can take it before the General Assembly. You can take Uncle Sam before a world court. But the only level you can do it on is the level of human rights. Civil rights keeps you under his restrictions, under his jurisdiction. Civil rights keeps you in his pocket. Civil rights means you're asking Uncle Sam to treat you right. Human rights are something you were born with. Human rights are your God-given rights. Human rights are the rights that are recognized by all nations of this earth. And any time any one violates your human rights, you can take them to the world court. Uncle Sam's hands are dripping with blood, dripping with the blood of the black man in this country. He's the earth's number-one hypocrite. He has the audacity—yes, he

has—imagine him posing as the leader of the free world. The free world!—and you over here singing "We Shall Overcome." Expand the civil-rights struggle to the level of human rights, take it into the United Nations, where our African brothers can throw their weight on our side, where our Latin-American brothers can throw their weight on our side, and where 800 million Chinamen are sitting there waiting to throw their weight on our side.

Let the world know how bloody his hands are. Let the world know the hypocrisy that's practiced over here. Let it be the ballot or the bullet. Let him know that it must be the ballot or the bullet.

When you take your case to Washington, D.C., you're taking it to the criminal who's responsible; it's like running from the wolf to the fox. They're all in cahoots together. They all work political chicanery and make you look like a chump before the eyes of the world. Here you are walking around in America, getting ready to be drafted and sent abroad, like a tin soldier, and when you get over there, people ask you what are you fighting for, and you have to stick your tongue in your cheek. No, take Uncle Sam to court, take him before the world.

By ballot I only mean freedom. Don't you know—I disagree with Lomax on this issue—that the ballot is more important than the dollar? Can I prove it? Yes. Look in the UN. There are poor nations in the UN; yet those poor nations can get together with their voting power and keep the rich nations from making a move. They have one nation—one vote, everyone has an equal vote. And when those brothers from Asia, and Africa and the darker parts of this earth get together, their voting power is sufficient to hold Sam in check. Or Russia in check. Or some other section of the earth in check. So, the ballot is most important.

Right now, in this country, if you and I, 22 million African-Americans—that's what we are—Africans who are in America. You're nothing but Africans. Nothing but Africans. In fact, you'd get farther calling yourself African instead of Negro. Africans don't catch hell. You're the only one catching hell. They don't have to pass civil-rights bills for Africans. An African can go anywhere he wants right now. All you've got to do is tie your head up. That's right, go anywhere you want. Just stop being a Negro. Change your name to Hoogagagooba. That'll show you how silly the white man is. You're dealing with a silly man. A friend of mine who's very dark put a turban on his head and went into a restaurant in Atlanta before they called themselves desegregated. He went into a white restaurant, he sat down, they served him, and he said, "What would happen if a Negro came in here?" And there he's sitting, black as night, but because he had his head wrapped up the waitress looked back at him and says, "Why, there wouldn't no nigger dare come in here."

So, you're dealing with a man whose bias and prejudice are making him lose his mind, his intelligence, every day. He's frightened. He looks around and sees what's taking place on this earth, and he sees that the pendulum of time is swinging in your direction. The dark people are waking up. They're losing their fear of the white man. No place where he's fighting right now is he winning. Everywhere he's fighting, he's fighting someone your and my complexion. And they're beating him. He can't win any more. He's won his last battle. He failed to win the Korean War. He couldn't win it. He had to sign a truce. That's a loss. Any time Uncle Sam, with all his machinery for warfare, is held to a draw by some rice-eaters, he's lost the battle. He had to sign a truce. America's not supposed to sign a truce. She's supposed to be bad. But she's not bad any more. She's bad as long as she can use her hydrogen bomb, but she can't use hers for fear Russia might use hers. Russia can't use hers, for fear that Sam might use his. So, both of them are weaponless. They can't use the weapon because each's weapon nullifies the other's. So the only place where action can take place is on the ground. And the white man can't win another war fighting on the ground. Those days are over. The black man knows it, the brown man knows it, the red man knows it, and the yellow man knows it. So they engage him in guerrilla warfare. That's not his style. You've got to have heart to be a guerrilla warrior, and he hasn't got any heart. I'm telling you now.

I just want to give you a little briefing on guerrilla warfare because, before you know it, before you know it—It takes heart to be a guerrilla warrior because you're on your own. In conventional warfare you have tanks and a whole lot of other people with you to back you up, planes over your head and all that kind of stuff. But a guerrilla is on his own. All you have is a rifle, some sneakers and a bowl of rice, and that's all you need—and a lot of heart. The Japanese on some of those islands in the Pacific, when the American soldiers landed, one Japanese sometimes could hold the whole army off. He'd just wait until the sun went down, and when the sun went down they were all equal. He would take his little blade and slip from bush to bush, and from American to American. The white soldiers couldn't cope with that. Whenever you see a white soldier that fought in the Pacific, he has the shakes, he has a nervous condition, because they scared him to death.

The same thing happened to the French up in French Indochina. People who just a few years previously were rice farmers got together and ran the heavily-mechanized French army out of Indochina. You don't need it—modern warfare today won't work. This is the day of the guerrilla. They did the same thing in Algeria. Algerians, who were nothing but Bedouins, took a rifle and sneaked off to the hills, and de Gaulle and all of his highfalutin' war machinery couldn't defeat those guerrillas. Nowhere on this earth does the white man win in a guerrilla warfare. It's not his speed. Just as guerrilla warfare is prevailing in Asia and in parts of Africa and in parts of Latin America, you've got to be mighty naive, or you've got to play the black man cheap, if you don't think some day he's going to wake up and find that it's got to be the ballot or the bullet.

I would like to say, in closing, a few things concerning the Muslim Mosque, Inc., which we established recently in New York City. It's true we're Muslims and our religion is Islam, but we don't mix our religion with our politics and our economics and our social and civil activities—not any more. We keep our religion in our mosque. After our religious services are over, then as Muslims we become involved in political action, economic action and social and civic action. We become involved with anybody, anywhere, any time and in any manner that's designed to eliminate the evils, the political, economic and social evils that are afflicting the people of our community.

The political philosophy of black nationalism means that the black man should control the politics and the politicians in his own community; no more. The black man in the black community has to be re-educated into the science of politics so he will know what politics is supposed to bring him in return. Don't be throwing out any ballots. A ballot is like a bullet. You don't throw your ballots until you see a target, and if that target is not within your reach, keep your ballot in your pocket. The political philosophy of black nationalism is being taught in the Christian church. It's being taught in the NAACP. It's being taught in CORE meetings. It's being taught in SNCC [Student Nonviolent Coordinating Committee] meetings. It's being taught in Muslim meetings. It's being taught where nothing but atheists and agnostics come together. It's being taught everywhere. Black people are fed up with the dillydallying, pussyfooting, compromising approach that we've been using toward getting our freedom. We want freedom *now*, but we're not going to get it saying "We Shall Overcome." We've got to fight until we overcome.

The economic philosophy of black nationalism is pure and simple. It only means that we should control the economy of our community. Why should white people be running all the stores in our community? Why should white people be running the banks of our community? Why should the economy of our community be in the hands of the white man? Why? If a black man can't move his store into a white community, you tell me why a white man should move his store into a black community. The philosophy of black nationalism involves a re-education program in the black community in regards to economics. Our people have to be made to see that any time you take your dollar out of your community and spend it in a community where you don't live, the community where you live will get poorer and poorer, and the community where you spend your money will get richer and richer. Then you wonder why where you live is always a ghetto or a slum area. And where you and I are concerned, not only do we lose it when we spend it out of the community, but the white man has got all our stores in the community tied up; so that though we spend it in the community, at sundown the man who runs the store takes it over across town somewhere. He's got us in a vise.

So the economic philosophy of black nationalism means in every church, in every civic organization, in every fraternal order, it's time now for our people to become conscious of the importance of controlling the economy of our community. If we own the stores, if we operate the businesses, if we try and establish some industry in our own community, then we're developing to the position where we are creating employment for our own kind. Once you gain control of your own community, then you don't have to picket and boycott and beg some cracker downtown for a job in his business.

The social philosophy of black nationalism only means that we have to get together and remove the veils, the vices, alcoholism, drug addiction, and other evils that are destroying the moral fiber of our community. We ourselves have to lift the level of our community, the standard of our community to a higher level, make our own society beautiful so that we will be satisfied in our own social circles and won't be running around here trying to knock our way into a social circle where we're not wanted.

So I say, in spreading a gospel such as black na-

tionalism, it is not designed to make the black man re-evaluate the white man—you know him already—but to make the black man re-evaluate himself. Don't change the white man's mind—you can't change his mind, and that whole thing about appealing to the moral conscience of America—America's conscience is bankrupt. She lost all conscience a long time ago. Uncle Sam has no conscience. They don't know what morals are. They don't try and eliminate an evil because it's evil, or because it's illegal, or because it's immoral; they eliminate it only when it threatens their existence. So you're wasting your time appealing to the moral conscience of a bankrupt man like Uncle Sam. If he had a conscience, he'd straighten this thing out with no more pressure being put upon him. So it is not necessary to change the white man's mind. We have to change our own mind. You can't change his mind about us. We've got to change our own minds about each other. We have to see each other with new eyes. We have to see each other as brothers and sisters. We have to come together with warmth so we can develop unity and harmony that's necessary to get this problem solved ourselves. How can we do this? How can we avoid jealousy? How can we avoid the suspicion and the divisions that exist in the community? I'll tell you how.

I have watched how Billy Graham comes into a city, spreading what he calls the gospel of Christ, which is only white nationalism. That's what he is. Billy Graham is a white nationalist; I'm a black nationalist. But since it's the natural tendency for leaders to be jealous and look upon a powerful figure like Graham with suspicion and envy, how is it possible for him to come into a city and get all the cooperation of the church leaders? Don't think because they're church leaders that they don't have weaknesses that make them envious and jealous—no, everybody's got it. It's not an accident that when they want to choose a cardinal [as Pope] over there in Rome, they get in a closet so you can't hear them cussing and fighting and carrying on.

Billy Graham comes in preaching the gospel of Christ, he evangelizes the gospel, he stirs everybody up, but he never tries to start a church. If he came in trying to start a church, all the churches would be against him. So, he just comes in talking about Christ and tells everybody who gets Christ to go to any church where Christ is; and in this way the church cooperates with him. So we're going to take a page from his book.

Our gospel is black nationalism. We're not trying to threaten the existence of any organization, but we're spreading the gospel of black nationalism. Anywhere there's a church that is also preaching and practicing the gospel of black nationalism, join that church. If the NAACP is preaching and practicing the gospel of black nationalism, join the NAACP. If CORE is spreading and practicing the gospel of black nationalism, join CORE. Join any organization that has a gospel that's for the uplift of the black man. And when you get into it and see them pussyfooting or compromising, pull out of it because that's not black nationalism. We'll find another one.

And in this manner, the organizations will increase in number and in quantity and in quality, and by August, it is then our intention to have a black nationalist convention which will consist of delegates from all over the country who are interested in the political, economic and social philosophy of black nationalism. After these delegates convene, we will hold a seminar, we will hold discussions, we will listen to everyone. We want to hear new ideas and new solutions and new answers. And at that time, if we see fit then to form a black nationalist party, we'll form a black nationalist party. If it's necessary to form a black nationalist army, we'll form a black nationalist army. It'll be the ballot or the bullet. It'll be liberty or it'll be death.

It's time for you and me to stop sitting in this country, letting some cracker senators, Northern crackers and Southern crackers, sit there in Washington, D.C., and come to a conclusion in their minds that you and I are supposed to have civil rights. There's no white man going to tell me anything about *my* rights. Brothers and sisters, always remember, if it doesn't take senators and congressmen and presidential proclamations to give freedom to the white man, it is not necessary for legislation or proclamation or Supreme Court decisions to give freedom to the black man. You let that white man know, if this is a country of freedom, let it be a country of freedom; and if it's not a country of freedom, change it.

We will work with anybody, anywhere, at any time, who is genuinely interested in tackling the problem head-on, nonviolently as long as the enemy is nonviolent, but violent when the enemy gets violent. We'll work with you on the voter-registration drive, we'll work with you on rent strikes, we'll work with you on school boycotts—I don't believe in any kind of integration; I'm not even worried about it because I know you're not going to get it anyway; you've got to be ready to die if you try and force yourself on the white man, because he'll get just as violent as those crackers in Mississippi, right here in Cleveland. But we will still work with you on the school boycotts because we're against a segregated school system. A segregated school system produces children who, when they graduate, graduate with crippled minds. But this does not mean that a school is segregated because it's all black. A segregated school means a school that is controlled by people who have no real interest in it whatsoever.

Let me explain what I mean. A segregated district or community is a community in which people live, but outsiders control the politics and the economy of that community. They never refer to the white section as a segregated community. It's the all-Negro section that's a segregated community. Why? The white man controls his own school, his own bank, his own economy, his own politics, his own everything, his own community—but he also controls yours. When you're under someone else's control, you're segregated. They'll always give you the lowest or the worst that there is to offer, but it doesn't mean you're segregated just because you have your own. You've got to *control* your own. Just like the white man has control of his, you need to control yours.

You know the best way to get rid of segregation? The white man is more afraid of separation than he is of integration. Segregation means that he puts you away from him, but not far enough for you to be out of his jurisdiction; separation means you're gone. And the white man will integrate faster than he'll let you separate. So we will work with you against the segregated school system because it's criminal, because it is absolutely destructive, in every way imaginable, to the minds of the children who have to be exposed to that type of crippling education.

Last but not least, I must say this concerning the great controversy over rifles and shotguns. The only thing that I've ever said is that in areas where the government has proven itself either unwilling or unable to defend the lives and the property of Negroes, it's time for Negroes to defend themselves. Article number two of the constitutional amendments provides you and me the right to own a rifle or a shotgun. It is constitutionally legal to own a shotgun or a rifle. This doesn't mean you're going to get a rifle and form battalions and go out looking for white folks, although you'd be within your rights—I mean, you'd be justified; but that would be illegal and we don't do anything illegal. If the white man doesn't want the black man buying rifles and shotguns, then let the government do its job. That's all. And don't let the white man come to you and ask you what you think about what Malcolm says—why, you old Uncle Tom. He would never ask you if he thought you were going to say, "Oh, man!" No, he is making a Tom out of you.

So, this doesn't mean forming rifle clubs and going out looking for people, but it is time, in 1964, if you are a man, to let that man know. If he's not going to do his job in running the government and providing you and me with the protection that our taxes are supposed to be for, since he spends all those billions for his defense budget, he certainly can't begrudge you and me spending $12 or $15 for a single-shot, or double-action. I hope you understand. Don't go out shooting people, but any time, brothers and sisters, and especially the men in this audience—some of you wearing Congressional Medals of Honor, with shoulders this wide, chests this big, muscles that big—any time you and I sit around and read where they bomb a church and murder in cold blood, not some grownups, but four little girls while they were praying ...

[*The next few words on the tape are inaudible.*]

Why, this man—he can find Eichmann hiding down in Argentina somewhere. Let two or three American soldiers, who are minding somebody else's business way over in South Vietnam, get killed, and he'll send battleships, sticking his nose in their business. He wanted to send troops down to Cuba and make them have what he calls free elections—this old cracker who doesn't have free elections in his own country. No, if you never see me another time in your life, if I die in the morning, I'll die saying one thing: the ballot or the bullet, the ballot or the bullet.

If a Negro in 1964 has to sit around and wait for some cracker senator to filibuster when it comes to the rights of black people, why, you and I should hang our heads in shame. You talk about a march on Washington in 1963, you haven't seen anything. There's some more going down in '64. And this time they're not going like they went last year. They're not going singing "We Shall Overcome." They're not going with white friends. They're not going with placards already painted for them. They're not going with round-trip tickets. They're going with one-way tickets.

And if they don't want that non-violent army going down there, tell them to bring the filibuster to a halt. The black nationalists aren't going to wait. Lyndon B. Johnson is the head of the Democratic Party. If he's for civil rights, let him go into the Senate next week and declare himself. Let him go in there right now and declare himself. Let him go in there and denounce the Southern branch of his party. Let him go in there right now and take a moral stand—right now, not later. Tell him, don't wait until election time. If he waits too long, brothers and sisters, he will be responsible for letting a condition develop in this country which will create a climate that will bring seeds up out of the ground with vegetation on the end of them looking like something these people never dreamed of. In 1964, it's the ballot or the bullet. Thank you.

Lyndon B. Johnson

We Shall Overcome
(March 15, 1965)

The Civil Rights Act of 1964 was concerned primarily with access to public accommodations. Important as it was, it left untouched some of the most basic economic and political grievances, the most fundamental of which was denial of the right to vote. In many of the Southern states, fewer than half the blacks of voting age were registered, because administrative machination and intimidation prevented them from the exercise of a right granted by the Constitution. Lyndon Johnson was deeply committed to voting rights, believing that the need to appeal for black votes would naturally create the pressure to accomplish most other civil rights goals. As majority leader of the Senate, he had steered to passage the Civil Rights Act of 1957—the first legislation in this area since Reconstruction—which was concerned primarily with voting rights. But it had been watered down to secure its passage, and its actual effects were far less profound than many of its supporters had hoped. Fresh from his 1964 election victory, Johnson pledged in the next year's State of the Union address to eliminate "every remaining obstacle."

He did not say, however, when—or even if—he planned to introduce legislation for this purpose. Most likely, he intended to go slow, to give Congress and the country time to digest the Civil Rights Act of 1964. But events in Alabama forced his hand. Hoping for a violent response that would arouse the conscience of the North, Martin Luther King deliberately chose Selma, Alabama, as the place for a major voting campaign. Only 2 percent of voting-age blacks were registered, and the sheriff was not characterized by tact or discretion in dealing with black demonstrators. As the climax of his campaign, King planned a fifty-mile march from Selma to the capital at Montgomery. Gov. George Wallace banned the march as disruptive to highway traffic, and Alabama state troopers attacked the marchers with tear gas and clubs. This scene was shown on national television and helped to create a constituency for new voting rights laws. Pressure grew with the news that a white minister from Boston had been beaten to death, and that a white mother from Detroit had been shot in her car by members of the Ku Klux Klan.

Johnson took advantage of this national mood. A week after the attack on the Selma marchers, he went on national television to preview and plead for a new voting rights law. Its details were sent to Congress soon thereafter. Johnson's voting rights speech is often described as his most moving and eloquent, and several of its features deserve notice. Johnson identified civil rights as the paramount issue facing the nation, arguing that if the country solved all its problems except for this one, it still would have failed. He linked civil rights to the issues of education and poverty, suggesting that the nation needed both to open the gates of opportunity and to see to it that people were able to walk through. He personalized his appeal, reminiscing about his years as a teacher in a poor rural school and how he now had a chance to help break through the cycle of poverty and ignorance. Most significantly, he endorsed and proclaimed the motto of the civil rights movement, "We shall overcome." That this line was repeated by a Southerner made the effect all the more powerful.

The voting rights bill, which gave the federal government the power to oversee registration when racial discrimination was suspected, moved quickly through Congress and was signed into law in August. Compared with earlier civil rights bills, Southern opposition seemed weak and almost half-hearted. The act permanently changed the political complexion of the South, leading to a dramatic increase in the number of black voters and black elected officials, and requiring that erstwhile segregationists such as George Wallace openly appeal for black votes in order to win. Paradoxically, however, Selma also signaled the coming fragmentation of the civil rights movement. Even as he was arousing Northern whites, King was criticized by militant blacks for not provoking a confrontation with the federal government itself. He would not again be the single recognized spokesman for a united movement. Nor would Johnson again lend the weight of his office to an appeal focused on the moral principle that the nation was hurt by its failure to assure equal rights. When riots broke out in the cities of the north, the focus of the issue was altogether different.

Mr. Speaker, Mr. President, Members of the Congress:—I speak tonight for the dignity of man and the destiny of democracy.

I urge every member of both parties, Americans of all religions and of all colors, from every section of this country, to join me in that cause.

At times history and fate meet at a single time in a single place to shape a turning point in man's unending search for freedom. So it was at Lexington and Concord. So it was a century ago at Appomattox. So it was last week in Selma, Alabama.

There, long-suffering men and women peacefully protested the denial of their rights as Americans. Many were brutally assaulted. One good man, a man of God, was killed.

There is no cause for pride in what has happened in Selma. There is no cause for self-satisfaction in the long denial of equal rights of millions of Americans. But there is cause for hope and for faith in our democracy in what is happening here tonight.

For the cries of pain and the hymns and protests of oppressed people have summoned into convocation all the majesty of this great Government—the Government of the greatest Nation on earth.

Our mission is at once the oldest and the most basic of this country: to right wrong, to do justice, to serve man.

In our time we have come to live with moments of great crisis. Our lives have been marked with debate about great issues; issues of war and peace, issues of prosperity and depression. But rarely in any time does an issue lay bare the secret heart of America itself.

Rarely are we met with a challenge, not to our growth or abundance, our welfare or our security, but rather to the values and the purposes and the meaning of our beloved Nation.

The issue of equal rights for American Negroes is such an issue. And should we defeat every enemy, should we double our wealth and conquer the stars, and still be unequal to this issue, then we will have failed as a people and as a nation.

For with a country as with a person, "What is a man profited, if he shall gain the whole world, and lose his own soul?"

There is no Negro problem. There is no Southern problem. There is no Northern problem. There is only an American problem. And we are met here tonight as Americans—not as Democrats or Republicans—we are met here as Americans to solve that problem.

This was the first nation in the history of the world to be founded with a purpose. The great phrases of that purpose still sound in every American heart, North and South: "All men are created equal"—"government by consent of the governed"—"give me liberty or give me death." Well, those are not just clever words, or those are not just empty theories. In their name Americans have fought and died for two centuries, and tonight around the world they stand there as guardians of our liberty, risking their lives.

Those words are a promise to every citizen that he shall share in the dignity of man. This dignity cannot be found in a man's possessions; it cannot be found in his power, or in his position. It really rests on his right to be treated as a man equal in opportunity to all others. It says that he shall share in freedom, he shall choose his leaders, educate his children, and provide for his family according to his ability and his merits as a human being.

To apply any other test—to deny a man his hopes because of his color or race, his religion or the place of his birth—is not only to do injustice, it is to deny America and to dishonor the dead who gave their lives for American freedom.

THE RIGHT TO VOTE

Our fathers believed that if this noble view of the rights of man was to flourish, it must be rooted in democracy. The most basic right of all was the right to choose your own leaders. The history of this country, in large measure, is the history of the expansion of that right to all of our people.

Many of the issues of civil rights are very complex and most difficult. But about this there can and should be no argument. Every American citizen must have an equal right to vote. There is no reason which can excuse the denial of that right. There is no duty which weighs more heavily on us than the duty we have to ensure that right.

Yet the harsh fact is that in many places in this country men and women are kept from voting simply because they are Negroes.

Every device of which human ingenuity is capable has been used to deny this right. The Negro citizen may go to register only to be told that the day is wrong, or the hour is late, or the official in charge is absent. And if he persists, and if he manages to present himself to the registrar, he may be disqualified because he did not spell out his middle name or because he abbreviated a word on the application.

And if he manages to fill out an application he is given a test. The registrar is the sole judge of whether he passes this test. He may be asked to recite the entire Constitution, or explain the most complex provisions of State law. And even a college degree cannot be used to prove that he can read and write.

For the fact is that the only way to pass these barriers is to show a white skin.

Experience has clearly shown that the existing process of law cannot overcome systematic and ingenious discrimination. No law that we now have on the books—and I have helped to put three of them there—can ensure the right to vote when local officials are determined to deny it.

In such a case our duty must be clear to all of us. The Constitution says that no person shall be kept from voting because of his race or his color. We have all sworn an oath before God to support and to defend that Constitution. We must now act in obedience to that oath.

GUARANTEEING THE RIGHT TO VOTE

Wednesday I will send to Congress a law designed to eliminate illegal barriers to the right to vote.

The broad principles of that bill will be in the hands of the Democratic and Republican leaders tomorrow. After they have reviewed it, it will come here formally as a bill. I am grateful for this opportunity to come here tonight at the invitation of the leadership to reason with my friends, to give them my views, and to visit with my former colleagues.

I have had prepared a more comprehensive analysis of the legislation which I had intended to transmit to the clerk tomorrow but which I will submit to the clerks tonight. But I want to really discuss with you now briefly the main proposals of this legislation.

This bill will strike down restrictions to voting in all elections—Federal, State, and local—which have been used to deny Negroes the right to vote.

This bill will establish a simple, uniform standard which cannot be used, however ingenious the effort, to flout our Constitution.

It will provide for citizens to be registered by officials of the United States Government if the State officials refuse to register them.

It will eliminate tedious, unnecessary lawsuits which delay the right to vote.

Finally, this legislation will ensure that properly registered individuals are not prohibited from voting.

I will welcome the suggestions from all of the Members of Congress—I have no doubt that I will get some—on ways and means to strengthen this law and to make it effective. But experience has plainly shown that this is the only path to carry out the command of the Constitution.

To those who seek to avoid action by their National Government in their own communities; who want to and who seek to maintain purely local control over elections, the answer is simple:

Open your polling places to all your people.

Allow men and women to register and vote whatever the color of their skin.

Extend the rights of citizenship to every citizen of this land.

THE NEED FOR ACTION

There is no constitutional issue here. The command of the Constitution is plain.

There is no moral issue. It is wrong—deadly wrong—to deny any of your fellow Americans the right to vote in this country.

There is no issue of States rights or national rights. There is only the struggle for human rights.

I have not the slightest doubt what will be your answer.

The last time a President sent a civil rights bill to the Congress it contained a provision to protect voting rights in Federal elections. That civil rights bill was passed after 8 long months of debate. And when that bill came to my desk from the Congress for my signature, the heart of the voting provision had been eliminated.

This time, on this issue, there must be no delay, no hesitation and no compromise with our purpose.

We cannot, we must not, refuse to protect the right of every American to vote in every election that he may desire to participate in. And we ought not and we cannot and we must not wait another 8 months before we get a bill. We have already waited a hundred years and more, and the time for waiting is gone.

So I ask you to join me in working long hours—nights and weekends, if necessary—to pass this bill. And I don't make that request lightly. For from the window where I sit with the problems of our country I recognize that outside this chamber is the outraged conscience of a nation, the grave concern of many nations, and the harsh judgment of history on our acts.

WE SHALL OVERCOME

But even if we pass this bill, the battle will not be over. What happened in Selma is part of a far larger movement which reaches into every section and State of America. It is the effort of American Negroes to secure for themselves the full blessings of American life.

Their cause must be our cause too. Because it is not just Negroes, but really it is all of us, who must overcome the crippling legacy of bigotry and injustice.

And we shall overcome.

As a man whose roots go deeply into Southern soil I know how agonizing racial feelings are. I know how difficult it is to reshape the attitudes and the structure of our society.

But a century has passed, more than a hundred years, since the Negro was freed. And he is not fully free tonight.

It was more than a hundred years ago that Abraham Lincoln, a great President of another party, signed the Emancipation Proclamation, but emancipation is a proclamation and not a fact.

A century has passed, more than a hundred years, since equality was promised. And yet the Negro is not equal.

A century has passed since the day of promise. And the promise is unkept.

The time of justice has now come. I tell you that I believe sincerely that no force can hold it back. It is right in the eyes of man and God that it should come. And when it does, I think that day will brighten the lives of every American.

For Negroes are not the only victims. How many white children have gone uneducated, how many white families have lived in stark poverty, how many white lives have been scarred by fear, because we have wasted our energy and our substance to maintain the barriers of hatred and terror?

So I say to all of you here, and to all in the Nation tonight, that those who appeal to you to hold on to the past do so at the cost of denying you your future.

This great, rich, restless country can offer opportunity and education and hope to all: black and white, North and South, sharecropper and city dweller. These are the enemies: poverty, ignorance, disease. They are the enemies and not our fellow man, not our neighbor. And these enemies too, poverty, disease and ignorance, we shall overcome.

AN AMERICAN PROBLEM

Now let none of us in any sections look with prideful righteousness on the troubles in another section, or on the problems of our neighbors. There is really no part of America where the promise of equality has been fully kept. In Buffalo as well as in Birmingham, in Philadelphia as well as in Selma, Americans are struggling for the fruits of freedom.

This is one Nation. What happens in Selma or in Cincinnati is a matter of legitimate concern to every American. But let each of us look within our own hearts and our own communities, and let each of us put our shoulder to the wheel to root out injustice wherever it exists.

As we meet here in this peaceful, historic chamber tonight, men from the South, some of whom were at Iwo Jima, men from the North who have carried Old Glory to far corners of the world and brought it back without a stain on it, men from the East and from the West, are all fighting together without regard to religion, or color, or region, in Viet-Nam. Men from every region fought for us across the world 20 years ago.

And in these common dangers and these common sacrifices the South made its contribution of honor and gallantry no less than any other region of the great Republic—and in some instances, a great many of them, more.

And I have not the slightest doubt that good men from everywhere in this country, from the Great Lakes to the Gulf of Mexico, from the Golden Gate to the harbors along the Atlantic, will rally together now in this cause to vindicate the freedom of all Americans. For all of us owe this duty; and I believe that all of us will respond to it.

Your President makes that request of every American.

PROGRESS THROUGH THE DEMOCRATIC PROCESS

The real hero of this struggle is the American Negro. His actions and protests, his courage to risk safety and even to risk his life, have awakened the conscience of this Nation. His demonstrations have been designed to call attention to injustice, designed to provoke change, designed to stir reform.

He has called upon us to make good the promise of America. And who among us can say that we would have made the same progress were it not for his persistent bravery, and his faith in American democracy.

For at the real heart of battle for equality is a deep-seated belief in the democratic process. Equality depends not on the force of arms or tear gas but upon the force of moral right; not on recourse to violence but on respect for law and order.

There have been many pressures upon your President and there will be others as the days come and go. But I pledge you tonight that we intend to fight this battle where it should be fought: in the courts, and in the Congress, and in the hearts of men.

We must preserve the right of free speech and the right of free assembly. But the right of free speech does not carry with it, as has been said, the right to holler fire in a crowded theater. We must preserve the right to free assembly, but free assembly does not carry with it the right to block public thoroughfares to traffic.

We do have a right to protest, and a right to march under conditions that do not infringe the constitutional rights of our neighbors. And I intend to protect all those rights as long as I am permitted to serve in this office.

We will guard against violence, knowing it strikes from our hands the very weapons which we seek—progress, obedience to law, and belief in American values.

In Selma as elsewhere we seek and pray for peace. We seek order. We seek unity. But we will not accept the peace of stifled rights, or the order imposed by fear, or the unity that stifles protest. For peace cannot be purchased at the cost of liberty.

In Selma tonight, as in every—and we had a good day there—as in every city, we are working for just and peaceful settlement. We must all remember that after this speech I am making tonight, after the police and the FBI and the Marshals have all gone, and after you have promptly passed this bill, the people of Selma and the other cities of the Nation must still live and work together. And when the attention of the Nation has gone elsewhere they must try to heal the wounds and to build a new community.

This cannot be easily done on a battleground of violence, as the history of the South itself shows. It is in recognition of this that men of both races have shown such an outstandingly impressive responsibility in recent days—last Tuesday, again today.

RIGHTS MUST BE OPPORTUNITIES

The bill that I am presenting to you will be known as a civil rights bill. But, in a larger sense, most of the program I am recommending is a civil rights program. Its object is to open the city of hope to all people of all races.

Because all Americans just must have the right to vote. And we are going to give them that right.

All Americans must have the privileges of citizenship regardless of race. And they are going to have those privileges of citizenship regardless of race.

But I would like to caution you and remind you that to exercise these privileges takes much more than just legal right. It requires a trained mind and a healthy body. It requires a decent home, and the chance to find a job, and the opportunity to escape from the clutches of poverty.

Of course, people cannot contribute to the Nation if they are never taught to read or write, if their bodies are stunted from hunger, if their sickness goes untended, if their life is spent in hopeless poverty just drawing a welfare check.

So we want to open the gates to opportunity. But we are also going to give all our people, black and white, the help that they need to walk through those gates.

THE PURPOSE OF THIS GOVERNMENT

My first job after college was as a teacher in Cotulla, Tex., in a small Mexican-American school. Few of them could speak English, and I couldn't speak much Spanish. My students were poor and they often came to class without breakfast, hungry. They knew even in their youth the pain of prejudice. They never seemed to know why people disliked them. But they knew it was so, because I saw it in their eyes. I often walked home late in the afternoon, after the classes were finished, wishing there was more that I could do. But all I knew was to teach them the little that I knew, hoping that it might help them against the hardships that lay ahead.

Somehow you never forget what poverty and hatred can do when you see its scars on the hopeful face of a young child.

I never thought then, in 1928, that I would be standing here in 1965. It never even occurred to me in my fondest dreams that I might have the chance to help the sons and daughters of those students and to help people like them all over this country.

But now I do have that chance—and I'll let you in on a secret—I mean to use it. And I hope that you will use it with me.

This is the richest and most powerful country which ever occupied the globe. The might of past empires is little compared to ours. But I do not want to be the President who built empires, or sought grandeur, or extended dominion.

I want to be the President who educated young children to the wonders of their world. I want to be the President who helped to feed the hungry and to prepare them to be taxpayers instead of taxeaters.

I want to be the President who helped the poor to find their own way and who protected the right of every citizen to vote in every election.

I want to be the President who helped to end hatred among his fellow men and who promoted love among the people of all races and all regions and all parties.

I want to be the President who helped to end war among the brothers of this earth.

And so at the request of your beloved Speaker and the Senator from Montana; the majority leader, the Senator from Illinois; the minority leader, Mr. McCulloch, and other Members of both parties, I came here tonight—not as President Roosevelt came down one time in person to veto a bonus bill, not as President Truman came down one time to urge the passage of a railroad bill—but I came down here to ask you to share this task with me and to share it with the people that we both work for. I want this to be the Congress, Republicans and Democrats alike, which did all these things for all these people.

Beyond this great chamber, out yonder in 50 States, are the people that we serve. Who can tell what deep and unspoken hopes are in their hearts tonight as they sit there and listen. We all can guess, from our own lives, how difficult they often find their own pursuit of happiness, how many problems each little family has. They look most of all to themselves for their futures. But I think that they also look to each of us.

Above the pyramid on the great seal of the United States it says—in Latin—"God has favored our undertaking."

God will not favor everything that we do. It is rather our duty to divine His will. But I cannot help believing that He truly understands and that He really favors the undertaking that we begin here tonight.

Stokely Carmichael

Berkeley Speech
(October 1966)

Just as the civil rights movement of the 1960's was achieving its greatest successes, militant blacks were increasingly questioning its very premises—that integration was a good thing, that whites and blacks had interests in common, and that whites were able to speak for blacks. Among those challenging these beliefs, few were more vocal than Stokely Carmichael. He had been engaged in voter registration drives, freedom rides, and organizing strategies for civil rights since 1960, but had come to question the more traditional civil rights groups' policy of nonviolence and to favor a black political party that would not need the help of whites.

Carmichael was elected to chair the Student Nonviolent Coordinating Committee (SNCC) in May of 1966. He called for blacks to "begin building independent political, economic, and cultural institutions that they will control and use as instruments of social change in this country." The next month, he joined a march from Memphis to Jackson that had been organized by James Meredith, who in 1962 had been the first black student admitted to the University of Mississippi. Meredith had been shot, though not killed, and civil rights leaders came to Mississippi to complete his march. They quickly found themselves in disagreement about whether nonviolence was appropriate. While in jail in Greenwood, Mississippi, following his arrest along the march, Carmichael issued the rallying cry for a new stage in the civil rights movement, proclaiming, "We want black power!"

The "black power" slogan had been used before, by author Richard Wright and by Congressman Adam Clayton Powell. But it was Carmichael who made it famous, especially as a counter to "freedom now" and "we shall overcome." The slogan was ambiguous, and Carmichael was questioned from all sides as to what he meant. Black

Power seemed to imply rejection of and separation from the social and economic system into which blacks had sought integration. What had been seen as a consensual, national value was redefined as a white value from which blacks were alienated. Some believed that Black Power was primarily a call for solidarity among blacks; some saw it as seeking to fill a power vacuum in the black community; and some saw it as a bid to wrest power from whites. Moreover, the slogan at least on some level implied belligerence and the threat of violence.

Perhaps most significantly, the Black Power slogan raised the issue of blacks' right to define their own identity; it was a demand for control of one's own self-concept. Carmichael argued that blacks would always be in a dependent relationship as long as whites could determine their identity. He believed that for blacks to appeal to white power structures as the way to bring about change was both ineffective and demeaning, and that real change required that blacks develop the necessary economic and political muscle themselves. That would happen only if blacks were inspired by pride in their accomplishments and capabilities as blacks, and such inspiration began with self-definition.

Carmichael delivered many speeches in which he tried to explain Black Power to predominantly white audiences. The forerunner of what became his standard speech was delivered at Berkeley in October 1966. Two years before, the campus at the University of California had been the site of the first of the student protest movements of the 1960's. Some of the idealism that had characterized the Free Speech Movement, however, had since been eroded.

Carmichael's speech illustrates the rhetorical tension inherent in his assignment. To "explain" Black Power, in a sense, presumes that it must be made comprehensible *to whites*, but that assumption perpetuates the very dependency relationship that Black Power seeks to change. On the other hand, to threaten whites might provoke a strong backlash. So Carmichael sought largely to *proclaim* Black Power in a way that rendered whites irrelevant to the attainment of blacks' goals. They could understand and sympathize, but there was little they could do to help. Carmichael emphasized that American society was racist and that that very racism prevented whites from effective self-condemnation. His message differed from Martin Luther King's in that he did not preach nonviolence and he did not advocate integrating blacks into white society, calling instead for a transformation of society itself.

The themes developed in this speech were expanded in a book published in 1967 and written jointly by Carmichael and Charles V. Hamilton. The authors emphasized that the first step toward Black Power was for blacks to redefine themselves. The program Carmichael advocated, he believed, would speak to the needs of young black people both in the rural South and in the urban ghettos. By contrast, Carmichael saw the more traditional civil rights movement as appealing primarily to middle-class whites and to offer no possibilities for action to people who were facing violence and racism. The call for Black Power refocused the issues and caused many traditional leaders to take a more militant stance.

It's a privilege and an honor to be in the white intellectual ghetto of the West. This is a student conference, as it should be, held on a campus, and we'll never be caught up in intellectual masturbation on the question of Black Power. That's a function of the people who are advertisers but call themselves reporters. Incidentally, for my friends and members of the press, my self-appointed white critics, I was reading Mr. Bernard Shaw two days ago, and I came across a very important quote that I think is most apropos to you. He says, "All criticism is an autobiography." Dig yourself. OK.

The philosophers Camus and Sartre raise the question of whether or not a man can condemn himself. The black existentialist philosopher who is pragmatic, Frantz Fanon, answered the question. He said that man could not. Camus and Sartre don't answer the question. We in SNCC tend to agree with Fanon—a man cannot condemn himself. If he did, he would then have to inflict punishment upon himself. An example is the Nazis. Any of the Nazi prisoners who, after he was caught and incarcerated, admitted that he committed crimes, that he killed all the many people he killed, had to commit suicide. The only ones able to stay alive were the ones who never admitted that they committed a crime against people—that is, the ones who rationalized that Jews were not human beings and deserved to be killed, or that they were only following orders. There's another, more recent example provided by the officials and the population—the white population—of Neshoba County, Mississippi (that's where Philadelphia is). They could not condemn Sheriff Rainey, his deputies, and the other fourteen men who killed three human beings. They could not because they elected Mr. Rainey to do precisely what he did; and condemning him would be condemning themselves.

In a much larger view, SNCC says that white America cannot condemn herself for her criminal acts against black America. So black people have done it— you stand condemned. The institutions that function in this country are clearly racist; they're built upon racism. The questions to be dealt with then are: How can black people inside this country move? How can white people who say they're not part of those institutions begin to move? And how then do we begin to clear away the obstacles that we have in this society, to make us live like human beings?

Several people have been upset because we've said that integration was irrelevant when initiated by blacks, and that in fact it was an insidious subterfuge for the maintenance of white supremacy. In the past six years or so, this country has been feeding us a "thalidomide drug of integration," and some Negroes have been walking down a dream street talking about sitting next to white people. That does not begin to solve the problem. We didn't go to Mississippi to sit next to Ross Barnett [former Governor of Mississippi], we did not go to sit next to Jim Clark [sheriff of Selma, Alabama], we went to get them out of our way. People ought to understand that; we were never fighting for the right to integrate, *we were fighting against white supremacy.* In order to understand white supremacy we must dismiss the fallacious notion that white people can give anybody his freedom. A man is born free. You may enslave a man after he is born free, and that is in fact what this country does. It enslaves blacks after they're born. The only thing white people can do *is stop denying black people their freedom.*

I maintain that every civil rights bill in this country was passed for white people, not for black people. For example, I am black. I know that. I also know that while I am black I am a human being. Therefore I have the right to go into any public place. White people didn't know that. Every time I tried to go into a public place they stopped me. So some boys had to write a bill to tell that white man, "He's a human being; don't stop him." That bill was for the white man, not for me. I knew I could vote all the time and that it wasn't a privilege but my right. Every time I tried I was shot, killed or jailed, beaten or economically deprived. So somebody had to write a bill to tell white people, "When a black man comes to vote, don't bother him." That bill was for white people. I know I can live anyplace I want to live. It is white people across this country who are incapable of allowing me to live where I want. You need a civil rights bill, not me. The failure of the civil rights bill isn't because of Black Power or because of the Student Nonviolent Coordinating Committee or because of the rebellions that are occurring in the major cities. That failure is due to the whites' incapacity to deal with their own problems inside their own communities.

And so in a sense we must ask, How is it that black people move? And what do we do? But the question in a much greater sense is, How can white people who are the majority, and who are responsible for making democracy work, make it work? They have failed miserably on this point. They have never made democracy work, be it inside the United States, Vietnam, South Africa, the Philippines, South America, Puerto Rico, or wherever America has been. We not only condemn the country for what it has done internally, but we must condemn it for what it does externally. We see this country trying to rule the world, and someone must stand up and start articulating that this country is not God, and that it cannot rule the world.

The white supremacist attitude, which you have either consciously or subconsciously,is running rampant through society today. For example, missionaries were sent to Africa with the attitude that blacks were automatically inferior. As a matter of fact, the first act the missionaries did when they got to Africa was to make us cover up our bodies, because they said it got them excited. We couldn't go bare-breasted any more because they got excited! When the missionaries came to civilize us because we were uncivilized, to educate us because we were uneducated, and to give us some literate studies because we were illiterate, they charged a price. The missionaries came with the Bible, and we had the land: when they left, they had the land, and we still have the Bible. That's been the rationalization for Western civilization as it moves across the world—stealing, plundering and raping everybody in its path. Their one rationalization is that the rest of the world is uncivilized and they are in fact civilized. But the West is un-civ-i-lized. And that still runs on today, you see, because now we have "modern-day missionaries," and they come into our ghettos—they Head Start, Upward Lift, Bootstrap, and Upward Bound us into white society. They don't want to face the real problem. A man is poor for one reason and one reason only—he does not have money. If you want to get rid of poverty, you give people money. And you ought not to tell me about people who don't work, and that you can't give people money if they don't work, because if that were true, you'd have to start stopping Rockefeller, Kennedy, Lyndon Baines Johnson, Lady Bird Johnson, the whole of Standard Oil, the Gulf Corporation, all of them, including probably a large number of the board of trustees of this university. The question, then, is not whether or not one can work; it's *Who has power to make his or her acts legitimate*? That is all. In this country that power is invested in the hands of white people, and it makes their acts legitimate.

We are now engaged in a psychological struggle in this country about whether or not black people have the right to use the words they want to use without white people giving their sanction. We maintain the use of the words Black Power—let them address themselves to that. We are not going to wait for white people to sanction Black Power. We're tired of waiting; every time black people try to move in this country, they're forced to defend their position beforehand. It's time that white people do that. They ought to start defending themselves as to why they have oppressed and exploited us. A man was picked as a slave for one reason—the color of his skin. Black was automatically inferior, inhuman, and therefore fit for slavery, so the question of whether or not we are individually suppressed is nonsensical, and it's a downright lie. We are op-pressed as a group because we are black, not because we are lazy or apathetic, not because we're stupid or we stink, not because we eat watermelon or have good rhythm. We are oppressed because we are black.

In order to escape that oppression we must wield the group power we have, not the individual power that this country sets as the criterion under which a man may come into it. That's what is called integration. "You do what I tell you to do and we'll let you sit at the table with us." Well, if you believe in integration, you can come live in Watts, send your children to the ghetto schools. Let's talk about that. If you believe in integration, then we're going to start adopting us some white people to live in our neighborhoods. So it is clear that this question is not one of integration or segregation. We cannot afford to be concerned about the 6 per cent of black children in this country whom you allow to enter white schools. We are going to be concerned about the 94 per cent. You ought to be concerned about them too. But are we willing to be concerned about the black people who will never get to Berkeley, never get to Harvard, and cannot get an education, the ones you'll never get a chance to rub shoulders with and say, "Why, he's almost as good as we are; he's not like the others"? The question is, How can white society begin to move to see black people as human beings? I am black, therefore I am. Not: I am black and I must go to college to prove myself. I am black, therefore I am. And don't deprive me of anything and say to me that you must go to college before you gain access to X, Y, and Z. That's only a rationalization for suppression.

The political parties of this country do not meet the needs of the people on a day-to-day basis. How can we build new political institutions that will become the political expressions of people? How can you build political institutions that will begin to meet the needs of Oakland, California? The need of Oakland, California, is not 1,000 policemen with submachine guns. They need that least of all. How can we build institutions that will allow those people to function on a day-to-day basis, so that they can get decent jobs and have decent houses, and they can begin to participate in the policy and make the decisions that affect their lives? That's what they need, not Gestapo troops, because this is not 1942, and if you play like Nazis, we're not going to play Jew this time around. Get hip to that. Can white people move inside their own community and start tearing down racism where in fact it exists? It is you who live in Cicero and stopped us from living there. White people stopped us from moving into Grenada, Miss. White people make sure that we live in the ghettos of this country. White institutions do that. They must change. In order for America to really live on a basic principle of human relationships, a new society must be born. Racism must die. The economic exploitation by this country of non-white people around the world must also die.

There are several programs in the South where whites are trying to organize poor whites so they can begin to move around the question of economic exploitation and political disfranchisement. We've all heard the theory several times. But few people are willing to go into it. The question is, Can the white activist stop trying to be a Pepsi generation who comes alive in the black community, and be a man who's willing to move into the white community and start organizing where the organization is needed? Can he do that? Can the white activist disassociate himself from the clowns who waste time parrying with each other and start talking about the problems that are facing people in this state? You must start inside the white community. Our political position is that we don't think the Democratic Party represents the needs of black people. We know that it does not. If, in fact, white people believe that they're going to move inside that structure, how are they going to organize around a concept of whiteness based on true brotherhood and on stopping economic exploitation in order to form a coalition base for black people to hook up with? You cannot build a coalition based on national sentiment. If you want a coalition to address itself to real changes in this country, white people must start building those institutions inside the white community. And that's the real question facing the white activists today. Can they tear down the institutions that have put us all in the trick bag we've been into for the last hundreds of years? Frederick Douglass said that the youth should fight to be leaders today. God knows we need to be leaders today, because the men who run this country are sick. We must begin to start building those institutions and to fight to articulate our position, to fight to be able to control our universities (we need to be able to do that), to fight to control the basic institutions that perpetuate racism by destroying them and building new ones. That's the real question that faces us today, and it is a dilemma because most of us don't know how to work.

Most white activists run into the black community as an excuse. We cannot have white people working in the black community—on psychological grounds. The fact is that all black people question whether or not they are equal to whites, since every time they start to do something, white people are around showing them how to do it. If we are going to eliminate that for the generation that comes after us, then black people must be in positions of power, doing and articulating for themselves. That's not reverse racism; it is moving onto healthy ground; it is becoming what the philosopher Sartre says, an "antiracist racist." And this country can't understand that. What we have in SNCC is antiracist racism. We are against racists. If everybody who's white sees himself as racist and sees us against him, he's speaking from his own guilt.

We do not have the power in our hands to change the institution of war in this country—to begin to re-create it so that they learn to leave the Vietnamese people alone. The only power we have is the power to say, "Hell, no!" to the draft.

The war in Vietnam is illegal and immoral. The question is, What can we do to stop that war? What can we do to stop the people who, in the name of America, are killing babies, women, and children? We have to say to ourselves that there's a higher law than the law of a fool named Rusk; there's a higher law than the law of a buffoon named Johnson. It's the law of each of us. We will not murder anybody who they say kill, and if we decide to kill, *we're* going to decide who it shall be. This country will only stop the war in Vietnam when the young men who are made to fight it begin to say, "Hell, no, we ain't going."

The peace movement has been a failure because it hasn't gotten off the college campuses where everybody has a 2S and is not afraid of being drafted anyway. The problem is how you can move out of that into the white ghettos of this country and articulate a position for those white youth who do not want to go. You cannot do that. It is sometimes ironic that many of the peace groups have begun to call SNCC violent and say they can no longer support us, when we are in fact the most militant organization for peace or civil rights or human rights against the war in Vietnam in this country today. There isn't one organization that has begun to meet our stand on the war in Vietnam. We not only say we are against the war in Vietnam; we are against the draft. No man has the right to take a man for two years and train him to be a killer. Any black man fighting in the war in Vietnam is nothing but a black mercenary. Any time a black man leaves the country where he can't vote to supposedly deliver the vote to somebody else, he's a black mercenary. Any time a black man leaves this country, gets shot in Vietnam on foreign ground, and returns home and you won't give him a burial place in his own homeland, he's a black mercenary. Even if I believed the lies of Johnson, that we're fighting to give democracy to the people in Vietnam, as a black man living in this country I wouldn't fight to give this to anybody. We have to use our bodies and our minds in the only way that we see fit. We must begin, as the philosopher Camus says, to come alive by saying "No." This country is a nation of thieves. It stole everything it has, beginning with black people. The U.S. cannot justify its existence as the policeman of the world any longer. The marines are at ready disposal to bring democracy, and if the Vietnamese don't want democracy, well then, "We'll just wipe them out, because they don't deserve to live if they won't have our way of life."

There is a more immediate question: What do you do on your campus? Do you raise questions about the hundred black students who were kicked off campus a couple of weeks ago? Eight hundred? And how does that question begin to move? Do you begin to relate to people outside the ivory tower and university walls? Do you think you're capable of building those human relationships as the country now stands? You're fooling yourself. It is impossible for white and black people to talk about building a relationship based on humanity when the country is the way it is, when the institutions are clearly against us.

We have found all the myths of the country to be nothing but downright lies. We were told that if we worked hard we would succeed, and if that were true we would own this country lock, stock, and barrel. We have picked the cotton for nothing; we are the maids in the kitchens of liberal white people; we are the janitors, the porters, the elevator men; we sweep up your college floors. We are the hardest workers and the lowest paid. It is nonsensical for people to talk about human relationships until they are willing to build new institutions. Black people are economically insecure. White liberals are economically secure. Can you begin to build an economic coalition? Are the liberals willing to share their salaries with the economically insecure black people they so much love? Then if you're not, are you willing to start building new institutions that will provide economic security for black people? That's the question *we* want to deal with!

American students are perhaps the most politically unsophisticated students in the world. Across every country of the world, while we were growing up,

students were leading the major revolutions of their countries. We have not been able to do that. They have been politically aware of their existence. In South America our neighbors have one every 24 hours just to remind us that they are politically aware. But we have been unable to grasp it because we've always moved in the field of morality and love while people have been politically jiving with our lives. You can't move morally against men like Brown and Reagan. You can't move morally against Lyndon Baines Johnson because he is an immoral man. He doesn't know what it's all about. So you've got to move politically. We have to develop a political sophistication that doesn't parrot ("The two-party system is the best system in the world"). We have to raise questions about whether we need new types of political institutions in this country, and we in SNCC maintain that we need them now. Any time Lyndon Baines Johnson can head a party that has in it Bobby Kennedy, Wayne Morse, Eastland, Wallace, and all those other supposed-to-be-liberal cats, there's something wrong with that party. They're moving politically, not morally. If that party refuses to seat black people from Mississippi and goes ahead and seats racists like Eastland and his clique, it's clear to me that they're moving politically, and that one cannot begin to talk morality to people like that.

We must question the values of this society, and I maintain that black people are the best people to do that since we have been excluded from that society. We ought to think whether or not we want to become a part of that society. That's precisely what the Student Nonviolent Coordinating Committee is doing. We are raising questions about this country. I do not want to be a part of the American pie. The American pie means raping South Africa, beating Vietnam, beating South America, raping the Philippines, raping every country you've been in. I don't want any of your blood money. I don't want to be part of that system. We are the generation who has found this country to be a world power and the wealthiest country in the world. We must question whether or not we want this country to continue being the wealthiest country in the world at the price of raping everybody else. And because black people are saying we do not now want to become a part of you, we are called reverse racists. Ain't that a gas?

White society has caused the failure of nonviolence. I was always surprised at Quakers who came to Alabama and counseled me to be nonviolent, but didn't have the guts to tell James Clark to be nonviolent. That's where nonviolence needs to be preached—to Jim

Clark, not to black people. White people should conduct their nonviolent schools in Cicero where they are needed, not among black people in Mississippi. Six-foot-two men kick little black children in Grenada—can you conduct nonviolent schools there? Can you name one black man today who has killed anybody white and is still alive? Even after a rebellion, when some black brothers throw bricks and bottles, ten thousand of them have to pay the price. When the white policeman comes in, anybody who's black is arrested because we all look alike.

The youth of this country must begin to raise those questions. We are going to have to change the foreign policy of this country. One of the problems with the peace movement is that it is too caught up in Vietnam, and if America pulled out the troops from Vietnam this week, next week you'd have to get another peace movement for Santo Domingo. *We have to hook up with black people around the world; and that hookup must not only be psychological, but real.* If South America were to rebel today, and black people were to shoot the hell out of all the white people there, as they should, Standard Oil would crumble tomorrow. If South Africa were to go today, Chase Manhattan Bank would crumble tomorrow. If Zimbabwe, which is called Rhodesia by white people, were to go tomorrow, General Electric would cave in on the East Coast. How do we stop those institutions that are so willing to fight against "Communist aggression" but close their eyes against racist oppression? We're not talking about a policy of aid or sending Peace Corps people in to teach people how to read and write and build houses while we steal their raw materials from them. Because that's all this country does. What underdeveloped countries need is information about how to become industrialized, so they can keep their raw materials where they have them, produce goods, sell them to this country for the price it's supposed to pay. Instead, America keeps selling goods back to them for a profit and keeps sending our modern day missionaries there, calling them the sons of Kennedy. And if the youth are going to participate in that program, how do you begin to control the Peace Corps?

This country assumes that if someone is poor, they are poor because of their own individual blight, or because they weren't born on the right side of town, or they had too many children, or went in the army too early, or because their father was a drunk, or they didn't care about school—they made a mistake. That's a lot of nonsense. Poverty is well calculated in this coun-

try, and the reason why the poverty program won't work is because the calculators of poverty are administering it.

How can you, as the youth in this country, move to start carrying those things out? Move into the white community. We have developed a movement in the black community. The white activist has miserably failed to develop the movement inside of his community. Will white people have the courage to go into white communities and start organizing them? That's the question for the white activist. We won't get caught up in questions about power. This country knows what power is. It knows what Black Power is because it deprived black people of it for over four hundred years. White people associate Black Power with violence because of their own inability to deal with blackness. If we had said "Negro power" nobody would get scared. Everybody would support it. If we said power for colored people, everybody'd be for that, but it is the word "black" that bothers people in this country, and that's their problem, not mine. That's the lie that says anything black is bad.

You're all a college and university crowd. You've taken your basic logic course. You know about major premise, minor premise. People have been telling you anything all black is bad. Let's make that our major premise.

Major premise: Anything all black is bad.

Minor premise or particular premise: I am all black.

Therefore ... I'm never going to be put in that bag; I'm all black and I'm all good. Anything all black is not necessarily bad. Anything all black is only bad when you use force to keep whites out. Now that's what white people have done in this country, and they're projecting their same fears and guilt on us, and we won't have it. Let them handle their own affairs and their own guilt. Let them find their own psychologists. We refuse to be the therapy for white society any longer. We have gone stark, raving mad trying to do it.

I look at Dr. King on television every single day, and I say to myself: "Now there is a man who's desperately needed in this country. There is a man full of love. There is a man full of mercy. There is a man full of compassion" But every time I see Lyndon on television, I say, "Martin, baby, you got a long way to go."

If we were to be real and honest, we would have to admit that most people in this country see things black and white. We live in a country that's geared that way. White people would have to admit that they are afraid to go into a black ghetto at night. They're afraid because they'd be "beat up," "lynched," "looted," "cut up," etc. It happens to black people inside the ghetto every day, incidentally. Since white people are afraid of that, they get a man to do it for them—a policeman. Figure his mentality. The first time a black man jumps, that white man's going to shoot him. Police brutality is going to exist on that level. The only time I hear people talk about nonviolence is when black people move to defend themselves against white people. Black people cut themselves every night in the ghetto—nobody talks about nonviolence. White people beat up black people every day—nobody talks about nonviolence. But as soon as black people start to move, the double standard comes into being. You can't defend yourself. You show me a black man who advocates aggressive violence who would be able to live in this country. Show him to me. Isn't it hypocritical for Lyndon to talk about how you can't accomplish anything by looting and you must accomplish it by the legal ways? What does he know about legality? Ask Ho Chi Minh.

We must wage a psychological battle on the right for black people to define themselves as they see fit, and organize themselves as they see fit. We don't know whether the white community will allow for that organizing, because once they do they must also allow for the organizing inside their own community. It doesn't make a difference, though—we're going to organize our way. The question is how we're going to organize our way. The question is how we're going to facilitate those matters, whether it's going to be done with a thousand policemen with submachine guns, or whether it's going to be done in a context where it's allowed by white people warding off those policemen. Are white people who call themselves activists ready to move into the white communities on two counts, on building new political institutions to destroy the old ones that we have, and to move around the concept of white youth refusing to go into the army? If so, then we can start to build a new world. We must urge you to fight now to be the leaders of today, not tomorrow. This country is a nation of thieves. It stands on the brink of becoming a nation of murderers. We must stop it. We must stop it. We must stop it.

We are on the move for our liberation. We're tired of trying to prove things to white people. We are tired of trying to explain to white people that we're not going to hurt them. We are concerned with getting the things we want, the things we have to have to be able to function. The question is, Will white people overcome their racism and allow for that to happen in this country? If not, we have no choice but to say very clearly, "Move on over, or we're going to move on over you."

Eldridge Cleaver

Political Struggle in America
(March 1968)

Until the mid-1960's, the goal of civil rights advocates had been clear: to secure the integration of blacks into a presumably good society. By mid-decade, however, the movement had fragmented. Some continued to favor the traditional goal; some now found it necessary to fundamentally reform society itself; and others considered white society to be beyond hope of salvation and advocated various forms of separatism. This last group included not only the Black Muslims but more militant groups as well. Among the most militant was the Black Panther Party for Self-Defense.

The Panthers were founded by Huey P. Newton and Bobby Seale in October of 1966. The party was dedicated to end what it regarded as the white man's robbery of the black community, and professed adherence to Marxism, self-defense, and black nationalism. Panthers followed the teachings of Malcolm X that called for separatism either by returning to Africa or by exclusive occupation of parts of the United States. The Panthers established themselves almost as a vigilante police force in Oakland, California, where members would patrol the police. They received national attention when they came en masse to a session of the California state assembly.

Eldridge Cleaver, one of the Panthers' principal speakers, grew up in the ghetto of Los Angeles and was imprisoned for various crimes. While in prison, he became politically conscious and became a follower of Malcolm X. He joined the Black Panthers in 1966 and became minister of information. Cleaver assumed power within the Panthers when founder Huey P. Newton was jailed for manslaughter. Cleaver saw the potential for depicting Newton as a martyr and for using his arrest as a way for the Panthers to align with other radical organizations. He advocated separatism, but was less concerned with physical separation than escape from the mindset of colonialism. He used the metaphor of the "mother country" to describe the white establishment, and "colony" to refer to the black community.

The speech reprinted here was delivered at the peak of the Panthers' visibility and power. It preaches black nationalism and invokes the rhetoric of revolution to advocate separation from the "mother country." In the speech, Cleaver announced a tentative merger between the Panthers and the Student Nonviolent Coordinating Committee (SNCC), headed by Stokely Carmichael, James Forman, and H. Rap Brown. The announced merger signified the growing power of the Panthers, since SNCC had been the major black leftist organization. The call for merger was also evidence of the fragmentation within the movement during the middle and late 1960's.

Six days after this speech was delivered, on Huey Newton's birthday, a merger meeting was held in the Oakland Auditorium. The flimsiness of Cleaver's program became clear at that time. He continued to refer to a merger, but Forman spoke only of an "alliance," and Carmichael recanted his support of Marxist ideology. Cleaver went on to become the Peace and Freedom Party Presidential candidate but he was involved during the campaign in a shootout with the police. Alternately in and out of jail, he finally jumped bail and fled to Algeria, where he resumed the title of minister of education for the Panthers. By the time Newton was released from prison in 1970, little of the party was left; by 1980, it was gone.

In the climate of the 1990's it is hard to read calls for revolution and to take them seriously. The temptation is to dismiss texts such as Cleaver's as proving only that the 1960's were exuberant and hyperbolic. But the tone and sentiments of Cleaver's speech capture the way many people felt at the time: on the front lines, struggling against a government and society that were imperialist and repressive. The sense of desperation implicit in the rhetorical stance captures well the cynicism, bitterness, and frustrations of the time.

I think the first thing we have to realize, really get into our minds, is that it is a reality when you hear people say that there's a "black colony" and a "white mother country." I think you really have to get that distinction clear in your minds in order to understand that there are two different sets of political dynamics functioning in this country. If you don't make that distinction, then a lot of the activities going on in this country will be non-sensical. For instance, if there's a homogeneous country and everyone here is a citizen of that country, when it comes to participating in the politics of this country, it makes a lot of sense to insist that black people participate in electoral politics and all the other forms of politics as we have known them. But if you accept the analysis that the black colony is separate and distinct from the mother country, then a lot of other forms of political struggle are indicated.

I think that most black revolutionaries or militants or what have you have generally accepted this distinction. A lot of people seem reluctant to accept this distinction. I know that in your education you were given to believe the melting pot theory, that people have come from all over the world and they've been put into this big pot and they've been melted into American citizens. In terms of the white immigrants who came to this country, this is more or less true. But in this stew that's been produced by these years and years of stirring the pot, you'll find that the black elements, the black components have not blended well with the rest of the ingredients. And this is so because of the forms of oppression that have been generated—black people have been blocked out of this, and blocked out of that, and not allowed to participate in this, and excluded from that. This has created a psychology in black people where they have now turned all the negative exclusions to their advantage.

I mean the same things that were used to our disadvantage are now being turned around to our advantage. The whole thing about condemning blackness and developing an inferior image of everything black has now been turned completely around because I think the slogan of Black Power was a recognition of the change in the psychology of black people, that in fact they have seized upon their blackness and rallied around the elements or the points at which they were oppressed. They have turned the focal point of the oppression into the focal point of the struggle for national liberation.

Now, when people decide in their own minds that they are going to separate themselves from a country or from a political situation, a lot of dynamics and a lot of directions flow from that basic distinction. For example, people are talking these days about going to the United Nations and seeking membership in the United Nations for Afro-America. And when you look at the criteria for nationhood, you'll find that the only place that black people fall short in terms of this standard is the one where the land question comes up. They say that a nation is defined as a people sharing a common culture, a common language, a common history, and a common land situation. Now, that land question was a hang-up for a long time, simply because the black people in this country were dispersed throughout the population of the mother country. People couldn't begin to deal with the question of how to build a nation on someone else's land. It presents a very sticky problem.

In the history of the liberation struggle in this country, the two outstanding efforts that we remember in history were the Marcus Garvey movement and the Nation of Islam under Elijah Muhammed. I consider their fundamental mistake was that they projected goals that they were unable to fulfill. Marcus Garvey said that he was going to take black people back to Africa. In fact, he wasn't in a position to do that, technically speaking in terms of resources. It falls down to a question of resources, because I think that if Marcus Garvey had been able to come over here with enough ships and enough technical resources, he would have succeeded, because he did have a very tight grip on the minds and imaginations of black people, and he could have had enough of them with him to make his dream a reality. Elijah Muhammed said that he wanted to have a part of this country, that he would accept some of these states. Well, the way he approached the question I think, was sure to doom it to be unfulfilled because he was asking the white power structure to give him several states. He offered no alternative means of obtaining these states other than come down from the sky and give them to us. Well, black people have been waiting for help to come from abroad and from the sky,

from underground, and from anywhere, and it hasn't come. So that we began to feel that we were in a bag where nothing could happen.

The beautiful thing about the slogan Black Power was that it implemented the dictum laid down by Kwame Nkrumah, in which he said, "Seek ye first the political kingdom, and other things will be added unto you." It's very important to realize that in moving to gain power, you do not conceal or repudiate the land question, you hold it in abeyance. What you're saying is that we must first get ourselves organized, and then we can get some of this land. It's very important to realize that 20,000,000 people or 30,000,000 people, what have you—we're going to have to take a count because the government has been lying to us about everything else they do so we can assume that they are lying about that, so we can say that there might be 30,000,000, 40,000,000 we might even be a majority, I don't know; but I am quite sure that there are more than the 20,000,000 that the government wants to give us. But, we can say that it's possible to organize 20,000,000 or 30,000,000 people right here. Even though we are dispersed throughout the mother country, it is possible to set up political forms where we can have representatives in the full sense of the word, like ambassadors going to other countries.

You can see from the experience of Malcolm and from the experience of Stokely that governments around the world are hip enough to the political realities of our situation to recognize and to accept our representatives in every sense of the word. I mean, Stokely Carmichael, when he went to Havana, received the same respect, or maybe even a little more, as delegates from other countries. Black people recognize this and they know that there is a way through the international machinery to cope with the situation.

I think it's very important to realize that there is a way to move. So that today black people are talking about going to the United Nations, asking the United Nations for a UN supervised plebiscite throughout the colony. Black people have never been able through any mechanism to express what their will is. People have come along and spoken in the name of black people; they have said black people want to be separated; but no where at no time have black people been given the chance to register their own position. I think it's very important that we decide this once and for all, because as black people we are able to wage a campaign on this subject: do you want to be a part of America, do you want to be integrated into America, or do you want to be separated from America, do you want to be a nation, do you want to have your ambassadors, your representatives seated in the United Nations, as a full member of the General Assembly, do you want to have your ambassadors accepted around the world? I think it would be very hard for the black people to say no, particularly when the argument of the government is going to be that black people don't need those things because they are already American citizens. Because then we come back and say, Well, if we're citizens, what about this, and what about that? And, at the very least, what it will do is to put tremendous pressure on the Babylonians, and they need all the pressure we can give them.

Now, a lot of people don't want to see this country and its structure basically change. They want to think the United States of America is an eternal entity. When you look at history, you'll find that great empires have had their boundaries changed, have had their political structures rearranged, and some of them, like Rome, lasted for 500, 600 years, and the people thought nothing could ever destroy this. It's gone. The Egyptian Empire—all the empires as you look down through history, you will find that a day of reckoning came down and the whole situation was rearranged. Americans cannot envision a situation where the same thing could happen here. I think that black people have already envisioned that this, in fact, could happen, because if we were to get organized in this fashion and then be able to bring international leverage against the United States, we could have those questions decided in our favor in an international forum. I think that by then Mao Tse-tung would be at the UN, I think he would vote for us, I don't think he would sustain LBJ's argument. I think that Fidel Castro would vote for us. I think Charles De Gaulle may say something about that. I don't think he would just turn thumbs down on us, so that there are a lot of areas that we have to get into and explore. Now what that means is that there are realities out here today and will be in the future.

One thing about the coalition with the Peace and Freedom Party: we approached this whole thing from the point of view of international relations. We feel that our coalition is part of our foreign policy. That is how we look at it, that is how we are moving on it and thinking about it.

A lot of people feel just as Mike Parker said: We are endangering them as well as ourselves by coalescing with the white radicals, particularly here in Berke-ley. Berkeley, as far as we can see, has a foul reputation among a lot of black cats, especially black cats associated with the NCNP. Bobby Seale, myself, and several other members of the Black Panther Party spent about a week in Los Angeles, and we were put through a lot of changes by black cats who didn't relate to the Peace and Freedom Party. They told us rather frankly that we had become tools of the white racists who had refused to accept the 50% bit in Chicago and they wanted to know what we were trying to do, were we trying to undercut what other blacks were trying to around the country? Our reply to that was that we had made a functional coalition with the Peace and Freedom Party and that we feel that we have 100% say so over our affairs. I mean we don't allow Mike Parker and Bob Avakian to come in and dictate to us what is going to happen in terms of what we want to do. They have not tried to do that, and they are not going to try, and they had better not try. And in the same way, we do not come in and try to dictate to them what they are going to do, although we have been accused of that, but that is not the way it goes.

We recognize that we have a powerful interest in seeing a white radical movement develop into something that we can relate to. There are many things that we cannot do by ourselves. And then, there are many things that the white radical movement cannot do by itself. So we recognize that, and we are not going to be running around trying to stab each other in the back, or put each other in trickbags. It is not going to work from our point of view and we hope it won't work from your point of view because we have an interest in seeing that you develop a stable organization and a stable movement.

Now, one very important thing that we are working towards is how to unify the black population in this country within a national structure. The structure has to be inclusive enough to pull in all black people. In the past, when a new organization came on the scene, it sought to eliminate existing organizations. It was going to move every other organization out and it was going to take over and do this thing. We say that this is a mistake. What we have done is worked out a merger with SNCC. The Black Panther Party for Self-Defense and SNCC are going to merge into a functional organization that can move nationally. We are moving into a period now where the Black Panther Party for Self-Defense has consolidated enough of a base to move things nationally. SNCC has already established national contact as well as international contact.

It is very important to realize that SNCC is composed virtually of black hippies, you might say, of black college students who have dropped out of the black middle class. And because that is their origin and that is where they came from, they cannot relate to the black brother on the block in a political fashion. They can relate to him, they can talk to him, they can communicate with him much better than, say, Roy Wilkins ever could. But, they are not able to move him *en masse* to the point where he could be organized and involved in political functions.

Now, the beauty and the genius of what Bobby Seale and Huey Newton have done is that they are able to move the last man on the totem pole. That is very important, because until that man can move, we really can't do that thing. SNCC has seen that the Black Panther Party is able to get to that man. So what they have done is made their apparatus available to us and there's no hangup; we can move into that. Most people don't know this, but a lot of the rhetoric you hear from Stokely Carmichael and Rap Brown these days, especially when Rap Brown first started speaking, was adopted precisely because they had come to the West Coast and spent a little time with the Black Panthers out here. That is very important, and if you see them you ask them to tell you about that, that they were greatly influenced by the Panthers. I mean that their lines were already moving in that direction because of the political pressures they were forced to deal with, but they hadn't yet made that step, they hadn't taken that leap. But coming out here and seeing the Panthers moving, seeing brothers carrying guns on the street, talking about the gun, violence, and revolution had a certain impact on their minds and they went back talking about that. So now we can say that SNCC—actually, I shouldn't even be going into this until February 17th at the Oakland Auditorium. This is when we are going to do this officially. I think it is very important that you be there so that you can see and hear for yourself what these people have to say, unless you want to depend on the newspapers, and you really don't want to get into that. So, let's just say that we are involved in trying to create models in the vanguard set so that people around the country will see how we can move.

Now, we have done two important things, I think. One, we have made this coalition with the Peace and Freedom Party; and two, we have merged with SNCC.

When people look at that they can say that in the Era of Black Power, we have got to merge and merge into larger units until we have a national structure. In terms of our relationship with the white community, we can move with functional coalitions.

It is very important that we all hold up our end of the bargain—and don't think that by using us you can get away with something, because, in fact, you will only destroy what you are trying to build for yourself. Black people have only one way to protect themselves, particularly politically, and that is to be capable of implementing and inflicting a political consequence. If we cannot inflict a political consequence, then we will in fact become nothing. So, that if the Peace and Freedom Party ever tries to misuse us, we have to be in a position to hurt the Peace and Freedom Party. We have to keep the political relationship such that if we were to pull out of it, that would be very costly to the Peace and Freedom Party. We must maintain that, we must be able to inflict a consequence, and we intend to be able to do that, and it is very important that that happens. White radicals who are like the vanguard in the white community should recognize that and then move to help us get in that position—because without that you are not going to be able to convince people that they should even relate to this whole effort.

As Mike Parker said, we are also catching a lot of hell—the word is purgatory, rather, it is not hell—about this coalition. Because a lot of people have begun to feel that we can be trusted, they have taken a wait-and-see attitude to find out how this coalition comes down, to see if we, in fact, do become puppets. People all around the country are asking—if you could look at our mail or listen to our phone calls—you would know about all the people who have asked, "Hey, what is this you are doing out there? What do you think you're doing, man, explain that to me." We feel that we are able to explain that, and as I said, Bobby is going to be going on a nation-wide tour and is going to be explaining that, I am going on a nation-wide tour and other members of the Party are going to be going on these tours. We are going to be explaining it and SNCC is going to be explaining it, and I think that we are going to be able to do it. It is very important that the Peace and Freedom Party be able to relate to that, because when we move nationally we will have to talk about the Peace and Freedom Party and then they will have grounds for moving into areas that we have already organized. So it is going to become extremely important that we realize what we are doing. And the thing that we need from the white mother country is technical assistance—technical assistance to the colony, dig it?

I think we have a good thing going. I want to see it continue to develop and broaden and deepen because we are all involved in this and there is no way out. We have got to do it, because time is against us, a lot of people are against us, and I know that I am out of time, so I think I will cool it right here.

Martin Luther King, Jr.

I've Been to the Mountaintop
(April 3, 1968)

Black Power pulled virtually all civil rights advocates in a more militant direction. After the passage of the Voting Rights Act, the movement shifted its attention to northern cities, where it encountered problems more intractable than the legally sanctioned segregation of the South. The issues were not ones of voter registration or gaining access to a lunch counter. They involved economic concerns—jobs, housing, welfare, and the like. Nonviolence proved to be relatively ineffective in addressing these issues, and there was at least some evidence that a more militant stance might succeed. Younger blacks, in particular, were impatient with the call for nonviolent civil disobedience and were attracted to the more assertive proclamations of Black Power.

To militant blacks, Martin Luther King was not an effective leader. They ridiculed him as "De Lawd" or dismissed him as an anachronism. But King himself was changing during the mid-1960's. He brought his campaign to Chicago, where he was not effective. The political machine had a great capacity to absorb criticism without undertaking major reform. But King stayed north, and he continued to focus on such economic issues as a boycott of stores discriminating against blacks and agreements for minority hiring. In his 1967 address to the Southern Christian Leadership Conference, King still advocated integration—but his definition of that term had changed since 1963. No longer assuming that the assimilation of blacks into white society was the goal, King now spoke of transformation of both white and black America and the achievement of a new synthesis. He still talked about nonviolence, but he gave more emphasis to the movement's goals and less to its methods as ends in themselves.

During the winter of 1967–1968, King planned to follow the March on Washington with a Poor People's Campaign, including a tent city to be erected in Washington to dramatize the plight of the poor and homeless. King was heavily involved in planning for this event, but he decided that he must interrupt his preparations in order to try to mediate a strike by sanitation workers in Memphis. The strike had lasted for two months and involved a vulnerable group: men working at wages that left them below the poverty line, who had no strike fund or other source of supplemental income, and who had been a relatively docile group who accepted their place in society. Moreover, since it was still cold, the uncollected garbage did not create odors that would have pressured the two sides to come to agreement. King's task, then, was to inspire and rally the garbage workers not to abandon their protest until an agreement had been reached.

This purpose prompted King's speech on the night of April 3, 1968. It is an eerie speech, and not just because it foreshadows King's tragic death the following day. King takes a panoramic view of the whole time, reviews the progress and problems of civil rights, and concludes that—if given a choice—there is no other age in which he would rather live. He speaks of what he has achieved, yet draws back from the temptation to see the struggle only in personal terms. It is in this context that King proclaims that, like Moses, he has seen the promised land and knows that his people will enter, whether or not he is with them. The analogy to Moses has other, unintended implications. If King is Moses, then the civil rights leaders who question his judgment or oppose him are the rebellious priests who must be cast aside.

The speech is widely remembered as a prophecy of King's own death. It is that, to be sure, but it also is an interesting and rich text in its own right. It reveals how King sought to deal with a very difficult situation, and it indexes the change in his thought and action that had transpired since the March on Washington.

Thank you very kindly, my friends. As I listened to Ralph Abernathy and his eloquent and generous introduction, and then thought about myself, I wondered who he was talking about. [*Laughter*] It is always good to have your closest friend and associate to say something good about you. And Ralph Abernathy is the best friend that I have in the world.

I'm delighted to see each of you here tonight in spite of a storm warning. You reveal that you are determined [*Voice says, "Come on, talk to us."*] I would go on even to the great heyday of the Roman Empire, and I would see developments around there through various emperors and leaders, but I wouldn't stop there. [*Voice says, "Keep on."*] I would even come up to the day of the Renaissance, and get a quick picture of all that the Renaissance did for the cultural and aesthetic life of man, but I wouldn't stop there. I would even go by the way that the man for whom I'm named had his habitat, and I would watch Martin Luther as he tacks his 95 Theses on the door at the Church of Wittenberg, but I wouldn't stop there. I would come on up even to 1863, and watch a vacillating President by the name of Abraham Lincoln finally come to the conclusion that

he had to sign the Emancipation Proclamation, but I wouldn't stop there. [*applause*] I would even come up to early 'thirties, and see a man grappling with the problems of the bankruptcy of his nation, and come with an eloquent cry that "We have nothing to fear but fear itself," but I wouldn't stop there. Strangely enough I would turn to the Almighty and say, "If you allow me to live just a few years in the second half of the twentieth century, I will be happy." [*applause*]

Now that's a strange statement to make because the world is all messed up, the nation is sick, trouble is in the land, confusion all around. That's a strange statement. But I know somehow that only when it is dark enough can you see the stars. And I see God working in this period of the twentieth century in a way that men in some strange way are responding. Something is happening in our world. The masses of people are rising up, and wherever they are assembled today, whether they are in Johannesburg, South Africa; Nairobi, Kenya; Accra, Ghana; New York City; Atlanta, Georgia; Jackson, Mississippi; or Memphis, Tennessee, the cry is always the same: "We want to be free!" [*Applause. Thunder sounds in the background*]

And another reason that I'm happy to live in this period is that we have been forced to a point where we are going to have to grapple with the problems that men have been trying to grapple with through history but the demands didn't force them to do it. Survival demands that we grapple with them. Men for years now have been talking about war and peace but now no longer can they just talk about it. It is no longer the choice between violence and nonviolence in this world, it's nonviolence or nonexistence. That is where we are today. [*Applause*] And also in the human rights revolution, if something isn't done and done in a hurry to bring the colored peoples of the world out of their long years of poverty, their long years of hurt and neglect, the whole world is doomed. [*Applause. Voice says, "All right."*] Now I'm just happy that God has allowed me to live in this period, to see what is unfolding, and I'm happy that He has allowed me to be in Memphis.(applause)

I can remember ... I can remember when Negroes were just going around as Ralph has said so often, scratching where they didn't itch and laughing when they were not tickled. (applause) But that day is all over. [*Applause*] We mean business now, and we are determined to gain our rightful place in God's world. [*Applause*] And that's all this whole thing is about. We aren't engaged in any negative protests and in any negative arguments with anybody. We are saying that "We are determined to be men, we are determined to be people." We are saying, [*Applause*]...we are saying that "We are God's children." And if we are God's children we don't have to live like we are forced to live.

Now what does all of this mean in this great period of history? It means that we've got to stay together. We've got to stay together and maintain unity. You know, whenever Pharaoh wanted to prolong the period of slavery in Egypt, he had a favorite, favorite formula for doing it. What was that? He kept the slaves fighting among themselves. [*Applause*] But whenever the slaves get together, something happens in Pharaoh's court and he cannot hold the slaves in slavery. When the slaves get together, that's the beginning of getting out of slavery. [*Applause*] Now let us maintain unity.

Secondly, let us keep the issues where they are. [*Voice says, "Right."*] The issue is injustice. The issue is the refusal of Memphis to be fair and honest in its dealings with its public servants who happen to be sanitation workers. [*Applause*] Now we've got to keep attention on that. That's always the problem with a little

violence. You know what happened the other day, and the press dealt only with the window-breaking. I read the articles. They very seldom got around to mentioning the fact that one thousand three hundred sanitation workers are on strike, and that Memphis is not being fair to them, and that Mayor Loeb is in dire need of a doctor. [*Cheers and applause*] They didn't get around to that.

Now we're gonna march again and we've gotta march again in order to put the issue where it is supposed to be, and force everybody to see that there are thirteen hundred of God's children here suffering, sometimes goin' hungry, going through dark and dreary nights wondering how this thing is gonna come out. That's the issue. And we've got to say to the nation, "We know how it's coming out." For when people get caught up with that which is right and they are willing to sacrifice for it, there is no stopping point short of victory! [*Applause*]

We aren't going to let any mace stop us. We are masters in our nonviolent movement in disarming police forces. They don't know what to do. I've seen them so often. I remember, in Birmingham, Alabama, when we were in that majestic struggle there, we would move out of the 16th Street Baptist Church day after day. By the hundreds we would move out, and Bull Connor would tell them to send the dogs forth, and they did come. But we just went before the dogs singing, "Ain't gonna let nobody turn me around." [*Cheers*] Bull Connor next would say, "Turn the firehoses on." And I said to you the other night Bull Connor didn't know history. He knew a kind of physics that somehow didn't relate to the transphysics that we knew about, and that was the fact that there was a certain kind of fire that no water could put out. [*Applause. Voice says, "Tell it like it is."*] And we went before the firehoses. We had known water. If we were Baptist or some other denominations we had been immersed, if we were Methodists and some others we had been sprinkled, but we knew water. That couldn't stop us. [*Applause*] And we just went on before the dogs and we would look at them, and we'd go on before the water hoses and we would look at it, and we'd just go on singing "Over my head I see freedom in the air." And then we would be thrown in the paddy wagons, and sometimes we were stacked in there like sardines in a can. And they would throw us in and old Bull would say, "Take 'em off," and they did. And we would just go on in the paddy wagons singin' "We Shall Overcome." And every now and then we'd get in jail and we'd see the jailers looking through the windows being moved by our prayers, and being moved by our words and our songs. And there was a power there which Bull Connor couldn't adjust to. And so we ended up transforming Bull into a steer, and we won our struggle in Birmingham. [*Applause*]

And we've got to go on in Memphis just like that. I call upon you to be with us when we go out Monday.

Now about injunctions—we have an injunction and we are going into court tomorrow morning to fight this illegal, unconstitutional injunction. All we say to America is, "Be true to what you said on paper." [*Applause*] If I lived in China or even Russia or any totalitarian country, maybe I could understand some of these illegal injunctions. Maybe I could understand the denial of certain basic first amendment privileges because they haven't committed themselves to that over there. But somewhere I read of the freedom of assembly. Somewhere I read of the freedom of speech. Somewhere I read of the freedom of the press. Somewhere I read that the greatness of America is the right to protest for right. And so just as I say, we aren't going to let any injunction turn us around. We are going on. We need all of you.

And you know, what's beautiful to me is to see all of these ministers of the gospel. It's a marvelous picture. Who is it that is supposed to articulate the longings and aspirations of the people more than the preacher? Somehow the preacher must have a kind of fire shut up in his bones, [*Voice says, "Yes, Sir."*] and whenever injustice is around he must tell it. [*Voices say, "Yeah."*] Somehow the preacher must be an Amos, who said, "When God speaks, who can but prophesy." Again with Amos, "Let justice roll down like waters, and righteousness like a mighty stream." Somehow the preacher must say with Jesus, "The spirit of the Lord is upon me because He has anointed me." And He's anointed me to deal with the problems of the poor. And I want to commend the preachers, under the leadership of these noble men: James Lawson, one who has been in this struggle for many years, he's been to jail for struggling, he's been kicked out of Vanderbilt University for this struggling, but he's still going on fighting for the rights of his people. [*Applause*] Reverend Ralph Jackson, Billy Kyles, I could just go right on down the list but time will not permit. But I want to thank all of 'em, and I want to you to thank them, because so often preachers aren't concerned about anything but themselves. [*Voices of agreement*]

And I'm always happy to see a relevant ministry. It's all right to talk about long white robes over yonder in all of its symbolism, but ultimately people want some suits and dresses and shoes to wear down here. [*Cheers and applause. Voice says, "Yes, yes, yes."*] It's all right to talk about streets flowing with milk and honey, but God has commanded us to be concerned about the slums down here and His children who can't eat three square meals a day. [*Applause*] It's all right to talk about the New Jerusalem, but one day God's preacher must talk about the New York, the New Atlanta, the New Philadelphia, the New Los Angeles, the New Memphis, Tennessee. [*Applause*] This is what we have to do.

Now the other thing we'll have to do is this: Always anchor our external direct action with the power of economic withdrawal. Now we are poor people. Individually, we are poor when you compare us with white society in America. We are poor. Never stop ... forget that collectively, that means all of us together, collectively we are richer than all the nations in the world with the exception of nine. Did you ever think about that? [*Voice says, "Right on."*] After you leave the United States, Soviet Russia, Great Britain, West Germany, France—and I could name the others—the American Negro collectively is richer than most nations of the world. We have an annual income of more than thirty billion dollars a year, which is more than all of the exports of the United States, and more than the national budget of Canada. Did you know that? That's power right there if we know how to pool it. [*Applause*]

We don't have to argue with anybody. We don't have to curse and go around acting bad with our words. We don't need any bricks and bottles. We don't need any Molotov cocktails. We just need to go around to these stores, [*Voice says, "Yes sir"*] and to these massive industries in our country and say, "God sent us by here to say to you that you're not treating His children right. [*Voice says, "That's right"*] And we've come by here to ask you to make the first item on your agenda fair treatment where God's children are concerned. Now if you are not prepared to do that we do have an agenda that we must follow. And our agenda calls for withdrawing economic support from you." [*Applause*]

So as the result of this we are asking you tonight to go out and tell your neighbors not to buy Coca Cola in Memphis. [*Applause*] Go by and tell them not to buy Sealtest milk, [*Applause*] tell them not to buy—what is the other bread?—Wonder bread. What is the other bread, Jesse? Tell them not to buy Hart's bread. As Jesse Jackson has said, "Up to now only the garbage men have been feeling pain. Now we must kind of redistribute the pain." [*Applause*] We are choosing these companies because they haven't been fair in their hiring policies, and we are choosing them because they can begin the process of saying they are going to support the needs and the rights of these men who are on strike, and then they can move on downtown and tell Mayor Loeb to do what is right. [*Applause*]

And not only that. We've got to strengthen black institutions. I call upon you to take your money out of the banks downtown and deposit your money in Tri-State Bank. [*Applause*] We want a bank-in movement in Memphis. Go by the savings and loan associations. I'm not asking you something we don't do ourselves in S.C.L.C. Judge Hooks and others will tell you that we have an account here in the savings and loan association from the Southern Christian Leadership Conference. We are telling you to follow what we are doing, put your money there. You have six or seven black insurance companies here in the city of Memphis. Take out your insurance there, we want to have an insurance-in. [*Applause*]

Now these are some practical things that we can do. We begin the process of building a greater economic base, and at the same time we are putting pressure where it really hurts. And I ask you to follow through here. [*Applause*]

Now let me say as I move to my conclusion that we've got to give ourselves to this struggle until the end. Nothing would be more tragic than to stop at this point in Memphis. We've got to see it through. [*Applause*] And when we have our march you need to be there. If it means leaving work, if it means leaving school, be there. [*Applause*] Be concerned about your brother. You may not be on strike, but either we go up together or we go down together. [*Applause*] Let us develop a kind of dangerous unselfishness.

One day a man came to Jesus and he wanted to raise some questions about some vital matters of life. At points he wanted to trick Jesus [*Voice says, "That's right"*] and show him that he knew a little more than Jesus knew, and throw him off base. Jesus showed him up because he was a lawyer and he was raising a question that any lawyer should know. And finally the man didn't want to give up and he said to Jesus, "Who is my neighbor?" Now that question could have easily ended up in a philosophical and theological debate. But Jesus immediately pulled that question from mid-air, and placed it on a dangerous curve between Jerusalem and Jericho. [*Chuckles of appreciation from crowd.*] And

he talked about a certain man who fell among thieves. And you remember that a Levite [*Voices say, "Sure"*] and a priest passed by on the other side. They didn't stop to help him. And finally a man of another race came by. [*Voices say, "Sure"*] He got down from his beast, decided not to be compassionate by proxy, but he got down with him, administered first aid, and helped the man in need. Jesus ended up saying, this was the good man, this was the great man, because he had the capacity to project the "I" into the "thou," and to be concerned about his brother.

Now you know we use our imagination a great deal to try to determine why the priest and the Levite didn't stop. At times we say they were busy going to a church meeting, an ecclesiastical gatherin', and they had to get on down to Jerusalem so they wouldn't be late for their meeting. At other times we would speculate that there was a religious law that one who was engaged in religious ceremonials was not to touch a human body twenty-four hours before the ceremony. And every now and then we begin to wonder whether maybe they were not going down to Jerusalem—or down to Jericho rather—to organize a Jericho Road Improvement Association. [*Laughter*] That's a possibility. Maybe they felt that it was better to deal with the problem from the causal root rather than to get bogged down with an individual effect.

But I'm going to tell you what my imagination tells me. It's possible that those men were afraid. You see, the Jericho road is a dangerous road. [*Voice says, "That's right. That's right."*] I remember when Mrs. King and I were first in Jerusalem. We rented a car and drove from Jerusalem down to Jericho. And as soon as we got on that road I said to my wife, "I can see why Jesus used this as the setting for his parable."It's a winding, meandering road. [*Voice says, "Yeah, yeah."*] It's really conducive for ambushing. You start out in Jerusalem, which is about twelve hundred miles—or rather twelve hundred feet—above sea level, and by the time you get down to Jericho fifteen or twenty minutes later you are about twenty-two hundred feet below sea level. That's a dangerous road. In the days of Jesus it came to be known as the Bloody Pass. You know it's possible that the priest and the Levite looked over to that man on the ground and wondered if the robbers were still around. [*Voices agree, "Yeah."*] Or it's possible that they felt that the man on the ground was merely faking [*Voice says, "Uh-huh"*] and he was acting like he had been robbed and hurt in order to seize them over there, lull them there for quick and easy seizure. [*Voices agree, "Yeah."*] And so the first question that the priest asked, the first question that the Levite asked, was, "If I stop to help this man, what will happen to me?" But then the good Samaritan came by, and he reversed the question: "If I do not stop to help this man, what will happen to him?"

That's the question before you tonight. Not, "If I stop to help the sanitation workers, what will happen to my job?" Not, "If I stop to help the sanitation workers, what will happen to all of the hours that I usually spend in my office every day and every week as a pastor?" The question is not, "If I stop to help this man in need, what will happen to me?" The question is, "If I do *not* stop to help the sanitation workers, what will happen to them?" That's the question. [*Long applause*]

Let us rise up tonight with a greater readiness. Let us stand with a greater determination. And let us move on, in these powerful days, these days of challenge, to make America what it ought to be. We have an opportunity to make America a better nation, and I want to thank God once more for allowing me to be here with you. [*Voice says, "Yes sir."*]

You know, several years ago I was in New York City, autographing the first book that I had written. And while sitting there autographing books, a demented black woman came up, and the only question I heard from her was, "Are you Martin Luther King?" And I was looking down writing, and I said, "Yes." The next minute I felt something beating on my chest. Before I knew it, I had been stabbed by this demented woman. I was rushed to Harlem Hospital. It was a dark Saturday afternoon. And that blade had gone through, and the X-rays revealed that the tip of the blade was on the edge of my aorta, the main artery, and once that's punctured you drown in your own blood. That's the end of you. It came out in the *New York Times* the next morning that if I had merely sneezed, I would have died.

Well, about four days later they allowed me after the operation, after my chest had been opened and the blade had been taken out, to move around in the wheelchair in the hospital. They allowed me to read some of the mail that came in, and from all over the states and the world kind letters came in. I read a few but one of them I will never forget. I had received one from the President and the Vice-President. I've forgotten what those telegrams said. [*Voice says, "Go ahead, now. Go ahead."*] I had received a visit and a letter from the governor of New York but I've forgotten what that letter said. [*Voice says, "Yes sir"*] But there was

another letter [*Voices say, "All right"*] that came from a little girl, a young girl, who was a student at the White Plains High School, and I looked at that letter and I'll never forget it. It said simply, "Dear Dr. King, I am a ninth grade student at the White Plains High School." She said, "While it should not matter, I would like to mention that I'm a white girl. I read in the paper of your misfortune and of your suffering, and I read that if you had sneezed you would have died. I'm simply writing you to say that I'm so happy that you didn't sneeze."

And I want to say tonight ... [*Applause*] I want to say tonight that I too am happy that I didn't sneeze, because if I had sneezed [*Voice says, "All right"*] I wouldn't have been around here in 1960 when students all over the South started sitting in at lunch counters. And I knew that as they were sitting in they were really standing up for the best in the American dream and taking the whole nation back to those great wells of democracy which were dug deep by the founding fathers in the Declaration of Independence and the Constitution. If I had sneezed [*Crowd replies, "Yeah"*] I wouldn't have been around here in 1961 when we decided to take a ride for freedom and ended segregation in interstate travel. If I had sneezed [*Crowd says, "Yes"*] I wouldn't have been around here in 1962 when Negroes in Albany, Georgia, decided to straighten their backs up. And whenever men and women straighten their backs up they are going somewhere because a man can't ride your back unless it is bent. If I had sneezed [*Long applause*] ... if I had sneezed I wouldn't have been here in 1963, when the black people of Birmingham, Alabama, aroused the conscience of this nation and brought into being the civil rights bill. If I had sneezed, [*Applause*] I wouldn't have had a chance later in that year in August to try to tell America about a dream that I had had. If I had sneezed, [*Applause*] I wouldn't have been down in Selma, Alabama, to see the great movement there. If I had sneezed, I wouldn't have been in Memphis to see a community rally around those brothers and sisters who are suffering. [*Voices say, "Yes sir."*] I'm so happy that I didn't sneeze.

And they were telling me ... [*Applause*] Now it doesn't matter now. [*Voice says, "Go ahead."*] It really doesn't matter what happens now. I left Atlanta this morning, and as we got started on the plane—there were six of us—the pilot said over the public address system, "We are sorry for the delay, but we have Dr. Martin Luther King on the plane, and to be sure that all of the bags were checked and to be sure that nothing would be wrong on the plane, we had to check out everything carefully, and we've had the plane protected and guarded all night."

And then I got into Memphis, and some began to say the threats, or talk about the threats that were out of what would happen to me from some of our sick white brothers. Well, I don't know what will happen now. We've got some difficult days ahead. But it really doesn't matter with me now because I've been to the mountaintop. [*Applause*] And I don't mind. Like anybody I would like to live a long life. Longevity has its place, but I'm not concerned about that now. I just want to do God's will, and He's allowed me to go up to the mountain, and I've looked over and I've seen the Promised Land. I may not get there with you, but I want you to know tonight that we as a people will get to the Promised Land. [*Applause*] So I'm happy tonight, I'm not worried about anything, I'm not fearing any man. Mine eyes have seen the glory of the coming of the Lord. [*Long applause, cheers.*]

John Bell Williams

School Desegregation Problems
(January 3, 1970)

The 1954 Supreme Court decision in *Brown v. Board of Education* held that legally enforced school segregation was unconstitutional; a subsequent decision the following year stipulated that schools be desegregated with "all deliberate speed." Although many school districts, especially in the border states, complied quickly with the Court's order, across the South there was a widespread pattern of resistance. Some districts ignored the Supreme Court decision until specific legal challenges were advanced against their own systems. Others developed means to evade the decision, ranging from freedom-of-choice plans that abolished neighborhood schools to the closing of the public schools altogether. In many communities private schools were established to thwart desegregation; these were sometimes supported with tax funds.

For all these reasons, the pace of desegregation was slow. In 1969, fifteen years after *Brown*, 233 Southern school districts, many in Mississippi, had yet to be desegregated at all; many more remained segregated de facto even if not de jure. Continued litigation resulted in the case of *Alexander v. Holmes County Board of Education*, decided by the Supreme Court in October of 1969. In that decision, the Court ordered thirty-three districts in Mississippi to desegregate "at once" and to operate integrated systems "now and hereafter." The pace of "all deliberate speed" was no longer acceptable; districts were given only until December 31, 1969, to implement desegregation plans.

John Bell Williams, a former congressman and a conservative on racial matters, was governor of Mississippi at the time. He was enraged by the Court's decision, which he believed was itself discrimination, since Mississippi was challenged but de facto segregation in the North was not. He proposed that Mississippi file desegregation suits in Northern and Eastern cities. His motive, of course, was not to achieve integration there but to expose what he believed to be the hypocrisy of Northern society in order to create pressure from the North and East to induce the Supreme Court to modify its own rule. Even the Mississippi legislature opposed this move. Williams also proposed a statewide system of private schools for white children, and requested legislative approval for income tax credits for private school expenditures. Finally, Williams indicated that he would support teachers who refused new assignments prompted by the Court order. Although he explicitly challenged the Court's decision itself, he also implicitly challenged the Court's right to rule, believing that education was solely the business of the state. He thus re-enacted the conflict between states' rights and federal power that traces back to the 1790's.

This speech was among the last gasps of resistance to school desegregation. It relies on the underlying theories of interposition and nullification that supported the tariff protests during the nineteenth century and the "massive resistance" of the 1950's, and it attempts to apply them to the current situation. Although many were still persuaded by these appeals, the times had passed Williams by. Even if they did not like blacks, his constituents came to realize that racial discrimination was a loss to the economy of Mississippi and to its public image. The legislature adjourned its 1970 session without granting tax incentives for white parents to send their children to private schools and without developing an antibusing plan—both real defeats for Williams. The governor vetoed over $4 million in federal funds for Project Head Start, on the grounds that they were targeted to blacks and therefore discriminated against whites. His veto was overridden by President Nixon, as the Head Start legislation permitted, in a showdown in which the President prevailed.

Within four years of this speech, the South had a new generation of moderate governors, most prominently Jimmy Carter of Georgia, who proclaimed that the age of segregation was over and that Southerners were moving on to matters of greater significance. Williams's speech remains as the illustration of a lost cause.

Ladies and gentlemen, friends and fellow Mississippians:—I speak to you in a fateful hour in the life of our State. I have requested this time that I may visit in your homes, through the medium of television and radio, that we may discuss a mutual problem—the most important one facing us in our State, and one that concerns the future of the things nearest and dearest to our hearts—our children.

In the course of my discussion, I will try to be as deliberate and objective as possible—though for me, as well as you, the subject is one which understandably tends to arouse emotions. But I ask you to reason with me, at a time when reason must outweigh emotion, and calm must prevail over hysteria. This is not a time for histrionics or emotional tirades. It is a time when we must keep our heads, or risk losing our childrens' future.

The moment that we have resisted for fifteen years—that we have fought hopefully to avoid; at least

to delay—is finally at hand. We have reached the moment of decision.

The children of Mississippi, white and black, have been denied the right to attend the school of their choice by an arbitrary edict of the United States Supreme Court. From the sanctuary of their secluded chambers, isolated from the practical problems of every day living, protected from the normal experiences of regular social contact among all races and economic strata, they have arrogated unto themselves the power to sit as sole and final arbiters of our children's welfare and as self-appointed dictators of our children's futures. Through a series of decisions, the high court has taken away from the people the right and the responsibility to run their own schools and to safeguard the best interests of their own children.

In the years since 1954, when the Supreme Court first overstepped its judicial authority to assume law-making powers, the full resources of the State of Mississippi have been constantly employed in a struggle to salvage our Constitutional right to operate our own schools, in our own way, with our own money, for the best interests of our own children, of whatever race or economic status.

During these fifteen years, our Governors, our Attorneys General, our Legislatures, our School Boards, their attorneys and administrators, our Congressional Delegations in Washington, and our other State and local officials have stood foursquare, shoulder to shoulder, in fighting an uphill battle against these forces who would thus dissolve our freedoms.

Throughout these fifteen years, Mississippi has been used as a proving ground for every kind of radical so-called "civil rights" experiment that could be dreamed up by the witch doctors of the pseudo-liberal left and their fellow revolutionaries. These elements have had the full support of fawning Federal Administrations fearing the power of their strategically located and rigidly controlled bloc votes. Even Presidents of the United States, dreading the wrath of their vengeance, have cravenly yielded to their demands, however unreasonable or unconstitutional. They have furnished them troops, money, and legal aid, and they have placed entire departments of the Federal Government at their disposal. Even before Lyndon Johnson led the cheers for these radicals by chanting their theme song, "We Shall Overcome," to a joint session of the United States Congress, the Southern States—and Mississippi in particular—have been open, defenseless, marked, and singular targets for all the vitriolic hate and abuse that could be heaped upon us by anyone with a politically motivated cause.

Mississippi has faced trying times before. Our people suffered the terrible ordeal of Civil War fought on our own ground. We were dragged through the terrible days of the Reconstruction. Yet we survived, and from the carnage of that era rose a greater and finer State and People. As an agricultural state, we survived the era of five-cent cotton, and furnished more than our share of young men to the defense of this Nation in times of war. We have walked through the shadows, each time to emerge into the sunlight of a finer age and better civilization.

We did not weather these crises by the easy expedient of surrender. In every instance we knew setbacks and reverses, yet we never yielded in our determination to survive, and we did survive, and we maintained our honor and self-respect.

In times of great stress and strife it is customary,

and properly so, that the people look to their elected officials—and more especially to their Chief Executive—to provide the leadership, and to suggest the course that might accomplish their escape from the dilemma.

By the same token, the people have the right to expect their leaders to be open and candid with them; that their leaders will give an honest assessment of the situation confronting them—no matter how good or how bad it might be.

That is why I speak to you tonight.

When the District of Columbia public schools were fully integrated overnight into a unitary school system in 1955, President Eisenhower proclaimed that these schools should serve as a "model of integration" for other states to follow. At that time, Washington's public school racial population was about the same proportion existing in our State.

The result of that experiment became obvious in less than a year, when standards deteriorated drastically, police patrols were dispatched to keep peace in the schools, and whites began to flee these schools by the thousands.

In 1954, Washington numbered among its schools some of the finest in the country. In scholastic achievement, nearly half of the schools were rated in the top five per cent of all schools in the nation.

Today, the Washington public schools are segregated again—not by law—but by the practical fact that nearly all the white children have fled the school system, and it is now more than 96 per cent black. No longer does Washington brag about the high standards in its schools—indeed they cannot—because the former high standards are no more. They fell victim long ago to the axe of a blind social experiment that has failed miserably. Instead of becoming a "showcase" of successful integration, the District of Columbia School System has become a national disgrace. All of this has been freely admitted by Dr. Carl Hansen, who was Superintendent of the Washington Schools throughout the period of change and for quite some time thereafter, in testimony before a number of federal courts.

The tragic case of the Washington schools is the only precedent available by which we can judge the possible effects on our school system. Except for the obvious advantage they had over our schools in having the full financial support of the federal establishment—which we do not have—the situations are parallel. The story of the Washington schools is one we might well contemplate. And the story has been the same wherever it was tried under similar circumstances.

Now *our* public schools have been forced into the same dire, serious, troublesome and impossible predicament. Quality public education in a great portion of our State has been made an impossibility under conditions inflicted on our public schools by a vindictive, autocratic, arbitrary Supreme Court.

I am frank to tell you that our arsenal of legal and legislative weapons has been exhausted. I would be less than honest if I were to suggest that there might be some magic formula that could be applied; some radical or spectacular maneuver that could be employed; or hope of some last minute reprieve that might come to provide escape for the calamity certain to befall our public schools in their next semester's operations.

This is not to infer that our best legal efforts will not be expended in the hope of relief in the future. We will not surrender nor yield in our continued efforts to provide escape for our people from this cruel yoke of judicial tyranny.

The results of great legal research and expertise have already gone into the records of these Federal Courts, though they have chosen thus far to ignore them. Yet, sooner or later, an appellate Court will find itself in a position where it has no choice but to give full review, and take appropriate notice of these facts. When that time comes, we must be given relief.

We will give legal support to our teachers whose individual and employment rights are being violated by these arbitrary actions, and we will enter suits on behalf of our aggrieved students whose constitutional freedoms have been usurped by these orders of the high courts.

We will institute litigation to compel equal application of these judicial laws to other areas of the country which now, because of their politically strategic positions, enjoy immunity from their application.

We will continue to fight—as long as these intolerable conditions endure—for the right of our children to be given a quality education, whether in public or private schools, or both.

But in facing the immediate ordeal, I am compelled to repeat—as distasteful as it is to contemplate—there is no panacea for a statewide solution prior to the opening of our schools for the next semester.

It is easy for each of us to say what should be done. At this point, the crux of the problem is not so much "what should be done"; but rather, "what can be done."

The Courts have directed the immediate establishment of what they call a "unitary" system; yet they have not defined what they mean by the term "unitary." They have said that we must forcibly integrate our systems fully and completely overnight, and when practical difficulties in accomplishing this were raised, even by federal agencies themselves, we were told to do it by the numbers.

Let us explore, for a moment, the courses available to us as a State.

We can acquiesce in total surrender to their orders, and suffer the obvious consequences: a sudden deterioration in the quality of education; and immediate lowering of standards; interminable disciplinary problems; and a destruction of teacher and pupil morale everywhere.

We could brazenly shout defiance of the Federal Government and the Court orders; yet we know from experience the futility of that course, and we know that such a course would avail nothing more than additional grief and strife.

We could close our public schools entirely, or keep them open in the fond hope that a brighter day might dawn which would see a return of their control to our own people through their school boards. Shall we abandon public education and rely entirely on setting up a private school system?

In my contemplation of the various alternatives, I am strongly of the opinion that we must preserve our public school system as an absolute necessity for the good of all. While a majority of our public schools will find it extremely difficult to survive under the onus of the court orders, it must be recognized, also, that in a substantially large area of our State the problem is not acute. With such a divergence of conditions, it becomes necessary that we mold into one objective the many and varied alternatives and suggested plans of action. Such a plan, to be workable, must contemplate a continued strong and vibrant system of public education.

In the light of the burden placed on our public schools by the Supreme Court, their preservation in many areas of our State is not going to be an easy matter. Nor is it going to be an easy matter to establish private schools as a workable alternative, though I shall ask the Legislature to seek ways and means of rendering assistance toward this end. In the recent Special Session of the Legislature, loans were authorized to assist children in obtaining an education in private and parochial schools, only to run headlong into an injunction against the laws' operation by the Federal Courts. While this is yet to be heard on its merits, there is little doubt that the Court, following its usual arbitrary line of decisions in this area, will render them invalid.

It will be my intention in the next Session to renew my request to the Legislature that it authorize tax credits for taxpayers who donate moneys to educational institutions, whether public or private. We will explore other possible avenues by which we can encourage and assist in the creation and operation of private schools throughout our State.

To those who would hold that in seeking to lend support to private schools in our State I am concurrently seeking the demise of public schools, I would caution a moment's reflection.

If you will recall, the main thrust of my Administration at the outset was to upgrade public education in Mississippi, and to update our dangerous and antiquated system of highways. Even in this, our educational needs were given first priority. With the courageous cooperation of the Legislature, we brought a new day to our schools, our teachers, and to public education. For the first time within my memory, the needs of public education in our State had been given first priority on the agenda of a new Administration's goals. In line with my recommendation, the Legislature enacted into law the most comprehensive and far-reaching program of public school improvement in the history of our State.

In order to accomplish these improvements, I had to recommend additional taxes to defray the additional costs. I shouldered this responsibility and recommended these increases, knowing full well that it would cost me dearly in loss of whatever popularity I may have enjoyed at the time. Yet it had to be done, and the Legislature recognized that it had to be done, and they assumed their responsibility also, at no little risk to their political futures.

I do not think it necessary for me to proclaim further my support for quality education in our public schools—my record speaks for itself.

If our public schools system is destroyed, it will not be your Governor who brings it about. I did not seek this office to preside over the destruction of public education in our State, nor do I want to see the fruits of my Administration go down the drain and into the sewers of power politics.

If our public school system suffers—and it will—it will not be because of our people's lack of support of the principle of public education. The fact is that our people have always supported our public school system, even to the extent of devoting a greater propor-tion of our tax revenues for public school support than any other State in the Union.

On the other hand, a strong private school system may very well supplement and add strength to our public schools. There is no doubt but that a strong system of public schools will have to be the ultimate primary vehicle for providing the education for both white and black children; but this is not to say that it must be the only system, and each must respect the rights and responsibilities of the other.

Parents must decide for themselves what type of school their child will attend. In many cases, parents—unable to defray the cost of private schools for their children—and unwilling to place their children in the public schools under existing circumstances, will have no choice but to keep their children out of school for the semester. Parents must be left free from extraneous pressures and coercion in exercising their right to choose what is best for their children.

But whatever the situation, and whatever course is chosen in January, it may have to be altered, perhaps even reversed, in September. We cannot permit our people to become polarized, or committed irrevocably to any particular position at this point—for times change, and what may be today may be gone tomorrow. No one can say what our circumstances may be in September, or next January, and we would be utterly foolish if we tried to burn our bridges behind us.

It is senseless to engage in name-calling, vilification, and categorizing because of the present decision of any individual family.

Our fight has been for freedom of choice, and that fight will continue on and on until we have gained an ultimate victory. To restrict parents in exercising the choices remaining to them after the Court's decision—whether to patronize public or private schools or to withdraw their children—is wholly inconsistent with the freedom of choice concept, and handicaps us greatly in advancing that principle.

Our schools rightfully belong to us, yet we no longer control them. They are now under the complete control of the majority of the Fifth Circuit Court of Appeals, backed up by the Supreme Court. Judging by recent orders of the Fifth Circuit Court of Appeals, they intend to retain absolute control, and through force and threats, run them without regard to our wishes or the best educational advantages of our children, white or black.

The task at hand is monumental. It brings into immediate focus the problems confronting 148 public school districts, 795 school board members, 970 attendance centers, 40,000 public school teachers and staff personnel, 600,000 enrolled students, and an indeterminate number of parents and guardians.

In addition to this, Mississippi has about 100 private schools in operation throughout the State, and this number is growing rapidly.

Instead of rivalry between the two school systems—one seeking to gain advantage at the expense of the other—it is my hope that there might be, instead, a spirit of cooperation to the end that all of our children may be given the best education within our power to provide. For instance, it might be well for our school administrators, in communities where the needs are great and the facilities limited, to make arrangements with legitimate private school administrators for the use of their physical facilities at times and hours when they are not required for public school purposes. The same spirit of cooperation, in my opinion, should exist between our churches and private schools, even as it exists now between our churches and the public schools. The preservation of quality public education for our children is a challenge that demands the full cooperation of all people in Mississippi, regardless of faith or race or philosophy. I have every confidence to believe that the administrators and supporters of the private school system will in turn support to the fullest the efforts of public school administrators in seeking return of the people's control over the public schools.

In passing, let me say that we owe a great debt of gratitude to those members of our school boards who have served through the years with skill, devotion and courage.

These boards have fought a good fight to preserve and maintain the quality and integrity of our public schools. They have done so without compensation and at great personal risk and sacrifice—and in many cases, without the sympathetic understanding of the public. I ask you, the public, to join in petitioning them to remain at their posts of duty even in the face of the difficult conditions visited upon them, and to pledge our continued support and encouragement for their efforts. Let us remember that even the parents who may decide to withdraw their children from the public schools still have an economic interest, as taxpayers, in seeing these schools operated efficiently and economically. Whatever may come, it is absolutely essential that good people serve on our school boards.

There is no limit to what free men of goodwill in voluntary association can accomplish. There is likewise no limit to the damage which can be visited on us by irresponsible actions of a small minority heli-bent on dividing our people and frustrating honest and intelligent efforts to bring order out of disorder. The ultimate answer depends upon us. We became free, and we can stay free by doing for ourselves, but in doing for ourselves, we must also work with others in resolving this common problem.

Like many of you, I am a parent. I have two children in our Mississippi public schools. Their year and a half in public school here has been the happiest of their school careers. Yet the school they attend is under a court order, and no one knows at this point what changes will be forced on it in the next semester. They do not know whether they will be separated arbitrarily from their friends and teachers even if they are permitted to return to the same school. They do not know, even, whether they will be reassigned to that school, or summarily reassigned to another school on the other side of town simply to help create some kind of predetermined racial balance by the numbers as ordered by the courts and H.E.W.

As a parent, I share your dilemma. Like you, Mrs. Williams and I face a dread and serious decision within our own family. Like you, we will try to reach a decision that will serve the best educational interests of our children.

The court orders apply to our school boards and administrators. They are the only people who must follow these orders under penalty of prosecution.

You, as parents, are free to follow whatever course you may deem best for your children. You are under no legal compulsion to place your children in any particular school, though the Courts have denied you the freedom to enroll your children in the school of your choice.

As Governor, I will not presume to suggest which of these three options should be followed by any particular parents. Different situations confront parents in the several school districts. The decision must be yours as parents, to be made in the light of conditions that prevail in your particular school or community, and should be made in the best interests of your children.

I would say this, however. While it is your right to exercise whatever option you choose for your child, it is likewise the right of your neighbor to do the same for his child. No parent should be subjected to criticism or recrimination for choosing to send his child to a particular school.

It is my hope that we can stand up to this crisis

unified as one in a determination to preserve the peace and dignity of our State. How the people of our State react in this time of great emergency and trial, how we deport ourselves in the face of adversity, will determine whether we may ever expect relief.

As earnestly and emphatically as I can, I want to urge restraint on our people. Most of us resent this denial of our rights by the Courts, and it follows that tempers usually rise under these conditions. Let us remember that the public schools, after all, are still public property, and willful damage or destruction of these properties is senseless: it is like cutting off a nose to spite the face. Nothing can be gained through violent acts of any kind; that has been proven time and time again.

So let us accept the inevitable fact that we are going to suffer one way or the other, both white and black, as a result of the Court's decrees. With God's help, let us make the best of a bad situation, and show to the world that we still have the same indomitable spirit that characterized our valiant ancestors who endured the rigors and hardships of reconstruction to emerge undaunted in their struggle for dignity and self-determination.

To this end, I seek the support, the cooperation, and sympathetic understanding of all Mississippians, of all races and philosophies.

As we emerge into the dawn of a new decade, let us petition the Guidance and Blessings for Divine Providence; that whatever we do, whatever decisions we make, and whatever course we choose will be right; that we will not despair, but face the future with hope, with an unbounded determination that these next ten years will witness a return of our government to its ancient landmarks of Constitutional liberty; and that freedom, under God, will become—once again—the hallmark of America's greatness.

The New Frontier and the Great Society

John F. Kennedy

Inaugural Address
(January 20, 1961)

The 1960 Presidential election was the closest in American history. Less than one vote per precinct separated the victor, John F. Kennedy, from his rival, Richard M. Nixon. Moreover, the Congress elected in 1960 was, if anything, more conservative than its predecessor. The Democrats held a nominal majority, but effective control was in the hands of a coalition of Republicans and conservative Southern Democrats. The election followed a campaign not marked by sharp distinctions between the candidates on the issues. It was hard to discern any mandate in the election results, and it was clear that the new administration had little room in which to maneuver.

The modern inaugural address attempts to proclaim and celebrate national unity after a hard-fought campaign, to inspire listeners to believe in themselves and in their country, and to suggest in a general way the program of the new administration. Kennedy's inaugural adapts these functions to the political circumstances of 1961. Virtually all of the speech is concerned with foreign affairs, an atypical placement of emphasis. But if there was consensus on any belief, it was that the United States had to play the role of leader of the free world against communism. If there was a lingering doubt about Kennedy, even after the matters of his wealth and religion had been settled, it was whether he was experienced enough to "stand up to Khrushchev" in confrontation. Kennedy accordingly emphasized firmness and resolve, and he concentrated on foreign affairs. The pledge to "pay any price, bear any burden," which would seem troubling in later years, was reassuring to the doubters of 1961.

As for a forecast of the administration's program, it was ambiguous. The inaugural address reflects the ambivalence of the time, captured in such delicately balanced antitheses as "Let us never negotiate out of fear. But let us never fear to negotiate." In these and other phrases, one may find portents both of confrontations over Berlin and Cuba and of moves toward détente.

Finally, the inaugural repeats the call for self-sacrifice that characterized much of Kennedy's campaign rhetoric. Proclaiming that the present offered unparalleled challenges and opportunities, insisting that he would not trade places with any other generation, Kennedy issued the call for which the speech is most known: "Ask not what your country can do for you—ask what you can do for your country."

The speech was greatly praised by analysts at the time, both for its content and for its eloquence and style. Its careful use of cumulation, parallel structure, and antithesis was atypical of American rhetoric. It did, indeed, inspire people and coalesce energy for the difficult tasks the new President saw in the near future. It did celebrate unity amid diversity, it did link the current concerns with history and tradition, and it did offer a good measure of hope. Although later readers would shrink from some of the commitments it implied, it was pre-eminently a speech of its time. It still is one of the few contemporary texts almost always named in a list of American oratorical masterpieces.

Vice President Johnson, Mr. Speaker, Mr. Chief Justice, President Eisenhower, Vice President Nixon, President Truman, Reverend Clergy, fellow citizens:— We observe today not a victory of party but a celebration of freedom—symbolizing an end as well as a beginning—signifying renewal as well as change. For I have sworn before you and Almighty God the same solemn oath our forebears prescribed nearly a century and three quarters ago.

The world is very different now. For man holds in his mortal hands the power to abolish all forms of human poverty and all forms of human life. And yet the same revolutionary beliefs for which our forebears fought are still at issue around the globe—the belief that the rights of man come not from the generosity of the state but from the hand of God.

We dare not forget today that we are the heirs of that first revolution. Let the word go forth from this time and place, to friend and foe alike, that the torch has been passed to a new generation of Americans—born in this century, tempered by war, disciplined by a hard and bitter peace, proud of our ancient heritage—and unwilling to witness or permit the slow undoing of those human rights to which this nation has always been committed, and to which we are committed today at home and around the world.

Let every nation know, whether it wishes us well or ill, that we shall pay any price, bear any burden, meet any hardship, support any friend, oppose any foe to assure the survival and the success of liberty.

This much we pledge—and more.

To those old allies whose cultural and spiritual origins we share, we pledge the loyalty of faithful friends. United, there is little we cannot do in a host of cooperative ventures. Divided, there is little we can do—for we dare not meet a powerful challenge at odds and split asunder.

To those new states whom we welcome to the ranks of the free, we pledge our word that one form of colonial control shall not have passed away merely to be replaced by a far more iron tyranny. We shall not always expect to find them supporting our view. But we shall always hope to find them strongly supporting their own freedom—and to remember that, in the past, those who foolishly sought power by riding the back of the tiger ended up inside.

To those peoples in the huts and villages of half the globe struggling to break the bonds of mass misery, we pledge our best efforts to help them help themselves, for whatever period is required—not because the communists may be doing it, not because we seek their votes, but because it is right. If a free society cannot help the many who are poor, it cannot save the few who are rich.

To our sister republics south of our border, we offer a special pledge—to convert our good words into good deeds—in a new alliance for progress—to assist free men and free governments in casting off the chains of poverty. But this peaceful revolution of hope cannot become the prey of hostile powers. Let all our neighbors know that we shall join with them to oppose aggression or subversion anywhere in the Americas.

And let every other power know that this Hemisphere intends to remain the master of its own house.

To that world assembly of sovereign states, the United Nations, our last best hope in an age where the instruments of war have far outpaced the instruments of peace, we renew our pledge of support—to prevent it from becoming merely a forum for invective—to strengthen its shield of the new and the weak—and to enlarge the area in which its writ may run.

Finally, to those nations who would make themselves our adversary, we offer not a pledge but a request: that both sides begin anew the quest for peace, before the dark powers of destruction unleashed by science engulf all humanity in planned or accidental self-destruction.

We dare not tempt them with weakness. For only when our arms are sufficient beyond doubt can we be certain beyond doubt that they will never be employed.

But neither can two great and powerful groups of nations take comfort from our present course—both sides overburdened by the cost of modern weapons, both rightly alarmed by the steady spread of the deadly atom, yet both racing to alter that uncertain balance of terror that stays the hand of mankind's final war.

So let us begin anew—remembering on both sides that civility is not a sign of weakness, and sincerity is always subject to proof. Let us never negotiate out of fear. But let us never fear to negotiate.

Let both sides explore what problems unite us instead of belaboring those problems which divide us.

Let both sides, for the first time, formulate serious and precise proposals for the inspection and control of arms—and bring the absolute power to destroy other nations under the absolute control of all nations.

Let both sides seek to invoke the wonders of science instead of its terrors. Together let us explore the stars, conquer the deserts, eradicate disease, tap the ocean depths and encourage the arts and commerce.

Let both sides unite to heed in all corners of the earth the command of Isaiah—to "undo the heavy burdens ... (and) let the oppressed go free."

And if a beach-head of cooperation may push back the jungle of suspicion, let both sides join in creating a new endeavor, not a new balance of power, but a new world of law, where the strong are just and the weak secure and the peace preserved.

All this will not be finished in the first one hundred days. Nor will it be finished in the first one thousand days, nor in the life of this Administration, nor even perhaps in our lifetime on this planet. But let us begin.

In your hands, my fellow citizens, more than mine, will rest the final success or failure of our course. Since this country was founded, each generation of Americans has been summoned to give testimony to its national loyalty. The graves of young Americans who answered the call to service surround the globe.

Now the trumpet summons us again—not as a call to bear arms, though arms we need—not as a call to battle, though embattled we are—but a call to bear the burden of a long twilight struggle, year in and year out, "rejoicing in hope, patient in tribulation"—a struggle against the common enemies of man: tyranny, poverty, disease and war itself.

Can we forge against these enemies a grand and global alliance, North and South, East and West, that can assure a more fruitful life for all mankind? Will you join in that historic effort?

In the long history of the world, only a few generations have been granted the role of defending freedom in its hour of maximum danger. I do not shrink from this responsibility—I welcome it. I do not believe that any of us would exchange places with any other people or any other generation. The energy, the faith, the devotion which we bring to this endeavor will light our country and all who serve it—and the glow from that fire can truly light the world.

And so, my fellow Americans: ask not what your country can do for you—ask what you can do for your country.

My fellow citizens of the world: ask not what America will do for you, but what together we can do for the freedom of man.

Finally, whether you are citizens of America or citizens of the world, ask of us here the same high standards of strength and sacrifice which we ask of you. With a good conscience our only sure reward, with history the final judge of our deeds, let us go forth to lead the land we love, asking His blessing and His help, but knowing that here on earth God's work must truly be our own.

John F. Kennedy

Response to the Bay of Pigs
(April 20, 1961)

Kennedy's most humiliating defeat occurred less than three months into his term, with the failure of the mission of Cuban exiles to land at the Bay of Pigs and from there to launch an invasion that would topple Fidel Castro. This covert plan had been developed during the closing months of the Eisenhower administration, but Kennedy knew about it, approved it, and failed to test the underlying assumptions of his proposal. And it was Kennedy who accepted responsibility for the operation's failure.

Shortly after Castro came to power in 1959, he began to align himself with communism and to develop strong ties with the Soviet Union. This behavior made most Americans see him as a serious threat. Communism was widely regarded as monolithic, so Castro became seen as Khrushchev's underling, trying to export the Soviet system into the Western hemisphere from his strategically located home just ninety miles from the Florida coast. Ridding the free world of this threat became a high priority in American foreign policy and a serious issue during the 1960 Presidential campaign. John F. Kennedy had called for active American support for Cuban exiles seeking to topple Castro; he sounded this theme during one of the Presidential debates. In reply, Vice President Richard M. Nixon insisted that Kennedy's plan was irresponsible and would serve only to invite direct Soviet intervention.

But Nixon did not really believe what he said. In his memoirs he explained that he had to take the position he did, lest public attention be drawn to the planning already under way. The United States would arm and train Cuban refugees, always remaining distant enough from the operation so that its involvement could be denied plausibly. The refugees would land at the Bay of Pigs, make their way up into the mountains where they would gather additional help from among the disgruntled Cuban people, and then mount an all-out attack on Castro.

In retrospect, this plan was clearly flawed, both in its assumptions about Cuban geography and in its assumptions of the likelihood of obtaining additional recruits in the mountains. Kennedy could have kept it alive only by ordering an air strike, which could not be certain to hit the right targets and would invite Soviet intervention into the Western hemisphere. Kennedy chose to abort the operation, to give reasons for his action, and then to accept responsibility for the failed operation. He previously had accepted an invitation to address the American Society of Newspaper Editors, and used his speech there as the opportunity to publicly explain the debacle at the Bay of Pigs.

The speech illustrates how the task was accomplished within the framework of the cold war. What Kennedy had to explain was not why the invasion was undertaken but why he did not directly involve American forces so that it might have had a chance to succeed. The failure was explained not as misjudgment but as fidelity to an American tradition of restraint, which was, however, "not inexhaustible." The lesson of the Bay of Pigs, as developed in this speech, is that Communist forces are stronger than supposed and warrant a more vigilant scrutiny by the American government. Then the President enlarged the nature of the struggle by equating Communist activities in Cuba with Communist subversion elsewhere. In this way he was able to transform the speech to the newspaper editors from a defensive explanation of failure into a rally for even greater military strength. The cold war assumption of a Communist monolith permitted Kennedy to redefine the rhetorical situation to which his speech was a response.

In the immediate context, Kennedy's maneuver was successful. The combination of accepting responsibility for the decisions, hinting that America might be less restrained in the future, and explaining Cuba as a piece in a much larger puzzle, evoked public support and silenced criticism. Kennedy's public approval rating reached its all-time high after the Bay of Pigs. The very next day, at a press conference, the President was able to deflect questions about Cuba by referring to his speech to the newspaper editors. It is difficult to imagine that Castro was much reassured by this speech. Although the evidence is only speculative, it is not unreasonable that the fear of a possible future American invasion that it aroused had something to do with his decision to request the installation of Soviet missiles—the first step leading to the missile crisis of 1962.

Mr. Catledge, members of the American Society of Newspaper Editors, ladies and gentlemen:—The President of a great democracy such as ours, and the editors of great newspapers such as yours, owe a common obligation to the people: an obligation to present the facts, to present them with candor, and to present them in perspective. It is with that obligation in mind that I have decided in the last 24 hours to discuss briefly at this time the recent events in Cuba.

On that unhappy island, as in so many other arenas of the contest for freedom, the news has grown worse instead of better. I have emphasized before that this was a struggle of Cuban patriots against a Cuban dictator. While we could not be expected to hide our sympathies, we made it repeatedly clear that the armed forces of this country would not intervene in any way.

Any unilateral American intervention, in the absence of an external attack upon ourselves or an ally, would have been contrary to our traditions and to our international obligations. But let the record show that our restraint is not inexhaustible. Should it ever appear that the inter-American doctrine of non-interference merely conceals or excuses a policy of nonaction—if the nations of this Hemisphere should fail to meet their commitments against outside Communist penetration—then I want it clearly understood that this Government will not hesitate in meeting its primary obligations which are to the security of our Nation!

Should that time ever come, we do not intend to be lectured on "intervention" by those whose character was stamped for all time on the bloody streets of Budapest! Nor would we expect or accept the same outcome which this small band of gallant Cuban refugees must have known that they were chancing, determined as they were against heavy odds to pursue their courageous attempts to regain their Island's freedom.

But Cuba is not an island unto itself; and our concern is not ended by mere expressions of nonintervention or regret. This is not the first time in either ancient or recent history that a small band of freedom fighters has engaged the armor of totalitarianism.

It is not the first time that Communist tanks have rolled over gallant men and women fighting to redeem the independence of their homeland. Nor is it by any means the final episode in the eternal struggle of liberty against tyranny, anywhere on the face of the globe, including Cuba itself.

Mr. Castro has said that these were mercenaries. According to press reports, the final message to be relayed from the refugee forces on the beach came from the rebel commander when asked if he wished to be evacuated. His answer was: "I will never leave this country." That is not the reply of a mercenary. He has gone now to join in the mountains countless other guerrilla fighters, who are equally determined that the dedication of those who gave their lives shall not be forgotten, and that Cuba must not be abandoned to the Communists. And we do not intend to abandon it either!

The Cuban people have not yet spoken their final piece. And I have no doubt that they and their Revolutionary Council, led by Dr. Cardona—and members of the families of the Revolutionary Council, I am informed by the Doctor yesterday, are involved themselves in the Islands—will continue to speak up for a free and independent Cuba.

Meanwhile we will not accept Mr.Castro's attempts to blame this nation for the hatred which his onetime supporters now regard his repression. But there are from this sobering episode useful lessons for us all to learn. Some may be still obscure,and await further information. Some are clear today.

First, it is clear that the forces of communism are not to be underestimated, in Cuba or anywhere else in the world. The advantages of a police state—its use of mass terror and arrests to prevent the spread of free dissent—cannot be overlooked by those who expect the fall of every fanatic tyrant. If the self-discipline of the free cannot match the iron discipline of the mailed fist—in economic, political, scientific and all the other kinds of struggles as well as the military—then the peril to freedom will continue to rise.

Secondly, it is clear that this Nation, in concert with all the free nations of this hemisphere, must take an ever closer and more realistic look at the menace of external Communist intervention and domination in Cuba. The American people are not complacent about Iron Curtain tanks and planes less than 90 miles from their shore. But a nation of Cuba's size is less a threat to our survival than it is a base for subverting the survival of other free nations throughout the hemisphere. It is not primarily our interest or our security but theirs which is now, today, in the greater peril. It is for their sake as well as our own that we must show our will.

The evidence is clear—and the hour is late. We and our Latin friends will have to face the fact that we cannot postpone any longer the real issue of survival of freedom in this hemisphere itself. On that issue, unlike perhaps some others, there can be no middle ground. Together we must build a hemisphere where freedom can flourish; and where any free nation under outside attack of any kind can be assured that all of our resources stand ready to respond to any request for assistance.

Third, and finally, it is clearer than ever that we face a relentless struggle in every corner of the globe that goes far beyond the clash of armies or even nuclear armaments. The armies are there, and in large number. The nuclear armaments are there. But they serve primarily as the shield behind which subversion, infiltration, and a host of other tactics steadily advance, picking off vulnerable areas one by one in situations which do not permit our own armed intervention.

Power is the hallmark of this offensive—power and discipline and deceit. The legitimate discontent of yearning people is exploited. The legitimate trappings of self-determination are employed. But once in power, all talk of discontent is repressed, all self-determination disappears, and the promise of a revolution of hope is betrayed, as in Cuba, into a reign of terror. Those who on instruction staged automatic "riots" in the streets of free nations over the efforts of a small group of young Cubans to regain their freedom should recall the long roll call of refugees who cannot now go back—to Hungary, to North Korea, to North Viet-Nam, to East Germany, or to Poland, or to any of the other lands from which a steady stream of refugees pours forth, in eloquent testimony to the cruel oppression now holding sway in their homeland.

We dare not fail to see the insidious nature of this new and deeper struggle. We dare not fail to grasp the new concepts, the new tools, the new sense of urgency we will need to combat it—whether in Cuba or South Viet-Nam. And we dare not fail to realize that this struggle is taking place every day, without fanfare, in thousands of villages and markets—day and night—and in classrooms all over the globe.

The message of Cuba, of Laos, of the rising din of Communist voices in Asia and Latin America—these messages are all the same. The complacent, the self-indulgent, the soft societies are about to be swept away with the debris of history. Only the strong, only the industrious, only the determined,only the courageous, only the visionary who determine the real nature of our struggle can possibly survive.

No greater task faces this country or this administration. No other challenge is more deserving of our every effort and energy. Too long we have fixed our eyes on traditional military needs, on armies prepared to cross borders, on missiles poised for flight. Now it should be clear that this is no longer enough—that our security may be lost piece by piece, country by country, without the firing of a single missile or the crossing of a single border.

We intend to profit from this lesson. We intend to reexamine and reorient our forces of all kinds—our tactics and our institutions here in this community. We intend to intensify our efforts for a struggle in many ways more difficult than war, where disappointment will often accompany us.

For I am convinced that we in this country and in the free world possess the necessary resource, and the skill, and the added strength that comes from a belief in the freedom of man. And I am equally convinced that history will record the fact that this bitter struggle reached its climax in the late 1950's and the early 1960's. Let me then make clear as the President of the United States that I am determined upon our system's survival and success, regardless of the cost and regardless of the peril!

John F. Kennedy

The Berlin Crisis
(July 25, 1961)

The Kennedy Presidency was marked by a series of international crises, but none was potentially more serious in its consequences than Berlin. At the end of World War II, pending a formal peace treaty, Germany was divided into four occupation zones, controlled by Britain, France, the United States, and the Soviet Union. The capital city of Berlin, which lay within the Soviet zone, was similarly divided. When the emergence of the cold war made a peace treaty unlikely, the British, French, and American zones were merged to create the Federal Republic of Germany, whose capital was Bonn. The Soviet zone became the German Democratic Republic (East Germany). The three western zones in Berlin were merged to form West Berlin, sometimes described as an oasis of freedom 110 miles behind the Iron Curtain.

Western access rights to Berlin stemmed from their nations' status as occupying powers, since World War II had not been formally ended. Periodically, the Soviet Union or its satellite East German government sought to test those rights. The most dramatic test came in 1948 when the land routes from West Germany to Berlin were blocked. The Western response was the Berlin airlift, the use of airplanes to bring food and needed supplies to the people of West Berlin. The airlift was conducted on a massive scale and lasted for almost a year; it finally broke the Berlin blockade.

Throughout the 1950's, the Soviet Union threatened to sign a separate peace treaty with East Germany. If concluded, such an agreement would bring a formal state of peace to East Germany, and—from the Soviet perspective—would remove the legal basis by which the Western powers claimed rights of access over East German territory in order to reach Berlin. Viewed from the East, any Western attempts to reach the city would be belligerent acts justifying a military response.

From the perspective of the West, however, the loss of West Berlin was unthinkable. Not only did prevailing thought view *any* gain of territory by Communists as a threat to freedom everywhere, but Berlin had special political and symbolic significance. It was a showplace for the economic transformation that had taken place in West Germany and stood in stark contrast to the East. And it had become the symbol of the East-West confrontation and the willingness of the Western nations to resist the onslaught of Communism—"the great testing place," as President Kennedy would say, "of Western courage and will." Moreover, the West would not have acknowledged the legality of a separate peace between the Soviet Union and East Germany. From their point of view, the attempt to seal access to Berlin would itself be a hostile act. And under the treaty establishing the North Atlantic Treaty Organization, an attack on one of its members would be construed as an attack upon all. In short, any confrontation over Berlin had the potential for rapid escalation into a third world war.

A common Soviet tactic was to threaten to sign a separate peace treaty if a formal treaty were not agreed upon by a certain date. President Eisenhower received such an ultimatum in 1958. These threats might be seen as opening moves in complex international bargaining and negotiation, often on unrelated issues. Conciliatory gestures or satisfactory agreements on whatever matters were being discussed would cause the deadline to pass without incident.

When Kennedy received an ultimatum in 1961, however, he did not perceive that his situation permitted any conciliatory move. Within months, he had experienced the debacle of the Bay of Pigs and the neutralization of Laos. He had been bullied by Soviet premier Nikita Khrushchev at their Vienna summit conference in June. He feared, and with reason, that he and his country would be seen as weak, unwilling to stand firm in the face of Soviet threats. If there was any place where firmness was required, clearly it was Berlin.

The President's speech to the nation, delivered from his office over radio and television on July 25, 1961, is an excellent example of a President's rhetorical response to international crisis. It describes the American position as responding to unjustified Soviet provocation. It reviews postwar history and describes the basis for the American position. It generalizes from the situation in West Berlin to the worldwide struggle between freedom and communism. And it announces specific actions, which themselves have both military and symbolic value—they strengthen our defenses and also signal that the United States is serious and is not going to back away from a threat to Berlin. The support requested was quickly obtained, and only with that foundation laid did Kennedy believe that he could open discussions leading to a resolution of the crisis through discussion and diplomacy.

Good evening:—Seven weeks ago tonight I returned from Europe to report on my meeting with Premier Khrushchev and the others. His grim warnings about the future of the world, his aide memoire on Berlin, his subsequent speeches and threats which he and his agents have launched, and the increase in the Soviet military budget that he has announced, have all prompted a series of decisions by the Administration and a series of consultations with the members of the NATO organization. In Berlin, as you recall, he intends to bring to an end, through a stroke of the pen, *first* our legal rights to be in West Berlin—and *secondly* our ability to make good on our commitment to the two million free people of that city. That we cannot permit.

We are clear about what must be done—and we intend to do it. I want to talk frankly with you tonight about the first steps that we shall take. These actions will require sacrifice on the part of many of our citizens. More will be required in the future. They will require, from all of us, courage and perseverance in the years to come. But if we and our allies act out of strength and unity of purpose—with calm determination and steady nerves—using restraint in our words as well as our weapons—I am hopeful that both peace and freedom will be sustained.

The immediate threat to free men is in West Berlin. But that isolated outpost is not an isolated problem. The threat is worldwide. Our effort must be equally wide and strong, and not be obsessed by any single manufactured crisis. We face a challenge in Berlin, but there is also a challenge in Southeast Asia, where the borders are less guarded, the enemy harder to find, and the dangers of communism less apparent to those who have so little. We face a challenge in our own hemisphere, and indeed wherever else the freedom of human beings is at stake.

Let me remind you that the fortunes of war and diplomacy left the free people of West Berlin, in 1945, 110 miles behind the Iron Curtain.

This map makes very clear the problem that we face. The white is West Germany—the East is the area controlled by the Soviet Union, and as you can see from the chart, West Berlin is 110 miles within the area which the Soviets now dominate—which is immediately controlled by the so-called East German regime.

We are there as a result of our victory over Nazi Germany—and our basic rights to be there, deriving from that victory, include both our presence in West Berlin and the enjoyment of access across East Germany. These rights have been repeatedly confirmed and recognized in special agreements with the Soviet Union. Berlin is not a part of East Germany, but a separate territory under the control of the allied powers. Thus our rights there are clear and deep-rooted. But in addition to those rights is our commitment to sustain—and defend, if need be—the opportunity for more than two million people to determine their own future and choose their own way of life.

II.

Thus, our presence in West Berlin, and our access thereto, cannot be ended by any act of the Soviet government. The NATO shield was long ago extended to cover West Berlin—and we have given our word that an attack upon that city will be regarded as an attack upon us all.

For West Berlin—lying exposed 110 miles inside East Germany, surrounded by Soviet troops and close to Soviet supply lines—has many roles. It is more than a showcase of liberty, a symbol, an island of freedom in a Communist sea. It is even more than a link with the Free World, a beacon of hope behind the Iron Curtain, an escape hatch for refugees.

West Berlin is all of that. But above all it has now become—as never before—the great testing place of Western courage and will, a focal point where our solemn commitments stretching back over the years since 1945, and Soviet ambitions now meet in basic confrontation.

It would be a mistake for others to look upon Berlin, because of its location, as a tempting target. The United States is there; the United Kingdom and France are there; the pledge of NATO is there—and the people of Berlin are there. It is as secure, in that sense, as the rest of us—for we cannot separate its safety from our own.

I hear it said that West Berlin is militarily untenable. And so was Bastogne. And so, in fact, was Stalingrad. Any dangerous spot is tenable if men—brave men—will make it so.

We do not want to fight—but we have fought before. And others in earlier times have made the same dangerous mistake of assuming that the West was too selfish and too soft and too divided to resist invasions of freedom in other lands. Those who threaten to unleash the forces of war on a dispute over West Berlin should recall the words of the ancient philosopher: "A man who causes fear cannot be free from fear."

We cannot and will not permit the Communists to drive us out of Berlin, either gradually or by force. For the fulfillment of our pledge to that city is essential to the morale and security of Western Germany, to the unity of Western Europe, and to the faith of the entire Free World. Soviet strategy has long been aimed, not merely at Berlin, but at dividing and neutralizing all of Europe, forcing us back on our own shores. We must meet our oft-stated pledge to the free peoples of West Berlin—and maintain our rights and their safety, even in the face of force—in order to maintain the confidence of other free peoples in our word and our resolve. The strength of the alliance on which our security depends is dependent in turn on our willingness to meet our commitments to them.

III.

So long as the Communists insist that they are preparing to end by themselves unilaterally our rights in West Berlin and our commitments to its people,we must be prepared to defend those rights and those commitments. We will at all times be ready to talk, if talk will help. But we must also be ready to resist with force, if force is used upon us. Either alone would fail. Together, they can serve the cause of freedom and peace.

The new preparations that we shall make to defend the peace are part of the long-term build-up in our strength which has been underway since January. They are based on our needs to meet a world-wide threat, on a basis which stretches far beyond the present Berlin crisis. Our primary purpose is neither propaganda nor provocation—but preparation.

A first need is to hasten progress toward the military goals which the North Atlantic allies have set for themselves. In Europe today nothing less will suffice. We will put even greater resources into fulfilling those goals, and we look to our allies to do the same.

The supplementary defense build-ups that I asked from the Congress in March and May have already started moving us toward these and our other defense goals. They included an increase in the size of the Marine Corps, improved readiness of our reserves, expansion of our air and sea lift, and stepped-up procurement of needed weapons, ammunition, and other items. To insure a continuing invulnerable capacity to deter or destroy any aggressor, they provided for the strengthening of our missile power and for putting 50% of our B-52 and B-47 bombers on a ground alert which would send them on their way with 15 minutes' warning.

These measures must be speeded up, and still others must now be taken. We must have sea and air lift capable of moving our forces quickly and in large numbers to any part of the world.

But even more importantly, we need the capability of placing in any critical area at the appropriate time a force which, combined with those of our allies, is large enough to make clear our determination and our ability to defend our rights at all costs—and to meet all levels of aggressor pressure with whatever levels of force are required. We intend to have a wider choice than humiliation or all-out nuclear action.

While it is unwise at this time either to call up or send abroad excessive numbers of these troops before they are needed, let me make it clear that I intend to take, as time goes on, whatever steps are necessary to make certain that such forces can be deployed at the appropriate time without lessening our ability to meet our commitments elsewhere.

Thus, in the days and months ahead, I shall not hesitate to ask the Congress for additional measures, or exercise any of the executive powers that I possess to meet this threat to peace. Everything essential to the security of freedom must be done; and if that should require more men, or more taxes, or more controls, or other new powers, I shall not hesitate to ask them. The measures proposed today will be constantly studied, and altered as necessary. But while we will not let panic shape our policy, neither will we permit timidity to direct our program.

Accordingly, I am now taking the following steps:

(1) I am tomorrow requesting the Congress for the current fiscal year an additional $3,247,000,000 of appropriations for the Armed Forces.

(2) To fill out our present Army Divisions, and to make more men available for prompt deployment, I am requesting an increase in the Army's total authorized strength from 875,000 to approximately 1 million men.

(3) I am requesting an increase of 29,000 and 63,000 men respectively in the active duty strength of the Navy and the Air Force.

(4) To fulfill these manpower needs, I am ordering that our draft calls be doubled and tripled in the coming months; I am asking the Congress for authority to order to active duty certain ready reserve units and individual reservists, and to extend tours of duty; and, under that authority, I am planning to order to active duty a number of air transport squadrons and Air National Guard tactical air squadrons, to give us the airlift capacity and protection that we need. Other reserve forces will be called up when needed.

(5) Many ships and planes once headed for retirement are to be retained or reactivated, increasing our airpower tactically and our sealift, airlift,and anti-submarine warfare capability. In addition, our strategic air power will be increased by delaying the deactivation of B-47 bombers.

(6) Finally, some $1.8 billion—about half of the total sum—is needed for the procurement of non-nuclear weapons, ammunition and equipment.

The details on all these requests will be presented to the Congress tomorrow. Subsequent steps will be taken to suit subsequent needs. Comparable efforts for the common defense are being discussed with our NATO allies. For their commitment and interest are as precise as our own.

And let me add that I am well aware of the fact that many American families will bear the burden of these requests. Studies or careers will be interrupted; husbands and sons will be called away; incomes in some cases will be reduced. But these are burdens which must be borne if freedom is to be defended—Americans have willingly borne them before—and they will not flinch from the task now.

IV.

We have another sober responsibility. To recognize the possibilities of nuclear war in the missile age, without our citizens knowing what they should do and where they should go if bombs begin to fall, would be a failure of responsibility. In May, I pledged a new start on Civil Defense. Last week, I assigned, on the recommendation of the Civil Defense Director, basic responsibility for this program to the Secretary of Defense, to make certain it is administered and coordinated with our continental defense efforts at the highest civilian level. Tomorrow, I am requesting of the Congress new funds for the following immediate objectives: to identify and mark space in existing structures—public and private—that could be used for fall-out shelters in case of attack; to stock those shelters with food, water, first-aid kits and other minimum essentials for survival; to increase their capacity; to improve our air-raid warning and fall-out detection systems, including a new household warning system which is now under development; and to take other measures that will be effective at an early date to save millions of lives if needed.

In the event of an attack, the lives of those families which are not hit in a nuclear blast and fire can still be saved—*if* they can be warned to take shelter and *if* that shelter is available. We owe that kind of insurance to our families—and to our country. In contrast to our friends in Europe, the need for this kind of protection is new to our shores. But the time to start is now. In the coming months, I hope to let every citizen know what steps he can take without delay to protect his family in case of attack. I know that you will want to do no less.

V.

The addition of $207 million in Civil Defense appropriations brings our total new defense budget requests to $3.454 billion, and a total of $47.5 billion for the year.

This is an increase in the defense budget of $6 billion since January, and has resulted in official estimates of a budget deficit of over $5 billion. The Secretary of the Treasury and other economic advisers assure me, however, that our economy has the capacity to bear this new request.

We are recovering strongly from this year's recession. The increase in this last quarter of our year of our total national output was greater than that for any postwar period of initial recovery. And yet, wholesale prices are actually lower than they were during the recession, and consumer prices are only 1/4 of 1% higher than they were last October. In fact, this last quarter was the first in eight years in which our production has increased without an increase in the overall-price index. And for the first time since the fall of 1959, our gold position has improved and the dollar is more respected abroad. These gains, it should be stressed, are being accomplished with Budget deficits far smaller than those of the 1958 recession.

This improved business outlook means improved revenues; and I intend to submit to the Congress in January a budget for the next fiscal year which will be strictly in balance. Nevertheless, should an increase in taxes be needed—because of events in the next few months—to achieve that balance, or because of subsequent defense rises, those increased taxes will be requested in January.

Meanwhile, to help make certain that the current deficit is held to a safe level, we must keep down all expenditures not thoroughly justified in budget requests. The luxury of our current post-office deficit must be ended. Costs in military procurement will be closely scrutinized—and in this effort I welcome the cooperation of the Congress. The tax loopholes I have specified—on expense accounts, overseas income, dividends, interest, cooperatives and others—must be closed.

I realize that no public revenue measure is welcomed by everyone. But I am certain that every American wants to pay his fair share, and not leave the burden of defending freedom entirely to those who bear arms. For we have mortgaged our very future on this defense—and we cannot fail to meet our responsibilities.

VI.

But I must emphasize again that the choice is not merely between resistance and retreat, between atomic holocaust and surrender. Our peace-time military posture is traditionally defensive; but our diplomatic posture need not be. Our response to the Berlin crisis will not be merely military or negative. It will be more than merely standing firm. For we do not intend to leave it to others to choose and monopolize the forum and the framework of discussion. We do not intend to abandon our duty to mankind to seek a peaceful solution.

As signers of the UN Charter, we shall always be prepared to discuss international problems with any and all nations that are willing to talk—and listen—with reason. If they have proposals—not demands—we shall hear them. If they seek genuine understanding—not concessions of our rights—we shall meet with them. We have previously indicated our readiness to remove any actual irritants in West Berlin, but the freedom of that city is not negotiable. We cannot negotiate with those who say "What's mine is mine and what's yours is negotiable." But we are willing to consider any arrangement or treaty in Germany consistent with the maintenance of peace and freedom, and with the legitimate security interests of all nations.

We recognize the Soviet Union's historical concern about their security in Central and Eastern Europe, after a series of ravaging invasions, and we believe arrangements can be worked out which will help to meet those concerns, and make it possible for both security and freedom to exist in this troubled area.

For it is not the freedom of West Berlin which is "abnormal" in Germany today, but the situation in that entire divided country. If anyone doubts the legality of our rights in Berlin, we are ready to have it submitted to international adjudication. If anyone doubts the extent to which our presence is desired by the people of West Berlin, compared to East German feelings about their regime, we are ready to have that question submitted to a free vote in Berlin and, if possible, among all the German people. And let us hear at that time from the two and one-half million refugees who have fled the Communist regime in East Germany—voting for Western-type freedom with their feet.

The world is not deceived by the Communist attempt to label Berlin as a hot-bed of war. There is peace in Berlin today. The source of world trouble and tension is Moscow, not Berlin. And if war begins, it will have begun in Moscow and not Berlin.

For the choice of peace or war is largely theirs, not ours. It is the Soviets who have stirred up this crisis. It is they who are trying to force a change. It is they who have opposed free elections. It is they who have rejected an all-German peace treaty, and the rulings of

international law. And as Americans know from our history on our own old frontier, gun battles are caused by outlaws, and not by officers of the peace.

In short, while we are ready to defend our interests, we shall also be ready to search for peace—in quiet exploratory talks—in formal or informal meetings. We do not want military considerations to dominate the thinking of either East or West. And Mr. Khrushchev may find that his invitation to other nations to join in a meaningless treaty may lead to *their* inviting *him* to join in the community of peaceful men, in abandoning the use of force, and in respecting the sanctity of agreements.

VII.

While all of these efforts go on, we must not be diverted from our total responsibilities, from other dangers, from other tasks. If new threats in Berlin or elsewhere should cause us to weaken our program of assistance to the developing nations who are also under heavy pressure from the same source, or to halt our efforts for realistic disarmament, or to disrupt or slow down our economy, or to neglect the education of our children, then those threats will surely be the most successful and least costly maneuver in Communist history. For we can afford all these efforts, and more—but we cannot afford *not* to meet this challenge.

And the challenge is not to us alone. It is a challenge to every nation which asserts its sovereignty under a system of liberty. It is a challenge to all those who want a world of free choice. It is a special challenge to the Atlantic Community—the heartland of human freedom.

We in the West must move together in building military strength. We must consult one another more closely than ever before. We must together design our proposals for peace, and labor together as they are pressed at the conference table. And together we must share the burdens and the risks of this effort.

The Atlantic Community, as we know it, has been built in response to challenge: the challenge of European chaos in 1947, of the Berlin blockade in 1948, the challenge of Communist aggression in Korea in 1950. Now, standing strong and prosperous, after an unprecedented decade of progress, the Atlantic Community will not forget either its history or the principles which gave it meaning.

The solemn vow each of us gave to West Berlin in

time of peace will not be broken in time of danger. If we do not meet our commitments to Berlin, where will we later stand? If we are not true to our word there, all that we have achieved in collective security, which relies on these words, will mean nothing. And if there is one path above all others to war, it is the path of weakness and disunity.

Today, the endangered frontier of freedom runs through divided Berlin. We want it to remain a frontier of peace. This is the hope of every citizen of the Atlantic Community; every citizen of Eastern Europe; and, I am confident, every citizen of the Soviet Union. For I cannot believe that the Russian people—who bravely suffered enormous losses in the Second World War—would now wish to see the peace upset once more in Germany. The Soviet government alone can convert Berlin's frontier of peace into a pretext for war.

The steps I have indicated tonight are aimed at avoiding that war. To sum it all up: we seek peace—but we shall not surrender. That is the central meaning of this crisis, and the meaning of your government's policy.

With your help, and the help of other free men, this crisis can be surmounted. Freedom can prevail—and peace can endure.

I would like to close with a personal word. When I ran for the Presidency of the United States, I knew that this country faced serious challenges, but I could not realize—nor could any man realize who does not bear the burdens of this office—how heavy and constant would be those burdens.

Three times in my life-time our country and Europe have been involved in major wars. In each case serious misjudgments were made on both sides of the intentions of others, which brought about great devastation.

Now, in the thermonuclear age, any misjudgment on either side about the intentions of the other could rain more devastation in several hours than has been wrought in all the wars of human history.

Therefore I, as President and Commander-in-Chief, and all of us as Americans, are moving through serious days. I shall bear this responsibility under our Constitution for the next three and one-half years, but I am sure that we all, regardless of our occupations, will do our very best for our country, and for our cause. For all of us want to see our children grow up in a country at peace, and in a world where freedom endures.

I know that sometimes we get impatient, we wish for some immediate action that would end our perils. But I must tell you that there is no quick and easy solution. The Communists control over a billion people, and they recognize that if we should falter, their success would be imminent.

We must look to long days ahead, which if we are courageous and persevering can bring us what we all desire.

In these days and weeks I ask for your help, and your advice. I ask for your suggestions, when you think we could do better.

All of us, I know, love our country, and we shall all do our best to serve it.

In meeting my responsibilities in these coming months as President, I need your good will, and your support—and above all, your prayers.

Thank you, and good night.

John F. Kennedy

Cuban Missile Crisis
(October 22, 1962)

Eighteen months after the Bay of Pigs, Cuba again preoccupied the news, with the most dramatic crisis of the Kennedy Presidency or, for that matter, of United States history since the Second World War. Perhaps fearing an American invasion, Fidel Castro of Cuba sought even stronger ties between his government and the Soviet Union. For weeks it had been rumored that the Soviet Union was placing offensive missiles in Cuba, ninety miles from Florida and within striking range of much of the United States. Soviet diplomats denied that their country was doing any such thing, and, lacking contrary evidence, the Kennedy administration dismissed the rumors—much to the dismay of several Republican senators who had been sounding the alarm. Meanwhile, Kennedy had ordered continued surveillance of Cuba by reconnaissance flights. By mid-October 1962, photographic evidence confirmed the preparation of missile sites in Cuba.

Their discovery precipitated an intense debate within the administration over what the American response should be. United Nations ambassador Adlai Stevenson proposed a diplomatic solution: dismantling obsolete American missiles in Turkey in exchange for the removal of Soviet missiles from Cuba. In fact, Kennedy several months earlier had ordered the removal of the missiles from Turkey, and was angered to discover that nothing had been done. Most participants in the deliberation, however, believed that the threat to the United States was so severe and menacing that the matter was not subject to negotiation. They simply had to be removed, with no other preconditions. Besides, to negotiate the matter would be to concede that the presence of Soviet missiles in Cuba was as much justified as the presence of American missiles in Turkey. The options most seriously discussed were all unilateral: an invasion of Cuba, an air strike against the missile sites, or a blockade to prevent delivery of the remaining materials and to force dismantling of the sites.

One key element of the deliberations was the President's wish to be the one to announce the discovery of the sites, so that the United States would take the initiative rather than respond to a discovery announced by someone else. For this reason, he maintained the appearance of a normal schedule. He met with the Soviet ambassador to the United States, who denied that offensive missiles were being placed in Cuba. He traveled to Chicago for a previously scheduled political address, using the pretext of a cold to return to Washington when his advisers were approaching the point of decision. When the press began to discover parts of the story, Kennedy appealed successfully to have the story squelched until after his own speech, so that the Soviets would not be alerted to American discovery of the missiles. The speech announcing the President's actions was not shared even with the congressional leaders until very shortly before its presentation. As a result, Kennedy's nationally televised address of October 22 was the first public confirmation of the impending missiles in Cuba.

The speech follows the same basic pattern as the Berlin speech of 1961, which may characterize crisis rhetoric in general. A short narrative characterizes the United States as a victim who must now respond in a defensive way to unprovoked hostile acts. Specific responses are enumerated, with a prefatory note that these are *initial* responses and can be augmented if it is warranted. An offer is made to discuss outstanding issues in any international forum, but not under threat resulting from the emplacement of the missiles. The people of Cuba are told that the missiles are not in their interest, and Americans are urged to support the President's proposals as the alternative to "surrender or submission."

One feature of the language of this speech is especially noteworthy. Kennedy decided on a blockade, partly because it could be augmented by an air strike later if necessary. But he did not use the term *blockade*, since under international law a blockade is an act of war. Instead, perhaps thinking of Franklin D. Roosevelt's 1937 "Quarantine the Aggressor" speech, Kennedy described what would occur with the more benign term *quarantine.*

The steps leading to the end of the crisis are well known—the exchanges of papers, proposals, and conversations, the decision to ignore a harsh message from Nikita Khrushchev and to reply instead to a more moderate one, the turning back of a ship carrying contraband, and finally the word that a settlement had been reached: dismantling of the missiles and their return to the Soviet Union, in return for an American pledge not to invade the island. The missile crisis has affected American public discourse from that day to this. Recent scholarship begins to question whether the crisis was real, pointing out that Kennedy would have been willing to trade the Turkish missiles if necessary to avert war. But to everyone alive at the time, the crisis was real and the tension palpable. It is no exaggeration to say that its final resolution produced a great collective sigh of relief all around the globe.

Good evening, my fellow citizens:— This Government, as promised, has maintained the closest surveillance of the Soviet military buildup on the island of Cuba. Within the past week, unmistakable evidence has established the fact that a series of offensive missile sites is now in preparation on that imprisoned island. The purpose of these bases can be none other than to provide a nuclear strike capability against the Western Hemisphere.

Upon receiving the first preliminary hard information of this nature last Tuesday morning at 9 a.m., I directed that our surveillance be stepped up. And having now confirmed and completed our evaluation of the evidence and our decision on a course of action, this Government feels obliged to report this new crisis to you in fullest detail.

The characteristics of these new missile sites indicate two distinct types of installations. Several of them include medium range ballistic missiles, capable of carrying a nuclear warhead for a distance of more than 1,000 nautical miles. Each of these missiles, in short, is capable of striking Washington, D.C., the Panama Canal, Cape Canaveral, Mexico City, or any other city in the southeastern part of the United States, in Central America, or in the Caribbean area.

Additional sites not yet completed appear to be designed for intermediate range ballistic missiles—capable of traveling more than twice as far—and thus capable of striking most of the major cities in the Western Hemisphere, ranging as far north as Hudson Bay, Canada, and as far south as Lima, Peru. In addition, jet bombers, capable of carrying nuclear weapons, are now being uncrated and assembled in Cuba, while the necessary air bases are being prepared.

This urgent transformation of Cuba into an important strategic base—by the presence of these large, long-range, and clearly offensive weapons of sudden mass destruction—constitutes an explicit threat to the peace and security of all the Americas, in flagrant and deliberate defiance of the Rio Pact of 1947, the traditions of this Nation and hemisphere, the joint resolution of the 87th Congress, the Charter of the United Nations, and my own public warnings to the Soviets on September 4 and 13. This action also contradicts the repeated assurances of Soviet spokesmen, both publicly and privately delivered, that the arms buildup in Cuba would retain its original defensive character, and that the Soviet Union had no need or desire to station strategic missiles on the territory of any other nation.

The size of this undertaking makes clear that it has been planned for some months. Yet only last month, after I had made clear the distinction between any introduction of ground-to-ground missiles and the existence of defensive antiaircraft missiles, the Soviet Government publicly stated on September 11 that, and I quote, "the armaments and military equipment sent to Cuba are designed exclusively for defensive purposes," that, and I quote the Soviet Government, "there is no need for the Soviet Government to shift its weapons ... for a retaliatory blow to any other country, for

instance Cuba," and that, and I quote their government, "the Soviet Union has so powerful rockets to carry these nuclear warheads that there is no need to search for sites for them beyond the boundaries of the Soviet Union." That statement was false.

Only last Thursday, as evidence of this rapid offensive buildup was already in my hand, Soviet Foreign Minister Gromyko told me in my office that he was instructed to make it clear once again, as he said his government had already done, that Soviet assistance to Cuba, and I quote, "pursued solely the purpose of contributing to the defense capabilities of Cuba," that, and I quote him, "training by Soviet specialists of Cuban nationals in handling defensive armaments was by no means offensive, and if it were otherwise," Mr. Gromyko went on, "the Soviet Government would never become involved in rendering such assistance." That statement also was false.

Neither the United States of America nor the world community of nations can tolerate deliberate deception and offensive threats on the part of any nation, large or small. We no longer live in a world where only the actual firing of weapons represents a sufficient challenge to a nation's security to constitute maximum peril. Nuclear weapons are so destructive and ballistic missiles are so swift, that any substantially increased possibility of their use or any sudden change in their deployment may well be regarded as a definite threat to peace.

For many years, both the Soviet Union and the United States, recognizing this fact, have deployed strategic nuclear weapons with great care, never upsetting the precarious status quo which insured that these weapons would not be used in the absence of some vital challenge. Our own strategic missiles have never been transferred to the territory of any other nation under a cloak of secrecy and deception; and our history—unlike that of the Soviets since the end of World War II—demonstrates that we have no desire to dominate or conquer any other nation or impose our system upon its people. Nevertheless, American citizens have become adjusted to living daily on the bull's-eye of Soviet missiles located inside the U.S.S.R. or in submarines.

In that sense, missiles in Cuba add to an already clear and present danger—although it should be noted the nations of Latin America have never previously been subjected to a potential nuclear threat.

But this secret, swift, and extraordinary buildup of Communist missiles—in an area well known to have a special and historical relationship to the United States and the nations of the Western Hemisphere, in violation of Soviet assurances, and in defiance of American and hemispheric policy—this sudden, clandestine decision to station strategic weapons for the first time outside of Soviet soil—is a deliberately provocative and unjustified change in the status quo which cannot be accepted by this country, if our courage and our commitments are ever to be trusted again by either friend or foe.

The 1930's taught us a clear lesson: aggressive conduct, if allowed to go unchecked and unchallenged, ultimately leads to war. This nation is opposed to war. We are also true to our word. Our unswerving objective, therefore, must be to prevent the use of these missiles against this or any other country, and to secure their withdrawal or elimination from the Western Hemisphere.

Our policy has been one of patience and restraint, as befits a peaceful and powerful nation, which leads a worldwide alliance. We have been determined not to be diverted from our central concerns by mere irritants and fanatics. But now further action is required—and it is under way; and these actions may only be the beginning. We will not prematurely or unnecessarily risk the costs of worldwide nuclear war in which even the fruits of victory would be ashes in our mouth—but neither will we shrink from that risk at any time it must be faced.

Acting, therefore, in the defense of our own security and of the entire Western Hemisphere, and under the authority entrusted to me by the Constitution as endorsed by the resolution of the Congress, I have directed that the following *initial* steps be taken immediately:

First: To halt this offensive buildup, a strict quarantine on all offensive military equipment under shipment to Cuba is being initiated. All ships of any kind bound for Cuba from whatever nation or port will, if found to contain cargoes of offensive weapons, be turned back. This quarantine will be extended, if needed, to other types of cargo and carriers. We are not at this time, however, denying the necessities of life as the Soviets attempted to do in their Berlin blockade of 1948.

Second: I have directed the continued and increased close surveillance of Cuba and its military buildup. The foreign ministers of the OAS, in their communique of October 6, rejected secrecy on such matters in this hemisphere. Should these offensive military preparations continue, thus increasing the threat to the hemisphere, further action will be justified. I have directed the Armed Forces to prepare for any eventualities; and I trust that in the interest of both the Cuban people and the Soviet technicians at the sites, the hazards to all concerned of continuing this threat will be recognized.

Third: It shall be the policy of this Nation to regard any nuclear missile launched from Cuba against any nation in the Western Hemisphere as an attack by the Soviet Union on the United States, requiring a full retaliatory response upon the Soviet Union.

Fourth: As a necessary military precaution, I have reinforced our base at Guantanamo, evacuated today the dependents of our personnel there, and ordered additional military units to be on a standby alert basis.

Fifth: We are calling tonight for an immediate meeting of the Organ of Consultation under the Organization of American States, to consider this threat to hemispheric security and to invoke articles 6 and 8 of the Rio Treaty in support of all necessary action. The United Nations Charter allows for regional security arrangements—and the nations of this hemisphere decided long ago against the military presence of outside powers. Our other allies around the world have also been alerted.

Sixth: Under the Charter of the United Nations, we are asking tonight that an emergency meeting of the Security Council be convoked without delay to take action against this latest Soviet threat to world peace. Our resolution will call for the prompt dismantling and withdrawal of all offensive weapons in Cuba, under the supervision of U.N. observers, before the quarantine can be lifted.

Seventh and finally: I call upon Chairman Khrushchev to halt and eliminate this clandestine, reckless, and provocative threat to world peace and to stable relations between our two nations. I call upon him further to abandon this course of world domination, and to join in an historic effort to end the perilous arms race and to transform the history of man. He has an opportunity now to move the world back from the abyss of destruction—by returning to his government's own words that it had no need to station missiles outside its own territory, and withdrawing these weapons from Cuba—by refraining from any action which will widen or deepen the present crisis—and then by participating in a search for peaceful and permanent solutions.

This Nation is prepared to present its case against

the Soviet threat to peace, and our own proposals for a peaceful world, at any time and in any forum—in the OAS, in the United Nations, or in any other meeting that could be useful—without limiting our freedom of action. We have in the past made strenuous efforts to limit the spread of nuclear weapons. We have proposed the elimination of all arms and military bases in a fair and effective disarmament treaty. We are prepared to discuss new proposals for the removal of tensions on both sides—including the possibilities of a genuinely independent Cuba, free to determine its own destiny. We have no wish to war with the Soviet Union—for we are a peaceful people who desire to live in peace with all other peoples.

But it is difficult to settle or even discuss these problems in an atmosphere of intimidation. That is why this latest Soviet threat—or any other threat which is made either independently or in response to our actions this week—must and will be met with determination. Any hostile move anywhere in the world against the safety and freedom of peoples to whom we are committed—including in particular the brave people of West Berlin—will be met by whatever action is needed.

Finally, I want to say a few words to the captive people of Cuba, to whom this speech is being directly carried by special radio facilities. I speak to you as a friend, as one who knows of your deep attachment to your fatherland, as one who shares your aspirations for liberty and justice for all. And I have watched and the American people have watched with deep sorrow how your nationalist revolution was betrayed—and how your fatherland fell under foreign domination. Now your leaders are no longer Cuban leaders inspired by Cuban ideals. They are puppets and agents of an international conspiracy which has turned Cuba against your friends and neighbors in the Americas—and turned it into the first Latin American country to become a target for nuclear war—the first Latin American country to have these weapons on its soil.

These new weapons are not in your interest. They contribute nothing to your peace and well-being. They can only undermine it. But this country has no wish to cause you to suffer or to impose any system upon you. We know that your lives and land are being used as pawns by those who deny your freedom.

Many times in the past, the Cuban people have risen to throw out tyrants who destroyed their liberty. And I have no doubt that most Cubans today look forward to the time when they will be truly free—free from foreign domination, free to choose their own leaders, free to select their own system, free to own their own land, free to speak and write and worship without fear or degradation. And then shall Cuba be welcomed back to the society of free nations and to the associations of this hemisphere.

My fellow citizens: let no one doubt that this is a difficult and dangerous effort on which we have set out. No one can foresee precisely what course it will take or what costs or casualties will be incurred. Many months of sacrifice and self-discipline lie ahead—months in which both our patience and our will will be tested—months in which many threats and denunciations will keep us aware of our dangers. But the greatest danger of all would be to do nothing.

The path we have chosen for the present is full of hazards, as all paths are—but it is the one most consistent with our character and courage as a nation and our commitments around the world. The cost of freedom is always high—but Americans have always paid it. And one path we shall never choose, and that is the path of surrender or submission.

Our goal is not the victory of might, but the vindication of right—not peace at the expense of freedom, but both peace *and* freedom, here in this hemisphere, and, we hope, around the world. God willing, that goal will be achieved.

Thank you and good night.

John F. Kennedy

American University Speech
(June 10, 1963)

The Cuban missile crisis chastened both Kennedy and Soviet premier Nikita Khrushchev. Each was aware of how perilously close the world had come to nuclear conflagration. New evidence, disclosed on the twenty-fifth anniversary of the missile crisis, suggested that Kennedy would have been willing, after all, to trade off the Turkish missiles if war had been his only alternative. Nevertheless, the potential for miscalculation on both sides was great. Each leader had hard-line advisers who were urging an aggressive stance, and each was vulnerable to domestic pressures as well. Having come to the brink of war inspired both leaders to work harder to preserve peace.

Politically, too, the missile crisis gave Kennedy room to maneuver. If there had been any doubt of his ability to "stand up to Khrushchev," he had dispelled it in the supreme test. No longer need he worry about his youth, or inexperience, or his control over the situation. These changed circumstances enabled him to make conciliatory moves without worrying that he would be assailed at home for doing so. During 1963 the United States and the Soviet Union announced an increased schedule of cultural exchanges and the installation of a "hot line" linking the White House and the Kremlin. Kennedy worked especially hard to secure a nuclear test ban treaty; this too was negotiated and ratified during 1963. Commentators described a new spirit of détente characterizing Soviet-American relations.

In this spirit, Kennedy delivered the commencement address at American University in June 1963. It is difficult to overstate the change that this speech represents from the way American Presidents had viewed world affairs almost since 1945. Previously the key value in the hierarchy had been "freedom" and Presidents spoke of what America must do to remain a bulwark against communism. In this speech, while clearly reaffirming that communism has no appeal, Kennedy distinguished between communism as an ideological system and the Soviet Union as a world power. Now "peace" became the key term, subsuming ideological differences. Paraphrasing Woodrow Wilson, Kennedy called on his listeners to "make the world safe for diversity." The speech not only called for a test ban treaty but urged listeners to reconsider their basic attitudes toward the Soviet Union. Like the Yale speech of the year before, it was a call for changed ways of thinking, for which a commencement address was an appropriate occasion.

Reaction to the speech was quite favorable both at home and abroad. Kennedy's quest for a test ban treaty was realized when the treaty was initialed in Moscow in late summer and ratified by the Senate in the fall. On a "nonpolitical" speaking tour of the West, Kennedy had planned to talk about water conservation. His audiences were lackluster until he mentioned the test ban treaty and its contribution to world peace. Then listeners would be attentive and would signal enthusiastic approval. Kennedy took the hint, and increasingly made "peace" and "diversity" his key themes during the fall of 1963.

Still, one must not think that Kennedy discarded all the cold war habits of mind. His conversion to détente was less complete than this analysis suggests. Barely two weeks after the American University speech, Kennedy traveled to Berlin. Facing the Wall, which East Germany had erected in 1961, he proclaimed that the proudest boast was "Ich bin ein Berliner." Overcome with the emotion of the moment and with the enthusiasm of the crowd, he strongly implied that it was not possible to trust the Russians and that the notion of peaceful coexistence was a will-o-the-wisp. The contrast between the American University and Berlin speeches does not mean that Kennedy was hypocritical, nor that he had changed his mind. Rather, the juxtaposition of the speeches suggests the uneasiness and ambivalence with which Kennedy revised cold war thought. Such ambivalence is natural and appropriate when one is calling into question the habits of mind that had been developed over twenty years.

President Anderson, members of the faculty, board of trustees, distinguished guests, my old colleague, Senator Bob Byrd, who has earned his degree through many years of attending night law school, while I am earning mine in the next 30 minutes, ladies and gentlemen:—It is with great pride that I participate in this ceremony of the American University, sponsored by the Methodist Church, founded by Bishop John Fletcher Hurst, and first opened by President Woodrow Wilson in 1914. This is a young and growing university, but it has already fulfilled Bishop Hurst's enlightened hope for the study of history and public affairs in a city devoted to the making of history and to the conduct of the public's business. By sponsoring this institution of higher learning for all who wish to learn, whatever their color or their creed, the Methodists of this area and the Nation deserve the Nation's thanks, and I commend all those who are today graduating.

Professor Woodrow Wilson once said that every man sent out from a university should be a man of his nation as well as a man of his time, and I am confident that the men and women who carry the honor of graduating from this institution will continue to give from their lives, from their talents, a high measure of public service and public support.

"There are few earthly things more beautiful than a university," wrote John Masefield, in his tribute to English universities—and his words are equally true today. He did not refer to spires and towers, to campus greens and ivied walls. He admired the splendid beauty of the university, he said, because it was "a place where those who hate ignorance may strive to know, where those who perceive truth may strive to make others see."

I have, therefore, chosen this time and this place to discuss a topic on which ignorance too often abounds and the truth is too rarely perceived—yet it is the most important topic on earth: world peace.

What kind of peace do I mean? What kind of peace do we seek? Not a Pax Americana enforced on the world by American weapons of war. Not the peace of the grave or the security of the slave. I am talking about genuine peace, the kind of peace that makes life on earth worth living, the kind that enables men and nations to grow and to hope and to build a better life for their children—not merely peace for Americans but peace for all men and women—not merely peace in our time but peace for all time.

I speak of peace because of the new face of war. Total war makes no sense in an age when great powers can maintain large and relatively invulnerable nuclear forces and refuse to surrender without resort to those forces. It makes no sense in an age when a single nuclear weapon contains almost ten times the explosive force delivered by all of the allied air forces in the Second World War. It makes no sense in an age when the deadly poisons produced by a nuclear exchange would be carried by wind and water and soil and seed to the far corners of the glove and to generations yet unborn.

Today the expenditure of billions of dollars every year of weapons acquired for the purpose of making sure we never need to use them is essential to keeping the peace. But surely the acquisition of such idle stockpiles—which can only destroy and never create—is not the only, much less the most efficient, means of assuring peace.

I speak of peace, therefore, as the necessary rational end of rational men. I realize that the pursuit of peace is not as dramatic as the pursuit of war—and frequently the words of the pursuer fall on deaf ears. But we have no more urgent task.

Some say that it is useless to speak of world peace or world law or world disarmament—and that it will be useless until the leaders of the Soviet Union adopt a more enlightened attitude. I hope they do. I believe we can help them do it. But I also believe that we must reexamine our own attitude—as individuals and as a Nation—for our attitude is as essential as theirs. And every graduate of this school, every thoughtful citizen who despairs of war and wishes to bring peace, should begin by looking inward—by examining his own attitude toward the possibilities of peace,toward the Soviet Union, toward the course of the cold war and toward freedom and peace here at home.

First: Let us examine our attitude toward peace itself. Too many of us think it is impossible. Too many think it unreal. But that is a dangerous, defeatist belief. It leads to the conclusion that war is inevitable—that

mankind is doomed—that we are gripped by forces we cannot control.

We need not accept that view. Our problems are manmade—therefore, they can be solved by man. And man can be as big as he wants. No problem of human destiny is beyond human beings. Man's reason and spirit have often solved the seemingly unsolvable—and we believe they can do it again.

I am not referring to the absolute, infinite concept of universal peace and good will of which some fantasies and fanatics dream. I do not deny the value of hopes and dreams but we merely invite discouragement and incredulity by making that our only and immediate goal.

Let us focus instead on a more practical, more attainable peace—based not on a sudden revolution in human nature but on a gradual evolution in human institutions—on a series of concrete actions and effective agreements which are in the interest of all concerned. There is no single, simple key to this peace—no grand or magic formula to be adopted by one or two powers. Genuine peace must be the product of many nations, the sum of many acts. It must be dynamic, not static, changing to meet the challenge of each new generation. For peace is a process—a way of solving problems.

With such a peace, there will still be quarrels and conflicting interests, as there are within families and nations. World peace, like community peace, does not require that each man love his neighbor—it requires only that they live together in mutual tolerance, submitting their disputes to a just and peaceful settlement. And history teaches us that enmities between nations, as between individuals, do not last forever. However our likes and dislikes may seem, the tide of time and events will often bring surprising changes in the relations between nations and neighbors.

So let us persevere. Peace need not be impracticable, and war need not be inevitable. By defining our goal more clearly, by making it seem more manageable and less remote, we can help all peoples to see it, to draw hope from it, and to move irresistibly toward it.

Second: Let us reexamine our attitude toward the Soviet Union. It is discouraging to think that their leaders may actually believe what their propagandists write. It is discouraging to read a recent authoritative Soviet text on *Military Strategy* and find, on page after page, wholly baseless and incredible claims—such as the allegation that "American imperialist circles are preparing to unleash different types of wars ... that there is a very real threat of a preventive war being unleashed by American imperialists against the Soviet Union ... [and that] the political aims of the American imperialists are to enslave economically and politically the European and other capitalist countries ... [and] to achieve world domination ... by means of aggressive wars."

Truly, as it was written long ago: "The wicked flee when no man pursueth." Yet it is sad to read these Soviet statements—to realize the extent of the gulf between us. But it is also a warning—a warning to the American people not to fall into the same trap as the Soviets, not to see only a distorted and desperate view of the other side, not to see conflict as inevitable, accommodation as impossible, and communication as nothing more than an exchange of threats.

No government or social system is so evil that its people must be considered as lacking in virtue. As Americans, we find communism profoundly repugnant as a negation of personal freedom and dignity. But we can still hail the Russian people for their many achievements—in science and space, in economic and industrial growth, in culture and in acts of courage.

Among the many traits the peoples of our two countries have in common, none is stronger than our mutual abhorrence of war. Almost unique, among the major world powers, we have never been at war with each other. And no nation in the history of battle ever suffered more than the Soviet Union suffered in the course of the Second World War. At least 20 million lost their lives. Countless millions of homes and farms were burned or sacked. A third of the nation's territory, including nearly two thirds of its industrial base, was turned into a wasteland—a loss equivalent to the devastation of this country east of Chicago.

Today, should total war ever break out again—no matter how—our two countries would become the primary targets. It is an ironic but accurate fact that the two strongest powers are the two in the most danger of devastation. All we have built, all we have worked for, would be destroyed in the first 24 hours. And even in the cold war, which brings burdens and dangers to so many countries, including this Nation's closest allies—our two countries bear the heaviest burdens. For we are both devoting massive sums of money to weapons that could be better devoted to combating ignorance, poverty, and disease. We are both caught up in a vicious and dangerous cycle in which suspicion on one side breeds suspicion on the other, and new weapons beget counterweapons.

In short, both the United States and its allies, and the Soviet Union and its allies, have a mutually deep interest in a just and genuine peace and in halting the arms race. Agreements to this end are in the interests of the Soviet Union as well as ours—and even the most hostile nations can be relied upon to accept and keep those treaty obligations, and only those treaty obligations, which are in their own interest.

So, let us not be blind to our differences—but let us also direct attention to our common interests and to the means by which those differences can be resolved. And if we cannot end now our differences, at least we can help make the world safe for diversity. For, in the final analysis, our most basic common link is that we all inhabit this small planet. We all breathe the same air. We all cherish our children's future. And we are all mortal.

Third: Let us reexamine our attitude toward the cold war, remembering that we are not engaged in a debate, seeking to pile up debating points. We are not here distributing blame or pointing the finger of judgment. We must deal with the world as it is, and not as it might have been had the history of the last 18 years been different.

We must, therefore, persevere in the search for peace in the hope that constructive changes within the Communist bloc might bring within reach solutions which now seem beyond us. We must conduct our affairs in such a way that it becomes in the Communist's interest to agree on a genuine peace. Above all, while defending our own vital interests, nuclear powers must avert those confrontations which bring an adversary to a choice of either a humiliating retreat or a nuclear war. To adopt that kind of course in the nuclear age would be evidence only of the bankruptcy of our policy—or of a collective death-wish for the world.

To secure these ends, America's weapons are nonprovocative, carefully controlled, designed to deter, and capable of selective use. Our military forces are committed to peace and disciplined in self-restraint. Our diplomats are instructed to avoid unnecessary irritants and purely rhetorical hostility.

For we can seek a relaxation of tensions without relaxing our guard. And, for our part, we do not need to use threats to prove that we are resolute. We do not need to jam foreign broadcasts out of fear our faith will be eroded. We are unwilling to impose our system on any unwilling people—but we are willing and able to engage in peaceful competition with any people on earth.

Meanwhile, we seek to strengthen the United Nations, to help solve its financial problems, to make it a more effective instrument for peace, to develop it into a genuine world security system—a system capable of resolving disputes on the basis of law, of insuring the security of the large and the small, and of creating conditions under which arms can finally be abolished.

At the same time we seek to keep peace inside the non-Communist world, where many nations, all of them our friends, are divided over issues which weaken Western unity, which invite Communist intervention or which threaten to erupt into war. Our efforts in West New Guinea, in the Congo, in the Middle East, and in the Indian sub-continent, have been persistent and patient despite criticism from both sides. We have also tried to set an example for others—by seeking to adjust small but significant differences with our own closest neighbors in Mexico and in Canada.

Speaking of other nations, I wish to make one point clear. We are bound to many nations by alliances. Those alliances exist because our concern and theirs substantially overlap. Our commitment to defend Western Europe and West Berlin, for example, stands undiminished because of the identity of our vital interests. The United States will make no deal with the Soviet Union at the expense of other nations and other peoples, not merely because they are our partners, but also because their interests and ours converge.

Our interests converge, however, not only in defending the frontiers of freedom, but in pursuing the paths of peace. It is our hope—and the purpose of allied policies—to convince the Soviet Union that she, too, should let each nation choose its own future, so long as that choice does not interfere with the choices of others. The Communist drive to impose their political and economic system on others is the primary cause of world tension today. For there can be no doubt that, if all nations could refrain from interfering in the self-determination of others, the peace would be much more assured.

This will require a new effort to achieve world law—a new context for world discussions. It will require increased understanding between the Soviets and ourselves. And increased understanding will require increased contact and communication. One step in this direction is the proposed arrangement for a direct line between Moscow and Washington, to avoid on each side the dangerous delays, misunderstandings, and misreadings of the other's actions which might occur at a time of crisis.

We have also been talking in Geneva about other first-step measures of arms control, designed to limit the intensity of the arms race and to reduce the risks of accidental war. Our primary long-range interest in Geneva, however, is general and complete disarmament—designed to take place by stages, permitting parallel political developments to build the new institutions of peace which would take the place of arms. The pursuit of disarmament has been an effort of this Government since the 1920's. It has been urgently sought by the past three administrations. And however dim the prospects may be today, we intend to continue this effort—to continue it in order that all countries, including our own, can better grasp what the problems and possibilities of disarmament are.

The one major area of these negotiations where the end is in sight, yet where a fresh start is badly needed, is in a treaty to outlaw nuclear tests. The conclusion of such a treaty, so near and yet so far, would check the spiraling arms race in one of its most dangerous areas. It would place the nuclear powers in a position to deal more effectively with one of the greatest hazards which man faces in 1963, the further spread of nuclear arms. It would increase our security—it would decrease the prospects of war. Surely this goal is sufficiently important to require our steady pursuit, yielding neither to the temptation to give up the whole effort nor the temptation to give up our insistence on vital and responsible safeguards.

I am taking this opportunity, therefore, to announce two important decisions in this regard.

First: Chairman Khrushchev, Prime Minister Macmillan, and I have agreed that high-level discussions will shortly begin in Moscow looking toward early agreement on a comprehensive test ban treaty. Our hopes must be tempered with the caution of history—but with our hopes go the hopes of all mankind.

Second: To make clear our good faith and solemn convictions on the matter, I now declare that the United States does not propose to conduct nuclear tests in the atmosphere so long as other states do not do so. We will not be the first to resume. Such a declaration is no substitute for a formal binding treaty, but I hope it will help us achieve one. Nor would such a treaty be a substitute for disarmament, but I hope it will help us achieve it.

Finally, my fellow Americans, let us examine our attitude toward peace and freedom here at home. The quality and spirit of our own society must justify and support our efforts abroad. We must show it in the dedication of our own lives—as many of you who are graduating today will have a unique opportunity to do, by serving without pay in the Peace Corps abroad or in the proposed National Service Corps here at home.

But wherever we are, we must all, in our daily lives, live up to the age-old faith that peace and freedom walk together. In too many of our cities today, the peace is not secure because freedom is incomplete.

It is the responsibility of the executive branch at all levels of government—local, State, and National—to provide and protect that freedom for all of our citizens by all means within their authority. It is the responsibility of the legislative branch at all levels, wherever that authority is not now adequate, to make it adequate. And it is the responsibility of all citizens in all sections of this country to respect the rights of all others and to respect the law of the land.

All this is not unrelated to world peace. "When a man's ways please the Lord," the Scriptures tell us, "he maketh even his enemies to be at peace with him." And is not peace, in the last analysis, basically a matter of human rights—the right to live out our lives without fear of devastation—the right to breathe air as nature provided it—the right of future generations to a healthy existence?

While we proceed to safeguard our national interests, let us also safeguard human interests. And the elimination of war and arms is clearly in the interest of both. No treaty, however much it may be to the advantage of all, however tightly it may be worded, can provide absolute security against the risks of deception and evasion. But it can—if it is sufficiently effective in its enforcement and if it is sufficiently in the interests of its signers—offer far more security and far fewer risks than an unabated, uncontrolled, unpredictable arms race.

The United States, as the world knows, will never start a war. We do not want a war. We do not now expect a war. This generation of Americans has already had enough—more than enough—of war and hate and oppression. We shall be prepared if others wish it. We shall be alert to try to stop it. But we shall also do our part to build a world of peace where the weak are safe and the strong are just. We are not helpless before that task or hopeless of its success. Confident and unafraid, we labor on—not toward a strategy of annihilation but toward a strategy of peace.

Everett M. Dirksen

Atomic Test Ban Treaty
(September 11, 1963)

Democrats controlled the United States Senate consistently from 1957 through 1980. When Minority Leader William Knowland was defeated in the 1958 midterm election, Republicans elected Everett McKinley Dirksen of Illinois to succeed him. Dirksen had been elected to the Senate in 1950 as a conservative Republican. He remained as minority leader until his death in 1969.

After the election of John F. Kennedy as President, Dirksen and House Minority Leader Charles Halleck of Indiana formed the Republican Joint Congressional Leadership Committee. Their goal was to make all the key policy decisions for congressional Republicans. After each weekly meeting, they held a press conference. These events brought greater visibility to Dirksen. They were dubbed the "Ev and Charlie Show" and were continued after Gerald Ford succeeded Halleck in 1965.

Despite his political opposition, however, Dirksen enjoyed a personal relationship of mutual respect with President Kennedy. He supported many of the administration's policies, especially with regard to foreign affairs. He stifled Republican criticism of the President after the Bay of Pigs debacle and offered his complete support in the Berlin crisis of 1961; he also supported Kennedy's actions in Vietnam and Laos. In domestic matters his support was sometimes even more critical, if Kennedy needed Republican votes to offset the defection of conservative Southerners. But Dirksen was sparing in his support; it often required either amendments to the legislation being considered or specific assurances that his reservations would be answered.

The Nuclear Test Ban Treaty was the result of a seventeen-nation disarmament conference that had been meeting in Geneva for many months. Following previous unsuccessful efforts at a test ban, both the Soviet Union and the United States had resumed atmospheric testing of nuclear weapons and there was widespread concern about radioactive fallout from these tests. Both superpowers and Great Britain were trying to achieve a halt of all nuclear testing but had been haggling for several months over issues such as the number and method of inspections to verify compliance with the treaty. As a compromise, a treaty was proposed to ban nuclear testing in the atmosphere, under water, and in space. Underground testing, however, could be continued since there was no danger of fallout. (Conveniently, underground testing was more advantageous to the United States.) The three major powers agreed to this treaty in late July 1963.

According to the Constitution, treaties must be ratified by a two-thirds vote of the Senate. While the treaty awaited Senate consideration, approximately one hundred nations ratified it. Nevertheless, American ratification was needed if the treaty was not to collapse. And ratification was hardly a sure thing, since some members of both parties were opposed.

Dirksen had his doubts. He questioned the "good faith" of the Soviet Union and asserted that the treaty was an open invitation for East Germany and Cuba (two particularly touchy places in the early 1960's) to begin testing. He urged Kennedy to resume atmospheric tests while the negotiations were in progress and he regarded Kennedy's unilateral suspension of tests in mid-1963 as a grave mistake. It is reasonable to surmise that Kennedy would have regarded Dirksen as an opponent of the treaty.

But a meeting with the President on September 4 allayed Dirksen's doubts about the treaty and convinced him that it was in the national interest. He then faced the task of convincing his Senate Republican colleagues to vote for the treaty. Although it was supported by prominent Republicans such as former President Eisenhower and former Vice President Nixon, as well as many military leaders, it also had formidable opponents, including senators on the Armed Services Committee and Sen. Barry Goldwater, a likely contender for the Presidency in 1964. Dirksen came out in favor of the treaty in a Senate speech on September 11 and engaged in private negotiations with individual senators.

It became evident during the fall that the treaty enjoyed strong public support. Reflecting that sentiment, the Senate ratified the treaty by a vote of 80–19. Twenty-five Republicans joined fifty-five Democrats to vote yes. Dirksen actually delivered a larger percentage of the Republican vote in favor of the treaty than did his Democratic counterparts in their own party. In turn, the nuclear test ban treaty became the key element in a climate of détente between the superpowers that has waxed and waned in the years since 1963.

Mr. Dirksen:—Mr. President, I envy Senators who have time to commit words to paper and to present a formal speech to the Senate. I make that statement in all modesty. First, I wish I had the talent for it; second, I wish I had time for it, because it makes an infinitely better RECORD. But, because of the pressures of a variety of work, I discover that I must be content with something of a synopsis that I had to dictate between telephone calls yesterday, and which Senators will find on their desks. So I apologize for the meager material that I have presented to Senators in a formal fashion.

As Senators know, I do not read a manuscript

very well; and I believe it is incumbent on me to search my heart and my mind and to talk topically as well as I can on the subject at hand.

At the outset, let me say that I shall support the treaty. It is no easy vote. In my office are probably 40,000 letters, and on my Capitol desk are petitions containing 10,000 names in opposition to the treaty. But I must equate those against the whole number of electors in my State. Moreover, I have admonished them over and over again that, regardless of the entreaties and presentations that have been made to me, I feel that I must follow a type of formula laid down by

Edmund Burke, the great parliamentarian and Prime Minister of Britain, when he said it was his business to consult with his people, but it would be a betrayal of his conscience and a disservice to them if he failed to exercise his independent judgment.

So today my statement that I shall support the treaty is an exercise of my independent judgment based upon what I think is best for my country.

I have been drenched by all the correspondence and material that have come to my desk. I have gone over 100 pounds of pamphlets, brochures, letters, and all types of printed material that had a bearing upon the issue that is before the Senate.

I doubt whether at any other time—except three—in nearly 30 years of experience in the House and in the Senate, I have been so beset with the views and expressions of people everywhere.

I believe the first occasion was in 1940. If I am in error by a year, I shall have to ask my distinguished friend the Senator from Georgia [Mr. RUSSELL] whether that was the year of the "cash and carry" neutrality debate. I think it was. I remember the intensity of feeling which existed everywhere in the country and how emotionally and passionately people committed their feelings to paper. That was one occasion.

The second occasion was the dismissal of Douglas MacArthur. That happened in the Truman administration. The commentators and others had managed to excite the country. At that time I received about 200,000 letters.

The third time was when I was a member of the Committee on Government Operations of the Senate, the committee of which the late Senator McCarthy was the chairman. That committee conducted the trial. I was a member of the committee. On that occasion, the country was excited. Senators will remember that it was late at night when the Senate voted on the question. As the proceeding had been under the klieg lights and television cameras for 7 weeks, obviously it evoked a tremendous interest everywhere in the land. I believe there are still thousands of letters which I received, which have not been opened. My office staff indicated that more than 250,000 letters were received.

Senators can conceive what it is to have someone "smite you hip and thigh," in an angry mood, and say, "I demand a personal answer."

I do not know how one could answer people personally under those circumstances without resorting to the robot machines and other devices which are designed to diminish the workload upon the shoulders of Senators.

So I find, under all circumstances, that this is one of such occasions. On the other occasions—one under Franklin Roosevelt, one under Truman, and one under Eisenhower—we managed to survive, and we went our own way.

I believe perhaps Shakespeare was essentially correct when he said, in "Hamlet":

There's a divinity that shapes our ends,
Rough-hew them how we will.

He might well have used the word "destiny." This could be, conceivably, a time of destiny for the country and for the world. Who am I to judge? Time and history will have to render that judgment.

But this is an important matter that engrosses our attention. I pray that I may be on the right side. I accept this assignment, and I accept the responsibility for my vote with a sense of gravity and concern.

Before the treaty was initialed, I was privileged to see a thermofax copy. I examined it as best I could. I rendered some offhand opinions at the time, some of which did not stand up. I saw them recited in an editorial the other day. One must expect that sort of thing in public life. But I do not let it bother me.

I said to my people, I said to the country publicly, and I said in the press gallery that I would take a hard look at the treaty. I said I would be diligent in examining its every implication, and that there would be only one standard by which to come to a vote, and that would be: What is best for the present and for the future of the United States of America, which has been so good to me as a citizen?

In pursuance of the assurance that I would take a hard look, I wanted to look at both sides, and I did look at both sides. I was concerned about a treaty with the Soviet Union. Who would not be?

I am no novice at the business of examining into the Soviet history and its record with respect to treaties. As a member of the Internal Security Subcommittee of the Senate Committee on the Judiciary I have had abundant opportunity to look. I referred even to the old Army data known as "Alert No. 5: Soviet Treaty Violations."

I examined the violation of an understanding with the Georgian Republic, now absorbed into the Soviet Union, as early as 1920.

I examined into the trade agreement with Britain, when there was assurance against propaganda. It was violated, and the trade agreement with Britain fell.

In 1922 there was a treaty of assurance and friendship with the country of Czechoslovakia, yet later it was violated, and Czechoslovakia was forced to cede territory to the Soviet Union.

There was a nonaggression pact with Turkey in 1925, and ultimately a tremendous effort to secure rights from Turkey on the Black Sea Straits.

There was a treaty with Afghanistan in 1926. We have recently been host to the Afghan royal King. Yet the Soviets made Afghanistan cede a piece of territory.

I have a special interest in Lithuania, because there are literally thousands of Baltic people—Lithuanians, Estonians, and Latvians—in Chicago. A treaty with Lithuania not only was made but also was extended, yet it did not prevent the Soviet Union from annexing Lithuania.

So I have gone through the whole lesson book to get that side of the story. I went further than that. I referred to the records of 1933, when, during the administration of Franklin Roosevelt, the Soviet Union was recognized, on the 16th of November, 1933.

It intrigues me some to read Maxim Litvinov's letter. He was the Soviet Commissar for Foreign Affairs. The letter was written in Washington. It was written to Franklin Roosevelt.

In the first paragraph he said:

> It will be the fixed policy of the Government of the Union of Soviet Socialist Republics—
> 1. To respect scrupulously the indisputable right of the United States to order its own life within its own jurisdiction in its own way and to refrain from interfering in any manner in the internal affairs of the United States, its territories or possessions.

Paragraph 2 is worthy of recording, because at times we forget these things. In paragraph 2 Mr. Litvinov wrote:

> To refrain, and to restrain all persons in Government service and all organizations of the Government or under its direct or indirect control, including the organizations in receipt of any financial assistance from it, from any act overt or covert liable in any way whatsoever to injure the tranquillity, prosperity, order, or security of the whole or any part of the United States, its territories or possessions, and in particular, from any act tending to incite or encourage armed intervention, or any agitation or propaganda having as an aim, the violation of the territorial integrity of the United States, its territories or possessions, or the bringing about by force of a change in the political or social order of the whole or any part of the United States, its territories or possessions.

These assurances go on and on. They were the foundation for the recognition of the Soviet Union by the United States in the first administration of Franklin Roosevelt, in November 1933.

I want those people who send me all this documentation and literature to know that sources of information are available. I want them to know that I have been rather diligent in carrying out the pledge I made to them.

Second, I was curious about the sudden change on the part of the Soviet Union. When Mr. Dean was still our representative to Geneva—and then there had been 400 sessions—I was still a member of the Joint Committee on Atomic Energy.

The day Mr. Dean left for Geneva, I said, "Mr. Dean, come back with something worth while and I will support it. Come back with something else and I will fight, and I will resist as best I can." So I served notice at that time.

Who would not be curious about the sudden change of heart? Is it China and the reported difficulties with the Soviet Union that have had some impact on Mr. Khrushchev? I do not know. But while I am about it, I want to give my own opinion of what I expect is a part of the Chinese situation. In 1953 China took a census. Probably a mistake was made. It took a little while to obtain corrected figures, and when that was done it announced to the world that the population of Red China was 583 million and that it was growing at a rate of 15 million or more each year. At that rate, China today has 730 million people. In 15 years she will have 1 billion people. Those 1 billion people will have to be fed.

A great many headaches, difficulties, and responsibilities have arisen, and will arise.

When I was in Burma, I visited about 10 miles down the Irrawaddy River and I was shown a great storage of rice. I was told that the rice was full of weevils. Then I was told that we sold 250,000 tons of Louisiana rice to Japan, and that it was their market. That is a surplus rice bowl. I flew over Thailand. I know the rice bowl in that area. I know the Laotian rice bowl. I remember being in that area when the French were fighting at Dien Bien Phu.

That is a large area; and the population of 1 billion must be fed. There is the pressure. Perhaps Mr. Khrushchev knows of that pressure. It may well be. Difficulties have been referred to with respect to these countries. There may be something real about it. It may be what was written on the parchments of history long ago when it was said, "It shall come to pass that when man is hungry he shall feed himself, and when he does he shall curse his king and his God."

There is nothing worse than a population pressure. What is to be done about it? Many countries have been through great hunger, and they have been impelled by a force that drove people not only to desperation, but to action.

That, of course, is a diversion; but I want people to know that I have tried to take a hard look. I have tried to fortify myself. I believe I have been diligent. The chairman of the Foreign Relations Committee can well say that I was present to listen to the testimony. The distinguished Senator from Mississippi can say that I was present to listen to Dr. Teller. In addition, Dr. Teller came to my office for a long visit. I sat with the Atomic Energy Commission under Director McCone. I have proceeded with diligence. I say that in modesty. I have tried to explore everything involved. I wanted to get the whole story.

I make that statement as I try to explain the question of treaty violations, evidences of lack of faith on the part of the Soviet Union, and the testimony of our leaders, like Secretary Rusk, Secretary McNamara, Dr. Teller, John McCone, and the Joint Chiefs of Staff. There is no question about the anxiety and concern on one side, and the counsel and advice stressed by those to whom we have committed the security and defense of our country.

Where do we turn in our difficulty if it is not to General Wheeler? Where do we turn to if it is not to Admiral McDonald? Where do we turn to if not to General Shoup, of the Marine Corps? Where do we turn to if not to the Chief of Staff of the Navy? They have been educated in our own schools, supported at public expense. We not only expect them to become competent in their field, but we also expect fidelity to duty, and we get it. They are ranged on one side, and history is ranged on the other. What choice does one take in the case of the treaty under those circumstances?

I detected one thing in every committee hearing I attended. I have detected it in much of the material that has come to my desk. I detected it in the letter that is attached to the 10,000 signatures that lie at the desk in my Capitol office. It was an overlay of concern, of anxiety, and of fear. It could be detected in the questions which arose, namely Where are we vis-a-vis the Soviet Union? Where are we in respect to heavy yield weapons? Where are we in respect to light yield weapons? What is the strategy? What is the pattern? What is the formula? Have we a readiness posture? Are we pre-

pared to resume testing if necessary? What shall we do in the event of abrogation? What shall we do if there is evidence of deviation from the treaty?

All these questions arise in anxious minds and hearts. One cannot hear such questions without having some sense of apprehension and concern, himself. What do we do about it?

I began to toy with the idea of a concurrent resolution expressing the sense of the Senate and the House. I conferred with the Parliamentarian. It had no place here, but it had only one purpose. It was to allay the sense of anxiety and fear I had detected on every ground.

I went to my friend the distinguished majority leader, and discussed the question with him. After thinking about it some more, I thought this was not the approach. Someone said, "Why did you include the House of Representatives?" After all, we must ascertain whether to implement the treaty or whether to implement a program. That was set out in the concurrent resolution. I drafted the resolution. I had it perfected, I thought. But I did not submit it. Then subsequently I went to the majority leader again. I said, "Mike, there is fear in the country. Why do people call at all hours of the night?"

One of the roughest scoldings I ever received was at 2 o'clock in the morning from a constituent of the distinguished Senator from Florida. I could not get him off the telephone. He said, "Don't you hang up on me. I am a taxpayer, and I am going to tell you off."

The number of telephone calls was legion. They came at the most awkward hours. I tried to accept all of them. Some of the callers would not wait, and it was a little difficult.

At long last I had two more discussions with the distinguished majority leader. I said, "MIKE, there is only one place where this question can be discussed at the top echelon, and that is with the Commander in Chief, the President of the United States." I said, "I have read the capitulation of Dr. Seaborg in the hearings. I thought it was excellent. But suppose the President had other ideas. I heard the Joint Chiefs of Staff when they expressed the hope that this would be done or that would be done or the other would be done."

I went to the upper office. It is rather difficult to get into that office. Sometimes I think it is easier to get a charge account at Tiffany's than to get into the upper office, where the Joint Committee on Atomic Energy meets. There I saw John McCone, who served as chairman of the Joint Committee on Atomic Energy under

Eisenhower, and who now serves as Director of Intelligence.

I listened keenly. He had certain recommendations, as the distinguished chairman of the Joint Committee, the Senator from Rhode Island [Mr. PASTORE], so well knows.

I followed through on this matter because of the fear that continued to beset me.

Then I had another meeting with the distinguished majority leader. I said, "MIKE, I think you ought to contact the President." The letter which I shall read a little later is not the result of the President calling me. It is the result of the work of the majority leader and the minority leader, who expressed a common fear, and who felt that they ought to talk with the Commander in Chief, because if there were to be assurances, they ought to come from the highest and most authoritative source, the President of the United States.

That was the foundation and background.

I should like to recite a few of the considerations which move me to support the treaty, not the least of which, of course, is the party position. I am a little old fashioned. I was here when Wendell Willkie appeared before a Senate committee, and when Tom Connally asked him a rather sharp question, Wendell Willkie said, "Oh, that is only campaign oratory." I was here as a public servant at that time. It is no campaign oratory in my book, when one's party goes to the country and asks the country to give to it the direction of the affairs of the country. That is either a covenant or it is not. If it is a covenant, it is made to be kept.

This was my party's platform in 1960:

> We are similarly ready to negotiate and to institute realistic methods and safeguards for disarmament, and for the suspension of nuclear tests. We advocate an early agreement—

Listen to that—

> We advocate an early agreement by all nations to forgo nuclear tests in the atmosphere, and the suspension of other tests as verification techniques permit. We support the President in any decision he may make to reevaluate the question of resumption of underground nuclear explosions testing, if the Geneva Conference falls to produce a satisfactory agreement.

That is what my party said to the country, as we rallied behind Richard Nixon. Out of 69 million votes we came within 113,000 of victory. Oh, yes, we have a party in this country. I do not subscribe lightly to party platforms. I have served on the platform committee of my party when such solemn words were indited. They become lures to get the people into one's corner. There is something grave and solemn about it. I accepted the platform plank in that spirit. We said:

> We advocate an early agreement by all nations to forgo nuclear tests in the atmosphere.

That is what we seek in the treaty today.

Second, 89 nations are now signatories to the treaty. Think of the propaganda weapon that we would give Nikita Khrushchev if we failed to stand up and ratify the treaty. He could go into all the areas of the world and say to their leaders, "Did I not tell you for many years that they are imperialists, capitalists, and warmongers? Here is the proof. They refused to subscribe to a cessation of testing of the hideous weapons that can snuff out so much life."

That would be a consideration in itself for supporting the treaty. Our arsenal of weapons is available. I shall touch on that later. It will be remembered that on the 23d of August former President Eisenhower sent a letter to the distinguished chairman of the Foreign Relations Committee. I have read it several times. He used the word "reservation." It bothered me. I decided to pursue it. I did so. Through one of his assistants I contacted him at Gettysburg. Was it an inadvertent use of the word, which is a word of art in this business, or did he really mean it? Did he know what a reservation really meant? It was not the significant thing in the mind of President Eisenhower. What he wanted to be sure of was that there would be an iron-clad assurance that our nuclear arsenal would be available for ourselves and for our allies if the need ever arose. I will deal with that point at a little greater length in connection with the President's letter.

Suppose there is deviation. Suppose there is abrogation. Will we be ready, and would we move into it? That was another point on which I wanted some assurances.

The President in his message to the Senate said it was a first step. So it is. The Chinese—and perhaps it comes from Confucius himself—have a saying: "The longest journey begins with the first step." A step must be made somehow, because a whole generation of Americans has grown up in the atmosphere and intensity of the cold war.

The bombs fell in August 1945. Suppose a youngster was 12 years old. Add 18 to that. That is 30 years. Consider the generation that has not known anything except the cold war.

We are devoting hundreds of millions of dollars to studies of mental retardation and mental health. Does anyone mean to tell me that those pressures do not have an effect upon a nation? When I was in Britain, and the V–1's and V–2's were falling during the late war, a prominent member of the House of Commons said, "If it keeps up, it will break the nervous system of our people."

Some think this is all remote. But it is not remote. There is an impingement of all these pressures, all these considerations, that are a part of the cold war. Yet a whole generation has grown up under them. How many more generations will grow up before we receive an answer to the question? That is a concern of mine; it must be a concern of every other Member of this body.

There has been some sentiment about the heavy-yield, high-megaton weapons as distinguished from those that we have; and one could detect a certain defeatism. I am not an expert in the field. I have never served on the Committee on Armed Services, which has the benefit of such information. I readily sit at the feet of those who are members of the committee, when I seek advice, information, and instruction. But I remember that in the war in which I was a soldier on the Western Front, our strength was on paper, but our cause was good, and we prevailed.

I remember when I helped to vote this country into World War II. Our air power was on paper. We made close distinctions between weapons that were in being and those that were being planned. So much was not in being. But our cause was good and we triumphed. Let it never be said that the Senator from Illinois has any spark of defeatism in his soul, no matter what the equation is as between weapon strengths, because I am pretty sure that our thermonuclear strength, coupled with our cause, will abide and prevail, as it has and as it must.

One other thing the President said: Do not expect too much of this treaty. I thought it sounded biased in the message, which contains 10 specifics. But the treaty will not necessarily stop war. We hope it will. We hope it is in the direction of peace. What else can we do except hope? But is there assurance? None. There are many things that the treaty will not do, and it is necessary to go back to what the President said in his message.

Abraham Lincoln had a rule, and I think it was a great rule. I jotted it down, so that I would have it correct. This is what he said:

The true rule in determining to embrace or reject anything is not whether it have any evil in it but whether it have more of evil than of good. There are few things wholly evil or wholly good. Almost everything especially of Government policy is an inseparable compound of the two so that our best judgment of the preponderance between them is continuously demanded.

That is the case in this instance. I have not heard anyone deny that there are risks in the treaty. But, as Lincoln said, every policy is a compound of risk and nonrisk, of good and evil. Which is the preponderant quality? That is why our judgment is demanded. So I must rationalize the problem in that fashion and on that basis predicate judgment.

With those concerns in my mind, and with those concerns in the mind of our distinguished majority leader, we spent 45 minutes with the President and expressed our concern. We made certain suggestions to him. In response, on September 10, he sent this letter, which reached me by hand last night at half-past 6. Let me read it to the Senate:

THE WHITE HOUSE,

Washington, D.C., September 10, 1963.

Hon. MIKE MANSFIELD,

Hon. EVERETT McKINLEY DIRKSEN,

U.S. Senate,

Washington, D.C.

DEAR SENATOR MANSFIELD AND SENATOR DIRKSEN: I am deeply appreciative of the suggestion which you made to me on Monday morning that it would be helpful to have a further clarifying statement about the policy of this administration toward certain aspects of our nuclear weapons defenses, under the proposed test ban treaty now before the Senate. I share your view that it is desirable to dispel any fears or concerns in the minds of Senators or of the people of our country on these matters. And while I believe that fully adequate statements have been made on these matters before the various committees of the Senate by the Secretary of State, the Secretary of Defense, the Director of Central Intelligence, the Chairman of the Atomic Energy Commission, and the Joint Chiefs of Staff, nevertheless I am happy to accept your judgment that it would be helpful if I restated what has already been said so that there may be no misapprehension.

In confidence that the Congress will share and support the policies of the administration in this field, I am happy to give these unqualified and unequivocal assurances to the Members of the Senate, to the entire Congress, and to the country:

1. Underground nuclear testing, which is permitted under the treaty, will be vigorously and diligently carried forward, and the equipment, facilities, personnel, and funds necessary for that purpose will be provided. As the Senate knows, such testing is now going on. While we must all hope that at some future time a more comprehensive treaty may become possible by changes in the policies of other nations, until that time our underground testing program will continue.

2. The United States will maintain a posture of readiness to resume testing in the environments prohibited by the present treaty, and it will take all the necessary steps to safeguard our national security in the event that there should be an abrogation or violation of any treaty provision. In particular, the United States retains the right to resume atmospheric testing forthwith—

That was a point I made with the President. I said, "It has got to be made"; and he put it in his letter—

if the Soviet Union should conduct tests in violation of the treaty.

3. Our facilities for the detection of possible violations of this treaty will be expanded and improved as required to increase our assurance against clandestine violation by others.

I hope particular attention will be given to this paragraph:

4. In response to the suggestion made by President Eisenhower to the Foreign Relations Committee on August 23, 1963, and in conformity with the opinion of the legal adviser of the Department of State, set forth in the report of the Committee on Foreign Relations, I am glad to emphasize again that the treaty in no way limits the authority of the Commander in Chief to use nuclear weapons for the defense of the United States and its allies, if a situation should develop requiring such a grave decision. Any decision to use such weapons would be made by the United States in accordance with its constitutional processes and would in no way be affected by the terms of the nuclear test ban treaty.

5. While the abnormal and dangerous presence of Soviet military personnel in the neighboring island of Cuba is not a matter which can be dealt with through the instrumentality of this treaty, I am able to assure the Senate that if that unhappy island should be used either directly or indirectly to circumvent or nullify this treaty, the United States will take all necessary action in response.

6. The treaty in no way changes the status of the authorities in East Germany. As the Secretary of State has made clear, "We do not recognize, and we do not intend to recognize, the Soviet occupation zone of East Germany as a state or as an entity possessing national sovereignty, or to recognize the local authorities as a government. Those authorities cannot alter these facts by the act of subscribing to the test ban treaty."

7. This Government will maintain strong weapons laboratories in a vigorous program of weapons development, in order to ensure that the United States will continue to have in the future a strength fully adequate for an effective national defense. In particular, as the Secretary of Defense has made clear, we will maintain strategic forces fully ensuring that this Nation will continue to be in a position to destroy any aggressor, even after absorbing a first strike by a surprise attack.

8. The United States will diligently pursue its programs for the further development of nuclear explosives for peaceful purposes by underground tests within the terms of the treaty, and as and when such developments make possible constructive uses of atmospheric nuclear explosions for peaceful purposes, the United States will seek international agreement under the treaty to permit such explosions.

I trust that these assurances may be helpful in dispelling any concern or misgivings which any member of the Senate or any citizen may have as to our determination to maintain the interests and security of the United States. It is not only safe but necessary, in the interest of this country and the interest of mankind, that this treaty should now be approved, and the hope for peace which it offers firmly sustained, by the Senate of the United States.

Once more, let me express my appreciation to you both for your visit and for your suggestions.

Sincerely,

JOHN KENNEDY.

Mr. President, late the other night I went back to refresh myself on a little history. One of the classic reports made in our generation was the one made by John Hersey, to the New Yorker, on what happened at Hiroshima. It makes one think. It came as an account from a Japanese preacher who long ago was educated at Emory University, in Atlanta, Ga. He did his undergraduate work there and developed great fluency in English. He was one of the principal witnesses when John Hersey went to Hiroshima to write that almost deathless account.

The B-29's had bombed nearly every Japanese town except Kyoto and Hiroshima. The Japanese called the B-29 "Mr. B," out of respect for the might and the power of that great wartime bomber.

As he relates the story, it was 8:15 in the morning of a bright, sunny day. The weather was a little humid and warm. At 8:15, things happened. Out of the 20th Air Wing, Col. Paul W. Tibbetts, Jr., flying that B-29, and with two escort observation planes, flew over the center of Hiroshima, a town of probably 375,000 persons. Then, for the first time, the whole bosom of God's earth was ruptured by a manmade contrivance that we call a nuclear weapon.

Oh, the tragedy. Oh, the dismay. Oh, the blood. Oh, the anguish. When the statisticians came to put the cold figures on paper, they were as follows: As a result of 1 bomb—66,000 killed; 69,000 injured; 62,000 structures destroyed. That was the result of that one bomb, made by man in the hope of stopping that war. Little did he realize what this thermonuclear weapon would do, and the anguish that would be brought into the hearts of men, women, and children. At Hiroshima it caused a mass incineration such as never before had been witnessed in the history of the whole wide world. The result was almost too catastrophic to contemplate.

In the accelerated march of history, how quickly we forget. But there is the account, for all to read; and it all happened at 8:15, on a bright and shining morning, when God's day began, and when, I suppose, hundreds of thousands of people were thinking that, despite the war, they had been privileged to live another day.

Mr. President, that happened 18 years ago last month. Since then, what have we done? What steps have we taken? How far have we moved?

The President calls this treaty a first step. What sort of steps have we taken, except steps to make the bombs that fell on Hiroshima and Nagasaki look like veritable toys when compared to the heavy-duty, heavy-yield weapons of today.

I want to take a first step, Mr. President. I am not a young man; I am almost as old as the oldest Member of the Senate, certainly am older than a great many Senators. One of my age thinks about his destiny a little. I should not like to have written on my tombstone, "He knew what happened at Hiroshima, but he did not take a first step."

God willing, Mr. President, and in the frame of my own party's platform and with the knowledge that the Soviet Union has violated treaties, there must still be enough faith, and enough confidence to make us willing to take a first step in this field.

If it fails, we will still be here. We have not forfeited caution. We have forfeited nothing. The President has given us assurances in regard to what is proposed to be done in underground testing in these and other environments and in regard to developing all the equipment necessary in order to maintain our strength against any aggressor on the face of the earth.

Mr. President, I believe it is just as well to conclude this slightly rambling discourse by reverting to the Chinese proverb. "The longest journey begins with a single step."

This is a first, single step. It is for destiny to write the answer. It is for history to render judgment. But with consummate faith and some determination, this may be the step that can spell a grander destiny for our country and for the world.

If there be risks, Mr. President, I am willing to assume them for my country.

So I support the treaty; and I will vote for approval of the treaty with no reservations whatsoever.

John F. Kennedy

Amherst College Speech
(October 26, 1963)

Robert Frost, sometimes identified as America's unofficial poet laureate, died in 1963. Kennedy had known him only late in life. Frost had been invited to the inaugural in 1961 and had a place on the program. He had composed a poem especially for the occasion but, because of a blinding sun reflecting off the snow, was unable to see the words on the paper and recited the familiar lines of "The Gift Outright" instead. The young President was moved by the words and emotion of the aging poet.

Amherst College, where Frost taught for over twenty years, planned to name its new library in his memory. Construction was to begin in October 1963. Amherst alumnus John J. McCloy, Kennedy's disarmament adviser, had invited the President to attend the groundbreaking for the library. Kennedy accepted and delivered brief remarks at the ceremony on October 26.

Earlier that same day, Amherst College bestowed an honorary degree on the President, and on that occasion he delivered the speech that is printed here. No great crisis of state prompted this speech; it addressed no urgent matters of domestic or foreign policy. Rather, Kennedy used the occasion to speak about the national character and purpose, taking advantage of the opportunity—much like that of a commencement speech—to use an academic setting to discuss enduring issues and to evoke a vision of an ideal future.

This speech is of interest for at least three reasons. First, Kennedy defined the occasion such that it naturally called forth remarks of the sort he wanted to give. Amherst was honoring Frost. The poet was an American hero, but not in the realm of diplomacy, war, politics, or even sports. As an artist and an academic, Frost was a hero of the spirit, a critic who pointed the way to "the deepest sources of our national strength." From this insight, Kennedy could proceed to discuss the true nature of heroism, the relationship between power and poetry, the role of the artist and critic in society, and a corresponding vision of the future.

Second, the Amherst College speech illustrates very well a frequent Kennedy stylistic figure, the use of antitheses. The complexity of his worldview was evident in his use of terms of positive value—such as the nation's size and strength—as the initial terms with which to contrast less well recognized values that were, in Kennedy's mind, equally important. We hear, for example, that "the men who create power make an indispensable contribution to the Nation's greatness, but the men who question power make a contribution just as indispensable," and "Our national strength matters, but the spirit which informs and controls our strength matters just as much." Sometimes the contrasts are even more sharply drawn, such as "when power corrupts, poetry cleanses." Kennedy does not negate the first term in the pair, but uses it to exalt the second, which is always less clear and more abstract.

Finally, because of the President's untimely death less than a month later, this speech serves as a valedictory message. Although it was not intended as one, it does share some of the characteristics of a farewell address, reviewing accomplishments, looking forward to a bright future, and issuing a challenge to one's listeners and fellow citizens. The speech warrants attention not only because it illustrates how a President shapes and articulates such a vision, but also because of the richness and vigor of the future in Kennedy's vision itself.

By their nature, speeches of this kind seldom lead to specific changes or policies; they function in what the ancients called the epideictic mode—ceremonial addresses that serve to establish, strengthen, and celebrate values, thereby giving the listeners a clearer sense of self and a nobler view of their individual and collective purpose.

Mr. McCloy, President Plimpton, Mr. MacLeish, distinguished guests, ladies and gentlemen:—I am very honored to be here with you on this occasion which means so much to this college and also means so much to art and the progress of the United States. This college is part of the United States. It belongs to it. So did Mr. Frost, in a large sense. And, therefore, I was privileged to accept the invitation somewhat rendered to me in the same way that Franklin Roosevelt rendered his invitation to Mr. MacLeish, the invitation which I received from Mr. McCloy. The powers of the Presidency are often described. Its limitations should occasionally be remembered. And therefore when the Chairman of our Disarmament Advisory Committee, who has labored so long and hard, Governor Stevenson's assistant during the very difficult days at the United Nations during the Cuban crisis, a public servant of so many years, asks or invites the President of the United States, there is only one response. So I am glad to be here.

Amherst has had many soldiers of the king since its first one, and some of them are here today: Mr. McCloy, who has long been a public servant; Jim Reed, who is the Assistant Secretary of the Treasury; President Cole, who is now our Ambassador to Chile; Mr. Ramey, who is a Commissioner of the Atomic Energy Commission; Dick Reuter, who is head of the Food for Peace. These and scores of others down through the years have recognized the obligations of the advantages which the graduation from a college such as this places upon them to serve not only their private interest but the public interest as well.

Many years ago, Woodrow Wilson said, what good is a political party unless it is serving a great national purpose? And what good is a private college or university unless it is serving a great national purpose? The library being constructed today, this college, itself—all of this, of course, was not done merely to give this school's graduates an advantage, an economic advantage, in the life struggle. It does do that. But in return for that, in return for the great opportunity which society gives the graduates of this and related schools, it seems to me incumbent upon this and other schools' graduates to recognize their responsibility to the public interest.

Privilege is here, and with privilege goes responsibility. And I think, as your president said, that it must be a source of satisfaction to you that this school's graduates have recognized it. I hope that the students who are here now will also recognize it in the future. Although Amherst has been in the forefront of extending aid to needy and talented students, private colleges, taken as a whole, draw 50 percent of their students from the wealthiest 10 percent of our Nation. And even State universities and other public institutions derive 25 percent of their students from this group. In March 1962, persons of 18 years or older who had not completed high school made up 46 percent of the total labor force, and such persons comprised 64 percent of those who were unemployed. And in 1958, the lowest fifth of the families in the United States had 4 1/2 percent of the total personal income, the highest fifth, 44 1/2 percent. There is inherited wealth in this country and also inherited poverty. And unless the graduates of this college and other colleges like it who are given a running start in life—unless they are willing to put back into our society those talents, the broad sympathy, the understanding, the compassion—unless they are willing to put those qualities back into the service of the Great Republic, then obviously the presuppositions upon which our democracy are based are bound to be fallible.

The problems which this country now faces are staggering, both at home and abroad. We need the service, in the great sense, of every educated man or woman to find 10 million jobs in the next 2 1/2 years, to govern our relations—a country which lived in isolation for 150 years, and is now suddenly the leader of the free world—to govern our relations with over 100 countries, to govern those relations with success so that the balance of power remains strong on the side of freedom, to make it possible for Americans of all different races and creeds to live together in harmony, to make it possible for a world to exist in diversity and freedom. All this requires the best of all of us.

Therefore, I am proud to come to this college whose graduates have recognized this obligation and to say to those who are now here that the need is endless, and I am confident that you will respond.

Robert Frost said:

Two roads diverged in a wood, and I—
I took the one less traveled by,

And that has made all the difference.

I hope that road will not be the less traveled by, and I hope your commitment to the Great Republic's interest in the years to come will be worthy of your long inheritance since your beginning.

This day devoted to the memory of Robert Frost offers an opportunity for reflection which is prized by politicians as well as by others, and even by poets, for Robert Frost was one of the granite figures of our time in America. He was supremely two things: an artist and an American. A nation reveals itself not only by the men it produces but also by the men it honors, the men it remembers.

In America, our heroes have customarily run to men of large accomplishments. But today this college and country honors a man whose contribution was not to our size but to our spirit, not to our political beliefs but to our insight, not to our self-esteem, but to our self-comprehension. In honoring Robert Frost, we therefore can pay honor to the deepest sources of our national strength. That strength takes many forms, and the most obvious forms are not always the most significant. The men who create power make an indispensable contribution to the Nation's greatness, but the men who question power make a contribution just as indispensable, especially when that questioning is disinterested, for they determine whether we use power or power uses us.

Our national strength matters, but the spirit which informs and controls our strength matters just as much. This was the special significance of Robert Frost. He brought an unsparing instinct for reality to bear on the platitudes and pieties of society. His sense of the human tragedy fortified him against self-deception and easy consolation. "I have been," he wrote, "one acquainted with the night." And because he knew the midnight as well as the high noon, because he understood the ordeal as well as the triumph of the human spirit, he gave his age strength with which to overcome despair. At bottom, he held a deep faith in the spirit of man, and it is hardly an accident that Robert Frost coupled poetry and power, for he saw poetry as the means of saving power from itself. When power leads man towards arrogance, poetry reminds him of his limitations. When power narrows the areas of man's concern, poetry reminds him of the richness and diversity of his existence. When power corrupts, poetry cleanses. For art establishes the basic human truth which must serve as the touchstone of our judgment.

The artist, however faithful to his personal vision

of reality, becomes the last champion of the individual mind and sensibility against an intrusive society and an officious state. The great artist is thus a solitary figure. He has, as Frost said, a lover's quarrel with the world. In pursuing his perceptions of reality, he must often sail against the currents of his time. This is not a popular role. If Robert Frost was much honored during his lifetime, it was because a good many preferred to ignore his darker truths. Yet in retrospect, we see how the artist's fidelity has strengthened the fibre of our national life.

If sometimes our great artists have been the most critical of our society, it is because their sensitivity and their concern for justice, which must motivate any true artist, makes him aware that our Nation falls short of its highest potential. I see little of more importance to the future of our country and our civilization than full recognition of the place of the artist.

If art is to nourish the roots of our culture, society must set the artist free to follow his vision wherever it takes him. We must never forget that art is not a form of propaganda; it is a form of truth. And as Mr. MacLeish once remarked of poets, there is nothing worse for our trade than to be in style. In free society art is not a weapon and it does not belong to the sphere of polemics and ideology. Artists are not engineers of the soul. It may be different elsewhere. But democratic society—in it, the highest duty of the writer, the composer, the artist is to remain true to himself and to let the chips fall where they may. In serving his vision of the truth, the artist best serves his nation. And the nation which disdains the mission of art invites the fate of Robert Frost's hired man, the fate of having "nothing to look backward to with pride, and nothing to look forward to with hope."

I look forward to a great future for America, a future in which our country will match its military strength with our moral restraint, its wealth with our wisdom, its power with our purpose. I look forward to an America which will not be afraid of grace and beauty, which will protect the beauty of our natural environment, which will preserve the great old American houses and squares and parks of our national past, and which will build handsome and balanced cities for our future.

I look forward to an America which will reward achievement in the arts as we reward achievement in business or statecraft. I look forward to an America which will steadily raise the standards of artistic accomplishment and which will steadily enlarge cultural opportunities for all of our citizens. And I look forward to an America which commands respect throughout the world not only for its strength but for its civilization as well. And I look forward to a world which will be safe not only for democracy and diversity but also for personal distinction.

Robert Frost was often skeptical about projects for human improvement, yet I do not think he would disdain this hope. As he wrote during the uncertain days of the Second War:

Take human nature altogether since time began...
And it must be a little more in favor of man,
Say a fraction of one percent at the very least...
Our hold on the planet wouldn't have so
    increased.

Because of Mr. Frost's life and work, because of the life and work of this college, our hold on this planet has increased.

Lyndon B. Johnson

The Forward Thrust of America
(November 27, 1963)

The assassination of President Kennedy thrust Lyndon B. Johnson into the office under particularly difficult circumstances. The shock and horror of the act itself created the need for a calming and reassuring influence. The possibility that the act was the work of a conspiracy, and that other government officials were targeted, made it necessary for the new President to demonstrate quickly that he was in control and that the machinery of government would continue to work, even amid national tragedy. Those who had supported and worked for President Kennedy had to be inspired to stay on. And the country needed to learn more about the new man at the helm.

Although he had been in public life for three decades, Lyndon Johnson was not well known. As Senate majority leader during the 1950's, he had exercised great power, but he had wielded it behind the scenes. Interpersonal persuasion rather than formal speeches was his forte. He had passed three years in the Vice Presidency in relative obscurity, dutifully serving Kennedy and attracting little attention in his own right. What was known about him, moreover, was not altogether favorable. His reputation was that of a parochial Texas politician, generally conservative, who was not above abandoning principle in order to win votes, just as he had abandoned his New Deal liberalism when his Texas constituency changed.

Johnson would be occupied through much of 1964 in addressing the rhetorical problems of the succession. He began immediately, meeting with Kennedy's cabinet and key advisers, urging them all to stay on and insisting that he needed them more than Kennedy had. He met with foreign diplomats who had come to Washington for the funeral, and assured them that he would continue Kennedy's foreign policy. He reviewed the situation in South Vietnam and determined to stay the course in that troubled land.

He gave his approval to proceed with plans for an antipoverty program, which would have been a centerpiece of Kennedy's 1964 legislative program. He met with scores of leaders from every sector of American society. This early burst of energy and activity itself conveyed the message of comfort and reassurance.

But Johnson had not yet made a public speech as President, save for his very brief remarks at Andrews Air Force Base immediately after the assassination. He asked to address a joint session of Congress on November 27. In many ways Congress was his natural home in Washington; he might seem more at ease speaking there than in the Oval Office, where the memories of Kennedy were so vivid; and the occasion still would permit national coverage by radio and television. The speech clearly reflects the influence of both Kennedy and Johnson writers and has many stylistic elements characteristic of each man.

The key theme of the speech is "continuity." Johnson early on established that he would be a caretaker for the Kennedy program, asserting in his opening line that he did not wish to be in the circumstance in which fate placed him—a particularly telling remark, since he had very much wanted the Presidency in 1960 through the normal means of an election. He stressed the two key items of the Kennedy legislative program, the tax cut and the civil rights bill, and urged that they be passed as memorials to the late President. Harking back to the Kennedy inaugural address with its call, "Let us begin," Johnson closed his speech with the theme, "Let us continue." For anyone who had doubts that the Kennedy efforts would be carried forward, this speech should have provided ample reassurance.

Interestingly, however, the speech also laid the foundation for a positive view of the Johnson Presidency in its own right. Johnson had many choices about how to define continuity, even after resolving to make that his central theme. He could have focused on diplomacy, on retention of personnel, on political symbolism, on his own conduct in the office, or on numerous other dimensions. Johnson, however, focused on continuity as the passage of Kennedy legislation currently before the Congress. In doing so he emphasized his own strength—mastery of congressional procedures and the ability to fashion a compromise and break a deadlock. He also created conditions that would enable critics later to say that he had succeeded with Congress where Kennedy himself had not been able to do so. Even while tying himself to Kennedy, then, the speech subtly permitted Johnson to lay the basis for going beyond Kennedy and earning acclaim in his own right.

The speech has many of the hallmarks of an inaugural address, in its call for unity and its evocation of basic national values. The circumstances of its delivery, however, make it a special inaugural and justify the more specific treatment of legislation and policies, and the explicit—and otherwise overdone—references to continuity in both substance and style.

Mr. Speaker, Mr. President, Members of the House, Members of the Senate, my fellow Americans:—All I have I would have given gladly not to be standing here today.

The greatest leader of our time has been struck down by the foulest deed of our time. Today John Fitzgerald Kennedy lives on in the immortal words and works that he left behind. He lives on in the mind and memories of mankind. He lives on in the hearts of his countrymen.

No words are sad enough to express our sense of loss. No words are strong enough to express our determination to continue the forward thrust of America that he began.

The dream of conquering the vastness of space—the dream of partnership across the Atlantic—and across the Pacific as well—the dream of a Peace Corps in less developed nations—the dream of education for all of our children—the dream of jobs for all who seek them and need them—the dream of care for our elderly—the dream of an all-out attack on mental illness—and above all, the dream of equal rights for all Americans, whatever their race or color—these and other American dreams have been vitalized by his drive and by his dedication.

And now the ideas and the ideals which he so nobly represented must and will be translated into effective action.

Under John Kennedy's leadership, this Nation has demonstrated that it has the courage to seek peace, and it has the fortitude to risk war. We have proved that we are a good and reliable friend to those who seek peace and freedom. We have shown that we can also be a formidable foe to those who reject the path of peace and those who seek to impose upon us or our allies the yoke of tyranny.

This Nation will keep its commitments from South Viet-Nam to West Berlin. We will be unceasing in the search for peace; resourceful in our pursuit of areas of agreement even with those with whom we differ; and generous and loyal to those who join with us in common cause.

In this age when there can be no losers in peace and no victors in war, we must recognize the obligation to match national strength with national restraint. We must be prepared at one and the same time for both the confrontation of power and the limitation of power. We must be ready to defend the national interest and to negotiate the common interest. This is the path that we shall continue to pursue. Those who test our courage will find it strong, and those who seek our friendship will find it honorable. We will demonstrate anew that the strong can be just in the use of strength; and the just can be strong in the defense of justice.

And let all know we will extend no special privilege and impose no persecution. We will carry on the fight against poverty and misery, and disease and ignorance, in other lands and in our own.

We will serve all the Nation, not one section or one sector, or one group, but all Americans. These are the United States—a united people with a united purpose.

Our American unity does not depend upon unanimity. We have differences; but now, as in the past, we can derive from those differences strength, not weakness, wisdom, not despair. Both as a people and a government, we can unite upon a program, a program which is wise and just, enlightened and constructive.

For 32 years Capitol Hill has been my home. I have shared many moments of pride with you, pride in the ability of the Congress of the United States to act, to meet any crisis, to distill from our differences strong programs of national action.

An assassin's bullet has thrust upon me the awesome burden of the Presidency. I am here today to say I need your help; I cannot bear this burden alone. I need the help of all Americans, and all America. This Nation has experienced a profound shock, and in this critical moment, it is our duty, yours and mine, as the Government of the United States, to do away with uncertainty and doubt and delay, and to show that we are capable of decisive action; that from the brutal loss of our leader we will derive not weakness, but strength; that we can and will act and act now.

From this chamber of representative government, let all the world know and none misunderstand that I rededicate this Government to the unswerving support of the United Nations, to the honorable and determined execution of our commitments to our allies, to the maintenance of military strength second to none, to the defense of the strength and the stability of the dollar, to the expansion of our foreign trade, to the reinforcement of our programs of mutual assistance and cooperation in Asia and Africa, and to our Alliance for Progress in this hemisphere.

On the 20th day of January, in 1961, John F. Kennedy told his countrymen that our national work would not be finished "in the first thousand days, nor in the life of this administration, nor even perhaps in our lifetime on this planet. But," he said, "let us begin."

Today, in this moment of new resolve, I would say to all my fellow Americans, let us continue.

This is our challenge—not to hesitate, not to pause, not to turn about and linger over this evil moment, but to continue on our course so that we may fulfill the destiny that history has set for us. Our most immediate tasks are here on this Hill.

First, no memorial oration or eulogy could more eloquently honor President Kennedy's memory than the earliest possible passage of the civil rights bill for which he fought so long. We have talked long enough in this country about equal rights. We have talked for one hundred years or more. It is time now to write the next chapter, and to write it in the books of law.

I urge you again, as I did in 1957 and again in 1960, to enact a civil rights law so that we can move forward to eliminate from this Nation every trace of discrimination and oppression that is based upon race or color. There could be no greater source of strength to this Nation both at home and abroad.

And second, no act of ours could more fittingly continue the work of President Kennedy than the early passage of the tax bill for which he fought all this long year. This is a bill designed to increase our national income and Federal revenues, and to provide insurance against recession. That bill, if passed without delay, means more security for those now working, more jobs for those now without them, and more incentive for our economy.

In short, this is no time for delay. It is a time for action—strong, forward-looking action on the pending education bills to help bring the light of learning to every home and hamlet in America—strong, forward-looking action on youth employment opportunities; strong, forward-looking action on the pending foreign aid bill, making clear that we are not forfeiting our responsibilities to this hemisphere or to the world, nor erasing Executive flexibility in the conduct of our foreign affairs—and strong, prompt, and forward-looking action on the remaining appropriation bills.

In this new spirit of action, the Congress can expect the full cooperation and support of the executive branch. And in particular, I pledge that the expenditures of your Government will be administered with the utmost thrift and frugality. I will insist that the Government get a dollar's value for a dollar spent. The Government will set an example of prudence and economy. This does not mean that we will not meet our unfilled needs or that we will not honor our commitments. We will do both.

As one who has long served in both Houses of the Congress, I firmly believe in the independence and the integrity of the legislative branch. And I promise you that I shall always respect this. It is deep in the marrow of my bones. With equal firmness, I believe in the capacity and I believe in the ability of the Congress, despite the divisions of opinions which characterize our Nation, to act—to act wisely, to act vigorously, to act speedily when the need arises.

The need is here. The need is now. I ask your help.

We meet in grief, but let us also meet in renewed dedication and renewed vigor. Let us meet in action, in tolerance, and in mutual understanding. John Kennedy's death commands what his life conveyed—that America must move forward. The time has come for Americans of all races and creeds and political beliefs to understand and to respect one another. So let us put an end to the teaching and the preaching of hate and evil and violence. Let us turn away from the fanatics of the far left and the far right, from the apostles of bitterness and bigotry, from those defiant of law, and those who pour venom into our Nation's bloodstream.

I profoundly hope that the tragedy and the torment of these terrible days will bind us together in new fellowship, making us one people in our hour of sorrow. So let us here highly resolve that John Fitzgerald Kennedy did not live—or die—in vain. And on this Thanksgiving eve, as we gather together to ask the Lord's blessing, and give Him our thanks, let us unite in those familiar and cherished words:

America, America,
God shed His grace on thee,
And crown they good
With brotherhood
From sea to shining sea.

Lyndon B. Johnson

The Great Society
(May 22, 1964)

The domestic programs of President Lyndon B. Johnson, ranging from Medicare to conservation, are often summarized by the term "Great Society." The term, however, was more than a convenient label. It was a core of concepts that the President articulated in speeches during 1964 and 1965, most prominently in the 1964 commencement speech at the University of Michigan.

Johnson, who felt the need for a slogan to describe his domestic program, had thought of "better deal," no doubt reflecting his own experience as a young New Deal congressman, but he had little success in making the term stick. Beginning in late April 1964, he spoke of "a great society" in at least eight speeches before the Ann Arbor address, but it was this speech—devoted almost entirely to describing the concept—that attracted widespread interest. The speech was crafted deliberately to look to the future instead of the past, to talk about new themes rather than repeat old issues. A university audience was deliberately chosen, not only because it is often the most appropriate for visionary remarks but also because Johnson's experience during the depression had convinced him of the power of youth to reshape the country.

The Ann Arbor speech described cities, countryside, and classrooms as the places where the Great Society would be built. While it enumerated particulars, the speech did not attempt a coherent conceptual definition of the phrase. Such a definition can be gleaned, though, from a series of Johnson speeches during 1964 and 1965. One central theme was a strong emphasis on the quality of life, often in contrast to purely quantitative and materialistic indices of well-being. A society characterized by quality is not overwhelmed by change but seeks actively to shape and direct change. A second theme was the need for special efforts in behalf of individuals and groups who were relatively unaffected by macroeconomic policy—the beginnings of the idea of affirmative action. Finally, the government had a special role to play, as stimulus and guarantor in meeting the other goals. Sensitizing the people to problems and needs was the job of government, and particularly of the President.

Speaking about the Great Society, however, was not just a way for Johnson to coin a phrase or talk expansively about the future; it also responded to specific rhetorical needs. The legislation Johnson sought was of two types. Some, such as Medicare or federal aid to education, had been proposed for years, but each was stymied by failure to resolve a particular troublesome issue. The need was to find symbols that would subsume these disputes and inspire people with a more elaborate view of the future that would make the specific differences seem petty and unimportant. Other measures, such as the War on Poverty and aid to the cities, involved subjects that had no pre-existing base of public support. And, because the ideas were new, there had been no gestation period during which interest groups might mobilize in their support. The need, therefore, was to arouse attention to the problems and to mobilize support for the Johnson programs, and these goals could be achieved through an inspirational vision of the future to which the programs were geared.

It is hard to assess the effect of the Ann Arbor speech in itself, except that it succeeded in calling widespread public attention to the "Great Society" phrase. Taken as a whole, however, Johnson's campaign for the Great Society was immensely successful. The legislation he sought moved through Congress in record time—aid to education within three months, the poverty program within five, and Medicare within six, for example. All told, eighty-nine major domestic bills were passed by the Congress during 1965 alone. And both Johnson and his programs enjoyed widespread public approval during 1964 and 1965.

Few of the Great Society programs, in practice, achieved their promise. Some critics saw the discrepancy between expectation and result as proof that the vision of the Great Society was itself utopian and impractical, a charge that Johnson vigorously denied. The legacy of the Great Society is a mixture of positive achievements and disappointed expectations. To what degree the programs were conceptually flawed, to what degree they were hurt by Johnson's inattention to administrative details, and to what degree they were casualties of underfunding caused by the Vietnam War—all these questions have been matters of disagreement almost since 1964.

President Hatcher, Governor Romney, Senators Mc-Namara and Hart, Congressmen Meader and Staebler, and other members of the fine Michigan delegation, members of the graduating class, my fellow Americans:—It is a great pleasure to be here today. This university has been coeducational since 1870, but I do not believe it was on the basis of your accomplishments that a Detroit high school girl said, "In choosing a college, you first have to decide whether you want a coeducational school or an educational school."

Well, we can find both here at Michigan, although perhaps at different hours.

I came out here today very anxious to meet the Michigan student whose father told a friend of mine that his son's education had been a real value. It stopped his mother from bragging about him.

I have come today from the turmoil of your Capital to the tranquility of your campus to speak about the future of your country.

The purpose of protecting the life of our Nation and preserving the liberty of our citizens is to pursue the happiness of our people. Our success in that pursuit is the test of our success as a Nation.

For a century we labored to settle and to subdue a continent. For half a century we called upon unbounded invention and untiring industry to create an order of plenty for all of our people.

The challenge of the next half century is whether

we have the wisdom to use that wealth to enrich and elevate our national life, and to advance the quality of our American civilization.

Your imagination, your initiative, and your indignation will determine whether we build a society where progress is the servant of our needs, or a society where old values and new visions are buried under unbridled growth. For in your time we have the opportunity to move not only toward the rich society and the powerful society, but upward to the Great Society.

The Great Society rests on abundance and liberty for all. It demands an end to poverty and racial injustice, to which we are totally committed in our time. But that is just the beginning.

The Great Society is a place where every child can find knowledge to enrich his mind and to enlarge his talents. It is a place where leisure is a welcome chance to build and reflect, not a feared cause of boredom and restlessness. It is a place where the city of man serves not only the needs of the body and the demands of commerce but the desire for beauty and the hunger for community.

It is a place where man can renew contact with nature. It is a place which honors creation for its own sake and for what it adds to the understanding of the race. It is a place where men are more concerned with the quality of their goals than the quantity of their goods.

But most of all, the Great Society is not a safe harbor, a resting place, a final objective, a finished work. It is a challenge constantly renewed, beckoning us toward a destiny where the meaning of our lives matches the marvelous products of our labor.

So I want to talk to you today about three places where we begin to build the Great Society—in our cities, in our countryside, and in our classrooms.

Many of you will live to see the day, perhaps 50 years from now, when there will be 400 million Americans—four-fifths of them in urban areas. In the remainder of this century urban population will double, city land will double, and we will have to build homes, highways, and facilities equal to all those built since this country was first settled. So in the next 40 years we must rebuild the entire urban United States.

Aristotle said: "Men come together in cities in order to live, but they remain together in order to live the good life." It is harder and harder to live the good life in American cities today.

The catalog of ills is long: there is the decay of the centers and the despoiling of the suburbs. There is not enough housing for our people or transportation for our traffic. Open land is vanishing and old landmarks are violated.

Worst of all, expansion is eroding the precious and time honored values of community with neighbors and communion with nature. The loss of these values breeds loneliness and boredom and indifference.

Our society will never be great until our cities are great. Today the frontier of imagination and innovation is inside those cities and not beyond their borders.

New experiments are already going on. It will be the task of your generation to make the American city a place where future generations will come, not only to live but to live the good life.

I understand that if I stayed here tonight I would see that Michigan students are really doing their best to live the good life.

This is the place where the Peace Corps was started. It is inspiring to see how all of you, while you are in this country, are trying so hard to live at the level of the people.

A second place where we begin to build the Great Society is in our countryside. We have always prided ourselves on being not only America the strong and America the free, but America the beautiful. Today that beauty is in danger. The water we drink, the food we eat, the very air that we breathe, are threatened with pollution. Our parks are overcrowded, our seashores overburdened. Green fields and dense forests are disappearing.

A few years ago we were greatly concerned about the "Ugly American." Today we must act to prevent an ugly America.

For once the battle is lost, once our natural splendor is destroyed, it can never be recaptured. And once man can no longer walk with beauty or wonder at nature his spirit will wither and his sustenance be wasted.

A third place to build the Great Society is in the classrooms of America. There your children's lives will be shaped. Our society will not be great until every young mind is set free to scan the farthest reaches of thought and imagination. We are still far from that goal.

Today, 8 million adult Americans, more than the entire population of Michigan, have not finished 5 years of school. Nearly 20 million have not finished 8 years of school. Nearly 54 million—more than one-quarter of all America—have not even finished high school.

Each year more than 100,000 high school graduates, with proved ability, do not enter college because they cannot afford it. And if we cannot educate today's youth, what will we do in 1970 when elementary school enrollment will be 5 million greater than 1960? And high school enrollment will rise by 5 million. College enrollment will increase by more than 3 million.

In many places, classrooms are overcrowded and curricula are outdated. Most of our qualified teachers are underpaid, and many of our paid teachers are unqualified. So we must give every child a place to sit and a teacher to learn from. Poverty must not be a bar to learning, and learning must offer an escape from poverty.

But more classrooms and more teachers are not enough. We must seek an educational system which grows in excellence as it grows in size. This means better training for our teachers. It means preparing youth to enjoy their hours of leisure as well as their hours of labor. It means exploring new techniques of teaching, to find new ways to stimulate the love of learning and the capacity for creation.

These are three of the central issues of the Great Society. While our Government has many programs directed at those issues, I do not pretend that we have the full answer to those problems.

But I do promise this: We are going to assemble the best thought and the broadest knowledge from all over the world to find those answers for America. I intend to establish working groups to prepare a series of White House conferences and meetings—on the cities, on natural beauty, on the quality of education, and on other emerging challenges. And from these meetings and from this inspiration and from these studies we will begin to set our course toward the Great Society.

The solution to these problems does not rest on a massive program in Washington, nor can it rely solely on the strained resources of local authority. They require us to create new concepts of cooperation, a creative federalism, between the National Capital and the leaders of local communities.

Woodrow Wilson once wrote: "Every man sent out from his university should be a man of his Nation as well as a man of his time."

Within your lifetime powerful forces, already loosed, will take us toward a way of life beyond the realm of our experience, almost beyond the bounds of our imagination.

For better or for worse, your generation has been appointed by history to deal with those problems and to lead America toward a new age. You have the chance never before afforded to any people in any age. You can help build a society where the demands of morality, and the needs of the spirit, can be realized in the life of the Nation.

So, will you join in the battle to give every citizen the full equality which God enjoins and the law requires, whatever his belief, or race, or the color of his skin?

Will you join in the battle to give every citizen an escape from the crushing weight of poverty?

Will you join in the battle to make it posssible for all nations to live in enduring peace—as neighbors and not as mortal enemies?

Will you join in the battle to build the Great Society, to prove that our material progress is only the foundation on which we will build a richer life of mind and spirit?

There are those timid souls who say this battle cannot be won; that we are condemned to a soulless wealth. I do not agree. We have the power to shape the civilization that we want. But we need your will, your labor, your hearts, if we are to build that kind of society.

Those who came to this land sought to build more than just a new country. They sought a new world. So I have come here today to your campus to say that you can make their vision our reality. So let us from this moment begin our work so that in the future men will look back and say: It was then, after a long and weary way, that man turned the exploits of his genius to the full enrichment of his life.

Thank you. Goodby.

Everett M. Dirksen

Nominating Speech for Barry Goldwater
(July 15, 1964)

Normally, the nominating speech at a national political convention is given by someone who is a strong and long-time supporter of the nominee. The speech is effusive in its praise of the candidate's personal qualities, his or her ability to deal with the issues of the day, and the assurance that he or she can defeat the candidate of the opposition party in the coming election. Virtues are magnified and blemishes ignored. The speech is not marked by temporizing or doubt.

In the face of these normal expectations, Republicans in 1964 faced an unusual situation. It was clear that the nomination would be won by Arizona senator Barry Goldwater, and equally clear that Goldwater was opposed by a large segment of the Republican party—either because people disagreed with his principles, or believed that he could not be elected, or both. Goldwater enjoyed strong, almost fanatical support among the newly emerging Republican middle-class voters in the South and West. But he had taken many unpopular positions both in the campaign and in the Senate, and these hurt his standing among the general electorate.

Goldwater had voted against the nuclear test ban treaty, against the 1964 tax cut, against the War on Poverty, against the Civil Rights Act of 1964, and against a motion to close debate to end the Southern filibuster that was blocking a vote on the Civil Rights Act. He could be credibly accused of having cast votes that threatened race relations, economic growth, and peace.

The nominating speech was to be delivered by Senate minority leader Everett McKinley Dirksen of Illinois, a strong partisan and loyalist as much to the party as to the nominee. Dirksen had his own disagreements with Goldwater. The minority leader had supported both the test ban treaty and the Civil Rights Act, for example, and had delivered Republican votes that had helped to pass both. He could hardly endorse Goldwater's stands on these important measures. He particularly feared that Goldwater's vote against the Civil Rights Act would harm the party in appealing to black voters. In an attempt to control the damage, Dirksen had worked to include in the party platform a plank pledging strong enforcement of that law.

Stripped of many of the usual appeals found in a nominating speech, then, Dirksen had to employ his skills of rhetorical invention to determine what approaches would be persuasive. The speech reflects his two dominant choices. First, he emphasized the virtues of the party, believing it to be more popular than the candidate. He tried to rally the faithful against succumbing to their own doubts or giving in to defeatism, and he appealed for party harmony. These sections of the speech were attempts to hold Republicans who considered defecting or who were convinced that the nomination was political suicide. Second, Dirksen emphasized those personal qualities of Goldwater that he thought would be appealing. Like a lawyer selecting the best arguments to include in his brief, Dirksen stressed Goldwater's courage in being willing to take unpopular positions, his conviction in upholding them, his integrity and conscience, and his unwavering devotion to constitutional principles as he understood them. This appeal attempts to transcend specific issue positions to emphasize traits of mind and character that Americans would value in a President. Along the way, Dirksen also tried to explain several of the questionable statements Goldwater had made, but this aspect of the speech was probably less successful.

This speech is significant not primarily for its historical value. Dirksen's words are not well remembered; what is recalled is that he was the loyal supporter of his party. Goldwater went down to one of the biggest electoral defeats in history, and in its wake many of his principles seemed to have been repudiated. Rather, the speech is important because it illustrates how a gifted rhetor finds the available appeals in a situation in which he is severely constrained and the normal conventions do not apply.

My friend and colleague Senator Morton, delegates, alternates, Republicans, and fellow countrymen:—In a few days, we shall return home. We shall have had the energizing fellowship of a spirited national convention. We shall carry with us the set of principles we have adopted, declaring where we stand. We shall have selected the leaders to command our forces. We shall be prepared to march to victory.

Let neither doubt nor defeatism impair our forces and our strength. Beyond the rough terrain of the intervening months lies the sweet, green valley of victory and that valley can be ours.

In this spirit, let me tell you briefly about a man. He is the grandson of a peddler, a peddler who was a proud, honorable and spirited man who left his ancestral home in Europe at an early age and came to this land a century ago. He arrived nine years before the Civil War—in 1852. Almost immediately he set across the nation to make a home on the hardy Frontier of the Far West. There he peddled his wares among the mining and lumber camps and the peoples of that western land. There were then but 31 states in the Union. There he eventually gained renown as a merchant and frontier leader and it is of his grandson I would speak to you. His name is Barry Goldwater.

I want to speak of him as the Whole Man moving toward whatever destiny may provide. There is today a strange and destructive cynicism which has fastened itself upon our thinking. It may be a kind of sadistic sport to hear a statement by one who marches at the head of the parade and then unleash some seemingly contrary sentiment which he may have uttered ten years before and to assail him for inconsistency. Our appraisal of the individual so often becomes fragmented instead of thinking of the whole man, impelled by conviction to say or do what at the moment should be said or done. Quoting only a part of what a man has said has become a favorite indoor sport. By this standard of appraisal, the man never lived, and the hero was never born who by singling out some vote, some utterance, some opinion cannot be crucified upon the cross erected by the cynics. It is time that in the larger and more tolerant spirit, we consider the whole man, his life, his actions, his works and his attributes measured against the problems, duties, and responsibilities which loom upon the horizon both at home and abroad.

Consider the moral COURAGE of this humble peddler's grandson, Barry Goldwater. When a poll was taken some years ago to select five former Senators whose portraits might adorn the unfilled ovals in the Senate reception room, those who participated selected Henry Clay and John C. Calhoun, Daniel Webster and Robert Marion LaFollette and Robert A. Taft. Their common attribute was courage in facing the challenges of their day and time. Each took to heart the thunderous admonition of the Lord to Joshua as he took command of that ancient host: "Have I not commanded thee. Be strong and of good courage. Be not afraid, neither be thou dismayed."

Already in 12 short years in the United States Senate, Barry Goldwater has repeatedly cast votes that won him no applause, that gained him nothing politically, that did nothing more than show the man's blazing courage in refusing to take the easy paths already so heavily trafficked by some of his colleagues.

In the days and years ahead, as we assess the fevers which beset us abroad and the problems which afflict us at home, it will take courage of a high order to make the decisions and to withstand the multitude if it beckon one on to an unsound course. The peddler's grandson has courage, and it is but a part of the whole man.

He is a man of CONSCIENCE. How commonly we think of conscience as the still small accusing voice to persuade the individual that a certain act or course of conduct is morally wrong. The true sensitive conscience does not wait until the act is about to be committed or the course of conduct is to be followed. It is always there to monitor the morals, the conduct, the actions of any man. It is like a fixed star in the firmament to light the way. What is deemed snap judgment is more often than not a judgment directed by an acute conscience which can operate faster than reason. And whether it be in the domain of peace or war, in rearmament or the scrapping of weapons, in domestic policy or internal security, conscience can be an unfailing guide. The peddler's grandson has a conscience to chart his course and when he committed the fruit of conscience to paper in a book called *The Conscience of a Conservative* four years ago, more than 2 1/2 million copies were sold—an incredible testament to the interest of the American people. Conscience is another indelible part of the whole man.

Whether in commerce or finance, in business or industry, in private or public service, there is such a thing as COMPETENCE. What is it but the right vision, the right touch, in the right way, at the right time? What man could be a jet pilot without this touch? But Barry Goldwater has demonstrated it over and over in his every activity. As Chief of Staff of his state National Guard, he brought about its desegration shortly after World War II and long before Civil Rights became a burning issue. He brought integration to his own retail enterprises. For his own employees he established the 5-day week and a health and life insurance plan. All this was done without fanfare or the marching of bands. My friends, in an age of self-congratulating Do-Gooders, Barry Goldwater stands out as a Good-Doer, and what a breath of fresh air that is! Yes, the grandson of that peddler who came to this land 112 years ago has demonstrated his competence in many fields.

In an age when gratitude is scant for services rendered, we so often overlook the CONTRIBUTION of time and effort which a man makes to his Party. Yet the whole man must be judged by his fidelity to his Party and his willingness to go forth and assist in making it a vital instrument. From the moment he came to the United States Senate more than 12 years ago until this good hour, I can name no man in the Republican Party who day after day, year after year has applied his talents and his zeal to the Republican cause as the grandson of that peddler. No weather was too foul, no journey too long, no sacrifice too great to take him forth on a mission for his Party and its candidates. He has raised money, he has made speeches and he has rallied organization support. And I ask you: Who will forget his great speech, in an hour dark for his supporters, to the 1960 Republican National Convention calling on them and all Republicans to help the Party unite? And who will forget his 126 speeches in 26 states in the next three months in support of the Nixon-Lodge ticket. I haven't forgotten it and I know you haven't either.

In my office is a set of silver spurs, mounted on a plaque as a token of appreciation for service to the Party. I doubt that I deserve them or the generous inscription on that plaque. As for the grandson of that peddler of long ago, surely he merits spurs of gold for the immeasurable effort, energy and sacrifice which he has devoted to his Party and to the espousal of Republican gospel. Yes, cheerful contribution has been one of the shining graces of this man and it has been performed with a spirit of dedication in his heart.

All of us were raised to love our COUNTRY, to take pride in its glorious history, and to defend it with our lives if necessary. We call it patriotism, a word once revered by all. Today it is the fashion of our critics to sneer at patriotism, to label positions of strength as extremism, to find other nation's points of view right more often than our own. Perhaps too long the bugles have sounded retreat in our relations with other lands.

Our diplomatic representative in Zanzibar is hustled to a dock at bayonet point and told to leave. Our embassy flag in Ghana is hauled down and desecrated. A nation like Panama, which would not exist today but for the United States, can abuse us with impunity. A bearded communist in Cuba can revile and insult us and confiscate the property of our citizens. There is such a thing as going the first mile and even the second mile of forebearance and tolerance but there is also such a thing as a Nation's honor and prestige and the rights of her citizens. Twenty centuries ago, the Apostle Paul needed but to say to the Roman Captain of the Guard when he was about to be scourged that he was a free-born Roman Citizen and immediately they loosed the thongs with which he was bound. We have come far since then. But why today are indignities so freely hurled at us as a nation, against our people, and against our flag? What, oh what, has become of that vital thrill, that pride in being an American? We heard so much about American prestige in the 1960 campaign. It was a phony issue then, but what a real issue it has become in four short years! The time is here for America to retrieve its self-respect. I believe that through firmness, through the sure hand, Barry Goldwater, the grandson of that immigrant frontier peddler, could retrieve it. This is part of the Whole Man.

Could there be a more devoted person to the CONSTITUTION than Barry Goldwater, the peddler's grandson? That document not only created the balanced structure of our government but became our charter of freedom as well. Barry Goldwater's grandfather could come here 112 years ago and share its protection and its benefits along with all others—the rich, the mighty, the poor, the humble. It has been the central core of Republican gospel. One hundred years ago, the Republican Party met in Baltimore, Maryland to re-

nominate Lincoln and adopt the platform of 1864. The very first pledge in that platform reads, "Resolved that it is the highest duty of every American citizen to maintain against all their enemies, the integrity of the Union and the permanent authority of the Constitution and laws of the United States." Today, no person can sit in the United States Senate without first holding up his hand and swearing before God that he "will support and defend the Constitution of the United States" and that he will bear true faith and allegiance to it.

But is the Constitution anything more than words on parchment until the human touch is applied and the minds of men indicate what it means? Seldom does a day go by but what some individual clothed in judicial robes sets forth his view of what it means as he interprets an ordinance, a resolution, an administrative order or a statute. Is it not proper that a legislator who has sworn to uphold and defend it and bear true faith to it is entitled to his own view whether any measure before the Congress squares with his estimate of the Constitution?

So it was that Barry Goldwater, grandson of an immigrant peddler, took his stand on the constitutionality of certain provisions in the most controversial law of the 1960's and in so doing, exhibited that quality of moral courage which has won him the admiration of the citizens of this land whether they agree with him or not. For a lifetime, with high fidelity, he has carried out his oath as a soldier and a Senator. With equal fidelity Barry Goldwater would discharge his Presidential oath to enforce and execute all the laws of the land.

We come then to one last consideration as we contemplate the courage, the conscience, the competence, the contribution to party service, the pride in country, the Constitutional devotion of Barry Goldwater, the grandson of an immigrant peddler. That consideration is the opportunity for an ideological CHOICE for the Republican Party and for the country.

For 20 years, the controversy on the conservative position has hovered over our Party like a menacing spectre. Simply expressed, it has meant that, like Bismarck whose Federated Germany withered away, like Britain's almost nonexistent Liberal Party, we should give an inch here, a foot there, and finally a mile to the socialist philosophy that has already debilitated three-fourths of the world.

Gradually the enervating effect of this divisive philosophy has become quite noticeable. Those strongly wedded to Republican policy and conservatism began to sit on their hands on election day or take a walk.

Others, perceiving no marked difference between the two parties came to take the ADA version of socialism straight. Still others, with high and fervent hopes, felt that this philosophical cleavage would be healed by the gentle hands of time; that complete unity of purpose and action would be restored; that with banners unfurled and trumpets sounding a common note we could inscribe the iridescent "V" of Victory upon our Republican shields once more.

But even as Paul of old wrote "For if the trumpet give an uncertain sound, who shall prepare himself to the battle?" So today in this convention there is a chance to make a choice. Ask yourselves: Why is it that this man, who so certainly has sounded the call to CONSERVATISM, should be subjected to the abuse which has been heaped upon him? Is it because he offers a choice, a clear-cut choice, that the Democratic Party, as now constituted, doesn't dare face? Is it because there is a fear that the American people, in their traditional sense of fair play, are beginning to grasp the truth this man utters? Delegates to this Convention, the tide is turning! Let's give it a chance.

With the platform as our chart and compass and with the militant son of an immigrant peddler as our leader, let's give 190 million Americans the choice they have been waiting for. Let's place before our people the cause of a Party which was born to preserve the Union, to save Constitutional government, and to keep government the servant and not the master of the people. Let's rededicate ourselves and our nation to those goals. It is in that spirit that I nominate my friend and colleague, Barry Goldwater of Arizona, to be the Republican candidate for President of the United States.

Barry Goldwater

Nomination Acceptance Speech
(July 16, 1964)

Richard Nixon had two major rivals for the 1960 Presidential nomination. Although neither man pressed his case all the way to the convention balloting, both Nelson Rockefeller and Barry Goldwater had challenged the Vice President. The two challengers respectively symbolized the liberal and conservative wings of the Republican party. Among Nixon's virtues in 1960 was that he was perceived as a centrist, able to bridge the ideological chasm represented by Rockefeller and Goldwater. Although he declined their support, Goldwater was endorsed by several of the Southern delegates. Rockefeller withdrew in 1960 in return for concessions made by Nixon with respect to the party platform.

After his narrow defeat at the hands of John F. Kennedy, Nixon sought a political comeback by running for the governorship of California in 1962. His defeat for that office humiliated him, seemingly ending his political career (he told the press, "You won't have Nixon to kick around anymore") and definitely removing him from the list of Republican contenders for 1964. It appeared that the battle for the nomination would be between Rockefeller and Goldwater, and that it would be an ideological struggle for the soul of the party.

Based on public opinion polls, Rockefeller initially had the upper hand. Goldwater was regarded as too extreme a conservative for the mainstream of Republican voters, and Rockefeller was thought able to attract support from independents and Democrats as well as moderate Republicans. Much of his lead evaporated, however, with his announcement that he was divorcing his wife of many years and with his subsequent remarriage. Even in the early 1960's, these quick and abrupt changes in marital relationship somehow called into question the stability of judgment needed in a President.

Kennedy had hoped to run for re-election against Goldwater. Although they were personal friends, the President hoped that the election would put to rest the right-wing threat to his administration, which had required that he proceed cautiously with his own programs. Goldwater's standing increased during the fall of 1963 and it seemed that Kennedy might get his wish. After the assassination, Lyndon Johnson especially courted business and captured some of the traditionally conservative vote. His accession renewed Republican interest in a moderate candidate—if not Rockefeller, then someone else. Henry Cabot Lodge, the American ambassador to South Vietnam and 1960 Vice Presidential candidate, made a surprisingly strong showing in the early primaries. Governor William Scranton of Pennsylvania was also considered. Rockefeller won the Oregon primary and threatened Goldwater in California.

A number of incautious statements during the primary campaign hurt Goldwater. He proposed selling the Tennessee Valley Authority, jeopardizing the availability of inexpensive electric power for many in the South. He urged that Social Security be made voluntary, threatening the income of many of the elderly. He advocated the use of atomic weapons to defoliate the jungles of Vietnam. In Europe, he would give to field commanders the authority to use nuclear weapons. He once stated that the Eastern seaboard should be sawed off and floated out to sea. In addition, he opposed both the test ban treaty and the Civil Rights Act.

The embarrassing public statements made Goldwater seem vulnerable, but he had been assiduously courting convention delegates at the grass-roots level. His organization was superior, and he amassed large numbers of delegates, often not selected by primaries, who were committed to him. His narrow victory in the California primary in June virtually assured him the nomination.

An acceptance speech normally serves to conciliate the defeated opponents, reunite the party, and inspire heightened effort with a vision of success in the fall campaign. But Goldwater's 1964 acceptance address did not conform to these expectations. It was an ideological statement of his own position, a strong attack against big government, and it took little notice of his Republican opponents. It is best remembered for the lines, "Extremism in the defense of liberty is no vice" and "Moderation in the pursuit of justice is no virtue." In themselves these statements are commendable, but in the context of 1964 they signaled rejection of the mainstream politics of coalition and compromise.

Goldwater went down to disastrous defeat in the fall election; Lyndon Johnson won the greatest percentage of the popular vote in history and the Congress was more than two-thirds Democratic. But the Republican party recovered quickly from defeat, and won the Presidency not only in 1968 but in five of the next six elections. And many of the ideas Goldwater espoused—though not the eccentric ones that marked his campaign—came into the mainstream in the 1980's, during the Presidency of Ronald Reagan.

My good friend and great Republican, Dick Nixon and your charming wife, Pat; my running mate—that wonderful Republican who has served us so well for so long—Bill Miller and his wife, Stephanie; to Thruston Morton, who's done such a commendable job in chairmaning this convention; to Mr. Herbert Hoover who I hope is watching, and to the great American and his wife, General and Mrs. Eisenhower. To my own wife, my family, and to all of my fellow Republicans here assembled, and Americans across this great nation:— From this moment, united and determined, we will go forward together dedicated to the ultimate and undeniable greatness of the whole man.

Together we will win.

I accept your nomination with a deep sense of humility. I accept, too, the responsibility that goes with it, and I seek your continued help and your continued guidance. My fellow Republicans, our cause is too great for any man to feel worthy of it. Our task would be too great for any man did he not have with him the heart and the hands of this great Republican party.

And I promise you tonight that every fibre of my being is consecrated to our cause, that nothing shall be lacking from the struggle that can be brought to it by enthusiasm, by devotion and plain hard work.

In this world no person, no party can guarantee anything, but what we can do and what we shall do is to deserve victory and victory will be ours. The Good Lord raised this mighty Republican, Republic to be a home for the brave and to flourish as the land of the free—not to stagnate in the swampland of collectivism, not to cringe before the bully of Communism.

Now my fellow Americans, the tide has been running against freedom. Our people have followed false prophets. We must, and we shall return to proven ways—not because they are old, but because they are true.

We must, and we shall, set the tide running again in the cause of freedom. And this party, with its every action, every word, every breath and every heart beat, has but a single resolve, and that is freedom.

Freedom made orderly for this nation by our constitutional government. Freedom under a government limited by laws of nature and of nature's God. Freedom balanced so that order lacking liberty will not become the slavery of the prison cell; balanced so that liberty lacking order will not become the license of the mob and of the jungle.

Now, we Americans understand freedom, we have earned it; we have lived for it, and we have died for it. This nation and its people are freedom's models in a searching world. We can be freedom's missionaries in a doubting world.

But, ladies and gentlemen, first we must renew freedom's mission in our own hearts and in our own homes.

During four futile years the Administration which we shall replace has distorted and lost that faith. It has talked and talked and talked and talked the words of freedom but it has failed and failed and failed in the works of freedom.

Now failure cements the wall of shame in Berlin; failures blot the sands of shame at the Bay of Pigs; failures marked the slow death of freedom in Laos; failures infest the jungles of Vietnam, and failures haunt the houses of our once great alliances and undermine the greatest bulwark ever erected by free nations, the NATO community.

Failures proclaim lost leadership, obscure purpose, weakening wills and the risk of inciting our sworn enemies to new aggressions and to new excesses.

And because of this Administration we are tonight a world divided. We are a nation becalmed. We have lost the brisk pace of diversity and the genius of individual creativity. We are plodding along at a pace set by centralized planning, red tape, rules without responsibility and regimentation without recourse.

Rather than useful jobs in our country, people have been offered bureaucratic make-work; rather than moral leadership, they have been given bread and circuses; they have been given spectacles, and yes, they've even been given scandals.

Tonight there is violence in our streets, corruption in our highest offices, aimlessness among our youth, anxiety among our elderly, and there's a virtual despair among the many who look beyond material success toward the inner meaning of their lives. And where examples of morality should be set, the opposite is seen. Small men seeking great wealth or power have too often and too long turned even the highest levels of public service into mere personal opportunity.

Now, certainly simple honesty is not too much to demand of men in government. We find it in most. Republicans demand it from everyone.

They demand it from everyone no matter how exalted or protected his position might be.

The growing menace in our country tonight, to personal safety, to life, to limb and property, in homes, in churches, on the playgrounds and places of business, particularly in our great cities, is the mounting concern or should be of every thoughtful citizen in the United States. Security from domestic violence, no less than from foreign aggression, is the most elementary and fundamental purpose of any government, and a government that cannot fulfill this purpose is one than cannot long command the loyalty of its citizens.

History shows us, demonstrates that nothing, nothing prepares the way for tyranny more than the failure of public officials to keep the streets safe from bullies and marauders.

Now we Republicans see all this as more—much more—than the result of mere political differences, or mere political mistakes. We see this as the result of a fundamentally and absolutely wrong view of man, his nature and his destiny.

Those who seek to live your lives for you, to take your liberty in return for relieving you of yours; those who elevate the state and downgrade the citizen, must see ultimately a world in which earthly power can be substituted for Divine Will. And this nation was founded upon the rejection of that notion and upon the acceptance of God as the author of freedom.

Now those who seek absolute power, even though they seek it to do what they regard as good, are simply demanding the right to enforce their own version of heaven on earth, and let me remind you they are the very ones who always create the most hellish tyranny.

Absolute power does corrupt, and those who seek it must be suspect and must be opposed. Their mistaken course stems from false notions, ladies and gentlemen, of equality. Equality, rightly understood as our founding fathers understood it, leads to liberty and to the emancipation of creative differences; wrongly understood, as it has been so tragically in our time, it leads first to conformity and then to despotism.

Fellow Republicans, it is the cause of Republicanism to resist concentrations of power, private or public, which enforce such conformity and inflict such despotism.

It is the cause of Republicanism to insure that power remains in the hands of the people—and, so help us God, that is exactly what a Republican President will do with the help of a Republican Congress.

It is further the cause of Republicanism to restore a clear understanding of the tyranny of man over man in the world at large. It is our cause to dispel the foggy thinking which avoids hard decisions in the delusion that a world of conflict will somehow resolve itself into a world of harmony, if we just don't rock the boat or irritate the forces of aggression—and this is hogwash.

It is, further, the cause of Republicanism to remind ourselves, and the world, that only the strong can remain free; that only the strong can keep the peace.

Now I needn't remind you, or my fellow Americans regardless of party, that Republicans have shouldered this hard responsibility and marched in this cause before. It was Republican leadership under Dwight Eisenhower that kept the peace, and passed along to this Administration the mightiest arsenal for defense the world has ever known.

And I needn't remind you that it was the strength and the believable will of the Eisenhower years that kept the peace by using our strength, by using it in the Formosa Strait, and in Lebanon, and by showing it courageously at all times.

It was during those Republican years that the thrust of Communist imperialism was blunted. It was during those years of Republican leadership that this world moved closer not to war but closer to peace than at any other time in the last three decades.

And I needn't remind you, but I will, that it's been during Democratic years that our strength to deter war has been stilled and even gone into a planned decline. It has been during Democratic years that we have weakly stumbled into conflicts, timidly refusing to draw our own lines against aggression, deceitfully refusing to tell even our own people of our full participation and tragically letting our finest men die on battlefields unmarked by purpose, unmarked by pride or the prospect of victory.

Yesterday it was Korea; tonight it is Vietnam. Make no bones of this. Don't try to sweep this under the rug. We are at war in Vietnam. And yet the President, who is the Commander in Chief of our forces, refuses to say, refuses to say mind you, whether or not the objective over there is victory, and his Secretary of Defense continues to mislead and misinform the American people and enough of it has gone by.

And I needn't remind you, but I will, it has been during Democratic years that a billion persons were cast into communist captivity and their fate cynically sealed.

Today—today in our beloved country we have an Administration which seems eager to deal with Communism in every coin known—from gold to wheat; from consulates to confidence, and even human freedom itself.

Now the Republican cause demands that we brand Communism as the principal disturber of peace in the world today. Indeed, we should brand it as the only significant disturber of the peace. And we must make clear that until its goals of conquest are absolutely renounced, and its relations with all nations tempered, Communism and the governments it now controls are enemies of every man on earth who is or wants to be free.

Now, we here in America can keep the peace only if we remain vigilant, and only if we remain strong. Only if we keep our eyes open and keep our guard up can we prevent war.

And I want to make this abundantly clear—I don't intend to let peace or freedom be torn from our grasp because of lack of strength, or lack of will—and that I promise you Americans.

I believe that we must look beyond the defense of freedom today to its extension tomorrow. I believe that the Communism which boasts it will bury us will instead give way to the forces of freedom. And I can see in the distant and yet recognizable future the outlines of a world worthy of our dedication, our every risk, our every effort, our every sacrifice along the way. Yes, a world that will redeem the suffering of those who will be liberated from tyranny.

I can see, and I suggest that all thoughtful men must contemplate, the flowering of an Atlantic civilization, the whole world of Europe reunified and free, trading openly across its borders, communicating openly across the world.

This is a goal far, far more meaningful than a moon shot.

It's a truly inspiring goal for all free men to set for themselves during the latter half of the twentieth century. I can see and all free men must thrill to the events of this Atlantic civilization joined by a straight ocean highway to the United States. What a destiny! What a destiny can be ours to stand as a great central pillar linking Europe, the Americas and the venerable and vital peoples and cultures of the Pacific.

I can see a day when all the Americas—North and South—will be linked in a mighty system—a system in which the errors and misunderstandings of the past will be submerged one by one in a rising tide of prosperity and interdependence.

We know that the misunderstandings of centuries are not to be wiped away in a day or wiped away in an hour. But we pledge, we pledge, that human sympathy—what our neighbors to the South call an attitude of sympatico—no less than enlightened self-interest will be our guide.

And I can see this Atlantic civilization galvanizing and guiding emergent nations everywhere. Now I know this freedom is not the fruit of every soil. I know that our own freedom was achieved through centuries by unremitting efforts by brave and wise men. And I know that the road to freedom is a long and a challenging road, and I know also that some men may walk away from it, that some men resist challenge, accepting the false security of governmental paternalism.

And I pledge that the America I envision in the years ahead will extend its hand in help in teaching and in cultivation so that all new nations will be at least encouraged to go our way; so that they will not wander down the dark alleys of tyranny or to the deadend streets of collectivism.

My fellow Republicans, we do no man a service by hiding freedom's light under a bushel of mistaken humility.

I seek an America proud of its past, proud of its ways, proud of its dreams and determined actively to proclaim them. But our examples to the world must, like charity, begin at home.

In our vision of a good and decent future, free and peaceful, there must be room, room for the liberation of the energy and the talent of the individual, otherwise our vision is blind at the outset.

We must assure a society here which while never abandoning the needy, or forsaking the helpless, nurtures incentives and opportunity for the creative and the productive.

We must know the whole good is the product of many single contributions. And I cherish the day when our children once again will restore as heroes the sort of men and women who, unafraid and undaunted, pursue the truth, strive to cure disease, subdue and make fruitful our natural environment, and produce the inventive engines of production, science and technology.

This nation, whose creative people have enhanced this entire span of history, should again thrive upon the greatness of all those things which we—we as individual citizens—can and should do.

During Republican years, this again will be a nation of men and women, of families proud of their role, jealous of their responsibilities, unlimited in their aspirations—a nation where all who can will be self-reliant.

We Republicans see in our constitutional form of government the great framework which assures the orderly but dynamic fulfillment of the whole man, and we see the whole man as the great reason for instituting orderly government in the first place.

We can see in private property and in economy based upon and fostering private property the one way to make government a durable ally of the whole man rather than his determined enemy.

We see in the sanctity of private property the only durable foundation for constitutional government in a free society.

And beyond that we see and cherish diversity of ways, diversity of thoughts, of motives, and accomplishments. We don't seek to live anyone's life for him. We only seek to secure his rights, guarantee him opportunity, guarantee him opportunity to strive with government performing only those needed and constitutionally sanctioned tasks which cannot otherwise be performed.

We, Republicans, seek a government that attends to its inherent responsibilities of maintaining a stable monetary and fiscal climate, encouraging a free and a competitive economy and enforcing law and order.

Thus do we seek inventiveness, diversity and creative difference within a stable order, for we Republicans define governments role where needed at many, many levels, preferably though the one closest to the people involved: our towns and our cities, then our counties, then our states then our regional contacts and only then the national government.

That, let me remind you, is the land of liberty built by decentralized power. On it also we must have balance between the branches of government at every level.

Balance, diversity, creative difference—these are the elements of Republican equation. Republicans agree, Republicans agree heartily, to disagree on many, many of their applications. But we have never disagreed on the basic fundamental issues of why you and I are Republicans.

This is a party—this Republican party is a party for free men. Not for blind followers and not for conformists.

Back in 1858 Abraham Lincoln said this of the Republican party, and I quote him because he probably could have said it during the last week or so: "It was composed of strained, discordant, and even hostile elements." End of quote.

Yet all of these elements agreed on one paramount objective: to arrest the progress of slavery, and place it in the course of ultimate extinction.

Today, as then, but more urgently and more broadly than then, the task of preserving and enlarging freedom at home and of safeguarding it from the forces of tyranny abroad is great enough to challenge all our resources and to require all our strength.

Anyone who joins us in all sincerity we welcome. Those, those who do not care for our cause, we don't expect to enter our ranks in any case. And let our Republicanism so focused and so dedicated not be made fuzzy and futile by unthinking and stupid labels.

I would remind you that extremism in the defense of liberty is no vice.

And let me remind you also that moderation in the pursuit of justice is no virtue!

By the beauty of the very system, we Republicans are pledged to restore and revitalize, the beauty of this Federal system of ours is in its reconciliation of diversity with unity. We must not see malice in honest differences of opinion, and no matter how great, so long as they are not inconsistent with the pledges we have given to each other in and through our Constitution.

Our Republican cause is not to level out the world or make its people conform in computer-regimented sameness. Our Republican cause is to free our people and light the way for liberty throughout the world. Ours is a very human cause for very humane goals. This party, its good people, and unquestionable devotion to freedom will not fulfill the purposes of this campaign which we launch here now until our cause has won the day, inspired the world, and shown the way to a tomorrow worthy of all our yesteryears.

I repeat, I accept your nomination with humbleness, with pride and you and I are going to fight for the goodness of our land. Thank you.

Richard M. Nixon

Welfare Reform
(August 8, 1969)

Until the depression of the 1930's, welfare was primarily a private responsibility, with assistance from state and local governments. This approach collapsed under the weight of the emergency. The New Deal sponsored the Federal Emergency Relief Act, but Franklin Roosevelt wanted to replace the dole with a combination of employment and training programs for those in the work force, and social insurance to anticipate and prepare for retirement. The Social Security Act of 1935 provided for categories of public assistance: for the aged, blind, disabled, and dependent children. The federal government shared in the cost but eligibility determinations and most matters of administration were in the hands of state and local government. The largest relief category was Old Age Assistance, but it was expected that this was a transitional program that the growth of Social Security would make superfluous.

In part, events transpired as predicted. Old Age Assistance dwindled, and aid to the blind and the disabled remained small and easily handled. What was not foreseen was the dramatic growth during the late 1950's and 1960's in Aid to Families with Dependent Children. AFDC had become the nation's largest welfare program, and it was subjected to a barrage of criticism. Liberals were concerned about the low payment levels and the vast discrepancies among states in both eligibility requirements and benefit rates. Conservatives were convinced that welfare stunted the incentive to work, since in some states AFDC was more lucrative than minimum-wage employment, and they feared that AFDC also sanctioned family breakup and illegitimate births. State and local governments complained of the financial burden of the program, particularly as the welfare rights movement of the 1960's increased costs by making more people aware of welfare benefits for which they were eligible. As growing numbers of AFDC recipients were inner-city blacks, the program became embroiled in the racial turmoil of the cities. Social workers complained that they were caught in a role conflict between enforcing eligibility requirements and delivering needed services, with the result that they were not able to do well at either.

By the mid-1960's, it was hard to find any political constituency in favor of welfare programs. So great was the antipathy that President Lyndon Johnson championed the War on Poverty as the antithesis of welfare programs. He sought to offer "a hand up, not a hand-out" and "to make taxpayers out of taxeaters." But that did not happen either. Many recipients of antipoverty programs and welfare checks were the same people. Like welfare, the poverty program became heavily involved in delivering services that did not have much impact on the actual poverty rate. And when the poverty program supported community groups that alerted the poor to their welfare rights, its effect was to expand rather than to reduce the welfare rolls.

During the mid-1960's, a collection of welfare liberals and libertarian conservatives sought to change the approach altogether. In place of welfare programs they advocated direct cash payments to the poor, removing the intermediate layers of bureaucracy and empowering the poor to make decisions about the allocation of their resources. President Johnson appointed a commission on income maintenance programs. The commission, though calling a guaranteed income both infeasible and beyond the nation's means, nonetheless argued that the idea warranted further study and experimentation.

Campaigning for President in 1968, Richard Nixon was not sure what to do about welfare, with one exception—he was altogether opposed to any form of a guaranteed income. He modified his thinking after assuming office, largely as a result of the persuasive efforts of a small group of advisers. They convinced Nixon that placing cash in the hands of the poor was a conservative solution and a way to weaken the power of big government. They suggested that payment levels could be set so as to preserve the incentive to work, and that, for the able-bodied, receipt of funds could be made contingent on accepting employment or training. Perhaps most intriguingly, they suggested that an income program offered Nixon a chance to leapfrog his opponents and confound his critics, establishing his own credentials as a humanitarian and reformer.

Nixon's speech on welfare reform, announcing his new proposals, was delivered in August of 1969. Although it is a fairly pedestrian speech on first reading, it gains in interest when set against the backdrop of administrative and public debate. Nixon redefined the issue as a matter not of welfare but of family assistance, replacing a heavily charged negative term with a positive and conservative value. In other ways as well, the speech blends liberal appeals about the goals of welfare with conservative fears about its operation. The President ultimately was unable to secure passage of his welfare reform proposals. But his speech of August 8 did succeed in reframing the discussion and in taking the issue away from his opponents. Nixon was a more complicated strategist than many had thought.

Good evening my fellow Americans:—As you know, I returned last Sunday night from a trip around the world—a trip that took me to eight countries in 9 days.

The purpose of this trip was to help lay the basis for a lasting peace, once the war in Vietnam is ended.

In the course of it, I also saw once again the vigorous efforts so many new nations are making to leap the centuries into the modern world.

Every time I return to the United States after such a trip, I realize how fortunate we are to live in this rich land. We have the world's most advanced industrial economy, the greatest wealth ever known to man, the fullest measure of freedom ever enjoyed by any people, anywhere.

Yet we, too, have an urgent need to modernize our institutions—and our need is no less than theirs.

We face an urban crisis, a social crisis—and at the same time, a crisis of confidence in the capacity of government to do its job.

A third of a century of centralizing power and responsibility in Washington has produced a bureaucratic monstrosity, cumbersome, unresponsive, ineffective.

A third of a century of social experiment has left us a legacy of entrenched programs that have outlived their time or outgrown their purposes.

A third of a century of unprecedented growth and change has strained our institutions, and raised serious questions about whether they are still adequate to the times.

It is no accident, therefore, that we find increasing skepticism—and not only among our young people, but among citizens everywhere—about the continuing capacity of government to master the challenges we face.

Nowhere has the failure of government been more tragically apparent than in its efforts to help the poor and especially in its system of public welfare.

TARGET: REFORMS

Since taking office, one of my first priorities has been to repair the machinery of government, to put it in shape for the 1970's. I have made many changes designed to improve the functioning of the executive branch. And I have asked Congress for a number of important structural reforms; among others, a wide-ranging postal reform, a comprehensive reform of the draft, a reform of unemployment insurance, a reform of our hunger programs, a reform of the present confusing hodge-podge of Federal grants-in-aid.

Last April 21, I sent Congress a message asking for a package of major tax reforms, including both the closing of loopholes and the removal of more than 2 million low-income families from the tax rolls altogether. I am glad that Congress is now acting on tax reform, and I hope the Congress will begin to act on the other reforms that I have requested.

The purpose of all these reforms is to eliminate unfairness; to make government more effective as well

as more efficient; and to bring an end to its chronic failure to deliver the service that it promises.

My purpose tonight, however, is not to review the past record, but to present a new set of reforms—a new set of proposals—a new and drastically different approach to the way in which government cares for those in need, and to the way the responsibilities are shared between the State and the Federal Government.

I have chosen to do so in a direct report to the people because these proposals call for public decisions of the first importance; because they represent a fundamental change in the Nation's approach to one of its most pressing social problems; and because, quite deliberately, they also represent the first major reversal of the trend toward ever more centralization of government in Washington, D.C. After a third of a century of power flowing from the people and the States to Washington it is time for a New Federalism in which power, funds, and responsibility will flow from Washington to the States and to the people.

During last year's election campaign, I often made a point that touched a responsive chord wherever I traveled.

I said that this Nation became great not because of what government did for people, but because of what people did for themselves.

This new approach aims at helping the American people do more for themselves. It aims at getting everyone able to work off welfare rolls and onto payrolls.

It aims at ending the unfairness in a system that has become unfair to the welfare recipient, unfair to the working poor, and unfair to the taxpayer.

This new approach aims to make it possible for people—wherever in America they live—to receive their fair share of opportunity. It aims to ensure that people receiving aid, and who are able to work, contribute their fair share of productivity.

This new approach is embodied in a package of four measures: First, a complete replacement of the present welfare system; second, a comprehensive new job training and placement program; third, a revamping of the Office of Economic Opportunity; and fourth, a start on the sharing of Federal tax revenues with the States.

Next week—in three messages to the Congress and one statement—I will spell out in detail what these measures contain. Tonight I want to explain what they mean, what they are intended to achieve, and how they are related.

WELFARE

Whether measured by the anguish of the poor themselves, or by the drastically mounting burden on the taxpayer, the present welfare system has to be judged a colossal failure.

Our States and cities find themselves sinking in a welfare quagmire, as caseloads increase, as costs escalate, and as the welfare system stagnates enterprise and perpetuates dependency.

What began on a small scale in the depression 30's has become a huge monster in the prosperous 60's. And the tragedy is not only that it is bringing States and cities to the brink of financial disaster, but also that it is failing to meet the elementary human, social, and financial needs of the poor.

It breaks up homes. It often penalizes work. It robs recipients of dignity. And it grows.

Benefit levels are grossly unequal—for a mother with three children, they range from an average of $263 a month in one State, down to an average of only $39 in another State. Now such an inequality as this is wrong; no child is "worth" more in one State than in another State. One result of this inequality is to lure thousands more into already overcrowded inner cities, as unprepared for city life as they are for city jobs.

The present system creates an incentive for desertion. In most States a family is denied welfare payments if a father is present—even though he is unable to support his family. Now, in practice, this is what often happens: A father is unable to find a job at all or one that will support his children. And so, to make the children eligible for welfare, he leaves home—and the children are denied the authority, the discipline, the love that come with having a father in the home. This is wrong.

The present system often makes it possible to receive more money on welfare than on a low-paying job. This creates an incentive not to work, and it also is unfair to the working poor. It is morally wrong for a family that is working to try to make ends meet to receive less than a family across the street on welfare. This has been bitterly resented by the man who works, and rightly so—the rewards are just the opposite of what they should be. Its effect is to draw people off payrolls and onto welfare rolls—just the opposite of what government should be doing. To put it bluntly and simply—any system which makes it more profitable for a man not to work than to work, or which encourages a man to desert his family rather than to stay with his family, is wrong and indefensible.

We cannot simply ignore the failures of welfare, or expect them to go away. In the past 8 years, 3 million more people have been added to the welfare rolls—and this in a period of low unemployment. If the present trend continues, another 4 million will join the welfare rolls by 1975. The financial cost will be crushing; and the human cost will be suffocating.

That is why tonight I, therefore, propose that we will abolish the present welfare system and that we adopt in its place a new family assistance system. Initially, this new system will cost more than welfare. But, unlike welfare, it is designed to correct the condition it deals with and, thus, to lessen the long-range burden and cost.

Under this plan, the so-called, "adult categories" of aid—aid to the aged, the blind, the disabled—would be continued, and a national minimum standard for benefits would be set, with the Federal Government contributing to its cost and also sharing the cost of additional State payments above that amount.

But the program now called "Aid to Families with Dependent Children"—the program we all normally think of when we think of "welfare"—would be done away with completely. The new family assistance system I propose in its place rests essentially on these three principles: equality of treatment across the Nation, a work requirement, and a work incentive.

Its benefits would go to the working poor, as well as the nonworking; to families with dependent children headed by a father, as well as to those headed by a mother; and a basic Federal minimum would be provided, the same in every State.

What I am proposing is that the Federal Government build a foundation under the income of every American family with dependent children that cannot care for itself—and wherever in America that family may live.

For a family of four now on welfare, with no outside income, the basic Federal payment would be $1,600 a year. States could add to that amount and most States would add to it. In no case would anyone's present level of benefits be lowered. At the same time, this foundation would be one on which the family itself could build. Outside earnings would be encouraged, not discouraged. The new worker could keep the first $60 a month of outside earnings with no reduction in his benefits; and beyond that, his benefits would be reduced by only 50 cents for each dollar earned.

By the same token, a family head already employed at low wages could get a family assistance supplement; those who work would no longer be discriminated against. For example, a family of five in which the father earns $2,000 a year—which is the hard fact of life for many families in America today—would get family assistance payments of $1,260, so that they would have a total income of $3,260. A family of seven earning $3,000 a year would have its income raised to $4,360.

Thus, for the first time, the government would recognize that it has no less an obligation to the working poor than to the nonworking poor; and for the first time, benefits would be scaled in such a way that it would always pay to work.

With such incentives, most recipients who can work will want to work. This is part of the American character.

But what of the others—those who can work but choose not to?

Well, the answer is very simple.

Under this proposal, everyone who accepts benefits must also accept work or training provided suitable jobs are available either locally or at some distance if transportation is provided. The only exceptions would be those unable to work and mothers of preschool children.

Even mothers of preschool children, however, would have the opportunity to work, because I am also proposing along with this a major expansion of day-care centers to make it possible for mothers to take jobs by which they can support themselves and their children.

This national floor under incomes for working or dependent families is not a "guaranteed income." Under the guaranteed income proposal, everyone would be assured a minimum income, regardless of how much he was capable of earning, regardless of what his need was, regardless of whether or not he was willing to work.

Now, during the presidential campaign last year, I opposed such a plan. I oppose it now and I will continue to oppose it, and this is the reason: A guaranteed income would undermine the incentive to work; the family assistance plan that I propose increases the incentive to work.

A guaranteed income establishes a right without any responsibilities; family assistance recognizes a need and establishes a responsibility. It provides help to those in need and, in turn, requires that those who

receive help work to the extent of their capabilities. There is no reason why one person should be taxed so that another can choose to live idly.

In States that now have benefit levels above the Federal floor, family assistance would help ease the State's financial burdens. But in 20 States—those in which poverty is most widespread—the new Federal floor would be above present average benefits and would mean a leap upward for many thousands of families that cannot care for themselves.

MANPOWER TRAINING

Now I would like to turn to the job training proposals that are part of our full opportunity concept. America prides itself on being a "land of opportunity." I deeply believe in this ideal, as I am sure everyone listening to me also believes in this ideal.

Full opportunity means the chance for upward mobility on every rung of the economic ladder—and for every American, no matter what the handicaps of birth.

The cold, hard truth is that a child born to a poor family has far less chance to make a good living than a child born to a middle-income family.

He is born poor; he is fed poorly; and if his family is on welfare, he starts life in an atmosphere of hand-out and dependency; often he receives little preparation for work and less inspiration. The wonder of the American character is that so many have the spark and the drive to fight their way up. But for millions of others, the burdens of poverty in early life snuff out that spark.

The new family assistance would provide aid for needy families. It would establish a work requirement and a work incentive, but these in turn require effective programs of job training and job placement—including a chance to qualify not just for any jobs, but for good jobs, that provide both additional self-respect and full self-support.

Therefore, I am also sending a message to Congress calling for a complete overhaul of the Nation's manpower training services.

The Federal Government's job training programs have been a terrible tangle of confusion and waste.

To remedy the confusion, arbitrariness, and rigidity of the present system, the new Manpower Training Act would basically do three things.

—It would pull together the jumble of programs

that presently exist, and equalize standards of eligibility.

—It would provide flexible funding—so that Federal money would follow the demands of labor and industry, and flow into those programs that people most want and most need.

—It would decentralize administration, gradually moving it away from the Washington bureaucracy and turning it over to States and localities.

In terms of its symbolic importance, I can hardly overemphasize this last point. For the first time, applying the principles of the New Federalism, administration of a major established Federal program would be turned over to the States and local governments, recognizing that they are in a position to do the job better.

For years, thoughtful Americans have talked of the need to decentralize Government. The time has come to begin.

Federal job training programs have grown to vast proportions, costing more than a billion dollars a year. Yet they are essentially local in character. As long as the Federal Government continues to bear the cost, they can perfectly well be run by States and local governments, and that way they can be better adapted to specific State and local needs.

The Manpower Training Act will have other provisions specifically designed to help move people off welfare rolls and onto payrolls:

—A computerized job bank would be established to match job seekers with job vacancies.

—For those on welfare, a $30 a month bonus would be offered as an incentive to go into job training.

—For heads of families now on welfare, 150,000 new training slots would be opened.

—As I mentioned previously, greatly expanded day-care center facilities would be provided for the children of welfare mothers who choose to work. However, these would be day-care centers with a difference. There is no single ideal to which this administration is more firmly committed than to the enriching of a child's first 5 years of life, and thus, helping lift the poor out of misery at a time when a lift can help the most. Therefore, these day-care centers would offer more than custodial care; they would also be devoted to the development of vigorous young minds and bodies. As a further dividend, the day-care centers would

offer employment to many welfare mothers themselves.

OFFICE OF ECONOMIC OPPORTUNITY

One common theme running through my proposals tonight is that of providing full opportunity for every American. A second theme is that of trying to equip every American to play a productive role and a third is the need to make Government itself workable—which means reshaping, reforming, innovating.

The Office of Economic Opportunity is basically an innovative agency, and thus it has a vital place in our efforts to develop new programs and apply new knowledge. But in order to do so effectively what it can do best, OEO itself needs reorganization.

This administration has completed a thorough study of OEO. We have assigned it a leading role in the effort to develop and test new approaches to the solving of social problems. OEO is to be a laboratory agency where new ideas for helping people are tried on a pilot basis. When they prove successful, they can be spun off to operating departments or agencies—just as the space agency, for example, spun off the weather satellite and the communications satellite when these proved successful. Then OEO will be free to concentrate on breaking even newer ground.

The OEO reorganization to be announced next week will stress this innovative role. It also will stress accountability, a clear separation of functions, and a tighter more effective organization of field operations.

REVENUE SHARING

We come now to a proposal which I consider profoundly important to the future of our Federal system of shared responsibilities. When we speak of poverty or jobs or opportunity or making government more effective or getting it closer to the people, it brings us directly to the financial plight of our States and cities.

We can no longer have effective government at any level unless we have it at all levels. There is too much to be done for the cities to do it alone, for Washington to do it alone, or for the States to do it alone.

For a third of a century, power and responsibility have flowed toward Washington, and Washington has taken for its own the best sources of revenue.

We intend to reverse this tide, and to turn back to

the States a greater measure of responsibility—not as a way of avoiding problems, but as a better way of solving problems.

Along with this would go a share of Federal revenues. I shall propose to the Congress next week that a set portion of the revenues from Federal income taxes be remitted directly to the States, with a minimum of Federal restrictions on how those dollars are to be used, and with a requirement that a percentage of them be channeled through for the use of local governments.

The funds provided under this program will not be great in the first year. But the principle will have been established, and the amounts will increase as our budgetary situation improves.

This start on revenue sharing is a step toward what I call the New Federalism. It is a gesture of faith in America's State and local governments and in the principle of democratic self-government.

With this revenue sharing proposal we follow through on a commitment I made in the last campaign. We follow through on a mandate which the electorate gave us last November.

In recent years, we all have concentrated a great deal of attention on what we commonly call the "crisis of the cities." These proposals I have made are addressed in part to that, but they also are focused much more broadly.

They are addressed to the crisis of government—to adapting its structures and making it manageable.

They are addressed to the crisis of poverty and need, which is rural as well as urban. This administration is committed to full opportunity on the farm as well as in the city; to a better life for rural America; to ensuring that government is responsive to the needs of rural America as well as urban America. These proposals will advance these goals.

I have discussed these four matters together because together they make both a package and a pattern. They should be studied together, debated together, and seen in perspective.

Now these proposals will be controversial, just as any new program is controversial. They also are expensive. Let us face that fact frankly and directly.

The first-year costs of the new family assistance program, including the child care centers and job training, would be $4 billion. I deliberated long and hard over whether we could afford such an outlay. I decided in favor of it for two reasons: First, because the costs will not begin until fiscal year 1971, when I expect the funds to be available within the budget; and second, be-

cause I concluded that this is a reform we cannot afford not to undertake. The cost of continuing the present system, in financial as well as human terms, is staggering if projected into the 1970's.

Revenue sharing would begin in the middle of fiscal 1971, at a half-year cost of a half billion dollars. This cuts into the Federal budget, but it represents relief for the equally hard-pressed States. It would help curb the rise in State and local taxes which are such a burden to millions of American families.

Overall, we would be spending more—in the short run—to help people who now are poor and who now are unready for work or unable to find work.

But I see it this way: Every businessman, every workingman knows what "start-up costs" are. They are a heavy investment made in early years in the expectation that they will more than pay for themselves in future years.

The investment in these proposals is a human investment; it also is a "start-up cost" in turning around our dangerous decline into welfarism in America. We cannot produce productive people with the antiquated, wheezing, overloaded machine we now call the welfare system.

If we fail to make this investment in work incentives now, if we merely try to patch up the system here and there, we will only be pouring good money after bad in ever-increasing amounts.

If we do invest in this modernization, the heavily burdened taxpayer at least will have the chance to see the end of the tunnel. And the man who now only looks ahead only to a lifetime of dependency will see hope—hope for a life of work and pride and dignity.

In the final analysis, we cannot talk our way out of poverty; we cannot legislate our way out of poverty; but this Nation can work its way out of poverty. What America needs now is not more welfare, but more "workfare."

The task of this Government, the great task of our people, is to provide the training for work, the incentive to work, the opportunity to work, and the reward for work. Together these measures are a first long step in that direction.

For those in the welfare system today who are struggling to fight their way out of poverty, these measures offer a way to independence through the dignity of work.

For those able to work, these measures provide new opportunities to learn work, to find work.

For the working poor—the forgotten poor—these

measures offer a fair share in the assistance given to the poor.

This new system establishes a direct link between the Government's willingness to help the needy and the willingness of the needy to help themselves.

It removes the present incentive not to work and substitutes an incentive to work; it removes the present incentive for families to break apart and substitutes an incentive for families to stay together.

It removes the blatant inequities and injustices and indignities of the welfare system.

It establishes a basic Federal floor so that children in any State can have at least the minimum essentials of life.

Together, these measures cushion the impact of welfare costs on States and localities, many of which have found themselves in fiscal crisis as costs have escalated.

They bring reason, order, and purpose into a tangle of overlapping programs, and show that Government can be made to work.

Poverty will not be defeated by a stroke of a pen signing a check, and it will not be reduced to nothing overnight with slogans or ringing exhortations.

Poverty is not only a state of income. It is also a state of mind, a state of health. Poverty must be conquered without sacrificing the will to work, for if we take the route of the permanent handout, the American character will itself be impoverished.

In my recent trip around the world, I visited countries in all stages of economic development; countries with different social systems, different economic systems, different political systems.

In all of them, however, I found that one event had caught the imagination of the people and lifted their spirits almost beyond measure: the trip of Apollo 11 to the moon and back. On that historic day, when the astronauts set foot on the moon, the spirit of Apollo truly swept through this world. It was a spirit of peace and brotherhood and adventure, a spirit that thrilled to the knowledge that man had dreamed the impossible, dared the impossible, and done the impossible.

Abolishing poverty, putting an end to dependency—like reaching the moon a generation ago—may seem to be impossible. But in the spirit of Apollo, we can lift our sights and marshal our best efforts. We can resolve to make this the year not that we reached the goal, but that we turned the corner—turned the corner from a dismal cycle of dependency toward a new birth of independence; from despair toward hope; from an ominously mounting impotence of government toward a new effectiveness of government, and toward a full opportunity for every American to share the bounty of this rich land.

Thank you and goodnight.

Vietnam

Lyndon B. Johnson

Gulf of Tonkin Incident
(August 4, 1964)

Presiding over a foreign war was not among Lyndon Johnson's objectives upon becoming President of the United States. But he shared the widespread public belief, nurtured by two decades of cold war, that the success of communism anywhere was a threat to freedom everywhere. He therefore viewed the deteriorating situation in South Vietnam with grave concern. He was also concerned, however, about public support for his policies. Ironically, the fear was not that the public would oppose the war—indeed, large-scale opposition did not develop until much later—but that war fever, once unleashed, would be uncontrollable. Johnson feared both that he would be unable to keep a limited war limited, and that the pressure to mobilize for war would jeopardize his cherished domestic programs. For most of his Presidency, Johnson was more worried about disappointing the "hawks" than about displeasing the "doves."

The delicate nature of his situation induced caution during Johnson's first few months in office. He slowly increased the number of American advisers in Vietnam, always eschewing the desire for any wider war. Meanwhile his advisers and staff developed contingency plans and speculated about alternative scenarios for increased American involvement should that appear necessary to stave off the defeat of South Vietnam. To intervene on a larger scale while keeping a stance of restraint required that American action be portrayed as specific reprisal for a hostile act, not a portent of a wider war. And the hostile act must evoke public sympathy and generate support for the President.

A circumstance that met these criteria developed in August 1964. Two American ships were alleged to have been attacked by North Vietnamese patrol boats while in international waters. Recent evidence calls into question whether the second attack actually occurred, and whether the mission of the American ships was truly benign. But these doubts were not harbored at the time. The incident in the Gulf of Tonkin was seen as both a threat and an insult to the United States, calling for retributive action against the North Vietnamese.

Several elements of the speech in which President Johnson announced his response are notable. First, he delivered it shortly before midnight, when most of his potential audience was asleep. Reducing the size of the audience was thought to lessen the risk that the speech would generate passionate desires to widen the war. Second, he explicitly characterized the American military response as a "reply" to specific conduct by the North Vietnamese. In this fashion, he both avenged the insult to American honor and conveyed that he was acting reluctantly, that North Vietnam was the aggressor and he was just acting in self-defense. Moreover, characterizing the American action as a "reply" seemed to suggest that the essence of a conflict was the exchange of messages. The purpose of American bombing was not military but communicative. It was a symbolic way to make a point. Finally, Johnson asked for a congressional resolution supporting his actions. Congressional authorization was not necessary, but—as Eisenhower had found during the 1950's—it was a useful device to prove that the country was united and to minimize the risk of defections later.

What became the Gulf of Tonkin Resolution had been drafted weeks earlier, held in reserve for just such a contingency. Within three days of this speech, both houses of Congress had acted. Passage by the House of Representatives was unanimous and there were but two dissenting votes in the Senate. Some of its supporters later maintained that they had been misled and had not intended to authorize greater American involvement in the war. But in the years ahead, Johnson frequently referred to the resolution as granting prior approval for whatever additional steps he thought were required. For the most part public opinion was with him, until Americans despaired of his ability to bring the war to a satisfactory conclusion within a reasonable time.

My fellow Americans:—As President and Commander in Chief, it is my duty to the American people to report that renewed hostile actions against United States ships on the high seas in the Gulf of Tonkin have today required me to order the military forces of the United States to take action in reply.

The initial attack on the destroyer *Maddox*, on August 2, was repeated today by a number of hostile vessels attacking two U.S. destroyers with torpedoes. The destroyers and supporting aircraft acted at once on the orders I gave after the initial act of aggression. We believe at least two of the attacking boats were sunk. There were no U.S. losses.

The performance of commanders and crews in this engagement is in the highest tradition of the United States Navy. But repeated acts of violence against the Armed Forces of the United States must be met not only with alert defense, but with positive reply. That reply is being given as I speak to you tonight. Air action is now in execution against gunboats and cer-

tain supporting facilities in North Viet-Nam which have been used in these hostile operations.

In the larger sense this new act of aggression, aimed directly at our own forces, again brings home to all of us in the United States the importance of the struggle for peace and security in southeast Asia. Aggression by terror against the peaceful villagers of South Viet-Nam has now been joined by open aggression on the high seas against the United States of America.

The determination of all Americans to carry out our full commitment to the people and to the government of South Viet-Nam will be redoubled by this outrage. Yet our response, for the present, will be limited and fitting. We Americans know, although others appear to forget, the risks of spreading conflict. We still seek no wider war.

I have instructed the Secretary of State to make this position totally clear to friends and to adversaries and, indeed, to all. I have instructed Ambassador Stevenson to raise this matter immediately and urgently before the Security Council of the United Nations. Finally, I have today met with the leaders of both parties in the Congress of the United States and I have informed them that I shall immediately request the Congress to pass a resolution making it clear that our Government is united in its determination to take all necessary measures in support of freedom and in defense of peace in southeast Asia.

I have been given encouraging assurance by these leaders of both parties that such a resolution will be promptly introduced, freely and expeditiously debated, and passed with overwhelming support. And just a few minutes ago I was able to reach Senator Goldwater and I am glad to say that he has expressed his support of the statement that I am making to you tonight.

It is a solemn responsibility to have to order even limited military action by forces whose overall strength is as vast and as awesome as those of the United States of America, but it is my considered conviction, shared throughout your Government, that firmness in the right is indispensable today for peace; that firmness will always be measured. Its mission is peace.

Lyndon B. Johnson

Johns Hopkins University Speech
(April 7, 1965)

In early February 1965, a Vietcong guerrilla attack on the officers' barracks at Pleiku killed eight and wounded over one hundred Americans. Lyndon Johnson again felt the need for reprisal, but unlike in the Gulf of Tonkin situation did not confine himself to a single specific action. Instead he ordered Operation Rolling Thunder, the first massive, sustained bombing of North Vietnam. This significant expansion of American participation in the war, which was accompanied by the dispatch of two Marine battalions—the first American ground troops—did not occasion a Presidential address. Only after questioning and criticism mounted, both at home and abroad, did Johnson speak out. The first "teach-in" was held in March at the University of Michigan. It was a marathon weekend of lectures and seminars about the war, and its success sparked plans for a national teach-in in May. The ranks of Senate critics of the war had grown, and such allied leaders as Charles de Gaulle of France were critical as well. To be sure, Johnson also was criticized for not doing enough. Although his ratings in the polls remained high, he was beginning to chafe under criticism from both ends of the political spectrum.

Johnson decided that the time had come for a major Presidential statement on Vietnam, in which he would set out his policy and—at least by implication—respond to his critics. He accepted an invitation to speak at Johns Hopkins University on April 7. The speech went through several drafts as White House writers fought over whether it was tilting too far to the hawks or the doves, and Johnson tried out portions of the speech as a way to share his thinking with important constituencies.

The speech ostensibly announced no new American policy but merely restated existing goals so that the American people could better understand the Johnson policy. It is important, however, for at least two reasons. It illustrates a blending of appeals to both hawks and doves, and it set the justification for the war in a wider context than had been used previously.

Sensitive to the fact that his critics came from both sides, the President sought to answer both. To those fearful that he was not firm enough, Johnson reaffirmed the American commitment to resist aggression. Because he was mindful of the European experience before World War II, he was convinced that unchecked aggression was the way to war. Moreover, there would be no welshing on an American commitment; the nation's honor was at stake. Finally, if the enemy forces continued to enlarge the war, the United States would respond in kind.

Meanwhile, however, Johnson was careful not to characterize the greater American role as signifying a change in our policy. He was still sensitive to the danger of provoking a war fever that he could not control. So he described American actions as only a shift in the means used to achieve the same ends. This theme also was intended to reassure doves that Johnson truly sought no wider war. Meanwhile, the greater appeal to the doves was the statement that America stood ready for "unconditional discussions." Liberal critics were urging Johnson to submit the conflict to international diplomacy; the President seemingly signaled his willingness to go along and to suggest, by implication, that any failure to convene talks would therefore rest with the Vietcong and North Vietnamese.

At the same time, Johnson expanded the justification for the war. It was not just a matter of stopping communism, thwarting aggression, or keeping one's word, important though those goals might be. It was also a necessary precondition to the real goals of nation-building and economic development of the Southeast Asian region. Johnson looked beyond the present to a day of peace when the Mekong River would be developed on the model of the Tennessee Valley Authority and when economic development would bring prosperity to all of Southeast Asia. To this end the United States pledged $1 billion toward the cost of the program. Liberals, Johnson hoped, would be more likely to support the war on *this* basis, and early reactions to the speech suggested that he was correct.

Still, each part of the speech could be criticized. Hawks could regard the development program as an unjustified giveaway, and doves could complain that the President still acted as though the struggle in Vietnam was an international conflict rather than a civil war in which America did not belong. The early responses to the speech proved fleeting, and criticism became more pronounced as the size of the war grew. Johnson did not deliver a nationally televised address on Vietnam again for some time. The final irony is that this speech was alluded to in 1975 by the victorious North Vietnamese, who demanded $1 billion in reparations payments from the United States. That certainly was not what Johnson had had in mind.

Mr. Garland, Senator Brewster, Senator Tydings, Members of the congressional delegation, members of the faculty of Johns Hopkins, student body, my fellow Americans:—Last week 17 nations sent their views to some two dozen countries having an interest in southeast Asia. We are joining those 17 countries and stating our American policy tonight which we believe will contribute toward peace in this area of the world.

I have come here to review once again with my own people the views of the American Government.

Tonight Americans and Asians are dying for a world where each people may choose its own path to change.

This is the principle for which our ancestors fought in the valleys of Pennsylvania. It is the principle for which our sons fight tonight in the jungles of Vietnam.

Viet-Nam is far away from this quiet campus. We have no territory there, nor do we seek any. The war is dirty and brutal and difficult. And some 400 young men, born into an America that is bursting with opportunity and promise, have ended their lives on Viet-Nam's steaming soil.

Why must we take this painful road?

Why must this Nation hazard its ease, and its interest, and its power for the sake of a people so far away?

We fight because we must fight if we are to live in a world where every country can shape its own destiny. And only in such a world will our own freedom be finally secure.

This kind of world will never be built by bombs or bullets. Yet the infirmities of man are such that force must often precede reason, and the waste of war, the works of peace.

We wish that this were not so. But we must deal with the world as it is, if it is ever to be as we wish.

THE NATURE OF THE CONFLICT

The world as it is in Asia is not a serene or peaceful place.

The first reality is that North Viet-Nam has attacked the independent nation of South Viet-Nam. Its object is total conquest.

Of course, some of the people of South Viet-Nam are participating in attack on their own government. But trained men and supplies, orders and arms, flow in a constant stream from north to south.

This support is the heartbeat of the war.

And it is a war of unparalleled brutality. Simple farmers are the targets of assassination and kidnapping. Women and children are strangled in the night because their men are loyal to their government. And helpless villages are ravaged by sneak attacks. Large-scale raids are conducted on towns, and terror strikes in the heart of cities.

The confused nature of this conflict cannot mask the fact that it is the new face of an old enemy.

Over this war—and all Asia—is another reality: the deepening shadow of Communist China. The rulers in Hanoi are urged on by Peking. This is a regime which has destroyed freedom in Tibet, which has attacked India, and has been condemned by the United Nations for aggression in Korea. It is a nation which is helping the forces of violence in almost every continent. The contest in Viet-Nam is part of a wider pattern of aggressive purposes.

WHY ARE WE IN VIET-NAM?

Why are these realities our concern? Why are we in South Viet-Nam?

We are there because we have a promise to keep. Since 1954 every American President has offered support to the people of South Viet-Nam. We have helped to build, and we have helped to defend. Thus, over many years, we have made a national pledge to help South Viet-Nam defend its independence.

And I intend to keep that promise.

To dishonor that pledge, to abandon this small and brave nation to its enemies, and to the terror that must follow, would be an unforgivable wrong.

We are also there to strengthen world order. Around the globe, from Berlin to Thailand, are people whose well-being rests, in part, on the belief that they can count on us if they are attacked. To leave Viet-Nam to its fate would shake the confidence of all these people in the value of an American commitment and in the value of America's word. The result would be increased unrest and instability, and even wider war.

We are also there because there are great stakes in the balance. Let no one think for a moment that retreat from Viet-Nam would bring an end to conflict. The battle would be renewed in one country and then another. The central lesson of our time is that the appetite of aggression is never satisfied. To withdraw from one battlefield means only to prepare for the next. We must say in southeast Asia—as we did in Europe—in the words of the Bible: "Hitherto shalt thou come, but no further."

There are those who say that all our effort there will be futile—that China's power is such that it is bound to dominate all southeast Asia. But there is no end to that argument until all of the nations of Asia are swallowed up.

There are those who wonder why we have a responsibility there. Well, we have it there for the same reason that we have a responsibility for the defense of Europe. World War II was fought in both Europe and Asia, and when it ended we found ourselves with continued responsibility for the defense of freedom.

OUR OBJECTIVE IN VIET-NAM

Our objective is the independence of South Viet-Nam, and its freedom from attack. We want nothing for ourselves—only that the people of South Viet-Nam be allowed to guide their own country in their own way.

We will do everything necessary to reach that objective. And we will do only what is absolutely necessary.

In recent months attacks on South Viet-Nam were stepped up. Thus, it became necessary for us to increase our response and to make attacks by air. This is not a change of purpose. It is a change in what we believe that purpose requires.

We do this in order to slow down aggression.

We do this to increase the confidence of the brave people of South Viet-Nam who have bravely borne this brutal battle for so many years with so many casualties.

And we do this to convince the leaders of North Viet-Nam—and all who seek to share their conquest—of a very simple fact:

We will not be defeated.

We will not grow tired.

We will not withdraw, either openly or under the cloak of a meaningless agreement.

We know that air attacks alone will not accomplish all of these purposes. But it is our best and prayerful judgment that they are a necessary part of the surest road to peace.

We hope that peace will come swiftly. But that is in the hands of others besides ourselves. And we must be prepared for a long continued conflict. It will require patience as well as bravery, the will to endure as well as the will to resist.

I wish it were possible to convince others with words of what we now find it necessary to say with guns and planes: Armed hostility is futile. Our resources are equal to any challenge. Because we fight for values and we fight for principles, rather than territory or colonies, our patience and our determination are unending.

Once this is clear, then it should also be clear that the only path for reasonable men is the path of peaceful settlement.

Such peace demands an independent South Viet-Nam—securely guaranteed and able to shape its own relationships to all others—free from outside interference—tied to no alliance—a military base for no other country.

These are the essentials of any final settlement.

We will never be second in the search for such a peaceful settlement in Viet-Nam.

There may be many ways to this kind of peace: in discussion or negotiation with the governments concerned; in large groups or in small ones; in the reaffirmation of old agreements or their strengthening with new ones.

We have stated this position over and over again, fifty times and more, to friend and foe alike. And we remain ready, with this purpose, for unconditional discussions.

And until that bright and necessary day of peace we will try to keep conflict from spreading. We have no desire to see thousands die in battle—Asians or Americans. We have no desire to devastate that which the people of North Viet-Nam have built with toil and sacrifice. We will use our power with restraint and with all the wisdom that we can command.

But we will use it.

This war, like most wars, is filled with terrible irony. For what do the people of North Viet-Nam want? They want what their neighbors also desire: food for their hunger; health for their bodies; a chance to learn; progress for their country; and an end to the bondage of material misery. And they would find all these things far more readily in peaceful association with others than in the endless course of battle.

A COOPERATIVE EFFORT FOR DEVELOPMENT

These countries of southeast Asia are homes for millions of impoverished people. Each day these people rise at dawn and struggle through until the night to wrestle existence from the soil. They are often wracked by disease, plagued by hunger, and death comes at the early age of 40.

Stability and peace do not come easily in such a land. Neither independence nor human dignity will ever be won, though, by arms alone. It also requires the work of peace. The American people have helped generously in times past in these works. Now there must be a much more massive effort to improve the life of man in that conflict-torn corner of our world.

The first step is for the countries of southeast Asia to associate themselves in a greatly expanded cooperative effort for development. We would hope that North Viet-Nam would take its place in the common effort just as soon as peaceful cooperation is possible.

The United Nations is already actively engaged in

development in this area. As far back as 1961 I conferred with our authorities in Viet-Nam in connection with their work there. And I would hope tonight that the Secretary General of the United Nations could use the prestige of his great office, and his deep knowledge of Asia, to initiate, as soon as possible, with the countries of that area, a plan for cooperation in increased development.

For our part I will ask the Congress to join in a billion dollar American investment in this effort as soon as it is underway.

And I would hope that all other industrialized countries, including the Soviet Union, will join in this effort to replace despair with hope, and terror with progress.

The task is nothing less than to enrich the hopes and the existence of more than a hundred million people. And there is much to be done.

The vast Mekong River can provide food and water and power on a scale to dwarf even our own TVA.

The wonders of modern medicine can be spread through villages where thousands die every year from lack of care.

Schools can be established to train people in the skills that are needed to manage the process of development.

And these objectives, and more, are within the reach of a cooperative and determined effort.

I also intend to expand and speed up a program to make available our farm surpluses to assist in feeding and clothing the needy in Asia. We should not allow people to go hungry and wear rags while our own warehouses overflow with an abundance of wheat and corn, rice and cotton.

So I will very shortly name a special team of outstanding, patriotic, distinguished Americans to inaugurate our participation in these programs. This team will be headed by Mr. Eugene Black, the very able former President of the World Bank.

In areas that are still ripped by conflict, of course development will not be easy. Peace will be necessary for final success. But we cannot and must not wait for peace to begin this job.

THE DREAM OF WORLD ORDER

This will be a disorderly planet for a long time. In Asia, as elsewhere, the forces of the modern world are shaking old ways and uprooting ancient civilizations. There will be turbulence and struggle and even violence. Great social change—as we see in our own country now—does not always come without conflict.

We must also expect that nations will on occasion be in dispute with us. It may be because we are rich, or powerful; or because we have made some mistakes; or because they honestly fear our intentions. However, no nation need ever fear that we desire their land, or to impose our will, or to dictate their institutions.

But we will always oppose the effort of one nation to conquer another nation.

We will do this because our own security is at stake.

But there is more to it than that. For our generation has a dream. It is a very old dream. But we have the power and now we have the opportunity to make that dream come true.

For centuries nations have struggled among each other. But we dream of a world where disputes are settled by law and reason. And we will try to make it so.

For most of history men have hated and killed one another in battle. But we dream of an end to war. And we will try to make it so.

For all existence most men have lived in poverty, threatened by hunger. But we dream of a world where all are fed and charged with hope. And we will help to make it so.

The ordinary men and women of North Viet-Nam and South Viet-Nam—of China and India—of Russia and America—are brave people. They are filled with the same proportions of hate and fear, of love and hope. Most of them want the same things for themselves and their families. Most of them do not want their sons to ever die in battle, or to see their homes, or the homes of others, destroyed.

Well, this can be their world yet. Man now has the knowledge—always before denied—to make this planet serve the real needs of the people who live on it.

I know this will not be easy. I know how difficult it is for reason to guide passion, and love to master hate. The complexities of this world do not bow easily to pure and consistent answers.

But the simple truths are there just the same. We must all try to follow them as best we can.

CONCLUSION

We often say how impressive power is. But I do not find it impressive at all. The guns and the bombs, the rockets and the warships, are all symbols of human failure. They are necessary symbols. They protect what we cherish. But they are witness to human folly.

A dam built across a great river is impressive.

In the countryside where I was born, and where I live, I have seen the night illuminated, and the kitchens warmed, and the homes heated, where once the cheerless night and the ceaseless cold held sway. And all this happened because electricity came to our area along the humming wires of the REA. Electrification of the countryside—yes, that, too, is impressive.

A rich harvest in a hungry land is impressive.

The sight of healthy children in a classroom is impressive.

These—not mighty arms—are the achievements which the American Nation believes to be impressive.

And, if we are steadfast, the time may come when all other nations will also find it so.

Every night before I turn out the lights to sleep I ask myself this question: Have I done everything that I can do to unite this country? Have I done everything I can to help unite the world, to try to bring peace and hope to all the peoples of the world? Have I done enough?

Ask yourselves that question in your homes—and in this hall tonight. Have we, each of us, all done all we could? Have we done enough?

We may well be living in the time foretold many years ago when it was said: "I call heaven and earth to record this day against you, that I have set before you life and death, blessing and cursing: therefore choose life, that both thou and thy seed may live."

This generation of the world must choose: destroy or build, kill or aid, hate or understand.

We can do all these things on a scale never dreamed of before.

Well, we will choose life. In so doing we will prevail over the enemies within man, and over the natural enemies of all mankind.

To Dr. Eisenhower and Mr. Garland, and this great institution, Johns Hopkins, I thank you for this opportunity to convey my thoughts to you and to the American people.

Good night.

Wayne Morse

Protests Against Vietnam Policy: An Undeclared War (October 19, 1965)

Steadily the Johnson administration had escalated the American presence in Vietnam. Following the incident in the Gulf of Tonkin in August 1964, retaliatory air strikes had been ordered against North Vietnam, but this reprisal was an isolated incident. The President was relatively successful in removing Vietnam as an issue in the 1964 election. An attack on American barracks at Pleiku stimulated an order early in 1965 for sustained bombing of the North. Beginning that spring, the role and number of American troops grew. From the 23,000 American "advisers" who had been in Vietnam at the end of 1964, the number rose to 125,000 by mid-1965. American troops were no longer limited to protecting the South Vietnamese but were authorized to engage in ground combat activities.

The escalation of the war continued to enjoy broad public support, but antiwar protest also was growing. It began on the campuses, where "teach-ins" in the spring of 1965 both provided information about the Johnson policy and inspired opposition to it. As draft calls rose to provide the increased number of troops needed, demonstrations and protests became commonplace, including the massing of bodies to block trains carrying troops and the public burning of draft cards—an action that Congress, in the fall of 1965, made a federal crime. Over the weekend of October 16, 1965, antiwar protests took place in thirty-eight American cities, including New York, Philadelphia, Chicago, Columbus, and Ann Arbor. Ten thousand people marched against the war in Berkeley; another ten thousand people marched in New York. The primary stimulus for these protests was the fact that the Johnson administration had labeled a ten-week effort to secure peace talks with North Vietnam a failure.

The antiwar protests were condemned by President Johnson and the military leaders, and also by leaders of the Senate, Democrats Mike Mansfield and Richard Russell and Republicans Everett Dirksen and Leverett Saltonstall. But several other influential senators had themselves begun to question American policy in Vietnam and to distance themselves from it. Most notable was Foreign Relations Committee chairman J. William Fulbright of Arkansas, who had maintained a public posture of support while growing increasingly critical in private. In September, Fulbright delivered a speech breaking with the administration's handling of the crisis in the Dominican Republic, and he moved closer to an open break on the Vietnam War. Other senators, including Eugene McCarthy and George McGovern, followed his lead; so did Mansfield, despite his disapproval of the protests.

These senators, however, initially had supported Johnson on the war. Not so Wayne Morse of Oregon, who had been one of only two senators to vote against the Gulf of Tonkin Resolution. Morse had the reputation of a political gadfly. Elected to the Senate as a Republican, he became first an independent and then a Democrat. His voting record was generally liberal but his actions and his reasoning were often unpredictable. His opposition to the war was consistent from the beginning. Since there had been no declaration of war by Congress, he believed that American military action was unconstitutional. He also doubted that the war was in the national interest and believed that it could not be won on acceptable terms. In opposing the Gulf of Tonkin Resolution, he had predicted that America would be involved in Vietnam for years and that the war would end in stalemate. In opposing the bombing of the North, he had predicted that Johnson's war policy, while currently popular, ultimately would discredit him and drive him from office.

On October 19, Morse took the Senate floor to speak about the protests of the previous weekend and the issues they raised about American policy in Vietnam. This speech is representative of early liberal dissent on the war, in that it gives great weight to matters of order and procedure as well as to the substance of American policy. Morse endorsed the right of American citizens to protest the war, but only by lawful means—thereby distancing himself and like-minded senators from those burning draft cards or engaging in acts of civil disobedience. He gave great stress to the illegality of American action and called on the President to ask Congress for a declaration of war. Morse certainly did not intend to support such a declaration, but he believed that raising the issue in this fashion would make clear the stakes. He thought that a Presidential request for a declaration of war would call Johnson's Vietnam policy into question both with our allies and with the American people. Inability to defend the policy thus would stimulate a change.

Few of Morse's aims in this speech were achieved. The President did not request a declaration of war, though many have speculated that Congress certainly would have complied if he had. And supporters of the war became less and less likely to distinguish between lawful and unlawful dissent. But Morse, in this speech as elsewhere, uttered statements that may strike today's reader as prophetic. "History will show," he said, "that after all the military victories which we shall win, and after that time has passed, we shall still have to occupy, occupy, and continue to occupy areas of Asia. Then, sooner or later, we will be driven out."

Mr. President,—the agitation in today's news about the nature of the Vietnam protests and the action of the U.S. Government to suppress them is indicative of the use of a straw man by both sides.

The youthful protestors who ignore the many means of peaceful and orderly protest open to them under the first amendment to the Constitution, are affording to the entire Nation the opportunity to dismiss all dissent from Government policy as lawless, reckless, and bordering on sedition.

The near hysteria with which these demonstrations are being met by Government officials suggests that they are anxious to tag all dissent as lawless, reckless, and bordering on sedition. To bring the full weight of Government police power down upon a few noticeable individuals can, they hope, spread disrepute to the whole idea of dissent or objection to a policy in Vietnam that is producing not peace but only war and the prospect of more war.

I do not doubt that the agitators on the one hand and their prosecutors on the other serve each other's purposes quite well. Many of the youths about whom the public has been reading so much in recent days have for their purpose little more than agitation, leading to jail. There are ample laws on the books to deal with anyone who evades or resists the draft, and these young men know that perfectly well. If that is their chosen means of expression, the law will deal with them.

And the administration, too, needs an extremist and violent faction against which to act, for then it can act with something like public support. No one can condone violation of the law in the form of evasion or resistance to selective service. For those who are bona fide conscientious objectors, the law permits an alternative to combat service. But the right to violate selective service laws because of a disagreement with the use to which they are put cannot gain support or approval in this country. Therefore, the administration is safe in cracking down on that type of dissent from its Vietnam war. I expect that in the weeks ahead, the Nation will be treated to a vast public relations campaign that will seek to create the impression that anyone who questions what is being done in Vietnam is a draft evader, or is the tool or dupe of Communists, or trying to further Communist objectives. A few prosecutions and a barrage of high-level statements will be central features of the campaign.

It is in these terms that the administration thinks it can best consolidate public support for its war.

RIGHT OF PROTEST IS PROTECTED BY CONSTITUTION

In this situation, it is well for those of us who believe our Vietnam policy is aiding the Communist cause in the long run to remember that there are ample means

of registering protest, means that are protected by the first amendment to the Constitution.

These means have been protected time and again by the Federal police power in the last decade when they were used in connection with civil rights. They take the form of peaceful, nonviolent protest. It is the sound of feet marching in protest, the use of the right of peaceful assembly, and of petition that are protected not only by the Federal courts, but by the same FBI and Justice Department that are now investigating the violation of draft laws and other forms of illegal or violent action in connection with Vietnam demonstrations.

What America needs to hear is the tramp, tramp, tramp of marching feet, in community after community, across the length and breadth of this land, in protest against the administration's unconstitutional and illegal war in South Vietnam. Those protests must be within the law. Those protests must not violate the law. But the administration must also act in keeping with the rights of the protesters under the first amendment.

Let me say to the administration that it owes a responsibility of seeing to it that, under the guarantees of the first amendment, the legal rights of the protesters are protected. I know there will be incidents. That always has happened from time immemorial when people have protested against what they considered to be unsound government policies. Those who violate the law must be held accountable to the law. But also I forewarn the administration that it cannot, because of the actions of some of these demonstrators who may be law violators, breach the rights of the legitimate protestors; that it has the obligation to see that the rights of the legitimate protesters are protected, even though the Government itself is violating the Constitution of this country.

Beyond that, there are the rights of dissent that are exercised in political debate, open and public forums, and eventually at the ballot box.

I say to this administration that it should keep its eye on the ballot box, for, in my judgment, there will be an exercise of public opinion at that ballot box in 1966 and 1968, if this administration does not reverse itself in its policy of international outlawry, that will awaken this administration to what I think is a great miscalculation on its part, if it thinks that at the grassroots of America the people want war and not peace.

These are means of protest and dissent that cannot be squelched by Federal police power. I am satisfied that the longer the war in Vietnam fails to produce peace, the more these methods of dissent will be used by the American people, no matter how much the Federal authorities try in the meantime to discredit opposition by condemning and campaigning against those who conveniently provide a grounds for criminal prosecution.

Those means should be used. They should be used by an American people that wishes to abide by the rule of law. They should be used by people who believe their Government should itself abide by the Constitution of the United States, which permits war to be pursued only upon a declaration of war by Congress, and by people who believe that the United States must take the lead in furthering, not destroying, the rule of law in relations among nations.

It can hardly be wondered at that an administration that engages in war in violation of the means outlined by the Constitution is met with protests taking the form of violation of the draft laws.

But jungle law is usually met by more jungle law. This will be true not only here at home, but among the nations of the world, who see the United States in flagrant violation of the United Nations Charter.

PEACEFUL PROTESTS SHOULD CONTINUE

These events of illegality being countered by more illegality should not deter the rest of us from continuing our quest for a return to the procedures of the Constitution and the United Nations Charter. We have ample means for making our views known. There is no need to resort to violence or violation of the law.

Some weeks ago I said as much to a group of young people who were organizing a Vietnam war protest in my home State of Oregon. They were planning a sit-in at the Portland post office last February, and while I recognize their status as adults able to choose their own course of action, I commented as I shall read.

At the time of the incident I discussed it on the floor of the Senate, and I discussed it last Friday in my speech on the floor of the Senate, but I did not have the telegram in my possession at the time.

As I said last Friday, the U.S. district attorney in Portland, Oreg., called me to report what these students were doing. He pointed out that it would be necessary for him to arrest them because, at 5 o'clock, he would have to close the building where they were protesting. He told me that he did not like to have to arrest them because that arrest would be on their record all

through their adulthood, and he did not think that they realized the great mistake they were making.

He said:

"I think they might listen to you."

I said:

"I am not going to establish the precedent of involving myself in every protest in which some of the protesters move outside the law and do not stay within the framework of their legal rights. But I will send, through you, a telegram to them, if you will read it, stating once and for all my position in regard to my dedicated belief that no protester has the right to violate the law."

I shall read the telegram. I do not know if it has had any effect on them as to their subsequent conduct, but the fact is that subsequent to reading the wire they left the building and proceeded thereafter to continue their protest within the law. The telegram reads as follows:

"I am concerned over the reports of commission of unlawful acts by a group of young people in Oregon in an attempt to dramatize their disagreement with U.S. policy in Vietnam.

"The use of so-called 'civil-disobedience' techniques is not only inappropriate but also highly ineffective in bringing about changes in national policy in a constitutional democracy. Students have a right freely to publicize their views in a lawful manner and may perform a service in making a reasonable presentation in an attempt to influence public opinion. But irresponsible and unlawful actions do not contribute to intelligent discussion of the issues and can only hurt the cause which is propounded.

"I do not doubt that the flouting of the Constitution and the United Nations Charter by the administration through its Vietnam policy will breed much more disrespect for the draft laws and for the obligations of citizens to stick to peaceful means of protest. A country that takes the law into its own hands is no example for its citizens to do differently."

But there is no justification, in my opinion, for any young man in this country to violate the law by burning draft cards, or by defying the draft; then the youth who is able to establish that he is a conscientious objector within the meaning of the existing law is not exempt from a substitute service.

Let there be no mistake. The Senator from Oregon holds no brief for these law violators who are using these means of protest against our war policies in South Vietnam. I condemn it. To those who protest within the law I say you must not be dissuaded by the scofflaws because we are going to have extremists in our administration who will smear the lawful along with the unlawful.

But there are many Americans who recognize where such a course is going to take this country if it continues in its course of action. Many of us recognize that it is this country that has the most to gain in world affairs by adhering to a standard of respect for the United Nations and for international agreements and insisting that others do the same. To the extent that we depart from that standard in our international conduct, we damage our long-range purposes and objectives.

We are fighting in Vietnam without benefit of a declaration of war. That alone cannot help but breed disrespect for our domestic laws among those who disagree with the policy. But we are fighting that war in violation of the United Nations Charter, and that is going to breed disrespect for peaceful settlement of disputes among all nations, not the least of them the new nations of the world we are so anxious to influence and to guide in the ways of adherence to the rule of law.

EFFECT ON MORALE OF U. S. FORCES

Much will be heard, and has already been heard, about dissent at home having a demoralizing effect upon American forces fighting in Vietnam. This argument has nothing to do with the rightness or wrongness, or success or failure, of a policy, but is supposed only to shut off comment. If it does, then the supremacy of the military over the civilian in government will truly be established in this country.

I hope the time will never come when the wisdom of sending American soldiers into a war situation will become a forbidden subject of discussion. I hope the time will never come when the purpose of sending American soldiers into battle will be a forbidden topic among the civilians who support them and who may eventually have to join them. I hope the time will never come when the objective to be achieved by war is no longer a fit matter of debate, because if it is, the men who think they have gone 10,000 miles away to serve American interests will have gone in vain.

I repeat my position in connection with supporting the fighting men in South Vietnam.

There have been Senators who have said, "Are you not pretty much boxed in, because you are in a po-

sition where you will have to vote against appropriations for the war in Vietnam?"

I have said that I shall vote for appropriations for the war in Vietnam only because it is my trust and duty to provide the maximum protection for our troops in whatever situation they find themselves. They are not there on their volition but on the volition of their civilian commanders.

I shall continue to protest the war. I shall continue to vote against giving the President any vote of confidence for what I think is his inexcusable course of action involving us in the war in South Vietnam in the absence of a declaration of war.

That has been my policy. I voted for the defense appropriation bill. I voted against the President's two requests for a vote of confidence. Although it was concealed, he frankly admitted that he sent up the request to compel a vote of confidence, and said at the time he did not need the $700 million, because he had transfer power. When he sent a bill based upon his need to finance the war in South Vietnam, I voted for the appropriation bill, but at the same time I filed again what I am filing this afternoon, my protest to his course of action in southeast Asia.

I repeat that protest, because it needs to be repeated, in view of the tremendous propaganda drive that is being conducted against those of us who are protesting the outlawry of our Government, the violation by our Government of our Constitution, the violation by our Government of the United Nations Charter.

The propaganda, of course, continues to mount. However, the senior Senator from Oregon will continue to protest, in the hope that at long last my country will return to the rule of law and that my country will return to keeping its pledges to its ideals in regard to the settlement of disputes that threaten the peace of the world through existing procedures which are designed to promote settlement by peaceful means, rather than by bullets.

That is the position which I stated last night at Princeton University, which I stated last Saturday in my own State, and which I have stated over and over again across the country, and will continue to state.

The views of those who are protesting the administration's course of action will never receive the attention or the emphasis that the propaganda of the administration, coming out by the reams from the Pentagon and the State Department and the White House, receives on the desks of American editors—the same editors who are remarkably silent on the censorship that has been imposed upon American war correspondents to a degree never before experienced in the history of American journalism and American foreign policy.

I can well understand why the guilty consciences of so many editors cause them to follow the propaganda line of the administration.

But there are some who do not, and I shall have something to say about editors who have demonstrated that they understand the importance of preserving another great constitutional freedom in this country—the freedom of the press. I shall discuss them briefly before I finish.

I wish to make clear once more my views as to why this administration is not declaring war. There are two main reasons, as I have said many times. The administration knows that to ask Congress for a declaration of war would start a historic debate at the grassroots of America. The administration would soon come to recognize that the American people want peace, not war.

Second, a declaration of war would completely change the international law relationships immediately with every noncombatant nation in the world. The administration knows that. The administration knows that those relationships with every other country would change overnight, if war were declared, because then the United States would be treated as a combatant. Other countries would have to deal with us as a combatant. That would cause great changes in trade policies. It would cause great changes, for example, in the relationship between the United States and the British Commonwealth in North Vietnam, and between the United States and Canada in North Vietnam.

It would change the relationships between the United States and France, the United States and Italy, and the United States and every other country in every area of the world that could be considered an area of the war. In my judgment, that, probably more than anything else, is of great concern to the administration.

But that does not justify the President of the United States making war without a declaration of war. That is why there is a need, not only for the officials of the executive branch of the Government, but for Members of Congress, as well, to reread that great war message of Woodrow Wilson of April 2, 1917, when he came before a joint session of Congress and read his recommendations for a declaration of war, stating in the message that he was without the constitutional authority to make war in the absence of a declaration of war. He was right. That is why I have recommended

that officials of the executive branch of the Government and Members of Congress again read the great war message of Franklin Delano Roosevelt following Pearl Harbor, when Franklin Roosevelt also pointed out that without a declaration of war he was without authority to make war, and recommended his reasons for asking for a declaration of war. That, from the very beginning of this historic debate, has been the position of the senior Senator from Oregon.

The effort to suppress debate about the Vietnam war is taking increasingly blatant forms. One reason why the talk about morale has become necessary is the lack of general support for the war at the grassroots of America. The only time support for the war can be gained is when it is described as forcing the Vietcong to negotiate. But they are not negotiating; and that calls for a scapegoat.

Read the polls. Read the interesting semantics. Read the way the questions are put in the polls, with a subtlety that is easily detected. The person questioned is left with the impression that the administration's policy is the way to attain peace.

A part of the burden of the argument of the senior Senator from Oregon is that making war will never attain peace. In my judgment, there is no battle in South Vietnam that the American military force we have there, which is now taking over the war, cannot win. As I have said many times, we are shooting fish in a barrel. Our so-called opposition is without an air force, it is without a navy, it is without heavy artillery, it is without tanks. Of course it cannot possibly stand up to American military force.

But when we finish winning, when we finish leveling, when we finish devastating South and North Vietnam, will we have won a peace? I am satisfied that history will say that we have removed for decades the possibility of winning a peace. History will show that after all the military victories which we shall win, and after that time has passed, we shall still have to occupy, occupy, and continue to occupy areas of Asia. Then, sooner or later, we will be driven out. That may occur 25 or 50 years from now.

But I do not want to leave that heritage to future generations of American boys and girls. That is why I have been urging the stopping of the killing. I have been urging multilateral support for peacekeeping. I have been urging that we bring in multilateral forces. I think we have been reduced now, with the failure of SEATO, and with the apparent impossibility of reconvening the 14-nation conference that established the

Geneva accords in the first place, to resorting to the Security Council of the United Nations, and from there, if there should be a veto, to the General Assembly. I am confident that if we have to go to the General Assembly, we will get an overwhelming majority of support for peacekeeping operations in South Vietnam.

I believe that that will lead, first, to a cease-fire, and then to the establishment of some form of administration for that area of the world, which can be called, for want of a better description, a United Nations trusteeship. But it will provide for a termination of hostilities. That is what the war hawks in the United States do not like. That is what the nationalists in the United States do not want. It is interesting how we talk about nationalism in Asia but so little about America's own nationalism.

Mr. President, our operations in southeast Asia are operations based upon nationalism, and nationalism, in my judgment, has no place in our foreign policy when it comes to the course of action which we are following in southeast Asia.

If we accept it on a multilateral approach, and change the status from that of warmaking to peacekeeping, of course the Communists will have a voice in the determination of operations during a period of time, for however many years it may take to finally determine what kind of system of government shall prevail.

Yes. I, too, would like to wishfully think the Communists off the earth. I, too, would like to go to sleep some night and wake up in the morning and have a dream come true during the night that there are no more Communists. However, they happen to be an ugly reality. We are not going to wishfully think them out of existence. We are never going to be able to shoot them out of existence, for the more shooting we do, the more Communists we make.

The U. S. shooting in southeast Asia, in my judgment, has increased the number of Communists in the world by the millions.

The underdeveloped areas of the world, with their mass of ignorant, illiterate people, with their youngsters and, in many instances, their starving people, with their diseased children, and with their longevity of 30 to 35 years do not intend to permit the United States to shoot its way into dominion and domination over any segment of Asia.

If we have not learned what the French, the British, the Dutch, and the Belgians and the other colonial powers have learned from the pages of history at such

a great cost in blood and material, then, let me say most respectfully, that we do not wish to learn. However, I believe that we have a trust, and I think that our trust is to keep faith with our ideals. Our trust is to practice our professings about morality.

We are a great people to ring church bells. However, we had better be on guard that the church bells do not start tolling the decline of America. I want to ring the church bells, too, but I want to ring them in jubilation over our practicing of the spiritual teachings from the pulpits of those churches.

In my judgment, we cannot reconcile America's foreign policy in South Vietnam with Christianity, nor, for that matter, with any other religion that believes in one Supreme Being.

I will not be silenced in this constant plea for peace as a substitute for the jungle law of military might that the United States is practicing in southeast Asia.

In my judgment, the only time that support for the war can be gained is when it is described as forcing the Vietcong to negotiate. However, they are not negotiating. That calls for a scapegoat in the administration's propaganda.

It is an American characteristic that when a U. S. foreign policy fails to achieve its goal, someone here at home must be blamed for it. We had to find Americans to blame for the takeover of China by the Communists, and then for the takeover of Cuba by Castro. By our standards, nothing abroad ever happens unless some American or group of Americans wills it. If an American policy flops, it is only because it was sabotaged by someone in the State Department, or was designed to fail in the first place, or was frustrated by some other Americans.

Today, we are seeing the failure of the "peace through war" policy in Vietnam being blamed upon those Americans who simply disagree that peace in Asia can be achieved by a unilateral American war effort. The longer the war is stalemated, the more blame will be placed upon those who thought it was misconceived in the first place.

But I am confident that the good sense and judgment of the American people will recognize that we are alone in this war in Asia, and that despite all our claims that we are saving Asia from communism, not a single major Asian country is fighting with us.

When the Pope made his appeal for peace, he did not make it to the Pentagon, or even the White House. He made it to the United Nations. Many of the phony sophisticates in high office are given to nodding at speeches like that of Pope Paul, and intimating that while the Pope had to say all that churchy stuff, it is really a question of who has the power to make their views prevail in the world. That is the attitude of the war hawks. That is the position of the warmongers. Like Stalin before them, many Americans are wont to ask how many divisions the Pope has.

But I do not believe that Pope Paul came to this country on a fool's errand. I think he knew the right place to come, the right words to say, and the right appeal to make to further the cause of peace. The United States stands outside the framework of the United Nations today. Until we get back in it with regard to Vietnam, we are not furthering the cause of peace any more than the Communists are.

It is regrettable that those who believe in lawful protest under the first amendment are bound to be smeared by two forces in this country. The first force is the small group of agitators or outright Communists who undoubtedly, whenever we have a situation of protest, would seek to termite their way into the foundation. However, our FBI knows who they are. Our intelligence service knows who they are.

They are such a small minority that those of us who believe that we have a trust and a duty to carry on our life under the first amendment must continue the protest. The senior Senator from Oregon intends to so continue.

Then, of course, we are smeared by the rightists and extremists within the administration and outside the administration who would seek to create the impression that, unless one bends his knee at the altar of the political expediency of this administration and sanctions what he considers to be wrongful acts in the field of foreign policy, he is guilty of some kind of sedition.

I have been called names before, and I have never surrendered to ad hominem arguments, and I do not intend to do so on this occasion. I intend to continue, short of a declaration of war, to protest, in the hope that, at long last, my administration will change its course of action and proceed to lay this whole threat to the peace of the world before the Security Council and call upon it, as the charter provides, to take jurisdiction over this threat to the peace of the world in Asia.

The general thesis of my remarks appears in an editorial published in this morning's *Washington Post*, entitled: "Demonstrators and the Law."

I shall read certain excerpts from the editorial and then, when I close, I shall have the entire editorial printed in the RECORD.

The editorial begins:

The Department of Justice is properly interested in and concerned about the possibility of a Communist conspiracy to obstruct the operation of the draft law. It ought to conduct an appropriate investigation, make arrests where warranted, and institute prosecutions where required.

The senior Senator from Oregon agrees. The senior Senator from Oregon wants to make very clear that where one can advance proof to show that we have those—not only Communists, but anyone else in the list of protesters—who are seeking to violate the law, they should be investigated and prosecuted.

The editorial continues:

The law is quite clear on the responsibilities of registered citizens, and burning draft cards and illegally avoiding service is not an acceptable way of expressing disagreement with Government policy.

The senior Senator from Oregon wants the RECORD to show that he agrees. However, that is a long way from the position taken by some that it would silence lawful protest. It is a long way from the position taken by some that no one should exercise the constitutional right under the first amendment to protest a foreign policy of his Government that he thinks is a grossly mistaken foreign policy.

The editorial continues:

What it ought not to do is to confuse illegal defiance and perfectly lawful demonstration. Nor should it use the fact that many of the weekend marchers against the war in Vietnam are known Communists to discredit the marchers who simply differ with Government policies, without being disloyal to the country.

Madam President (Mrs. Neuberger in the chair), I seriously doubt that many of the marchers are known Communists, and, if they are, let the FBI present the evidence. I have no doubt that there probably was a sprinkling of them among those marchers, but it is easy to build up to the false conclusion that because people march in protest to the foreign policy of this Government—within the law—that they are honeycombed with Communists.

The editorial continues:

Surely the overwhelming number of the demonstrators were not Communists and many probably withered at their association with Communists in the demonstrations. The coercive power of Government law-enforcement agencies must not be used to inhibit disagreement and dissent when the expression of that dissent is limited to perfectly lawful means.

The senior Senator from Oregon agrees and heartily applauds this wise observation by the editorial in the *Washington Post*.

The editorial continues:

As a practical matter, the Government should be careful to avoid giving the demonstrations the attention that ought to be reserved for major threats to national unity. Demonstrations as large as those held over the weekend could be mobilized to protest the manufacture of straight pins on almost any pleasant autumn day. The dissent in the country is relatively minor; but the Government risks exaggerating its significance by reacting too strongly.

I say most respectfully that in my judgment, the administration is over-reacting as a means of silencing all objections to its policy. The soundings at the grassroots of America indicate that the dissent is of great proportions, from coast to coast.

The editorial continues:

After a long and searching examination of the courses available in South Vietnam, the overwhelming majority of the American people have come to the conclusion that there is no acceptable alternative to the policy the Government is pursuing.

I do not think the *Washington Post* could be more mistaken, Madam President. In fact, even the polls, with their slanted and weighted consideration in favor of the administration's position, show a close division in this country in regard to public opinion vis-a-vis the administration policy in South Vietnam.

The *Post* says:

That majority is bound to be impatient with critics of that policy whose credentials, like those of the Communists, will not stand examination. It is likely to resent and prone to overreact to extremists who imply that their own country is indifferent to considerations of humanity. But whatever the majority's resentment, it must tolerate criticism from those who, in good faith, have a different point of view.

And so it must. And so, also for the sake of discussing a hypothesis, and accepting what I consider to be an unsound major premise factually, let us assume that a majority favors the administration's policy at the present time. One of the precious safeguards of freedom in this Republic is that a minority must not be suppressed in its lawful right to change into a majority. This great foreign policy issue is in a state of flux. This is one Senator who believes that when the American people get the facts—and this administration has not started to give the American people the facts about the war in South Vietnam—when they get the facts, in my judgment, an overwhelming majority of the American people will repudiate the administration's policy. I believe the repudiation will start at the ballot box in 1966, and continue at the ballot box in 1968. And it should, unless this administration changes what I consider to be its illegal, unconstitutional course of international outlawry in South Vietnam, along with the Communist nations, which are likewise engaged in outlawry, in their prosecution of a war. What they should be doing on both sides is submitting the issues of that war to the council table, under the procedures provided for in the United Nations Charter.

Until we are willing to try it, I do not accept the argument of those who say it will not work. We will never know until we try to make it work.

Martin Luther King, Jr.

Speech at Riverside Church
(April 4, 1967)

Despite the early objections of Sen. Wayne Morse and others, opposition to the Vietnam War was slow to materialize. Public opinion polls revealed strong support for President Johnson's handling of the war, and even the vocal opposition was concentrated among groups with little political power—among students on college campuses, for instance. Most Americans still accepted the cold war premise that any advance of communism must be steadfastly resisted, and most also believed that deference to the President on foreign affairs was warranted by the executive's possession of superior information. Moreover, most saw the war in Vietnam as essentially independent of decisions about domestic policy, economics, civil rights, or any other issue.

Slowly, however, prominent individuals from different walks of life spoke out against the war. In doing so, they lent credibility to the antiwar argument but also rendered themselves vulnerable to the charge that they were speaking about matters beyond their expertise. How the tension between these results was resolved, whether antiwar advocacy helped the protest or discredited the speaker, would depend on the nature of the situation and the speaker's mastery of rhetorical art.

Remaining silent on the war became increasingly troublesome for Dr. Martin Luther King, Jr. He could not reconcile his advocacy of nonviolent revolution at home with his government's support of violence abroad. He also regarded the war as directly injurious to the civil rights movement, not as an unrelated issue. He harbored his doubts privately for a time, but eventually concluded that the time had come for him to speak out. In a major address in New York City's Riverside Church, on April 4, 1967, King denounced the Johnson administration's policy in Vietnam, defended his right as a civil rights leader to speak out on the war, and argued that his civil rights and antiwar arguments were clearly related.

King saw the war as indicative of a fundamental flaw in American society; the nation had fallen far short of the American dream with which he had identified so eloquently. In this respect, the speech takes on a prophetic quality; King engaged in denunciation and counseled repentance. King challenged the view of Americans as benevolent and well-intentioned, suggesting instead that their foreign policy was hypocritical. He tried to see the war from the perspective of the North Vietnamese, suggesting that it was our action that had prompted the arms buildup in the North rather than the other way around.

King's preferred goal was American withdrawal, but he portrayed this goal not as a strategic or even a principled matter, but as an act of expiation for national sins. Few Americans enjoy being called to moral account in any case, and this argument was especially troublesome in light of the men, money, and materiel already committed to Vietnam. These sacrifices could not have been in vain, so the casualties became a warrant for continued American presence.

Since most people have come to the view that the Vietnam War was somehow a tragic mistake, King's indictments do not seem so radical. At the time, however, they were quite controversial. Most criticisms of the speech centered on King's disregard for the legacy of the American dream, and on his seeming ingratitude for attacking the very administration that had done so much to promote civil rights. Although there were some positive responses to the speech, it remained extremely controversial and King was criticized until his death. Once he determined to oppose the war, he took an extreme position, rejecting less radical dissent such as distinguishing between the American dream and the current government so that he could uphold the former while condemning the latter. These and other alternatives might have been more palatable politically.

But King was not a politician. His was a moral challenge, which may have required drawing the issues as starkly as possible, and making a direct frontal assault on the prevailing policy. His immediate audience, Clergy and Laymen Concerned About Vietnam, was interested in the moral dimensions of the issue, but most in the audience were not. Nevertheless, King's address has stood the test of time and remains as a powerful prophecy of things to come.

I come to this magnificent house of worship tonight because my conscience leaves me no other choice. I join you in this meeting because I am in deepest agreement with the aims and work of the organization which has brought us together: Clergy and Laymen Concerned About Vietnam. The recent statement of your executive committee are the sentiments of my own heart and I found myself in full accord when I read its opening lines: "A time comes when silence is betrayal." That time has come for us in relation to Vietnam.

The truth of these words is beyond doubt, but the mission to which they call us is a most difficult one. Even when pressed by the demands of inner truth, men do not easily assume the task of opposing their government's policy, especially in time of war. Nor does the human spirit move without great difficulty against all the apathy of conformist thought within one's own bosom and in the surrounding world. Moreover when the issues at hand seem as perplexing as they often do in the case of this dreadful conflict we are always on the verge of being mesmerized by uncertainty; but we must move on.

Some of us who have already begun to break the silence of the night have found that the calling to speak is often a vocation of agony, but we must speak. We must speak with all the humility that is appropriate to our limited vision, but we must speak. And we must rejoice as well, for surely this is the first time in our nation's history that a significant number of its religious leaders have chosen to move beyond the prophesying of smooth patriotism to the high grounds of a firm dissent based upon the mandates of conscience and the reading of history. Perhaps a new spirit is rising among us. If it is, let us trace its movements well and pray that our own inner being may be sensitive to its guidance, for we are deeply in need of a new way beyond the darkness that seems so close around us.

Over the past two years, as I have moved to break the betrayal of my own silence and to speak from the burnings of my own heart, as I have called for radical departures from the destruction of Vietnam, many persons have questioned me about the wisdom of my path. At the heart of their concerns this query has often loomed large and loud: Why are *you* speaking about the war, Dr. King? Why are *you* joining the voices of dissent? Peace and civil rights don't mix, they say. Aren't you hurting the cause of your people, they ask? And when I hear them, though I often understand the source of their concern, I have nevertheless been greatly saddened, for such questions mean that the inquirers have not really known me, my commitment or my calling. Indeed, their questions suggest that they do not know the world in which they live.

In the light of such tragic misunderstanding, I deem it of signal importance to try to state clearly, and I trust concisely, why I believe that the path from Dexter Avenue Baptist Church—the church in Montgomery, Alabama where I began my pastorate—leads clearly to this sanctuary tonight.

I come to this platform tonight to make a passionate plea to my beloved nation. This speech is not addressed to Hanoi or to the National Liberation Front. It is not addressed to China or to Russia.

Nor is it an attempt to overlook the ambiguity of the total situation and the need for a collective solution to the tragedy of Vietnam. Neither is it an attempt to make North Vietnam or the National Liberation Front paragons of virtue, nor to overlook the role they can play in a successful resolution of the problem. While they both may have justifiable reason to be suspicious of the good faith of the United States, life and history give eloquent testimony to the fact that conflicts are never resolved without trustful give and take on both sides.

Tonight, however, I wish not to speak with Hanoi and the NLF, but rather to my fellow Americans who, with me, bear the greatest responsibility in ending a conflict that has exacted a heavy price on both continents.

Since I am a preacher by trade, I suppose it is not surprising that I have seven major reasons for bringing Vietnam into the field of my moral vision. There is at the outset a very obvious and almost facile connection between the war in Vietnam and the struggle I, and others, have been waging in America. A few years ago there was a shining moment in that struggle. It seemed as if there was a real promise of hope for the poor—both black and white—through the Poverty Program. There were experiments, hopes, new beginnings. Then came the buildup in Vietnam and I watched the program broken and eviscerated as if it were some idle political plaything of a society gone mad on war, and I knew that America would never invest the necessary funds or energies in rehabilitation of its poor so long as adventures like Vietnam continued to draw men and skills and money like some demonic destructive suction tube. So I was increasingly compelled to see the war as an enemy of the poor and to attack it as such.

Perhaps a more tragic recognition of reality took place when it became clear to me that the war was doing far more than devastating the hopes of the poor at home. It was sending their sons and their brothers and their husbands to fight and to die in extraordinarily high proportions relative to the rest of the population. We were taking the black young men who had been crippled by our society and sending them 8,000 miles away to guarantee liberties in Southeast Asia which they had not found in Southwest Georgia and East Harlem. So we have been repeatedly faced with the cruel irony of watching Negro and white boys on TV screens as they kill and die together for a nation that has been unable to seat them together in the same schools. So we watch them in brutal solidarity burning the huts of a poor village but we realize that they would never live on the same block in Detroit. I could not be silent in the face of such cruel manipulation of the poor.

My third reason moves to an even deeper level of awareness, for it grows out of my experience in the ghettos of the north over the last three years—especially the last three summers. As I have walked among the desperate, rejected, and angry young men I have told them that Molotov cocktails and rifles would not solve their problems. I have tried to offer them my deepest compassion while maintaining my conviction that social change comes most meaningfully through non-violent action. But they asked—and rightly so—what about Vietnam? They asked if our own nation wasn't using massive doses of violence to solve its problems, to bring about the changes it wanted. Their questions hit home, and I knew that I could never again raise my voice against the violence of the oppressed in the ghettos without having first spoken clearly to the greatest purveyor of violence in the world today—my own government. For the sake of those boys, for the sake of this government, for the sake of the hundreds of thousands trembling under our violence, I cannot be silent.

For those who ask the question, "Aren't you a Civil Rights leader?" and thereby mean to exclude me from the movement for peace, I have this further answer. In 1957 when a group of us formed the Southern Christian Leadership Conference, we chose as our motto: "To save the soul of America." We were convinced that we could not limit our vision to certain rights for black people, but instead affirmed the conviction that America would never be free or saved from itself unless the descendants of its slaves were loosed completely from the shackles they still wear. In a way we were agreeing with Langston Hughes, that black bard of Harlem, who had written earlier:

"O, yes,
I say it plain,
America never was America to me,
And yet I swear this oath—
America will be!"

Now, it should be incandescently clear that no one who has any concern for the integrity and life of America today can ignore the present war. If America's soul becomes totally poisoned, part of the autopsy must read Vietnam. It can never be saved so long as it destroys the deepest hopes of men the world over. So it is that those of us who are yet determined that America *will* be are led down the path of protest and dissent, working for the health of our land.

As if the weight of such a commitment to the life and health of America were not enough, another burden of responsibility was placed upon me in 1964; and I cannot forget that the Nobel Prize for Peace was also a commission—a commission to work harder than I had ever worked before for the "brotherhood of man." This is a calling that takes me beyond national allegiances, but even if it were not present I would yet have to live with the meaning of my commitment to the ministry of Jesus Christ. To me the relationship of this ministry to the making of peace is so obvious that I sometimes marvel at those who ask me why I am speaking against the war. Could it be that they do not know that the good news was meant for all men—for communist and capitalist, for their children and ours, for black and for white, for revolutionary and conservative? Have they forgotten that my ministry is in obedience to the one who loved his enemies so fully that he died for them? What then can I say to the Viet Cong or to Castro or to Mao as a faithful minister of this one? Can I threaten them with death or must I not share with them my life?

Finally, as I try to delineate for you and for myself the road that leads from Montgomery to this place I would have offered all that was most valid if I simply said that I must be true to my conviction that I share with all men the calling to be a son of the Living God. Beyond the calling of race or nation or creed is this vocation of sonship and brotherhood, and because I believe that the Father is deeply concerned especially for his suffering and helpless and outcast children, I come tonight to speak for them.

This I believe to be the privilege and burden of all of us who deem ourselves bound by allegiances and loyalties which are broader and deeper than nationalism and which go beyond our nation's self-defined goals and positions. We are called to speak for the weak, for the voiceless, for victims of our nation and for those it calls enemy, for no document from human hands can make these humans any less our brothers.

And as I ponder the madness of Vietnam and search within myself for ways to understand and respond in compassion my mind goes constantly to the people of that peninsula. I speak now not of the soldiers of each side, not of the junta in Saigon, but simply of the people who have been living under the curse of war for almost three continuous decades now. I think of them too because it is clear to me that there will be no meaningful solution there until some attempt is made to know them and hear their broken cries.

They must see Americans as strange liberators. The Vietnamese people proclaimed their own independence in 1945 after a combined French and Japanese occupation, and before the communist revolution in China. They were led by Ho Chi Minh. Even though they quoted the American Declaration of Independence in their own document of freedom, we refused to recognize them. Instead, we decided to support France in its re-conquest of her former colony.

Our government felt then that the Vietnamese people were not "ready" for independence, and we again fell victim to the deadly western arrogance that has poisoned the international atmosphere for so long. With that tragic decision we rejected a revolutionary government seeking self-determination, and a government that had been established not by China (for whom the Vietnamese have no great love) but by clearly indigenous forces that included some communists. For the peasants this new government meant real land reform, one of the most important needs in their lives.

For nine years following 1945 we denied the people of Vietnam the right of independence. For nine years we vigorously supported the French in their abortive effort to re-colonize Vietnam.

Before the end of the war we were meeting 80% of the French war costs. Even before the French were defeated at Dien Bien Phu, they began to despair of the reckless action, but we did not. We encouraged them with our huge financial and military supplies to continue the war even after they had lost the will. Soon we would be paying almost the full costs of this tragic attempt at re-colonization.

After the French were defeated it looked as if independence and land reform would come again through the Geneva agreements. But instead there came the United States, determined that Ho should not unify the temporarily divided nation, and the peasants watched again as we supported one of the most vicious modern dictators—our chosen man, Premier Diem. The peasants watched and cringed as Diem ruthlessly routed out all opposition, supported their extortionist landlords and refused even to discuss reunification with the North. The peasants watched as all this was presided over by U.S. influence and then by increasing numbers of U.S. troops who came to help quell the insurgency that Diem's methods had aroused. When Diem was overthrown they may have been happy, but the long line of military dictatorships seemed to offer no real change—especially in terms of their need for land and peace.

The only change came from America as we increased our troop commitments in support of governments which were singularly corrupt, inept and without popular support. All the while the people read our leaflets and received regular promises of peace and democracy—and land reform. Now they languish under our bombs and consider us—not their fellow Vietnamese—the real enemy. They move sadly and apathetically as we herd them off the land of their fathers into concentration camps where minimal social needs are rarely met. They know they must move or be destroyed by our bombs. So they go—primarily women and children and the aged.

They watch as we poison their water, as we kill a million acres of their crops. They must weep as the bulldozers roar through their areas preparing to destroy the precious trees. They wander into the hospitals, with at least 20 casualties from American firepower for one Vietcong-inflicted injury. So far we may have killed a million of them—mostly children. They wander into the towns and see thousands of the children, homeless, without clothes, running in packs on the streets like animals. They see the children degraded by our soldiers, as they beg for food. They see the children selling their sisters to our soldiers, soliciting for their mothers.

What do the peasants think as we ally ourselves with the landlords and as we refuse to put any action into our many words concerning land reform? What do they think as we test out our latest weapons on them, just as the Germans tested out new medicine and new tortures in the concentration camps of Europe? Where are the roots of the independent Vietnam we claim to be building? Is it among these voiceless ones?

We have destroyed their two most cherished institutions: the family and the village. We have destroyed their land and their crops. We have cooperated in the crushing of the nation's only non-communist revolutionary political force—the unified Buddhist Church. We have supported the enemies of the peasants of Saigon. We have corrupted their women and children and killed their men. What liberators!

Now there is little left to build on—save bitterness. Soon the only solid physical foundations remaining will be found at our military bases and in the concrete of the concentration camps we call fortified hamlets. The peasants may well wonder if we plan to build our new Vietnam on such grounds as these? Could we blame them for such thoughts? We must speak for them and raise the questions they cannot raise. These too are our brothers.

Perhaps the more difficult but no less necessary task is to speak for those who have been designated as our enemies. What of the National Liberation Front—that strangely anonymous group we call VC or Communists? What must they think of us in America when they realize that we permitted the repression and cruelty of Diem which helped to bring them into being as a resistance group in the south? What do they think of our condoning the violence which led to their own taking up of arms? How can they believe in our integrity when now we speak of "aggression from the North" as if there were nothing more essential to the war? How can they trust us when now we charge them with violence after the murderous reign of Diem, and charge them with the violence while we pour every new weapon of death into their land? Surely we must understand their feelings even if we do not condone their actions. Surely we must see that the men we supported pressed them to their violence. Surely we must see that our own computerized plans of destruction simply dwarf their greatest acts.

How do they judge us when our officials know that their membership is less than 25 per cent communist and yet insist on giving them the blanket name? What must they be thinking when they know that we are aware of their control of major sections of Vietnam and yet we appear ready to allow national elections in which this highly organized political parallel government will have no part? They ask how we can speak of free elections when the Saigon press is censored and controlled by the military junta. And they are surely right to wonder what kind of new government we plan to help form without them—the only party in real touch with the peasants. They question our political goals and they deny the reality of a peace settlement from which they will be excluded. Their questions are frighteningly relevant. Is our nation planning to build on political myth again and then shore it up with the power of new violence?

Here is the true meaning and value of compassion and non-violence when it helps us to see the enemy's point of view, to hear his questions, to know his assessment of ourselves. For from his view we may indeed see the basic weaknesses of our own condition, and if we are mature, we may learn and grow and profit from the wisdom of the brothers who are called the opposition.

So, too, with Hanoi. In the North, where our bombs now pummel the land, and our mines endanger the waterways, we are met by a deep but understandable mistrust. To speak for them is to explain this lack of confidence in western words, and especially their distrust of American intentions now. In Hanoi are the men who led the nation to independence against the Japanese and the French, the men who sought membership in the French commonwealth and were betrayed by the weakness of Paris and the wilfulness of the colonial armies. It was they who led a second struggle against French domination at tremendous costs, and then were persuaded to give up the land they controlled between the 13th and 17th parallel as a temporary measure at Geneva. After 1954 they watched us conspire with Diem to prevent elections which would have surely brought Ho Chi Minh to power over a united Vietnam, and they realized they had been betrayed again.

When we ask why they do not leap to negotiate these things must be remembered. Also it must be clear that the leaders of Hanoi considered the presence of American troops in support of the Diem regime to have been the initial military breach of the Geneva Agreement concerning foreign troops, and they remind us that they did not begin to send in any large number of supplies or men until American forces had moved into the tens of thousands.

Hanoi remembers how our leaders refused to tell us the truth about the earlier North Vietnamese overtures for peace, how the President claimed that none existed when they had clearly been made. Ho Chi Minh has watched as America has spoken of peace and built up its forces, and now he has surely heard the increasing international rumors of American plans for an invasion of the North. He knows the bombing and shelling and mining we are doing are part of traditional pre-invasion strategy. Perhaps only his sense of humor and of irony can save him when he hears the most powerful nation of the world speaking of aggression as it drops thousands of bombs on a poor weak nation more than 8,000 miles away from its shores.

At this point I should make it clear that while I have tried in these last few minutes to give a voice to the voiceless on Vietnam and to understand the arguments of those who are called enemy, I am as deeply concerned about our own troops there as anything else. For it occurs to me that what we are submitting them to in Vietnam is not simply the brutalizing process that goes on in any war where armies face each other and seek to destroy. We are adding cynicism to the process of death, for they must know after a short period there that none of the things we claim to be fighting for are really involved. Before long they must know that their government has sent them into a struggle among Vietnamese, and the more sophisticated surely realize that we are on the side of the wealthy and the secure while we create a hell for the poor.

Somehow this madness must cease. We must stop now. I speak as a child of God and brother to the suffering poor of Vietnam. I speak for those whose land is being laid waste, whose homes are being destroyed, whose culture is being subverted. I speak for the poor of America who are paying the double price of smashed hopes at home and death and corruption in Vietnam. I speak as a citizen of the world, for the world as it stands aghast at the path we have taken. I speak as an American to the leaders of my own nation. The great initiative in this war is ours. The initiative to stop it must be ours.

This is the message of the great Buddhist leaders of Vietnam. Recently one of them wrote these words: "Each day the war goes on the hatred increases in the heart of the Vietnamese and in the hearts of those of humanitarian instinct. The Americans are forcing even their friends into becoming their enemies. It is curious that the Americans, who calculate so carefully on the possibilities of military victory, do not realize that in the process they are incurring deep psychological and political defeat. The image of America will never again be the image of revolution, freedom and democracy, but the image of violence and militarism."

If we continue there will be no doubt in my mind and in the mind of the world that we have no honorable intentions in Vietnam. It will become clear that our minimal expectation is to occupy it as an American colony and men will not refrain from thinking that our maximum hope is to goad China into a war so that we may bomb her nuclear installations. If we do not stop our war against the people of Vietnam immediately the world will be left with no other alternative than to see this as some horribly clumsy and deadly game we have decided to play.

The world now demands a maturity of America that we may not be able to achieve. It demands that we admit that we have been wrong from the beginning of our adventure in Vietnam, that we have been detrimental to the life of the Vietnamese people. The situation is one in which we must be ready to turn sharply from our present ways.

In order to atone for our sins and errors in Vietnam, we should take the initiative in bringing a halt to this tragic war. I would like to suggest five concrete things that our government should do immediately to begin the long and difficult process of extricating ourselves from this nightmarish conflict:

1. End all bombing in North and South Vietnam.
2. Declare a unilateral cease-fire in the hope that such action will create the atmosphere for negotiation.
3. Take immediate steps to prevent other battlegrounds in Southeast Asia by curtailing our military build-up in Thailand and our interference in Laos.
4. Realistically accept the fact that the National Liberation Front has substantial support in South Vietnam and must thereby play a role in any meaningful negotiations and in any future Vietnam government.
5. Set a date that we will remove all foreign troops from Vietnam in accordance with the 1954 Geneva Agreement.

Part of our ongoing commitment might well express itself in an offer to grant asylum to any Vietnamese who fears for his life under a new regime which included the Liberation Front. Then we must make what reparations we can for the damage we have done. We must provide the medical aid that is badly needed, making it available in this country if necessary.

Meanwhile we in the churches and synagogues have a continuing task while we urge our government to disengage itself from a disgraceful commitment. We must continue to raise our voices and our lives if our nation persists in its perverse ways in Vietnam. We must be prepared to match actions with words by seeking out every creative means of protest possible.

As we counsel young men concerning military service we must clarify for them our nation's role in Vietnam and challenge them with the alternative of conscientious objection. I am pleased to say that this is the path now being chosen by more than seventy students at my own Alma Mater, Morehouse College, and I recommend it to all who find the American course in Vietnam a dishonorable and unjust one. Moreover I would encourage all ministers of draft age to give up their ministerial exemptions and seek status as conscientious objectors. These are the times for real choices and not false ones. We are at the moment when our lives must be placed on the line if our nation is to survive its own folly. Every man of humane convictions must decide on the protest that best suits his convictions, but we must all protest.

There is something seductively tempting about stopping there and sending us all off on what in some circles has become a popular crusade against the war in Vietnam. I say we must enter that struggle, but I wish to go on now to say something even more disturbing. The war in Vietnam is but a symptom of a far deeper malady within the American spirit, and if we ignore this sobering reality we will find ourselves organizing clergy and laymen-concerned committees for the next generation. They will be concerned about Guatemala and Peru. They will be concerned about Thailand and Cambodia. They will be concerned about Mozambique and South Africa. We will be marching for these and a dozen other names and attending rallies without end unless there is a significant and profound change in American life and policy. Such thoughts take us beyond Vietnam, but not beyond our calling as sons of the living God.

In 1957 a sensitive American official overseas said that it seemed to him that our nation was on the wrong side of a world revolution. During the past 10 years we have seen emerge a pattern of suppression which now has justified the presence of U.S. military "advisors" in Venezuela. This need to maintain social stability for our investments accounts for the counter-revolutionary action of American forces in Guatemala. It tells why American helicopters are being used against guerrillas in Colombia and why American napalm and green beret forces have already been active against rebels in Peru. It is with such activity in mind that the words of the late John F. Kennedy come back to haunt us. Five years ago he said, "Those who make peaceful revolution impossible will make violent revolution inevitable."

Increasingly, by choice or by accident, this is the role our nation has taken—the role of those who make peaceful revolution impossible by refusing to give up the privileges and the pleasures that come from the immense profits of overseas investment.

I am convinced that if we are to get on the right side of the world revolution, we as a nation must undergo a radical revolution of values. We must rapidly begin the shift from a "thing-oriented" society to a "person-oriented" society. When machines and computers, profit motives and property rights are considered more important than people, the giant triplets of racism, materialism, and militarism are incapable of being conquered.

A true revolution of value will soon cause us to question the fairness and justice of many of our past and present policies. On the one hand we are called to play the Good Samaritan on life's roadside; but that will be only an initial act. One day we must come to see that the whole Jericho Road must be transformed so that men and women will not be constantly beaten and robbed as they make their journey on Life's highway. True compassion is more than flinging a coin to a beggar; it is not haphazard and superficial. It comes to see that an edifice which produces beggars needs re-structuring. A true revolution of values will soon look uneasily on the glaring contrast of poverty and wealth. With righteous indignation, it will look across the seas and see individual capitalists of the West investing huge sums of money in Asia, Africa and South America, only to take the profits out with no concern for the social betterment of the countries, and say: "This is not just." It will look at our alliance with the landed gentry of Latin America and say: "This is not just." The Western arrogance of feeling that it has everything to teach others and nothing to learn from them is not just. A true revolution of values will lay hands on the world order and say of war: "This way of settling differences is not just." This business of burning human beings with napalm, of filling our nation's homes with orphans and widows, of injecting poisonous drugs of hate into the veins of peoples normally humane, of sending men home from dark and bloody battlefields physically handicapped and psychologically deranged, cannot be reconciled with wisdom, justice, and love. A nation that continues year after year to spend more money on military defense than on programs of social uplift is approaching spiritual death.

America, the richest and most powerful nation in the world, can well lead the way in this revolution of values. There is nothing except a tragic death wish, to prevent us from re-ordering our priorities, so that the pursuit of peace will take precedence over the pursuit of war. There is nothing to keep us from molding a recalcitrant status-quo with bruised hands until we have fashioned it into a brotherhood.

This kind of positive revolution of values is our best defense against Communism. War is not the answer. Communism will never be defeated by the use of atomic bombs or nuclear weapons. Let us not join those who shout war and through their misguided passions urge the United States to relinquish its participation in the United Nations. These are days which demand wise restraint and calm reasonableness. We must not call everyone a Communist or an appeaser who advocates the seating of Red China in the United Nations and who recognizes that hate and hysteria are not the final answers to the problem of those turbulent days. We must not engage in a negative anti-Communism, but rather in a positive thrust for democracy, realizing that our greatest defense against Communism is to take offensive action in behalf of justice. We must with positive action seek to remove those conditions of poverty, insecurity and injustice which are the fertile soil in which the seed of Communism grows and develops.

These are revolutionary times. All over the globe men are revolting against old systems of exploitation and oppression and out of the wombs of a frail world new systems of justice and equality are being born. The shirtless and barefoot people of the land are rising up as never before. "The people who sat in darkness have seen a great light." We in the West must support these revolutions. It is a sad fact that, because of comfort, complacency, a morbid fear of Communism, and our proneness to adjust to injustice, the Western nations that initiated so much of the revolutionary spirit of the modern world have now become the arch anti-revolutionaries. This has driven many to feel that only Marxism has the revolutionary spirit. Therefore, Communism is a judgment against our failure to make democracy real and follow through on the revolutions that we initiated. Our only hope today lies in our ability to recapture the revolutionary spirit and go out into a sometimes hostile world declaring eternal hostility to poverty, racism, and militarism. With this powerful commitment we shall boldly challenge the status-quo and unjust mores and thereby speed the day when "every valley shall be exalted, and every mountain and hill shall be made low, and the crooked shall be made straight and the rough places plain."

A genuine revolution of values means in the final analysis that our loyalties must become ecumenical rather than sectional. Every nation must now develop an overriding loyalty to mankind as a whole in order to preserve the best in their individual societies.

This call for a world-wide fellowship that lifts neighborly concern beyond one's tribe, race, class and nation is in reality a call for an all-embracing and unconditional love for all men. This oft misunderstood and misinterpreted concept so readily dismissed by the Nietzsches of the world as a weak and cowardly force—has now become an absolute necessity for the survival of man. When I speak of love I am not speaking of some sentimental and weak response. I am speaking of that force which all of the great religions have seen as the supreme unifying principle of life. Love is somehow the key that unlocks the door which leads to ultimate reality. This Hindu-Moslem-Christian-Jewish-Buddhist belief about ultimate reality is beautifully summed up in the first epistle of Saint John:

"Let us love one another; for love is God and everyone that loveth is born of God and knoweth God. He that loveth not knoweth not God; for God is love. If we love one another, God dwelleth in us, and his love is perfected in us."

Let us hope that this spirit will become the order of the day. We can no longer afford to worship the God of Hate or bow before the altar of retaliation. The oceans of history are made turbulent by the ever-rising tides of hate. History is cluttered with the wreckage of nations and individuals that pursued this self-defeating path of hate. As Arnold Toynbee says: "Love is the ultimate force that makes for the saving choice of life and good against the damning choice of death and evil. Therefore the first hope in our inventory must be the hope that love is going to have the last word."

We are now faced with the fact that tomorrow is today. We are confronted with the fierce urgency of now. In this unfolding conundrum of life and history there is such a thing as being too late. Procrastination is still the thief of time. Life often leaves us standing bare, naked and dejected with a lost opportunity. The "tide in the affairs of men" does not remain at the flood; it ebbs. We may cry out desperately for time to pause in her passage, but time is deaf to every plea and rushes on. Over the bleached bones and jumbled residue of numerous civilizations are written the pathetic

words: "Too late." There is an invisible book of life that faithfully records our vigilance or our neglect. "The moving finger writes, and having written moves on...." We still have a choice today: non-violent co-existence or violent co-annihilation.

We must move past indecision to action. We must find new ways to speak for peace in Vietnam and justice throughout the developing world—a world that borders on our doors. If we do not act we shall surely be dragged down the long dark and shameful corridors of time reserved for those who possess power without compassion, might without morality, and strength without sight.

Now let us begin. Now let us re-dedicate ourselves to the long and bitter—but beautiful—struggle for a new world. This is the calling of the sons of God, and our brothers wait eagerly for our response. Shall we say the odds are too great? Shall we tell them the struggle is too hard? Will our message be that the forces of American life militate against their arrival as full men, and we send our deepest regrets? Or will there be another message, of longing, of hope, of solidarity with their yearnings, of commitment to their cause, whatever the cost? The choice is ours, and though we might prefer it otherwise we *must* choose in this crucial moment of human history.

As that noble bard of yesterday, James Russell Lowell eloquently stated:

ONCE TO EVERY NATION
"Once to every man and nation,
   Comes the moment to decide
In the strife of truth and falsehood
   For the good or evil side;
Some great cause God's new Messiah
   Offering each the gloom or blight
And the choice goes by forever
   Twixt that darkness and that light.
"Though the cause of evil prosper
   Yet 'tis truth alone is strong
Though her portion be the scaffold
   And upon the throne be wrong
Yet that scaffold sways the future
   And behind the dim unknown
Standeth God within the shadow
   Keeping watch above his own."

Eugene McCarthy

On Vietnam
(October 16, 1967)

By the fall of 1967, public impatience with the war in Vietnam had grown, even though the administration was optimistic in its predictions for the future. The Harris Poll reported that American support for the war had dropped from 72 percent to 58 percent between July and September. President Johnson's handling of the war met with the disapproval of 57 percent of the respondents in a Gallup Poll reported on October 9. These figures, however, masked the complex nature of public opinion. Some disapproved of the President's handling of the war because they favored de-escalation or withdrawal; others disapproved because they thought that Johnson was not prosecuting the war vigorously enough.

Among those known as "doves" because they wanted to de-escalate the war, protest activities intensified and were to be climaxed by a march on the Pentagon in late October. Meanwhile, others sought through the political process to reverse the course of the war. Americans for Democratic Action, a liberal group, in late September promised its support to the candidate who offered "the best prospect for a settlement of the Vietnam conflict," an implicit threat to the President. A vice chairman of ADA, Allard Lowenstein, organized a "dump Johnson" campaign and began to court other Democrats to run for President. Many younger liberals believed that the only way in which they could create an effective political effort against the war was to run an antiwar candidate for President.

Periodically throughout the war, President Johnson had halted the bombing of North Vietnam in the hope that this step might facilitate peace negotiations, but this hope had proved to be futile. In the fall of 1967, a bipartisan group of thirty members of Congress called upon the President to stop the bombing again. In response to this request, Secretary of State Dean Rusk held a press conference in which he asserted a new justification for staying firm in Vietnam. He implied that the issue was not just the survival of South Vietnam but the protection of Americans from China. In a decade or so, Rusk suggested, there would be "a billion Chinese on the mainland, armed with nuclear weapons, with no certainty about what their attitude toward the rest of Asia will be." To abandon Vietnam in the face of this threat, he suggested, would be to place the United States in danger. This argument made the American presence in Vietnam seem even more essential. It prompted a response on the Senate floor from Sen. Eugene McCarthy of Minnesota.

McCarthy was an atypical politician. By nature reserved and aloof, he shunned the rough-and-tumble of public political debate. He was often regarded as a philosopher, poet, or theologian who was in the political world but not really a part of it. He was considered a "dove" but a quiet one who seldom spoke out against the President's policy. He had voted for the Gulf of Tonkin Resolution in 1964 but did not believe that in doing so he was voting to endorse the war. His opposition evolved slowly.

McCarthy, however, could not accept Rusk's argument, reminiscent as it was of the early-twentieth-century stereotype of the "Yellow Peril." He criticized Rusk's remarks and challenged the premise of the widely accepted "domino theory": that the loss of any Southeast Asian country to communism would result in a whole series of Communist triumphs. He did not yet advocate withdrawal from Vietnam, however; he merely challenged the assumptions on which Johnson's Vietnam policy was based.

Nevertheless, McCarthy's Senate speech is a good index of the evolution of antiwar sentiment among political moderates. It made public McCarthy's break with the administration and provided evidence of yet another Democrat breaking with the President. It was the first step toward McCarthy's willingness to run for President on a platform promising to stop the war.

On October 26, McCarthy called for Rusk's resignation as a sign of a shift in the administration's policy direction on Vietnam. On November 9, he said that the time had come for the United States to consider whether the war was defensible on moral grounds. Finally, on November 30, after Robert Kennedy had refused to do so, McCarthy declared his candidacy for President and announced that he would enter some of the 1968 Presidential primaries to raise the issue of the war. If his effort did not prompt a policy change by the Johnson administration, he promised, then the challenge would go all the way to an active campaign for the Presidency.

Originally written off as a quixotic effort by college-age liberals, the McCarthy campaign caught fire in the 1968 New Hampshire primary, where the senator received 42 percent of the vote to Johnson's 49 percent. That showing prompted Robert Kennedy to enter the race and began a bitter campaign for the nomination, which McCarthy, after Kennedy's assassination, ultimately would lose to Vice President Hubert Humphrey.

STATEMENTS OF DEAN RUSK ON VIETNAM ANALYZED

Mr. President,—on Monday, October 12 the Secretary of State, Mr. Dean Rusk, opened his press conference with a statement which has been marked by editors and commentators as significant. They are not altogether in agreement as to what constitutes the significance, but generally it has been labeled as bold and clarifying. I do not see it as being any more bold than previous statements made by the Secretary nor any clearer since the style and language are those of the Secretary, unless the clarification is in the more simplified and restricted statement of our purpose and objectives in Vietnam. The Secretary did not speak of bringing the good life or the great society to Southeast Asia as a purpose of the war or of honoring the pledges of four Presidents, nor did he suggest that we cannot improve life in our own cities unless we make improvements in Vietnam. He said that we are in Vietnam in our own national interest and to honor our commitment.

> Our commitment is clear and our national interest is real- -

He said. I do not intend to reopen the question as to whether or not our commitment is clear since this point has been subject to serious debate and challenge for nearly a year and a half.

The Tonkin Gulf resolution in 1964 gave the President no power which he did not already have nor was it in any way an open-ended license for expansion and intensification of the war free from congressional restraint or criticism.

The President, in a recent press conference, indicated the purpose of that resolution. He said the purpose was to keep Congress in place and hold us committed in case there was a change in policy in Southeast Asia.

Our commitment under the SEATO Treaty signed in 1954 was a limited one, imposing a limited obligation upon us, an obligation which was contingent at least in part on the concurrent response of the other major nations in the treaty organizations. There is little to be gained from arguing these quasi-legal points. Any worthwhile debate must deal with the realities of Southeast Asia. The debate on Vietnam is not a matter of variations on a theme although the Secretary evidently wants to have it considered within those limits. It is a debate upon the theme itself and beyond that on the nature of the music which the State Department is playing.

Let me consider first the positive statements made by the Secretary. He said there is "no significant body of American opinion which would have us withdraw from Vietnam" and "no serious opinion among us which wishes to transform this struggle into a general war." I do not know whether this is an accurate statement or not, but in any case it is irrelevant since the debate on our policy in Vietnam falls between these two extremes.

Early in his remarks the Secretary speaks of the fate which Asian communism has planned for Southeast Asia. Asian communism, for that matter world communism, undoubtedly has a fate planned for Southeast Asia and for all the world, but the fact that it has

such plans does not necessarily mean that they are possible of realization or that we have to respond to every action as though the total plan were in operation and likely to be realized.

On the record, the Secretary has not shown himself to be the most accurate judge of Chinese intentions or potential or of the other forces running within the world. I quote from his May 18, 1951, speech before the China Institute in New York: he describes "greedy hands" of Russia stretching out to dismember China.

He said:

> China is being sacrificed to the ambitions of the communist conspiracy. China has been driven by foreign masters into an adventure of foreign aggression ... (Korea); the Peiping regime may be a colonial Russian government—a Slavic Manchukuo on a larger scale. It is not the government of China. It does not pass the first test. It is not Chinese.

He said of the Nationalist Chinese government:

> We believe it more authentically represents the views of the great body of the people of China, particularly their historical demand for independence from foreign control.

The debate on Vietnam is not, as the Secretary states, essentially over procedures for carrying out policies on which the Nation is united. This is a debate on matters of great substance over which the Nation is indeed deeply divided and concerned. The Secretary may speak as solemnly as he can—and he can speak solemnly—but the Members of Congress and the people of the country must continue to ask and seek answers to the question, "What is America's proper role in the world and what is the bearing of the policy in Vietnam on the fulfillment of that role?" We cannot permit the Secretary to dismiss, even solemnly, the United Nations and the recommendations of Members of the Senate including the majority leader, Senator MANSFIELD, with the easy remark:

> There are some problems about going through an exercise of futility ... to satisfy some critics among our own people.

Members of the Senate have a clear constitutional responsibility, which becomes personal because of their position, to be concerned over foreign policy, a responsibility which in the case of the Secretary of State exists only by delegation or proxy. As a matter of fact much of what has been done or what is being done in Vietnam may be a costly exercise in futility—that the bombing of North Vietnam for example, if we are to accept the recent testimony of the Secretary of Defense regarding the failure of that bombing to reduce significantly the supply of arms and men to the South, may be such an exercise; that the much publicized program of pacification, more recently labeled "revolutionary development," which is essentially an attempt to graft onto Asian society Western values and institutions and practices, may also be an exercise in futility.

The one rather clear conclusion from his remarks is that in his mind, the United States must establish and maintain an anti-Communist bastion in South Vietnam and that this is essential as a part of the overall strategy of containing China through encirclement and that all of this bears quite directly on our national interest, if not our survival. This is a continuing application of the strategic theory of John Foster Dulles and reflects in action the ancient fear of the yellow peril presented to us now in a new image of the Secretary of State in his words:

> Within the next decade or two there will be a billion Chinese on the Mainland, armed with nuclear weapons, with no certainty about what their attitude toward the rest of Asia will be.

If this is the specter that is haunting Asia, it is difficult to see how we will rid Asia of it even though we achieve an unpredictable and total victory in South Vietnam.

I fail to see the relationship between the 1 billion and nuclear weapons. We have in this country 200 million people, very nearly, but only one of them has control over nuclear weapons.

The Secretary seems to accept the Chinese Communists' belief that their doctrine of world revolution is applicable to the entire underdeveloped world. It must be encouraging to the Chinese propagandists to see this basic tenet of their political philosophy accepted and endorsed by the American Secretary of State.

I think, Mr. President, that we must ask ourselves: What is the real measure of the Chinese threat? What does it show on the record? There may be every reason to believe that the leaders in Peking are firmly convinced that their revolution will serve as a model for the developing world and for the eventual defeat of the industrial "cities" by the countryside of the "people," in reality, the Chinese experience has, with one significant exception, almost no relevance outside China. In no other country or part of the world do precisely the

same conditions exist under which the Chinese Communists achieved power. Mao was able to gain control of China because he gained leadership of the Chinese nationalist movement, consolidating, and leading it against a foreign invader in World War II. Only in Vietnam has this feat been duplicated. Ho Chi Minh is the only Communist leader in the underdeveloped world who was able to gain control of his country's nationalist movement at the time of resistance to a foreign invasion.

Throughout the underdeveloped world, Chinese attempts to promote their style of revolution have met with failure, largely because of internal forces, of which nationalism itself is the most important.

The failure of the Communist attempt to gain control of Indonesia in late 1965 was a disaster of major proportions. China's attack on India in 1962 and her support of Pakistan on the Kashmir issue have dealt a severe blow to whatever hopes Indian Communists might have had for capitalizing on India's internal problems and divisions.

In Japan the Communist Party has followed the Peking line at great cost, alienating the trade unions and the powerful Japanese Socialist Party. Even North Korea has proclaimed its "neutrality" in the Sino-Soviet Communist struggle. China's lack of success in Africa has also been noteworthy. The Government of Malawi had to get rid of some cabinet ministers for allegedly conspiring with the Chinese; Kenya expelled the New China News Agency correspondent "in the interests of national security"; Burundi, once regarded as safely in the Chinese camp, expelled Peking's diplomatic mission. In Latin America, the Chinese have had even less success. Even Fidel Castro, whose rise to power had been hailed in Peking as a demonstration of the validity of the Chinese analysis of the Latin American revolutionary situation, has also denounced China.

China continues to talk a world power game, but even with nuclear weapons, the evidence of internal economic difficulties, particularly the food-population problem, and the political struggle, which may be only a dress rehearsal for what will come after Mao passes from the scene, suggest that China's principal concern and effort will remain domestic and internal for a long time to come.

China's foreign policy objectives are of concern to us, but there is significant disagreement—which we must also acknowledge—about her ability to pursue these objectives successfully. She seeks recognition as a great power whose voice is heard in the world's councils. China, understandably, seeks to overcome the bitter legacy of a hundred years of humiliation by the West. Recognition as a great power is essentially a nationalist, rather than an ideological objective. All Chinese, Communist and non-Communist, agree on its importance.

China also seeks recovery of the "lost territories," Hong Kong, Macao, parts of Soviet Asia, Taiwan and the offshore islands, and land along the Sino-Indian frontier. This is also an essentially nationalist objective, shared by all Chinese. In Chinese eyes, it is not an expansionist position, for they consider that these territories were taken forcibly from China by the unequal treaties imposed on her during the 19th century, or in the case of Taiwan, were denied to her by the military power of the U.S. 7th Fleet.

China seeks to reestablish what she considers her traditional sphere of influence in Southeast Asia and to eradicate U.S. military power from the Asian mainland. Chinese political domination in that area has not been clear or consistent, at least not since the 10th century when Vietnam achieved "independence" from China. At times the relationship appears to have meant little more than tacit agreement not to aid China's enemies.

China's desire to eliminate U.S. power and influence from the Asian mainland, where it conforms to Communist ideological opposition to democratic philosophy, is basically nationalistic and there is little reason to believe that a non-Communist Chinese government would welcome a U.S. presence on the Asian mainland any more than the present government in Peking actually does.

Our policy in the Far East is based largely on unsubstantiated assumptions. First, we assume that revolutions throughout the less-developed world are a Chinese-inspired wave of the future and that Vietnam is a test case for guerrilla war and for wars of national liberation. There is no good reason for accepting this characterization of the war in Vietnam. The techniques of the Chinese revolution have not yet proved fully successful in China; they are a long way from inspiring revolution in other parts of the world. Second, we assert that the Southeast Asia situation is analogous to previous situations and experiences in Asia and in Europe. Military containment worked in Europe and in Korea, according to the theory; thus it is the method to be applied in Southeast Asia or in any other test area. But the conditions under which containment was effective in Europe and in Korea do not exist in Southeast Asia, which is marked by deep ethnic and social divisions; by instability, political and social; by deep antagonism to Western colonialism; and by a desire for change rather than for a return to the past.

Many of our problems today are the result of our unwillingness or inability in the past to anticipate what might be the shape of the world 20 years in the future. Few Americans expected in 1945 that 20 years later we would still have 225,000 troops in Europe. We have 55,000 troops in South Korea 14 years after the end of the fighting yet at the height of the Korean conflict, we never had as many troops committed as we have today in Vietnam. We must ask whether we are prepared to maintain from 100,000 to 200,000 troops in South Vietnam as well, for 15 or 20 years after the fighting stops. If we are not prepared to do so, the process must be reversed before temporary commitment assumes the character of a permanent establishment and an irritation in the changed context of another generation. We must begin now the adjustments of attitude which will be necessary if we are to reduce or liquidate our commitments in Asia.

The long-range question is whether the United States and China are on a collision course. The likelihood of confrontation, of ultimate showdown, is not immediate, and certainly is not inevitable.

With regret I must conclude that the Secretary, in his remarks, has added nothing constructive to the debate of American involvement in Southeast Asia by way of new facts, new policies, strategy, or understanding, but rather because of the posture, almost of defiance, careless of intentional abuse of the language, can serve only to raise the emotional level of the debate, obscure the issues upon which judgment should be made and cause further frustration and division within the country, I believe, as well as between the Congress and the executive branch of the Government.

Lyndon B. Johnson

Renunciation Speech
(March 31, 1968)

The ambiguities of Vietnam followed Lyndon Johnson throughout his Presidency. By the fall of 1967, things seemed to be looking up. Americans and the South Vietnamese were making military gains, military leaders were predicting imminent success, and twice as many people regarded themselves as hawks than as doves. To be sure, the cost of the war had slowed the Great Society and had begun to fuel inflation, but the domestic programs had not been abandoned for the duration.

These bright prospects, however, were shattered by the Tet offensive at the end of January 1968. On the occasion of the Vietnamese New Year, guerrillas struck simultaneously against the major cities and provincial capitals, including the seemingly impregnable U.S. Embassy in Saigon itself. The offensive ultimately was a military failure; all the attackers were routed within two or three weeks. But Tet dealt a severe psychological blow to the assumption that all was going well and that the enemy was facing imminent collapse. In larger numbers, Americans doubted that they had been told the truth and more sharply questioned whether the purposes for which the war was being fought were really worth the cost.

Newly appointed Secretary of Defense Clark Clifford undertook a complete review of American policy. Other factors also called for a review: the growing harm to the balance of payments caused by Vietnam spending and the position of the dollar, the surprisingly strong showing by Sen. Eugene McCarthy in the New Hampshire primary, and the subsequent entry of Sen. Robert F. Kennedy into the Presidential race; the fact that polls for the first time showed that a majority of the people opposed Johnson's war policy (although the opposition was divided equally between hawks and doves), and the disclosure in March that, in the aftermath of Tet, Gen. William Westmoreland—who had been optimistic the previous fall—had requested an increase of over 206,000 troops in Vietnam, almost a 50 percent increase in the number stationed there.

Such a volatile situation almost demands a Presidential speech, for Presidential discourse enables Americans to structure an ambiguous situation. Johnson announced a nationwide television address for Sunday, March 31. There ensued an intense internal controversy about what should be said. Johnson's informal speeches during March sounded hawkish, but a group of senior advisers from past administrations (the "Wise Men") tried to convince the President that the war was not winnable on acceptable terms, and urged him to disengage and cut his losses. Writers were working on two alternative drafts of the speech, one far more conciliatory and one calling for increased commitments and manpower. Only two days before delivery did the writer receive word that the "peace speech" was going to be used.

The "peace speech," though, was something of a misnomer. It reaffirmed American commitments and asserted that they had been successful. As a result, the nation was now able to operate without the additional 206,000 troops Westmoreland had requested. But there would be *some* additions, together with the pledge of more should it be needed. In a dramatic concession to antiwar protest, Johnson stopped aerial bombing over approximately 90 percent of the area of North Vietnam. But he did not stop it altogether and he insisted on a quid pro quo in future negotiations before he would stop it altogether.

The genius of this text is in its manipulation of ambiguities. Depending on one's wish, the speech can be read as an indicator of *continuity* or of major *change*. Antiwar protesters acknowledged it as a concession to them, but Johnson claimed that it was inspired because of Secretary of State Rusk's claim that Johnson's policy had been such a success that the American presence could be capped at its current size.

It was not the Vietnam section of the speech that was well remembered. Instead, it was the final section, in which Johnson startled the nation with the news that he was not a candidate for re-election, because the time he would spend in campaigning would be a distraction from the pursuit of peace. Evidence indicates that Johnson privately had decided on this course the previous fall but had delayed the announcement so that it might be used for maximum effect. Including it here—rather than a press conference or State of the Union address—tied Johnson's personal plans with his Vietnam policy. His personal political sacrifice lent weight and credibility to his statement that he was devoting all his energies to the pursuit of peace. What the Vietnam remarks on March 31 meant is still the subject of controversy. Johnson was probably as surprised as anyone when, within three days of this speech, the North Vietnamese agreed to open peace talks in Paris. Procedural disputes were arcane and protracted, and Johnson left office the following January with one-half million Americans still in uniform in Vietnam.

Good evening, my fellow Americans:—Tonight I want to speak to you of peace in Vietnam and Southeast Asia.

No other question so preoccupies our people. No other dream so absorbs the 250 million human beings who live in that part of the world. No other goal motivates American policy in Southeast Asia.

For years, representatives of our Government and others have traveled the world—seeking to find a basis for peace talks.

Since last September, they have carried the offer that I made public at San Antonio.

That offer was this:

That the United States would stop its bombardment of North Vietnam when that would lead promptly to productive discussions—and that we would assume that North Vietnam would not take military advantage of our restraint.

Hanoi denounced this offer, both privately and publicly. Even while the search for peace was going on, North Vietnam rushed their preparations for a savage assault on the people, the government, and the allies of South Vietnam.

Their attack—during the Tet holidays—failed to achieve its principal objectives.

It did not collapse the elected government of South Vietnam or shatter its army—as the Communists had hoped.

It did not produce a "general uprising" among the people of the cities as they had predicted.

The Communists were unable to maintain control of any of the more than 30 cities that they attacked. And they took very heavy casualties.

But they did compel the South Vietnamese and their allies to move certain forces from the countryside into the cities.

They caused widespread disruption and suffering. Their attacks, and the battles that followed, made refugees of half a million human beings.

The Communists may renew their attack any day.

They are, it appears, trying to make 1968 the year of decision in South Vietnam—the year that brings, if not final victory or defeat, at least a turning point in the struggle.

This much is clear:

If they do mount another round of heavy attacks, they will not succeed in destroying the fighting power of South Vietnam and its allies.

But tragically, this is also clear: Many men—on both sides of the struggle—will be lost. A nation that has already suffered 20 years of warfare will suffer once again. Armies on both sides will take new casualties. And the war will go on.

There is no need for this to be so.

There is no need to delay the talks that could bring an end to this long and this bloody war.

Tonight, I renew the offer I made last August—to stop the bombardment of North Vietnam. We ask that talks begin promptly, that they be serious talks on the substance of peace. We assume that during those talks Hanoi will not take advantage of our restraint.

We are prepared to move immediately toward peace through negotiations.

So, tonight, in the hope that this action will lead to early talks, I am taking the first step to deescalate the conflict. We are reducing—substantially reducing—the present level of hostilities.

And we are doing so unilaterally, and at once.

Tonight, I have ordered our aircraft and our naval vessels to make no attacks on North Vietnam, except in the area north of the demilitarized zone where the continuing enemy buildup directly threatens allied forward positions and where the movements of their troops and supplies are clearly related to that threat.

The area in which we are stopping our attacks includes almost 90 percent of North Vietnam's population, and most of its territory. Thus there will be no attacks around the principal populated areas, or in the food-producing areas of North Vietnam.

Even this very limited bombing of the North could come to an early end—if our restraint is matched by restraint in Hanoi. But I cannot in good conscience stop all bombing so long as to do so would immediately and directly endanger the lives of our men and our allies. Whether a complete bombing halt becomes possible in the future will be determined by events.

Our purpose in this action is to bring about a reduction in the level of violence that now exists.

It is to save the lives of brave men—and to save the lives of innocent women and children. It is to permit the contending forces to move closer to a political settlement.

And tonight, I call upon the United Kingdom and I call upon the Soviet Union—as cochairmen of the Geneva Conferences, and as permanent members of the United Nations Security Council—to do all they can to move from the unilateral act of deescalation that I have just announced toward genuine peace in Southeast Asia.

Now, as in the past, the United States is ready to send its representatives to any forum, at any time, to discuss the means of bringing this ugly war to an end.

I am designating one of our most distinguished Americans, Ambassador Averell Harriman, as my personal representative for such talks. In addition, I have asked Ambassador Llewellyn Thompson, who returned from Moscow for consultation, to be available to join Ambassador Harriman at Geneva or any other suitable place—just as soon as Hanoi agrees to a conference.

I call upon President Ho Chi Minh to respond positively, and favorably, to this new step toward peace.

But if peace does not come now through negotiations, it will come when Hanoi understands that our common resolve is unshakable, and our common strength is invincible.

Tonight, we and the other allied nations are contributing 600,000 fighting men to assist 700,000 South Vietnamese troops in defending their little country.

Our presence there has always rested on this basic belief: The main burden of preserving their freedom must be carried out by them—by the South Vietnamese themselves.

We and our allies can only help to provide a shield behind which the people of South Vietnam can survive and can grow and develop. On their efforts—on their determination and resourcefulness—the outcome will ultimately depend.

That small, beleaguered nation has suffered terrible punishment for more than 20 years.

I pay tribute once again tonight to the great courage and endurance of its people. South Vietnam supports armed forces tonight of almost 700,000 men—and I call your attention to the fact that this is the equivalent of more than 10 million in our own population. Its people maintain their firm determination to be free of domination by the North.

There has been substantial progress, I think, in building a durable government during these last 3 years. The South Vietnam of 1965 could not have survived the enemy's Tet offensive of 1968. The elected government of South Vietnam survived that attack—and is rapidly repairing the devastation that it wrought.

The South Vietnamese know that further efforts are going to be required:

—to expand their own armed forces,
—to move back into the countryside as quickly as possible,
—to increase their taxes,
—to select the very best men that they have for civil and military responsibility,
—to achieve a new unity within their constitutional government, and
—to include in the national effort all those groups who wish to preserve South Vietnam's control over its own destiny.

Last week President Thieu ordered the mobilization of 135,000 additional South Vietnamese. He plans to reach—as soon as possible—a total military strength of more than 800,000 men.

To achieve this, the Government of South Vietnam started the drafting of 19-year-olds on March 1st. On May 1st, the Government will begin the drafting of 18-year-olds.

Last month, 10,000 men volunteered for military service—that was two and a half times the number of volunteers during the same month last year. Since the middle of January, more than 48,000 South Vietnamese have joined the armed forces—and nearly half of them volunteered to do so.

All men in the South Vietnamese armed forces have had their tours of duty extended for the duration of the war, and reserves are now being called up for immediate active duty.

President Thieu told his people last week:

"We must make greater efforts and accept more sacrifices because, as I have said many times, this is our country. The existence of our nation is at stake, and this is mainly a Vietnamese responsibility."

He warned his people that a major national effort is required to root out corruption and incompetence at all levels of government.

We applaud this evidence of determination on the part of South Vietnam. Our first priority will be to support their effort.

We shall accelerate the reequipment of South Vietnam's armed forces—in order to meet the enemy's increased firepower. This will enable them progressively to undertake a larger share of combat operations against the Communist invaders.

On many occasions I have told the American people that we would send to Vietnam those forces that are required to accomplish our mission there. So, with that as our guide, we have previously authorized a force level of approximately 525,000.

Some weeks ago—to help meet the enemy's new offensive—we sent to Vietnam about 11,000 additional Marine and airborne troops. They were deployed by air in 48 hours, on an emergency basis. But the artillery, tank, aircraft, medical, and other units that were needed to work with and to support these infantry troops in combat could not then accompany them by air on that short notice.

In order that these forces may reach maximum combat effectiveness, the Joint Chiefs of Staff have recommended to me that we should prepare to send—during the next 5 months—support troops totaling approximately 13,500 men.

A portion of these men will be made available from our active forces. The balance will come from reserve component units which will be called up for service.

The actions that we have taken since the beginning of the year

—to reequip the South Vietnamese forces,

—to meet our responsibilities in Korea, as well as our responsibilities in Vietnam,

—to meet price increases and the cost of activating and deploying reserve forces,

—to replace helicopters and provide the other military supplies we need,

all of these actions are going to require additional expenditures.

The tentative estimate of those additional expenditures is $2.5 billion in this fiscal year, and $2.6 billion in the next fiscal year.

These projected increases in expenditures for our national security will bring into sharper focus the Nation's need for immediate action: action to protect the prosperity of the American people and to protect the strength and the stability of our American dollar.

On many occasions I have pointed out that, without a tax bill or decreased expenditures, next year's deficit would again be around $20 billion. I have emphasized the need to set strict priorities in our spending. I have stressed that failure to act and to act promptly and decisively would raise very strong doubts throughout the world about America's willingness to keep its financial house in order.

Yet Congress has not acted. And tonight we face the sharpest financial threat in the postwar era—a threat to the dollar's role as the keystone of international trade and finance in the world.

Last week, at the monetary conference in Stockholm, the major industrial countries decided to take a big step toward creating a new international monetary asset that will strengthen the international monetary system. I am very proud of the very able work done by Secretary Fowler and Chairman Martin of the Federal Reserve Board.

But to make this system work the United States just must bring its balance of payments to—or very close to—equilibrium. We must have a responsible fiscal policy in this country. The passage of a tax bill now, together with expenditure control that the Congress may desire and dictate, is absolutely necessary to protect this Nation's security, to continue our prosperity, and to meet the needs of our people.

What is at stake is 7 years of unparalleled prosperity. In those 7 years, the real income of the average American, after taxes, rose by almost 30 percent—a gain as large as that of the entire preceding 19 years.

So the steps that we must take to convince the world are exactly the steps we must take to sustain our own economic strength here at home. In the past 8 months, prices and interest rates have risen because of our inaction.

We must, therefore, now do everything we can to move from debate to action—from talking to voting. There is, I believe—I hope there is—in both Houses of the Congress—a growing sense of urgency that this situation just must be acted upon and must be corrected.

My budget in January was, we thought, a tight one. It fully reflected our evaluation of most of the demanding needs of this Nation.

But in these budgetary matters, the President does not decide alone. The Congress has the power and the duty to determine appropriations and taxes.

The Congress is now considering our proposals and they are considering reductions in the budget that we submitted.

As part of a program of fiscal restraint that includes the tax surcharge, I shall approve appropriate reductions in the January budget when and if Congress so decides that that should be done.

One thing is unmistakably clear, however: Our deficit just must be reduced. Failure to act could bring on conditions that would strike hardest at those people that all of us are trying so hard to help.

These times call for prudence in this land of plenty. I believe that we have the character to provide it, and tonight I plead with the Congress and with the people to act promptly to serve the national interest, and thereby serve all of our people.

Now let me give you my estimate of the chances for peace:

—the peace that will one day stop the bloodshed in South Vietnam,

—that will permit all the Vietnamese people to rebuild and develop their land,

—that will permit us to turn more fully to our own tasks here at home.

I cannot promise that the initiative that I have announced tonight will be completely successful in achieving peace any more than the 30 others that we have undertaken and agreed to in recent years.

But it is our fervent hope that North Vietnam, after years of fighting that have left the issue unresolved, will now cease its efforts to achieve a military victory and will join with us in moving toward the peace table.

And there may come a time when South Vietnamese—on both sides—are able to work out a way to settle their own differences by free political choice rather than by war.

As Hanoi considers its course, it should be in no doubt of our intentions. It must not miscalculate the pressures within our democracy in this election year.

We have no intention of widening this war.

But the United States will never accept a fake solution to this long and arduous struggle and call it peace.

No one can foretell the precise terms of an eventual settlement.

Our objective in South Vietnam has never been the annihilation of the enemy. It has been to bring about a recognition in Hanoi that its objective—taking over the South by force—could not be achieved.

We think that peace can be based on the Geneva Accords of 1954—under political conditions that permit the South Vietnamese—all the South Vietnamese—to chart their course free of any outside domination or interference, from us or from anyone else.

So tonight I reaffirm the pledge that we made at Manila—that we are prepared to withdraw our forces from South Vietnam as the other side withdraws its forces to the north, stops the infiltration, and the level of violence thus subsides.

Our goal of peace and self-determination in Vietnam is directly related to the future of all of Southeast Asia—where much has happened to inspire confidence during the past 10 years. We have done all that we knew how to do to contribute and to help build that confidence.

A number of its nations have shown what can be accomplished under conditions of security. Since 1966, Indonesia, the fifth largest nation in all the world, with a population of more than 100 million people, has had a government that is dedicated to peace with its neighbors and improved conditions for its own people. Political and economic cooperation between nations has grown rapidly.

I think every American can take a great deal of pride in the role that we have played in bringing this about in Southeast Asia. We can rightly judge—as responsible Southeast Asians themselves do—that the progress of the past 3 years would have been far less likely—if not completely impossible—if America's sons and others had not made their stand in Vietnam.

At Johns Hopkins University, about 3 years ago, I announced that the United States would take part in the great work of developing Southeast Asia, including the Mekong Valley, for all the people of that region. Our determination to help build a better land—a better land for men on both sides of the present conflict—has not diminished in the least. Indeed, the ravages of war, I think, have made it more urgent than ever.

So, I repeat on behalf of the United States again tonight what I said at Johns Hopkins—that North Vietnam could take its place in this common effort just as soon as peace comes.

Over time, a wider framework of peace and security in Southeast Asia may become possible. The new cooperation of the nations of the area could be a foundation-stone. Certainly friendship with the nations of such a Southeast Asia is what the United States seeks—and that is all that the United States seeks.

One day, my fellow citizens, there will be peace in Southeast Asia.

It will come because the people of Southeast Asia want it—those whose armies are at war tonight, and those who, though threatened, have thus far been spared.

Peace will come because Asians were willing to work for it—and to sacrifice for it—and to die by the thousands for it.

But let it never be forgotten: Peace will come also because America sent her sons to help secure it.

It has not been easy—far from it. During the past 4 1/2 years, it has been my fate and my responsibility to be Commander in Chief. I have lived—daily and nightly—with the cost of this war. I know the pain that it has inflicted. I know, perhaps better than anyone, the misgivings that it has aroused.

Throughout this entire, long period, I have been sustained by a single principle: that what we are doing now, in Vietnam, is vital not only to the security of Southeast Asia, but it is vital to the security of every American.

Surely we have treaties which we must respect. Surely we have commitments that we are going to keep. Resolutions of the Congress testify to the need to resist aggression in the world and in Southeast Asia.

But the heart of our involvement in South Vietnam—under three different Presidents, three separate administrations—has always been America's own security.

And the larger purpose of our involvement has always been to help the nations of Southeast Asia become independent and stand alone, self-sustaining, as members of a great world community—at peace with themselves, and at peace with all others.

With such an Asia, our country—and the world—will be far more secure than it is tonight.

I believe that a peaceful Asia is far nearer to reality because of what America has done in Vietnam. I believe that the men who endure the dangers of battle—fighting there for us tonight—are helping the entire world avoid far greater conflicts, far wider wars, far more destruction, than this one.

The peace that will bring them home someday will come. Tonight I have offered the first in what I hope will be a series of mutual moves toward peace.

I pray that it will not be rejected by the leaders of North Vietnam. I pray that they will accept it as a means by which the sacrifices of their own people may be ended. And I ask your help and your support, my fellow citizens, for this effort to reach across the battlefield toward an early peace.

Finally, my fellow Americans, let me say this:

Of those to whom much is given, much is asked. I cannot say and no man could say that no more will be asked of us.

Yet, I believe that now, no less than when the decade began, this generation of Americans is willing to "pay any price, bear any burden, meet any hardship, support any friend, oppose any foe to assure the survival and the success of liberty."

Since those words were spoken by John F. Kennedy, the people of America have kept that compact with mankind's noblest cause.

And we shall continue to keep it.

Yet, I believe that we must always be mindful of this one thing, whatever the trials and the tests ahead. The ultimate strength of our country and our cause will lie not in powerful weapons or infinite resources or boundless wealth, but will lie in the unity of our people.

This I believe very deeply.

Throughout my entire public career I have followed the personal philosophy that I am a free man, an American, a public servant, and a member of my party, in that order always and only.

For 37 years in the service of our Nation, first as a Congressman, as a Senator, and as Vice President, and now as your President, I have put the unity of the people first. I have put it ahead of any divisive partisanship.

And in these times as in times before, it is true that a house divided against itself by the spirit of faction, of party, of region, of religion, of race, is a house that cannot stand.

There is division in the American house now.

There is divisiveness among us all tonight. And holding the trust that is mine, as President of all the people, I cannot disregard the peril to the progress of the American people and the hope and the prospect of peace for all peoples.

So, I would ask all Americans, whatever their personal interests or concern, to guard against divisiveness and all its ugly consequences.

Fifty-two months and 10 days ago, in a moment of tragedy and trauma, the duties of this office fell upon me. I asked then for your help and God's, that we might continue America on its course, binding up our wounds, healing our history, moving forward in new unity, to clear the American agenda and to keep the American commitment for all of our people.

United we have kept that commitment. United we have enlarged that commitment.

Through all time to come, I think America will be a stronger nation, a more just society, and a land of greater opportunity and fulfillment because of what we have all done together in these years of unparalleled achievement.

Our reward will come in the life of freedom, peace, and hope that our children will enjoy through ages ahead.

What we won when all of our people united just must not now be lost in suspicion, distrust, selfishness, and politics among any of our people.

Believing this as I do, I have concluded that I should not permit the Presidency to become involved in the partisan divisions that are developing in this political year.

With America's sons in the fields far away, with America's future under challenge right here at home, with our hopes and the world's hopes for peace in the balance every day, I do not believe that I should devote an hour or a day of my time to any personal partisan causes or to any duties other than the awesome duties of this office—the Presidency of your country.

Accordingly, I shall not seek, and I will not accept, the nomination of my party for another term as your President.

But let men everywhere know, however, that a strong, a confident, and a vigilant America stands ready tonight to seek an honorable peace—and stands ready tonight to defend an honored cause—whatever the price, whatever the burden, whatever the sacrifice that duty may require.

Thank you for listening.

Good night and God bless all of you.

Hubert Humphrey

Salt Lake City Speech
(September 30, 1968)

Like the rest of the country, Vice President Hubert Humphrey listened in stunned silence on March 31, 1968, when President Lyndon Johnson announced that he would not be a candidate for re-election. During the next few weeks Humphrey examined his options, and on April 27 he announced his own candidacy for President. Immediately the Vice President faced two rhetorical problems. First, he suddenly felt the burden of responsibility for Johnson's Vietnam policy without having had real authority to influence it (and, indeed, having privately opposed large-scale bombing of North Vietnam). Somehow he had to distance himself from Johnson on Vietnam in order to win the allegiance of disgruntled Democrats. But therein lay his second problem. He could not go too far without repudiating his own role. And he needed to appeal to untapped delegate strength within the mainstream of Democratic voters, particularly organized labor, who largely *supported* Johnson on Vietnam.

During the spring and summer months, Humphrey tried two ways to escape his dilemma, and they both failed. First, he tried to transcend the issue by appealing to broad values of the political process itself. But his upbeat rhetoric about the American system simply did not correspond to the ghastly events of 1968—the murders of Martin Luther King, Jr., and Robert Kennedy, Humphrey's inept handling of protesters during the summer, and the brutal response of the Chicago police to demonstrations at the convention. Second, he tried to defend Johnson's record on Vietnam as a matter of personal and professional loyalty while hoping for a favorable break on the battlefield or at the negotiating table. But this approach created the impression that Humphrey was tied to Johnson on Vietnam, especially when he insisted on defeating a "peace plank" in the Democratic platform and approving a plank strongly supportive of the President. All he could manage in his acceptance speech was a tepid suggestion that "the policies of tomorrow need not be limited by the policies of yesterday."

Humphrey's first month of the fall campaign was dismal. He actually lowered his standing in the polls despite active campaigning. He was plagued by disruptive hecklers who shouted down his speeches and pre-empted his news coverage; he was short on both strategy and money; and the pall of the loser hung over him. Indeed, it was an open question whether Humphrey or third-party candidate George Wallace would finish last. In desperation he decided to make a half-hour television speech from Salt Lake City on September 30. There was bitter dispute among his advisers as to what he should say, and he finally dismissed his aides and outlined the speech himself.

The speech presents the critic with a puzzle. The policy it announces is only marginally different from that of Lyndon Johnson, especially when Humphrey threatened to resume bombing if the North Vietnamese were to show bad faith. It must be read very carefully to detect nuances such as Humphrey's endorsement of a bombing halt without preconditions. Yet the speech was widely perceived as the turning point of the campaign, the time when Humphrey emerged from Johnson's shadow and became his own man. Solving the puzzle requires examining the image or *persona* that the Vice President built through this speech. It suggested a candidate who, after a sputtering start to the campaign, was clearly in control. The absence of the Vice Presidential seal and the fact that Lyndon Johnson was not informed of the speech until moments before its delivery symbolized Humphrey's independence. Advisers resolved the ambiguity in the speech by explaining to the press that it was artifice, deliberately chosen to conceal the candidate's true intentions from those who still feared that Humphrey might be "soft on communism."

The speech had a tonic effect on the candidate and the campaign. He felt better about himself; the heckling at his rallies almost immediately ceased. By removing the Vietnam millstone, the Salt Lake City speech allowed Humphrey to return to his theme of trust in the political process. This theme enabled him to attack both Nixon and Wallace, and to woo traditional Democrats back to the fold. The race tightened during October and ended up "too close to call." Many factors contributed to that result, but the Salt Lake City speech was especially important in creating a Humphrey persona that allowed him to transform the campaign from one of despair to one of hope.

Tonight I want to share with you my thoughts as a citizen and a candidate for President of the United States. I want to tell you what I think about great issues which I believe face this nation.

I want to talk with you about Vietnam, and about another great issue in the search for peace in the world—the issue of stopping the threat of nuclear war.

After I have told you what I think, I want you to think.

And if you agree with me, I want you to help me.

For the past several weeks, I have tried to tell you what was in my heart and on my mind.

But sometimes that message has been drowned out by the voices of protesters and demonstrators.

I shall not let the violence and disorder of a noisy few deny me the right to speak or to destroy the orderly democratic process.

I have paid for this television time this evening to tell you my story uninterrupted by noise ... by protest ... or by second-hand interpretation.

When I accepted the Democratic party's nomination and platform, I said that the first reality that confronted this nation was the need for peace in Vietnam.

I have pledged that my first priority as President shall be to end the war and obtain an honorable peace.

For the past four years I have spoken my mind about Vietnam, frankly and without reservation, in the Cabinet and in the National Security Council—and directly to the President.

When the President has made his decisions, I have supported them.

He has been the Commander in Chief. It has been his job to decide. And the choices have not been simple or easy.

President Johnson will continue—until Jan. 20, 1969—to make the decisions in Vietnam. The voice at the negotiating table must be his. I shall not compete with that voice. I shall cooperate and help.

We all pray that his efforts to find peace will succeed.

But, 112 days from now, there will be a President ... a new Administration ... and new advisers.

If there is no peace by then, it must be their responsibility to make a complete reassessment of the situation in Vietnam—to see where we stand and to judge what we must do.

As I said in my acceptance speech: The policies of tomorrow need not be limited by the policies of yesterday.

We must look to the future. For neither vindication nor repudiation of our role in Vietnam will bring peace or be worthy of our country.

The American people have a right to know what I would do—if I am President—after Jan. 20, 1969, to keep my pledge to honorably end the war in Vietnam.

What are the chances for peace?

The end of the war is not yet in sight. But our chances for peace are far better today than they were a year or even a month ago.

On March 31, the war took on an entirely new dimension.

On that date President Johnson by one courageous act removed the threat of bombing from 90 per cent of the people, and 78 per cent of the land area, of North Vietnam.

On that date President Johnson sacrificed his own political career in order to bring negotiations that could lead to peace.

Until that time, the struggle was only on the battlefield.

Now our negotiators are face to face across the table with negotiators from North Vietnam.

A process has been set in course. And lest that process be set back, our perseverance at the conference table must be great as our courage has been in the war.

There have been other changes during these past few months.

The original Vietnam decision—made by President Eisenhower—was made for one basic reason.

President Eisenhower believed it was in our national interest that Communist subversion and aggression should not succeed in Vietnam.

It was his judgment—and the judgment of President Kennedy and President Johnson since then—that if aggression did succeed in Vietnam, there was a danger that we would become involved on a more dangerous scale in a wider area of Southeast Asia.

While we have stood with our allies in Vietnam, several things have happened.

Other nations of Southeast Asia—given the time we have bought for them—have strengthened themselves ... have begun to work together ... and are far more able to protect themselves against any future subversion or aggression.

In South Vietnam itself, a constitution has been written ... elections have been stepped up ... and the South Vietnamese Army has increased its size and capacity, and improved its equipment, training and performance—just as the Korean Army did during the latter stages of the Korean War.

So—in sharp contrast to a few months ago—we see peace negotiations going on.

We see a stronger Southeast Asia.

We see a stronger South Vietnam.

Those are the new circumstances which a new President will face in January.

In light of those circumstances—and assuming no marked change in the present situation—how would I proceed as President?

Let me first make clear what I would not do.

I would not undertake a unilateral withdrawal.

To withdraw would not only jeopardize the independence of South Vietnam and the safety of other Southeast Asian nations. It would make meaningless the sacrifices we have already made.

It would be an open invitation to more violence ... more aggression ... more instability.

It would, at this time of tension in Europe, cast doubt on the integrity of our word under treaty and alliance.

Peace would not be served by weakness or withdrawal.

Nor would I escalate the level of violence in either North or South Vietnam. We must seek to de-escalate.

The platform of my party says that the President should take reasonable risks to find peace in Vietnam. I shall do so.

North Vietnam, according to its own statements and those of others, has said it will proceed to prompt and good faith negotiations, if we stop the present limited bombing of the North.

We must always think of the protection of our troops.

As President, I would stop the bombing of the North as an acceptable risk for peace because I believe it could lead to success in the negotiations and thereby shorten the war. This would be the best protection for our troops.... In weighing that risk—and before taking action—I would place key importance on evidence—direct or indirect—by deed or word—of Communist willingness to restore the demilitarized zone between North and South Vietnam.

Now if the Government of North Vietnam were to show bad faith, I would reserve the right to resume the bombing.

Now secondly, I would take the risk that South Vietnamese would meet the responsibilities they say they are now ready to assume in their own self-defense.

I would move, in other words, toward de-Americanization of the war.

I would sit down with the leaders of South Vietnam to set a specific timetable by which American forces could be systematically reduced while South Vietnamese forces took over more and more of the burden.

The schedule must be a realistic one—one that would not weaken the over-all Allied defense posture. I am convinced such action would be as much in South Vietnam's interest as in ours.

What I am proposing is that it should be basic to our policy in Vietnam that the South Vietnamese take over more and more of the defense of their own country.

That would be an immediate objective of the Humphrey-Muskie Administration as I sought to end the war.

If the South Vietnamese Army maintains its present rate of improvement, I believe this will be possible next year—without endangering either our remaining troops or the safety of South Vietnam.

I do not say this lightly. I have studied this matter carefully.

Third, I would propose once more an immediate cease-fire—with United Nations or other international supervision and supervised withdrawal of all foreign forces from South Vietnam.

American troops are fighting in numbers in South Vietnam today only because North Vietnamese forces were sent to impose Hanoi's will on the South Vietnamese people by aggression.

We can agree to bring home our forces from South Vietnam, if the North Vietnamese agree to bring theirs home at the same time.

External forces assisting both sides could and should leave at the same time, and should not be replaced.

The ultimate key to an honorable solution must be free elections in South Vietnam—with all people, including members of the National Liberation Front and other dissident groups, able to participate in those elections if they were willing to abide by peaceful processes.

That, too, would mean some risk.

But I have never feared the risk of one man, one vote. I say: let the people speak. And accept their judgment, whatever it is.

The Government of South Vietnam should not be imposed by force from Hanoi or by pressure from Washington. It should be freely chosen by all the South Vietnamese people.

—A stopping the bombing of the North—taking account of Hanoi's actions and assurances of prompt good faith negotiations and keeping the option of resuming that bombing if the Communists show bad faith.

—Careful, systematic reduction of American troops in South Vietnam—a de-Americanization of the war—turning over to the South Vietnamese Army a greater share of the defense of its own country.

—An internationally supervised cease-fire—and supervised withdrawal of all foreign forces from South Vietnam.

—Free elections, including all people in South Vietnam willing to follow the peaceful process.

Those are risks I would take for peace.

I do not believe any of these risks would jeopardize our security or be contrary to our national interest.

There is, of course, no guarantee that all these things could be successfully done.

Certainly, none of them could be done if North Vietnam were to show bad faith.

But I believe there is a good chance these steps could be undertaken with safety for our men in Vietnam.

As President, I would be dedicated to carrying them out—as I would be dedicated to urging the Government of

South Vietnam to expedite all political, economic and social reforms essential to broadening popular participation including high priority to land reform... more attention to the suffering of refugees ... and constant Government pressure against inflation and corruption.

I believe all of these steps could lead to an honorable and lasting settlement, serving both our own national interest and the interests of the independent nations of Southeast Asia.

We have learned a lesson from Vietnam.

The lesson is not that we should turn our backs on Southeast Asia, or on other nations or peoples in less familiar parts of the world neighborhood.

The lesson is, rather, that we should carefully define our goals and priorities. And within those goals and priorities, that we should formulate policies which will fit new American guidelines.

Applying the lesson of Vietnam, I would insist as President that we review other commitments made in other times, that we carefully decide what is and is not in our national interest.

I do not condemn any past commitment.

I do not judge the decisions of past Presidents when, in good conscience, they made those decisions in what they thought were the interest of the American people.

But I do say, if I am President, I owe it to this nation to bring our men and resources in Vietnam back to America where we need them so badly, and to be sure we put first things first in the future.

Let me be clear: I do not counsel withdrawal from the world.

I do not swerve from international responsibility.

I only say that, as President, I would undertake a new strategy for peace in this world, based not on American omnipotence, but on American leadership, not only military and economic but moral.

That new strategy for peace would emphasize working through the United Nations ... strengthening and maintaining our key alliances for mutual security, particularly including **NATO** ... supporting international peacekeeping machinery ... and working with other nations to build new institutions and instruments for cooperation.

In a troubled and dangerous world we should seek not to march alone, but to lead in such a way that others will wish to join us.

Even as we seek peace in Vietnam, we must for our own security and well-being seek to halt and turn back the costly and even more dangerous arms race.

Five nations now have nuclear bombs.

The United States and the Soviet Union already possess enough weapons to burn and destroy every human being on this earth.

Unless we stop the arms race ... unless we stop 15 to 20 more nations from getting nuclear bombs and nuclear bomb technology within the next few years, this generation may be the last.

For 20 years we have lived under the constant threat that some irresponsible action or even some great miscalculation could blow us all up in the wink of an eye.

There is danger that we have become so used to the idea that we no longer think it abnormal—forgetting that our whole world structure depends for its stability on the precarious architecture of what Winston Churchill called the "balance of terror." This is no longer an adequate safeguard for peace.

There is a treaty now before the Senate which would stop the spread of nuclear weapons. That treaty must be ratified now.

If this nation cannot muster the courage to ratify this treaty—a treaty which in no way endangers our national security, but adds to it by keeping these weapons out of the hands of a Nasser, a Castro ... and many others—then there can be little hope for our future in this world. We must ratify this treaty.

I also believe that we must have the courage—while keeping our guard up and fulfilling our commitments to **NATO**—to talk with the Soviet Union as soon as possible about a freeze and a reduction of offensive and defensive nuclear missile systems.

To escalate the nuclear missile arms race is to raise the level of danger and total destruction. It is costly, menacing, fearsome and offers no genuine defense.

Beyond that, if I am President, I shall take the initiative to find the way—under carefully safeguarded, mutually acceptable international inspection—to reduce arms budgets and military expenditures systematically among all countries of the world.

Our country's military budget this year is $80-billion.

It is an investment we have to make under existing circumstances. It protects our freedom.

But if we can work with other nations so that we can all reduce our military expenditures together, with proper safeguards and inspection, then it will be a great day for humanity.

All of us will have moved further away from self-destruction. And all of us will have billions of dollars with which to help people live better lives.

The American people must choose the one man they believe can best face these great issues.

I would hope that Mr. Nixon, Mr. Wallace and I could express our views on Vietnam not only individually, but on the same public platform.

I call for this because—on the basis of our past records and past careers—there are great differences between our policies and programs.

Those views of Governor Wallace which I have seen reported indicate that he would sharply escalate the war.

Mr. Nixon's past record reveals his probable future policies.

In 1954—at the time of the French defeat at Dienbienphu—he advocated American armed intervention in Vietnam in aid of French colonialism. It was necessary for President Eisenhower to repudiate his proposal.

Since then, he has taken a line on Vietnam policy which I believe could lead to greater escalation of the war.

In January of this year, Mr. Nixon described as "bunk" the idea that free elections in South Vietnam were of importance.

In February of this year, when questioned about the use of nuclear weapons in Vietnam, Mr. Nixon said that a general "has to take the position that he cannot rule out the use of nuclear-weapons in extreme situations that might develop."

Since then, he has indicated he has a plan to end the war in Vietnam but will not disclose it until he becomes President.

If he has such a plan, he has an obligation to so inform President Johnson and the American people.

A few days ago the Republican Vice-Presidential nominee said there is not now and never has been a Nixon-Agnew plan for peace in Vietnam. It was, he said, a ploy "to maintain suspense."

And then he said: "Isn't that the way campaigns are run?"

I think we need some answers about this from Mr. Nixon.

Mr. Nixon's public record shows, also, consistent opposition to measures for nuclear arms controls.

He attacked Adlai Stevenson and myself for advocating a nuclear test ban treaty—a treaty to stop radioactive fallout from poisoning and crippling people the world over. He called our plan "a cruel hoax." We can be thankful that President Kennedy and the Congress did not follow his advice.

Today, he is asking for delay of ratification of a treaty carefully negotiated over several years and signed by 80 nations—the nuclear nonproliferation treaty designed to stop the spread of nuclear weapons.

I speak plainly: I do not believe the American Presidency can afford a return to leadership which would increase tension in the world; which would, on the basis of past statements, escalate the Vietnam war; and which would turn the clock back on progress that has been made at a great sacrifice to bring the great powers of the world into a saner relationship in this nuclear age.

On the great issues of Vietnam, of the arms race and of human rights in America, I have clear differences with Mr. Nixon and Mr. Wallace.

I call on both of these men to join me in open debate before the American people.

Let us put our ideas before the people. Let us offer ourselves for their judgment—as men and as leaders.

Let us appear together—in front of the same audiences or on the same television screens, and at the same time—to give the people a choice.

We must not let a President be elected by the size of his advertising budget.

We cannot let a President be elected without having met the issues before the people.

I am willing to put myself, my programs, my capacity for leadership, before the American people for their judgment.

I ask the Republican nominee and the third-party candidate to do the same.

I ask, before Election Day, that we be heard together as you have heard me alone tonight.

I appeal to the people—as citizens of a nation whose compassion and sense of decency and fair play have made it what Lincoln called "the last best hope on earth."

I appeal to you as a person who wants his children to grow up in that kind of country.

I appeal to you to express and vote your hopes and not your hates.

I intend, in these five weeks, to wage a vigorous, tireless and forthright campaign for the Presidency. I shall not spare myself, or those who will stand with me.

I have prepared myself. I know the problems facing this nation. I do not shrink from these problems. I challenge them. They were made by men. I believe they can be solved by men.

If you will give me your confidence and support, together we shall build a better America.

Richard M. Nixon

Vietnamization
(November 3, 1969)

Richard Nixon campaigned for the Presidency in 1968 on a pledge to end the war in Vietnam. He had a plan, he said, but would not reveal its details lest he disturb the delicate negotiations under way in Paris. Although he was ridiculed during the campaign for his claim to have a "secret plan," his stance of generalized opposition to the Johnson policies won him support from among Johnson critics, hawk and dove alike, who read into Nixon's general statements their own beliefs about what ought to be done.

Nixon's plan proceeded from the same premise that Johnson had recognized in 1968. The South Vietnamese army had been strengthened so that it could carry a greater share of the burden, gradually replacing American troops. The replacement schedule would have to be stretched out over a long period of time, so that the South Vietnamese forces would have ample time to be trained and prepared. And the replacement of American by Vietnamese troops was also accompanied by an increase in aerial bombing, including—we now know—the illegal bombing of Cambodia in an attempt to destroy Vietcong sanctuaries there. Nevertheless, to a public that equated curtailment of American troops with curtailment of the war, the Nixon plan certainly seemed to be disengagement. After four years of steadily increasing numbers of troops in Vietnam, the trend was now running the other way.

The first stage of the troop withdrawal was announced in the spring of 1969, but Nixon had not yet delivered a formal speech to set forth his views on the war. Meanwhile antiwar protest continued to grow. The conviction that the war had been a terrible mistake from which we should extricate ourselves as soon as possible quickly took hold among a larger part of the population. Moderates and conservatives joined radicals in their impatience with what appeared to be the glacial pace of Nixon's winding down the war. Antiwar demonstrations by the fall of 1969 were the largest yet. Under the rubric of a national "moratorium," simultaneous demonstrations were held nationwide in September and October, with an even longer and larger demonstration planned for November. Nixon, of course, could not cede the initiative to the protesters. If he was to coordinate American withdrawals with the growing capacity of the South Vietnamese, he would have to control the pace and timing of the withdrawals.

The November 3 speech was Nixon's attempt to articulate a general plan and to wrest the initiative from the protesters, mobilizing support from among those previously uninvolved and, with luck, dampening the size and strength of the November moratorium. The speech exploits some of the same ambiguities Johnson had discovered, so that Nixon was able to support both war and peace at the same time. He reaffirmed basic American commitments, indicated that the South Vietnamese armed forces had improved considerably, and announced that he had developed a withdrawal schedule but that he could not reveal it, lest he give aid and comfort to the enemy and subvert the Paris peace talks. Then he objected to domestic dissent against the war because it would send the wrong signal to North Vietnam and her allies, leading them to think that there was a deep division within the United States. He suggested that a vocal minority, if unchecked, could defeat him, and he rallied the previously inert "great silent majority" to come to his aid and support.

Judged by short-term criteria, the "Vietnamization" speech was eminently successful. Polls showed a general growth of support for the President. His descriptions of secret correspondence with Ho Chi Minh made it appear that he was pursuing all possible approaches to peace. Those who thought that not enough was being done were encouraged to see the North Vietnamese rather than the President as the culprit. The size of the November moratorium was reduced. Although the effects of the speech were not long lasting, it did appear to have gained for Nixon some valuable time. Immediately after the speech, television network commentators subjected it to critique. This "instant analysis," which had become common during the late 1960's, was the target for an attack by Vice President Spiro T. Agnew ten days after the "Vietnamization" speech. Agnew's speech shifted the focus to patterns of media coverage and away from the contents of Nixon's speech. The President and Vice President had gained some valuable breathing space, but the war clearly had become "Nixon's war."

Good evening, my fellow Americans:–Tonight I want to talk to you on a subject of deep concern to all Americans and to many people in all parts of the world–the war in Vietnam.

I believe that one of the reasons for the deep division about Vietnam is that many Americans have lost confidence in what their Government has told them about our policy. The American people cannot and should not be asked to support a policy which involves the overriding issues of war and peace unless they know the truth about that policy.

Tonight, therefore, I would like to answer some of the questions that I know are on the minds of many of you listening to me.

How and why did America get involved in Vietnam in the first place?

How has this administration changed the policy of the previous administration?

What has really happened in the negotiations in Paris and on the battlefront in Vietnam?

What choices do we have if we are to end the war?

What are the prospects for peace?

Now, let me begin by describing the situation I found when I was inaugurated on January 20.

–The war had been going on for 4 years.
–31,000 Americans had been killed in action.

—The training program for the South Vietnamese was behind schedule.

—540,000 Americans were in Vietnam with no plans to reduce the number.

—No progress had been made at the negotiations in Paris and the United States had not put forth a comprehensive peace proposal.

—The war was causing deep division at home and criticism from many of our friends as well as our enemies abroad.

In view of these circumstances there were some who urged that I end the war at once by ordering the immediate withdrawal of all American forces.

From a political standpoint this would have been a popular and easy course to follow. After all, we became involved in the war while my predecessor was in office. I could blame the defeat which would be the result of my action on him and come out as the peacemaker. Some put it to me quite bluntly: This was the only way to avoid allowing Johnson's war to become Nixon's war.

But I had a greater obligation than to think only of the years of my administration and of the next election. I had to think of the effect of my decision on the next generation and on the future of peace and freedom in America and in the world.

Let us all understand that the question before us is not whether some Americans are for peace and some Americans are against peace. The question at issue is not whether Johnson's war becomes Nixon's war.

The great question is: How can we win America's peace?

Well, let us turn now to the fundamental issue. Why and how did the United States become involved in Vietnam in the first place?

Fifteen years ago North Vietnam, with the logistical support of Communist China and the Soviet Union, launched a campaign to impose a Communist government on South Vietnam by instigating and supporting a revolution.

In response to the request of the Government of South Vietnam, President Eisenhower sent economic aid and military equipment to assist the people of South Vietnam in their efforts to prevent a Communist takeover. Seven years ago, President Kennedy sent 16,000 military personnel to Vietnam as combat advisers. Four years ago, President Johnson sent American combat forces to South Vietnam.

Now, many believe that President Johnson's decision to send American combat forces to South Vietnam was wrong. And many others—I among them—have been strongly critical of the way the war has been conducted.

But the question facing us today is: Now that we are in the war, what is the best way to end it?

In January I could only conclude that the precipitate withdrawal of American forces from Vietnam would be a disaster not only for South Vietnam but for the United States and for the cause of peace.

For the South Vietnamese, our precipitate withdrawal would inevitably allow the Communists to repeat the massacres which followed their takeover in the North 15 years before.

—They then murdered more than 50,000 people and hundreds of thousands more died in slave labor camps.

—We saw a prelude of what would happen in South Vietnam when the Communists entered the city of Hue last year. During their brief rule there, there was a bloody reign of terror in which 3,000 civilians were clubbed, shot to death, and buried in mass graves.

—With the sudden collapse of our support, these atrocities of Hue would become the nightmare of the entire nation—and particularly for the million and a half Catholic refugees who fled to South Vietnam when the Communists took over in the North.

For the United States, this first defeat in our Nation's history would result in a collapse of confidence in American leadership, not only in Asia but throughout the world.

Three American Presidents have recognized the great stakes involved in Vietnam and understood what had to be done.

In 1963, President Kennedy, with his characteristic eloquence and clarity, said: "... we want to see a stable government there, carrying on a struggle to maintain its national independence.

"We believe strongly in that. We are not going to withdraw from that effort. In my opinion, for us to withdraw from that effort would mean a collapse not only of South Viet-Nam, but Southeast Asia. So we are going to stay there."

President Eisenhower and President Johnson expressed the same conclusion during their terms of office.

For the future of peace, precipitate withdrawal would thus be a disaster of immense magnitude.

—A nation cannot remain great if it betrays its allies and lets down its friends.

—Our defeat and humiliation in South Vietnam without question would promote recklessness in the councils of those great powers who have not yet abandoned their goals of world conquest.

—This would spark violence wherever our commitments help maintain the peace—in the Middle East, in Berlin, eventually even in the Western Hemisphere.

Ultimately, this would cost more lives.

It would not bring peace; it would bring more war.

For these reasons, I rejected the recommendation that I should end the war by immediately withdrawing all of our forces. I chose instead to change American policy on both the negotiating front and battlefront.

In order to end a war fought on many fronts, I initiated a pursuit for peace on many fronts.

In a television speech on May 14, in a speech before the United Nations, and on a number of other occasions I set forth our peace proposals in great detail.

—We have offered the complete withdrawal of all outside forces within 1 year.

—We have proposed a cease-fire under international supervision.

—We have offered free elections under international supervision with the Communists participating in the organization and conduct of the elections as an organized political force. And the Saigon Government has pledged to accept the result of the elections.

We have not put forth our proposals on a take-it-or-leave-it basis. We have indicated that we are willing to discuss the proposals that have been put forth by the other side. We have declared that anything is negotiable except the right of the people of South Vietnam to determine their own future. At the Paris peace conference, Ambassador Lodge has demonstrated our flexibility and good faith in 40 public meetings.

Hanoi has refused even to discuss our proposals. They demand our unconditional acceptance of their terms, which are that we withdraw all American forces immediately and unconditionally and that we overthrow the Government of South Vietnam as we leave.

We have not limited our peace initiatives to public forums and public statements. I recognized, in January, that a long and bitter war like this usually cannot be settled in a public forum. That is why in addition to the public statements and negotiations I have explored every possible private avenue that might lead to a settlement.

Tonight I am taking the unprecedented step of disclosing to you some of our other initiatives for peace—initiatives we undertook privately and secretly because we thought we thereby might open a door which publicly would be closed.

I did not wait for my inauguration to begin my quest for peace.

—Soon after my election, through an individual who is directly in contact on a personal basis with the leaders of North Vietnam, I made two private offers for a rapid, comprehensive settlement. Hanoi's replies called in effect for our surrender before negotiations.

—Since the Soviet Union furnishes most of the military equipment for North Vietnam, Secretary of State Rogers, my Assistant for National Security Affairs, Dr. Kissinger, Ambassador Lodge, and I, personally, have met on a number of occasions with representatives of the Soviet Government to enlist their assistance in getting meaningful negotiations started. In addition, we have had extended discussions directed toward that same end with representatives of other governments which have diplomatic relations with North Vietnam. None of these initiatives have to date produced results.

—In mid-July, I became convinced that it was necessary to make a major move to break the deadlock in the Paris talks. I spoke directly in this office, where I am now sitting, with an individual who had known Ho Chi Minh [President, Democratic Republic of Vietnam] on a personal basis for 25 years. Through him I sent a letter to Ho Chi Minh.

I did this outside of the usual diplomatic channels with the hope that with the necessity of making statements for propaganda removed, there might be constructive progress toward bringing the war to an end. Let me read from that letter to you now.

Dear Mr. President:
I realize that it is difficult to communicate meaningfully across the gulf of four years of war. But precisely because of this gulf, I wanted to take this opportunity to reaffirm in all solemnity my desire to work for a just peace. I deeply believe that the war in Vietnam has gone on too long and delay in bringing it to an end can benefit no one—least of all the people of Vietnam....

The time has come to move forward at the conference table toward an early resolution of this tragic war. You will find us forthcoming and open-minded in a common effort to bring the blessings of peace to the brave people of Vietnam. Let history record that at this critical juncture, both sides turned their face toward peace rather than toward conflict and war.

I received Ho Chi Minh's reply on August 30, 3 days before his death. It simply reiterated the public position North Vietnam had taken at Paris and flatly rejected my initiative.

The full text of both letters is being released to the press.

—In addition to the public meetings that I have referred to, Ambassador Lodge has met with Vietnam's chief negotiator in Paris in 11 private sessions.

—We have taken other significant initiatives which must remain secret to keep open some channels of communication which may still prove to be productive.

But the effect of all the public, private, and secret negotiations which have been undertaken since the bombing halt a year ago and since this administration came into office on January 20, can be summed up in one sentence: No progress whatever has been made except agreement on the shape of the bargaining table.

Well now, who is at fault?

It has become clear that the obstacle in negotiating an end to the war is not the President of the United States. It is not the South Vietnamese Government.

The obstacle is the other side's absolute refusal to show the least willingness to join us in seeking a just peace. And it will not do so while it is convinced that all it has to do is to wait for our next concession, and our next concession after that one, until it gets everything it wants.

There can now be no longer any question that progress in negotiation depends only on Hanoi's deciding to negotiate, to negotiate seriously.

I realize that this report on our efforts on the diplomatic front is discouraging to the American people, but the American people are entitled to know the truth—the bad news as well as the good news—where the lives of our young men are involved.

Now let me turn, however, to a more encouraging report on another front.

At the time we launched our search for peace I recognized we might not succeed in bringing an end to

the war through negotiation. I, therefore, put into effect another plan to bring peace—a plan which will bring the war to an end regardless of what happens on the negotiating front.

It is in line with a major shift in U.S. foreign policy which I described in my press conference at Guam on July 25. Let me briefly explain what has been described as the Nixon Doctrine—a policy which not only will help end the war in Vietnam, but which is an essential element of our program to prevent future Vietnams.

We Americans are a do-it-yourself people. We are an impatient people. Instead of teaching someone else to do a job, we like to do it ourselves. And this trait has been carried over into our foreign policy.

In Korea and again in Vietnam, the United States furnished most of the money, most of the arms, and most of the men to help the people of those countries defend their freedom against Communist aggression.

Before any American troops were committed to Vietnam, a leader of another Asian country expressed this opinion to me when I was traveling in Asia as a private citizen. He said: "When you are trying to assist another nation defend its freedom, U.S. policy should be to help them fight the war but not to fight the war for them."

Well, in accordance with this wise counsel, I laid down in Guam three principles as guidelines for future American policy toward Asia:

—First, the United States will keep all of its treaty commitments.

—Second, we shall provide a shield if a nuclear power threatens the freedom of a nation allied with us or of a nation whose survival we consider vital to our security.

—Third, in cases involving other types of aggression, we shall furnish military and economic assistance when requested in accordance with our treaty commitments. But we shall look to the nation directly threatened to assume the primary responsibility of providing the manpower for its defense.

After I announced this policy, I found that the leaders of the Philippines, Thailand, Vietnam, South Korea, and other nations which might be threatened by Communist aggression, welcomed this new direction in American foreign policy.

The defense of freedom is everybody's business—not just America's business. And it is particularly the responsibility of the people whose freedom is threatened. In the previous administration, we Americanized the war in Vietnam. In this administration, we are Vietnamizing the search for peace.

The policy of the previous administration not only resulted in our assuming the primary responsibility for fighting the war, but even more significantly did not adequately stress the goal of strengthening the South Vietnamese so that they could defend themselves when we left.

The Vietnamization plan was launched following Secretary Laird's visit to Vietnam in March. Under the plan, I ordered first a substantial increase in the training and equipment of South Vietnamese forces.

In July, on my visit to Vietnam, I changed General Abrams' orders so that they were consistent with the objectives of our new policies. Under the new orders, the primary mission of our troops is to enable the South Vietnamese forces to assume the full responsibility for the security of South Vietnam.

Our air operations have been reduced by over 20 percent.

And now we have begun to see the results of this long overdue change in American policy in Vietnam.

—After 5 years of Americans going into Vietnam, we are finally bringing American men home. By December 15, over 60,000 men will have been withdrawn from South Vietnam—including 20 percent of all of our combat forces.

—The South Vietnamese have continued to gain in strength. As a result they have been able to take over combat responsibilities from our American troops.

Two other significant developments have occurred since this administration took office.

—Enemy infiltration, infiltration which is essential if they are to launch a major attack, over the last 3 months is less than 20 percent of what it was over the same period last year.

—Most important—United States casualties have declined during the last 2 months to the lowest point in 3 years.

Let me now turn to our program for the future.

We have adopted a plan which we have worked out in cooperation with the South Vietnamese for the complete withdrawal of all U.S. combat ground forces, and their replacement by South Vietnamese forces on an orderly scheduled timetable. This withdrawal will be made from strength and not from weakness. As South

Vietnamese forces become stronger, the rate of American withdrawal can become greater.

I have not and do not intend to announce the timetable for our program. And there are obvious reasons for this decision which I am sure you will understand. As I have indicated on several occasions, the rate of withdrawal will depend on developments on three fronts.

One of these is the progress which can be or might be made in the Paris talks. An announcement of a fixed timetable for our withdrawal would completely remove any incentive for the enemy to negotiate an agreement. They would simply wait until our forces had withdrawn and then move in.

The other two factors on which we will base our withdrawal decisions are the level of enemy activity and the progress of the training programs of the South Vietnamese forces. And I am glad to be able to report tonight progress on both of these fronts has been greater than we anticipated when we started the program in June for withdrawal. As a result, our timetable for withdrawal is more optimistic now than when we made our first estimates in June. Now, this clearly demonstrates why it is not wise to be frozen in on a fixed timetable.

We must retain the flexibility to base each withdrawal decision on the situation as it is at that time rather than on estimates that are no longer valid.

Along with this optimistic estimate, I must—in all candor—leave one note of caution.

If the level of enemy activity significantly increases we might have to adjust our timetable accordingly.

However, I want the record to be completely clear on one point.

At the time of the bombing halt just a year ago, there was some confusion as to whether there was an understanding on the part of the enemy that if we stopped the bombing of North Vietnam they would stop the shelling of cities in South Vietnam. I want to be sure that there is no misunderstanding on the part of the enemy with regard to our withdrawal program.

We have noted the reduced level of infiltration, the reduction of our casualties, and are basing our withdrawal decisions partially on those factors.

If the level of infiltration or our casualties increase while we are trying to scale down the fighting, it will be the result of a conscious decision by the enemy.

Hanoi could make no greater mistake than to assume that an increase in violence will be to its advantage. If I conclude that increased enemy action jeopardizes our remaining forces in Vietnam, I shall not hesitate to take strong and effective measures to deal with that situation.

This is not a threat. This is a statement of policy, which as Commander in Chief of our Armed Forces, I am making in meeting my responsibility for the protection of American fighting men wherever they may be.

My fellow Americans, I am sure you can recognize from what I have said that we really only have two choices open to us if we want to end this war.

—I can order an immediate, precipitate withdrawal of all Americans from Vietnam without regard to the effects of that action.

—Or we can persist in our search for a just peace through a negotiated settlement if possible, or through continued implementation of our plan for Vietnamization if necessary—a plan in which we will withdraw all of our forces from Vietnam on a schedule in accordance with our program, as the South Vietnamese become strong enough to defend their own freedom.

I have chosen this second course.

It is not the easy way.

It is the right way.

It is a plan which will end the war and serve the cause of peace—not just in Vietnam but in the Pacific and in the world.

In speaking of the consequences of a precipitate withdrawal, I mentioned that our allies would lose confidence in America.

Far more dangerous, we would lose confidence in ourselves. Oh, the immediate reaction would be a sense of relief that our men were coming home. But as we saw the consequences of what we had done, inevitable remorse and divisive recrimination would scar our spirit as a people.

We have faced other crises in our history and have become stronger by rejecting the easy way out and taking the right way in meeting our challenges. Our greatness as a nation has been our capacity to do what had to be done when we knew our course was right.

I recognize that some of my fellow citizens disagree with the plan for peace I have chosen. Honest and patriotic Americans have reached different conclusions as to how peace should be achieved.

In San Francisco a few weeks ago, I saw demonstrators carrying signs reading: "Lose in Vietnam, bring the boys home."

Well, one of the strengths of our free society is that any American has a right to reach that conclusion and to advocate that point of view. But as President of the United States, I would be untrue to my oath of office if I allowed the policy of this Nation to be dictated by the minority who hold that point of view and who try to impose it on the Nation by mounting demonstrations in the street.

For almost 200 years, the policy of this Nation has been made under our Constitution by those leaders in the Congress and the White House elected by all of the people. If a vocal minority, however fervent its cause, prevails over reason and the will of the majority, this Nation has no future as a free society.

And now I would like to address a word, if I may, to the young people of this Nation who are particularly concerned, and I understand why they are concerned, about this war.

I respect your idealism.

I share your concern for peace.

I want peace as much as you do.

There are powerful personal reasons I want to end this war. This week I will have to sign 83 letters to mothers, fathers, wives, and loved ones of men who have given their lives for America in Vietnam. It is very little satisfaction to me that this is only one-third as many letters as I signed the first week in office. There is nothing I want more than to see the day come when I do not have to write any of those letters.

—I want to end the war to save the lives of those brave young men in Vietnam.

—But I want to end it in a way which will increase the chance that their younger brothers and their sons will not have to fight in some future Vietnam someplace in the world.

—And I want to end the war for another reason. I want to end it so that the energy and dedication of you, our young people, now too often directed into bitter hatred against those responsible for the war, can be turned to the great challenges of peace, a better life for all Americans, a better life for all people on this earth.

I have chosen a plan for peace. I believe it will succeed.

If it does succeed, what the critics say now won't matter. If it does not succeed, anything I say then won't matter.

I know it may not be fashionable to speak of patriotism or national destiny these days. But I feel it is appropriate to do so on this occasion.

Two hundred years ago this Nation was weak and poor. But even then, America was the hope of millions in the world. Today we have become the strongest and richest nation in the world. And the wheel of destiny has turned so that any hope the world has for the survival of peace and freedom will be determined by whether the American people have the moral stamina and the courage to meet the challenge of free world leadership.

Let historians not record that when America was the most powerful nation in the world we passed on the other side of the road and allowed the last hopes for peace and freedom of millions of people to be suffocated by the forces of totalitarianism.

And so tonight—to you, the great silent majority of my fellow Americans—I ask for your support.

I pledged in my campaign for the Presidency to end the war in a way that we could win the peace. I have initiated a plan of action which will enable me to keep that pledge.

The more support I can have from the American people, the sooner that pledge can be redeemed; for the more divided we are at home, the less likely the enemy is to negotiate at Paris.

Let us be united for peace. Let us also be united against defeat. Because let us understand: North Vietnam cannot defeat or humiliate the United States. Only Americans can do that.

Fifty years ago, in this room and at this very desk, President Woodrow Wilson spoke words which caught the imagination of a war-weary world. He said: "This is the war to end war." His dream for peace after World War I was shattered on the hard realities of great power politics and Woodrow Wilson died a broken man.

Tonight I do not tell you that the war in Vietnam is the war to end wars. But I do say this: I have initiated a plan which will end this war in a way that will bring us closer to that great goal to which Woodrow Wilson and every American President in our history has been dedicated—the goal of a just and lasting peace.

As President I hold the responsibility for choosing the best path to that goal and then leading the Nation along it.

I pledge to you tonight that I shall meet this responsibility with all of the strength and wisdom I can command in accordance with your hopes, mindful of your concerns, sustained by your prayers.

Thank you and goodnight.

The Politics of the Seventies

——————————Richard M. Nixon——————————

Acceptance of the Republican Nomination for President
(August 8, 1968)

The turbulence of the sixties reached a crescendo in the election year 1968. A short four years before, Lyndon Johnson had been elected to the Presidency in his own right, swamping his conservative Republican opponent, Barry Goldwater, in a landslide victory at the polls. In the years that followed that triumph, however, the country was torn apart with racial strife and bitterly divided over the growing commitment to the war in Vietnam. By the end of 1967 almost a half-million American troops were fighting the bloody, slogging, seemingly endless war. The "living room war," brought into American homes on the television nightly news, made the conflict vivid and horribly real to American viewers. When the North Vietnamese launched an offensive at the beginning of Tet, a lunar New Year holiday in Vietnam, the spectacle of American bodies stretched out on the lawn of the United States Embassy in Saigon, and the brutal image of a high-ranking South Vietnamese officer shooting a bound captive in the head, shocked American audiences.

The Tet offensive, finally blunted, had a profound impact. While the President assured the press that the offensive was "a complete failure," skepticism over the war and suspicion of the administration intensified. Senator Aiken of Vermont, for example, observed caustically that "if this is a failure I hope the Viet Cong never have a major success," and Sen. Robert Kennedy's uneasiness with the progress of the war crystallized in a major attack on administration policy. Eugene McCarthy, the senator from Minnesota, took the politically unorthodox step of organizing a campaign for the Presidency, a campaign designed to unseat the sitting President of his own party, Lyndon Johnson. When McCarthy secured over 40 percent of the vote in the New Hampshire primary in the teeth of the opposition from the Democratic establishment, it became clear that Lyndon Johnson's leadership was to be seriously challenged.

As the year wore on, Robert Kennedy decided to enter the primary race, Johnson made the surprise decision not to seek re-election, and the Democratic race focused on Kennedy, McCarthy, and Vice President Hubert Humphrey. Meanwhile, on the Republican side, former Vice President Richard Nixon, with an impressive win in the New Hampshire primary, became the front-runner against Gov. George Romney of Michigan and Gov. Nelson Rockefeller of New York, whose indecision on whether or not to seek the nomination disheartened his supporters and weakened his candidacy.

Nixon had been narrowly defeated in his 1960 race against John F. Kennedy, and lost a bid for the governorship of California two years later. In the frustration of the moment, Nixon, angered by what he saw as unfriendly media coverage, announced his retirement from politics with the comment that newspeople would no longer "have Dick Nixon to kick around." Nixon moved to New York where he joined a law firm, but he did not, in fact, retire from politics. He maintained contacts with party leaders, issued statements on political issues, campaigned for Republican candidates, and spoke at fund-raisers. If anything, his activities strengthened his position among the party faithful.

By the time the Republican party gathered in Miami in early August, the political scene had changed. Robert Kennedy, mounting an aggressive primary campaign, had seemed to have success within his grasp, but following his win in the California primary he was assassinated while on his way to make a victory statement. Although McCarthy would still present a challenge, the likely Democratic candidate was Hubert Humphrey. Furthermore, racial tensions had been exacerbated by the assassination, in April, of Dr. Martin Luther King. His death set off a wave of rioting: there were 2,600 fires set in towns and cities across the country—over 700 in the nation's capital itself. Hundreds were arrested and thousands injured.

The Republican convention was, by most accounts, a boring affair, prompting the Associated Press to comment that "Richard Nixon rode to victory in a tedious ritual at Miami Beach." One surprise came when Nixon named Gov. Spiro Agnew, virtually unknown outside his home state of Maryland, as his running mate. During the convention, a riot broke out in a black ghetto in Miami and was quelled by local police with shotguns; the deaths of four blacks were reported. This violence, however, scarcely touched the convention itself where "boredom," Theodore White wrote, "lay on the convention like a mattress." Nixon, duly anointed as the party's candidate, addressed the delegates on August 8, in a speech that praised the peaceful record of the Eisenhower administration—clearly in contrast with the Vietnam years, belittled Democratic efforts at social reform, demanded a restoration of order and respect for law, and called for a return to the "lift of a driving [American] dream."

Mr. Chairman, delegates to this convention, my fellow Americans:—Sixteen years ago I stood before this convention to accept your nomination as the running mate of one of the greatest Americans of our time or any time—Dwight D. Eisenhower.

Eight years ago I had the highest honor of accepting your nomination for President of the United States.

Tonight I again proudly accept that nomination for President of the United States.

But I have news for you. This time there's a difference—this time we're going to win.

We're going to win for a number of reasons. First a personal one.

General Eisenhower, as you know, lies critically ill in the Walter Reed Hospital tonight. I have talked, however, with Mrs. Eisenhower on the telephone.

She tells me that his heart is with us. She says that there is nothing that he lives more for, and there is nothing that would lift him more than for us to win in November.

And I say let's win this one for Ike.

We're going to win because this great convention has demonstrated to the nation that the Republican party has the leadership, the platform and the purpose that America needs.

We're going to win because you have nominated as my running mate a statesman of the first rank who will be a great campaigner, and one who is fully qualified to undertake the new responsibilities that I shall give to the next Vice President of the United States.

And he is a man who fully shares my conviction and yours that after a period of 40 years when power has gone from the cities and the states to the Government in Washington, D.C., it's time to have power go back from Washington to the states and to the cities of this country all over America.

We're going to win because at a time that America cries out for the unity that this Administration has destroyed, the Republican party, after a spirited contest for its nomination for President and Vice President, stands united before the nation tonight.

And I congratulate Governor Reagan, I congratulate Governor Rockefeller, I congratulate Governor Romney, I congratulate all those who have made the hard fight that they have for this nomination, and I know that you will all fight even harder for the great victory our party is going to win in November because we're going to be together in that election campaign.

And a party that can unite itself will unite America.

My fellow Americans, most important we're going to win because our cause is right. We make history tonight not for ourselves but for the ages. The choice we make in 1968 will determine not only the future of America but the future of peace and freedom in the world for the last third of the 20th century, and the question that we answer tonight: can America meet this great challenge?

Let us listen to America to find the answer to that question.

As we look at America, we see cities enveloped in smoke and flame. We hear sirens in the night. We see Americans dying on distant battlefields abroad. We see Americans hating each other; fighting each other; killing each other at home.

And as we see and hear these things, millions of Americans cry out in anguish: Did we come all this way for this? Did American boys die in Normandy and Korea and in Valley Forge for this?

Listen to the answers to those questions.

It is another voice, it is a quiet voice in the tumult of the shouting. It is the voice of the great majority of Americans, the forgotten Americans, the non shouters, the non demonstrators. They're not racists or sick; they're not guilty of the crime that plagues the land; they are black, they are white; they're native born and foreign born; they're young and they're old.

They work in American factories, they run American businesses. They serve in government; they provide most of the soldiers who die to keep it free. They give drive to the spirit of America. They give lift to the American dream. They give steel to the backbone of America.

They're good people. They're decent people; they work and they save and they pay their taxes and they care.

Like Theodore Roosevelt, they know that this country will not be a good place for any of us to live in unless it's a good place for all of us to live in.

And this I say, this I say to you tonight, is the real voice of America. In this year 1968, this is the message it will broadcast to America and to the world.

Let's never forget that despite her faults, America is a great nation. And America is great because her people are great.

With Winston Churchill we say, we have not journeyed all this way, across the centuries, across the oceans, across the mountains, across the prairies because we are made of sugar candy.

America's in trouble today not because her people have failed but because her leaders have failed. And what America wants are leaders to match the greatness of her people.

And this great group of Americans—the forgotten Americans and others—know that the great question Americans must answer by their votes in November is this: Whether we will continue for four more years the policies of the last five years.

And this is their answer, and this is my answer to that question: When the strongest nation in the world can be tied up for four years in a war in Vietnam with no end in sight, when the richest nation in the world can't manage its own economy, when the nation with the greatest tradition of the rule of law is plagued by unprecedented lawlessness, when a nation that has been known for a century for equality of opportunity is torn by unprecedented racial violence, and when the President of the United States cannot travel abroad or to any major city at home without fear of a hostile demonstration—then it's time for new leadership for the United States of America.

Thank you. My fellow Americans, tonight I accept the challenge and the commitment to provide that new leadership for America and I ask you to accept it with me.

And let us accept this challenge not as a grim duty but as an exciting adventure in which we are privileged to help a great nation realize its destiny and let us begin by committing ourselves to the truth, to see it like it is and tell it like it is, to tell the truth, to speak the truth and to live the truth. That's what we will do.

We've had enough of big promises and little action. The time has come for an honest government in the United States of America.

And so tonight I do not promise the millennium in the morning. I don't promise that we can eradicate poverty and end discrimination and eliminate all danger of wars in the space of four or even eight years. But I do promise action. A new policy for peace abroad, a new policy for peace and progress at home.

Look at our problems abroad. Do you realize that we face the stark truth that we are worse off in every area of the world tonight than we were when President Eisenhower left office eight years ago? That's the record.

And there is only one answer to such a record of failure, and that is the complete house cleaning of those responsible for the failures and that record.

The answer is the complete reappraisal of America's policy in every section of the world. We shall begin with Vietnam.

We all hope in this room that there's a chance that current negotiations may bring an honorable end to that war. And we will say nothing during this campaign that might destroy that chance.

And if the war is not ended when the people choose in November, the choice will be clear. Here it is: For four years this administration has had at its disposal the greatest military and economic advantage that one nation has ever had over another in a war in history. For four years America's fighting men have set a record for courage and sacrifice unsurpassed in our history. For four years this Administration has had the support of the loyal opposition for the objective of seeking an honorable end to the struggle.

Never has so much military and economic and diplomatic power been used so ineffectively. And if after all of this time, and all of this sacrifice, and all of this support, there is still no end in sight, then I say the time has come for the American people to turn to new leadership not tied to the mistakes and policies of the past. That is what we offer to America.

And I pledge to you tonight that the first priority foreign policy objective of our next Administration will be to bring an honorable end to the war in Vietnam.

We shall not stop there. We need a policy to prevent more Vietnams. All of America's peace-keeping institutions and all of America's foreign commitments must be reappraised.

Over the past 25 years, America has provided more than $150-billion in foreign aid to nations abroad. In Korea, and now again in Vietnam, the United States furnished most of the money, most of the arms, most of the men to help the people of those countries defend themselves against aggression. Now we're a rich country, we're a strong nation, we're a populous nation but there are 200 million Americans and there are two billion people that live in the free world, and I say the time has come for other nations in the free world to bear their fair share of the burden of defending peace and freedom around this world.

What I call for is not a new isolationism. It is a new internationalism in which America enlists its allies and its friends around the world in those struggles in which their interest is as great as ours.

And now to the leaders of the Communist world we say, after an era of confrontations, the time has come for an era of negotiations.

Where the world super-powers are concerned there is no acceptable alternative to peaceful negotiation. Because this will be a period of negotiations we shall restore the strength of America so that we shall always negotiate from strength and never from weakness.

And as we seek through negotiations let our goals be made clear. We do not seek domination over any other country. We believe deeply in our ideas but we believe they should travel on their own power and not on the power of our arms. We shall never be belligerent. But we shall be as firm in defending our system as they are in expanding theirs.

We believe this should be an era of peaceful competition not only in the productivity of our factories but in the quality of our ideas. We extend the hand of friendship to all people. To the Russian people. To the Chinese people. To all people in the world. And we shall work toward the goal of an open world, open sky, open cities, open hearts, open minds. The next eight years my friends ...

This period in which we're entering—I think we will have the greatest opportunity for world peace, but also face the greatest danger of world war of any time in our history.

I believe we must have peace. I believe that we can have peace. But I do not underestimate the difficulty of this task.

Because, you see, the art of preserving peace is greater than that of waging war, and much more demanding.

But I am proud to have served in an Administration which ended one war and kept the nation out of other wars for eight years afterward.

And it is that kind of experience, and it is that kind of leadership, that America needs today and that we will give to America, with your help.

And as we commit the new policies for America tonight, let me make one further pledge—For five years hardly a day has gone by when we haven't read or heard a report of the American flag being spit on, and our embassy being stoned, a library being burned, or an ambassador being insulted some place in the world, and each incident reduced respect for the United States until the ultimate insult inevitably occurred.

And I say to you tonight that when respect for the United States of America falls so low that a fourth-rate military power like Korea will seize an American naval vessel in the high seas, it's time for new leadership to restore respect for the United States of America.

Thank you very much. My friends, America is a great nation. It is time we started to act like a great nation around the world.

It's ironic to note, when we were a small nation, weak militarily and poor economically, America was respected. And the reason was that America stood for something more powerful than military strength or economic wealth.

The American Revolution was a shining example of freedom in action which caught the imagination of the world, and today, too often, America is an example to be avoided and not followed.

A nation that can't keep the peace at home won't be trusted to keep the peace abroad. A President who isn't treated with respect at home will not be treated with respect abroad. A nation which can't manage its own economy can't tell others how to manage theirs.

If we are to restore prestige and respect for America abroad, the place to begin is at home—in the United States of America.

My friends, we live in an age of revolution in America and in the world. And to find the answers to our problems, let us turn to a revolution—a revolution that will never grow old, the world's greatest continuing revolution, the American Revolution.

The American Revolution was and is dedicated to progress. But our founders recognized that the first requisite of progress is order.

Now there is no quarrel between progress and order because neither can exist without the other.

So let us have order in America, not the order that suppresses dissent and discourages change but the order which guarantees the right to dissent and provides the basis for peaceful change.

And tonight it's time for some honest talk about the problem of order in the United States. Let us always respect, as I do, our courts and those who serve on them, but let us also recognize that some of our courts in their decisions have gone too far in weakening the peace forces as against the criminal forces in this country.

Let those who have the responsibility to enforce our laws, and our judges who have the responsibility to interpret them, be dedicated to the great principles of civil rights. But let them also recognize that the first civil right of every American is to be free from domestic violence. And that right must be guaranteed in this country.

And if we are to restore order and respect for law in this country, there's one place we're going to begin: We're going to have a new Attorney General of the United States of America.

I pledge to you that our new Attorney General will be directed by the President of the United States to launch a war against organized crime in this country.

I pledge to you that the new Attorney General of the United States will be an active belligerent against the loan sharks and the numbers racketeers that rob the urban poor in our cities.

I pledge to you that the new Attorney General will open a new front against the pill peddlers and the narcotics peddlers who are corrupting the lives of the children of this country.

Because, my friends, let this message come through clear from what I say tonight. Time is running out for the merchants of crime and corruption in American society. The wave of crime is not going to be the wave of the future in the United States of America.

We shall re-establish freedom from fear in America so that America can take the lead of re-establishing freedom from fear in the world.

And to those who say that law and order is the code word for racism, here is a reply: Our goal is justice—justice for every American. If we are to have respect for law in America, we must have laws that deserve respect. Just as we cannot have progress without order, we cannot have order without progress.

And so as we commit to order tonight, let us commit to progress.

And this brings me to the clearest choice among the great issues of this campaign.

For the past five years we have been deluged by Government programs for the unemployed, programs for the cities, programs for the poor, and we have reaped from these programs an ugly harvest of frustrations, violence and failure across the land. And now our opponents will be offering more of the same—more billions for Government jobs, Government housing, Government welfare. I say it's time to quit pouring billions of dollars into programs that have failed in the United States of America.

To put it bluntly, we're on the wrong road and it's time to take a new road to progress.

Again we turn to the American Revolution for our answers. The war on poverty didn't begin five years ago in this country, it began when this country began. It's been the most successful war on poverty in the history of nations. There's more wealth in America today, more broadly shared than in any nation in the world.

We are a great nation. And we must never forget how we became great. America is a great nation today, not because of what government did for people, but because of what people did for themselves over 190 years in this country.

And so it is time to apply the lessons of the American Revolution to our present problems.

Let us increase the wealth of America so we can provide more generously for the aged and for the needy and for all those who cannot help themselves.

But for those who are able to help themselves, what we need are not more millions on welfare rolls but more millions on payrolls in the United States of America.

Instead of Government jobs and Government housing and Government welfare, let Government use its tax and credit policies to enlist in this battle the greatest engine of progress ever developed in the history of man—American private enterprise.

Let us enlist in this great cause the millions of Americans in volunteer organizations who will bring a dedication to this task that no amount of money can ever buy.

And let us build bridges, my friends, build bridges to human dignity across that gulf that separates black America from white America.

Black Americans—no more than white Americans—do not want more Government programs which perpetuate dependency. They don't want to be a colony in a nation. They want the pride and the self-respect and the dignity that can only come if they have an equal chance to own their own homes, to own their own businesses, to be managers and executives as well as workers, to have a piece of the action in the exciting ventures of private enterprise.

I pledge to you tonight that we shall have new programs which will provide that equal chance. We make great history tonight. We do not fire a shot heard round the world, but we shall light the lamp of hope in millions of homes across this world in which there is no hope today.

And that great light shining out from America will again become a beacon of hope for all those in the world who seek freedom and opportunity.

My fellow Americans, I believe that historians will recall that 1968 marked the beginning of the American generation in world history. Just to be alive in America, just to be alive at this time is an experience unparalleled in history. Here's where the naction is.

Think: Thirty-two years from now most of the Americans living today will celebrate a New Year that comes once in a thousand years.

Eight years from now, in the second term of the next President, we will celebrate the 200th anniversary of the American Revolution.

And by our decision in this we—all of us here, all of you listening on television and radio—we will determine what kind of nation America will be on its 200th birthday. We will determine what kind of a world America will live in in the year 2000.

This is the kind of a day I see for America on that glorious fourth eight years from now: I see a day when Americans are once again proud of their flag; when once again at home and abroad it is honored as the world's greatest symbol of liberty and justice.

I see a day when the President of the United States is respected and his office is honored because it is worthy of respect and worthy of honor. I see a day when every child in the land, regardless of his background, has a chance for the best education that our wisdom and schools can provide, and an equal chance to go just as high as his talents will take him.

I see a day when life in rural America attracts people to the country rather than driving them away.

I see a day when we can look back on massive break-through in solving the problems of slums and pollution and crime which are choking our cities to death.

I see a day when our senior citizens and millions of others can plan for the future with the assurance that their government is not going to rob them of their savings by destroying the value of their dollar.

I see a day when we will again have freedom from fear in America and freedom from fear in the world. I see a day when every nation is at peace and the world is at peace and everyone on earth—those who hope, those who aspire, those who desire liberty will look to America as the shining example of dreams realized and dreams achieved.

My fellow Americans, this is the cause I ask you to vote for. This is the cause I ask you to work for. This is the cause I ask you to commit to not just for victory in November but beyond that to a new Administration because the time when one man or a few leaders could save America is gone. We need tonight nothing less than the total commitment and the total mobilization of the American people if we are to succeed.

Government can pass laws but respect for law can come only from people who take the law into their hearts and their minds and not into their hands.

Government can provide opportunity, but opportunity means nothing unless people are prepared to seize it.

A President can ask for reconciliation in the racial conflict that divides Americans, but reconciliation comes only from the hearts of people.

And tonight, therefore, as we make this commitment, let us look into our hearts, and let us look down into the faces of our children.

Is there anything in the world that should stand in their way? None of the old hatreds mean anything when you look down into the faces of our children. In their faces is our hope, our love and our courage.

Tonight, I see the face of a child. He lives in a great city, he's black or he's white, he's Mexican, Italian, Polish, none of that matters. What matters he's an American child.

That child in that great city is more important than any politician's promise. He is America, he is a poet, he is a scientist, he's a great teacher, he's a proud craftsman, he's everything we've ever hoped to be in everything we dare to dream about.

He sleeps the sleep of a child, and he dreams the dreams of a child. And yet when he awakens, he awakens to a living nightmare of poverty, neglect and despair.

He fails in school, he ends up on welfare. For him the American system is one that feeds his stomach and starves his soul. It breaks his heart. And in the end it may take his life on some distant battlefield.

To millions of children in this rich land this is their prospect, but this is only part of what I see in America.

I see another child tonight. He hears a train go by. At night he dreams of faraway places where he'd like to go. It seems like an impossible dream. But he is helped on his journey through life. A father who had to go to work before he finished the sixth grade sacrificed everything he had so that his sons could go to college.

A gentle Quaker mother with a passionate concern for peace, quietly wept when he went to war but she understood why he had to go.

A great teacher, a remarkable football coach, an inspirational minister encouraged him on his way. A courageous wife and loyal children stood by him in victory and also in defeat.

And in his chosen profession of politics, first there were scores, then hundreds, then thousands, and finally millions who worked for his success.

And tonight he stands before you, nominated for President of the United States of America.

You can see why I believe so deeply in the American dream.

For most of us the American revolution has been won, the American dream has come true. What I ask of you tonight is to help me make that dream come true for millions to whom it's an impossible dream today.

One hundred and eight years ago the newly elected President of the United States, Abraham Lincoln, left Springfield, Ill., never to return again.

He spoke to his friends gathered at the railroad station. Listen to his words:

"Today I leave you. I go to assume a greater task than devolved on General Washington. The Great God which helped him must help me. Without that great assistance I will surely fail. With it, I cannot fail."

Abraham Lincoln lost his life but he did not fail.

The next President of the United States will face challenges which in some ways will be greater than those of Washington or Lincoln, because for the first time in our nation's history an American President will face not only the problem of restoring peace abroad, but of restoring peace at home.

Without God's help, and your help, we will surely fail.

But with God's help and your help, we shall surely succeed.

My fellow Americans, the dark long night for America is about to end.

The time has come for us to leave the valley of despair and climb the mountain so that we may see the glory of the dawn, a new day for America, a new dawn for peace and freedom to the world.

Richard M. Nixon

First Inaugural Address
(January 20, 1969)

Two weeks after Richard Nixon's nomination by the Republican party in Miami, the Democrats gathered in Chicago. Their convention turned into a nightmare. A protest group, the Youth International Party, organized demonstrations; they were joined by over eighty peace groups that converged on Chicago for a massive peace protest. The result was a series of violent clashes, culminating in what was later called a "police riot," in which demonstrators were savagely beaten and teargassed. Senator Ribicoff, from the convention podium, denounced "the Gestapo tactics on the streets of Chicago," and was answered with a chorus of boos and curses and shaking fists from the Illinois delegation led by Chicago's political boss, Mayor Daley. All of this turmoil was played out on national television before a horrified American audience. The nomination of Vice President Hubert Humphrey seemed almost an anticlimax. Humphrey left Chicago saddled not only with the unpopularity of Lyndon Johnson, whom he had served as Vice President for four years, but also with the Daley image and all it represented for the more liberal Democrats now disillusioned, discouraged, and disinclined to support the party's nominee.

The campaign was further complicated by the independent candidacy of Gov. George Wallace of Alabama, whose naked appeals to racism and vicious attacks on protestors and "pointy-headed intellectuals" found a sympathetic audience, particularly in the deep South where resentments against the civil rights movement were intense. Humphrey started the election far behind in the polls; the August Gallup Poll put Nixon 16 points ahead of the Democratic nominee.

In fact, the positions of the two candidates on the issue of what to do in Vietnam were hard to distinguish—both called for some kind of solution that would get us out and both were vague about what that solution should be. Nixon had a "secret plan" that he claimed would be compromised if he spelled it out clearly, and Humphrey gradually moved from a loyal defense of present administration policy to the point where, in a speech in October in Salt Lake City, he could announce that he would take an "acceptable risk for peace" by stopping the bombing in Vietnam. As the election got closer, Wallace's support faded and Humphrey gained in the polls. Election night was a seesaw affair but ultimately Nixon triumphed. The popular vote was exceedingly close, 43.4 percent for Nixon to 42.7 percent for Humphrey, but Nixon captured 301 electoral votes to 191 for Humphrey and 45 for Wallace. The Democrats, however, retained control of both houses of Congress.

While campaigning in Ohio, Richard Nixon caught sight of a placard that read "Bring Us Together," and the new President-elect professed that this was to be his goal. It is hard to imagine a time in our history when such a goal was more challenging. Enraged by years of oppression and economic deprivation, blacks rioted, engulfing sections of America's major cities in flames; peace demonstrators in New York City were set upon by construction workers who beat them with their hard hats; the American flag was routinely desecrated as all formerly revered symbols and values seemed under attack. Hawks and doves reviled one another as Commie pinkos or superpatriotic pigs; the young seemed violently alienated from the old. It was clear, however, that if the country was ever to be brought together again, the war in Vietnam had first to be dealt with.

In his inaugural, President Nixon declared that one of the first things Americans had to do was to "lower our voices," in order to reduce the "fever of words" from which the country was suffering. While maintaining that his administration would continue to pursue social goals, the President argued that we were "approaching the limits of what government alone can do." From our "past agony," President Nixon drew the lesson that "without the people we can do nothing; with the people we can do everything." To achieve progress at home, however, would demand that "our wealth ... be transferred from the destruction of war abroad to the urgent needs of our people...." The inaugural address sought to assure Americans themselves, as well as friends and adversaries abroad, that the first priority of the new administration would be peace. "I shall consecrate my office, my energies and all the wisdom I can summon," Nixon asserted, "to the cause of peace among nations."

Senator Dirksen, Mr. Chief Justice, Mr. Vice President, President Johnson, Vice President Humphrey, my fellow Americans and my fellow citizens of the world community:—I ask you to share with me today the majesty of this moment. In the orderly transfer of power, we celebrate the unity that keeps us free.

Each moment in history is a fleeting time, precious and unique. But some stand out as moments of beginning, in which courses are set that shape decades or centuries.

This can be such a moment. Forces now are converging that make possible for the first time the hope that many of man's deepest aspirations can at last be realized.

The spiraling pace of change allows us to contemplate, within our own lifetime, advances that once would have taken centuries.

In throwing wide the horizons of space, we have discovered new horizons on earth.

For the first time, because the people of the world want peace and the leaders of the world are afraid of war, the times are on the side of peace.

Eight years from now America will celebrate its 200th anniversary as a nation. And within the lifetime of most people now living, mankind will celebrate that great new year which comes only once in a thousand years—the beginning of the third millennium.

What kind of a nation we will be, what kind of a

world we will live in, whether we shape the future in the image of our hopes, is ours to determine by our actions and our choices.

The greatest honor history can bestow is the title of peacemaker. This honor now beckons America—the chance to help lead the world at last out of the valley of turmoil and on to that high ground of peace that man has dreamed of since the dawn of civilization.

If we succeed, generations to come will say of us now living that we mastered our moment, that we helped make the world safe for mankind.

This is our summons to greatness.

And I believe the American people are ready to answer this call.

The second third of this century has been a time of proud achievement. We have made enormous strides in science and industry and agriculture. We have shared our wealth more broadly than ever, we learned at last to manage a modern economy to assure its continued growth.

We have given freedom new reach, we have begun to make its promise real for black as well as for white.

We see the hope of tomorrow in the youth of today. I know America's youth. I believe in them. We can be proud that they are better educated, more committed, more passionately driven by conscience than any generation in our history.

No people has ever been so close to the achievement of a just and abundant society, or so possessed of the will to achieve it.

And because our strengths are so great, we can afford to appraise our weaknesses with candor and to approach them with hope.

Standing in this same place a third of a century ago, Franklin Delano Roosevelt addressed the nation ravaged by depression gripped in fear. He could say in surveying the nation's troubles: "They concern, thank God, only material things."

Our crisis today is in reverse.

We find ourselves rich in goods, but ragged in spirit; reaching with magnificent precision for the moon, but falling into raucous discord on earth.

We are caught in war, wanting peace. We're torn by division, wanting unity. We see around us empty lives, wanting fulfillment. We see tasks that need doing, waiting for hands to do them.

To a crisis of the spirit, we need an answer of the spirit.

And to find that answer, we need only look within ourselves.

When we listen to "the better angels of our nature," we find that they celebrate the simple things, the basic things—such as goodness, decency, love, kindness.

Greatness comes in simple trappings.

The simple things are the ones most needed today if we are to surmount what divides us and cement what unites us. To lower our voices would be a simple thing.

In these difficult years, America has suffered from a fever of words; from inflated rhetoric that promises more than it can deliver; from angry rhetoric that fans discontents into hatreds; from bombastic rhetoric that postures instead of persuading.

We cannot learn from one another until we stop shouting at one another—until we speak quietly enough so that our words can be heard as well as our voices.

For its part, government will listen. We will strive to listen in new ways—to the voices of quiet anguish, the voices that speak without words, the voices of the heart—to the injured voices, the anxious voices, the voices that have despaired of being heard.

Those who have been left out we will try to bring in. Those left behind, we will help to catch up.

For all our people, we will set as our goal the decent order that makes progress possible and our lives secure.

As we reach toward our hopes, our task is to build on what has gone before—not turning away from the old, but turning toward the new.

In this past third of a century, government has passed more laws, spent more money, initiated more programs, than in all our previous history.

In pursuing our goals of full employment, better housing, excellence in education; in rebuilding our cities and improving our rural areas; in protecting our environment, enhancing the quality of life—in all these and more, we will and must press urgently forward.

We shall plan now for the day when our wealth can be transferred from the destruction of war abroad to the urgent needs of our people at home.

The American dream does not come to those who fall asleep.

But we are approaching the limits of what government alone can do.

Our greatest need now is to reach beyond government, to enlist the legions of the concerned and the committed. What has to be done has to be done by government and people together or it will not be done at all. The lesson of past agony is that without the people we can do nothing; with the people we can do everything.

To match the magnitude of our talks, we need the energies of our people—enlisted not only in grand enterprises, but more importantly in those small splendid efforts that make headlines in the neighborhood newspaper instead of the national journal.

With these, we can build a great cathedral of the spirit—each of us raising it one stone at a time, as he reaches out to his neighbor, helping, caring, doing.

I do not offer a life of uninspiring ease. I do not call for a life of grim sacrifice. I ask you to join in a high adventure—one as rich as humanity itself, and exciting as the times we live in.

The essence of freedom is that each of us shares in the shaping of his own destiny. Until he has been part of a cause larger than himself, no man is truly whole.

The way to fulfillment is in the use of our talents; we achieve nobility in the spirit that inspires that use.

As we measure what can be done, we shall promise only what we know we can produce; but as we chart our goals we shall be lifted by our dreams.

No man can be fully free while his neighbor is not. To go forward at all is to go forward together.

This means black and white together, as one nation, not two. The laws have caught up with our conscience. What remains is to give life to what is in the law: to insure at last that as all are born equal in dignity before God, all are born equal in dignity before man.

As we learn to go forward together at home, let us also seek to go forward together with all mankind.

Let us take as our goal: where peace is unknown, make it welcome; where peace is fragile, make it strong; where peace is temporary, make it permanent.

After a period of confrontation, we are entering an era of negotiation. Let all nations know that during this Administration our lines of communication will be open.

We seek an open world—open to ideas, open to the exchange of goods and people, a world in which no people, great or small, will live in angry isolation.

We cannot expect to make everyone our friend, but we can try to make no one our enemy.

Those who would be our adversaries, we invite to a peaceful competition—not in conquering territory or extending dominion, but in enriching the life of man.

As we explore the reaches of space, let us go to the new worlds together—not as new worlds to be conquered, but as a new adventure to be shared.

And with those who are willing to join, let us cooperate to reduce the burden of arms, to strengthen the structure of peace, to lift up the poor and the hungry.

But to all those who would be tempted by weakness, let us leave no doubt that we will be as strong as we need to be for as long as we need to be.

Over the past 20 years, since I first came to this Capitol as a freshman Congressman, I have visited most of the nations of the world.

I have come to know the leaders of the world, the great forces, the hatreds, the fears that divide the world.

I know that peace does not come through wishing for it—that there is no substitute for days and even years of patient and prolonged diplomacy.

I also know the people of the world.

I have seen the hunger of a homeless child, the pain of a man wounded in battle, the grief of a mother who has lost her son. I know these have no ideology, no race.

I know America. I know the heart of America is good.

I speak from my own heart, and the heart of my country, the deep concern we have for those who suffer and those who sorrow.

I have taken an oath today in the presence of God and my countrymen. To uphold and defend the Constitution of the United States. And to that oath, I now add this sacred commitment: I shall consecrate my office, my energies and all the wisdom I can summon, to the cause of peace among nations.

Let this message be heard by strong and weak alike.

The peace we seek—the peace we seek to win—is not victory over any other people, but the peace that comes with healing in its wings; with compassion for those who have suffered; with understanding for those who have opposed us; with the opportunity for all the peoples of this earth to choose their own destiny.

Only a few short weeks ago, we shared the glory of man's first sight of the world as God sees it, as a single sphere reflecting light in the darkness.

As Apollo astronauts flew over the moon's gray surface on Christmas Eve, they spoke to us of the beauty of earth and in that voice so clear across the lunar distance we heard them invoke God's blessing on its goodness.

In that moment, their view from the moon moved poet Archibald MacLeish to write: "To see the earth as it truly is, small and blue and beautiful in that eternal silence where it floats, is to see ourselves as riders on the earth together, brothers in that bright loveliness in the eternal cold—brothers who know now they are truly brothers."

In that moment of surpassing technological triumph, men turned their thoughts toward home and humanity—seeing in that far perspective that man's destiny on earth is not divisible; telling us that however far we reach into the cosmos our destiny lies not in the stars but on earth itself, in our own hands, in our own hearts.

We have endured a long night of the American spirit. But as our eyes catch the dimness of the first rays of dawn, let us not curse the remaining dark. Let us gather the light.

Our destiny offers not the cup of despair, but the chalice of opportunity. So let us seize it, not in fear, but in gladness and "riders on the earth together," let us go forward, firm in our faith, steadfast in our purpose, cautious of the dangers; but sustained by our confidence in the will of God and the promise of man.

Edward M. Kennedy

Incident at Chappaquiddick
(July 25, 1969)

Bright, aggressive, politically astute, and socially conscious, the "Kennedy clan" captivated some, alienated others, and fascinated most Americans throughout the sixties. The Kennedys had achieved the pinnacle of success with John's election to the Presidency and plummeted to the depths of despair with his assassination in 1963. His brother Robert, inheriting the mantle of leadership, was close to winning the Democratic nomination for President when he was shot and killed in Los Angeles in 1968. The third brother, "Ted" Kennedy, a United States senator from Massachusetts, was in 1969 emerging as a powerful force in his own right in Democratic politics. In January, he successfully challenged Sen. Russell Long of Louisiana for the Democratic whip's position in the Senate, and some talked of Edward Kennedy as a Presidential candidate to run against Nixon in 1972.

Kennedy's fortunes were dramatically altered, however, by a deadly accident on a little island off Cape Cod: Chappaquiddick. On July 18 he and some friends hosted a cookout on Chappaquiddick, separated by 250 feet of water from the larger Martha's Vineyard, for a group of young women who had worked in Robert's Presidential campaign the previous year. Senator Kennedy left the party with one of the women, Mary Jo Kopechne, to return, the senator later testified, to Edgartown on Martha's Vineyard. Traveling along a dirt road, the senator failed to negotiate a sharp turn and the car plunged over Dike Bridge, turned over, and landed on the bottom of the ten-foot channel beneath the bridge.

Kennedy later recounted how he had dived several times in an effort to free Ms. Kopechne. Unsuccessful and exhausted, he returned to the cookout and came back with two friends who also dove into the channel in an attempt to extricate Ms. Kopechne.

What happened next was most puzzling and most damaging to the senator. Kennedy had his friends drive him to the ferry where he impulsively jumped into the water and swam the narrow stretch back to Martha's Vineyard. He returned to his hotel, changed into dry clothes, and finally went to sleep. His friends Joseph Gargan and Paul Markham, who had driven him back to the scene of the accident the night before, picked up the senator at his hotel in the morning, horrified to learn that he had not notified the police. Returning to Chappaquiddick, Kennedy finally did call the police, almost eleven hours after the accident had happened, and after the wreck had already been discovered and Mary Jo's body recovered. The senator made a statement to the police and was subsequently charged with leaving the scene of an accident.

The story, of course, made the national news. Edward Kennedy went into seclusion at the family home in Hyannisport. There were questions about the senator's account of the incident. How, for example, could he have mistakenly taken the gravel road that led to the beach instead of staying on the road to the ferry when he was familiar with both roads? And his strange behavior following the accident, even if completely true, raised serious questions about Kennedy's judgment. A week later he appeared in court to plead guilty to the charge of leaving the scene, was given a suspended sentence, and had his driver's license revoked. That night, from his father's house, he delivered a radio and television address to the people of Massachusetts.

The speech itself was Kennedy's attempt to explain his actions and to salvage his political career. Much as Richard Nixon had left his fate to the determination of the electorate in the "Checkers" speech, Kennedy used the speech to appeal to the people of Massachusetts, asserting his willingness to resign from the Senate if the voters in his home state called for that action. The response, from both the public and the Massachusetts press, was overwhelmingly favorable to Kennedy. Nevertheless, his national image was tarnished and there seemed no question that, if the senator did have Presidential aspirations, they had been shelved indefinitely.

My fellow citizens:—I have requested this opportunity to talk to the people of Massachusetts about the tragedy which happened last Friday evening. This morning I entered a plea of guilty to the charge of leaving the scene of an accident. Prior to my appearance in court it would have been improper for me to comment on these matters. But tonight I am free to tell you what happened and to say what it means to me.

On the weekend of July 18 I was on Martha's Vineyard Island participating with my nephew Joe Kennedy—as for thirty years my family has participated—in the annual Edgartown sailing regatta. Only reasons of health prevented my wife from accompanying me.

On Chappaquiddick Island, off Martha's Vineyard, I attended on Friday evening, July 18, a cookout I had encouraged and helped sponsor for a devoted group of Kennedy campaign secretaries. When I left the party, around 11:15 P.M., I was accompanied by one of these girls, Miss Mary Jo Kopechne. Mary Jo was one of the most devoted members of the staff of Senator Robert Kennedy. She worked for him for four years and was broken up over his death. For this reason, and because she was such a gentle, kind and idealistic person, all of us tried to help her feel that she still had a home with the Kennedy family.

There is no truth, no truth whatever, to the widely circulated suspicions of immoral conduct that have been leveled at my behavior and hers regarding that evening. There has never been a private relationship between us of any kind. I know of nothing in Mary Jo's conduct on that or any other occasion—the same is true of the other girls at that party—that would lend any substance to such ugly speculation about their character. Nor was I driving under the influence of liquor.

Little over one mile away, the car that I was driving on an unlit road went off a narrow bridge which had no guardrails and was built on a left angle to the road. The car overturned in a deep pond and immediately filled with water. I remember thinking as the cold water rushed in around my head that I was for certain drowning. Then water entered my lungs and I actually felt the sensation of drowning. But somehow I struggled to the surface alive. I made immediate and repeated efforts to save Mary Jo by diving into the strong and murky current but succeeded only in increasing my state of utter exhaustion and alarm.

My conduct and conversations during the next several hours to the extent that I can remember them make no sense to me at all. Although my doctors informed me that I suffered a cerebral concussion as well as shock, I do not seek to escape responsibility for my actions by placing the blame either on the physical, emotional trauma brought on by the accident or on anyone else. I regard as indefensible the fact that I did not report the accident to the police immediately.

Instead of looking directly for a telephone after lying exhausted in the grass for an undetermined time, I walked back to the cottage where the party was being held and requested the help of two friends, my cousin Joseph Gargan and Paul Markham, and directed them to return immediately to the scene with me—this was some time after midnight—in order to undertake a new effort to dive down and locate Miss Kopechne. Their strenuous efforts, undertaken at some risks to their own lives, also proved futile.

All kinds of scrambled thoughts—all of them confused, some of them irrational, many of them which I cannot recall and some of which I would not have seriously entertained under normal circumstances—went through my mind during this period. They were reflected in the various inexplicable, inconsistent and inconclusive things I said and did, including such questions as whether the girl might still be alive somewhere out of that immediate area, whether some awful curse did actually hang over all the Kennedys, whether there was some justifiable reason for me to doubt what had happened and to delay my report, whether somehow the awful weight of this incredible incident might in some way pass from my shoulders. I was overcome, I'm frank to say, by a jumble of emotions—grief, fear, doubt, exhaustion, panic, confusion and shock.

Instructing Gargan and Markham not to alarm Mary Jo's friends that night, I had them take me to the ferry crossing. The ferry having shut down for the night, I suddenly jumped into the water and impulsively swam across, nearly drowning once again in the effort, and returned to my hotel about 2 A.M. and

collapsed in my room. I remember going out at one point and saying something to the room clerk.

In the morning, with my mind somewhat more lucid, I made an effort to call a family legal adviser, Burke Marshall, from a public telephone on the Chappaquiddick side of the ferry and belatedly reported the accident to the Martha's Vineyard police.

Today, as I mentioned, I felt morally obligated to plead guilty to the charge of leaving the scene of an accident. No words on my part can possibly express the terrible pain and suffering I feel over this tragic incident. This last week has been an agonizing one for me and the members of my family, and the grief we feel over the loss of a wonderful friend will remain with us the rest of our lives.

These events, the publicity, innuendo and whispers which have surrounded them and my admission of guilt this morning raise the question in my mind of whether my standing among the people of my state has been so impaired that I should resign my seat in the United States Senate. If at any time the citizens of Massachusetts should lack confidence in their senator's character or his ability, with or without justification, he could not in my opinion adequately perform his duty and should not continue in office.

The people of this state, the state which sent John Quincy Adams and Daniel Webster and Charles Sumner and Henry Cabot Lodge and John Kennedy to the United States Senate, are entitled to representation in that body by men who inspire their utmost confidence. For this reason, I would understand full well why some might think it right for me to resign. For me this will be a difficult decision to make.

It has been seven years since my first election to the Senate. You and I share many memories—some of them have been glorious, some have been very sad. The opportunity to work with you and serve Massachusetts has made my life worthwhile.

And so I ask you tonight, people of Massachusetts, to think this through with me. In facing this decision, I seek your advice and opinion. In making it, I seek your prayers. For this is a decision that I will have finally to make on my own.

It has been written a man does what he must in spite of personal consequences, in spite of obstacles and dangers and pressures, and that is the basis of all human morality. Whatever may be the sacrifices he faces, if he follows his conscience—the loss of his friends, his fortune, his contentment, even the esteem of his fellow man—each man must decide for himself the course he will follow. The stories of past courage cannot supply courage itself. For this, each man must look into his own soul.

I pray that I can have the courage to make the right decision. Whatever is decided and whatever the future holds for me, I hope that I shall be able to put this most recent tragedy behind me and make some further contribution to our state and mankind, whether it be in public or private life.

Thank you and good night.

Spiro T. Agnew

Television News Coverage
(November 13, 1969)

As Richard Nixon's first year in office progressed, it became increasingly apparent that the war in Vietnam was not to be brought to a speedy conclusion. Nixon's policy of "Vietnamization," a term coined by Secretary of Defense Melvin Laird, was designed to reduce the involvement of American troops in Vietnam; ground combat was gradually to be turned over to the South Vietnamese army while the United States stepped up the bombing war. At first, with troops returning home and American casualties reduced, the peace movement was somewhat blunted. By the fall of 1969, however, antiwar sentiment was channeled into plans for a massive demonstration, the Vietnam Moratorium, to be held on October 15. Two days before the scheduled protest the President announced that he would make a major statement on Vietnam on November 3. Clearly the President wished to defuse the impact of the demonstration, and, while the moratorium proceeded as planned, its tone was somewhat muted.

The President's address on November 3 gave little comfort to the peace movement; he dismissed protests as unnecessary since his Vietnamization plan called for "the complete withdrawal of all United States ground combat forces." It was clear, of course, that the fighting would not end and that Americans would still be involved in the air war. Furthermore, Nixon seemed to dismiss his critics almost contemptuously, preferring to rely on the wishes of the "silent majority" who he maintained supported him. He made it clear that he did not want peace without victory: "Let us be united for peace. Let us also be united against defeat." In an unmistakable jab at peace activists, the President asserted that "North Vietnam cannot defeat or humiliate the United States. Only Americans can do that."

At the conclusion of the television speech, Mr. Nixon's address was subjected to brief, but careful, scrutiny by news analysts and by some of his critics. These discussions immediately following the speech, "instant analysis and querulous criticism" as Vice President Agnew characterized them, were not generally favorable to the President. President Nixon, in common with most Presidents, was consistently irritated by the propensity of the media to interpret, question, and challenge statements that the President conceived as made directly from him to the American people. In Nixon's case, however, relations with the press had never been cordial, and the President bitterly resented the power of commentators to intervene between him and his intended audience. Furthermore, popular reactions to the President's speech seemed much more positive that those of media analysts. A Gallup Poll showed that 77 percent of his audience approved the speech and only 6 percent disapproved it. This appeared to be a propitious time to launch an attack on the national media.

Vice President Spiro Agnew was the obvious choice to undertake such a venture. It became clear early in the campaign that Agnew was capable of vicious, slashing attacks on "phony intellectuals who don't understand what we mean by hard work and patriotism." His rather baroque rhetoric subsequently was turned on critics of the war—"parasites of passion" and "ideological eunuchs"—who were "an effete corps of impudent snobs."

A little over a week after the President's speech, Agnew traveled to Des Moines, Iowa, to speak at a meeting of the Mid-West Regional Republican Committee. In a speech that asserted that the views of "a small group of men" who controlled the news represented "a concentration of power over American public opinion unknown in history," Agnew argued that these views "do not—and I repeat, not—represent the views of America." Although the Vice President was careful to say that he did not favor censorship, the chilling implication was clear: "... perhaps it is time that the networks were made more responsive to the views of the nation and more responsible to the people they serve." To many this sounded very much like a threat, a warning against actions and comments by the news media that the President considered politically unfair and popularly unsupported. The speech, obviously intended to isolate critics of the administration, put the media on the defensive and made them somewhat wary of critical responses to the President.

Tonight I want to discuss the importance of the television news medium to the American people. No nation depends more on the intelligent judgment of its citizens. No medium has a more profound influence over public opinion. Nowhere in our system are there fewer checks on vast power. So, nowhere should there be more conscientious responsibility exercised than by the news media. The question is, Are we demanding enough of our television news presentations? And are the men of this medium demanding enough of themselves?

Monday night a week ago, President Nixon delivered the most important address of his Administration, one of the most important of our decade. His subject was Vietnam. His hope was to rally the American peo-

ple to see the conflict through to a lasting and just peace in the Pacific. For 32 minutes, he reasoned with a nation that has suffered almost a third of a million casualties in the longest war in its history.

When the President completed his address—an address, incidentally, that he spent weeks in the preparation of—his words and policies were subjected to instant analysis and querulous criticism. The audience of 70 million Americans gathered to hear the President of the United States was inherited by a small band of network commentators and self-appointed analysts, the majority of whom expressed in one way or another their hostility to what he had to say.

It was obvious that their minds were made up in advance. Those who recall the fumbling and groping that followed President Johnson's dramatic disclosure of his intention not to seek another term have seen these men in a genuine state of nonpreparedness. This was not it.

One commentator twice contradicted the President's statement about the exchange of correspondence with Ho Chi Minh. Another challenged the President's abilities as a politician. A third asserted that the President was following a Pentagon line. Others, by the expression on their faces, the tone of their questions and the sarcasm of their responses, made clear their sharp disapproval.

To guarantee in advance that the President's plea for national unity would be challenged, one network trotted out Averell Harriman for the occasion. Throughout the President's message, he waited in the wings. When the President concluded, Mr. Harriman recited perfectly. He attacked the Thieu Government as unrepresentative; he criticized the President's speech for various deficiencies; he twice issued a call to the Senate Foreign Relations Committee to debate Vietnam once again; he stated his belief that the Vietcong or North Vietnamese did not really want military takeover of South Vietnam; and he told a little anecdote about a "very, very responsible" fellow he had met in the North Vietnamese delegation.

All in all, Mr. Harriman offered a broad range of gratuitous advice challenging and contradicting the policies outlined by the President of the United States. Where the President had issued a call for unity, Mr. Harriman was encouraging the country not to listen to him.

A word about Mr. Harriman. For 10 months he was America's chief negotiator at the Paris peace talks—a period in which the United States swapped some of the greatest military concessions in the history of warfare for an enemy agreement on the shape of the bargaining table. Like Coleridge's Ancient Mariner, Mr. Harriman seems to be under some heavy compulsion to justify his failure to anyone who will listen. And the networks have shown themselves willing to give him all the air time he desires.

Now every American has a right to disagree with the President of the United States and to express publicly that disagreement. But the President of the United States has a right to communicate directly with the people who elected him, and the people of this country have the right to make up their own minds and form their own opinions about a Presidential address without having a President's words and thoughts character-

ized through the prejudices of hostile critics before they can even be digested.

When Winston Churchill rallied public opinion to stay the course against Hitler's Germany, he didn't have to contend with a gaggle of commentators raising doubts about whether he was reading public opinion right, or whether Britain had the stamina to see the war through.

When President Kennedy rallied the nation in the Cuban missile crisis, his address to the people was not chewed over by a roundtable of critics who disparaged the course of action he'd asked America to follow.

The purpose of my remarks tonight is to focus your attention on this little group of men who not only enjoy a right of instant rebuttal to every Presidential address, but, more importantly, wield a free hand in selecting, presenting and interpreting the great issues in our nation.

First, let's define that power. At least 40 million Americans every night, it's estimated, watch the network news. Seven million of them view A.B.C., the remainder being divided between N.B.C. and C.B.S.

According to Harris polls and other studies, for millions of Americans the networks are the sole source of national and world news. In Will Rogers' observation, what you knew was what you read in the newspaper. Today for growing millions of Americans, it's what they see and hear on their television sets.

Now how is this network news determined? A small group of men, numbering perhaps no more than a dozen anchormen, commentators and executive producers, settle upon the 20 minutes or so of film and commentary that's to reach the public. This selection is made from the 90 to 180 minutes that may be available. Their powers of choice are broad.

They decide what 40 to 50 million Americans will learn of the day's events in the nation and in the world.

We cannot measure this power and influence by the traditional democratic standards, for these men can create national issues overnight.

They can make or break by their coverage and commentary a moratorium on the war.

They can elevate men from obscurity to national prominence within a week. They can reward some politicians with national exposure and ignore others.

For millions of Americans the network reporter who covers a continuing issue—like the ABM or civil rights—becomes, in effect, the presiding judge in a national trial by jury.

It must be recognized that the networks have

made important contributions to the national knowledge—for news, documentaries and specials. They have often used their power constructively and creatively to awaken the public conscience to critical problems. The networks made hunger and black lung disease national issues overnight. The TV networks have done what no other medium could have done in terms of dramatizing the horrors of war. The networks have tackled our most difficult social problems with a directness and an immediacy that's the gift of their medium. They focus the nation's attention on its environmental abuses—on pollution in the Great Lakes and the threatened ecology of the Everglades.

But it was also the networks that elevated Stokely Carmichael and George Lincoln Rockwell from obscurity to national prominence.

Nor is their power confined to the substantive. A raised eyebrow, an inflection of the voice, a caustic remark dropped in the middle of a broadcast can raise doubts in a million minds about the veracity of a public official or the wisdom of a Government policy.

One Federal Communications Commissioner considers the powers of the networks equal to that of local state and Federal Governments all combined. Certainly it represents a concentration of power over American public opinion unknown in history.

Now what do Americans know of the men who wield this power? Of the men who produce and direct the network news, the nation knows practically nothing. Of the commentators, most Americans know little other than that they reflect an urbane and assured presence seemingly well-informed on every important matter.

We do know that to a man these commentators and producers live and work in the geographical and intellectual confines of Washington, D.C., or New York City, the latter of which James Reston terms the most unrepresentative community in the entire United States.

Both communities bask in their own provincialism, their own parochialism.

We can deduce that these men read the same newspapers. They draw their political and social views from the same sources. Worse, they talk constantly to one another, thereby providing artificial reinforcement to their shared viewpoints.

Do they allow their biases to influence the selection and presentation of the news? David Brinkley states objectivity is impossible to normal human behavior. Rather, he says, we should strive for fairness.

Another anchorman on a network news show contends, and I quote: "You can't expunge all your private convictions just because you sit in a seat like this and a camera starts to stare at you. I think your program has to reflect what your basic feelings are. I'll plead guilty to that."

Less than a week before the 1968 election, this same commentator charged that President Nixon's campaign commitments were no more durable than campaign balloons. He claimed that, were it not for the fear of hostile reaction, Richard Nixon would be giving into, and I quote him exactly, "his natural instinct to smash the enemy with a club or go after him with a meat axe."

Had this slander been made by one political candidate about another, it would have been dismissed by most commentators as a partisan attack. But this attack emanated from the privileged sanctuary of a network studio and therefore had the apparent dignity of an objective statement.

The American people would rightly not tolerate this concentration of power in Government.

Is it not fair and relevant to question its concentration in the hands of a tiny, enclosed fraternity of privileged men elected by no one and enjoying a monopoly sanctioned and licensed by Government?

The views of the majority of this fraternity do not—and I repeat, not—represent the views of America.

That is why such a great gulf existed between how the nation received the President's address and how the networks reviewed it.

Not only did the country receive the President's address more warmly than the networks, but so also did the Congress of the United States.

Yesterday, the President was notified that 300 individual Congressmen and 50 Senators of both parties had endorsed his efforts for peace.

As with other American institutions, perhaps it is time that the networks were made more responsive to the views of the nation and more responsible to the people they serve.

Now I want to make myself perfectly clear. I'm not asking for Government censorship or any other kind of censorship. I'm asking whether a form of censorship already exists when the news that 40 million Americans receive each night is determined by a handful of men responsible only to their corporate employers and is filtered through a handful of commentators who admit to their own set of biases.

The questions I'm raising here tonight should

have been raised by others long ago. They should have been raised by those Americans who have traditionally considered the preservation of freedom of speech and freedom of the press their special provinces of responsibility.

They should have been raised by those Americans who share the view of the late Justice Learned Hand that right conclusions are more likely to be gathered out of a multitude of tongues than through any kind of authoritative selection.

Advocates for the networks have claimed a First Amendment right to the same unlimited freedoms held by the great newspapers of America.

(But the situations are not identical. Where *The New York Times* reaches 800,000 people, N.B.C., reaches 20 times that number on its evening news. [The average weekday circulation of the *Times* in October was 1,012,367; the average Sunday circulation was 1,523,558.] Nor can the tremendous impact of seeing television film and hearing commentary be compared with reading the printed page.)

A decade ago, before the network news acquired such dominance over public opinion, Walter Lippmann spoke to the issue. He said there's an essential and radical difference between television and printing. The three or four competing television stations control virtually all that can be received over the air by ordinary television sets. But besides the mass circulation dailies, there are weeklies, monthlies, out-of-town newspapers and books. If a man doesn't like his newspaper, he can read another from out of town or wait for a weekly news magazine. It's not ideal, but it's infinitely better than the situation in television.

There if a man doesn't like what the networks are showing, all he can do is turn them off and listen to a phonograph. Networks he stated which are few in number have a virtual monopoly of a whole media of communications.

The newspapers of mass circulation have no monopoly on the medium of print.

Now a virtual monopoly of a whole medium of communication is not something that democratic people should blindly ignore. And we are not going to cut off our television sets and listen to the phonograph just because the airways belong to the networks. They don't. They belong to the people.

As Justice Byron White wrote in his landmark opinion six months ago, it's the right of the viewers and listeners, not the right of the broadcasters, which is paramount.

Now it's argued that this power presents no danger in the hands of those who have used it responsibly. But, as to whether or not the networks have abused the power they enjoy, let us call as our first witness former Vice President Humphrey and the city of Chicago. According to Theodore White, television's intercutting of the film from the streets of Chicago with the current proceedings on the floor of the convention created the most striking and false political picture of 1968—the nomination of a man for the American Presidency by the brutality and violence of merciless police.

If we are to believe a recent report of the House of Representatives Commerce Committee, then television's presentation of the violence in the streets worked an injustice on the reputation of the Chicago police. According to the committee findings, one network in particular presented, and I quote, " a one-sided picture which in large measure exonerates the demonstrators and protesters." Film of provocations of police that was available never saw the light of day while the film of a police response which the protesters provoked was shown to millions.

Another network showed virtually the same scene of violence from three separate angles without making clear it was the same scene. And, while the full report is reticent in drawing conclusions, it is not a document to inspire confidence in the fairness of the network news.

Our knowledge of the impact of network news on the national mind is far from complete, but some early returns are available. Again, we have enough information to raise serious questions about its effect on a democratic society. Several years ago Fred Friendly, one of the pioneers of network news, wrote that its missing ingredients were conviction, controversy and a point of view. The networks have compensated with a vengeance.

And in the networks' endless pursuit of controversy, we should ask: What is the end value—to enlighten or to profit? What is the end result—to inform or to confuse? How does the ongoing exploration for more action, more excitement, more drama serve our national search for internal peace and stability.

Gresham's Law seems to be operating in the network news. Bad news drives out good news. The irrational is more controversial than the rational. Concurrence can no longer compete with dissent.

One minute of Eldridge Cleaver is worth 10 minutes of Roy Wilkins. The labor crisis settled at the negotiating table is nothing compared to the confrontation that results in a strike—or better yet, violence along the picket lines.

Normality has become the nemesis of the network news. Now the upshot of all this controversy is that a narrow and distorted picture of America often emerges from the televised news.

A single, dramatic piece of the mosaic becomes in the minds of millions the entire picture. And the American who relies upon television for his news might conclude that the majority of American students are embittered radicals. That the majority of black Americans feel no regard for their country. That violence and lawlessness are the rule rather than the exception on the American campus.

We know that none of these conclusions is true.

Perhaps the place to start looking for a credibility gap is not in the offices of the Government in Washington but in the studios of the networks in New York.

Television may have destroyed the old stereotypes, but has it not created new ones in their places?

What has this passionate pursuit of controversy done to the politics of progress through local compromise essential to the functioning of a democratic society?

The members of Congress or the Senate who follow their principles and philosophy quietly in a spirit of compromise are unknown to many Americans, while the loudest and most extreme dissenters on every issue are known to every man in the street.

How many marches and demonstrations would we have if the marchers did not know that the ever-faithful TV cameras would be there to record their antics for the next news show?

We've heard demands that Senators and Congressmen and judges make known all their financial connections so that the public will know who and what influences their decisions and their votes. Strong arguments can be made for that view.

But when a single commentator or producer, night after night, determines for millions of people how much of each side of a great issue they are going to see

and hear, should he not first disclose his personal views on the issue as well?

In this search for excitement and controversy, has more than equal time gone to the minority of Americans who specialize in attacking the United States—its institutions and its citizens?

Tonight I've raised questions. I've made no attempt to suggest the answers. The answers must come from the media men. They are challenged to turn their critical powers on themselves, to direct their energy, their talent and their conviction toward improving the quality and objectivity of news presentation.

They are challenged to structure their own civic ethics to relate to the great responsibilities they hold.

And the people of America are challenged, too, challenged to press for responsible news presentations. The people can let the networks know that they want their news straight and objective. The people can register their complaints on bias through mail to the networks and phone calls to local stations. This is one case where the people must defend themselves; where the citizen, not the Government, must be the reformer; where the consumer can be the most effective crusader.

By way of conclusion, let me say that every elected leader in the United States depends on these men of the media. Whether what I've said to you tonight will be heard and seen at all by the nation is not my decision, it's not your decision, it's their decision.

In tomorrow's edition of *The Des Moines Register*, you'll be able to read a news story detailing what I've said tonight. Editorial comment will be reserved for the editorial page, where it belongs.

Should not the same wall of separation exist between news and comment on the nation's networks?

Now, my friends, we'd never trust such power, as I've described, over public opinion in the hands of an elected Government. It's time we questioned it in the hands of a small and unelected elite.

The great networks have dominated America's airwaves for decades. The people are entitled to a full accounting of their stewardship.

Richard M. Nixon

Resignation Speech
(August 8, 1974)

In January of 1973, a year into Nixon's second term of office, the Vietnam War finally came to an end. For the moment, the South Vietnamese government remained in place, although it was soon to crumble, leading to reunification of the country under the Communist Hanoi regime. Certainly the peace was not a victorious one, but it was, at last, peace, and the domestic wounds inflicted by the bitter struggle slowly began to heal.

Although the Vietnam settlement was far from triumphant, Nixon had achieved other, more notable, foreign policy successes. After years of mutual hostility, the United States and the People's Republic of China were beginning to come to terms. Secret negotiations carried out by Secretary of State Henry Kissinger culminated in the President's trip to Peking in February 1972 and the issuance of a joint communiqué that began the process of normalization of relations between the two countries. A series of agreements between the USSR and the United States in May of the same year signaled the beginning of a thaw in the Cold War. The arms control agreements reached between the two superpowers did not halt the arms race, but they did recognize that it was not desirable to continue an uncontrolled weapons race.

Nixon's international triumphs were matched by a personal political victory at home later the same year. The Democrats nominated George McGovern, a dedicated, if lackluster, liberal whom his opponents managed to paint as a dangerous radical. His choice of a running mate, Sen. Thomas Eagleton of Missouri, proved disastrous when it was discovered that Eagleton had been hospitalized for psychiatric care; McGovern, who first declared himself "1000 percent" behind Eagleton, maladroitly maneuvered the senator off the ticket, replacing him with Sargent Shriver, the late John Kennedy's brother-in-law. The Democratic campaign seemed doomed from the start and consistent mismanagement made matters worse. President Nixon was re-elected by the largest popular vote margin in history and lost the electoral votes of only Massachusetts and the District of Columbia.

In the summer before the election, however, a seemingly insignificant burglary started a chain of events that was to lead to shocking revelations of illegal activities in the White House and, finally, to the resignation of the President of the United States. On the evening of June 16 a small group of men working for the Committee to Reelect the President (CREEP) were arrested after breaking into Democratic National Headquarters in the Watergate complex in Washington, D.C. At first, the break-in had little impact; a Gallup Poll in October showed that only half the voters had even heard about it. John McCord, a former CIA agent who ran security operations for CREEP, G. Gordon Liddy, and five men who had been involved in the break-in were indicted in September and the matter appeared closed. Presidential aides who had been frantically covering up the involvement of the President's closest advisers, even the President himself, in "security" operations of CREEP had made efforts to obstruct the FBI investigation and involve the CIA. McCord, apparently disturbed that the CIA would eventually be blamed, wrote a letter in December from his jail cell to Judge John J. Sirica disclosing that there were others involved in the affair, that perjury had been committed at the trial, and that political pressure was applied in order to prevent the truth from coming out. From there on, the cover-up began to unravel.

By May of 1973 the Senate had established a special investigating committee, chaired by the crusty senator Sam Ervin of North Carolina. The hearings of the Watergate Committee, carried on in the glare of television, gradually disclosed a series of covert and illegal activities carried on by the White House staff. John Dean, special counsel to the President who had been intimately involved in the cover-up, unburdened himself to the committee. As he explained in his opening testimony, "To one who was in the White House and became somewhat familiar with its interworkings, the Watergate matter was an inevitable outgrowth of a climate of excessive concern over the political impact of demonstrators, excessive concern over leaks, an insatiable appetite for political intelligence, all coupled with a do-it-yourself White House staff, regardless of the law." Through the hearings, the court trials, and the efforts of investigative reporters—notably Woodward and Bernstein of the *Washington Post*—accounts of wrongdoing and the abuse of power tumbled out. The American public learned of illegal campaign contributions, of efforts to use the FBI and the IRS to investigate and discredit political opponents, of clandestine bugs planted, of offices broken into and searched, as well as of numerous political "dirty tricks" played to sabotage the opposition.

Throughout it all, President Nixon had steadfastly maintained that he was personally unaware of much that had gone on and that he, himself, had moved to uncover the facts and remove those who had not acted properly. When it was disclosed that White House conversations had routinely been taped, and after a long legal battle to obtain the tapes was finally won, the President's culpability became more clear and moves to impeach him began to gain bipartisan support. Assured by Republican leaders in the House and Senate that impeachment was a virtual certainty, the President decided to resign. The speech he made to the country on the night of August 8, 1974, announced this decision. While acknowledging errors in judgment, Nixon refused to admit wrongdoing. At noon the next day, while Richard Nixon and his family were in the air on a flight to California, his resignation—the first by an American President—took effect as his successor, Gerald Ford, was sworn in as the thirty-eighth President of the United States.

Good evening. This is the 37th time I have spoken to you from this office in which so many decisions have been made that shape the history of this nation.

Each time I have done so to discuss with you some matters that I believe affected the national interest. And all the decisions I have made in my public life I have always tried to do what was best for the nation.

Throughout the long and difficult period of Watergate, I have felt it was my duty to persevere; to make every possible effort to complete the term of office to which you elected me.

In the past few days, however, it has become evident to me that I no longer have a strong enough political base in the Congress to justify continuing that effort.

As long as there was such a base, I felt strongly that it was necessary to see the constitutional process through to its conclusion; that to do otherwise would be unfaithful to the spirit of that deliberately difficult process, and a dangerously destabilizing precedent for the future.

But with the disappearance of that base, I now believe that the constitutional purpose has been served. And there is no longer a need for the process to be prolonged.

I would have preferred to carry through to the finish whatever the personal agony it would have involved, and my family unanimously urged me to do so.

But the interests of the nation must always come before any personal considerations. From the discussions I have had with Congressional and other leaders I have concluded that because of the Watergate matter I might not have the support of the Congress that I would consider necessary to back the very difficult decisions and carry out the duties of this office in the way the interests of the nation will require.

I have never been a quitter.

To leave office before my term is completed is opposed to every instinct in my body. But as President I must put the interests of America first.

America needs a full-time President and a full-time Congress, particularly at this time with problems we face at home and abroad.

To continue to fight through the months ahead for my personal vindication would almost totally absorb the time and attention of both the President and the Congress in a period when our entire focus should be on the great issues of peace abroad and prosperity without inflation at home.

Therefore, I shall resign the Presidency effective at noon tomorrow.

Vice President Ford will be sworn in as President at that hour in this office.

As I recall the high hopes for America with which we began this second term, I feel a great sadness that I will not be here in this office working on your behalf to achieve those hopes in the next two and a half years.

But in turning over direction of the Government to Vice President Ford I know, as I told the nation when I nominated him for that office 10 months ago, that the leadership of America will be in good hands.

In passing this office to the Vice President I also do so with the profound sense of the weight of responsibility that will fall on his shoulders tomorrow, and therefore of the understanding, the patience, the cooperation he will need from all Americans.

As he assumes that responsibility he will deserve the help and the support of all of us. As we look to the future, the first essential is to begin healing the wounds of this nation. To put the bitterness and divisions of the recent past behind us and to rediscover those shared ideals that lie at the heart of our strength and unity as a great and as a free people.

By taking this action, I hope that I will have hastened the start of that process of healing which is so desperately needed in America.

I regret deeply any injuries that may have been done in the course of the events that led to this decision. I would say only that if some of my judgments were wrong—and some were wrong—they were made in what I believed at the time to be the best interests of the nation.

To those who have stood with me during these past difficult months, to my family, my friends, the many others who've joined in supporting my cause because they believed it was right, I will be eternally grateful for your support.

And to those who have not felt able to give me

me say I leave with no bitterness
o have opposed me, because all of
_alysis have been concerned with the
good _. _untry however our judgments might
differ.

So let us all now join together in affirming that common commitment and in helping our new President succeed for the benefit of all Americans.

I shall leave this office with regret at not completing my term but with gratitude for the privilege of serving as your President for the past five and a half years.

These years have been a momentous time in the history of our nation and the world. They have been a time of achievement in which we can all be proud—achievements that represent the shared efforts of the administration, the Congress and the people. But the challenges ahead are equally great.

And they, too, will require the support and the efforts of a Congress and the people, working in cooperation with the new Administration.

We have ended America's longest war. But in the work of securing a lasting peace in the world, the goals ahead are even more far-reaching and more difficult. We must complete a structure of peace, so that it will be said of this generation—our generation of Americans—by the people of all nations, not only that we ended one war but that we prevented future wars.

We have unlocked the doors that for a quarter of a century stood between the United States and the People's Republic of China. We must now insure that the one-quarter of the world's people who live in the People's Republic of China will be and remain, not our enemies, but our friends.

In the Middle East, 100 million people in the Arab countries, many of whom have considered us their enemies for nearly 20 years, now look on us as their friends. We must continue to build on that friendship so that peace can settle at last over the Middle East and so that the cradle of civilization will not become its grave.

Together with the Soviet Union we have made the crucial breakthroughs that have begun the process of limiting nuclear arms. But, we must set as our goal, not just limiting, but reducing and finally destroying these terrible weapons so that they cannot destroy civilization.

And so that the threat of nuclear war will no longer hang over the world and the people, we have opened a new relation with the Soviet Union. We must continue to develop and expand that new relationship so that the two strongest nations of the world will live together in cooperation rather than confrontation.

Around the world—in Asia, in Africa, in Latin America, in the Middle East—there are millions of people who live in terrible poverty, even starvation. We must keep as our goal turning away from production for war and expanding production for peace so that people everywhere on this earth can at last look forward, in their children's time if not in our time, to having the necessities for a decent life.

Here in America we are fortunate that most of our people have not only the blessings of liberty but also the means to live full and good, and by the world's standards even abundant lives.

We must press on, however, toward a goal not only of more and better jobs but of full opportunity for every man, and of what we are striving so hard right now to achieve—prosperity without inflation.

For more than a quarter of a century in public life, I have shared in the turbulent history of this evening.

I have fought for what I believe in. I have tried, to the best of my ability, to discharge those duties and meet those responsibilities that were entrusted to me.

Sometimes I have succeeded. And sometimes I have failed. But always I have taken heart from what Theodore Roosevelt said about the man in the arena whose face is marred by dust and sweat and blood, who strives valiantly, who errs and comes short again and again because there is not effort without error and shortcoming, but who does actually strive to do the deed, who knows the great devotion, who spends himself in a worthy cause, who at the best knows in the end the triumphs of high achievements and with the worst if he fails, at least fails while daring greatly.

I pledge to you tonight that as long as I have a breath of life in my body I shall continue in that spirit. I shall continue to work for the great causes to which I have been dedicated throughout my years as a Congressman, a Senator, Vice President and President, the cause of peace—not just for America but among all nations—prosperity, justice and opportunity for all of our people.

There is one cause above all to which I have been devoted and to which I shall always be devoted for as long as I live.

When I first took the oath of office as President five and a half years ago, I made this sacred commitment; to consecrate my office, my energies and all the wisdom I can summon to the cause of peace among nations.

As a result of these efforts, I am confident that the world is a safer place today, not only for the people of America but for the people of all nations, and that all of our children have a better chance than before of living in peace rather than dying in war.

This, more than anything, is what I hoped to achieve when I sought the Presidency. This, more than anything, is what I hope will be my legacy to you, to our country, as I leave the Presidency.

To have served in this office is to have felt a very personal sense of kinship with each and every American. In leaving it, I do so with this prayer: May God's grace be with you in all the days ahead.

Gerald R. Ford

"Inaugural" Address
(August 9, 1974)

In the midst of the Watergate imbroglio, but unrelated to it, came the discovery that the Vice President of the United States, Spiro Agnew, had accepted bribes from construction companies when he was governor of Maryland. In October of 1973, pleading no contest to charges of federal tax evasion, Agnew agreed, as part of a plea bargain, to resign his office. Until 1967, when the Twenty-fifth Amendment to the Constitution was ratified, there had been no provision to fill the office of Vice President in the event it fell vacant. The new provision now stipulated that the President appoint a Vice President subject to congressional confirmation. Richard Nixon chose Gerald R. Ford.

The Michigan congressman had had a long political career in the House of Representatives. Soon after graduating from Yale Law School, Ford joined the navy and served throughout World War II on an aircraft carrier in the Pacific. Returning to Grand Rapids after the war, the young Ford established himself as a reform Republican, unseated the conservative congressional incumbent in the 1948 Republican primary, and went on to win election to the House in the fall.

By 1963, when he became Republican conference chairman, Ford was known as a serious and hard-working congressman. Although clearly a Republican loyalist, he was respected for his integrity by members of both parties. In 1965 he became minority leader of the House and gained national exposure in the sixties when he appeared at regular press conferences with his Senate counterpart, Everett Dirksen, in an effort to mount a sustained opposition to Democratic policies.

When Agnew resigned, Nixon needed to appoint to the Vice Presidency someone with an impeccable reputation who could secure the approval of the Democratic-controlled Congress. It was also clear that Nixon wanted a Vice President upon whose loyalty he could count and who would not seek to establish an independent political base. Ford seemed perfectly qualified on all these counts; his nomination was generally well received and he was easily confirmed, taking office on December 6, 1973.

Although the Watergate revelations were clearly damaging to President Nixon, there was little speculation about impeachment at this time and most observers fully expected the President to serve out his term. Ford maintained a low profile in the months ahead and held on to his conviction that the President was telling the whole truth about Watergate. As the facts about Nixon's involvement began to surface, however, it became more and more likely that Ford would succeed the man who had appointed him.

President Nixon's resignation propelled Gerald Ford, who had never been elected to a national office, into the highest office in the land. Within less than two years, the agony of Vietnam had been ended and the pain of Watergate had been endured. Ford now proclaimed that "our long national nightmare is over," and asked, "as we bind up the internal wounds," that Americans "restore the golden rule to our political process," letting "brotherly love purge our hearts of suspicion and hate."

Mr. Chief Justice, my dear friends, my fellow Americans:—The oath that I have taken is the same oath that was taken by George Washington and by every President under the Constitution. But I assume the Presidency under extraordinary circumstances never before experienced by Americans. This is an hour of history that troubles our minds and hurts our hearts.

Therefore, I feel it is my first duty to make an unprecedented compact with my countrymen. Not an inaugural address, not a fireside chat, not a campaign speech, just a little straight talk among friends. And I intend it to be the first of many.

I am acutely aware that you have not elected me as your President by your ballots. So I ask you to confirm me as your President with your prayers. And I hope that such prayers will also be the first of many.

NO 'SECRET PROMISES'

If you have not chosen me by secret ballot, neither have I gained office by any secret promises. I have not campaigned either for the Presidency or the Vice Presidency. I have not subscribed to any partisan platform. I am indebted to no man and only to one woman, my dear wife.

As I begin this very difficult job, I have not sought this enormous responsibility, but I will not shirk it. Those who nominated and confirmed me as Vice President were my friends and are my friends. They were of both parties, elected by all the people and acting under the Constitution in their name.

It is only fitting then that I should pledge to them and to you that I will be the President of all the people.

Thomas Jefferson said the people are the only sure reliance for the preservation of our liberty. And down the years, Abraham Lincoln renewed this American article of faith asking is there any better way for equal hopes in the world.

I intend on next Monday to request of the Speaker of the House of Representatives and the President pro tempore of the Senate the privilege of appearing before the Congress to share with my former colleagues and with you, the American people, my views on the priority business of the nation and to solicit your views and their views.

And may I say to the Speaker and the others, if I could meet with you right after this—these remarks—I would appreciate it.

A SEARCH FOR PEACE

Even though this is late in an election year there is no way we can go forward except together and no way anybody can win except by serving the people's urgent needs.

We cannot stand still or slip backward. We must go forward now together.

To the peoples and the governments of all friendly nations and I hope that could encompass the whole world, I pledge an uninterrupted and sincere search for peace. America will remain strong and united.

But its strength will remain dedicated to the safety and sanity of the entire family of man as well as to our own precious freedom.

I believe that truth is the glue that holds governments together, not only our Government but civilization itself. That bond, though strained, is unbroken at home and abroad.

In all my public and private acts as your President, I expect to follow my instincts of openness and candor with full confidence that honesty is always the best policy in the end.

My fellow Americans, our long national nightmare is over. Our Constitution works. Our great republic is a government of laws and not of men. Here, the people rule.

But there is a higher power, by whatever name we honor him, who ordains not only righteousness but love, not only justice but mercy.

As we bind up the internal wounds of Watergate, more painful and more poisonous than those of foreign wars, let us restore the golden rule to our political process. And let brotherly love purge our hearts of suspicion and of hate.

In the beginning, I asked you to pray for me. Before closing, I ask again your prayers for Richard Nixon and for his family. May our former President who brought peace to millions find it for himself.

May God bless and comfort his wonderful wife and daughters whose love and loyalty will forever be a shining legacy to all who bear the lonely burden of the White House.

I can only guess at those burdens although I witnessed at close hand the tragedies that befell three Presidents and the lesser trials of others.

With all the strength and all the good sense I have gained from life, with all the confidence my family, my friends and dedicated staff impart to me and with the goodwill of countless Americans I have encountered in recent visits to 40 states, I now solemnly reaffirm my promise I made to you last Dec. 6 to uphold the Constitution, to do what is right as God gives me to see the right and to do the very best I can for America.

God helping me, I will not let you down.

Thank you.

Barbara Jordan

Keynote Speech to the Democratic National Convention
(July 12, 1976)

In July of 1974, when the House Judiciary Committee was considering the impeachment of Richard Nixon, the country was introduced to a black congresswoman from Texas, Barbara Jordan. Ms. Jordan's clear, forceful eloquence captured national attention. Although she, as a black and as a woman, had once felt left out of the original Constitution, she explained that "through the process of amendment, interpretation, and court decision I have finally been included in 'We, the people.'" With the faith she had in the Constitution, the Houston congresswoman vowed that she was "not going to sit here and be an idle spectator to the diminution, the subversion, the destruction of the Constitution" through the abuse of power evident in the Watergate matter.

Two years later, Barbara Jordan was a logical choice to present one of the keynote speeches to the Democratic national convention meeting in New York City. Having been praised for her "solemn eloquence," as *Time* magazine put it, during the Judiciary Committee hearings, she stood as a symbolic reminder of the Republican disgrace. "Watergate," the Republican congressman from Virginia, M. Caldwell Butler, admitted, "is our shame," and the Watergate albatross clearly hung about the neck of the Republican party two years after Nixon had been forced from office. Even more, Barbara Jordan projected the image of the new Democratic party, a party that embraced blacks and women and reaffirmed its old commitment to protecting the interests of the poor, the downtrodden, the powerless common person.

Jordan's performance was hailed by delegates and the general public alike, a difficult feat for a speaker addressing as partisan an audience as a national political convention. Her success, according to Professor Wayne Thompson, came about "because her *method*—seemingly objective and high minded—won the respect of [the general audience] and set off no adverse reactions; while her *conclusions,* favorable to her own party, pleased the delegates, alternates, and spectators."

Certainly Jordan appealed to the highest American motives and values when she spoke against the tendency of the country to move toward "a collection of interest groups." Her prescription for seeking the common good was to "address and master the future together. It can be done if we restore the belief that we share a sense of national community, that we share a common national endeavor." Her call for political accountability and the highest standards of political rectitude for those who would serve the nation was a call particularly adapted to the time in which it was made and, indeed, relevant to all time in the political life of the nation.

One hundred and forty-four years ago, members of the Democratic Party first met in convention to select a Presidential candidate. Since that time, Democrats have continued to convene once every four years and draft a party platform and nominate a Presidential candidate. And our meeting this week is a continuation of that tradition.

But there is something different about tonight. There is something special about tonight. What is different? What is special? I, Barbara Jordan, am a keynote speaker.

A lot of years passed since 1832, and during that time it would have been most unusual for any national political party to ask that a Barbara Jordan deliver a keynote address ... but tonight here I am. And I feel that notwithstanding the past that my presence here is one additional bit of evidence that the American Dream need not forever be deferred.

Now that I have this grand distinction what in the world am I supposed to say?

I could easily spend this time praising the accomplishments of this party and attacking the Republicans but I don't choose to do that.

I could list the many problems which Americans have. I could list the problems which cause people to feel cynical, angry, frustrated: problems which include lack of integrity in government; the feeling that the individual no longer counts; the reality of material and spiritual poverty; the feeling that the grand American experiment is failing or has failed. I could recite these problems and then I could sit down and offer no solutions. But I don't choose to do that either.

The citizens of America expect more. They deserve and they want more than a recital of problems.

We are a people in a quandary about the present.

We are a people in search of our future. We are a people in search of a national community.

We are a people trying not only to solve the problems of the present: unemployment, inflation ... but we are attempting on a larger scale to fulfill the promise of America. We are attempting to fulfill our national purpose; to create and sustain a society in which all of us are equal.

Throughout our history, when people have looked for new ways to solve their problems, and to uphold the principles of this nation, many times they have turned to political parties. They have often turned to the Democratic Party.

What is it, what is it about the Democratic Party that makes it the instrument that people use when they search for ways to shape their future? Well I believe the answer to that question lies in our concept of governing. Our concept of governing is derived from our view of people. It is a concept deeply rooted in a set of beliefs firmly etched in the national conscience, of all of us.

Now what are these beliefs?

First, we believe in equality for all and privileges for none. This is a belief that each American regardless of background has equal standing in the public forum, all of us. Because we believe this idea so firmly, we are an inclusive rather than an exclusive party. Let everybody come.

I think it no accident that most of those emigrating to America in the 19th century identified with the Democratic Party. We are a heterogeneous party made up of Americans of diverse backgrounds.

We believe that the people are the source of all governmental power; that the authority of the people is to be extended, not restricted. This can be accomplished only by providing each citizen with every opportunity to participate in the management of the government. They must have that.

We believe that the government which represents the authority of all the people, not just one interest group, but all the people, has an obligation to actively underscore, actively seek to remove those obstacles which would block individual achievement ... obstacles emanating from race, sex, economic condition. The government must seek to remove them.

We are a party of innovation. We do not reject our traditions, but we are willing to adapt to changing circumstances, when change we must. We are willing to suffer the discomfort of change in order to achieve a better future.

We have a positive vision of the future founded on the belief that the gap between the promise and reality of America can one day be finally closed. We believe that.

This my friends, is the bedrock of our concept of governing. This is a part of the reason why Americans have turned to the Democratic Party. These are the foundations upon which a national community can be built.

Let's all understand that these guiding principles cannot be discarded for short-term political gains. They represent what this country is all about. They are indigenous to the American idea. And these are principles which are not negotiable.

In other times, I could stand here and give this kind of exposition on the beliefs of the Democratic Party and that would be enough. But today that is not enough. People want more. That is not sufficient reason for the majority of the people of this country to vote Democratic. We have made mistakes. In our haste to do all things for all people, we did not foresee the full consequences of our actions. And when the people raised their voices, we didn't hear. But our deafness was only a temporary condition, and not an irreversible condition.

Even as I stand here and admit that we have made mistakes I still believe that as the people of America sit in judgment on each party, they will recognize that our mistakes were mistakes of the heart. They'll recognize that.

And now we must look to the future. Let us heed the voice of the people and recognize their common sense. If we do not, we not only blaspheme our political heritage, we ignore the common ties that bind all Americans.

Many fear the future. Many are distrustful of their leaders, and believe that their voices are never heard. Many seek only to satisfy their private work wants. To satisfy private interests.

But this is the great danger America faces. That we will cease to be one nation and become instead a collection of interest groups: city against suburb, region against region, individual against individual. Each seeking to satisfy private wants.

If that happens, who then will speak for America?

Who then will speak for the common good?

This is the question which must be answered in 1976.

Are we to be one people bound together by common spirit sharing in a common endeavor or will we become a divided nation?

For all of its uncertainty, we cannot flee the future. We must not become the new puritans and reject our society. We must address and master the future together. It can be done if we restore the belief that we share a sense of national community, that we share a common national endeavor. It can be done.

There is no executive order; there is no law that can require the American people to form a national community. This we must do as individuals and if we do it as individuals, there is no President of the United States who can veto that decision.

As a first step, we must restore our belief in ourselves. We are a generous people so why can't we be generous with each other? We need to take to heart the words spoken by Thomas Jefferson:

Let us restore to social intercourse that harmony and that affection without which liberty and even life are but dreary things.

A nation is formed by the willingness of each of us to share in the responsibility for upholding the common good.

A government is invigorated when each of us is willing to participate in shaping the future of this nation.

In this election year we must define the common good and begin again to shape a common good and begin again to shape a common future. Let each person do his or her part. If one citizen is unwilling to participate, all of us are going to suffer. For the American idea, though it is shared by all of us, is realized in each one of us.

And now, what are those of us who are elected public officials supposed to do? We call ourselves public servants but I'll tell you this: we as public servants must set an example for the rest of the nation. It is hypocritical for the public official to admonish and exhort the people to uphold the common good if we are derelict in upholding the common good. More is required of public officials than slogans and handshakes and press releases. More is required. We must hold ourselves strictly accountable. We must provide the people with a vision of the future.

If we promise as public officials, we must deliver. If we as public officials propose, we must produce. If we say to the American people it is time for you to be sacrificial; sacrifice. If the public official says that, we (public officials) must be the first to give. We must be. And again, if we make mistakes, we must be willing to admit them. We have to do that. What we have to do is strike a balance between the idea that government should do everything and the idea, the belief, that government ought to do nothing. Strike a balance.

Let there be no illusions about the difficulty of forming this kind of a national community. It's tough, difficult, not easy. But a spirit of harmony will survive in America only if each of us remembers that we share a common destiny. If each of us remembers when self-interest and bitterness seem to prevail, that we share a common destiny.

I have confidence that we can form this kind of national community.

I have confidence that the Democratic Party can lead the way. I have that confidence. We cannot improve on the system of government handed down to us by the founders of the Republic, there is no way to improve upon that. But what we can do is to find new ways to implement that system and realize our destiny.

Now, I began this speech by commenting to you on the uniqueness of a Barbara Jordan making the keynote address. Well I am going to close my speech by quoting a Republican President and I ask you that as you listen to these words of Abraham Lincoln, relate them to the concept of a national community in which every last one of us participates: As I would not be a slave, so I would not be a master. This expresses my idea of Democracy. Whatever differs from this, to the extent of the difference is no Democracy.

Jimmy Carter

The Crisis of Confidence
(July 15, 1979)

In 1970 Georgia inaugurated as its new governor James Earl Carter, a graduate of Annapolis, a navy veteran, and a successful agribusinessman who had served in the Georgia state senate. He had failed in his attempt in 1966 to unseat the blatantly racist governor Lester Maddox; in 1970, however, after an intense grass-roots campaign, he defeated former governor Carl Sanders, generally regarded as a liberal. Denounced by the *Atlanta Constitution* as an "ignorant, racist, backward, ultra-conservative, rednecked South Georgia peanut farmer," Carter surprised enemies and supporters alike by announcing in his inaugural address that "no poor, rural, weak, or black person should ever again have to bear the additional burden of being deprived of the opportunity for an education, a job, or simple justice." "The time for racial discrimination," he declared, "is over." As a new voice of Southern moderation, Carter gained national attention.

As chairman of the Democratic Campaign Committee in 1974, Carter also gained national exposure and stature within his own party as he traveled throughout the country raising funds and speaking on behalf of Democratic candidates. Following the election, in December 1974, the governor announced his campaign for the Presidency. A seemingly unlikely candidate, Carter proved to be a tireless, energetic campaigner. His lack of extensive governmental experience became a virtue in those post-Watergate years when professional politicians and Washington insiders were viewed with popular suspicion. Carter was a "born-again" Christian, stressing personal integrity, honesty, responsiveness to the people, and compassion for their problems. He captured the nomination and then the election, defeating President Ford in a close race.

President Carter found, however, that while being an outsider enhanced his attractiveness as a candidate, it did not serve him well in dealing with the Washington political establishment. The Watergate experience had raised questions about the power of the Presidency itself—the "imperial Presidency" as it was frequently alluded to—and the growing tendency of the executive branch to overreach itself at the expense of the legislative wing of government. Congress was in no mood to be deferential to the new President, especially one who had been elected by a narrow margin in an election with a strikingly low voter turnout. The President confronted Congress on the issue of what he saw as unnecessary water projects being funded throughout the country and finally had to give in to save other aspects of his legislative program. Efforts at tax reform were frustrated by congressional action. Carter's belief that inflation was one of the most serious domestic problems and had to be countered with a balanced budget led him to a greater toleration for unemployment and a willingness to sacrifice social welfare spending, a stance that alienated liberals in his own party.

His foreign policy, although admirably grounded in idealistic principles and vigorously defensive of international human rights, seemed to lack strategic coherence. While the President did strengthen Sino-American relations and successfully brokered the Camp David accords between Israel and Egypt, his triumph in securing ratification of the Panama Canal Treaty appeared a hollow one as it did not gain him much popular support in the long run. Further, relations with the USSR remained strained; he failed to influence Russian policy in Afghanistan, and the grain embargo he imposed on the Soviet Union appeared to many Americans to hurt Midwestern farmers more than it did the Soviets.

Two-and-a-half years into his Presidency, Carter clearly saw that he, his administration, and the country itself were in trouble. The President's popularity in the polls was steadily and drastically declining. Immediate problems brought about by energy shortages were pressing and apparent. It was an unusual and painful experience for Americans, used to abundance in virtually all things, to have to wait in long lines to get—if they were lucky—gasoline for their cars, to worry about whether they could obtain enough oil to heat their homes or electricity to provide the air-conditioned comfort to which they had become accustomed. Even more potentially disastrous, energy shortages disrupted industrial processes and threatened jobs; energy costs fueled rising inflation. President Carter planned to speak to the nation about the crisis on July 5, 1979, in order to outline his energy program. Then, deciding that he needed wider consultation before addressing the problem, the President summoned 135 political, business, labor, educational, and religious leaders to the Presidential retreat at Camp David to solicit their advice. He emerged from these discussions to speak to an estimated audience of over sixty million Americans over radio and television.

From the Oval Office on the evening of July 15, President Carter delivered the speech that follows. In it he sought to address what he saw as "a fundamental threat to American democracy," namely, "a crisis in confidence." The President called for united action, declared that "energy will be the immediate test of our ability to unite this Nation," and set out to explain the principles that would govern his own specific energy program. This unusual speech—"almost a sermon," Frank Reynolds of ABC called it—was generally praised by the media and seemed to check the downward plunge in the President's popularity. It was not long, however, before Carter's critics began to question whether or not the crisis in confidence was not of the President's own doing, whether it was not, in fact, a crisis in leadership.

Good evening.—This is a special night for me. Exactly 3 years ago, on July 15, 1976, I accepted the nomination of my party to run for President of the United States. I promised you a President who is not isolated from the people, who feels your pain, and who shares your dreams and who draws his strength and his wisdom from you.

During the past 3 years I've spoken to you on many occasions about national concerns, the energy crisis, reorganizing the Government, our Nation's economy, and issues of war and especially peace. But over those years the subjects of the speeches, the talks, and the press conferences have become increasingly narrow, focused more and more on what the isolated world of Washington thinks is important. Gradually, you've heard more and more about what the Government thinks or what the Government should be doing and less and less about our Nation's hopes, our dreams, and our vision of the future.

Ten days ago I had planned to speak to you again about a very important subject—energy. For the fifth time I would have described the urgency of the problem and laid out a series of legislative recommendations to the Congress. But as I was preparing to speak, I began to ask myself the same question that I now know has been troubling many of you. Why have we not been able to get together as a nation to resolve our serious energy problem?

It's clear that the true problems of our Nation are much deeper—deeper than gasoline lines or energy shortages, deeper even than inflation or recession. And I realize more than ever that as President I need your help. So, I decided to reach out and listen to the voices of America.

I invited to Camp David people from almost every segment of our society—business and labor, teachers and preachers, Governors, mayors, and private citizens. And then I left Camp David to listen to other Americans, men and women like you. It has been an extraordinary 10 days, and I want to share with you what I've heard.

First of all, I got a lot of personal advice. Let me quote a few of the typical comments that I wrote down.

This from a southern Governor: "Mr. President, you are not leading this Nation—you're just managing the Government."

"You don't see the people enough any more."

"Some of your Cabinet members don't seem loyal. There is not enough discipline among your disciples."

"Don't talk to us about politics or the mechanics of government, but about an understanding of our common good."

"Mr. President, we're in trouble. Talk to us about blood and sweat and tears."

"If you lead, Mr. President, we will follow."

Many people talked about themselves and about the condition of our Nation. This from a young woman in Pennsylvania: "I feel so far from government. I feel like ordinary people are excluded from political power."

And this from a young Chicano: "Some of us have suffered from recession all our lives."

"Some people have wasted energy, but others haven't had anything to waste."

And this from a religious leader: "No material shortage can touch the important things like God's love for us or our love for one another."

And I like this one particularly from a black woman who happens to be the mayor of a small Mississippi town: "The big-shots are not the only ones who are important. Remember, you can't sell anything on Wall Street unless someone digs it up somewhere else first."

This kind of summarized a lot of other statements: "Mr. President, we are confronted with a moral and a spiritual crisis."

Several of our discussions were on energy, and I have a notebook full of comments and advice. I'll read just a few.

"We can't go on consuming 40 percent more energy than we produce. When we import oil we are also importing inflation plus unemployment."

"We've got to use what we have. The Middle East has only 5 percent of the world's energy, but the United States has 24 percent."

And this is one of the most vivid statements: "Our neck is stretched over the fence and OPEC has a knife."

"There will be other cartels and other shortages. American wisdom and courage right now can set a path to follow in the future."

This was a good one: "Be bold, Mr. President. We may make mistakes, but we are ready to experiment."

And this one from a labor leader got to the heart of it: "The real issue is freedom. We must deal with the energy problem on a war footing."

And the last that I'll read: "When we enter the moral equivalent of war, Mr. President, don't issue us BB guns."

These 10 days confirmed my belief in the decency

and the strength and the wisdom of the American people, but it also bore out some of my longstanding concerns about our Nation's underlying problems.

I know, of course, being President, that government actions and legislation can be very important. That's why I've worked hard to put my campaign promises into law—and I have to admit, with just mixed success. But after listening to the American people I have been reminded again that all the legislation in the world can't fix what's wrong with America. So, I want to speak to you first tonight about a subject even more serious than energy or inflation. I want to talk to you right now about a fundamental threat to American democracy.

I do not mean our political and civil liberties. They will endure. And I do not refer to the outward strength of America, a nation that is at peace tonight everywhere in the world, with unmatched economic power and military might.

The threat is nearly invisible in ordinary ways. It is a crisis of confidence. It is a crisis that strikes at the very heart and soul and spirit of our national will. We can see this crisis in the growing doubt about the meaning of our own lives and in the loss of a unity of purpose for our Nation.

The erosion of our confidence in the future is threatening to destroy the social and the political fabric of America.

The confidence that we have always had as a people is not simply some romantic dream or a proverb in a dusty book that we read just on the Fourth of July. It is the idea which founded our Nation and has guided our development as a people. Confidence in the future has supported everything else—public institutions and private enterprise, our own families, and the very Constitution of the United States. Confidence has defined our course and has served as a link between generations. We've always believed in something called progress. We've always had a faith that the days of our children would be better than our own.

Our people are losing that faith, not only in government itself but in the ability as citizens to serve as the ultimate rulers and shapers of our democracy. As a people we know our past and we are proud of it. Our progress has been part of the living history of America, even the world. We always believed that we were part of a great movement of humanity itself called democracy, involved in the search for freedom, and that belief has always strengthened us in our purpose. But just as we are losing our confidence in the future, we are also beginning to close the door on our past.

In a nation that was proud of hard work, strong families, close-knit communities, and our faith in God, too many of us now tend to worship self-indulgence and consumption. Human identity is no longer defined by what one does, but by what one owns. But we've discovered that owning things and consuming things does not satisfy our longing for meaning. We've learned that piling up material goods cannot fill the emptiness of lives which have no confidence or purpose.

The symptoms of this crisis of the American spirit are all around us. For the first time in the history of our country a majority of our people believe that the next 5 years will be worse than the past 5 years. Two-thirds of our people do not even vote. The productivity of American workers is actually dropping, and the willingness of Americans to save for the future has fallen below that of all other people in the Western world.

As you know, there is a growing disrespect for government and for churches and for schools, the news media, and other institutions. This is not a message of happiness or reassurance, but it is the truth and it is a warning.

These changes did not happen overnight. They've come upon us gradually over the last generation, years that were filled with shocks and tragedy.

We were sure that ours was a nation of the ballot, not the bullet, until the murders of John Kennedy and Robert Kennedy and Martin Luther King, Jr. We were taught that our armies were always invincible and our causes were always just, only to suffer the agony of Vietnam. We respected the Presidency as a place of honor until the shock of Watergate.

We remember when the phrase "sound as a dollar" was an expression of absolute dependability, until 10 years of inflation began to shrink our dollar and our savings. We believed that our Nation's resources were limitless until 1973, when we had to face a growing dependence on foreign oil.

These wounds are still very deep. They have never been healed.

Looking for a way out of this crisis, our people have turned to the Federal Government and found it isolated from the mainstream of our Nation's life. Washington, D.C., has become an island. The gap between our citizens and our Government has never been so wide. The people are looking for honest answers, not easy answers; clear leadership, not false claims and evasiveness and politics as usual.

What you see too often in Washington and elsewhere around the country is a system of government that seems incapable of action. You see a Congress twisted and pulled in every direction by hundreds of well-financed and powerful special interests. You see every extreme position defended to the last vote, almost to the last breath by one unyielding group or another. You often see a balanced and a fair approach that demands sacrifice, a little sacrifice from everyone, abandoned like an orphan without support and without friends.

Often you see paralysis and stagnation and drift. You don't like it, and neither do I. What can we do?

First of all, we must face the truth, and then we can change our course. We simply must have faith in each other, faith in our ability to govern ourselves, and faith in the future of this Nation. Restoring that faith and that confidence to America is now the most important task we face. It is a true challenge of this generation of Americans.

One of the visitors to Camp David last week put it this way: "We've got to stop crying and start sweating, stop talking and start walking, stop cursing and start praying. The strength we need will not come from the White House, but from every house in America."

We know the strength of America. We are strong. We can regain our unity. We can regain our confidence. We are the heirs of generations who survived threats much more powerful and awesome than those that challenge us now. Our fathers and mothers were strong men and women who shaped a new society during the Great Depression, who fought world wars, and who carved out a new charter of peace for the world.

We ourselves are the same Americans who just 10 years ago put a man on the Moon. We are the generation that dedicated our society to the pursuit of human rights and equality. And we are the generation that will win the war on the energy problem and in that process rebuild the unity and confidence of America.

We are at a turning point in our history. There are two paths to choose. One is a path I've warned about tonight, the path that leads to fragmentation and self-interest. Down that road lies a mistaken idea of freedom, the right to grasp for ourselves some advantage over others. That path would be one of constant conflict between narrow interests ending in chaos and immobility. It is a certain route to failure.

All the traditions of our past, all the lessons of our heritage, all the promises of our future point to another path, the path of common purpose and the restoration of American values. That path leads to true freedom for our Nation and ourselves. We can take the first steps down that path as we begin to solve our energy problem.

Energy will be the immediate test of our ability to unite this Nation, and it can also be the standard around which we rally. On the battlefield of energy we can win for our Nation a new confidence, and we can seize control again of our common destiny.

In little more than two decades we've gone from a position of energy independence to one in which almost half the oil we use comes from foreign countries, at prices that are going through the roof. Our excessive dependence on OPEC has already taken a tremendous toll on our economy and our people. This is the direct cause of the long lines which have made millions of you spend aggravating hours waiting for gasoline. It's a cause of the increased inflation and unemployment that we now face. This intolerable dependence on foreign oil threatens our economic independence and the very security of our Nation.

The energy crisis is real. It is worldwide. It is a clear and present danger to our Nation. These are facts and we simply must face them.

What I have to say to you now about energy is simple and vitally important.

Point one: I am tonight setting a clear goal for the energy policy of the United States. Beginning this moment, this Nation will never use more foreign oil than we did in 1977—never. From now on, every new addition to our demand for energy will be met from our own production and our own conservation. The generation-long growth in our dependence on foreign oil will be stopped dead in its tracks right now and then reversed as we move through the 1980's, for I am tonight setting the further goal of cutting our dependence on foreign oil by one-half by the end of the next decade—a saving of over 4 1/2 million barrels of imported oil per day.

Point two: To ensure that we meet these targets, I will use my Presidential authority to set import quotas. I'm announcing tonight that for 1979 and 1980, I will forbid the entry into this country of one drop of foreign oil more than these goals allow. These quotas will ensure a reduction in imports even below the ambitious levels we set at the recent Tokyo summit.

Point three: To give us energy security, I am asking for the most massive peacetime commitment of funds and resources in our Nation's history to develop America's own alternative sources of fuel—from coal, from oil shale, from plant products for gasohol, from unconventional gas, from the Sun.

I propose the creation of an energy security corporation to lead this effort to replace 2 1/2 million barrels of imported oil per day by 1990. The corporation will issue up to $5 billion in energy bonds, and I especially want them to be in small denominations so that average Americans can invest directly in America's energy security.

Just as a similar synthetic rubber corporation helped us win World War II, so will we mobilize American determination and ability to win the energy war. Moreover, I will soon submit legislation to Congress calling for the creation of this Nation's first solar bank, which will help us achieve the crucial goal of 20 percent of our energy coming from solar power by the year 2000.

These efforts will cost money, a lot of money, and that is why Congress must enact the windfall profits tax without delay. It will be money well spent. Unlike the billions of dollars that we ship to foreign countries to pay for foreign oil, these funds will be paid by Americans to Americans. These funds will go to fight, not to increase, inflation and unemployment.

Point four: I'm asking Congress to mandate, to require as a matter of law, that our Nation's utility companies cut their massive use of oil by 50 percent within the next decade and switch to other fuels, especially coal, our most abundant energy source.

Point five: To make absolutely certain that nothing stands in the way of achieving these goals, I will urge Congress to create an energy mobilization board which, like the War Production Board in World War II, will have the responsibility and authority to cut through the redtape, the delays, and the endless roadblocks to completing key energy projects.

We will protect our environment. But when this Nation critically needs a refinery or a pipeline, we will build it.

Point six: I'm proposing a bold conservation program to involve every State, county, and city and every average American in our energy battle. This effort will permit you to build conservation into your homes and your lives at a cost you can afford.

I ask Congress to give me authority for mandatory conservation and for standby gasoline rationing. To further conserve energy, I'm proposing tonight an extra $10 billion over the next decade to strengthen our public transportation systems. And I'm asking you for your good and for your Nation's security to take no unnecessary trips, to use carpools or public transportation whenever you can, to park your car one extra day per week, to obey the speed limit, and to set your thermostats to save fuel. Every act of energy conservation like this is more than just common sense—I tell you it is an act of patriotism.

Our Nation must be fair to the poorest among us, so we will increase aid to needy Americans to cope with rising energy prices. We often think of conservation only in terms of sacrifice. In fact, it is the most painless and immediate way of rebuilding our Nation's strength. Every gallon of oil each one of us saves is a new form of production. It gives us more freedom, more confidence, that much more control over our own lives.

So, the solution of our energy crisis can also help us to conquer the crisis of the spirit in our country. It can rekindle our sense of unity, our confidence in the future, and give our Nation and all of us individually a new sense of purpose.

You know we can do it. We have the natural resources. We have more oil in our shale alone than several Saudi Arabias. We have more coal than any nation on Earth. We have the world's highest level of technology. We have the most skilled work force, with innovative genius, and I firmly believe that we have the national will to win this war.

I do not promise you that this struggle for freedom will be easy. I do not promise a quick way out of our Nation's problems, when the truth is that the only way out is an all-out effort. What I do promise you is that I will lead our fight, and I will enforce fairness in our struggle, and I will ensure honesty. And above all, I will act.

We can manage the short-term shortages more effectively and we will, but there are no short-term solutions to our long-range problems. There is simply no way to avoid sacrifice.

Twelve hours from now I will speak again in Kansas City, to expand and to explain further our energy program. Just as the search for solutions to our energy shortages has now led us to a new awareness of our Nation's deeper problems, so our willingness to work for those solutions in energy can strengthen us to attack those deeper problems.

I will continue to travel this country, to hear the people of America. You can help me to develop a national agenda for the 1980's. I will listen and I will act. We will act together. These were the promises I made 3 years ago, and I intend to keep them.

Little by little we can and we must rebuild our confidence. We can spend until we empty our treasuries, and we may summon all the wonders of science.

But we can succeed only if we tap our greatest resources—America's people, America's values, and America's confidence.

I have seen the strength of America in the inexhaustible resources of our people. In the days to come, let us renew that strength in the struggle for an energy secure nation.

In closing, let me say this: I will do my best, but I will not do it alone. Let your voice be heard. Whenever you have a chance, say something good about our country. With God's help and for the sake of our Nation, it is time for us to join hands in America. Let us commit ourselves together to a rebirth of the American spirit. Working together with our common faith we cannot fail.

Thank you and good night.

Edward M. Kennedy

Principles of the Democratic Party
(August 12, 1980)

The death of Mary Jo Kopechne at Chappaquiddick in the summer of 1969 and Edward Kennedy's subsequent plea of guilty to the charge of leaving the scene of an accident raised serious questions about the Massachusetts senator's character and judgment. Responding to his televised explanation of events, the citizens of Massachusetts gave Kennedy the positive reaction that encouraged him to retain his Senate seat and to seek re-election. Although his vote totals were short of the mark set in 1964, he still managed to win the 1970 contest with a very comfortable 63 percent of the vote. He returned to the Senate, but was ousted from his post as Democratic whip by Sen. Robert Byrd of West Virginia.

Gradually, however, as Chappaquiddick faded into history, Ted Kennedy began to regain his position as a national Democratic leader. Re-elected to a third term in the Senate in 1976 with a commanding 70 percent of the vote, Kennedy gradually accrued seniority and, with it, leadership of important Senate committees, such as the Judiciary Committee and the health subcommittee. He spoke out on national and international issues, and consistently received wide media attention.

Increasingly, Kennedy became the most prominent Democratic spokesman for liberal causes. He spoke for and sought to address the needs of the elderly and the unemployed, of women and ethnic minorities, of consumers and middle-income taxpayers. He urged President Carter to take dramatic initiatives in tax reform, bombarding him with suggestions of ways to plug loopholes and eliminate corporate tax shelters. One of the senator's most cherished goals was to provide a national health insurance plan. Struggling behind the scenes with what he saw as Carter's timid and lukewarm support for a comprehensive health care system, Kennedy tried to negotiate compromise legislation. When negotiations finally broke down, the Massachusetts senator publicly attacked the Democratic President for his piecemeal approach to health care.

In the summer of 1978, a Gallup Poll showed that Democrats preferred Kennedy to President Carter by 54 to 32 percent and, once again, Edward Kennedy was being discussed as a Presidential contender. Kennedy, however, publicly demurred, telling a *Time* reporter that "this isn't the time." The time, however, was fast approaching. By 1979 Carter was obviously in political trouble. Moreover, with the rise of Ronald Reagan, it seemed that the Republican party would shift more dramatically to the right. Who was there to speak for "the people left out of the system"? Kennedy undertook one of the hardest political tasks to accomplish: to deny a sitting President the nomination of his own party.

In the end, it proved too monumental a job even for the hard-driving Kennedys. Neither the senator's rhetoric nor his campaign soared. With seizure of the American hostages in Iran, public opinion supported the President in the time of national trial. Kennedy's drubbing in the Iowa caucuses failed to provide him with the momentum he needed to make his candidacy appear more plausible, and while he did engender enthusiasm and garner support in urban areas, his challenge to the President did not seriously threaten Carter's renomination. Although he fought right up until the last minute, the senator's bid had clearly failed by the time the party faithful gathered in New York City.

Kennedy's was still a voice to be heard, however, and he did still speak for a large segment of traditionally liberal Democrats. His address to the convention on August 12, 1980, was a plea on behalf of this wing of the party, a plea to stand unequivocally for the "great traditions" of the Democratic party: "to speak for those who have no voice, to remember those who are forgotten, to respond to the frustrations and fulfill the aspirations of all Americans seeking a better life in a better land." As he himself had done throughout the campaign, Kennedy urged Democrats to "keep our rudder true" even when sailing against the wind, and to remember that, despite setbacks, "the work goes on, the cause endures, the hope still lives, and the dream shall never die."

Well, things worked out a little different than I thought, but let me tell you, I still love New York. My fellow Democrats and my fellow Americans: I have come here tonight not to argue for a candidacy, but to affirm a cause.

I am asking you to renew the commitment of the Democratic Party to economic justice. I am asking you to renew our commitment to a fair and lasting prosperity that can put America back to work.

This is the cause that brought me into the campaign and that sustained me for nine months, across a hundred thousand miles, in forty different states. We had our losses; but the pain of our defeats is far, far less than the pain of the people I have met. We have learned that it is important to take issues seriously, but never to take ourselves too seriously.

The serious issue before us tonight is the cause for which the Democratic Party has stood in its finest hours—the cause that keeps our party young—and makes it, in the second century of its age, the largest political party in this Republic and the longest lasting political party on this Planet.

Our cause has been, since the days of Thomas Jefferson, the cause of the common man—and the common woman. Our commitment has been, since the days of Andrew Jackson, to all those he called "the humble members of society—the farmers, mechanics, and laborers." On this foundation, we have defined our values, refined our policies, and refreshed our faith.

Now I take the unusual step of carrying the cause and the commitment of my campaign personally to our national convention. I speak out of a deep sense of urgency about the anguish and anxiety I have seen across America. I speak out of a deep belief in the ideals of the

Democratic Party, and in the potential of that party and of a President to make a difference. I speak out of a deep trust in our capacity to proceed with boldness and a common vision that will feel and heal the suffering of our time—and the division of our party.

The economic plank of this platform on its face concerns only material things; but is also a moral issue that I raise tonight. It has taken many forms over many years. In this campaign, and in this country that we seek to lead, the challenge in 1980 is to give our voice and our vote for these fundamental Democratic principles:

Let us pledge that we will never misuse unemployment, high interest rates, and human misery as false weapons against inflation.

Let us pledge that employment will be the first priority of our economic policy.

Let us pledge that there will be security for all who are now at work. Let us pledge that there will be jobs for all who are out of work—and we will not compromise on the issue of jobs.

These are not simplistic pledges. Simply put, they are the heart of our tradition; they have been the soul of our party across the generations. It is the glory and the greatness of our tradition to speak for those who have no voice, to remember those who are forgotten, to respond to the frustrations and fulfill the aspirations of all Americans seeking a better life in a better land.

We dare not forsake that tradition. We cannot let the great purposes of the Democratic Party become the bygone passages of history. We must not permit the Republicans to seize and run on the slogans of prosperity.

We heard the orators at their convention all trying to talk like Democrats. They proved that even Republican nominees can quote Franklin Roosevelt to their own purpose. The Grand Old Party thinks it has found a great new trick. But forty years ago, an earlier generation of Republicans attempted that same trick. And Franklin Roosevelt himself replied, "Most Republican leaders ... have bitterly fought and blocked the forward surge of average men and women in their pursuit of happiness. Let us not be deluded that overnight those leaders have suddenly become the friends of average men and women.... You know, very few of us are that gullible."

And four years later, when the Republicans tried that trick again, Franklin Roosevelt asked: "Can the Old Guard pass itself off as the New Deal? I think not. We have all seen many marvelous stunts in the circus—but no performing elephant could turn a handspring without falling flat on its back."

The 1980 Republican convention was awash with crocodile tears for our economic distress but it is by their long record and not their recent words that you shall know them.

The same Republicans who are talking about the crisis of unemployment have nominated a man who once said—and I quote: "Unemployment insurance is a prepaid vacation plan for freeloaders." And that nominee is no friend of labor.

The same Republicans who are talking about the problems of the inner cities have nominated a man who said—and I quote: "I have included in my morning and evening prayers everyday the prayer that the federal government not bail out New York." And that nominee is no friend of this city and of our great urban centers.

The same Republicans who are talking about security for the elderly have nominated a man who said just four years ago that participation in Social Security "should be made voluntary." And that nominee is no friend of the senior citizen.

The same Republicans who are talking about preserving the environment have nominated a man who last year made the preposterous statement, and I quote: "Eighty percent of air pollution comes from plants and trees." And that nominee is no friend of the environment.

And the same Republicans who are invoking Franklin Roosevelt have nominated a man who said in 1976—and these are his exact words: "Fascism was really the basis of the New Deal." And that nominee, whose name is Ronald Reagan, has no right to quote Franklin Delano Roosevelt.

The great adventure which our opponents offer is a voyage into the past. Progress is our heritage, not theirs. What is right for us as Democrats is also the right way for Democrats to win.

The commitment I seek is not to outworn views, but to old values that will never wear out. Programs may sometimes become obsolete, but the ideal of fairness always endures. Circumstances may change, but the work of compassion must continue. It is surely correct that we cannot solve problems by throwing money at them; but it is also correct that we dare not throw our national problems onto a scrap heap of inattention and indifference. The poor may be out of political fashion, but they are not without human needs. The middle-class may be angry, but they have not lost the dream that all Americans can advance together.

The demand of our people in 1980 is not for smaller government or bigger government, but for better government. Some say that government is always bad, and that spending for basic social programs is the root of our economic evils. But we reply: The present inflation and recession cost our economy $200 billion a year. We reply: Inflation and unemployment are the biggest spenders of all.

The task of leadership in 1980 is not to parade scapegoats or to seek refuge in reaction but to match our power to the possibilities of progress.

While others talked of free enterprise, it was the Democratic Party that acted—and we ended excessive regulation in the airline and trucking industry. We restored competition to the marketplace. And I take some satisfaction that this deregulation was legislation that I sponsored and passed in the Congress of the United States.

As Democrats, we recognize that each generation of Americans has a rendezvous with a different reality. The answers of one generation become the questions of the next generation. But there is a guiding star in the American firmament. It is as old as the revolutionary belief that all people are created equal—and as clear as the contemporary condition of Liberty City and the South Bronx. Again and again, Democratic leaders have followed that star—and they have given new meaning to the old values of liberty and justice for all.

We are the party of the New Freedom, the New Deal, and the New Frontier. We have always been the party of hope. So this year, let us offer new hope—new hope to an America uncertain about the present, but unsurpassed in its potential for the future.

To all those who are idle in the cities and industries of America, let us provide new hope for the dignity of useful work. Democrats have always believed that a basic civil right of all Americans is the right to earn their own way. The party of the people must always be the party of full employment.

To all those who doubt the future of our economy, let us provide new hope for the reindustrialization of America. Let our vision reach beyond the next election or the next year to a new generation of prosperity. If we could rebuild Germany and Japan after World War II, then surely we can reindustrialize our own nation and revive our inner cities in the 1980s.

To all those who work hard for a living wage, let us provide new hope that the price of their employment shall not be an unsafe workplace and death at an earlier age.

To all those who inhabit our land, from California to the New York Island, from the Redwood Forest to the Gulfstream waters, let us provide new hope that prosperity shall not be purchased by poisoning the air, the rivers and the natural resources that are the greatest gift of this continent. We must insist that our children and grandchildren shall inherit a land which they can truly call America the beautiful.

To all those who see the worth of their work and their savings taken by inflation, let us offer new hope for a stable economy. We must meet the pressures of the present by invoking the full power of government to master increasing prices. In candor, we must say that the federal budget can be balanced only by policies that bring us to a balanced prosperity of full employment and price restraint.

And to all those overburdened by an unfair tax structure, let us provide new hope for real tax reform. Instead of shutting down classrooms, let us shut off tax shelters.

Instead of cutting out school lunches, let us cut off tax subsidies for expensive business lunches that are nothing more than food stamps for the rich.

The tax cut of our Republican opponents takes the name of tax reform in vain. It is a wonderfully Republican idea that would redistribute income in the wrong direction. It is good news for any of you with incomes over $200,000 a year. For the few of you, it offers a pot of gold worth $14,000. But the Republican tax cut is bad news for middle income families. For the many of you, they plan a pittance of $200 a year. And that is not what the Democratic Party means when we say tax reform.

The vast majority of Americans cannot afford this panacea from a Republican nominee who has denounced the progressive income tax as the invention of Karl Marx. I am afraid he has confused Karl Marx with Theodore Roosevelt, the obscure Republican President who sought and fought for a tax system based on ability to pay. Theodore Roosevelt was not Karl Marx—and the Republican tax scheme is not tax reform.

Finally, we cannot have a fair prosperity in isolation from a fair society.

So I will continue to stand for national health insurance. We must not surrender to the relentless medical inflation that can bankrupt almost anyone—and that may soon break the budgets of government at every level.

Let us insist on real controls over what doctors and hospitals can charge. Let us resolve that the state of a family's health shall never depend on the size of a family's wealth.

The President, the Vice President, and the Members of Congress have a medical plan that meets their needs in full. Whenever Senators and Representatives catch a little cold, the Capitol physician will see them immediately, treat them promptly, and fill a prescription on the spot. We do not get a bill even if we ask for it. And when do you think was the last time a Member of Congress asked for a bill from the federal government?

I say again, as I have said before: if health insurance is good enough for the President, the Vice President, and the Congress of the United States, then it is good enough for all of you and for every family in America.

There were some who said we should be silent about our differences on issues during this convention. But the heritage of the Democratic Party has been a history of democracy. We fight hard because we care deeply about our principles and purposes. We did not flee this struggle. And we welcome this contrast with the empty and expedient spectacle last month in Detroit where no nomination was contested, no question was debated and no one dared to raise any doubt or dissent.

Democrats can be proud that we chose a different course—and a different platform.

We can be proud that our party stands for investment in safe energy instead of a nuclear future that may threaten the future itself. We must not permit the neighborhoods of America to be permanently shadowed by the fear of another Three Mile Island.

We can be proud that our party stands for a fair housing law to unlock the doors of discrimination once and for all. The American house will be divided against itself so long as there is prejudice against any American family buying or renting a home.

And we can be proud that our party stands plainly, publicly, and persistently for the ratification of the Equal Rights Amendment. Women hold their rightful place at our convention; and women must have their rightful place in the Constitution of the United States. On this issue, we will not yield, we will not equivocate, we will not rationalize, explain, or excuse. We will stand for E.R.A. and for the recognition at long last that our nation had not only founding fathers, but founding mothers as well.

A fair prosperity and a just society are within our vision and our grasp. We do not have every answer.

There are questions not yet asked, waiting for us in the recesses of the future.

But of this much we can be certain, because it is the lesson of all our history:

Together a President and the people can make a difference. I have found that faith still alive wherever I have traveled across the land. So let us reject the counsel of retreat and the call to reaction. Let us go forward in the knowledge that history only helps those who help themselves.

There will be setbacks and sacrifices in the years ahead. But I am convinced that we as a people are ready to give something back to our country in return for all it has given us. Let this be our commitment: Whatever sacrifices must be made will be shared—and shared fairly. And let this be our confidence at the end of our journey and always before us shines that ideal of liberty and justice for all.

In closing, let me say a few words to all those I have met and all those who have supported me at this convention and across the country.

There were hard hours on our journey. Often we sailed against the wind, but always we kept our rudder true. There were so many of you who stayed the course and shared our hope. You gave your help; but even more, you gave your hearts. Because of you, this has been a happy campaign. You welcomed Joan and me and our family into your homes and neighborhoods, your churches, your campuses, and your union halls. When I think back on all the miles and all the months and all the memories, I think of you. I recall the poet's words, and I say: "What golden friends I had."

Among you, my golden friends across this land, I have listened and learned.

I have listened to Kenny Dubois, a glassblower in Charleston, West Virginia, who has ten children to support, but has lost his job after 35 years, just three years short of qualifying for his pension.

I have listened to the Trachta family, who farm in Iowa and who wonder whether they can pass the good life and the good earth on to their children.

I have listened to a grandmother in East Oakland, who no longer has a phone to call her grandchildren, because she gave it up to pay the rent on her small apartment.

I have listened to young workers out of work, to students without the tuition for college, and to families without the chance to own a home. I have seen the closed factories and the stalled assembly lines of Anderson, Indiana and South Gate, California. I have seen too many—far too many—idle men and women desperate to work. I have seen too many—far too many—working families desperate to protect the value of their wages from the ravages of inflation.

Yet I have also sensed a yearning for new hope among the people in every state where I have been. I felt it in their handshakes; I saw it in their faces. I shall never forget the mothers who carried children to our rallies. I shall always remember the elderly who have lived in an America of high purpose and who believe it can all happen again.

Tonight, in their name, I have come here to speak for them. For their sake, I ask you to stand with them. On their behalf, I ask you to restate and reaffirm the timeless truth of our party.

I congratulate President Carter on his victory here. I am confident that the Democratic Party will reunite on the basis of Democratic principles—and that together we will march toward a Democratic victory in 1980.

And someday, long after this convention, long after the signs come down, and the crowds stop cheering, and the bands stop playing, may it be said of our campaign that we kept the faith. May it be said of our party in 1980 that we found our faith again.

May it be said of us, both in dark passages and in bright days, in the words of Tennyson that my brothers quoted and loved—and that have special meaning for me now:

I am a part of all that I have met ...
Tho much is taken, much abides ...
That which we are, we are—
One equal temper of heroic hearts ... strong in will
To strive, to seek, to find, and not to yield.

For me, a few hours ago, this campaign came to an end. For all those whose cares have been our concern, the work goes on, the cause endures, the hope still lives, and the dream shall never die.

Social Protest and Turmoil

Mario Savio

Speech at Berkeley
(December 2, 1964)

Student protests, which marked much of the late 1960's, began in the fall of 1964 on the campus of the University of California at Berkeley. These demonstrations were an outgrowth of student involvement in the civil rights movement. The summer of 1964 had been designated Freedom Summer, and thousands of students from the north and west traveled south to work in the civil rights struggle and especially to register blacks to vote. Freedom Summer was marked by the tragic murder of three civil rights workers in Mississippi. Beyond that, however, students who were involved in the cause were often radicalized themselves. They had seen a presumably good society systematically repress and discriminate against its citizens. Some participants were led to question not only the sincerity of the nation's commitment to civil rights but the wisdom of authority in general.

As often happens, the Berkeley protests can be traced to an incident relatively small in its own right. A section of the campus had been used for some time for the distribution of political literature and for political solicitation. This activity had been banned for some time by university rule, but the ban had not been enforced. In the fall of 1964 the university administration determined to enforce it.

In defiance of the ban, students continued to solicit and distribute literature. They held an all-night sit-in, modeled after the Southern civil rights sit-ins, in October 1964. The university suspended eight students after that episode. When the police were called in to clear the plaza, Mario Savio, a Berkeley student, stood on top of the police car and delivered an impromptu address to the assembled students, defining the issues, the focus of rebellion, and the relationships among students, police, and administration.

Savio gave voice to what previously had been an inchoate protest. He defined the situation in ideological terms and as a confrontation between opposing forces. His remarks were marked by defiance of authority and the issuance of threats and ultimata—the first time that this sort of rhetoric had been used by students against their universities. In defining the issue, Savio effectively enlarged the struggle. It was not a trivial matter of distributing literature, but the fundamental right of freedom of speech, that was at stake. Students did not shed this right on a public university campus; hence, the administration's restrictions should be defied. That such rules would be made in the first place was a sign that the university had become a depersonalized bureaucracy. In championing free speech, Savio was also championing the right of students to be heard and to participate in decisions about their own education, rather than being regarded as cogs in a machine.

Defining the issues in this fashion enlarged the potential audience, attracting the attention of people strongly committed to the principle of freedom of speech even if not to the specific issues in the demonstration. The Berkeley protesters named themselves the Free Speech Movement and gained the support of more moderate students and many of the faculty. Attendance at the rallies grew.

The speech reprinted here was delivered by Mario Savio outside Sproul Hall, the main administration building on the Berkeley campus, on December 2, 1964. No doubt inspired by Savio's address, over one thousand students marched into Sproul Hall and staged a sit-in. Gov. Edmund G. Brown summoned the police, who arrested over seven hundred students. In response, the Free Speech Movement called for a strike, which was widely supported by students and faculty. The administration was forced to capitulate.

The Berkeley pattern would be repeated during the next several years on campuses the country over. Protesters would adopt a stance of resistance, defiance, and confrontation. The challenge for the university administration was to determine how to react. Some adopted hard-line strategies that served only to radicalize the moderates who were appalled by the use of force against their fellow students. Other administrators were more subtle and made some concessions to defuse the protest while trying to isolate the radicals from the moderates. Although the protests—over causes ranging from dormitory regulations to the Vietnam War—may not have led to fundamental social change, they unquestionably changed the roles of students, faculty, and administrators on college and university campuses.

Last summer I went to Mississippi to join the struggle there for civil rights. This fall I am engaged in another phase of the same struggle, this time in Berkeley. The two battlefields may seem quite different to some observers, but this is not the case. The same rights are at stake in both places—the right to participate as citizens in democratic society and the right to due process of law. Further, it is a struggle against the same enemy. In Mississippi an autocratic and powerful minority rules, through organized violence, to suppress the vast, virtually powerless, majority. In California, the privileged minority manipulates the University bureaucracy to suppress the students' political expression. That "respectable" bureaucracy masks the financial plutocrats; that impersonal bureaucracy is the efficient enemy in a "Brave New World."

In our free speech fight at the University of California, we have come up against what may emerge as the greatest problem of our nation—depersonalized, unresponsive bureaucracy. We have encountered the organized status quo in Mississippi, but it is the same in Berkeley. Here we find it impossible usually to meet with anyone but secretaries. Beyond that, we find functionaries who cannot make policy but can only hide behind the rules. We have discovered total lack of response on the part of the policy makers. To grasp a situation which is truly Kafkaesque, it is necessary to understand the bureaucratic mentality. And we have learned quite a bit about it this fall, more outside the classroom than in.

As bureaucrat, an administrator believes that nothing new happens. He occupies an ahistorical point of view. In September, to get the attention of this bureaucracy which had issued arbitrary edicts suppressing student political expression and refused to discuss its action, we held a sit-in on the campus. We sat around a police car and kept it immobilized for over thirty-two hours. At last, the administrative bureaucracy agreed to negotiate. But instead, on the following Monday, we discovered that a committee had been appointed, in accordance with usual regulations, to resolve the dispute. Our attempt to convince any of the administrators that an event had occurred, that something new had happened, failed. They saw this simply as something to be handled by normal university procedures.

The same is true of all bureaucracies. They begin as tools, means to certain legitimate goals, and they end up feeding their own existence. The conception that bureaucrats have is that history has in fact come to an end. No events can occur now that the Second World War is over which can change American society substantially. We proceed by standard procedures as we are.

The most crucial problems facing the United States today are the problem of automation and the problem of racial injustice. Most people who will be put out of jobs by machines will not accept an end to events, this historical plateau, as the point beyond which no change occurs. Negroes will not accept an end to history here. All of us must refuse to accept history's final judgment that in America there is no place in society for people whose skins are dark. On campus, students are not about to accept it as fact that the university has ceased evolving and is in its final state of perfection, that students and faculty are respectively raw material and employees, or that the University is to be autocratically run by unresponsive bureaucrats.

Here is the real contradiction: the bureaucrats hold history as ended. As a result significant parts of the population both on campus and off are dispossessed, and these dispossessed are not about to accept this ahistorical point of view. It is out of this that the conflict has occurred with the university bureaucracy and will continue to occur until that bureaucracy becomes responsive or until it is clear the university cannot function.

The things we are asking for in our civil rights protests have a deceptively quaint ring. We are asking for the due process of law. We are asking for our actions to be judged by committees of our peers. We are asking that regulations ought to be considered as arrived at legitimately only from the consensus of the governed. These phrases are all pretty old, but they are not being taken seriously in America today, nor are they being taken seriously on the Berkeley campus.

I have just come from a meeting with the Dean of Students. She notified us that she was aware of certain violations of university regulations by certain organizations. University friends of SNCC, which I represent, was one of these. We tried to draw from her some statement on these great principles: consent of the governed, jury of one's peers, due process. The best she could do was to evade or to present the administration party line. It is very hard to make any contact with the human being who is behind these organizations.

The university is the place where people begin seriously to question the conditions of their existence and raise the issue of whether they can be committed to the society they have been born into. After a long period of apathy during the fifties, students have begun not only to question but, having arrived at answers, to act on those answers. This is part of a growing understanding among many people in America that history has not ended, that a better society is possible, and that it is worth dying for.

This free speech fight points up a fascinating aspect of contemporary campus life. Students are permitted to talk all they want so long as their speech has no consequences.

One conception of the university, suggested by a classical Christian formulation, is that it be in the world but not of the world. The conception of Clark Kerr, by contrast, is that the university is part and parcel of this particular stage in the history of American society; it stands to serve the need of American industry; it is a factory that turns out a certain product needed by industry or government. Because speech does often have consequences which might alter this perversion of higher education, the university must put itself in a position of censorship. It can permit two kinds of speech: speech which encourages continuation of the status quo, and speech which advocates changes in it so radical as to be irrelevant in the foreseeable future. Someone may advocate radical change in all aspects of American society, and this I am sure he can do with impunity. But if someone advocates sit-ins to bring about changes in discriminatory hiring practices, this can not be permitted because it goes against the status quo of which the university is a part. And that is how the fight began here.

The administration of the Berkeley campus has admitted that external, extra-legal groups have pressured the university not to permit students on campus to organize picket lines, not to permit on campus any speech with consequences. And the bureaucracy went along. Speech with consequences, speech in the area of civil rights, speech which some might regard as illegal, must stop.

Many students here at the university, many people in society, are wandering aimlessly about. Strangers in their own lives, there is no place for them. They are people who have not learned to compromise, who for example have come to the university to learn to question, to grow, to learn—all the standard things that sound like clichés because no one takes them seriously. And they find at one point or other that for them to become part of society, to become lawyers, ministers, businessmen, people in government, that very often they must compromise those principles which were most dear to them. They must suppress the most creative impulses that they have; this is a prior condition for being part of the system. The university is well structured, well tooled, to turn out people with all the sharp edges worn off, the well-rounded person. The university is well equipped to produce that sort of person, and this means that the best among the people who enter must for four years wander aimlessly much of the time questioning why they are on campus at all, doubting whether there is any point in what they are doing, and looking toward a very bleak existence afterward in a game in which all of the rules have been made up, which one cannot really amend.

It is a bleak scene, but it is all a lot of us have to look forward to. Society provides no challenge. American society in the standard conception it has of itself is simply no longer exciting. The most exciting things going on in America today are movements to change America. America is becoming ever more the utopia of sterilized, automated contentment. The "futures" and "careers" for which American students now prepare are for the most part intellectual and moral wastelands. This chrome-plated consumers' paradise would have us grow up to be well-behaved children. But an important minority of men and women coming to the front today have shown that they will die rather than be standardized, replaceable, and irrelevant.

Shirley Chisholm

For the Equal Rights Amendment
(May 21, 1969)

In 1923, barely three years after the Nineteenth Amendment extended the right to vote to women, the Equal Rights Amendment was first introduced in Congress. Its supporters, led by Alice Paul of the National Women's party, believed that the right of suffrage was not a sufficient remedy for the fact that the law, at both the national and state levels, regarded men and women differently. A constitutional amendment stating that "equality of rights under the law shall not be denied or abridged by the United States or by any state on account of sex" would provide the basis to challenge laws that were discriminatory on the basis of gender. Although the amendment was introduced in almost every Congress thereafter, it usually languished in committee. The Senate in 1950 and 1953 passed a version of the amendment that contained a rider permitting protective legislation for women, in large part nullifying the effect of the ERA. In the House, Judiciary Committee chairman Emanuel Celler refused even to hold hearings on the ERA between 1948 and 1971; it finally reached the House floor by a discharge petition that removed it from the committee's control.

The civil rights movement of the 1960's gave added impetus to the cause of equal rights for women. The word *sex* was inserted into Title VII of the Civil Rights Act of 1964 by an unlikely combination of women's rights advocates who were genuinely committed, and civil rights opponents who thought that it would trivialize and defeat the bill altogether. Increased sensitivity to minority rights caused many to view the social role of women as in some measure analogous to that of blacks. These and other considerations reinvigorated the women's movement in the late 1960's and increased the urgency with which supporters viewed the need for the Equal Rights Amendment.

Among the speeches that sought to make the issue more urgent was one delivered on the House floor by Rep. Shirley Chisholm of New York. Chisholm was the first black woman elected to the House; she had served previously in the New York state legislature after several years as a nursery school teacher. In her first year in Congress, she challenged the seniority system that, she said, concentrated power in a small group of "old men from the Southern oligarchy." She opposed increases in defense spending and focused on disadvantaged Americans in identifying her spending priorities. In speaking out on the ERA and other topics, she also challenged the congressional norm that first-year members should be seen and not heard. Chisholm went on to make an unsuccessful race for the Democratic Presidential nomination in 1972.

The appeals contained in Chisholm's speech are typical of those that helped to raise public consciousness about the ERA. It was passed by the House in 1970 and again in 1971; the Senate concurred in 1972 and sent the amendment to the states for ratification. Many states responded immediately, and quick approval was widely expected. But ERA opponents were able to stop the tide by portraying ERA supporters as radical proponents of women's liberation, by raising the specter of women in combat roles in the armed forces, by asserting that the ERA would require unisex bathrooms and that it would legalize same-sex marriages, and in general by equating legal equality with sexual sameness. The seven-year deadline for ratification arrived in 1979 with the ERA three states short of the necessary thirty-eight. Legislation was passed to extend the deadline until 1982, but no new states ratified during the ensuing three years and a few tried to rescind their earlier approval. No sooner had the ratification effort failed than the ERA was again introduced in the Congress so that the process might begin anew.

Mrs. Chisholm. Mr. Speaker—when a young woman graduates from college and starts looking for a job, she is likely to have a frustrating and even demeaning experience ahead of her. If she walks into an office for an interview, the first question she will be asked is, "Do you type?"

There is a calculated system of prejudice that lies unspoken behind that question. Why is it acceptable for women to be secretaries, librarians, and teachers, but totally unacceptable for them to be managers, administrators, doctors, lawyers, and Members of Congress.

The unspoken assumption is that women are different. They do not have executive ability, orderly minds, stability, leadership skills, and they are too emotional.

It has been observed before, that society for a long time, discriminated against another minority, the blacks, on the same basis—that they were different and inferior. The happy little homemaker and the contented "old darky" on the plantation were both stereotypes produced by prejudice.

As a black person, I am no stranger to race prejudice. But the truth is that in the political world I have been far oftener discriminated against because I am a woman than because I am black.

Prejudice against blacks is becoming unacceptable although it will take years to eliminate it. But it is doomed because, slowly, white America is beginning to admit that it exists. Prejudice against women is still acceptable. There is very little understanding yet of the immorality involved in double pay scales and the classification of most of the better jobs as "for men only."

More than half of the population of the United States is female. But women occupy only 2 percent of the managerial positions. They have not even reached the level of tokenism yet. No women sit on the AFL–CIO council or Supreme Court. There have been only two women who have held Cabinet rank, and at present there are none. Only two women now hold ambassadorial rank in the diplomatic corps. In Congress, we are down to one Senator and 10 Representatives.

Considering that there are about 3 1/2 million more women in the United States than men, this situation is outrageous.

It is true that part of the problem has been that women have not been aggressive in demanding their rights. This was also true of the black population for many years. They submitted to oppression and even co-operated with it. Women have done the same thing. But now there is an awareness of this situation particularly among the younger segment of the population.

As in the field of equal rights for blacks, Spanish-Americans, the Indians, and other groups, laws will not change such deep-seated problems overnight. But they can be used to provide protection for those who are most abused, and to begin the process of evolutionary change by compelling the insensitive majority to reexamine its unconscious attitudes.

It is for this reason that I wish to introduce today a proposal that has been before every Congress for the last 40 years and that sooner or later must become part of the basic law of the land—the equal rights amendment.

Let me note and try to refute two of the commonest arguments that are offered against this amendment. One is that women are already protected under the law and do not need legislation. Existing laws are not adequate to secure equal rights for women. Sufficient proof of this is the concentration of women in lower paying, menial, unrewarding jobs and their incredible scarcity in the upper level jobs. If women are already equal, why is it such an event whenever one happens to be elected to Congress?

It is obvious that discrimination exists. Women do not have the opportunities that men do. And women that do not conform to the system, who try to break with the accepted patterns, are stigmatized as "odd" and "unfeminine." The fact is that a woman who aspires to be chairman of the board, or a Member of the House, does so for exactly the same reasons as any man. Basically, these are that she thinks she can do the job and she wants to try.

A second argument often heard against the equal rights amendment is that it would eliminate legislation that many States and the Federal Government have enacted giving special protection to women and that it would throw the marriage and divorce laws into chaos.

As for the marriage laws, they are due for a sweeping reform, and an excellent beginning would be to wipe the existing ones off the books. Regarding special protection for working women, I cannot understand why it should be needed. Women need no protection that men do not need. What we need are laws to protect working people, to guarantee them fair pay, safe working conditions, protection against sickness and layoffs, and provision for dignified, comfortable retirement. Men and women need these things equally. That one sex needs protection more than the other is a male supremacist myth as ridiculous and unworthy of respect as the white supremacist myths that society is trying to cure itself of at this time.

Wendell Chino

Indian Affairs
(October 6, 1969)

The growing ethnic consciousness of the late 1960's also was felt by American Indians, who may have been the most long-standing victims of racism. During the nineteenth century native Americans were regarded either as savages to be exterminated or as primitives whose removal from their tribal lands and resettlement further west would be for their own good. At the same time, the Indian tribes were regarded as foreign nations with whom the United States negotiated by treaty. The status of Indians as a nation within a nation was inherently ambiguous and would have led to misunderstandings even if the settlers' greed, racial prejudice, and deceit had not provided additional cause for mistrust.

The Bureau of Indian Affairs was established in the early nineteenth century, originally within the War Department, but was later moved to the Interior Department in an attempt to allocate all Indian concerns to one agency and to signal that government policy toward native Americans would be oriented to preservation rather than extermination. Whatever the motives underlying policy, however, its actual operation was not benign. Reservations preserved Indian lands and culture, but they also isolated Indians from the mainstream economy and insulated society at large from the serious economic, health, and education problems of the native American population. These same problems left those Indians living in urban areas ill-equipped to function in American society and likely to be victims of discrimination.

Viewed through the lenses of ethnic and group consciousness of the 1960's, these problems were likely to be defined as problems of power. The condition of the Indians, in some ways, was not unlike that of blacks trapped in urban ghettos. According to this view, the Bureau of Indian Affairs was not an advocate of Indian interests but a witting or unwitting agent in the exploitation of Native Americans. Gaining power, then, required placing the Bureau of Indian Affairs under Indians' control and transforming it into a means for their empowerment.

The incoming Nixon administration was also concerned with the status of the bureau, even if for different reasons. A report on the bureau had recommended major restructuring, moving the agency out of the Interior Department and placing it either in the Executive Office of the President or in the Department of Health, Education, and Welfare. The long-time commissioner, although a Republican, was seen by Interior Secretary Walter J. Hickel as an agent of the Kennedy and Johnson administrations and hence as a candidate for replacement.

One possible contender for the commissioner's position was Wendell Chino, the president of the Mescalero Apache Tribe. He chaired the New Mexico Commission on Indian Affairs and was president of the National Congress of American Indians. He delivered this speech as the keynote address at the twenty-fifth annual convention of the National Congress of American Indians, in Albuquerque, New Mexico. It is an attempt to make salient the needs of native Americans and to impress on white America the urgency of solutions. It illustrates the role of rhetoric in pressing the claims of the relatively powerless.

By the time of this speech, another Indian, L. R. Bruce, had been appointed commissioner. Secretary Hickel denied charges that the administration was insensitive to Indian affairs and reported that Bruce had been given a charge to restructure the bureau in order to make it fully responsive to Indian needs. Although the administration was criticized for not consulting Indians before making the appointment, Bruce promised the National American Indian Conference that the bureau would be reorganized and that he would consult young Indians as he sought to turn the bureau's direction more toward service. He acted to shorten lines of communication between the bureau and the reservations, to make changes in the personnel and authority of area directors and superintendents, and to bring Indians into executive positions. These efforts all met with mixed reactions.

In the face of the agony of the Vietnam war, revolution for relevance, and revolution of racial hatred, our country has made tremendous progress in the fields of science and technology. We can send a man to the moon, we can go to the depths of the sea and probe its darkness. We have learned to harness the energy of the sun and use its energy, and we can build giant computers. So—we stop and take stock of our achievements—a technology that very few nations of the world can match. In spite of progress and advancements—we are failing in, and have neglected our primary duty to our people, and especially among our people—the American Indian.

I share the very deep common concern we all feel and have felt for these troubled and terrible conditions in our country and the world. Today, we, the American Indian people are faced with many problems—political,

economic, financial, racial, and many more. As an individual, I am a concerned citizen of this country—the country, which, in spite of its failings, that I love so very much. Indeed, I want to do everything that I can to promote its welfare and to see that it does not neglect its people.

Therefore, I want to address myself to: Indian Affairs—what has been done and what is remaining to be done.

From that first historic encounter between the American Indians and the "white men," our Indian lands have been diminished, leaving only certain allotted lands and established reservations as the remaining land base for the American Indians.

The Congress of the United States assumed responsibility for the Indian people. That responsibility included their education, health, and their general welfare. After almost two hundred years, we are even more cognizant of this responsibility and the commitment to our people and the great job which still needs to be done.

In addition to the concern and the responsibility of the Federal Government, certain Indian-interest groups and non-Indian individuals have made numerous reports on the administration of Indian affairs. We have been studied to death by reports and task forces representing the expenditure of vast sums of money. With this expenditure to improve our conditions you would think that we ought to be better off than we are today with all the reports and recommendations made in our behalf, suggesting ways and means of improving our conditions and welfare.

The changes in the Administration of this country have made the Indian people and their problems a political football resulting in vacillating policies. Some Administrations advocated keeping the status quo by leaving Indian matters and policies like they have been for a good many years. Some Administrations have initiated action requiring premature withdrawals of Federal services to the Indian people in several states—perhaps in more of the states, if the National Congress of American Indians and their friends had not intervened in certain cases in behalf of the Indian people. A review of the present condition of certain "terminated tribes" does not speak well of the Federal Government and its termination policy.

In view of these seemingly adverse and weak efforts by all parties concerned, we need now to look ahead and ask ourselves, What needs to be done in Indian affairs?

Since all of the studies and reviews reflect the weakness of the Bureau of Indian Affairs and the reticence of the Congress to deeply concern itself with the Indian people and their problems, then, in line with our theme, we must become involved! There is no other recourse but to stress the need for a strong, positive leadership among our Indian Tribes, pueblos and groups. If you see a need or a job that is waiting to be accomplished—put your hands to the plow, then having put your hands to the plow, request assistance if you need it. The need of this hour among Indian people is for strong, positive leadership that must come to grips with local problems—leadership that must be heard on state and national levels. It is not enough to speak only of our ills and the shortcomings of the Bureau of Indian Affairs—let us provide the leadership to provide the motivation and the stimulation to attack those areas needing our time, energy and effort.

Whether we are reservation or urban Indians—radicals or conservatives, we are Indians—let us not knock one another or seek personal aggrandizement. Let us, with common interest and energy make united efforts to attack those problems affecting our people. Unite we must—lest we divide and lose our strength.

Another thing that needs special attention is to secure from the Congress, an annual appropriation that is realistic, and large enough to attack and combat our problems. At the present rate of appropriation for Indian programs, it will take centuries to accomplish the task mutually facing all of us.

Turning our attention to the new national Administration, I have some remarks to address to it:

The "New Federalism" advocated by the new Administration has no appeal or interest for me as presently enunciated and I'll tell you why. The concept of the New Federalism that I hear is that all grants-in-aid and all Federal funding of projects and programs are going to be channeled through the states. By channeling funds through the states, the Federal Government will be abrogating its responsibility, a primary and a constitutional responsibility, to the several states for administration. I do believe that this form of the New Federalism will not work to the benefit of the American Indians, in fact, it will work against them. It will put all of us out in the cold!

New Federalism could work for the Indian people if it is handled in the right way. For New Federalism to work among the Indian tribes, those tribes must be dealt with on the same basis as the several states. Federal assistance must be granted to the Indian tribes in the same way that it is granted to the states—directly! For Federal Indian help to be channeled through the states will result in only tokenism. We need only to look at the administration of funds appropriated under the Omnibus Crime Law. Have any of our tribes really gained or received *any* benefits from this law, a law which grants funds to the several states for administration? At Mescalero, we have not received one iota of service or benefit from the Federal grant to the state of New Mexico.

Instead of New Federalism and tokenism for Indian people, there must come and there must be direct funding to tribes for Indian programs. The Indian desks now existing in the various departments of the Government must remain and continue; in fact, we need more of them.

The Congress of the United States must, without question, proceed immediately to enact Senate Concurrent Resolution 34, a resolution enunciating a new national Indian policy which is being spearheaded by Senator McGovern and his other senatorial colleagues. This proposed national Indian policy statement by the Congress concerning the First American must be enunciated very clearly and positively. It is a new policy that will lay to rest all the hidden and known fears manifest to us because we just do not know where we stand in our unique relationship with the Federal Government. I do not believe that this decade should come to a close without a marked improvement for our Indian people!

The Congress, through this resolution, and its disavowal of the Termination policy will restore the confidence of the Indian people in the Federal Government, making it possible for the Indian tribes and the Federal Government to go forward together to brighter future for our people and all people of this great country. The Indian must have the right of self-determination on the selection of his way of life!...

Let us not be lulled into accepting programs from the states!

Most of our Indian people do not now have, nor have we ever had political or legal relations with state governments. We do not now receive state assistance in any form except for those Federal funds given to the states specifically for Indians. Our experience with the states' administration of Federal funds in behalf of Indians has not been good. Only recently have we been allowed the vote in many states and today few of our Indian people do vote in state elections and have no power base in the state political machines.

The first Congress of the United States reserved unto itself, the power to deal and negotiate with Indian tribes, showing a wisdom thereby which was not fully appreciated until recent times. The Indian tribes were then, and are now legally considered as pseudosovereign nations—exercising the powers of residual sovereignty. As early as 1775, Article IX of the Articles of Confederation asserted: "The United States in Congress assembled shall also have the sole and exclusive right and power of ... regulating the trade and managing all affairs with the Indians...." This Article was approved in Congress in 1777. In 1787, the Constitution clearly established the Federal relationship to Indian tribes in the "commerce clause," which reads in part ... "to regulate commerce with foreign nations, and among the several states, *and with the Indian tribes*."

Subsequently, Congress passed a series of Federal laws "to regulate trade and intercourse with the Indian tribes, and to preserve peace on the frontier," such laws were commonly known as the Indian Trade and Intercourse Acts which served to further clarify the *absolute* relationship between the Federal Government and the Indian tribes, *and excluded the interference of any state*. The Federal Government was anxious then to promote Indian friendship and prosperity because it needed the might of the Indian warriors allied with the Government in the fight against European colonialism. The few thousand American whites could not stand against several million Indians at their backs and several million Europeans at their shores.

Recently, a brief article appeared, stating, and I quote—"Approximately $525 million has been allotted by the Government for Indian Affairs for fiscal 1970. If that money were given directly to the heads of Indian households, they would be receiving an annual income of almost $6,000. (There are about 100,000 Indian heads of households and not more than a half million Indians in the United States.) At present, their average annual income is under $2,000." End of quotation. That is a nice thought, but the writer failed to realize that the major portion or share of the $525 million will go to maintain, sustain and perpetuate an empire of the Federal Government—the empire of the Bureau of Indian Affairs. Parenthetically, we have offered, through our NCAI position paper, ideas that we believe could provide solutions to the problem of getting more funds into the hands of the tribes, and the elimination of a bureaucracy.

This great country which we call the United States of America would not have been created without Indian participation and Indian help. During the Revolutionary War, the Federal Army invited the assistance, the cooperation and the participation of the Six Nation Confederacy, the Delawares, Wyandots, Chippewas, the Ottawas and the Shawnees to protect the northern and western fronts, and the Cherokees, Choctaws, Creeks and Chickasaws to protect the southern front against the invasion of the British army.

The Indians did such an outstanding job that it resulted in total victory for the United Colonies. Thus, was the foundation of this country saved by the Indians. Had the Federal Army been defeated, then, there would never have been a United States of America. The early colonists looked to the Iroquois Confederacy for the formation and framing of the United States Constitution—one of the greatest and mightiest documents this world has ever known. Again, it was Indian help and Indian influence through the Iroquois Confederacy that provided the mold for the Constitution of the United States of America.

In the war with Japan, the Japanese could not decode the Navajo language, this was one code that they could not break. What a vital role the Indian language played in the Second World War—not to mention the large percentage of Indians who served in that war.

This is the kind of Indian involvement that we need. We will not accept anything less!

Now, how sad, how ironic, that our people—the American Indians, who have certainly played a viable and vital role in the shaping of this great country—can be given only lip service by the leaders of our country, and in many cases, by the leaders of our states.

We are sick, tired, and disappointed with tokenism, political platitudes and promises that were never intended to be kept! It is going to take more than lip service from our Government, more than political tokenism from the leaders of our country to improve and accomplish the needed programs existing among our people today.

What about the pledges given to the American Indians at last year's convention in Omaha, Nebraska? How many, can we truthfully say have been kept or fulfilled to the satisfaction of our Indian people? We are sad that all of our pleading, prodding, and requests have been shrugged off and fallen on deaf ears to be ignored.

Our pleas on behalf of our people aren't shallow or slight, they affect the basic well-being of our people. Our request for better and greater service is not welfare or tokenism! We are asking that the historic commitment of 1775 to the Indian people be fulfilled in this century.

Finally—I say to our Indian leaders and our Indian people, let *your* people see *you* take an active part in Indian affairs, and be involved in salvaging the ideals of our people, the traditions of our people. Fight the non-Indian values that would destroy our culture, and *oppose* the platitudes of our time and of the dominant society. Our mutual concern and protection will preserve and sustain our Indian heritage and culture for generations to come.

Thank you.

Wilma Scott Heide

Revolution: Tomorrow Is Now!
(February 17, 1973)

The National Organization for Women, which became the most prominent organization in the contemporary women's movement, was founded in the summer of 1966 by Betty Friedan and two dozen delegates to the conference of state commissions of the Equal Employment Opportunity Commission. Concerned that the national EEOC was not interested in sex discrimination, and incensed when conference officials kept from the floor a resolution demanding that EEOC enforce the sex clause of Title VII of the Civil Rights Act of 1964, dissidents decided that a new organization was needed to advance women's issues in the same way that the National Association for the Advancement of Colored People had done for blacks. The first organizing meeting was held in October 1966; several hundred women and men were present.

By the early 1970's NOW had grown to 30,000 members, with chapters in all fifty states. Friedan was succeeded as president by Aileen Hernandez, and she by Wilma Scott Heide. Heide, a Philadelphia sociologist and nurse, was elected in 1971 and re-elected at the 1973 convention at which she also delivered the keynote address. During her presidency, NOW brought to the attention of the EEOC the problem of gender discrimination in eligibility for promotions at the American Telephone and Telegraph Company, the nation's largest private employer. Portrayal of women on television was also a concern of NOW. Perhaps most prominently, the organization lobbied for ratification of the Equal Rights Amendment.

The ERA was passed by Congress and sent to the states in March of 1972. By the end of the year, twenty-one of the required thirty-eight states already had ratified it. Momentum seemed to be on the side of the ERA. Another victory for the women's movement was the Supreme Court decision in *Roe v. Wade*, issued just three weeks before the NOW convention. Despite a complicated concept of "trimesters" of pregnancy, this decision effectively legalized abortion in virtually all cases.

The women's movement, however, from the outset had been beset by controversy over whether its primary task was improvement of the educational and employment opportunities for women, thereby enabling them to participate more fully in society, or whether its principal duty was to remake society in order to eliminate sexism. During the late 1960's the movement appeared at times to be split into moderate and militant factions. By the early 1970's unity was a more important goal, and movement leaders sought a synthesis of militant and moderate positions. One effect of the search for synthesis was the radicalization of NOW.

This tendency was evident in the actions of the 1973 convention. One resolution voted to condemn Nixon administration policies on the grounds that they were not in the interest of minorities. Another endorsed repeal of all laws that made prostitution a criminal offense, complaining that women prostitutes were persecuted while the participation of men was ignored. Yet another pledged NOW to work against discrimination based on sexual preference in housing, employment, child custody, credit, and public accommodations. In short, NOW adopted much of the revolutionary rhetoric of the more radical wing of the feminist movement.

The word *revolution* was very much in the air in the early 1970's. In the spring of 1972, NOW had published a pamphlet called *Revolution: The Time is NOW*. A week before Heide's speech, the chair of the National Women's Political Caucus referred to the women's movement as a "revolution without arms." The excitement of what seemed rapid change made the word the common property of the civil rights and student protest movements as well as of the women's movement. Heide's speech reflects the same emphasis on confrontational and revolutionary rhetoric. She called for the end of "white male dominance of society" and pledged "creative, dramatic actions."

The persistence of strident rhetoric, even when NOW seemed to be winning on the major issues, may have been a source of the downfall of ERA. Opposition began to mount during 1973, and a key tactic of opponents was to portray all supporters as radical militants, thereby alienating moderate voters from ERA. The momentum for this political litmus test of the women's movement slowed perceptibly. Only nine more states ratified the ERA during 1973, three during 1974, one during 1975, and one during 1977. Both the initial seven-year deadline and a three-year extension expired without success. In retrospect, it appears that the rhetoric of confrontation, which served the movement well in its earlier years and which is represented here in Heide's keynote speech, began to affect the image of the movement adversely and to cause the term *feminist* to take on some of the unfavorable connotations that would impair the women's movement during the late 1970's and 1980's.

Eleanor Roosevelt, who I'd like to think would be with us in spirit, once wrote: "We face the future fortified only with the lessons we have learned from the past. It is today that we must create the world of the future.... In a very real sense, Tomorrow is NOW."

We return to the birthplace of NOW in our nation's capital to declare that feminism is a bona fide occupational qualification (b.f.o.q.) for every human en-

deavor. Every social issue, every public policy, every institution of our society needs feminist analyses and leadership and we will provide it as a basic requirement for a humanist world. What we are about is a profound universal behavioral Revolution: Tomorrow is NOW!

It is for any remaining status quoters, via institutions or persons, who would deny us by behavior or priorities to justify (if they can) any humaneness, legality or justice of their recalcitrance. For the news media, we insist that you communicate to the world that our lively discussions of issues, our diversity of views and styles, our disagreements are transcended by our togetherness that sexism is a societal disease and feminism is caring enough to cure it. What feminists in NOW have lovingly and vibrantly put together, no news media *or* other forces can put asunder. The no longer silent majority *will be* heard with our own voices as we choose to articulate our values and intentions.

Our diversity is our richness; NOW members' creativity and commitment are our greatest resources and a source of daily inspiration to me. Such seeking of funds as we do to support our revolution and the revolutionaries accommodates our fund-raising to our politics, never vice versa. It's a matter of individual and organizational integrity.

As a further matter of integrity, feminism includes the freedom and power to love ourselves *and* each other as women, as men and as women and men loving each other as persons and embracing such children as we choose to have or have had in that love. No particular sexuality preference, if any, is either a requirement of or a barrier to feminism in NOW. That orientation, in my view, is the sine qua non for getting on with the business of educating and being educated by our children vis á vis the full potential of human sexuality. We do not equate normal with natural and in neither do we see bases for praise or censure. Our sexuality is; that is its own validity and though often vital is not the totality of our identity. I would propose that philosophy as a societal imperative to help hang up our sex hang-ups. Though we've resolved this in NOW, we have *yet* to exhibit the courage of our convictions. This Conference must move beyond resolution to action programs for NOW and society.

What we are about is love in its deepest, most abiding sense. If we did not care, we would not be here; indeed, if we did not care, NOW would not be.

It is about daring to care that I want to share some thoughts. In the process. I trust you will note a fundamental belief that every person, at some time, if not always, wants to be humane and courageous in our human interrelationships. It has been said that where there's the will, there's the way; at least equally true must be the maxim that where there is the way, there is the will. Our institutions of religion, family, law, education, health, economics, politics and child rearing have not provided the way, thus superhuman trans-

cending will has been necessary to be courageous and humane. Most of us are not superhuman. Thus, we must create human institutions responsive to our needs; we are less daughters, and sons, of the American revolution than we are designers of the American revolution of feminism which is spreading throughout the world.

In daring to care, we must care *enough* to dare to know poverty in gut-level, existential terms and/or feelings else we will never reach or be reached by our poor sisters or brothers and *all* women are somehow poor in a male-dominated society as is society itself. We must dare to know that economic poverty means *if* to eat as much as what to eat, it means *if* anything to wear as much as what to wear; it means *if* adequate housing and schooling not the luxury of where to live or attend school. It means knowing the ghetto of one's home *and* the ghettos of our minds. It means also knowing the damning luxury of ennui of some affluent women who dilettante at still acceptable band aid volunteerism instead of radical feminism, e.g. to change the conditions their auxiliary status perpetuates.

Recommending the professionalization of volunteerism in Nixon's centers for voluntary action and most other establishment volunteerism without a contract to pay the ostensible "beneficiaries," potentially those most able to lead and needy of change, makes healthy redirection of effort more apparent than real. Co-optation by the existing system comes in many guises. We would do well to study and be wary of some of the current fashions in volunteerism that acknowledge the symptoms of subservience (since NOW adopted its position on change-directed volunteerism in preference to status quo efforts) but some of these current fashions still assure that the unhealthy donor-donee power relationships will be solidified.

Just as the poor, the majority of whom are women of all races and ages and our dependent children, must have whatever is necessary to survive and thrive as a basic right so must these poor know that even, if not especially, our affluent sisters and brothers must become psychologically if not economically liberated from materialism for humanism to begin. We all have so much to learn from each other.

First, we must all survive and to do that, we must get the affluent off public welfare by virtue of vested lobbying and unequal access to public funds and private profits often in obscene amounts. The real empowerment of women augurs more for the elimination of poverty than any so-called welfare reform advanced so far by any political system in any country. All we are saying is: give feminism a chance.

Johnnie Tillmon of the National Welfare Rights Organization is correct: every woman not economically independent or confident of and prepared for her capacity to be so may be just one man away from "welfare." Which brings me to the "housewife" syndrome though I do not accept that *anyone* can marry a house. Ponder the term "househusband." No wonder so many women are so alienated and dropped out from society and say in shy self-deprecation: "I'm *just* a housewife" though their and much of our labor and love have powered and emotionally supported men and children and such economic–political–social–educational–religious institutions of society as we have. There is the homemaker role for men or women and its devaluation is not created by feminists but by such phenomena as the U.S. Labor Department's Dictionary of Occupational Titles that still gives the homemaker the lowest classification of 23,000 + titles and insensitively describes it as of "no significant function except the serving function." I am delighted that NOW feminists from Wisconsin are addressing that significant and related problems.

We must reach out more to our sisters who currently accept the term "housewife" and offer alternatives of personhood to things like: HOW (The Happiness of Womanhood), MOM (Men Our Masters), Pussycats (a pet is not a person), and Fascinating Womanhood to make being a person who is a woman truly dynamic. The less respect one receives as a person, the more one values the superficial "respect" accorded as a woman. Dana Densmore has correctly called chivalry "The Iron Fist in the Velvet Glove."

If the life career of support of a fragile male ego is innate and healthy, why train so assiduously for what is natural and why do women of many traditional marriages have such a disproportionate rate of mental illness especially depression? Wait'll Barbie Doll, their plastic model, becomes a feminist! These, our potential allies and surely our sisters already affected enough by feminism to speak out publicly and assertively (*so unfeminine*) about *something* for the first time in their lives, will eventually experience raised consciousness and you know what that means. Scratch the surface of any woman—and somewhere there's a feminist.

What of the men in NOW or who could be? I'm tempted to say: "Bless their ever-loving hearts!" But that would be matronizing and I no way exclude men from the need and potential of human liberation from sexism. Feminism is more difficult for most men to live, if not to think about. Shall we have commissions on the status and roles of men or commissions on sex role policy as has been suggested? Shall we examine if men qua men are fit for leadership, at least those men victims of the masculine mystique (mistake)? Can those people conditioned to violence as the final assertion of "manhood" (currently synonymous with nationhood) be permitted to exercise power?

Is aggressiveness against people a consequence of incompatibility of one's transcending human mystique with the constraints of the stereotyped "masculine" and the consequent accommodating "feminine?" I think so. Shall we give academy awards for performances of women and men living lives of private and/or public desperation to adjust to expectations often foreign to their individuality and then retire them from their acts and habilitate them for personhood?

Most men have not had the potentially humanizing experience of child care, the gut-level issue of feminism and of society, in my view. Why not see that *every* boy who wants one has a doll (not G.I. Joe) and be supported as he plays with it in anticipatory socialization for his parent role, *if* he *and* a woman so choose. We *can* care enough about children to assure them the right to be wanted, the right to paternal and/or maternal care and the right to supplemental child care to broaden theirs and their parents' horizons and to provide our children adult models of caring, daring, competent, sensitive adults cured of masculinity and femininity and committed to humanity. That might really strengthen such families as we choose.

On the subject of the family, is the white patriarchal model of family itself or nation state viable? Should it be? The black family has inaccurately been called matriarchal. Matriarchy denotes power but women and power have been virtually mutually exclusive. Minority women who finesse/transcend racism and sexism are superb individual role models for us all. However, their institutionalized exclusion from power is no less than white women's. For Moynihan in his infamous study "The Negro Family; the Case for National Action" to consider matriarchy pathological is the epitome of misogyny. It is the white patriarchy of the Moynihans and their boss that is the manifest pathology of our time and all time as I suspect Indira Gandhi will have the 'guts' to inform "our" Ambassador of racism and sexism when and if he indeed goes to India.

We've had affirmative action programs for white men for centuries; we just haven't called them that. It's time we get together as women of all races and minority men and educate ourselves and each other on the interrelationships of racism and sexism and then educate the rest of society: white men that *they* are the minority. Some minority women may be understandably attracted to the physical comforts of the "kept woman" but my black and brown sisters and brothers can no more afford the "feminine mystique" life style than can I. We all need less of the feminine mystique and more of a joint feminist-humanist manifesto (or should we call it womanifesto—that includes man?)

We will come together as we of NOW have in creating and giving leadership and womanpower to the National Women's Political Caucus and its counterparts all over the U.S. to acknowledge that a white male club is not a democracy. We are coming together as women of all races and minority men to rank down General Mills for its sexism and racism. NOW and other human rights groups, by direct action and pressure on the Equal Employment Opportunity Commission (EEOC) and the Office of Federal Contract Compliance (OFCC), created the conditions and compliance of A.T. & T., that's "Pa" Bell (not "Ma" Bell), with (civil rights) law and (executive) order. Even as 'Pa' Bell still owes women employees of all races at A.T. & T. a remaining $3,962,000,000 for illegal economic disadvantages, still the $38,000,000 settlement is a landmark for other industries to beware. Already 'Pa' Bell is bragging about some behavioral changes that they were forced to institute. Who says we can't legislate morality; we've been doing it for centuries *when* we have the laws *and* the enforcement.

We have begun, often in coalitions with other civil rightists, to rid the airwaves of the unhealthy pollution of sexism and racism, both anti-human. We aren't sure yet if the Federal Communications Commission, F.C.C., is part of the solution or part of the problem, but we are assuming that they are educable at least more than their bosses who are introducing legislation that would make broadcasters even less accountable to the public and make access to the public forum more difficult for the excluded peoples, most of whom are women.

We must gain access to the public forum (preferably without interruption for thousands of years) for many of the significant questions have yet to be asked and the dramatic actions have yet to be taken to create the institutional, behavioral changes to which we are committed. Following are only a few of the questions:

Are men smart and humane enough to manage a home and loving child care or can they too be educated for these important roles?

Are people unbalanced with the masculine mystique qualified for responsible leadership?

If medicine were sanctioned for administration to people who are aggressive (not just to achieve goals) but against people as has been suggested, who would be the candidates? Without sanctioning such, even *that* would be more humane than psychosurgery that uses women and others powerless as subjects and considers women's adjustment to the "feminine mystique" as success.

If women are "natural" Secretaries (and typing is not a secondary sex characteristic of all females), why not Secretary of Labor, of Defense, of Health, Education and Welfare, Transportation, Commerce, Housing and Urban Development, Interior and Agriculture?

If the best communication is indeed "telewoman." why not a woman for Postmaster or Postperson or Postone General?

If women "intuitively" sense and value the good of the whole—family or community and the justice of this, then are not women the "naturals" for Attorney Generals and Supreme Court Justices? While the recent U.S. Supreme Court decision vis á vis abortion may represent *something* of our "emancipation proclamation," can we continue to depend on the sufferance and largesse of men only for this and related overdue decisions?

If black defendants have a right to determine if jurors and/or judges are racists (and I support this approach) must not women of all races demand non-sexist judges and juries and police of both sexes?

If power corrupts and absolute power corrupts absolutely, is not the corollary true i.e. that weakness tends to corrupt and impotence corrupts absolutely?

If any religion is to be fully human and thus more humane, should we not send sympathy letters (as I have) to the Pope and his counterparts for their myopia in failing to yet realize that the rebirth of feminism means "*She* Is Risen?"

If education is to fully educate the full human family, must we not insist that feminism be a bona fide occupational qualification for educators whether in our schools, our homes, our art or our literature?

If, and it's a big if, contests for models in America are healthy, how about a *Ms.* America program with feminist criteria for the ideal; if it's what's up front that counts, why not advance whole women not just our breasts? Can we not recognize that ageism as it currently dehumanizes especially women denies us all of wise, brave, mature models of courage and caring? Is it too immodest of me to observe the relevant facts that the current president of NOW is over 40, "overweight" (actually a liberated body), but not "over the hill?"

If veteran's preference is fair to aid those endangered or disadvantaged by national demands, are not women also disadvantaged by institutional sexism, minorities by racism, the poor by classism and all women endangered by childbirth and rape? Do we not need additional concepts of the veteran and benefits accordingly?

Can we wage war like physical atomic giants and consider peace like intellectual midgets equating a partial cease-fire with peace when a fundamental cause of war is the ultimate expression of violence from the masculine mystique and the adoring feminine mystique that sustains it? Must we not develop the transcending human mystique not as the nirvana but as a search for wholeness of persons and society?

Must not we expect the "think tankers" like at the Center for the Study of Democratic Institutions to see that undemographic institutions are undemocratic and futurists like of The World Future Society to begin to transcend current cultural biases to project a feminist-humanist world? Some of us from NOW are working in a Women's Coalition for the Third Century to do just that.

Should we, as women, continue to obey laws made mostly, if not entirely, by men, enforced by men, judged by men? Is this or should it not be unconstitutional? Is there not taxation without representation involved here and is that not tyranny? Should we not test this in the courts and in our lives? Our founding fathers in The Declaration of Independence (where *were* the mothers?) wrote that when government does not represent people, those people have not only the right, but the *duty*, to throw off such government. This government has never, nor does it yet, represent women as people let alone include us beyond tokenism. Shall we in NOW gather our forces and obey that dictum in the Declaration of Independence?

If a President impounds funds appropriated by Congress, gives public support to church teaching and promises public aid to sectarian schools does he not violate the separation of powers and separation of church and state he is sworn to uphold? When he vetoes health, education, child care and/or welfare legislation and/or funds as politically unsuitable or inflationary (while defense money is not called inflationary) is this not a corrupt use of veto power?

Can the foreign policy of this or any other nation continue to be a foreign affair to most women as is what it means to live life as a woman a foreign affair to most policy makers and yet expect to develop fully human let alone humane policy from roughly (literally) one half the population? Can population policy alone address itself to population choice and quality (while we still have the chance) with the women majority of the population only tokenly represented, if that?

Dear God, Heavenly Mother, Parent or Spirit, what *do* some men want? To possess women is not to incorporate the so-called "feminine" part of their nature they may need and covet (often covertly and deviously). Or is god an *idea* of the divine we can become ourselves by transcending the feminine only or masculine only to incorporate the best of each traits in ourselves to develop humane and courageous personhood and society?

To ask these and more questions and to create the behavioral actions they imply, let's remember the words of our foremother Susan B. Anthony, whose birth and courage we honor with the date and theme of our Conference: "Cautious, careful people always casting about to preserve their reputation or social standards never can bring about a reform (let alone a revolution—W.S.H.). Those who are really in earnest must be willing to be anything or nothing in the world's estimation and publicly and privately, in season and out, avow their sympathies with despised ideas and their advocates and bear the consequences."

The Equal Rights Amendment Blood Money program is one sample of dramatic action to behaviorally communicate that we will not only figuratively but literally give our blood to assure that women are included in the basic legal document of this alleged democracy.

If broadcasters and the Federal Communications Commission do not develop adequate feminist consciousness and effective affirmative action (as they have not yet) by the important license challenge and denial method, then perhaps we must educate by station and network takeover actions to assure them we are in earnest.

Heaven and feminists know the corporate world needs the authentic voice and talents of women beyond tokenism not only for fair employment but to challenge some products and services they produce, the dehumanization of much work/job design, and the sexploitive advertising with which they still bombard us. If our writing, speeches, protest by selective buying/non-buying continue to be substantively non-persuasive, some continuous sit-ins, teach-ins, consultins are obviously necessary.

Creative, dramatic actions, it appears, may continue to be necessary vis á vis toys, films, male-only athletic programs with public funds, otherwise uneducable school boards and departments of education, public education textbook publishers, guidance counselors, airlines, unions, national and local committees of political parties, federal cabinet level practices, and sexist social agencies. Women tithing for women and women leading an exodus from misogynous churches are great educators as is refusing to donate for United Funds united only in giving an average of twice as much to male programs (like Scouts and the Y) as to female programs.

When did Congress begin to take us seriously on the Equal Rights Amendment? When about 20 of us from Pennsylvania NOW interrupted a Senate Subcommittee on constitutional amendments February 17, 1970! When did the Office of Federal Contract Compliance of the U.S. Labor Department begin to implement Executive Order 11375 and issue Order #4 with goals and timetables to be applied to women? When we repeatedly visited, sat in the Labor Secretary's office and got on or took over their closed circuit television program in 14 cities in July, 1970! When did *New York Times* and others desegregate want ads? When NOW picketed! When did Southern Bell obey a court order to give sister Lorena Weeks her job? When NOW demonstrated all over the country! We could share thousands of other examples that when polite letters, proffered meetings, documented evidence, detailed offensiveness to our personhood do not penetrate and/or produce significant behavioral change, then it is irresponsible of us not to change our behavior and tactics.

For a manual for wave-makers, I recommend to your attention, the warmly humane and full of good humor book by NOW Board member Tish Sommers: "The Not-So-Helpless Female." Here is a practical how-to that recognizes that the processes of change are central to the quality of change itself.

In urging the courage of our convictions, I truly regret the necessity. It seems part of my personal preference to quietly persuade, softly negotiate change, cite the justice of our case. Yet, we haven't always the "luxury" of relative passivity or even limited activity. Our militancy and programs to get out into what has been "man's world" must be seen as a rejection of nearly total passivity through self-denial and vicarious half-lives. That so-called "man's world" is our world and

it's in trouble. We're hell-bent or heaven-bent (depending on one's view) to join it, determine the action and redirect it, share it, lead it—differently we hope but participate we *will*.

Even as we confront institutions, practices, and people, we must develop methods of non-adversarial human interrelationships. Even as we discuss NOW and its structure, leadership and its potential and limitations, *whatever* the structure is only justified if it facilitates the functions of achieving our common goals. We must continue to experiment with new values and styles of leadership only now in embrionic stages of creation. We have yet to adequately facilitate the local and national participation and leadership in NOW independent of personal economic resources. Leaderlessness, absence of structure, and impoverishment from inadequate dues imposes a tyranny that is even less healthy. Our challenge is to develop the values, resources, and caring, sharing participation and leadership opportunities that promotes corporate responsibility and reparations from institutions that "rip us off" in grievous sex-ploitation to positively fund our healthy activities.

The NOW finance committee and NOW's tax-deductible (for donors) Legal Defense and Education Fund as well as our public advertising ad campaign have begun that vital process. We are learning and teaching each other and society how to share the wealth (women never have and we don't want to control it exclusively) and educate society to the *wealth* of value in what NOW feminism is *really* all about and can mean for women, men and all of our children.

To challenge and change sexist institutions to become feminist-humanist institutions, it is unrealistic to think that vital local action alone and/or *only* "doing our own thing" negates the imperative for strong national organization. The resistance to change is not only organized, it is universally institutionalized. Healthy local, state and national organization is, of course, not mutually exclusive, it is mutually supportive and vital. And the world is our stage as evidenced by our June International Feminist Planning Conference. We have or could have the whole world in our hands and our heads and our hearts.

No other movement however just, overdue, needful of national commitment examines as does feminism the most basic of human power interrelationships, that between woman and men. Only those women and men free enough from stereotyped notions of "femininity" and "masculinity" to be secure about our common humanity are as yet liberated enough to move with the level of self-confidence to create a gynandrous society and world. For that, the power of love must exceed the love of power. Love is the only "game" in which two or more can play and everyone wins.

For feminism to be viable (and it is), then we must empower girls themselves and as women; we must prepare boys to find it livable as men and succeeding generations of children to thrive in its warmth, choices, and vitality. Even with the end of feigned or real innocence for women is the end of the age of guilty privilege of male "birthrights" denied to women and girls. The masks are off: this drama is for *real*.

As your president these past 18 months, I am one of thousands of us privileged to experience the joy, the risks, the gratifications, bone weariness, tragedies and triumphs of activist feminism. There are women and men and children in our lives and whose lives we touch who may never know how profoundly we care about ourselves and them and the quality of the world we must share and make livable for all. We are self-helpers with the courage of our commitment.

Let us, of course, commit ourselves to the ratification of the Equal Rights Amendment by August 26 of this year (if humanly possible). On that date let us celebrate not only the vote won by our brave foremothers and still living sisters but a truly democratic constitution. Further, if we all believe, as I do, that feminism is a bona fide occupational qualification for every human endeavor, then I ask that by August 26, 1973 we develop a feminist womanifesto applicable to every organization, institution, agency, social unit, individual of our society. On that date, whatever else we demonstrate, let us not fear to demonstrate by our presentation of womanifestos everywhere that feminism has universal potential and imperatives.

To date, we have taught men to be brave and women to care. NOW, men must become brave enough to care about the equality and thus the quality of our common life. NOW, women must care enough to bravely assert our talents and intentions not only to rock the cradle but rock the boats and share equally in guiding the ship of state of all our institutions.

Edwin Markham once wrote: "You drew a circle that shut me out; Rebel, heretic, a thing to flout. But love and I had the wit to win. We drew a circle that took you in." Just as the Reverend Dr. Martin Luther King, Jr. insisted that whites must be included in our other related behavioral revolution, so will we include men, even Richard Nixon, whom I (for the third time in a January 17 letter) offered the opportunity to meet with us. We do not want partnership in the world that is but offer the Nixons of the world partnership in what we are creating.

The (other) President has rejected our offer (at least for the suggested dates). In reality, Nixon and his other more or less powerful counterparts are hereby publicly challenged: 'Ask not what you can do for feminism (that's obvious: raise your consciousness and commitment of resources) but ask what feminism can do for you and for this heretofore "man's" world! Men are demonstrably unable, without the equal partnership of women at every level of public life, to fully conceptualize let alone solve our deepest problems that have their roots in sexism, racism, poverty and organized violence. Indeed, the very absence of women may *be the problem* itself. Even more than the brotherhood of all men may we need the sisterhood of all women and together to create the integrated humane family.

That would indeed be a behavioral Revolution: Tomorrow *is* NOW. Let's get on with it today. *And* in the process, please know you have my hands, my head, my heart, and my love.

Jesse Helms

The Uniting of the Silent Majority
(May 15, 1982)

The pace of social change during the late 1960's and early 1970's was too fast for some. Others were fundamentally opposed to its direction, and still others felt resentment at being left behind. These various frustrations helped to energize conservatives; by the early 1980's the movements for social change took place on the right of the political spectrum rather than the left. The issues for the new right included taxpayers' revolts, opposition to forced busing for school integration, opposition to abortion, and efforts to reinstate prayer in public schools.

The phrase *the silent majority* was used by President Richard Nixon in the speech on Vietnamization found in this volume. He appealed to those patriotic middle-class Americans who subscribed to traditional values but whose views remained unexpressed and drowned out by the protest of the late 1960's. Although Nixon had Vietnam specifically in mind, the "silent majority" became energized and articulate on a wide range of domestic issues.

One of the most vigorous spokesmen for this constituency was Jesse Helms, U.S. senator from North Carolina. The Republican Helms was originally elected to the Senate in 1972. He was a proponent of smaller government and tax cuts but he especially concerned himself with a group of "family issues"—pornography, prayer in the schools, and especially abortion. He led an unsuccessful attempt to propose a constitutional amendment declaring that personhood begins at the moment of conception. In 1982, he also led an unsuccessful filibuster to block the renewal of the Voting Rights Act. Helms's thesis was that people become part of what they condone. He saw the liberal elites in the judiciary and the media as proposing the destruction of Western values, and he believed that to acquiesce in the actions of these bodies was to become part of the problem. Instead, active resistance was called for.

This speech was delivered as the commencement address at Grove City College, a small school near Pittsburgh. Its significance does not rest in any specific action that it triggered or to which it responded, but in its encapsulation of the key themes of the new right. It was delivered at a time when the election of Ronald Reagan seemed to many extreme conservatives to be a vindication of their agenda and the precursor of major changes. Like many leftist speakers, Helms sought to characterize as "revolutionary" the fact that the silent majority had been aroused from its silence and was defending society against the onslaught.

One major theme of the speech is the opposition between family and government for the dominant social role. The liberal revolution, Helms argued, has been stopped in its tracks because it has come to be perceived as antifamily. More generally, Helms suggested that conservatives differed from liberals in kind and not just in degree. Until that fact was widely appreciated, the meaning of the 1980 election would not be understood and the agenda of the new right would not be realized.

The speech captures the thinking of a conservative leader at what seemed to be a propitious time. Certainly Ronald Reagan continued to espouse the themes of the new right. Increasingly, however, those themes became largely symbolic issues. Leaders alluded to them in a bid for the conservative vote in election campaigns, but they did not press hard for the legislative agenda of the new right. Reagan left office with most of the policies disliked by the right still intact; occasionally Helms wondered whether Reagan was sufficiently committed to the cause. On the other hand, the Supreme Court appointments made by President Reagan may help to assure the dominance of the new right agenda long after his term of office.

Mr. President, distinguished faculty members, alumni, friends of Grove City College—and, most especially, members of the graduating class:—While it is an honor to have been invited to share this memorable occasion with you, I suppose that there have been few commencement speakers who have not contemplated in advance the remark, years ago, by an irreverent classmate who speculated that if all the commencement speakers in America were laid end-to-end—that would be fine.

If it'll help my case any, let me say at the outset that I am very proud of you young people. I am proud of this great institution—Grove City College which has earned a position in the front ranks of colleges and universities in this country whose fidelity to the principles of freedom and free enterprise has never been compromised.

That raises questions, of course, about the configuration of higher education in the United States—questions that I suspect you already have considered.

It is good that there is a will, a capacity, to question, to be inquisitive, to analyze the things going on around us. That was part of the genius of the creation of America—our Founding Fathers dared to question, to assess, to evaluate. Out of all that they decided that true freedom had really never been tried in the history of mankind, and they decided to give it a try. And they produced the Miracle of America as a heritage that we are trying to revive and preserve today.

All of us have a duty to ask questions—even foolish questions. But occasionally I over-reach myself when I indulge in questions too perfunctory and too lacking in substance.

Mrs. Helms, awhile back, called just before I left the Senate one evening and asked that I stop by the supermarket for a few items on my way home.

I did, and as I was entering the store, out came an attractive young housewife who lives just up the street from us. Just as she stepped out the door onto the sidewalk, one of the two enormous grocery bags she was carrying burst, and potatoes rolled all over the place.

In a flash, both she and I were down on our knees, gathering up potatoes.

And what did I say? You guessed it, I asked a foolish question.

To be precise, I said, "Oh, mercy, your bag burst, didn't it?"

The young lady paused, looked at me, smiled faintly, and replied, "Oh, no, Senator. I always like to roll my potatoes home."

On the other hand, there are truly substantive rhetorical questions.

America, quo vadis?

Where are we headed as a nation?

Are we conducting ourselves as Americans should?

What are we condoning?

And: Do we not become a part of what we condone?

If I perceive our nation today, I find myself wondering if all of us—any of us—maintain a sufficiently adequate awareness that all of us have been designated as keepers of the same flame in protecting and preserving the concepts of freedom and free enterprise.

You who are being graduated today are more aware of that than most. The very purpose of Grove City College is to provide the inspiration to see those values through to another generation.

So, you are now a part of a continuum that reached back to the wildernesses of Judaea, to the porticoes of Athens, and the schools of medieval Europe whence have come the religious, political, moral and ethical values that we know as the Western tradition.

This is an ancient tradition, and an honorable one, but just because something is ancient and honorable doesn't assure that it is indestructible.

Indeed, the argument can very plausibly be made that we live in a time when the characteristic values of the West are collapsing, disintegrating, decomposing. This is hardly surprising because these values have fallen victims to neglect and indifference on the part of those who have most benefited from them and of assault and battery on the part of those who should be their staunchest defenders.

That is why I presume to ask you, on this very special day, to consider the proposition that we become part of what we condone. In this regard, much of what passes for education in our time is not education at all but indoctrination and the aim of it is to reconcile the individual with the destruction or repudiation of the moral and ethical patrimony that has sustained the West for thousands of years.

In our country, the most determined and implacable proponents of this destruction are the liberal elites in the judiciary, and in the media particularly, who have carried on for the past three decades a ferocious assault on the fundamental institution of the family—which is, need I say, the very basis of the social order. So the issue before us today is, simply stated, whether the government or the family should be the formative social principle in America.

The attack on the family went on for years and there really wasn't any sustained or organized opposition to it. Americans have traditionally been too busy making the most of the opportunities our system has always provided to concern themselves unduly with slow encroachments on that system.

But in the last decade, Americans have begun to see how their homes, their families, their children have been targeted for revolutionary change by leftists and liberals. That is why a groundswell of opposition has arisen to stop that revolution right in its tracks.

You may recall, as I do, watching the election returns on November 4, 1980, and observing the astonishment and chagrin of our leading pundits and commentators in the media when one by one the leading liberals in the Congress went down to defeat. They hadn't a clue this was coming. This was an unaccountable phenomenon by their lights, but it was not unaccountable to people in touch with grass roots America.

The experts then decided that what had happened was a sort of coup d'etat by an entity known as the "New Right," allegedly composed of a coalition of single issue voters. Immediately there began a counter-attack by the press, and on the airwaves, and in the pulpits, against this fearful menace and against the issues that brought it to the fore. This counter-attack is going to fail, in my estimation, because you cannot destroy ideals of justice, freedom and equity by slandering and maligning the people who hold those ideals.

Now if I may say so, one of the great handicaps we have to deal with in this country is that we are accustomed to think and talk about politics in terms and categories that the liberals have laid down. So it is with this expression "the New Right." Left and right are terms derived from revolutionary politics in Europe, terms that refer to how strongly a particular group wishes to push down on the accelerator of mandated social change.

Conservative Americans don't belong in this spectrum at all. Their concern is with values that are pre-political values that derive from the nature of man and from the moral law. Liberals and leftists apparently just can't conceive of any such category of people who find things worth preserving in the status quo, and so they have the habit of referring to such anomalous people as "far right," "right wing extremists" and so on. Conservatives just don't differ in degree from liberals—they differ *in kind*, and until that point is better understood, the vast significance of the 1980 elections will not be properly appreciated.

Now let us examine some of the so-called social issues that so galvanized grassroots America a year and a half ago. Let us consider first the tax revolt, the organized resistance of the wage earning, tax-paying families of America who have seen their assets eroded by the indirect tax called inflation as through inflation also they are elevated to higher tax brackets. Today many families find it impossible to live on the wages of one breadwinner, and almost impossible to live on the wages of two. This was not the case 15 years ago before our government opted for the fiscal and monetary policies that were to transfer the assets for the productive to the non-productive.

Secondly, we have the phenomenon of forced busing. It is here that the division—between elitist judges and bureaucrats on the one hand, and the American family on the other—is perhaps most strongly drawn. This is a scheme that is based on assumptions that are racist to the core and shows the fundamental contempt that left-wing ideologies have for ordinary people.

There are not many judges or bureaucrats or newspaper publishers who would put their own children on buses early in the morning to be taken to a distant, unfamiliar (and, under the circumstances, a very likely hostile) part of town just to fill some social planner's quotas of the proper racial mix. This is the fate that they mete out to the working middle class. And more than anything else it has served to discredit the myth that liberals are the champions of the people against the wealthy and powerful.

An issue related to forced busing in that it is aimed at the same victims is that of the abolition of voluntary prayer or Bible reading in the public schools. The campaign to restore this basic First Amendment right to public school children is a profoundly populist cause. The American people support it seven, eight, and nine to one. We are not talking about any sort of mandatory prayer or religious indoctrination by the public schools, but of allowing the opportunity to those who wish to do so to invoke the blessing of the Almighty on their daily work.

In 1981 the Supreme Court ruled that a public school classroom could not display a copy of the Ten Commandments on the wall. The irony was not lost on millions of parents that the same court whose decisions unleashed a tidal wave of pornography on this country would find a copy of the Ten Commandments unsettling to young minds. After all, these are parents who have watched in dismay as the public schools, in many places, have become transformed into howling wildernesses in which delinquency, violence, arson, vandalism and the drug culture have flourished.

How, they rightly ask, are good citizens and good human beings to emerge from totally permissive surroundings in which the *only prohibited activity* is to invoke the blessings of God or to make any reference to the spiritual and moral teachings that have been an abiding feature in our culture for thousands of years?

Clearly the American people, who have seen the results of educating a generation in the amoral atmosphere of the public schools want to have the opportunity for voluntary prayer reinstated in those schools, and they will not be daunted by pettifogging legalistic objections. There is nothing so invincible, the adage tells us, as an idea whose time has come. And now we come to the premier social issue, that of human life itself. The most salient and distinguishing feature of Western culture is the great emphasis it has always placed on the intrinsic worth and value of every human life.

This tradition was dramatically repudiated on January 22, 1973, when the Supreme Court struck down the laws of the 50 states, the District of Columbia and the Commonwealth of Puerto Rico having to do with abortion, the deliberate termination of innocent human life.

What really happened here, of course, is that the court simply established another category of individuals to whom the Bill of Rights did not apply.

As the author of a Constitutional Amendment that would secure the protection of the laws to all human life regardless of its condition of dependency, I have heard every rationalization that the human mind can devise. I know what fear and need and desperation can do to anyone's judgement and with all my heart I sympathize with those in fear and need.

But who has cause for greater fear—and who has greater need than the unborn child who cannot claim from the law even a fraction of the protection that applies to the snail darter or the furbish lousewort.

The media will tell you that the American people are "divided" on this subject. But it is obvious that the media are not divided on this subject at all. They are overwhelmingly and insistently supportive of the deliberate termination of innocent human life.

I think it is incorrect to say that the American people are divided on this subject. They know instinctively what abortion is, and what it does. Prior to 1973 there was not a legislature in America that could or would have dared to eliminate the legal prohibitions on abortion. This was one item on the liberal agenda that would not make it through the legislatures. And even today, the hysterical tone and frenetic nature of the pro-abortion movement, the deliberate obscurantism of the position, the semantic obfuscations, the pseudo science they invoke—all these things reflect a fundamental irrationality.

I rest my case with the American people, for, no matter how they have been brainwashed to see abortion not as an evil but as a positive good, in their hearts they know it is wrong.

The Irish poet William Butler Yeats wrote some celebrated lines describing the turmoil set loose upon the world at a time when "the best lack all conviction, and the worst are full of passionate intensity." Another poet used a different image in describing "truth forever on the scaffold, and error ever on the throne." That is the terrible dilemna of this world of ours where evil does so much damage—but where the toleration of evil does even more.

For more than a generation, we have been told by a garrulous array of experts that the toleration of evil is, on the contrary, a very great virtue. Indeed, our foreign policy has been predicated on finding ways to tolerate and co-exist with evil. Those of us who as a matter of conscience have been stalwart anti-communists through the 1960's and '70's, when detente was the order of the day, know a little about what it is like to swim against the current of the times.

That is why it is so encouraging to see the beginnings of a resurgence of the moral and ethical values and the patriotic fervor that sustained this country for 200 years. It is encouraging to see the erstwhile silent majority silent no longer about the values closest to their hearts. For what, as the Scriptures ask, does it profit a man if he gain the whole world, yet suffer the loss of his soul?

So, the battle for the soul of America is in progress.

Who will win the battle? I can't answer that—but you can, and you will. And you will answer it, in your generation, on the basis of that inevitable yardstick which measures how much we will condone.

I am optimistic.

In the solitude of the nights, I find myself retracing the footsteps of long ago—and hearing, again and again, the voices of little ones, now grown and gone.

I recall that Easter weekend three decades ago when our family embarked on a journey across our state to attend a sunrise service on a mountain top in western Northern Carolina.

On a majestic mountain ridge, a group of perhaps a hundred gathered in the pre-dawn darkness, just minutes before the first of the Easter morning sun began to peep over yonder mountain, burning away the chill that had settled like a net during the night.

Indelible upon my mind is the memory of our little girl, possessing all the charming impatience that goes along with being four years old. She couldn't see over the heads of the adults all around her. She couldn't see around them.

But she wanted to see—and began to improvise. She spotted a boulder to one side, but her little legs—and the slick soles of her new Easter patent-leather shoes—frustrated her efforts to scramble up to her own private vantage point. So she implored her Daddy to help her.

A good idea is infectious, and her seven-year-old sister found it appealing also. So Daddy did what Daddies almost always do—I yielded to the blandishments. I climbed up first, then with whispered cautions to "hold hands tight" I extended my hand to the seven-year-old who, in turn, held tight to the hand of her little sister.

And there we were—the three of us on top of the boulder at the precise moment that the rays of the sun slashed through the darkness.

The assembled group burst almost immediately into a familiar hymn—but not before that little girl, exulting in her achievement, spoke a profound philosophy that I shall remember always.

"You see, Daddy," she said triumphantly, "I'll betcha if we all hold hands tight, we could go anywhere!"

Isn't that it? Isn't that the very essence of our gathering here today—to signal our awareness that if we hold hands tight, with God who gave us liberty, and with truth that set us free, and with honor and decency and courage, we can go anywhere.

Or we can rekindle our faith—we can climb that boulder. If we hold hands tight.

It's up to us.

Lowell Weicker

Prayer in Public Schools
(September 19, 1982)

In the early 1960's, the United States Supreme Court outlawed organized prayer in public schools as a violation of the separation of church and state. Prior to that time, it had been common practice to open the school day by including a brief prayer as part of the opening exercises. The Supreme Court's decision was unpopular. Although most of the country eventually became reconciled to this decision, it gave ammunition to groups seeking the impeachment of Chief Justice Earl Warren, and it gave momentum to an effort to amend the Constitution in order to reverse the decision. Calls for such an amendment to permit voluntary organized prayer in public schools were made by conservatives throughout the late 1960's and 1970's.

When President Carter sought the creation of a separate Department of Education in the late 1970's, Sen. Jesse Helms of North Carolina tried to attach a school prayer amendment to that bill. Backers of the education department removed the Helms measure, which was then passed separately by the Senate but allowed to die in the House. What gave renewed energy to the amendment effort was the election in 1980 of Ronald Reagan, who had campaigned on a platform including many elements of the conservative social agenda.

In May of 1982 President Reagan announced that he would support a constitutional amendment to permit voluntary prayer in public schools and announced that the Justice Department was drafting such an amendment. Meanwhile, a long-promised Senate debate on abortion, which began in August, was quickly turned into a filibuster that ranged over the issue of school prayer as well, and especially over the scope of the federal courts' authority. The filibuster was led by Republican senators Robert Packwood of Oregon and Lowell Weicker of Connecticut. Weicker contended that the Senate was "not in such a big rush that we'll leave the Constitution behind," but a Helms aide countered that the amendment's opponents were filibustering only because they lacked the votes to kill it outright.

While the issue was on the Senate floor, Weicker was invited to give the sermon at the United Church on the Green in New Haven, Connecticut, at the regular Sunday morning services. He was invited by the regular minister in keeping with the Congregational tradition that government leaders were offered the opportunity to speak from the pulpit. He drew on a wide variety of materials from his personal life and from the fields of politics, law, and religion to illuminate his theme that prayer in public schools, while on the surface appealing, was potentially dangerous.

The Senate had scheduled a vote on cloture in an attempt to stop the filibuster. The cloture attempt was unsuccessful and the Senate then voted to kill the Helms proposal in order to get on with the concluding business of the session. Rejection of the Helms amendment was seen as a watershed in the efforts to enact legislation embodying the social agenda of the far right. Helms did not reintroduce his measure the following year. Two other constitutional amendments were proposed to the Senate, however. One backed by President Reagan would have permitted "'voluntary,' organized recited prayer," and one by Sen. Orrin Hatch of Utah would have allowed silent prayer or meditation. The Senate Judiciary Committee sent both bills to the floor without recommendation. Neither was adopted. President Reagan continued to champion school prayer in his speeches, but there was no further effort to enact the appropriate legislation.

It is a great honor for me to join you in worship this morning. Reverend Hay has reminded me that it is an old Congregational tradition for government leaders to speak from the pulpit. Forgive me if today I avail myself of this tradition to speak out against what used to be another old Congregational practice: theocracy, the fusion of Church and State into one authority. Until its disestablishment in 1818, nearly two hundred years after the Pilgrims came in search of religious liberty, Congregationalism was Connecticut's official creed.

I don't mean to cast stones but simply to cite facts. On this issue, my ancestors took much the same path. A great-uncle of mine was Archbishop of Canterbury. Nevertheless, I have come to believe with Mark Twain that established religion "means death to human liberty and paralysis to human thought." No greater mischief can be created than to combine the power of religion with the power of government. History has shown us that time and time again. The union of the two is as bad for religion as it is for government. It gives rise to tyrants and inquisitions. It is what drove many of our ancestors to these shores. That is why clergy, lay people, and public officeholders alike must fight radical rewrites of the First Amendment which are masquerading as good old-fashioned morality.

I want to speak in particular today about prayer in our public schools. The idea is very appealing on its surface. Indeed, it summons up reassuring images of freckle-faced Norman Rockwell children with their heads bowed and hands clasped in prayer. But as inspiring as it sounds, prayer in school has the potential for doing real damage—to children and their families, to the cause of true religion, and to the ideal of separation of Church and State our founders embraced.

Today's Gospel lesson goes to the heart of the issue, which is that prayer is—or should be—a personal act of devotion, not an official function. I would like to reread a part of that passage from the Sermon on the Mount, this time from the Phillips translation: "And when you pray don't be like the play actors. They love to stand and pray in the synagogues and street corners so that people may see them at it. Believe me, they have had all the reward they are going to get. But when you pray, go into your room, shut the door and pray to your Father privately. Your Father who sees all private things will reward you."

It seems to me that the kind of prayer Jesus is recommending here is not the sort the school prayer supporters have in mind. He advocates a one-on-one personal dialogue with God, not some kind of officially-sanctioned formula blared through a public address system. Now, to be sure, people are concerned about falling church attendance and the fewer and fewer applicants to seminaries and well they might be. But making prayer a government program won't help matters. Government itself is still in the midst of a crisis of confidence. Look at how few people exercise their right to vote and participate in government. I have never seen a merger between two weak companies that ever worked, and that is what is being attempted here. In this country, government and religion, each must stand on its own two feet. If they cannot, then we must shake them up. We must not yoke them together. When the blind lead the blind, they both fall in the ditch.

If getting the American people closer to God is their goal, why make government the go-between? It reminds me of the Old Testament story of the Tower of Babel. There you had civil leaders commissioning a public works project to bring people closer to God. In the end, of course, the tower not only failed at that but it so insulted God that he made sure such a thing could not happen again by causing the people to speak different languages and scattering them to the wind.

Do I encourage my fellow citizens to pray? Certainly. And I hope that when they do, they will keep those of us in the U.S. Senate in mind. But I do not believe it is up to a Representative or a Senator or even the President to espouse or encourage any one religion or even religion in general. It is not my job to do the convincing, to take up on Monday on the floor of the Senate where the rabbi left off on Saturday or the priest or minister left off on Sunday.

My job is simply this: to make certain that every individual is free to practice the articles of his or her faith, whatever they may be, without fear of reprisal.

Similarly, I believe that our public schools are meant to educate our children, teaching them a healthy respect for people of differing beliefs and disbeliefs. They were never intended to indoctrinate them or inculcate a certain set of beliefs. That is the work of parents and Sunday School teachers and Hebrew School teachers.

There is an old Spanish proverb which says "an ounce of mother is worth a pound of clergy." I would add that both are worth a ton of politicians where prayer is concerned. These days we talk a lot about strengthening families. But we will not do so by imposing some doctrine from without, particularly if that doctrine is alien to the family's own beliefs or traditions.

President Kennedy's comment on the 1962 Supreme Court decision barring prayer in the New York public school system was right on the button. "We have in this case a very easy remedy," he said. "And that is to pray ourselves. And I think it would be a welcome reminder to every American family that we can pray a good deal more at home, we can attend our churches with a good deal more fidelity, and we can make the true meaning of prayer more important in the lives of all our children."

School prayer supporters contend that the prayer they want could be voluntary and vaguely enough worded to embrace all beliefs. But there is nothing voluntary about school attendance; that is compulsory. And what six-year-old is going to stand up and insist on his or her constitutional right to be excused when the prayer is recited? At that age and older, peer pressure is intense. When everybody stands, you stand. When everyone bows their head, you bow your head. When everyone mumbles words, you mumble words. So, in a very real sense, neither is the exercise of the prayer voluntary to a young child.

As E. B. White wrote to Senator Margaret Chase Smith when this issue came up in 1966, "In an atmosphere of 'voluntary' prayer, pupils coming from homes where other faiths prevail will feel an embarrassment by their non-participation; in the eyes of their schoolmates they will be 'queer' or 'different' or 'irreligious.' Such a stigma for a child can be emotionally disturbing, and although we no longer hang and burn our infidels and our witches, a schoolchild who is left out in the cold during a prayer session suffers scars that are very real."

The Reverend Jerry Falwell, founder of the Moral Majority, recently made a very telling remark. He told reporters that because Moral Majority members represented a variety of denominations " if (they) ever opened a Moral Majority meeting with prayer, silent or otherwise, (they) would disintegrate." Well, just what does he expect to happen to our school systems, many of which are equally pluralistic in makeup?

What sort of prayer do they plan to recite: Protestant? Catholic? Jewish? Buddhist? Mormon? Depending on the community in question each of these religions could be in the majority. Is the prayer to be addressed to God, Jehovah, Buddha or the Virgin Mary? Or is it to be a meaningless mishmash of every religion known to man?

M. William Howard, the former president of the National Council of Churches, put it well recently when he said that religious people do not want "a least common denominator prayer addressed to whom it may concern." That is part of the reason why sixty major religious leaders have come out against school prayer.

These leaders are also motivated by a strong sense of our history and our destiny as a free people. In his book, *The Making of the President 1960*, Theodore White wrote: "America as a civilization began with religion. The first and earliest migrants from Europe, who shaped America's culture, law, tradition and ethics, were those who came from England—and they came when English civilization was in torment over the manner in which Englishmen might worship Christ.... It was with remembered bitterness they distilled, though not without struggle, that first great landmark in America's unique civilization, that first of the creative American compromises that was to set America apart from the old world: freedom of worship."

If you go to Plymouth, Massachusetts, today, you will find it teeming with tourists. They crowd around the rock with cameras. They clamber on board the Mayflower Two. They patiently file through the first Pilgrim house. How many of them, I wonder, relate what happened at Plymouth to their lives today? On the hill overlooking the sea, there is a monument bearing the names of those 102 English Calvinists who were persecuted because they denied the ecclesiastical authority of the King. There is also this dedication: "to the forefathers in recognition of their labors, sacrifices and sufferings for the cause of civil and religious liberty."

Religious liberty. If you ask me, that was the real rock upon which our country was built.

That was 1620. Unfortunately, not even a century passed before the persecuted became the persecutors. In 1692, for instance, entrenched Puritan hostility to freedom of thought and speech helped cause the deaths of 19 men and women during the Salem witch trials.

In 1802, Thomas Jefferson wrote to the Danbury, Connecticut, Baptist Association: "Believing with you that religion is a matter which lies solely between Man and his God ... I contemplate with sovereign reverence that act of the whole American people which declared that their legislature should 'make no law respecting an establishment of religion, or prohibiting the free exercise thereof,' thus building a wall of separation between Church and State."

Historians have since discovered that this letter was no casual piece of correspondence. Jefferson had the then Attorney General Levi Lincoln study it before mailing it. Why, twenty years after the adoption of the Constitution and the Bill of Rights, did Jefferson feel compelled to address the establishment issue? Because in many parts of the country people weren't taking the First Amendment seriously. As I noted earlier, the Congregationalists had official backing in Connecticut, much to the annoyance of the Danbury Baptists no doubt.

So, the current disregard for the First Amendment and the penchant for religious segregation is nothing new. Even after the last state religion was disestablished, Protestantism was still the unofficial national religion—to the detriment of all other faiths. It was a touchy matter to be a Jew or a Mormon. As recently as 1960 it was widely believed that Roman Catholics should not hold high public office. President Kennedy's election helped tear that barrier down. But prejudices persist.

And I believe that school prayer only serves to reinforce those prejudices. I attended a private school where not only prayer but worship was mandatory, and believe me it was Protestant in form. My Jewish friends either had to attend these services or stand in the park. The same held true for my Catholic friends. And we looked on them as something different just as they must have looked on themselves.

Of my children, and there are eight of them, some go to public schools, some to private They have not had the same experience. On the other hand, I think they probably have a more profound understanding of the world around them and a greater love and a greater beauty to their lives than I. When I see them working with a group of retarded children, giving of their free time, I can't help suspecting that that really is a form of worship far more exhilarating and far more meaningful than sitting in a pew with hands folded. It is certainly different, far different, from what I did. But according to the matters in which I believe, I think maybe they are closer to Heaven than I am.

The Apostle Paul wrote that "faith without works is dead." And in the Old Testament text read this morning, Isaiah seems to be saying that prayer without actions to match is not heard. It has always struck me how many Biblical passages the Moral Majority chooses to ignore when it sets its legislative priorities. This 58th chapter of Isaiah is one such passage. Isaiah is explaining why the Lord is ignoring Israel's many prayers, fasts, and solemn observances. As I read it, the people's piousness is an abomination to God until they first act on His social agenda. Isaiah writes: "Is not this the fast that I have chosen? to loose the bands of wickedness, to undo the heavy burdens, to let the oppressed go free? Is it not to deal thy bread to the hungry, and that thou bring the poor that are cast out to thy house?"

This, I believe, should be the agenda for each of us as individuals, and indeed for me as a Senator. It pains me to see the Congress diverted onto these moral crusades when there is so much real suffering in our land, when so many people are losing their livelihoods and so many going without the necessities of life. And when there are so many people denied the justice which should be accorded them by law.

Let us rededicate ourselves to taking up this agenda. Let us get involved in our public and private lives to shape a fairer society. Then, and only then, does God promise to hear our prayers. "Then shalt thou call, and the Lord shall answer," writes Isaiah. "Thou shalt cry and He shall say, Here I am."

Mario Cuomo

Religious Belief and Public Morality:
A Catholic Governor's Perspective
(September 13, 1984)

Few social issues of the 1970's or 1980's had the same intensity as the question of abortion. The Supreme Court's 1973 decision in *Roe v. Wade* held, in effect, that laws could not prohibit abortions during the period before the fetus was viable outside the womb. This decision was at odds with much conservative thought and particularly with the teaching of the Catholic church that human life begins at conception. Not perhaps since the debates about slavery were the moral positions so sharply drawn. One side, calling itself "pro-life," held that the sanctity of human life required protection of the unborn and defined abortion as murder. The other, using the term "pro-choice," emphasized that the question of when the fetus became a person was difficult and inconclusive, and gave primary emphasis to the woman's right to make the difficult moral and ethical choices that inevitably were involved. Substantive and procedural notions of morality were at odds. The attempt by the Supreme Court to use the concept of viability as a "middle ground" only added to the heat of controversy, and the dispute often led to stalemate characterized by mutual recriminations and invective.

The abortion issue posed especially difficult dilemmas for Catholic politicians who wished to be both true to their faith and respectful of the pro-choice sentiments of the majority of the population. If they personally opposed abortion, believing it to be murder, and yet opposed laws to ban abortion, on the ground that the majority of the population was pro-choice, they easily could be accused of hypocrisy and perhaps even subjected to church discipline. If, on the other hand, they attempted to legislate their personal convictions, they risked violating the pervasive American commitment to separation of church and state. During the 1960 campaign, John F. Kennedy responded to similar fears by saying, in effect, that his Catholicism was incidental to his performance in public office and that he did not look to the church for guidance in political matters. On the question of abortion, however, the distinctions between the personal and the public seemed hardly so clear.

Mario Cuomo, governor of New York, was among the prominent Catholic politicians to feel the force of this dilemma. He maintained that, while he was personally opposed to abortion, as a public servant and a Democrat he supported the pro-choice position. In part because of his eloquence, Cuomo had assumed national prominence in the Democratic party and had been selected to deliver the keynote speech at the 1984 national convention.

The party's Vice Presidential nominee, Rep. Geraldine Ferraro, was also Catholic and held the same views as Cuomo, for the same reasons. Although there was little that the President or Vice President could do about abortion, it was an important symbolic issue. Ferraro's views attracted criticism from Catholics, even within her own congressional district. For example, a parish priest in Queens cancelled Ferraro's speaking engagement there because of her stance on abortion.

As the views of Ferraro and Cuomo, two prominent New York Catholic politicians, became linked, Catholic leaders began to criticize them both. Archbishop John O'Connor of New York asserted that he did not believe that a Catholic "in good conscience" could vote for a political candidate who either advocated abortion or advocated leaving the decision on abortion to the woman. O'Connor particularly complained that Cuomo favored using state Medicaid funds to pay for abortions. In response, the governor accused the archbishop of mixing politics and religion and breaking down the division between church and state. He had no responsibility, the governor insisted, for persuading his constituents to adopt his personal view. For the time being, O'Connor backed down, but Catholic criticism of Cuomo continued and the United States Catholic Conference issued a statement condemning him for his views.

Cuomo accepted an invitation to deliver the John A. O'Brien Lecture in the Department of Theology at the University of Notre Dame, as a forum to address the issue. He risked alienating his Catholic constituents if he directly opposed church teaching or challenged the authority of the church. On the other hand, he risked alienating non-Catholic constituents if he acknowledged the superior authority of the church over matters of public policy. The speech illustrates Cuomo's attempt to negotiate this difficult dilemma.

In general, the governor sought to distinguish between the moral and the political aspect of the issue. He stated that abortion was not a failure of government, since government did not force women to have abortions. He acknowledged that overtly political activity on the part of religious leaders was not proscribed, but he believed that most Americans found it somehow inappropriate. Consequently, his personal opposition to abortion did not require that he champion abortion restrictions as a matter of policy or law. Interestingly, he compared his own reticence to mix religion and politics with that of nineteenth-century Catholics who remained aloof from the battles over slavery.

The speech was widely praised, even among Catholic theologians. The fact that they might "agree to disagree" was considered a victory for Cuomo, since the teaching of the church presumably is subject to only one interpretation. But the issue has certainly not disappeared. The clash between "pro-life" and "pro-choice" groups also marked the 1988 election, and in 1990 O'Connor, having been elevated to cardinal, suggested that Catholic politicians who were not anti-abortion might be subject to excommunication. Although Cuomo's speech did not resolve the issue, it does illustrate the delicate position of a speaker who faces a fundamental moral choice and wishes to find a middle ground between extremes.

I would like to begin by drawing your attention to the title of this lecture: "Religious Belief and Public Morality: A Catholic Governor's Perspective." I was not invited to speak on "Church and State" generally. Certainly not "Mondale vs. Reagan." The subject assigned is difficult enough. I will try not to do more than I've been asked.

It's not easy to stay contained. Certainly, although everybody talks about a wall of separation between church and state, I've seen religious leaders scale that wall with all the dexterity of olympic athletes. In fact, I've seen so many candidates in churches and synagogues that I think we should change election day from Tuesdays to Saturdays and Sundays.

I am honored by this invitation, but the record shows that I am not the first Governor of New York to appear at an event involving Notre Dame. One of my great predecessors, Al Smith, went to the Army–Notre Dame football game each time it was played in New York.

His fellow Catholics expected Smith to sit with Notre Dame; protocol required him to sit with Army because it was the home team. Protocol prevailed. But not without Smith noting the dual demands on his affections. "I'll take my seat with Army," he said, "but I commend my soul to Notre Dame!"

Today I'm happy to have no such problem. Both my seat and my soul are with Notre Dame. And as long as Father McBrien doesn't invite me back to sit with him at the Notre Dame–St. John's basketball game, I'm confident my loyalties will remain undivided.

In a sense, it's a question of loyalty that Father McBrien has asked me here today to discuss. Specifically, must politics and religion in America divide our loyalties? Does the "separation between church and state" imply separation between religion and politics? Between morality and government? Are these different propositions? Even more specifically, what is the relationship of my Catholicism to my politics? Where does the one end and other begin? Or are the two divided at all? And if they're not, should they be?

Hard questions.

No wonder most of us in public life—at least until recently—preferred to stay away from them, heeding the biblical advice that if "hounded and pursued in one city," we should flee to another.

Now, however, I think that it is too late to flee. The questions are all around us, and answers are coming from every quarter. Some of them have been simplistic, most of them fragmentary, and a few, spoken with a purely political intent, demagogic.

There has been confusion and compounding of confusion, a blurring of the issue, entangling it in personalities and election strategies, instead of clarifying it for Catholics, as well as others.

Today I would like to try to help correct that.

I can offer you no final truths, complete and unchallengeable. But it's possible this one effort will provoke other efforts—both in support and contradiction of my position—that will help all of us understand our differences and perhaps even discover some basic agreement.

In the end, I'm convinced we will all benefit if suspicion is replaced by discussion, innuendo by dialogue; if the emphasis in our debate turns from a search for talismanic criteria and neat but simplistic answers to an honest—more intelligent—attempt at describing the role religion has in our public affairs, and the limits placed on that role.

And if we do it right—if we're not afraid of the truth even when the truth is complex—this debate, by clarification, can bring relief to untold numbers of confused—even anguished—Catholics, as well as to many others who want only to make our already great democracy even stronger than it is.

I believe the recent discussion in my own State has already produced some clearer definition. In early summer, newspaper accounts had created the impression in some quarters that official church spokespeople would ask Catholics to vote for or against specific candidates on the basis of their political position on the abortion issue. I was one of those given that impression. Thanks to the dialogue that ensued over the summer—only partially reported by the media—we learned that the impression was not accurate.

Confusion had presented an opportunity for clarification, and we seized it. Now all of us are saying one thing—in chorus—reiterating the statement of the National Conference of Catholic Bishops that they will not "take positions for or against political candidates" and that their stand on specific issues should not be perceived "as an expression of political partisanship."

Of course the bishops will teach—they must—more and more vigorously and more and more extensively. But they have said they will not use the power of their position, and the great respect it receives from all Catholics, to give an imprimatur to individual politicians or parties.

Not that they couldn't if they wished to—some religious leaders do; some are doing it at this very moment.

Not that it would be a sin if they did—God doesn't insist on political neutrality. But because it is the judgment of the bishops, and most of us Catholic lay people, that it is not wise for prelates and politicians to be tied too closely together.

I think that getting this consensus was an extraordinarily useful achievement.

Now, with some trepidation and after much prayer, I take up your gracious invitation to continue the dialogue in the hope that it will lead to still further clarification.

Let me begin this part of the effort by underscoring the obvious. I do not speak as a theologian; I do not have that competence. I do not speak as a philosopher; to suggest that I could, would be to set a new record for false pride. I don't presume to speak as a "good" person except in the ontological sense of that word. My principal credential is that I serve in a position that forces me to wrestle with the problems you've come here to study and debate.

I am by training a lawyer and by practice a politician. Both professions make me suspect in many quarters, including among some of my own co-religionists. Maybe there's no better illustration of the public perception of how politicians unite their faith and their profession than the story they tell in New York about "Fishhooks" McCarthy, a famous Democratic leader on the lower East Side, and right-hand man to Al Smith.

"Fishhooks," the story goes, was devout. So devout that every morning on his way to Tammany Hall to do his political work, he stopped into St. James Church on Oliver Street in downtown Manhattan, fell on his knees, and whispered the same simple prayer: "Oh, Lord, give me health and strength. We'll steal the rest."

"Fishhooks" notwithstanding, I speak here as a politician. And also as a Catholic, a lay person baptized and raised in the pre–Vatican II Church, educated in Catholic schools, attached to the Church first by birth, then by choice, now by love. An old-fashioned Catholic who sins, regrets, struggles, worries, gets confused and most of the time feels better after confession.

The Catholic Church is my spiritual home. My heart is there, and my hope.

There is, of course, more to being a Catholic than a sense of spiritual and emotional resonance. Catholicism is a religion of the head as well as the heart, and to be a Catholic is to say "I believe" to the essential core of dogmas that distinguishes our faith.

The acceptance of this faith requires a lifelong struggle to understand it more fully and to live it more truly, to translate truth into experience, to practice as well as to believe.

That's not easy: applying religious belief to everyday life often presents difficult challenges.

It's always been that way. It certainly is today. The America of the late twentieth century is a consumer society, filled with endless distractions, where faith is more often dismissed than challenged, where the ethnic and other loyalties that once fastened us to our religion seem to be weakening.

In addition to all the weaknesses, dilemmas and temptations that impede every pilgrim's progress, the Catholic who holds political office in a pluralistic democracy—who is elected to serve Jews and Muslims, atheists and Protestants, as well as Catholics—bears special responsibility. He or she undertakes to help create conditions under which all can live with a maximum of dignity and with a reasonable degree of freedom; where everyone who chooses may hold beliefs different from specifically Catholic ones—sometimes contradictory to them; where the laws protect people's right to divorce, to use birth control and even to choose abortion.

In fact, Catholic public officials take an oath to preserve the Constitution that guarantees this freedom. And they do so gladly. Not because they love what others do with their freedom, but because they realize that in guaranteeing freedom for all, they guarantee our right to be Catholics: our right to pray, to use the sacraments, to refuse birth control devices, to reject abortion, not to divorce and remarry if we believe it to be wrong.

The Catholic public official lives the political truth most Catholics through most of American history have accepted and insisted on: the truth that to assure our freedom we must allow others the same freedom, even if occasionally it produces conduct by them which we would hold to be sinful.

I protect my right to be a Catholic by preserving your right to believe as a Jew, a Protestant or non-believer, or as anything else you choose.

We know that the price of seeking to force our beliefs on others is that they might some day force theirs on us.

This freedom is the fundamental strength of our unique experiment in government. In the complex interplay of forces and considerations that go into the making of our laws and policies, its preservation must be a pervasive and dominant concern.

But insistence on freedom is easier to accept as a general proposition than in its applications to specific situations. There are other valid general principles firmly embedded in our Constitution, which, operating at the same time, create interesting and occasionally troubling problems. Thus, the same amendment of the Constitution that forbids the establishment of a State Church affirms my legal right to argue that my religious belief would serve well as an article of our universal public morality. I may use the prescribed processes of government—the legislative and executive and judicial processes—to convince my fellow citizens—Jews and Protestants and Buddhists and non-believers—that what I propose is as beneficial for them as I believe it is for me; that it is not just parochial or narrowly sectarian but fulfills a human desire for order, peace, justice, kindness, love, any of the values most of us agree are desirable even apart from their specific religious base or context.

I am free to argue for a governmental policy for a nuclear freeze not just to avoid sin but because I think my democracy should regard it as a desirable goal.

I can, if I wish, argue that the State should not fund the use of contraceptive devices not because the Pope demands it but because I think that the whole community—for the good of the whole community—should not sever sex from an openness to the creation of life.

And surely, I can, if so inclined, demand some kind of law against abortion not because my Bishops say it is wrong but because I think that the whole community, regardless of its religious beliefs, should agree on the importance of protecting life—including life in the womb, which is at the very least potentially human and should not be extinguished casually.

No law prevents us from advocating any of these things: I am free to do so.

So are the Bishops. And so is Reverend Falwell.

In fact, the Constitution guarantees my right to try. And theirs. And his.

But should I? Is it helpful? Is it essential to human dignity? Does it promote harmony and understanding? Or does it divide us so fundamentally that it threatens our ability to function as a pluralistic community?

When should I argue to make my religious value your morality? My rule of conduct your limitation?

What are the rules and policies that should influence the exercise of this right to argue and promote?

I believe I have a salvific mission as a Catholic. Does that mean I am in conscience required to do everything I can as Governor to translate all my religious values into the laws and regulations of the State of New York or the United States? Or be branded a hypocrite if I don't?

As a Catholic, I respect the teaching authority of the bishops.

But must I agree with everything in the bishops' pastoral letter on peace and fight to include it in party platforms?

And will I have to do the same for the forthcoming pastoral on economics even if I am an unrepentant supply sider?

Must I, having heard the Pope renew the Church's ban on birth control devices, veto the funding of contraceptive programs for non-Catholics or dissenting Catholics in my State? I accept the Church's teaching on abortion. Must I insist you do? By law? By denying you Medicaid funding? By a constitutional amendment? If so, which one? Would that be the best way to avoid abortions or to prevent them?

These are only some of the questions for Catholics. People with other religious beliefs face similar problems.

Let me try some answers.

Almost all Americans accept some religious values as a part of our public life. We are a religious people, many of us descended from ancestors who came here expressly to live their religious faith free from coercion or repression. But we are also a people of many religions, with no established church, who hold different beliefs on many matters.

Our public morality, then—the moral standards we maintain for everyone, not just the ones we insist on in our private lives—depends on a consensus view of right and wrong. The values derived from religious belief will not—and should not—be accepted as part of the public morality unless they are shared by the pluralistic community at large, by consensus.

That values happen to be religious values does not deny them acceptability as a part of this consensus. But it does not require their acceptability, either.

The agnostics who joined the civil rights struggle were not deterred because that crusade's values had been nurtured and sustained in black Christian churches. Those on the political left are not perturbed today by the religious basis of the clergy and lay people who join them in the protest against the arms race and hunger and exploitation.

The arguments start when religious values are

used to support positions which would impose on other people restrictions they find unacceptable. Some people do object to Catholic demands for an end to abortion, seeing it as a violation of the separation of church and state. And some others, while they have no compunction about invoking the authority of the Catholic bishops in regard to birth control and abortion, might reject out of hand their teaching on war and peace and social policy.

Ultimately, therefore, the question "whether or not we admit religious values into our public affairs" is too broad to yield a single answer. "Yes," we create our public morality through consensus and in this country that consensus reflects to some extent religious values of a great majority of Americans. But "no," all religiously based values don't have an *a priori* place in our public morality. The community must decide if what is being proposed would be better left to private discretion than public policy; whether it restricts freedoms, and if so to what end, to whose benefit; whether it will produce a good or bad result; whether overall it will help the community or merely divide it.

The right answers to these questions can be elusive. Some of the wrong answers, on the other hand, are quite clear. For example, there are those who say there is a simple answer to *all* these questions; they say that by history and practice of our people we were intended to be—and should be—a Christian country in law.

But where would that leave the non-believers? And whose Christianity would be law, yours or mine?

This "Christian nation" argument should concern—even frighten—two groups: non-Christians and thinking Christians.

I believe it does.

I think it's already apparent that a good part of this nation understands—if only instinctively—that anything which seems to suggest that God favors a political party or the establishment of a state church, is wrong and dangerous.

Way down deep the American people are afraid of an entangling relationship between formal religions—or whole bodies of religious belief—and government. Apart from constitutional law and religious doctrine, there is a sense that tells us it's wrong to presume to speak for God or to claim God's sanction of our particular legislation and His rejection of all other positions. Most of us are offended when we see religion being trivialized by its appearance in political throw-away pamphlets.

The American people need no course in philosophy or political science or church history to know that God should not be made into a celestial party chairman.

To most of us, the manipulative invoking of religion to advance a politician or a party is frightening and divisive. The American people will tolerate religious leaders taking positions for or against candidates, although I think the Catholic bishops are right in avoiding that position. But the American people are leery about large religious organizations, powerful churches or synagogue groups engaging in such activities—again, not as a matter of law or doctrine, but because our innate wisdom and democratic instinct teaches us these things are dangerous.

Today there are a number of issues involving life and death that raise questions of public morality. They are also questions of concern to most religions. Pick up a newspaper and you are almost certain to find a bitter controversy over any one of them; Baby Jane Doe, the right to die, artificial insemination, embryos in vitro, abortion, birth control ... not to mention nuclear war and the shadow it throws across all existence.

Some of these issues touch the most intimate recesses of our lives, our roles as someone's mother or child or husband; some affect women in a unique way. But they are also public questions, for all of us.

Put aside what God expects—assume if you like there is no God—then the greatest thing still left to us is life. Even a radically secular world must struggle with the questions of when life begins, under what circumstances it can be ended, when it must be protected, by what authority; it too must decide what protection to extend to the helpless and the dying, to the aged and the unborn, to life in all its phases.

As a Catholic, I have accepted certain answers as the right ones for myself and my family, and because I have, they have influenced me in special ways, as Matilda's husband, as a father of five children, as a son who stood next to his own father's death bed trying to decide if the tubes and needles no longer served a purpose.

As a Governor, however, I am involved in defining policies that determine *other* people's rights in these same areas of life and death. Abortion is one of these issues, and while it is one issue among many, it is one of the most controversial and affects me in a special way as a Catholic public official.

So let me spend some time considering it.

I should start, I believe, by noting that the Catholic Church's actions with respect to the interplay of religious values and public policy make clear that there is no inflexible moral principle which determines what our *political* conduct should be. For example, on divorce and birth control, without changing its moral teaching, the Church abides the civil law as it now stands, thereby accepting—without making much of a point of it—that in our pluralistic society we are not required to insist that *all* our religious values be the law of the land.

Abortion is treated differently.

Of course there are differences both in degree and quality between abortion and some of the other religious positions the Church takes: abortion is a "matter of life and death," and degree counts. But the differences in approach reveal a truth, I think, that is not well enough perceived by Catholics and therefore still further complicates the process for us. That is, while we always owe our bishops' words respectful attention and careful consideration, the question whether to engage the political system in a struggle to have it adopt certain articles of our belief as part of public morality, is not a matter of doctrine: it is a matter of prudential political judgment.

Recently, Michael Novak put it succinctly: "Religious judgment and political judgment are both needed," he wrote. "But they are not identical."

My church and my conscience require me to believe certain things about divorce, birth control and abortion. My church does not order me—under pain of sin or expulsion—to pursue my salvific mission according to a precisely defined political plan.

As a Catholic I accept the church's teaching authority. While in the past some Catholic theologians may appear to have disagreed on the morality of some abortions (it wasn't, I think, until 1869 that excommunication was attached to all abortions without distinction), and while some theologians still do, I accept the bishops' position that abortion is to be avoided.

As Catholics, my wife and I were enjoined never to use abortion to destroy the life we created, and we never have. We thought Church doctrine was clear on this, and—more than that—both of us felt it in full agreement with what our hearts and our consciences told us. For me life or fetal life in the womb should be protected, even if five of nine Justices of the Supreme Court and my neighbor disagree with me. A fetus is different from an appendix or a set of tonsils. At the very least, even if the argument is made by some scientists or some theologians that in the early stages of fetal development we can't discern human life, the full potential of human life is indisputably there. That—to my less subtle mind—by itself should demand respect, caution, indeed... reverence.

But not everyone in our society agrees with me and Matilda.

And those who don't—those who endorse legalized abortions—aren't a ruthless, callous alliance of anti-Christians determined to overthrow our moral standards. In many cases, the proponents of legal abortion are the very people who have worked with Catholics to realize the goals of social justice set out in papal encyclicals: the American Lutheran Church, the Central Conference of American Rabbis, the Presbyterian Church in the United States, B'nai B'rith Women, the Women of the Episcopal Church. These are just a few of the religious organizations that don't share the Church's position on abortion.

Certainly, we should not be forced to mold Catholic morality to conform to disagreement by non-Catholics however sincere or severe their disagreement. Our bishops should be teachers not pollsters. They should not change what we Catholics believe in order to ease our consciences or please our friends or protect the Church from criticism.

But if the breadth, intensity and sincerity of opposition to church teaching shouldn't be allowed to shape our Catholic morality, it can't help but determine our ability—our realistic, political ability—to translate our Catholic morality into civil law, a law not for the believers who don't need it but for the disbelievers who reject it.

And it is here, in our attempt to find a political answer to abortion—an answer beyond our private observance of Catholic morality—that we encounter controversy within and without the Church over how and in what degree to press the case that our morality should be everybody else's, and to what effect.

I repeat, there is no Church teaching that mandates the best political course for making our belief everyone's rule, for spreading this part of our Catholicism. There is neither an encyclical nor a catechism that spells out a political strategy for achieving legislative goals.

And so the Catholic trying to make moral and prudent judgments in the political realm must discern which, if any, of the actions one could take would be best.

This latitude of judgment is not something new in

the Church, not a development that has arisen only with the abortion issue. Take, for example, the question of slavery. It has been argued that the failure to endorse a legal ban on abortions is equivalent to refusing to support the cause of abolition before the Civil War. This analogy has been advanced by the bishops of my own state.

But the truth of the matter is, few if any Catholic bishops spoke for abolition in the years before the Civil War. It wasn't, I believe, that the bishops endorsed the idea of some humans owning and exploiting other humans; Pope Gregory XVI, in 1840, had condemned the slave trade. Instead it was a practical political judgment that the bishops made. They weren't hypocrites; they were realists. At the time, Catholics were a small minority, mostly immigrants, despised by much of the population, often vilified and the object of sporadic violence. In the face of a public controversy that aroused tremendous passions and threatened to break the country apart, the bishops made a pragmatic decision. They believed their opinion would not change people's minds. Moreover they knew that there were southern Catholics, even some priests, who owned slaves. They concluded that under the circumstances arguing for a constitutional amendment against slavery would do more harm than good, so they were silent. As they have been, generally, in recent years, on the question of birth control. And as the Church has been on even more controversial issues in the past, even ones that dealt with life and death.

What is relevant to this discussion is that the bishops were making judgments about translating Catholic teachings into public policy, not about the moral validity of the teachings. In so doing they grappled with the unique political complexities of their time. The decision they made to remain silent on a constitutional amendment to abolish slavery or on the repeal of the Fugitive Slave Law wasn't a mark of their moral indifference: it was a measured attempt to balance moral truths against political realities. Their decision reflected their sense of complexity, not their diffidence. As history reveals, Lincoln behaved with similar discretion.

The parallel I want to draw here is not between or among what we Catholics believe to be moral wrongs. It is in the Catholic response to those wrongs. Church teaching on slavery and abortion is clear. But in the application of those teachings—the exact way we translate them into action, the specific laws we propose, the exact legal sanctions we seek—there was and is no one, clear, absolute route that the Church says, as a matter of doctrine, we must follow.

The bishops' pastoral, "The Challenge of Peace," speaks directly to this point. "We recognize," the bishops wrote, "that the Church's teaching authority does not carry the same force when it deals with technical solutions involving particular means as it does when it speaks of principles or ends. People may agree in abhorring an injustice, for instance, yet sincerely disagree as to what practical approach will achieve justice. Religious groups are entitled as others to their opinion in such cases, but they should not claim that their opinions are the only ones that people of good will may hold."

With regard to abortion, the American bishops have had to weigh Catholic moral teaching against the fact of a pluralistic country where our view is in the minority, acknowledging that what is ideally desirable isn't always feasible, that there can be different political approaches to abortion besides unyielding adherence to an absolute prohibition.

This is in the American-Catholic tradition of political realism. In supporting or opposing specific legislation the Church in this country has never retreated into a moral fundamentalism that will settle for nothing less than total acceptance of its views.

Indeed, the bishops have already confronted the fact that an absolute ban on abortion doesn't have the support necessary to be placed in our Constitution. In 1981, they put aside earlier efforts to describe a law they could accept and get passed, and supported the Hatch Amendment instead.

Some Catholics felt the bishops had gone too far with that action, some not far enough. Such judgments were not a rejection of the bishops' teaching authority: the bishops even disagreed among themselves. Catholics are allowed to disagree on these technical political questions without having to confess.

Respectfully, and after careful consideration of the position and arguments of the bishops, I have concluded that the approach of a constitutional amendment is not the best way for us to seek to deal with abortion.

I believe that legal interdicting of abortion by either the federal government or the individual states is not a plausible possibility and even if it could be obtained, it wouldn't work. Given present attitudes, it would be "Prohibition" revisited, legislating what couldn't be enforced and in the process creating a disrespect for law in general. And as much as I admire the bishops' hope that a constitutional amendment against abortion would be the basis for a full, new bill of rights for mothers and children, I disagree that this would be the result.

I believe that, more likely, a constitutional prohibition would allow people to ignore the causes of many abortions instead of addressing them, much the way the death penalty is used to escape dealing more fundamentally and more rationally with the problem of violent crime.

Other legal options that have been proposed are, in my view, equally ineffective. The Hatch Amendment, by returning the question of abortion to the states, would have given us a checkerboard of permissive and restrictive jurisdictions. In some cases people might have been forced to go elsewhere to have abortions and that might have eased a few consciences but it wouldn't have done what the Church wants to do—it wouldn't have created a deep-seated respect for life. Abortions would have gone on, millions of them.

Nor would a denial of Medicaid funding for abortion achieve our objectives. Given *Roe v. Wade*, it would be nothing more than an attempt to do indirectly what the law says cannot be done directly; worse, it would do it in a way that would burden only the already disadvantaged. Removing funding from the Medicaid program would not prevent the rich and middle classes from having abortions. It would not even assure that the disadvantaged wouldn't have them; it would only impose financial burdens on poor women who want abortions.

Apart from that unevenness, there is a more basic question. Medicaid is designed to deal with health and medical needs. But the arguments for the cutoff of Medicaid abortion funds are not related to those needs. They are moral arguments. If we assume health and medical needs exist, our personal view of morality ought not to be considered a relevant basis for discrimination.

We must keep in mind always that we are a nation of laws—when we like those laws, and when we don't.

The Supreme Court has established a woman's constitutional right to abortion. The Congress has decided the federal government should not provide federal funding in the Medicaid program for abortion. That, of course, does not bind states in the allocation of their own state funds. Under the law, the individual states need not follow the federal lead, and in New York I believe we *cannot* follow that lead. The equal protection clause in New York's Constitution has been interpreted by the courts as a standard of fairness that would preclude us from denying only the poor—indirectly, by a cutoff of funds—the practical use of the constitutional right given by *Roe v. Wade*.

In the end, even if after a long and divisive struggle we were able to remove all Medicaid funding for abortion and restore the law to what it was—if we could put most abortions out of our sight, return them to the backrooms where they were performed for so long—I don't believe our responsibility as Catholics would be any closer to being fulfilled than it is now, with abortion guaranteed by the law as a woman's right.

The hard truth is that abortion isn't a failure of government. No agency or department of government forces women to have abortions, but abortion goes on. Catholics, the statistics show, support the right to abortion in equal proportion to the rest of the population. Despite the teaching in our homes and schools and pulpits, despite the sermons and pleadings of parents and priests and prelates, despite all the effort at defining our opposition to the sin of abortion, collectively we Catholics apparently believe—and perhaps act—little differently from those who don't share our commitment.

Are we asking government to make criminal what we believe to be sinful because we ourselves can't stop committing the sin?

The failure here is not Caesar's. This failure is our failure, the failure of the entire people of God.

Nobody has expressed this better than a bishop in my own state, Joseph Sullivan, a man who works with the poor in New York City, is resolutely opposed to abortion and argues, with his fellow bishops, for a change of law. "The major problem the Church has is internal," the Bishop said last month in reference to abortion. "How do we teach? As much as I think we're responsible for advocating public policy issues, our primary responsibility is to teach our own people. We haven't done that. We're asking politicians to do what we haven't done effectively ourselves."

I agree with the Bishop. I think our moral and social mission as Catholics must begin with the wisdom contained in the words "Physician, heal thyself." Unless we Catholics educate ourselves better to the values that define—and can ennoble—our lives, following those teachings better than we do now, unless we set an example that is clear and compelling, then we will never convince this society to change the civil laws to protect what we preach is precious human life.

Better than any law or rule or threat of punishment would be the moving strength of our own good example, demonstrating our lack of hypocrisy, proving the beauty and worth of our instruction.

We must work to find ways to avoid abortions without otherwise violating our faith. We should provide funds and opportunity for young women to bring their child to term, knowing both of them will be taken care of if that is necessary; we should teach our young men better than we do now their responsibilities in creating and caring for human life.

It is this duty of the Church to teach through its practice of love that Pope John Paul II has proclaimed so magnificently to all peoples. "The Church," he wrote in *Redemptor Hominis* (1979), "which has no weapons at her disposal apart from those of the spirit, of the word and of love, cannot renounce her proclamation of 'the word ... in season and out of season.' For this reason she does not cease to implore ... everybody in the name of God and in the name of man: Do not kill! Do not prepare destruction and extermination for each other! Think of your brothers and sisters who are suffering hunger and misery! Respect each one's dignity and freedom!"

The weapons of the word and of love are already available to us: we need no statute to provide them.

I am not implying that we should stand by and pretend indifference to whether a woman takes a pregnancy to its conclusion or aborts it. I believe we should in all cases try to teach a respect for life. And I believe with regard to abortion that, despite *Roe v. Wade*, we can, in practical ways. Here, in fact, it seems to me that all of us can agree.

Without lessening their insistence on a woman's right to an abortion, the people who call themselves "pro-choice" can support the development of government programs that present an impoverished mother with the full range of support she needs to bear and raise her children, to have a real choice. Without dropping their campaign to ban abortion, those who gather under the banner of "pro-life" can join in developing and enacting a legislative bill of rights for mothers and children, as the bishops have already proposed.

While we argue over abortion, the United States' infant mortality rate places us sixteenth among the nations of the world. Thousands of infants die each year because of inadequate medical care. Some are born with birth defects that, with proper treatment, could be prevented. Some are stunted in their physical and mental growth because of improper nutrition.

If we want to prove our regard for life in the womb, for the helpless infant—if we care about women having real choices in their lives and not being driven to abortions by a sense of helplessness and despair

about the future of their child—then there is work enough for all of us. Lifetimes of it.

In New York, we have put in place a number of programs to begin this work, assisting women in giving birth to healthy babies. This year we doubled Medicaid funding to private-care physicians for prenatal and delivery services.

The state already spends 20 million dollars a year for prenatal care in out-patient clinics and for in-patient hospital care.

One program in particular we believe holds a great deal of promise. It's called "new avenues to dignity," and it seeks to provide a teenage mother with the special service she needs to continue with her education, to train for a job, to become capable of standing on her own, to provide for herself and the child she is bringing into the world.

My dissent, then, from the contention that we can have effective and enforceable legal prohibitions on abortion is by no means an argument for religious quietism, for accepting the world's wrongs because that is our fate as "the poor banished children of Eve."

Let me make another point.

Abortion has a unique significance but not a preemptive significance.

Apart from the question of the efficacy of using legal weapons to make people stop having abortions, we know our Christian responsibility doesn't end with any one law or amendment. That it doesn't end with abortion. Because it involves life and death, abortion will always be a central concern of Catholics. But so will nuclear weapons. And hunger and homelessness and joblessness, all the forces diminishing human life and threatening to destroy it. The "seamless garment" that Cardinal Bernardin has spoken of is a challenge to all Catholics in public office, conservatives as well as liberals.

We cannot justify our aspiration to goodness simply on the basis of the vigor of our demand for an elusive and questionable civil law declaring what we already know, that abortion is wrong.

Approval or rejection of legal restrictions on abortion should not be the exclusive litmus test of Catholic loyalty. We should understand that whether abortion is outlawed or not, our work has barely begun: the work of creating a society where the right to life doesn't end at the moment of birth; where an infant isn't helped into a world that doesn't care if it's fed properly, housed decently, educated adequately; where the blind or retarded child isn't condemned to exist rather than empowered to live.

The bishops stated this duty clearly in 1974, in their statement to the Senate Sub-Committee considering a proposed amendment to restrict abortions. They maintained such an amendment could not be seen as an end in itself. "We do not see a constitutional amendment as the final product of our commitment or of our legislative activity," they said. "It is instead the constitutional base on which to provide support and assistance to pregnant women and their unborn children. This would include nutritional, prenatal, child birth and postnatal care for the mother, and also nutritional and pediatric care for the child through the first year of life.... We believe that all of these should be available as a matter of right to all pregnant women and their children."

The bishops reaffirmed that view in 1976, in 1980, and again this year when the United States Catholic Committee asked Catholics to judge candidates on a wide range of issues—on abortion, yes; but also on food policy, the arms race, human rights, education, social justice and military expenditures.

The bishops have been consistently "pro-life" in the full meaning of that term, and I respect them for that.

The problems created by the matter of abortion are complex and confounding. Nothing is clearer to me than my inadequacy to find compelling solutions to all of their moral, legal and social implications. I—and many others like me—are eager for enlightenment, eager to learn new and better ways to manifest respect for the deep reverence for life that is our religion and our instinct. I hope that this public attempt to describe the problems as I understand them will give impetus to the dialogue in the Catholic community and beyond, a dialogue which could show me a better wisdom than I've been able to find so far.

It would be tragic if we let that dialogue become a prolonged, divisive argument that destroys or impairs our ability to practice any part of the morality given us in the Sermon on the Mount, to touch, heal and affirm the human life that surrounds us.

We Catholic citizens of the richest, most powerful nation that has ever existed are like the steward made responsible over a great household: from those to whom so much has been given, much shall be required. It is worth repeating that ours is not a faith that encourages its believers to stand apart from the world, seeking their salvation alone, separate from the salvation of those around them.

We speak of ourselves as a body. We come together in worship as companions, in the ancient sense of that word, those who break bread together, and who are obliged by the commitment we share to help one another, everywhere, in all we do, and in the process, to help the whole human family. We see our mission to be "the completion of the work of creation."

This is difficult work today. It presents us with many hard choices.

The Catholic Church has come of age in America. The ghetto walls are gone, our religion no longer a badge of irredeemable foreignness. This new-found status is both an opportunity and a temptation. If we choose, we can give in to the temptation to become more and more assimilated into a larger, blander culture, abandoning the practice of the specific values that made us different, worshipping whatever gods the marketplace has to sell while we seek to rationalize our own laxity by urging the political system to legislate on others a morality we no longer practice ourselves.

Or we can remember where we come from, the journey of two millennia, clinging to our personal faith, to its insistence on constancy and service and on hope. We can live and practice the morality Christ gave us, maintaining His truth in this world, struggling to embody His love, practicing it especially where that love is most needed, among the poor and the weak and the dispossessed. Not just by trying to make laws for others to live by, but by living the laws already written for us by God, in our hearts and in our minds.

We can be fully Catholic; proudly, totally at ease with ourselves, a people in the world, transforming it, a light to this nation. Appealing to the best in our people not the worst. Persuading not coercing. Leading people to truth by love. And still, all the while, respecting and enjoying our unique pluralistic democracy. And we can do it even as politicians.

The Politics of the Eighties

—Ronald Reagan—

Acceptance of the Republican Nomination for President
(July 17, 1980)

As he approached the 1980 election campaign, President Carter confronted several political problems. The energy shortage of the summer of 1979, characterized especially by long lines at gasoline stations, was unsettling. Carter's explanation, in the "crisis of confidence" speech, that the public's lack of moral fortitude somehow was the root cause, left many angry and confused. Even more serious was the fact that economic conditions had worsened since Carter took office. The interest rate rose to 13 percent in February 1980 and then to 16 percent in March. Between April 1979 and April 1980 the consumer price index meanwhile rose by 18 percent. These numbers were especially damning for the President, because during his 1976 campaign he had coined the term *misery index* for the sum of the inflation and unemployment rates; his own index was worse than that of Gerald Ford four years earlier.

Carter seemed to offer little hope in responding to these problems. His State of the Union message proclaimed that restraining inflation would be his top domestic priority, but he thought that the solution would require federal budget cuts that would be unsettling. In March he announced an anti-inflation program that would require "pain" and "discipline." A national poll found that fears about the economy, especially rising unemployment, were seriously undermining confidence in the President; in June only 18 percent of its sample approved of Carter's handling of the economy whereas 74 percent indicated disapproval.

The same weakening of confidence in President Carter could be seen in the international sphere. After the takeover of the American embassy in Tehran in November 1979, there had been an initial outpouring of support for the President. As the hostage crisis wore on without a solution, that support eroded—especially after April 1980, when Carter authorized and then, because of equipment failure, aborted a military attempt to free the hostages. This rescue mission was perceived as a bungled effort. Likewise, an American vote in the United Nations to rebuke Israel for expanding settlements in occupied territories, later disavowed as a mistake, suggested lack of effective control at the helm.

Adding to the Democrats' woes was the increasingly conservative mood of the country, evidenced by the growing promise of such causes as a constitutional amendment to restore prayers in schools, a strong defense, opposition to abortion, and opposition to the Equal Rights Amendment. In the economic sphere, the prevailing wisdom was challenged by a theory of "supply side economics" that was touted especially by conservative Republicans. This theory held that the economy could be revived by cutting business taxes and providing subsidies for business investment and subsidies to spur industrial productivity, which in turn would produce enough economic growth to restore the tax revenue lost by the cuts. Finally, although President Carter was assured of renomination, the Democratic party was badly divided as a result of the challenge presented by the strong campaign of Sen. Edward M. Kennedy.

The Republicans were divided too. Although by May the field had been narrowed to Ronald Reagan and George Bush, there had been several contenders for the nomination. One of them, John Anderson, Republican congressman from Illinois, had announced his intention to run as an independent, and there were fears that he would siphon enough votes from liberal and moderate Republicans that Carter would be re-elected. Many thought Reagan too old, or too conservative, to have a chance at winning in November.

But the Republican nomination was Reagan's. He had sought it for some time, making a late entry into the race in 1968 and then mounting a formidable challenge to Gerald Ford in 1976. His political career began with his election as governor of California in 1966, following many years as a movie actor, and his strong conservatism and anticommunism have changed little since then.

Reagan used his acceptance speech for the traditional purposes of reuniting the party and inspiring the faithful to make every possible effort for the campaign. But he also tried to reorient the party toward traditional values and to renew such standard Republican issues as smaller government, stronger defense, and more latitude for business. In a reversal of the political landscape of the New Deal, he sought to portray his values as the dominant values of Americans, and to criticize the Democrats as representing special interests. The speech is organized around key words that name Reagan's fundamental values. It closes with a silent prayer as a way to advocate the issue of prayer in schools. Responding directly to the charge that the American people were beset by a "malaise," Reagan called for Americans to "recapture our destiny" and to "renew the American spirit and sense of purpose."

Reagan's acceptance speech foreshadowed the appeals that would characterize his campaign. For his part, President Carter stressed his own experience and Reagan's naïveté and potential dangerousness. The race appeared to be fairly close until the last week. Following their single Presidential debate and the realization that no progress had been made in freeing the American hostages in Iran, Reagan surged ahead. He won in a landslide, carrying all but five states and the District of Columbia.

Thank you very much. We're using up prime time. Thank you very much. You're singing our song. Well, the first thrill tonight was to find myself for the first time in a long time in a movie on prime time.

But this, as you can imagine, is the second big thrill.

Mr. Chairman, Mr. Vice-President-to-be, this convention, my fellow citizens of this great nation:

With a deep awareness of the responsibility conferred by your trust, I accept your nomination for the Presidency of the United States. I do so with deep gratitude. And I think also I might interject on behalf of all of us our thanks to Detroit and the people of Michigan and to this city for the warm hospitality we've enjoyed.

And I thank you for your wholehearted response

to my recommendation in regard to George Bush as the candidate for Vice President.

I'm very proud of our party tonight. This convention has shown to all America a party united, with positive programs for solving the nation's problems, a party ready to build a new consensus with all those across the land who share a community of values embodied in these words: family, work, neighborhood, peace and freedom.

Now I know we've had a quarrel or two but only as to the method of attaining a goal. There was no argument here about the goal. As President, I will establish a liaison with the 50 Governors to encourage them to eliminate, wherever it exists, discrimination against women. I will monitor Federal laws to insure their implementation and to add statutes if they are needed.

More than anything else, I want my candidacy to unify our country, to renew the American spirit and sense of purpose. I want to carry our message to every American, regardless of party affiliation, who is a member of this community of shared values.

Never before in our history have Americans been called upon to face three grave threats to our very existence, any one of which could destroy us. We face a disintegrating economy, a weakened defense and an energy policy based on the sharing of scarcity.

The major issue in this campaign is the direct political, personal, and moral responsibility of Democratic Party leadership—in the White House and in the Congress—for this unprecedented calamity which has befallen us. They tell us they've done the most that humanly could be done. They say that the United States has had its day in the sun, that our nation has passed its zenith. They expect you to tell your children that the American people no longer have the will to cope with their problems; that the future will be one of sacrifice and few opportunities.

My fellow citizens, I utterly reject that view. The American people, the most generous on earth, who created the highest standard of living, are not going to accept the notion that we can only make a better world for others by moving backward ourselves. And those who believe we can have no business leading this nation.

I will not stand by and watch this great country destroy itself under mediocre leadership that drifts from one crisis to the next, eroding our national will and purpose. We have come together here because the American people deserve better from those to whom they entrust our nation's highest offices, and we stand united in our resolve to do something about it.

We need a rebirth of the American tradition of leadership at every level of government and in private life as well. The United States of America is unique in world history because it has a genius for leaders—many leaders—on many levels.

But back in 1976, Mr. Carter said, "Trust me." And a lot of people did. And now, many of those people are out of work. Many have seen their savings eaten away by inflation. Many others on fixed incomes, especially the elderly, have watched helplessly as the cruel tax of inflation wasted away their purchasing power. And, today, a great many who trusted Mr. Carter wonder if we can survive the Carter policies of national defense.

"Trust me" government asks that we concentrate our hopes and dreams on one man; that we trust him to do what's best for us. But my view of government places trust not in one person or one party, but in those values that transcend persons and parties. The trust is where it belongs—in the people. The responsibility to live up to that trust is where it belongs, in their elected leaders. That kind of relationship, between the people and their elected leaders, is a special kind of compact.

Three-hundred-and-sixty years ago, in 1620, a group of families dared to cross a mighty ocean to build a future for themselves in a new world. When they arrived at Plymouth, Massachusetts, they formed what they called a "compact," an agreement among themselves to build a community and abide by its laws.

This single act—the voluntary binding together of free people to live under the law—set the pattern for what was to come.

A century and a half later, the descendants of those people pledged their lives, their fortunes, and their sacred honor to found this nation. Some forfeited their fortunes and their lives; none sacrificed honor.

Four score and seven years later, Abraham Lincoln called upon the people of all America to renew their dedication and their commitment to a government of, for and by the people.

Isn't it once again time to renew our compact of freedom; to pledge to each other all that is best in our lives; all that gives meaning to them—for the sake of this, our beloved and blessed land?

Together, let us make this a new beginning. Let us make a commitment to care for the needy; to teach our children the values handed down to us by our families; to have the courage to defend those values and virtues and the willingness to sacrifice for them.

Let us pledge to restore, in our time, the American spirit of voluntary service, of cooperation, of private and community initiative; a spirit that flows like a deep and mighty river through the history of our nation.

As your nominee, I pledge to you to restore to the Federal Government the capacity to do the people's work without dominating their lives. I pledge to you a Government that will not only work well but wisely, its ability to act tempered by prudence, and its willingness to do good balanced by the knowledge that government is never more dangerous than when our desire to have it help us blinds us to its great power to harm us.

You know, the first Republican President once said, "While the people retain their virtue and their vigilance, no Administration by any extreme of wickedness or folly can seriously injure the Government in the short space of four years."

If Mr. Lincoln could see what's happened in these last three and a half years, he might hedge a little on that statement. But with the virtues that are our legacy as a free people and with the vigilance that sustains liberty, we still have time to use our renewed compact to overcome the injuries that have been done to America these past three and a half years.

First, we must overcome something the present Administration has cooked up: a new and altogether indigestible economic stew, one part inflation, one part high unemployment, one part recession, one part runaway taxes, one part deficit spending seasoned with an energy crisis. It's an economic stew that has turned the national stomach.

Ours are not problems of abstract economic theory. These are problems of flesh and blood; problems that cause pain and destroy the moral fiber of real people who should not suffer the further indignity of being told by the Government that it is all somehow their fault. We do not have inflation because—as Mr. Carter says—we've lived too well.

The head of a Government which has utterly refused to live within its means and which has, in the last few days, told us that this coming year's deficit will be $60 billion, dares to point the finger of blame at business and labor, both of which have been engaged in a losing struggle just trying to stay even.

High taxes, we are told, are somehow good for us, as if, when government spends our money it isn't inflationary, but when we spend it, it is.

Those who preside over the worst energy shortage in our history tell us to use less so that we will run out of oil, gasoline and natural gas a little more slowly. Well, now, conservation is desirable, of course, but we must not waste energy. But conservation is not the sole answer to our energy needs.

America must get to work producing more energy. The Republican program for solving economic problems is based on growth and productivity.

Large amounts of oil and natural gas lay beneath our land and off our shores, untouched because the present Administration seems to believe the American people would rather see more regulation, more taxes and more controls than more energy.

Coal offers a great potential. So does nuclear energy, produced under rigorous safety standards. It could supply electricity for thousands of industries and millions of jobs and homes. It must not be thwarted by a tiny minority opposed to economic growth which often finds friendly ears in regulatory agencies for its obstructionist campaigns.

Now make no mistake. We will not permit the safety of our people or our environmental heritage to be jeopardized, but we are going to reaffirm that the economic prosperity of our people is a fundamental part of our environment.

Our problems are both acute and chronic, yet all we hear from those in positions of leadership are the same tired proposals for more Government tinkering, more meddling and more control—all of which led us to this sorry state in the first place.

Can anyone look at the record of this Administration and say, "Well done"? Can anyone compare the state of our economy when the Carter Administration took office with where we are today and say, "Keep up the good work"? Can anyone look at our reduced standing in the world today and say, "Let's have four more years of this"?

I believe the American people are going to answer these questions, as you've answered them, in the first week of November and their answer will be, "No—we've had enough." And then it will be up to us—beginning next January 20—to offer an Administration and Congressional leadership of competence and more than a little courage.

We must have the clarity of vision to see the difference between what is essential and what is merely desirable; and then the courage to bring our Government back under control.

It is essential that we maintain both the forward momentum of economic growth and the strength of the safety net between those in our society who need help. We also believe it is essential that the integrity of all aspects of Social Security be preserved.

Beyond these essentials, I believe it is clear our Federal Government is overgrown and overweight. Indeed, it is time our Government should go on a diet. Therefore, my first act as chief executive will be to impose an immediate and thorough freeze on Federal hiring. Then, we are going to enlist the very best minds from business, labor and whatever quarter to conduct a detailed review of every department, bureau and agency that lives by Federal appropriation.

And we are also going to enlist the help and ideas of many dedicated and hard-working Government employees at all levels who want a more efficient Government just as much as the rest of us do. I know that many of them are demoralized by the confusion and waste they confront in their work as a result of failed and failing policies.

Our instructions to the groups we enlist will be simple and direct. We will remind them that Government programs exist at the sufferance of the American taxpayer and are paid for with money earned by working men and women and programs that represent a waste of their money—a theft from their pocketbooks—must have that waste eliminated or that program must go. It must go by Executive Order where possible, by Congressional action where necessary.

Everything that can be run more effectively by state and local government we shall turn over to state and local government, along with the funding sources to pay for it. We are going to put an end to the money merry-go-round where our money becomes Washington's money, to be spent by states and cities exactly the way the Federal bureaucrats tell us it has to be spent.

I will not accept the excuse that the Federal Government has grown so big and powerful that it is beyond the control of any President, any administration or Congress. We are going to put an end to the notion that the American taxpayer exists to fund the Federal Government. The Federal Government exists to serve the American people and to be accountable to the American people. On January 20, we are going to reestablish that truth.

Also on that date we are going to initiate action to get substantial relief for our taxpaying citizens and action to put people back to work. None of this will be based on any new form of monetary tinkering or fiscal sleight-of-hand. We will simply apply to government the common sense that we all use in our daily lives.

Work and family are at the center of our lives, the foundation of our dignity as a free people. When we deprive people of what they have earned, or take away their jobs, we destroy their dignity and undermine their families. We can't support families unless there are jobs; and we can't have jobs unless the people have both money to invest and the faith to invest it.

These are concepts that stem from an economic system that for more than 200 years has helped us master a continent, create a previously undreamed-of prosperity for our people and has fed millions of others around the globe and that system will continue to serve us in the future if our Government will stop ignoring the basic values on which it was built and stop betraying the trust and good will of the American workers who keep it going.

The American people are carrying the heaviest peacetime tax burden in our nation's history—and it will grow even heavier, under present law, next January. We are taxing ourselves into economic exhaustion and stagnation, crushing our ability and incentive to save, invest and produce.

This must stop. We must halt this fiscal self-destruction and restore sanity to our economic system.

I've long advocated a 30 percent reduction in income tax rates over a period of three years. This phased tax reduction would begin with a 10 percent "down payment" tax cut in 1981, which the Republicans in Congress and I have already proposed.

A phased reduction of tax rates would go a long way toward easing the heavy burden on the American people. But we shouldn't stop there.

Within the context of economic conditions and appropriate budget priorities during each fiscal year of my Presidency, I would strive to go further. This would include improvement in business depreciation taxes so we can stimulate investment in order to get plants and equipment replaced, put more Americans back to work and put our nation back on the road to being competitive in world commerce. We will also work to reduce the cost of government as a percentage of our gross national product.

The first task of national leadership is to set realistic and honest priorities in our policies and our budget, and I pledge that my administration will do that.

When I talk of tax cuts, I am reminded that every major tax cut in this century has strengthened the economy, generated renewed productivity and ended up yielding new revenues for the Government by creating new investment, new jobs and more commerce among our people.

The present Administration has been forced by the Republicans to play follow-the-leader with regard to a tax cut. But in this election year we must take with the proverbial "grain of salt" any tax cut proposed by those who have already given us the greatest tax increase in our nation's history.

When those in leadership give us tax increases and tell us we must also do with less, have they thought about those who've always had less—especially the minorities? This is like telling them that just as they step on the first rung of the ladder of opportunity, the ladder is being pulled out from under them. That may be the Democratic leadership's message to the minorities, but it won't be our message. Ours, ours will be: We have to move ahead, but we're not going to leave anyone behind.

Thanks to the economic policies of the Democratic Party, millions of Americans find themselves out of work. Millions more have never even had a fair chance to learn new skills, hold a decent job or secure for themselves and their families a share in the prosperity of this nation.

It's time to put America back to work, to make our cities and towns resound with the confident voices of men and women of all races, nationalities and faiths bringing home to their families a paycheck they can cash for honest money.

For those without skills, we'll find a way to help them get new skills.

For those without job opportunities we'll stimulate new opportunities, particularly in the inner cities where they live.

For those who've abandoned hope, we'll restore hope and we'll welcome them into a great national crusade to make America great again.

When we move from domestic affairs, and cast our eyes abroad, we see an equally sorry chapter in the record of the present Administration:

—A Soviet combat brigade trains in Cuba, just 90 miles from our shores.

—A Soviet army of invasion occupies Afghanistan, further threatening our vital interests in the Middle East.

—America's defense strength is at its lowest ebb in a generation, while the Soviet Union is vastly outspending us in both strategic and conventional arms.

—Our European allies, looking nervously at the growing menace from the East, turn to us for leadership and fail to find it.

—And incredibly, more than 50, as you've been told from this platform so eloquently already, more than 50 of our fellow Americans have been held captive for over eight years—eight months—by a dictatorial foreign power that holds us up to ridicule before the world.

Adversaries large and small test our will and seek to confound our resolve, but we are given weakness when we need strength; vacillation when the times demand firmness.

The Carter Administration lives in the world of make-believe. Every day, drawing up a response to that day's problems, troubles, regardless of what happened yesterday and what'll happen tomorrow.

But you and I live in a real world, where disasters are overtaking our nation without any real response from Washington.

This is make-believe, self-deceit and, above all, transparent hypocrisy.

For example, Mr. Carter says he supports the volunteer Army, but he lets military pay and benefits slip so low that many of our enlisted personnel are actually eligible for food stamps. Re-enlistment rates drop and, just recently, after he fought all week against a proposed pay increase for our men and women in the military, he then helicoptered out to our carrier the U.S.S. *Nimitz*, which was returning from long months of duty in the Indian Ocean, and told the crew of that ship that he advocated better pay for them and their comrades. Where does he really stand, now that he's back on shore?

Well, I'll tell you where I stand. I do not favor a peacetime draft or registration, but I do favor pay and benefit levels that will attract and keep highly motivated men and women in our volunteer forces and back them up with an active reserve trained and ready for instant call in case of emergency.

You know, there may be a sailor at the helm of the ship of state, but the ship has no rudder. Critical decisions are made at times almost in comic fashion, but who can laugh?

Who was not embarrassed when the Administration handed a major propaganda victory in the United Nations to the enemies of Israel, our staunch Middle East ally for three decades, and then claimed that the American vote was a "mistake," a "failure of communication" between the President, his Secretary of State and the U.N. Ambassador?

Who does not feel a growing sense of unease as

our allies, facing repeated instances of an amateurish and confused Administration, reluctantly conclude that America is unwilling or unable to fulfill its obligations as leader of the free world?

Who does not feel rising alarm when the question in any discussion of foreign policy is no longer, "Should we do something?" but "Do we have the capacity to do anything?"

The Administration which has brought us to this state is seeking your endorsement for four more years of weakness, indecision, mediocrity, and incompetence. No. No. No American should vote until he or she has asked: Is the United States stronger and more respected now than it was three-and-a-half years ago? Is the world safer, a safer place in which to live?

It is the responsibility of the President of the United States, in working for peace, to insure that the safety of our people cannot successfully be threatened by a hostile foreign power. As President, fulfilling that responsibility will be my No. 1 priority.

We're not a warlike people. Quite the opposite. We always seek to live in peace. We resort to force infrequently and with great reluctance—and only after we've determined that it is absolutely necessary. We are awed—and rightly so—by the forces of destruction at loose in the world in this nuclear era.

But neither can we be naive or foolish. Four times in my lifetime America has gone to war, bleeding the lives of its young men into the sands of island beachheads, the fields of Europe and the jungles and rice paddies of Asia. We know only too well that war comes not when the forces of freedom are strong, it is when they are weak that tyrants are tempted.

We simply cannot learn these lessons the hard way again without risking our destruction.

Of all the objectives we seek, first and foremost is the establishment of lasting world peace. We must always stand ready to negotiate in good faith, ready to pursue any reasonable avenue that holds forth the promise of lessening tensions and furthering the prospects of peace. But let our friends and those who may wish us ill take note: the United States has an obligation to its citizens and to the people of the world never to let those who would destroy freedom dictate the future course of life on this planet. I would regard my election as proof that we have renewed our resolve to preserve world peace and freedom. That this nation will once again be strong enough to do that.

Now this evening marks the last step, save one, of a campaign that has taken Nancy and me from one end

of this great nation to the other, over many months and thousands and thousands of miles. There are those who question the way we choose a President, who say that our process imposes difficult and exhausting burdens on those who seek the office. I have not found it so.

It is impossible to capture in words the splendor of this vast continent which God has granted as our portion of His creation. There are no words to express the extraordinary strength and character of this breed of people we call Americans.

Everywhere we've met thousands of Democrats, Independents and Republicans from all economic conditions, walks of life bound together in that community of shared values of family, work, neighborhood, peace and freedom. They are concerned, yes, they're not frightened. They're disturbed, but not dismayed. They are the kind of men and women Tom Paine had in mind when he wrote, during the darkest days of the American Revolution, "We have it in our power to begin the world over again."

Nearly 150 years after Tom Paine wrote those words, an American President told the generation of the Great Depression that it had a "rendezvous with destiny." I believe this generation of Americans today also has a rendezvous with destiny.

Tonight, let us dedicate ourselves to renewing the American compact. I ask you not simply to "trust me," but to trust your values—our values—and to hold me responsible for living up to them. I ask you to trust that American spirit which knows no ethnic, religious, social, political, regional or economic boundaries; the spirit that burned with zeal in the hearts of millions of immigrants from every corner of the earth who came here in search of freedom.

Some say that spirit no longer exists. But I've seen it—I've felt it—all across the land, in the big cities, the small towns and in rural America. It's still there, ready to blaze into life if you and I are willing to do what has to be done; we have to do the practical things, the down-to-earth things, such as creating policies that will stimulate our economy, increase productivity and put America back to work.

The time is now to limit Federal spending; to insist on a stable monetary reform and to free ourselves from imported oil.

The time is now to resolve that the basis of a firm and principled foreign policy is one that takes the world as it is and seeks to change it by leadership and example, not by harangue, harassment or wishful thinking.

The time is now to say that we shall seek new friendships and expand others and improve others, but we shall not do so by breaking our word or casting aside old friends and allies.

And the time is now to redeem promises once made to the American people, by another candidate, in another time and another place. He said:

"For three long years I have been going up and down this country preaching that government—Federal, state and local—costs too much. I shall not stop that preaching. As an immediate program of action, we must abolish useless offices. We must eliminate unnecessary functions of government.

"We must consolidate subdivisions of government and, like the private citizen, give up luxuries which we can no longer afford." And then he said:

"I propose to you, my friends, and through you, that government of all kinds, big and little, be made solvent and that the example be set by the President of the United States and his Cabinet."

That was Franklin Delano Roosevelt's words as he accepted the Democratic nomination for President in 1932.

The time is now, my fellow Americans, to recapture our destiny, to take it into our own hands. And to do this it will take many of us, working together. I ask you tonight, all over this land, to volunteer your help in this cause so that we can carry our message throughout the land.

Isn't it time that we, the people, carry out these unkept promises? That we pledge to each other and to all America on this July day 48 years later, that now we intend to do just that.

I have thought of something that's not a part of my speech and worried over whether I should do it. Can we doubt that only a Divine Providence placed this land, this island of freedom, here as a refuge for all those people in the world who yearn to breathe free? Jews and Christians enduring persecution behind the Iron Curtain; the boat people of Southeast Asia, Cuba, and of Haiti; the victims of drought and famine in Africa, the freedom fighters of Afghanistan, and our own countrymen held in savage captivity.

I'll confess that I've been a little afraid to suggest what I'm going to suggest. I'm more afraid not to. Can we begin our crusade joined together in a moment of silent prayer?

God bless America.

Thank you.

Ronald Reagan

National Security
(March 23, 1983)

In campaigning for the Presidency in 1980, Ronald Reagan had stressed the need to strengthen America's defenses and to increase the defense budget. Substantial increases were proposed each year, even though Congress had also granted his request for tax reductions and even though he was active in seeking to limit or cut spending on many domestic programs. Many in Congress objected to the continuing military buildup. In the spring of 1983, the President's budget request for the next fiscal year was still before Congress, embroiled in controversy.

In March, Reagan delivered an address to the nation in an attempt to rally support for his military budget proposals. He called for a change in the underlying theory of American nuclear defense and offered the prospect that the spending required for this Strategic Defense Initiative would help to ensure peace. Since the early 1960's, American policy had been based on the theory of "mutually assured destruction." According to this theory, nuclear attack by the Soviet Union was deterred by the knowledge that the United States even after attack would have sufficient nuclear strength to retaliate and destroy the Soviet Union. Soviet strategists were thought to believe that the same knowledge on the American side deterred the United States from launching a nuclear strike. Sometimes characterized as a "balance of terror," this mutual capacity for destruction ironically served to keep the peace.

In proposing to change this strategy, Reagan reopened a debate from the late 1960's and early 1970's on the creation of antiballistic missile systems. Reagan's Strategic Defense Initiative involved developing aerospace technology to destroy ballistic missiles after they have been launched and before they reach their targets, thereby saving millions of lives in the event of a nuclear attack. As Reagan saw it, such a system would both strengthen American military security and make the world safer. It would render the United States relatively invulnerable to Soviet attack, and by developing a shield against nuclear weapons it would render them obsolete. Although the development of this system was a new step in the arms race, Reagan saw it as clearly defensive rather than offensive.

Reagan made the decision to develop the Strategic Defense Initiative with relatively little consultation within the government. He was influenced by a presentation by the Heritage Foundation, a conservative organization, advocating the use of directed-energy and computer technology to develop a defense against ballistic missiles. Edward Teller, the inventor of the hydrogen bomb, urged Reagan to pursue this military strategy.

The speech proved to be highly controversial. Many scientific experts argued that the technology that Reagan assumed was in fact unachievable, and that the chances of intercepting a ballistic missile in midflight were very small. Other scientists argued that the system, if deployed, would damage many of the satellites in orbit around the earth. Some diplomats and politicians argued that the program would violate the Anti-Ballistic Missile Treaty with the Soviet Union, according to which only two antiballistic missile defense systems were permitted each country—one for its capital and one for another location of its choice. Perhaps the most serious objection was the charge that by abandoning the theory of mutually assured destruction, the United States would be destabilizing world peace. If the Strategic Defense Initiative worked, the United States would no longer be vulnerable to Soviet nuclear retaliation, and therefore might launch a nuclear attack against the Soviet Union. Recognizing this fact, the Soviet Union would be more likely to make a pre-emptive nuclear strike while the system was still under construction. Reagan had offered to share the technology with the Soviet Union once the United States had developed the system, but even if this offer were genuine, there still would be a margin of Soviet vulnerability in the interim.

Both this speech and the Strategic Defense Initiative soon became known not by their formal title but as "Star Wars," a reference to a popular science fiction movie of the time. Democratic senator Daniel K. Inouye bestowed this label on the program, charging in his response to Reagan's speech that the President was using a "Star Wars scenario" to arouse fear of the Soviet Union among the American people in order to distract them from the failure of the administration's economic program. Even House Republican leader Robert Michel criticized the speech for conveying a "rather macho image" and suggested that Reagan's efforts to convince Congress to approve his military budget were not succeeding. Conservatives generally supported the President for casting aside the "unilateral" limitations of the antiballistic missile treaty, whereas liberals saw the Strategic Defense Initiative as unnecessary, unworkable, and provocative.

Reagan continued to advocate SDI. The initial research and development expenditures were relatively small, and Congress appropriated at least some of the funds requested without ever committing itself to the full-scale development of the system. In 1984, Democratic Presidential candidate Walter Mondale chastised Reagan for taking nuclear war "to the heavens," but with no apparent success. In his 1986 State of the Union address, Reagan proclaimed that the security shield he was proposing "can one day render nuclear weapons obsolete and free mankind from the prison of nuclear terror." But the program Reagan actually supported was less comprehensive than that, and may have been intended mainly as a "bargaining chip" to induce the Soviet Union to agree to substantial reductions in each side's nuclear arsenal. Reagan did propose total nuclear disarmament within ten years, and the Soviet Union agreed in principle, but the agreement was not achieved largely because of disagreements over the Strategic Defense Initiative. These disagreements continued to stall arms reduction talks, even as doubts about technology, the emergence of the Iran-Contra affair, the 1988 election campaign, and the collapse of the Communist threat all weakened interest in deployment of the SDI.

My fellow Americans, thank you for sharing your time with me tonight.

The subject I want to discuss with you, peace and national security, is both timely and important. Timely, because I've reached a decision which offers a new hope for our children in the 21st century, a decision I'll tell you about in a few minutes. And important because there's a very big decision that you must make for yourselves. This subject involves the most basic duty that any President and any people share, the duty to protect and strengthen the peace.

At the beginning of this year, I submitted to the Congress a defense budget which reflects my best judgment of the best understanding of the experts and specialists who advise me about what we and our allies must do to protect our people in the years ahead. That budget is much more than a long list of numbers, for behind all the numbers lies America's ability to prevent the greatest of human tragedies and preserve our free way of life in a sometimes dangerous world. It is part of a careful, long-term plan to make America strong again after too many years of neglect and mistakes.

Our efforts to rebuild America's defenses and strengthen the peace began 2 years ago when we requested a major increase in the defense program. Since then, the amount of those increases we first proposed has been reduced by half, through improvements in management and procurement and other savings.

The budget request that is now before the Congress has been trimmed to the limits of safety. Further deep cuts cannot be made without seriously endangering the security of the Nation. The choice is up to the men and women you've elected to the Congress, and that means the choice is up to you.

Tonight, I want to explain to you what this defense debate is all about and why I'm convinced that the budget now before the Congress is necessary, responsible, and deserving of your support. And I want to offer hope for the future.

But first, let me say what the defense debate is not about. It is not about spending arithmetic. I know that in the last few weeks you've been bombarded with numbers and percentages. Some say we need only a 5-percent increase in defense spending. The so-called al-ternate budget backed by liberals in the House of Representatives would lower the figure to 2 to 3 percent, cutting our defense spending by $163 billion over the next 5 years. The trouble with all these numbers is that they tell us little about the kind of defense program America needs or the benefits and security and freedom that our defense effort buys for us.

What seems to have been lost in all this debate is the simple truth of how a defense budget is arrived at. It isn't done by deciding to spend a certain number of dollars. Those loud voices that are occasionally heard charging that the Government is trying to solve a security problem by throwing money at it are nothing more than noise based on ignorance. We start by considering what must be done to maintain peace and review all the possible threats against our security. Then a strategy for strengthening peace and defending against those threats must be agreed upon. And, finally, our defense establishment must be evaluated to see what is necessary to protect against any or all of the potential threats. The cost of achieving these ends is totaled up, and the result is the budget for national defense.

There is no logical way that you can say, let's spend x billion dollars less. You can only say, which part of our defense measures do we believe we can do without and still have security against all contingencies? Anyone in the Congress who advocates a percentage or a specific dollar cut in defense spending should be made to say what part of our defenses he would eliminate, and he should be candid enough to acknowledge that his cuts mean cutting our commitments to allies or inviting greater risk or both.

The defense policy of the United States is based on a simple premise: The United States does not start fights. We will never be an aggressor. We maintain our strength in order to deter and defend against aggression—to preserve freedom and peace.

Since the dawn of the atomic age, we've sought to reduce the risk of war by maintaining a strong deterrent and by seeking genuine arms control. "Deterrence" means simply this: making sure any adversary who thinks about attacking the United States, or our allies, or our vital interests, concludes that the risks to him outweigh any potential gains. Once he understands that, he won't attack. We maintain the peace through our strength; weakness only invites aggression.

This strategy of deterrence has not changed. It still works. But what it takes to maintain deterrence has changed. It took one kind of military force to deter an attack when we had far more nuclear weapons than any other power; it takes another kind now that the Soviets, for example, have enough accurate and powerful nuclear weapons to destroy virtually all of our missiles on the ground. Now, this is not to say that the Soviet Union is planning to make war on us. Nor do I believe a war is inevitable—quite the contrary. But what must be recognized is that our security is based on being prepared to meet all threats.

There was a time when we depended on coastal forts and artillery batteries, because, with the weaponry of that day, any attack would have had to come by sea. Well, this is a different world, and our defenses must be based on recognition and awareness of the weaponry possessed by other nations in the nuclear age.

We can't afford to believe that we will never be threatened. There have been two world wars in my lifetime. We didn't start them and, indeed, did everything we could to avoid being drawn into them. But we were ill-prepared for both. Had we been better prepared, peace might have been preserved.

For 20 years the Soviet Union has been accumulating enormous military might. They didn't stop when their forces exceeded all requirements of a legitimate defensive capability. And they haven't stopped now. During the past decade and a half, the Soviets have built up a massive arsenal of new strategic nuclear weapons—weapons that can strike directly at the United States.

As an example, the United States introduced its last new intercontinental ballistic missile, the Minute Man III, in 1969, and we're now dismantling our even older Titan missiles. But what has the Soviet Union done in these intervening years? Well, since 1969 the Soviet Union has built five new classes of ICBM's, and upgraded these eight times. As a result, their missiles are much more powerful and accurate than they were several years ago, and they continue to develop more, while ours are increasingly obsolete.

The same thing has happened in other areas. Over the same period, the Soviet Union built 4 new classes of submarine-launched ballistic missiles and over 60 new missile submarines. We built 2 new types of submarine

missiles and actually withdrew 10 submarines from strategic missions. The Soviet Union built over 200 new Backfire bombers, and their brand new Blackjack bomber is now under development. We haven't built a new long-range bomber since our B-52's were deployed about a quarter of a century ago, and we've already retired several hundred of those because of old age. Indeed, despite what many people think, our strategic forces only cost about 15 percent of the defense budget.

Another example of what's happened: In 1978 the Soviets had 600 intermediate-range nuclear missiles based on land and were beginning to add the SS-20—a new, highly accurate, mobile missile with 3 warheads. We had none. Since then the Soviets have strengthened their lead. By the end of 1979, when Soviet leader Brezhnev declared "a balance now exists," the Soviets had over 800 warheads. We still had none. A year ago this month, Mr. Brezhnev pledged a moratorium, or freeze, on SS-20 deployment. But by last August, their 800 warheads had become more than 1,200. We still had none. Some freeze. At this time Soviet Defense Minister Ustinov announced "approximate parity of forces continues to exist." But the Soviets are still adding an average of 3 new warheads a week, and now have 1,300. These warheads can reach their targets in a matter of a few minutes. We still have none. So far, it seems that the Soviet definition of parity is a box score of 1,300 to nothing, in their favor.

So, together with our NATO allies, we decided in 1979 to deploy new weapons, beginning this year, as a deterrent to their SS-20's and as an incentive to the Soviet Union to meet us in serious arms control negotiations. We will begin that deployment late this year. At the same time, however, we're willing to cancel our program if the Soviets will dismantle theirs. This is what we've called a zero-zero plan. The Soviets are now at the negotiating table—and I think it's fair to say that without our planned deployments, they wouldn't be there.

Now, let's consider conventional forces. Since 1974 the United States has produced 3,050 tactical combat aircraft. By contrast, the Soviet Union has produced twice as many. When we look at attack submarines, the United States has produced 27 while the Soviet Union has produced 61. For armored vehicles, including tanks, we have produced 11,200. The Soviet Union has produced 54,000—nearly 5 to 1 in their favor. Finally, with artillery, we've produced 950 artillery and rocket launchers while the Soviets have produced more than 13,000—a staggering 14-to-1 ratio.

There was a time when we were able to offset superior Soviet numbers with higher quality, but today they are building weapons as sophisticated and modern as our own.

As the Soviets have increased their military power, they've been emboldened to extend that power. They're spreading their military influence in ways that can directly challenge our vital interests and those of our allies.

The following aerial photographs, most of them secret until now, illustrate this point in a crucial area very close to home: Central America and the Caribbean Basin. They're not dramatic photographs. But I think they help give you a better understanding of what I'm talking about.

This Soviet intelligence collection facility, less than a hundred miles from our coast, is the largest of its kind in the world. The acres and acres of antennae fields and intelligence monitors are targeted on key U.S. military installations and sensitive activities. The installation in Lourdes, Cuba, is manned by 1,500 Soviet technicians. And the satellite ground station allows instant communications with Moscow. This 28-square-mile facility has grown by more than 60 percent in size and capability during the past decade.

In western Cuba, we see this military airfield and it complement of modern, Soviet-built Mig-23 aircraft. The Soviet Union uses this Cuban airfield for its own long-range reconnaissance missions. And earlier this month, two modern Soviet antisubmarine warfare aircraft began operating from it. During the past 2 years, the level of Soviet arms exports to Cuba can only be compared to the levels reached during the Cuban missile crisis 20 years ago.

This third photo, which is the only one in this series that has been previously made public, shows Soviet military hardware that has made its way to Central America. This airfield with is MI-8 helicopters, anti-aircraft guns, and protected fighter sites is one of a number of military facilities in Nicaragua which has received Soviet equipment funneled through Cuba, and reflects the massive military buildup going on in that country.

On the small island of Grenada, at the southern end of the Caribbean chain, the Cubans, with Soviet financing and backing, are in the process of building an airfield with a 10,000-foot runway. Grenada doesn't even have an air force. Who is it intended for? The Caribbean is a very important passageway for our international commerce and military lines of communication. More than half of all American oil imports now pass through the Caribbean. The rapid buildup of Grenada's military potential is unrelated to any conceivable threat to this island country of under 110,000 people and totally at odds with the pattern of other eastern Caribbean States, most of which are unarmed.

The Soviet-Cuban militarization of Grenada, in short, can only be seen as power projection into the region. And it is in this important economic and strategic area that we're trying to help the Governments of El Salvador, Costa Rica, Honduras, and others in their struggles for democracy against guerrillas supported through Cuba and Nicaragua.

These pictures only tell a small part of the story. I wish I could show you more without compromising our most sensitive intelligence sources and methods. But the Soviet Union is also supporting Cuban military forces in Angola and Ethiopia. They have bases in Ethiopia and South Yemen, near the Persian Gulf oil fields. They've taken over the port that we built at Cam Ranh Bay in Vietnam. And now for the first time in history, the Soviet Navy is a force to be reckoned with in the South Pacific.

Some people may still ask: Would the Soviets ever use their formidable military power? Well, again, can we afford to believe they won't? There is Afghanistan. And in Poland, the Soviets denied the will of the people and in so doing demonstrated to the world how their military power could also be used to intimidate.

The final fact is that the Soviet Union is acquiring what can only be considered an offensive military force. They have continued to build far more intercontinental ballistic missiles than they could possibly need simply to deter an attack. Their conventional forces are trained and equipped not so much to defend against an attack as they are to permit sudden, surprise offensives of their own.

Our NATO allies have assumed a great defense burden, including the military draft in most countries. We're working with them and our other friends around the world to do more. Our defensive strategy means we need military forces that can move very quickly, forces that are trained and ready to respond to any emergency.

Every item in our defense program—our ships, our tanks, our planes, our funds for training and spare parts—is intended for one all-important purpose: to keep the peace. Unfortunately, a decade of neglecting our military forces had called into question our ability to do that.

When I took office in January 1981, I was appalled by what I found: American planes that couldn't fly and American ships that couldn't sail for lack of spare parts and trained personnel and insufficient fuel and ammunition for essential training. The inevitable result of all this was poor morale in our Armed Forces, difficulty in recruiting the brightest young Americans to wear the uniform, and difficulty in convincing our most experienced military personnel to stay on.

There was a real question then about how well we could meet a crisis. And it was obvious that we had to begin a major modernization program to ensure we could deter aggression and preserve the peace in the years ahead.

We had to move immediately to improve the basic readiness and staying power of our conventional forces, so they could meet—and therefore help deter—a crisis. We had to make up for lost years of investment by moving forward with a long-term plan to prepare our forces to counter the military capabilities our adversaries were developing for the future.

I know that all of you want peace, and so do I. I know too that many of you seriously believe that a nuclear freeze would further the cause of peace. But a freeze now would make us less, not more, secure and would raise, not reduce, the risks of war. It would be largely unverifiable and would seriously undercut our negotiations on arms reduction. It would reward the Soviets for their massive military buildup while preventing us from modernizing our aging and increasingly vulnerable forces. With their present margin of superiority, why should they agree to arms reductions knowing that we were prohibited from catching up?

Believe me, it wasn't pleasant for someone who had come to Washington determined to reduce government spending, but we had to move forward with the task of repairing our defenses or we would lose our ability to deter conflict now and in the future. We had to demonstrate to any adversary that aggression could not succeed, and that the only real solution was substantial, equitable, and effectively verifiable arms reduction—the kind we're working for right now in Geneva.

Thanks to your strong support, and bipartisan support from the Congress, we began to turn things around. Already, we're seeing some very encouraging results. Quality recruitment and retention are up dramatically—more high school graduates are choosing military careers, and more experienced career personnel are choosing to stay. Our men and women in uniform at last are getting the tools and training they need to do their jobs.

Ask around today, especially among our young people, and I think you will find a whole new attitude toward serving their country. This reflects more than just better pay, equipment, and leadership. You the American people have sent a signal to these young people that it is once again an honor to wear the uniform. That's not something you measure in a budget, but it's a very real part of our nation's strength.

It'll take us longer to build the kind of equipment we need to keep peace in the future, but we've made a good start.

We haven't built a new long-range bomber for 21 years. Now we're building the B-1. We hadn't launched one new strategic submarine for 17 years. Now we're building one Trident submarine a year. Our land-based missiles are increasingly threatened by the many huge, new Soviet ICBM's. We're determining how to solve that problem. At the same time, we're working in the START and INF negotiations with the goal of achieving deep reductions in the strategic and intermediate nuclear arsenals of both sides.

We have also begun the long-needed modernization of our conventional forces. The Army is getting its first new tank in 20 years. The Air Force is modernizing. We're rebuilding our Navy, which shrank from about a thousand ships in the late 1960's to 453 during the 1970's. Our nation needs a superior navy to support our military forces and vital interests overseas. We're now on the road to achieving a 600-ship navy and increasing the amphibious capabilities of our marines, who are now serving the cause of peace in Lebanon. And we're building a real capability to assist our friends in the vitally important Indian Ocean and Persian Gulf region.

This adds up to a major effort, and it isn't cheap. It comes at a time when there are many other pressures on our budget and when the American people have already had to make major sacrifices during the recession. But we must not be misled by those who would make defense once again the scapegoat of the Federal budget.

The fact is that in the past few decades we have seen a dramatic shift in how we spend the taxpayer's dollar. Back in 1955, payments to individuals took up only about 20 percent of the Federal budget. For nearly three decades, these payments steadily increased and, this year, will account for 49 percent of the budget. By contrast, in 1955 defense took up more than half of the Federal budget. By 1980 this spending had fallen to a low of 23 percent. Even with the increase that I am requesting this year, defense will still amount to only 28 percent of the budget.

The calls for cutting back the defense budget come in nice, simple arithmetic. They're the same kind of talk that led the democracies to neglect their defenses in the 1930's and invited the tragedy of World War II. We must not let that grim chapter of history repeat itself through apathy or neglect.

This is why I'm speaking to you tonight—to urge you to tell your Senators and Congressmen that you know we must continue to restore our military strength. If we stop in midstream, we will send a signal of decline, of lessened will, to friends and adversaries alike. Free people must voluntarily, through open debate and democratic means, meet the challenge that totalitarians pose by compulsion. It's up to us, in our time, to choose and choose wisely between the hard but necessary task of preserving peace and freedom and the temptation to ignore our duty and blindly hope for the best while the enemies of freedom grow stronger day by day.

The solution is well within our grasp. But to reach it, there is simply no alternative but to continue this year, in this budget, to provide the resources we need to preserve the peace and guarantee our freedom.

Now, thus far tonight I've shared with you my thoughts on the problems of national security we must face together. My predecessors in the Oval Office have appeared before you on other occasions to describe the threat posed by Soviet power and have proposed steps to address that threat. But since the advent of nuclear weapons, those steps have been increasingly directed toward deterrence of aggression through the promise of retaliation.

This approach to stability through offensive threat has worked. We and our allies have succeeded in preventing nuclear war for more than three decades. In recent months, however, my advisers, including in particular the Joint Chiefs of Staff, have underscored the necessity to break out of a future that relies solely on offensive retaliation for our security.

Over the course of these discussions, I've become more and more deeply convinced that the human spirit must be capable of rising above dealing with other nations and human beings by threatening their existence. Feeling this way, I believe we must thoroughly examine every opportunity for reducing tensions and for introducing greater stability into the strategic calculus on both sides.

One of the most important contributions we can make is, of course, to lower the level of all arms, and particularly nuclear arms. We're engaged right now in several negotiations with the Soviet Union to bring about a mutual reduction of weapons. I will report to you a week from tomorrow my thoughts on that score. But let me just say, I'm totally committed to this course.

If the Soviet Union will join with us in our effort to achieve major arms reduction, we will have succeeded in stabilizing the nuclear balance. Nevertheless, it will still be necessary to rely on the specter of retaliation, on mutual threat. And that's a sad commentary on the human condition. Wouldn't it be better to save lives than to avenge them? Are we not capable of demonstrating our peaceful intentions by applying all our abilities and our ingenuity to achieving a truly lasting stability? I think we are. Indeed, we must.

After careful consultation with my advisers, including the Joint Chiefs of Staff, I believe there is a way. Let me share with you a vision of the future which offers hope. It is that we embark on a program to counter the awesome Soviet missile threat with measures that are defensive. Let us turn to the very strengths in technology that spawned our great industrial base and that have given us the quality of life we enjoy today.

What if free people could live secure in the knowledge that their security did not rest upon the threat of instant U.S. retaliation to deter a Soviet attack, that we could intercept and destroy strategic ballistic missiles before they reached our own soil or that of our allies?

I know this is a formidable, technical task, one that may not be accomplished before the end of this century. Yet, current technology has attained a level of sophistication where it's reasonable for us to begin this effort. It will take years, probably decades of effort on many fronts. There will be failures and setbacks, just as there will be successes and breakthroughs. And as we proceed, we must remain constant in preserving the nuclear deterrent and maintaining a solid capability for flexible response. But isn't it worth every investment necessary to free the world from the threat of nuclear war? We know it is.

In the meantime, we will continue to pursue real reductions in nuclear arms, negotiating from a position of strength that can be ensured only by modernizing our strategic forces. At the same time, we must take steps to reduce the risk of a conventional military conflict escalating to nuclear war by improving our non-nuclear capabilities.

America does possess—now—the technologies to attain very significant improvements in the effectiveness of our conventional, non-nuclear forces. Proceeding boldly with these new technologies, we can significantly reduce any incentive that the Soviet Union may have to threaten attack against the United States or its allies.

As we pursue our goal of defensive technologies, we recognize that our allies rely upon our strategic offensive power to deter attacks against them. Their vital interests and ours are inextricably linked. Their safety and ours are one. And no change in technology can or will alter that reality. We must and shall continue to honor our commitments.

I clearly recognize that defensive systems have limitations and raise certain problems and ambiguities. If paired with offensive systems, they can be viewed as fostering an aggressive policy, and no one wants that. But with these considerations firmly in mind, I call upon the scientific community in our country, those who gave us nuclear weapons, to turn their great talents now to the cause of mankind and world peace, to give us the means of rendering these nuclear weapons impotent and obsolete.

Tonight, consistent with our obligations of the ABM treaty and recognizing the need for closer consultation with our allies, I'm taking an important first step. I am directing a comprehensive and intensive effort to define a long-term research and development program to begin to achieve our ultimate goal of eliminating the threat posed by strategic nuclear missiles. This could pave the way for arms control measures to eliminate the weapons themselves. We seek neither military superiority nor political advantage. Our only purpose—one all people share—is to search for ways to reduce the danger of nuclear war.

My fellow Americans, tonight we're launching an effort which holds the promise of changing the course of human history. There will be risks, and results take time. But I believe we can do it. As we cross this threshold, I ask for your prayers and your support.

Thank you, good night, and God bless you.

Jesse Jackson

The Rainbow Coalition
(July 17, 1984)

Although Shirley Chisholm's name was placed in nomination in 1972, Jesse Jackson was the first African-American to mount a serious challenge for the Democratic Presidential nomination. He had worked with Martin Luther King in the civil rights movement of the 1960's and achieved national prominence through his leadership of Operation PUSH in Chicago. He was considered an eloquent, moving speaker who was popular in the black community but who had had difficulties in attracting significant support from whites. He was an early supporter of Rep. Harold Washington's bid for mayor of Chicago and viewed Washington's victory in a three-way race as a sign of the political empowerment of African-Americans.

Jackson entered the 1984 Presidential contest as a Democrat and had a strong showing in the primaries. In most states, he ran third behind former Vice President Walter Mondale and Sen. Gary Hart. He won the South Carolina convention and the primaries in Louisiana and the District of Columbia, and came in second in Virginia. Although he clearly would not receive the party's nomination, his achievement was impressive and warranted recognition at the national convention.

Although there was much to celebrate about Jackson's achievement, he also had engaged in controversial activities for which many thought he needed to apologize. He had met with Yasir Arafat, leader of the Palestine Liberation Organization, at a time when American policy considered the PLO to be a terrorist organization with which no dialogue was permitted. He championed a platform that included the diplomatic recognition of Fidel Castro, a renunciation of first use of nuclear weapons, and a 20 percent cut in the military budget. These positions went well beyond the mainstream of Democrats and caused Jackson problems in broadening the base of his appeal. He called his constituency the "rainbow coalition," but critics charged that only one hue was featured. He also complained about the rules for delegate selection, alleging that the requirement for runoff elections discriminated against blacks.

Jackson's most serious difficulty, however, involved his relationships with American Jews. In 1979, when Andrew Young, ambassador to the United Nations, was forced to resign because he had held unauthorized meetings with PLO leaders, Jackson attributed the resignation to Jewish pressure. Early in the 1984 campaign, in a conversation with a newspaper reporter, Jackson disparaged Jews as "Hymies" and New York City as "Hymietown." He first denied and then acknowledged having made the remark. The reporter, who was African-American, was then severely criticized by Minister Louis Farrakhan of the Nation of Islam for being overly critical of Jackson. Farrakhan had a history of anti-Semitism and, although Jackson spoke to a state B'nai B'rith convention in an attempt to forge a reconciliation with American Jews, he refused to disassociate himself from the controversial Farrakhan. He tried unsuccessfully to have the Democratic platform endorse "an independent state for Palestinians" and only in late June did he dispute a specific Farrakhan statement that the creation of the State of Israel was an "outlaw act."

There was considerable speculation that Mondale, once assured of the nomination, might select Jackson as his running mate. When he did not, citing deep differences between Jackson and himself, many in the black community were disappointed. But supporters and opponents of Jackson also recognized that he had a promising political future especially if he could heal the wounds within the party.

This speech, delivered to the 1984 Democratic convention, is especially interesting because Jackson both celebrated his triumph and acknowledged his mistakes. It was no abject apology, however. Jackson stressed his own agenda, including civil rights, the Middle East, and apartheid, and to some degree he distanced both his personality and his constituency from the party. At the same time, he suggested the possibility of reconciliation if it were achieved by transcending differences. The speech also illustrates Jackson's talents at language and especially the rhythm and cadence of his delivery.

In the speech, Jackson asked for symbolic first-ballot support. It is likely that he changed very few votes. But he did establish his constituency as an important part of the party that could not be taken for granted, and he assured his own future political prospects. Jackson made another run for the Presidency in 1988. He lost again, and his difficulty especially in appealing to Jews was evident again. But the 1988 campaign clearly was more mature and sophisticated than that of 1984 and showed greater awareness of the need for coalition-building rather than confrontation. His showing in the primaries was better than that of 1984 and enabled him to demand procedural changes that will provide him and his supporters with an even stronger voice in the party during the 1990's.

Tonight we come together bound by our faith in a mighty God, with genuine respect for our country, and inheriting the legacy of a great party—a Democratic Party—which is the best hope for redirecting our nation on a more humane, just and peaceful course.

This is not a perfect party. We are not a perfect people. Yet, we are called to a perfect mission: our mission, to feed the hungry, to clothe the naked, to house the homeless, to teach the illiterate, to provide jobs for the jobless, and to choose the human race over the nuclear race.

We are gathered here this week to nominate a candidate and write a platform which will expand, unify, direct and inspire our party and the nation to fulfill this mission.

My constituency is the damned, disinherited, disrespected and the despised.

They are restless and seek relief. They've voted in

record numbers. They have invested the faith, hope and trust that they have in us. The Democratic Party must send them a signal that we care. I pledge my best not to let them down.

There is the call of conscience, redemption, expansion, healing and unity. Leadership must heed the call of conscience, redemption, expansion, healing and unity, for they are the key to achieving our mission.

Time is neutral and does not change things.

With courage and initiative leaders change things. No generation can choose the age or circumstance in which it is born, but through leadership it can choose to make the age in which it is born an age of enlightenment—an age of jobs, and peace, and justice.

Only leadership—that intangible combination of gifts, discipline, information, circumstance, courage, timing, will, and divine inspiration—can lead us out of the crisis in which we find ourselves.

Leadership can mitigate the misery of our nation. Leadership can part the waters and lead our nation in the direction of the Promised Land. Leadership can lift the boats stuck at the bottom.

I have had the rare opportunity to watch seven men, and then two, pour out their souls, offer their service and heed the call of duty to direct the course of our nation.

There is a proper season for everything. There is a time to sow and a time to reap. There is a time to compete, and a time to cooperate.

I ask for your vote on the first ballot as a vote for a new direction for this party and this nation; a vote for conviction, a vote for conscience.

But I will be proud to support the nominee of this convention for the president of the United States of America.

I have watched the leadership of our party develop and grow. My respect for both Mr. Mondale and Mr. Hart is great.

I have watched them struggle with the cross-winds and cross-fires of being public servants, and I believe that they will both continue to try to serve us faithfully. I am elated by the knowledge that for the first time in our history a woman, Geraldine Ferraro, will be recommended to share our ticket.

Throughout this campaign, I have tried to offer leadership to the Democratic Party and the nation.

If in my high moments, I have done some good, offered some service, shed some light, healed some wounds, rekindled some hope or stirred someone from apathy and indifference, or in any way along the way

helped somebody, then this campaign has not been in vain.

For friends who loved and cared for me, and for a God who spared me, and for a family who understood, I am eternally grateful.

If in my low moments, in word, deed or attitude, through some error of temper, taste or tone, I have caused anyone discomfort, created pain, or revived someone's fears, that was not my truest self.

If there were occasions when my grape turned into a raisin and my joy bell lost its resonance, please forgive me. Charge it to my head and not to my heart. My head is so limited in its finitude; my heart is boundless in its love for the human family. I am not a perfect servant. I am a public servant. I'm doing my best against the odds. As I develop and serve, be patient. God is not finished with me yet.

This campaign has taught me much: that leaders must be tough enough to fight, tender enough to cry, human enough to make mistakes, humble enough to admit them, strong enough to absorb the pain, and resilient enough to bounce back and keep on moving. For leaders, the pain is often intense. But you must smile through your tears and keep moving with the faith that there is a brighter side somewhere.

I went to see Hubert Humphrey three days before he died. He had just called Richard Nixon from his dying bed, and many people wondered why. And, I asked him.

He said, "Jesse, from this vantage point, with the sun setting in my life, all of the speeches, the political conventions, the crowds and the great fights are behind me now. At a time like this you are forced to deal with your irreducible essence, forced to grapple with that which is really important to you. And what I have concluded about life," Hubert Humphrey said, "when all is said and done, we must forgive each other, and redeem each other, and move on."

Our party is emerging from one of its most hard-fought battles for the Democratic Party's presidential nomination in our history. But our healthy competition should make us better, not bitter. We must use the insight, wisdom and experience of the late Hubert Humphrey as a balm for the wounds in our party, this nation and the world. We must forgive each other, redeem each other, regroup and move on.

Our flag is red, white and blue, but our nation is rainbow—red, yellow, brown, black and white—we're all precious in God's sight. America is not like a blanket—one piece of unbroken cloth, the same color, the same texture, the same size. America is more like a quilt—many patches, many pieces, many colors, many sizes, all woven and held together by a common thread.

The white, the Hispanic, the black, the Arab, the Jew, the woman, the Native American, the small farmer, the businessperson, the environmentalist, the peace activist, the young, the old, the lesbian, the gay, and the disabled make up the American quilt.

Even in our fractured state, all of us count and fit somewhere. We have proven that we can survive without each other. But we have not proven that we can win or make progress without each other. We must come together.

From Fannie Lou Hamer in Atlantic City in 1964 to the Rainbow Coalition in San Francisco today, from the Atlantic to the Pacific, we have experienced pain but progress as we ended American apartheid laws; we got public accommodations; we secured voting rights; we obtained open housing, as young people got the right to vote, we lost Malcolm, Martin, Medgar, Bobby and John and Viola.

The team that got us here must be expanded, not abandoned. Twenty years ago, tears welled up in our eyes as the bodies of Schwerner, Goodman and Chaney were dredged from the depths of a river in Mississippi. Twenty years later, our communities, black and Jewish, are in anguish, anger and pain.

Feelings have been hurt on both sides. There is a crisis in communications. Confusion is in the air. We cannot afford to lose our way. We may agree to agree, or agree to disagree on issues; we must bring back civility to these tensions.

We are co-partners in a long and rich religious history—the Judeo-Christian traditions. Many blacks and Jews have a shared passion for social justice at home and peace abroad. We must seek a revival of the spirit, inspired by a new vision and new possibility. We must return to higher ground. We are bound by Moses and Jesus, but also connected to Islam and Mohammed.

These three great religions—Judaism, Christianity and Islam—were all born in the revered and holy city of Jerusalem. We are bound by Dr. Martin Luther King, Jr. and Rabbi Abraham Heschel, crying out from their graves for us to reach common ground. We are bound by shared blood and shared sacrifices. We are much too intelligent, much too bound by our Judeo-Christian heritage, much too victimized by racism, sexism, militarism and anti-Semitism, much too threatened as historical scapegoats to go on divided one from another. We must turn from finger-pointing to clasped hands. We

must share our burdens and our joys with each other once again. We must turn to each other and not on each other and choose higher ground. Twenty years later, we cannot be satisfied by just restoring the old coalition. Old wine skins must make room for new wine. We must heal and expand. The Rainbow coalition is making room for Arab-Americans. They too know the pain and hurt of racial and religious rejection. They must not continue to be made pariahs. The Rainbow coalition is making room for Hispanic Americans who this very night are living under the threat of the Simpson-Mazoli bill, and farm workers from Ohio who are fighting the Campbell Soup Company with a boycott to achieve legitimate workers rights.

The Rainbow is making room for the Native Americans, the most exploited people of all, a people with the greatest moral claim amongst us. We support them as they seek the restoration of their ancient land and claim amongst us. We support them as they seek the restoration of land and water rights, as they seek to preserve their ancestral homelands and the beauty of a land that was once all theirs. They can never receive a fair share for all that they have given us, but they must finally have a fair chance to develop their great resources and to preserve their people and their culture.

The Rainbow Coalition includes Asian-Americans, now being killed in our streets—scapegoats for the failures of corporate, industrial and economic policies. The Rainbow is making room for the young Americans. Twenty years ago, our young people were dying in a war for which they could not even vote. But 20 years later, Young America has the power to vote in great numbers. Young America must be politically active in 1984. The choice is war or peace. We must make room for Young America.

The Rainbow includes disabled veterans. The color scheme fits in the Rainbow. The disabled have their handicap revealed and their genius concealed, while the able-bodied have their genius revealed and their disability concealed. But ultimately we must judge people by their values and their contribution. Don't leave anybody out. I would rather have Roosevelt in a wheelchair than Reagan on a horse.

The Rainbow is making room for small farmers. They have suffered tremendously under the Reagan regime. They will either receive 90 percent parity or 100 percent charity. We must address their concerns and make room for them. The Rainbow includes lesbians and gays. No American citizen ought be denied equal protection under the law.

We must be unusually committed and caring as we expand our family to include new members. All of us must be tolerant and understanding as the fears and anxieties of the rejected and of the party leadership express themselves in many different ways. Too often what we call hate—as if it were deeply rooted in some philosophy or strategy—is simply ignorance, anxiety, paranoia, fear and insecurity. To be strong leaders, we must be long-suffering as we seek to right the wrongs of our party and our nation. We must expand our party, heal our party, and unify our party. That is our mission in 1984.

We are often reminded that we live in a great nation—and we do. But it can be greater still. The Rainbow is mandating a new definition of greatness. We must not measure greatness from the mansion down, but from the manger up.

Jesus said that we should not be judged by the bark we wear but by the fruit we bear. Jesus said that we must measure greatness by how we treat the least of these.

President Reagan says the nation is in recovery. Those 90,000 corporations that made a profit last year but paid no federal taxes are recovering. The 37,000 military contractors who have benefited from Reagan's more than doubling the military budget in peacetime, surely they are recovering. The big corporations and rich individuals who received the bulk of the three-year, multibillion tax cut from Mr. Reagan are recovering. But no such recovery is under way for the least of these. Rising tides don't lift all boats, particularly those stuck on the bottom.

For the boats stuck at the bottom there is the misery index. This administration has made life more miserable for the poor. Its attitude has been contemptuous. Its policies and programs have been cruel and unfair to working people. They must be held accountable in November for increasing infant mortality among the poor. In Detroit, one of the great cities of the Western world, babies are dying at the same rate as Honduras, the most underdeveloped nation in our hemisphere.

This administration must be held accountable for policies that contribute to the growing poverty in America. Under President Reagan, there are now 34 million people in poverty, 15 percent of our nation. Twenty-three million are white, 11 million black, Hispanic, Asian and others. Mostly women and children. By the end of this year, there will be 41 million people in poverty. We cannot stand idly by. We must fight for change, now.

Under this regime we look at Social Security. The 1981 budget cuts included nine permanent Social Security benefits cuts totaling $20 billion over five years.

Small businesses have suffered under Reagan tax cuts. Only 18 percent of total business tax cuts went to them—82 percent to big business.

Health care under Mr. Reagan has been sharply cut.

Education under Mr. Reagan has been cut 25 percent.

Under Mr. Reagan there are now 9.7 million female head families. They represent 16 percent of all families, half of all of them are poor. Seventy percent of all poor children live in a house headed by a woman, where there is no man.

Under Mr. Reagan, the administration has cleaned up only 6 of 546 priority toxic waste dumps.

Farmers' real net income was only about half its level in 1979.

Many say that the race in November will be decided in the South. President Reagan is depending on the conservative South to return him to office. But the south, I tell you, is unnaturally conservative. The South is the poorest region in our nation and, therefore, has the least to conserve. In his appeal to the South, Mr. Reagan is trying to substitute flags and prayer cloths for food, and clothing, and education, health care and housing. But President Reagan who asks us to pray, and I believe in prayer—I've come this way by the power of prayer. But we must watch false prophecy.

He cuts energy assistance to the poor, cuts breakfast programs from children, cuts lunch programs from children, cuts job training from children and then says, when at the table, "let us pray." Apparently he is not familiar with the structure of a prayer. You thank the Lord for the food that you are about to receive, not the food that just left.

I think that we should pray. But don't pray for the food that left, pray for the man that took the food to leave. We need a change. We need a change in November.

Under President Reagan, the misery index has risen for the poor, but the danger index has risen for everybody.

Under this administration we've lost the lives of our boys in Central America, in Honduras, in Grenada, in Lebanon.

A nuclear standoff in Europe. Under this administration, one-third of our children believe they will die in a nuclear war. The danger index is increasing in this world.

With all the talk about defense against Russia, the Russian submarines are closer and their missiles are more accurate. We live in a world tonight more miserable and a world more dangerous.

While Reaganomics and Reaganism is talked about often, so often we miss the real meaning. Reaganism is a spirit. Reaganism represents the real economic facts of life.

In 1980, Mr. George Bush, a man with reasonable access to Mr. Reagan, did an analysis of Mr. Reagan's economic plan. Mr. Bush concluded Reagan's plan was "voodoo economics." He was right. Third-party candidate John Anderson said that the combination of military spending, tax cuts and a balanced budget by '84 could be accomplished with blue smoke and mirrors. They were both right.

Mr. Reagan talks about a dynamic recovery. There is some measure of recovery, three and a half years later. Unemployment has inched just below where it was when he took office in 1981. But there are still 8.1 million people officially unemployed, 11 million working only part-time jobs. Inflation has come down, but let's analyze for a moment who has paid the price for this superficial economic recovery.

Mr. Reagan curbed inflation by cutting consumer demand. He cut consumer demand with conscious and callous fiscal and monetary policy. He used the federal budget to deliberately induce unemployment and curb social spending. He then waged and supported tight monetary policies of the Federal Reserve Board to deliberately drive up interest rates—again to curb consumer demand created through borrowing.

Unemployment reached 10.7 percent; we experienced skyrocketing interest rates; our dollar inflated abroad; there were record bank failures; record farm foreclosures; record business bankruptcies; record budget deficits; record trade deficits; Mr. Reagan brought inflation down by destabilizing our economy and disrupting family life.

He promised in 1980 a balanced budget, but instead we now have a record $200 billion budget deficit. Under President Reagan, the cumulative budget deficit for his four years is more than the sum total of deficits from George Washington to Jimmy Carter combined. I tell you, we need a change.

How is he paying for these short-term jobs? Reagan's economic recovery is being financed by deficit spending—$200 billion a year. Military spending, a major cause of this deficit, is projected over the next five years to be nearly $2 trillion, and will cost about $40,000 for every taxpaying family.

When the government borrows $200 billion annually to finance the deficit, this encourages the private sector to make its money off of interest rates as opposed to development and economic growth. Even money abroad—we don't have enough money domestically to finance the debt, so we are now borrowing money abroad, from foreign banks, government and financial institutions—$40 billion in 1983, $70 to $80 billion in 1984 (40 percent of our total); over $100 billion (50 percent of our total) in 1985.

By 1989, it is projected that 50 percent of all individual income taxes will be going to pay just for the interest on that debt. The U.S. used to be the largest exporter of capital, but under Mr. Reagan we will quite likely become the largest debtor nation. About two weeks ago, on July 4, we celebrated our Declaration of Independence. Yet every day, supply side economics is making our nation more economically dependent and less economically free. Five to six percent of our gross national product is now being eaten up with President Reagan's budget deficit.

To depend on foreign military powers to protect our national security would be foolish, making us dependent and less secure. Yet Reaganomics has us increasingly dependent on foreign economic sources. This consumer-led but deficit-financed recovery is unbalanced and artificial.

We have a challenge as Democrats: support a way out. Democracy guarantees opportunity, not success. Democracy guarantees the right to participate, not a license for either the majority or a minority to dominate. The victory for the rainbow coalition in the platform debates today was not whether we won or lost; but that we raised the right issues. We can afford to lose the vote; issues are negotiable. We cannot afford to avoid raising the right questions. Our self-respect and our moral integrity were at stake. Our heads are perhaps bloodied but not bowed. Our backs are straight. We can go home and face our people. Our vision is clear. When we think, on this journey from slaveship to championship, we've gone from the planks of the boardwalk in Atlantic City in 1964 to fighting to have the right planks in the platform in San Francisco in '84. There is a deep abiding sense of joy in our soul, despite the tears in our eyes. For while there are missing planks, there is a solid foundation upon which to build. Our party can win. But we must provide hope that will inspire people to struggle and achieve; provide a plan to show the way out of our dilemma, and then lead the way.

In 1984, my heart is made to feel glad because I know there is a way out. Justice. The requirement for rebuilding America is justice. The linchpin of progressive politics in our nation will not come from the North; they in fact will come from the South. That is why I argue over and over again—from Lynchburg, Va., down to Texas, there is only one black congressperson out of 115. Nineteen years later, we're locked out of the Congress, the Senate and the governor's mansion. What does this large black vote mean? Why do I fight to end second primaries and fight gerrymandering and (unintelligible) at large. Why do we fight over that? Because you cannot hold someone in the ditch and linger there with them. If we want a change in the nation, reinforce that Voting Rights Act—we'll get 12 to 20 black, Hispanic, female and progressive congresspersons from the South. We can save the cotton, but we've got to fight the boll weevil—we got to make a judgement. It's not enough to hope ERA will pass; how can we pass ERA? If blacks vote in great numbers, progressive whites win. It's the only way progressive whites win. If blacks vote in great numbers, Hispanics win. If blacks, Hispanics and progressive whites vote, women win. When women win, children win. When women and children win, workers win. We must all come up together. We must come up together.

I tell you, with all of our joy and excitement, we must not save the world and lose our souls; we should never short-circuit enforcement of the Voting Rights Act at every level. If one of us rises, all of us must rise. Justice is the way out. Peace is a way out. We should not act as if nuclear weaponry is negotiable and debatable. In this world in which we live, we dropped the bomb on Japan and felt guilty. But in 1984, other folks also got bombs. This time, if we drop, six minutes later, we, too, will be destroyed. It's not about dropping the bomb on everybody. We must choose developed minds over guided missiles, and think it out and not fight it out. It's time for a change.

Our foreign policy must be characterized by mutual respect, not by gunboat diplomacy, big stick diplomacy and threats. Our nation at its best feeds the hungry. Our nation at its worse will mine the harbors of Nicaragua; at its worst, will try to overthrow that government; at its worst, will cut aid to American education and increase aid to El Salvador; at its worst our nation will have partnership with South Africa. That's a moral disgrace. It's a moral disgrace. It's a moral disgrace.

When we look at Africa, we cannot just focus on apartheid in southern Africa. We must fight for trade with Africa, and not just aid to Africa. We cannot stand idly by and say we will not relate to Nicaragua unless they have elections there and then embrace military regimes in Africa, overthrowing Democratic governments in Nigeria and Liberia and Ghana. We must fight for democracy all around the world, and play the game by one set of rules.

Peace in this world. Our present formula for peace in the Middle East is inadequate; it will not work. There are 22 nations in the Middle East. Our nation must be able to talk and act and influence all of them. We must build upon Camp David and measure human rights by one yardstick and as we (unintelligible) too many interests and too few friends.

There is a way out. Jobs. Put Americans back to work. When I was a child growing up in Greenville, S.C., the Rev. (unintelligible) who used to preach every so often a sermon about Jesus. He said, if I be lifted up, I'll draw all men unto me. I didn't quite understand what he meant as a child growing up. But I understand a little better now. If you raise up truth, it's magnetic. It has a way of drawing people. With all this confusion in this convention—there is bright lights and parties and big fun—we must raise up the simple proposition: if we lift up a program to feed the hungry, they'll come running. If we lift up a program to study war no more, our youth will come running. If we lift up a program to put American back to work, an alternative to welfare and despair, they will come working. If we cut that military budget without cutting our defense, and use that money to rebuild bridges and put steelworkers back to work, and use that money, and provide jobs for our citizens, and use that money to build schools and train teachers and educate our children, and build hospitals and train doctors and train nurses, the whole nation will come running to us.

As I leave you now, vote in this convention and get ready to go back across this nation in a couple of days, in this campaign, I'll try to be faithful by my promise. I'll live in the old barrios, and ghettos and reservations, and housing projects. I have a message for our youth. I challenge them to put hope in their brains, and not dope in their veins. I told them like Jesus, I, too, was born in a slum, but just because you're born in a slum, does not mean the slum is born in you, and you can rise above it if your mind is made up. I told them in every slum, there are two sides. When I see a broken window, that's the slummy side. Train that youth to be a glazier, that's the sunny side. When I see a missing brick, that's the slummy side. Let that child in the union, and become a brickmason, and build, that's the sunny side. When I see a missing door, that's the slummy side. Train some youth to become a carpenter, that's the sunny side. When I see the vulgar words and hieroglyphics of destitution on the walls, that's the slummy side. Train some youth to be a painter, an artist—that's the sunny side. We need this place looking for the sunny side because there's a brighter side somewhere. I am more convinced than ever that we can win. We'll vault up the rough side of the mountain, we can win. I just want young America to do me one favor.

Exercise the right to dream. You must face reality—that which is. But then dream of the reality that ought to be, that must be. Live beyond the pain of reality with the dream of a bright tomorrow. Use hope and imagination as weapons of survival and progress. Use love to motivate you and obligate you to serve the human family.

Young American, dream. Choose the human race over the nuclear race. Bury the weapons and don't burn the people. Dream of a new value system. Teachers, who teach for life, and not just for a living, teach because they can't help it. Dream of lawyers more concerned with justice than a judgeship. Dream of doctors more concerned with public health than personal wealth. Dream (sic) preachers and priests who will prophesy and not just profiteer. Preach and dream. Our time has come.

Our time has come. Suffering breeds character. Character breeds faith. And in the end, faith will not disappoint.

Our time has come. Our faith, hope and dreams will prevail. Our time has come. Weeping has endured for the night. And, now joy cometh in the morning.

Our time has come. No graves can hold our body down.

Our time has come. No lie can live forever.

Our time has come. We must leave racial battleground and come to economic common ground and moral higher ground. America, our time has come.

We've come from disgrace to Amazing Grace, our time has come.

Give me your tired, give me your poor, your huddled masses who yearn to breathe free and come November, there will be a change because our time has come.

Thank you and God bless you.

———— Geraldine Ferraro ————

Acceptance of the Democratic Nomination for Vice President
(July 19, 1984)

On June 30, 1983, one year to the day after the Equal Rights Amendment failed to gain ratification, the National Organization for Women (NOW) scheduled a press conference on how to defeat President Reagan in 1984. The following month, 2,000 delegates to a National Women's Political Caucus forum were told by Texas governor Mark White that they could elect the President. These two events reflected the emergence of what was labeled the "gender gap"—the fact that women were significantly less supportive of President Reagan than were men.

The idea of naming a woman as the Vice Presidential candidate was suggested by NOW president Judy Goldsmith in October of 1983 and caught fire among the delegates to the NOW convention. An early poll reported that 26 percent of a national sample would be more likely to vote Democratic if the ticket included a woman, 16 percent would be less likely, and 52 percent believed that the gender of the Vice Presidential candidate would make no difference. (A later poll indicated that the net effect would be virtually zero.) Walter Mondale actively sought NOW's endorsement for the Democratic nomination; he received it in December of 1983. At the same time, Rep. Geraldine A. Ferraro was being discussed as a potential Vice Presidential candidate.

Ferraro, a representative from New York, was a lawyer and a respected member of Congress. Her district in Queens tended to be more conservative than her voting record, but her record was more conservative than Mondale's. She was Catholic and of Italian ancestry. She was named to chair the Platform Committee for the 1984 Democratic national convention. Her first major endorsement for Vice President came in May 1984 from Speaker of the House Thomas P. O'Neill.

Mondale, like the other Democratic aspirants for the Presidency, had pledged to

NOW and other groups that he was committed to "considering" a woman for Vice President. He planned to interview several potential candidates and to make his choice known before the Democratic convention. Ferraro was among those interviewed, as was San Francisco mayor Dianne Feinstein. In late June, the National Women's Political Caucus interviewed a sample of Democratic convention delegates and reported that 74 percent favored a woman on the ticket and only 10 percent opposed.

The growing clamor for a woman as the Vice Presidential candidate put Mondale in a dilemma. If he chose a woman, he would be accused of caving in to pressure from a special interest group; if he did not, he was courting trouble with the women's vote. A survey of convention delegates suggested that by a slight margin they preferred Sen. Gary Hart over Ferraro. Nevertheless, Mondale announced on July 12, just before the start of the Democratic convention, that Ferraro was his choice.

Immediate reaction to the selection was mixed. Older voters, married men, and Southerners were most negative; women and urban dwellers, most positive. Republicans criticized Ferraro's inexperience, especially in foreign affairs. The *New York Times* reported that the Democrats' chances were weakened among rural whites, who objected to the Ferraro choice, and among blacks, who were upset that Jackson was not on the ticket. Others, however, thought that the selection would energize the Democrats' campaign and increase their chances of coming from behind to defeat President Reagan.

Like any Vice Presidential acceptance speech, Ferraro's is not especially notable for its content. It espouses such traditional Democratic issues as keeping Social Security intact, working toward peace, and looking after the poor and oppressed. It repeatedly mentions the theme of "family values," as did Governor Cuomo's keynote address, but emphasizes the woman's perspective and equates the children of America with the future of America. The speech downplays the selection of a woman as Vice Presidential nominee but indicates that it sent the message that "there are no doors we cannot unlock."

Nevertheless, much of the significance of the speech lay in the speaker. Ferraro was the first woman to be selected by either major party as a Presidential or Vice Presidential nominee. Her speech symbolized the victory that was inherent in this selection. It also exemplified a new phase in the women's movement, one that was less confrontational, radical, or separatist, more cooperative with men, and more embracing of the potential political importance of motherhood.

Unfortunately, the acceptance speech was Ferraro's apex in the campaign. Immediately after the convention, controversy arose over the personal finances of her husband and her own involvement in his business and financial dealings. The initial refusal of Ferraro's husband to reveal his income tax records added to the controversy that lasted for the entire campaign. Additionally, Ferraro became embroiled in a dispute over abortion, publicly disagreeing with Archbishop John O'Connor of New York over the meaning and significance of Catholic teaching on the issue. Religion became an issue even earlier in the campaign when Ferraro stated that she did not consider President Reagan to be a good Christian because his social policies were unfair. This accusation backfired and hurt Ferraro. She engaged in an inconclusive television debate with Vice President George Bush, in which she sometimes found herself on the defensive about foreign policy and defense.

The Mondale-Ferraro ticket carried only Minnesota and the District of Columbia, although it is not likely that Ferraro's selection had much effect on that outcome. One month later, a House committee found her guilty of violating the Ethics in Government Act because of her failure to report her husband's finances, although the committee concluded that such violations were not intentional. Ferraro's appearance on the 1984

Democratic ticket broke an important barrier for women but did so at the cost of severe personal stress for the candidate.

Ladies and gentlemen of the convention:—My name is Geraldine Ferraro. I stand before you to proclaim tonight: America is the land where dreams can come true for all of us.

As I stand before the American people and think of the honor this great convention has bestowed upon me, I recall the words of Dr. Martin Luther King Jr., who made America stronger by making America more free.

He said: "Occasionally in life there are moments which cannot be completely explained by words. Their meaning can only be articulated by the inaudible language of the heart."

Tonight is such a moment for me.

My heart is filled with pride.

My fellow citizens, I proudly accept your nomination for vice president of the United States.

And I am proud to run with a man who will be one of the great presidents of this century, Walter F. Mondale.

Tonight, the daughter of a woman whose highest goal was a future for her children talks to our nation's oldest party about a future for us all.

Tonight, the daughter of working Americans tells all Americans that the future is within our reach—if we're willing to reach for it.

Tonight, the daughter of an immigrant from Italy has been chosen to run for [vice] president in the new land my father came to love.

Our faith that we can shape a better future is what the American dream is all about. The promise of our country is that the rules are fair. If you work hard and play by the rules, you can earn your share of America's blessings.

Those are the beliefs I learned from my parents. And those are the values I taught my students as a teacher in the public schools of New York City.

At night, I went to law school. I became an assistant district attorney, and I put my share of criminals behind bars. I believe: If you obey the law, you should be protected. But if you break the law, you should pay for your crime.

When I first ran for Congress, all the political experts said a Democrat could not win in my home district of Queens. But I put my faith in the people and the values that we shared. And together, we proved the political experts wrong.

In this campaign, Fritz Mondale and I have put our faith in the people. And we are going to prove the experts wrong again.

We are going to win, because Americans across this country believe in the same basic dream.

Last week, I visited Elmore, Minn., the small town where Fritz Mondale was raised. And soon Fritz and Joan will visit our family in Queens.

Nine hundred people live in Elmore. In Queens, there are 2,000 people on one block. You would think we would be different, but we're not.

Children walk to school in Elmore past grain elevators; in Queens, they pass by subway stops. But, no matter where they live, their future depends on education—and their parents are willing to do their part to make those schools as good as they can be.

In Elmore, there are family farms; in Queens, small businesses. But the men and women who run them all take pride in supporting their families through hard work and initiative.

On the Fourth of July in Elmore, they hang flags out on Main Street; in Queens, they fly them over Grand Avenue. But all of us love our country, and stand ready to defend the freedom that it represents.

Americans want to live by the same set of rules. But under this administration, the rules are rigged against too many of our people.

It isn't right that every year, the share of taxes paid by individual citizens is going up, while the share paid by large corporations is getting smaller and smaller. The rules say: Everyone in our society should contribute their fair share.

It isn't right that this year Ronald Reagan will hand the American people a bill for interest on the national debt larger than the entire cost of the federal government under John F. Kennedy.

Our parents left us a growing economy. The rules say: We must not leave our kids a mountain of debt.

It isn't right that a woman should get paid 59 cents on the dollar for the same work as a man. If you play by the rules, you deserve a fair day's pay for a fair day's work.

It isn't right that—that if trends continue—by the year 2000 nearly all of the poor people in America will be women and children. The rules of a decent society say, when you distribute sacrifice in times of austerity, you don't put women and children first.

It isn't right that young people today fear they won't get the Social Security they paid for, and that older Americans fear that they will lose what they have already earned. Social Security is a contract between the last generation and the next, and the rules say: You don't break contracts. We're going to keep faith with older Americans.

We hammered out a fair compromise in the Congress to save Social Security. Every group sacrificed to keep the system sound. It is time Ronald Reagan stopped scaring our senior citizens.

It isn't right that young couples question whether to bring children into a world of 50,000 nuclear warheads.

That isn't the vision for which Americans have struggled for more than two centuries. And our future doesn't have to be that way.

Change is in the air, just as surely as when John Kennedy beckoned America to a new frontier, when Sally Ride rocketed into space and when Rev. Jesse Jackson ran for the office of president of the United States.

By choosing a woman to run for our nation's second highest office, you sent a powerful signal to all Americans. There are no doors we cannot unlock. We will place no limits on achievement.

If we can do this, we can do anything.

Tonight, we reclaim our dream. We're going to make the rules of American life work fairly for all Americans again.

To an Administration that would have us debate all over again whether the Voting Rights Act should be renewed and whether segregated schools should be tax exempt, we say, Mr. President: Those debates are over.

On the issue of civil, voting rights and affirmative action for minorities, we must not go backwards. We must—and we will—move forward to open the doors of opportunity.

To those who understand that our country cannot prosper unless we draw on the talents of all Americans, we say: We will pass the Equal Rights Amendment. The issue is not what America can do for women, but what women can do for America.

To the Americans who will lead our country into the 21st century, we say: We will not have a

Supreme Court that turns the clock back to the 19th century.

To those concerned about this strength of American family values, as I am I say: We are going to restore those values—love, caring, partnership—by including, and not excluding, those whose beliefs differ from our own. Because our own faith is strong, we will fight to preserve the freedom of faith for others.

To those working Americans who fear that banks, utilities, and large special interests have a lock on the White House, we say: Join us; let's elect a people's president; and let's have government by and for the American people again.

To an Administration that would savage student loans and education at the dawn of a new technological age, we say: You fit the classic definition of a cynic; you know the price of everything, but the value of nothing.

To our students and their parents, we say: We will insist on the highest standards of excellence because the jobs of the future require skilled minds.

To young Americans who may be called to our country's service, we say: We know your generation of Americans will proudly answer our country's call, as each generation before us.

This past year, we remembered the bravery and sacrifice of Americans at Normandy. And we finally paid tribute—as we should have done years ago—to that unknown soldier who represents all the brave young Americans who died in Vietnam.

Let no one doubt, we will defend America's security and the cause of freedom around the world. But we want a president who tells us what America is fighting for, not just what we are fighting against. We want a president who will defend human rights—not just where it is convenient—but wherever freedom is at risk—from Chile to Afghanistan, from Poland to South Africa.

To those who have watched this administration's confusion in the Middle East, as it has tilted first toward one and then another of Israel's long-time enemies and wondered, "Will America stand by her friends and sister democracy?" We say: America knows who her friends are in the Middle East and around the world.

America will stand with Israel always.

Finally, we want a President who will keep America strong, but use that strength to keep America and the world at peace. A nuclear freeze is not a slogan: It is a tool for survival in the nuclear age. If we leave our children nothing else, let us leave them this Earth as we found it—whole and green and full of life.

I know in my heart that Walter Mondale will be that president.

A wise man once said, "Every one of us is given the gift of life, and what a strange gift it is. If it is preserved jealously and selfishly, it impoverishes and saddens. But if it is spent for others, it enriches and beautifies."

My fellow Americans: We can debate policies and programs. But in the end what separates the two parties in this election campaign is whether we use the gift of life—for others or only ourselves.

Tonight, my husband, John, and our three children are in this hall with me. To my daughters, Donna and Laura, and my son, John Jr., I say: My mother did not break faith with me ... and I will not break faith with you. To all the children of America, I say: The generation before ours kept faith with us, and like them, we will pass on to you a stronger, more just America.

Thank you.

Marion G. (Pat) Robertson

A New Vision for America
(September 17, 1986)

The first effort to organize evangelical Christians into a national political force was made during the mid-1970's. The goal was to politicize evangelicals and then to mobilize them to elect evangelicals who shared a conservative political agenda. A development that furthered these goals was the increasing popularity of television evangelists. Preachers such as Jerry Falwell, Jimmy Swaggart, James Robison, and Jim Bakker began to attract attention outside the narrow realm of religious broadcasting. In the 1976 campaign, Republican political strategists had urged that conservative Protestants and Catholics become more active politically, and the success of Ronald Reagan in the 1980 election campaign seemed to many evangelicals to suggest the effectiveness of their efforts.

In general, the new Christian right sees itself as contending against the forces of secular humanism and liberal Christianity. The call to return America to a former position of moral strength assumes that Biblical values originally were at the center of the national experience but have been displaced by liberal and humanistic values. The sermons and other speeches delivered by evangelical Christians follow the general form of the jeremiad, a speech that warns of impending doom and urges repentance before it is too late.

The best known organization of the new Christian right was the Moral Majority, founded by Jerry Falwell in 1979, and it was quickly successful in fund-raising and membership. In fact, the Moral Majority was often seen as synonymous with the entire new Christian right.

The Reverend Marion G. (Pat) Robertson was one of the most prominent "televangelists" of the early 1980's. He was the head of the Christian Broadcasting Network (CBN) and of CBN University, and also of the Freedom Council, a conservative organization. Robertson hosted *The 700 Club*, a fundamentalist religious program shown nightly on CBN. He was an active speaker for the religious right and claimed Biblical support for such conservative political positions as reinstatement of school prayer, outlawing of abortion, opposition to the Equal Rights Amendment and to day-care legislation and other efforts that encourage separation of children from their mothers, support for a strengthened defense, and staunch anticommunism.

It was widely rumored that Robertson himself had political aspirations. During the summer of 1986, he began fund-raising activities. Keeping his religious image, he announced that he was praying about whether to seek the 1988 Republican Presidential nomination, but he formed an exploratory committee in July. In September, he delivered a television address on the 199th anniversary of the ratification of the Constitution, announcing his intention to run for President if three million Americans signed petitions within a year urging him to do so. The speech reaffirms Robertson's themes of moral decay and the need for national renewal. Delivered at Constitution Hall in Washington, the speech was broadcast via satellite hookup to hundreds of rented halls across the country. A collection was taken at the end of the speech.

On October 1, 1987, Robertson announced that he had received the necessary signatures and that he was entering the race. At that time he resigned his Baptist ministry and severed his ties with the Christian Broadcasting Network, in order to avoid the question of religious influence on his Presidential bid. Most Republicans dismissed the prospect of a Robertson candidacy as quixotic, but extensive grass-roots organizing produced surprising results in the Michigan delegate selection contests and in the Iowa caucuses, where Robertson finished second to Robert Dole and was ahead of George Bush.

As more attention was paid to Robertson, some of his controversial statements and actions came to light. Republican congressman Paul McCloskey charged that Robertson had attempted to use the influence of his father, Virginia senator A. Willis Robertson, to avoid combat duty during the Korean War; Robertson sued McCloskey for libel but the suit was thrown out of court. Robertson acknowledged that his first child was conceived out of wedlock but assured audiences that Jesus Christ had forgiven him. In a 1985 interview he had said that only devout Jews and Christians were fit to govern. He claimed to have turned away hurricanes by invoking God's power, and in 1982 he had predicted the end of the world.

Robertson followed his Iowa success with second-place finishes in the Minnesota caucuses and the South Dakota primary. These results reflected the strong organizing effort of his campaign, his fervent following, and his success in raising campaign funds. Robertson had rejected federal matching funds and thereby had freed his campaign from spending limitations during the primaries. Still, Robertson believed that his best chance would be in the South, where evangelical Christianity was strongest and where a large number of primaries were scheduled for the same day. But he was out-organized in the South by George Bush. After predicting that he would win the South Carolina primary, Robertson received only 16 percent of the vote. Bush swept sixteen primaries on "Super Tuesday" and by early April Robertson was no longer an active candidate for President.

Even though Robertson's candidacy ultimately was unsuccessful, his 1986 speech captures the thought and belief of the new Christian right at a time when it was especially powerful in the Republican party. Its prominence appeared to wane after the 1988 election, but the prospect of a spirited clash on issues central to its agenda could well lead to a resurgence.

On September 17, 1987, just 199 years ago today, 391 men meeting in solemn assembly at Independence Hall in Philadelphia voted their approval of a document drafted on behalf of the people of the United States to "form a more perfect union, establish justice, insure domestic tranquility, provide for the common defense, promote the general welfare, and secure the blessings of liberty to ourselves and our posterity."

In 1788 the first elections were held under this newly drafted Constitution and in 1789 our first president, George Washington, placed his hand upon the Holy Bible and swore a solemn oath that to the best of his ability he would "preserve, protect, and defend the Constitution of the United States."

Tonight we meet in Constitution Hall and in 220 halls across our fifty states in equally solemn assembly on this 199th Anniversary of the founding document of our nation.

The Constitution adopted on this date moved a nation from the brink of anarchy to the threshold of stability and prosperity. A vision was born on this date of a nation united—a nation whose official motto was *E Pluribus Unum*—out of many one. The vision born on September 17 was of *one nation—under God—with liberty and justice for all.*

These men knew all too well that there was only one source of our liberty. Tonight we do well to listen to their words:

> Our First President who had presided over the Constitutional Convention in his farewell address declared, "Reason and experience forbid us to expect public morality in the absence of religious principle."

> Our Second President, John Adams, whose wisdom was key to the drafting of our Constitution said, "We have not government armed with power capable of contending with human passions unbridled by morality and religion. Our Constitution was made only for a moral and religious people. It is wholly inadequate to the government of any other."

> And our Third President, Thomas Jefferson, the author of our Declaration of Independence, gave us solemn warning, "And can the liberties of a nation be thought secure, when we have removed their only firm basis—a conviction in the minds of the people that these liberties are the gift of God? And they are not to be violated but with His wrath."

Yet despite these warnings, we have permitted during the past twenty-five years an assault on our faith and values that would have been unthinkable to past generations of Americans. We have taken virtually all mention of God from our classrooms and textbooks. Using public funds we have begun courses in so called "values clarification" which tend to undermine our historic Judeo-Christian faith. We have taken the Holy Bible from our young and replaced it with the thoughts of Charles Darwin, Karl Marx, Sigmund Freud, and John Dewey.

A small elite of lawyers, judges, and educators have given us such a tortured view of the establishment of religion clause of the First Amendment to our Constitution that it has been called by one United States Senator "an intellectual scandal."

Instead of absolutes, our youth have been given situational ethics and the life centered curriculum. Instead of a clear knowledge of right and wrong, they have been told "if it feels good do it." Instead of self-restraint they are often taught self-gratification and hedonism.

Our motion pictures, our television, our radio, our youth concerts, with a few outstanding exceptions, seem to have a single message—*God is out, casual sex, infidelity and easy divorce, the recreational use of drugs, and radical lifestyles are in.*

We have sown the wind—now we are reaping the whirlwind.

—Illegal drugs are being sold to fourth grade school children. Half of our high school children have tried marijuana. We are under assault by a tidal wave of drugs estimated to have a value of $120 billion annually.

—There are 1,000,000 illegitimate pregnancies to unwed teenagers every year in our country. Of these, 400,000 babies are aborted—yet 600,000 babies are born each year to youngsters hardly old enough to be away from their parents. In the black community, according to a CBS report, 60% of all births are to women without a man in residence.

—On the darker side of society an estimated 1/4 of all our children are sexually assaulted while they are growing up, and each year between 1.2 and 1.5 million teenagers are either runaways or throwaways. And to match our new sexual freedom this year there will be an estimated 8.6 million new cases of venereal disease in our country, and the dread incurable killer AIDS may have already infected 1,000,000 Americans.

—Our schools, with what is called "progressive education," have become progressively worse. We have in our society 27 million functional illiterates. Each year we add 2.3 million to their number. Instead of being the most literate nation on earth, we rank number 14 among the developed nations in literacy and we are falling fast.

Now in 1986 the same liberal elites that gave us the problem deny the cause and tell us that this is a problem for government. Ladies and gentlemen, what we are facing is *not a governmental problem, it is a moral problem.*

Human cruelty, human selfishness, alcoholism, drug addiction, and sexual promiscuity will always bring poverty and the disintegration of society.

The answer for us does not lie in institutionalizing aberrant behavior—whether that behavior is substance abuse or sexual perversion. And certainly the answer does not lie in once again penalizing the productive sector of our society with high taxes and wasteful spending.

Ladies and gentlemen, *the answer lies in a new rise of faith and freedom that will give to every American a vision of hope—a vision of opportunity—*a vision that will take us past these troubled days and show us the promise that lies ahead for each of us.

Even as the framers of our Constitution gave our forefathers a vision of a new land blessed with liberty, I would like for all of us on this special day to hold out A NEW VISION FOR AMERICA—A NEW VISION of hope for ourselves and our posterity.

Our children and our grandchildren are our greatest treasure. First of all we owe them a secure and loving family environment. We owe them strong homes and a mother and father who care for them, spend time with them, and truly love them. We owe to them the excitement and future potential offered by education and job training that is second to none in the world.

To accomplish this goal we must guarantee—

1 New tougher discipline in drug and alcohol free schools. For our children and grandchildren we will eliminate once and for all from our land the mob supported drugs and pornography which is destroying and debasing their dream of the future.

2 We will insure to them a return to a basic broad based phonics approach to reading. Our children must learn basic language and basic math. They must know the facts of history—the facts of geography—the facts of science. The "progressive education" advocated by John Dewey and his followers is a colossal failure and must be abandoned.

3 For our children's and grandchildren's sake we must insure that control of education is returned to their parents and caring teachers in local communities, and taken away from a powerful union; with leftist tendencies.

4 There can be no education without morality, and there can be no lasting morality without religion. For the sake of our children, we must bring God back to the classrooms of America!

Of course some would say, wouldn't that upset the atheists in our midst. Studies done for us by George Gallup show that 94% of all Americans believe in God. Only 6% are atheists. Ladies and gentlemen, I passionately believe that the atheists among us should have every right of citizenship—the right to print, to broadcast, to speak, to persuade, to own businesses, to organize politically, to run for office—but I do not believe that the 94% of us who believe in God have any duty whatsoever to dismantle our entire public affirmation of faith in God just to please a tiny minority who don't believe in anything.

And ladies and gentlemen, as we struggle to see a new birth of faith and freedom in our nation, we pledge ourselves without reservation to maintain religious liberty for all people. Speaking for myself, and I am sure for all of you, we affirm that we will preserve, protect, and defend with all our strength the First Amendment to the Constitution of the United States as it was given us by the founders of our nation.

Several weeks ago my lovely daughter-in-law gave birth to a red-headed, blue-eyed baby boy. My first grandson. As I looked down at that little fellow, I knew we had placed on his tiny shoulders a share of a $2.3 trillion national debt. As I thought more about it, I realized that before he began kindergarten he would owe a share of $3 trillion.

Why have we done this to him? Was our nation at war? Not recently. Were we in the throes of a great depression? Hardly. Was there some natural calamity to justify such extraordinary spending? None that I am aware of. In times of extraordinary prosperity we have become the first generation ever to plunder the patrimony of its children and grandchildren. We have robbed them to pay for our wasteful excesses.

Why then did we do it? We did it because Federal spending is out of control. We did it because we have a Congress controlled by politicians who lack the will to say no to the clamor of special interest groups. We did it because we have as a people forgotten the words of John Kennedy who said, "Ask not what your country can do for you, but rather ask what you can do for your country."

We must have a new vision of lean, efficient government—freed from the bloated excesses of the past—providing for the people those things they cannot do for themselves. Gone will be wasteful procurement; gone will be unnecessary departments and agencies; gone will be the frenzy to spend budget allocations before the next appropriation comes due; gone will be tax paid subsidies to the rich; and gone will be the hordes of favor seekers who have come for their piece of what Donald Lambro calls "Fat City."

Government will guarantee to every citizen the right *to pursue* happiness. No longer will it try to *guarantee happiness* for every citizen.

Government will be our servant not our master. The Federal Budget will be balanced and we will lay the foundation for a new era of prosperity.

Ladies and gentlemen, in 1978 I was shocked when America's trade deficit hit what was then an alarming $33 billion.

Now, eight years later, that trade deficit is projected this year to reach a staggering $168 billion.

We cannot sit idly by and watch the industrial might of America overcome by foreign competition.

Fine honest men and women who have labored all their lives to produce our steel—our automobiles—our television sets—our petroleum—are now out of work.

We are told not to worry because we are moving from an industrial to a service and information economy. But I do worry, because I know and you know, that in order to survive, an economy must produce tangible goods. No economy can survive which buys its goods from other countries and sells services and information on computer screens to itself.

Our new vision of America must include a partnership between the government, American business, and the American working men and women. We can no

longer count each other as adversaries, but allies in a worldwide struggle. We are all Americans and working together with our great reservoir of ingenuity, hard work, and the entrepreneurial spirit we will make *"made in America"* synonymous with *"the best in the world."*

We believe in free trade and open markets. We are against protective walls to shield outmoded or monopolistic industries.

But we also believe in fair trade—and we serve due notice on the Japanese and our other trading partners....

Either give us free and fair access to your markets—or we will shut down America's markets to you.

One year ago this Spring I visited a refugee camp in Honduras near the Nicaraguan border. I took my camera crew inside a dark tent with a dirt floor. Sitting on a rough cot was a Nicaraguan woman less than five feet tall.

She told a tale of horror at the hands of the Sandinistas. Her husband had been a bus driver. The Sandinistas accused him of being sympathetic to the Contras. Without a trial they seized him, and before her eyes they dismembered his body. Then they raped her and lowered her into a well half-dead with shock and fear. She regained consciousness, struggled out of her confinement, and made her way across the border to freedom.

As I think about this little woman, I realize that she is just one victim of the communist tyranny that since 1917 has claimed through war, starvation, murder, and torture an estimated 250 million lives.

President Abraham Lincoln wrote these unforgettable words, "Familiarize yourself with the chains of bondage and you prepare your own limbs to wear them."

Can we craft a new vision for our own society while ignoring the chains of bondage of one billion of our fellow human beings?

Can we allow armed aggression from outside or armed aggression from within a country to extinguish freedom for its people? Can we turn a deaf ear to the cries for material help from those brave freedom fighters in Angola, in Afghanistan, in Mozambique, in Nicaragua, who would take to the field of battle at the risk of their own lives to bring freedom and democracy to their people?

We must be strong enough to resist any further spread of communist tyranny. We must hold forth the dream that one day this terrible blight on the world will fall through its own corruption and violation of human nature. *And while we wait we must make it our goal that no longer will communist tyranny be financed by loans and credits from bankers and industrialists in the free world.*

Yes, together we share a dream.... A new vision for America. A vision of a great nation. A shining city on a hill. The undisputed leader of the free world. And together as we join our hands, our hearts, and our voices as one—we will once again see this great land truly one nation under God!

NOW A PERSONAL WORD

For the past three years, people have come to me and said, "your vision for America is our vision, will you be our champion and stand tall for the values millions of us share. Will you run for the presidency of the United States?"

What began as a trickle has become a torrent. Tens of thousands of wonderful people on their feet saying "*Go for it.*"

But those across America who know me know that this is not enough. The question for me on this or for that matter on any major decision is simple. "What is God's will for me in this?"

Let me assure you that deep in my heart I know God's will for me in this crucial decision and I have His further assurance that He will care for, continue, and enlarge the ministry of CBN which is so dear to my heart.

So now to all of you assembled on this 17th of September, I give you my decision.

If by September 17th, 1987, one year from today, three million registered voters have signed petitions telling me that they will pray—that they will work—that they will give toward my election, then I will run as a candidate for the nomination of the Republican Party for the office of President of the United States of America.

Ronald Reagan

Iran Arms and Contra Aid Controversy
(March 4, 1987)

Few events of the 1980's will seem more difficult to comprehend than the "Iran-Contra affair," as it was widely labeled. Before the affair was revealed in November of 1986, Ronald Reagan had been one of the most popular Presidents in history. News of "Iran-Contra" seriously eroded that popularity, led half the nation to believe that he was lying, put him on the defensive for much of his last two years in office, and followed him into retirement.

The story of Iran-Contra is complex. The shah of Iran, who had been returned to the throne in the early 1950's with American assistance, was overthrown in 1978. The following year, while he was in the United States for medical treatment, Iranian students seized the American embassy in Tehran and held more than fifty Americans hostage, demanding the extradition of the shah. The hostages were held for more than a year, even after the shah died. The students were supported by many in the Iranian government and especially by Ayatollah Khomeini, the political and religious leader of Iran, who referred to the United States as the "great Satan." Neither diplomatic nor military efforts by the Carter administration succeeded in obtaining the release of the hostages, and his failure to rescue them contributed to Carter's defeat in the 1980 Presidential election. Only in his last hours in office were negotiations completed for their release.

President Reagan, responding to this situation, insisted that his administration under no circumstances would negotiate with terrorists. Iran and Iraq had been at war since 1980, and Lebanon experienced civil war during the early 1980's. Muslim fundamentalists, following Khomeini's teaching, engaged in terrorist attacks on Americans throughout the Middle East. Six Americans were captured and held hostage by Lebanese allies of Iran. To some critics of President Reagan, the "no negotiation" policy had failed to deter terrorism and now created a stalemate that blocked the hostages' release.

At the same time Reagan was refusing to negotiate, however, the United States, through Israel, had been sending arms to Iran as part of a secret operation intended to gain the release of American hostages in Lebanon. This secret operation, which began about the time of the 1984 elections, was revealed in a Lebanese newspaper in November of 1986, shortly after one American hostage was released for no apparent reason. In a public statement acknowledging the operation, Reagan insisted that no laws were broken. But the public's trust in his administration, and in his knowledge about foreign policy, declined, especially when the facts seemed to contradict the "no negotiation" stance.

Three weeks later, Reagan revealed that the American arms were being sold to Iran at a profit, and that part of the profit had been secretly diverted to support the "Contra" rebels in Nicaragua. The Contras resistance group, encouraged by Reagan, was trying to overthrow the government of President Daniel Ortega. Although American conservatives strongly supported the Contras, they were controversial in Congress and among the public at large, with some arguing that they were no better than the ruling Sandinistas with respect to support for democracy or human rights. Reagan had asked for funds for Contra aid but had been refused; in fact, Congress had specifically prohibited foreign aid funds from being used to support the Contras. By using funds from a covert and controversial program to support an activity that Congress already had rejected, Reagan appeared to have doubly violated the public trust. His administration's effectiveness was compromised and his personal popularity plummeted, for the first time in his Presidency.

In an attempt to arrest his declining fortunes, Reagan appointed an independent investigative commission chaired by former Sen. John G. Tower of Texas. To many the investigation was reminiscent of the Watergate scandal. The key questions were, first, whether Reagan had authorized the Iran-Contra activities; second, if not, whether he knew about them; and third, if so, when he knew. Reagan maintained that he was ignorant of the events until they were brought to light after the fact.

The Tower commission submitted its report in early 1987. It concluded that Reagan had been regularly briefed on the Iranian operation in such a way that he could claim ignorance of the details if the plan were found out. It also portrayed the President as confused and remote, but ultimately as responsible for the events. Reagan delivered this speech in response to the Tower commission's report.

This speech is a contemporary example of the classical genre of *apologia*—the speech of self-defense by a person whose character has been attacked. Reagan faced a dilemma. If he said that he did not know what was going on, that position would undercut his image as a powerful leader in control of his administration. But if he did know what was occurring, then he would seem untrustworthy for deceiving the public about the American stance toward terrorism and contemptuous of the democratic process for failing to heed the congressional strictures against funding the Contras. In the speech, Reagan distanced himself from the conflict and denied knowledge of the diversion of funds. But he admitted that he had made a mistake, and combined taking responsibility with trying to transcend the issue by referring to his personal concern for the hostages. Nearly half the speech is devoted not to the matters uncovered by the Tower commission but to the question of what to do next.

The speech was moderately successful in stopping the erosion of Reagan's support. Congressional hearings on the Iran-Contra affair were held during the summer, but they failed to uncover specific evidence of Presidential knowledge or involvement. In any case, there was little public interest in steps that might lead to impeachment proceedings for the second time in two decades. Interest in the Iran-Contra affair waned during the 1988 election campaign, and criminal trials of the individuals directly responsible did not take place until after Reagan had retired from the Presidency in 1989.

My fellow Americans:—I've spoken to you from this historic office on many occasions and about many things. The power of the Presidency is often thought to reside within this Oval Office. Yet it doesn't rest here; it rests in you, the American people, and in your trust. Your trust is what gives a President his powers of leadership and his personal strength, and it's what I want to talk to you about this evening.

For the past 3 months, I've been silent on the revelations about Iran. And you must have been thinking: "Well, why doesn't he tell us what's happening? Why doesn't he just speak to us as he has in the past when we've faced troubles or tragedies?" Others of you, I guess, were thinking: "What's he doing hiding out in the White House?" Well, the reason I haven't spoken to you before now is this: You deserve the truth. And as frustrating as the waiting has been, I felt it was improper to come to you with sketchy reports, or possibly even erroneous statements, which would then have to be corrected, creating even more doubt and confusion. There's been enough of that.

I've paid a price for my silence in terms of your trust and confidence. But I've had to wait, as you have, for the complete story. That's why I appointed Ambassador David Abshire as my special counsellor to help get out the thousands of documents to the various investigations. And I appointed a special review board, the Tower board, which took on the chore of pulling the truth together for me and getting to the bottom of things. It has now issued its findings.

I'm often accused of being an optimist, and it's true I had to hunt pretty hard to find any good news in the Board's report. As you know, it's well-stocked with criticisms, which I'll discuss in a moment; but I was very relieved to read this sentence: "... the Board is convinced that the President does indeed want the full story to be told." And that will continue to be my pledge to you as the other investigations go forward.

I want to thank the members of the panel: former Senator John Tower, former Secretary of State Edmund Muskie, and former national security adviser Brent Scowcroft. They have done the Nation, as well as me personally, a great service by submitting a report of such integrity and depth. They have my genuine and enduring gratitude.

I've studied the Board's report. Its findings are honest, convincing, and highly critical; and I accept them. And tonight I want to share with you my thoughts on these findings and report to you on the actions I'm taking to implement the Board's recommendations.

First, let me say I take full responsibility for my own actions and for those of my administration. As angry as I may be about activities undertaken without my knowledge, I am still accountable for those activities. As disappointed as I may be in some who served me, I'm still the one who must answer to the American people for this behavior. And as personally distasteful as I find secret bank accounts and diverted funds—well, as the Navy would say, this happened on my watch.

Let's start with the part that is the most controversial. A few months ago I told the American people I did not trade arms for hostages. My heart and my best intentions still tell me that's true, but the facts and the evidence tell me it is not. As the Tower board reported, what began as a strategic opening to Iran deteriorated, in its implementation, into trading arms for hostages. This runs counter to my own beliefs, to administration policy, and to the original strategy we had in mind. There are reasons why it happened, but no excuses. It was a mistake.

I undertook the original Iran initiative in order to develop relations with those who might assume leadership in a post-Khomeini government. It's clear from the Board's report, however, that I let my personal concern for the hostages spill over into the geo-political strategy of reaching out to Iran. I asked so many questions about the hostages' welfare that I didn't ask enough about the specifics of the total Iran plan.

Let me say to the hostage families: We have not given up. We never will. And I promise you we'll use every legitimate means to free your loved ones from captivity. But I must also caution that those Americans who freely remain in such dangerous areas must know that they're responsible for their own safety.

Now, another major aspect of the Board's findings regards the transfer of funds to the Nicaraguan *con-*

tras. The Tower board wasn't able to find out what happened to this money, so the facts here will be left to the continuing investigations of the court-appointed Independent Counsel and the two congressional investigating committees. I'm confident the truth will come out about this matter, as well. As I told the Tower board, I didn't know about any diversion of funds to the *contras.* But as President, I cannot escape responsibility.

Much has been said about my management style, a style that's worked successfully for me during 8 years as Governor of California and for most of my Presidency. The way I work is to identify the problem, find the right individuals to do the job, and then let them go to it. I've found this invariably brings out the best in people. They seem to rise to their full capability, and in the long run you get more done.

When it came to managing the NSC staff, let's face it, my style didn't match its previous track record. I've already begun correcting this. As a start, yesterday I met with the entire professional staff of the National Security Council. I defined for them the values I want to guide the national security policies of this country. I told them that I wanted a policy that was as justifiable and understandable in public as it was in secret. I wanted a policy that reflected the will of the Congress as well as of the White House. And I told them that there'll be no more freelancing by individuals when it comes to our national security.

You've heard a lot about the staff of the National Security Council in recent months. Well, I can tell you, they are good and dedicated government employees, who put in long hours for the Nation's benefit. They are eager and anxious to serve their country.

One thing still upsetting me, however, is that no one kept proper records of meetings or decisions. This led to my failure to recollect whether I approved an arms shipment before or after the fact. I did approve it; I just can't say specifically when. Well, rest assured, there's plenty of recordkeeping now going on at 1600 Pennsylvania Avenue.

For nearly a week now, I've been studying the Board's report. I want the American people to know that this wrenching ordeal of recent months has not been in vain. I endorse every one of the Tower board's recommendations. In fact, I'm going beyond its recommendations so as to put the house in even better order.

I'm taking action in three basic areas: personnel, national security policy, and the process for making sure that the system works. First, personnel—I've brought in an accomplished and highly respected new team here at the White House. They bring new blood, new energy, and new credibility and experience.

Former Senator Howard Baker, my new Chief of Staff, possesses a breadth of legislative and foreign affairs skills that's impossible to match. I'm hopeful that his experience as minority and majority leader of the Senate can help us forge a new partnership with the Congress, especially on foreign and national security policies. I'm genuinely honored that he's given up his own Presidential aspirations to serve the country as my Chief of Staff.

Frank Carlucci, my new national security adviser, is respected for his experience in government and trusted for his judgment and counsel. Under him, the NSC staff is being rebuilt with proper management discipline. Already, almost half the NSC professional staff is comprised of new people.

Yesterday I nominated William Webster, a man of sterling reputation, to be Director of the Central Intelligence Agency. Mr. Webster has served as Director of the FBI and as a U.S. District Court judge. He understands the meaning of "rule of law."

So that his knowledge of national security matters can be available to me on a continuing basis, I will also appoint John Tower to serve as a member of my Foreign Intelligence Advisory Board. I am considering other changes in personnel, and I'll move more furniture, as I see fit, in the weeks and months ahead.

Second, in the area of national security policy, I have ordered the NSC to begin a comprehensive review of all covert operations. I have also directed that any covert activity be in support of clear policy objectives and in compliance with American values. I expect a covert policy that if Americans saw it on the front page of their newspaper, they'd say, "That makes sense." I have had issued a directive prohibiting the NSC staff itself from undertaking covert operations—no ifs, ands, or buts. I have asked Vice President Bush to reconvene his task force on terrorism to review our terrorist policy in light of the events that have occurred.

Third, in terms of the process of reaching national security decisions, I am adopting in total the Tower report's model of how the NSC process and staff should work. I am directing Mr. Carlucci to take the necessary steps to make that happen. He will report back to me on further reforms that might be needed. I've created the post of NSC legal adviser to assure a greater sensitivity to matters of law.

I am also determined to make the congressional oversight process work. Proper procedures for consultation with the Congress will be followed, not only in letter but in spirit. Before the end of March, I will report to the Congress on all the steps I've taken in line with the Tower board's conclusions.

Now, what should happen when you make a mistake is this: You take your knocks, you learn your lessons, and then you move on. That's the healthiest way to deal with a problem. This in no way diminishes the importance of the other continuing investigations, but the business of our country and our people must proceed. I've gotten this message from Republicans and Democrats in Congress, from allies around the world, and—if we're reading the signals right—even from the Soviets. And of course, I've heard the message from you, the American people.

You know, by the time you reach my age, you've made plenty of mistakes. And if you've lived your life properly—so, you learn. You put things in perspective. You pull your energies together. You change. You go forward.

My fellow Americans, I have a great deal that I want to accomplish with you and for you over the next 2 years. And the Lord willing, that's exactly what I intend to do.

Good night, and God bless you.

Michael S. Dukakis

Acceptance of the Democratic Nomination for President
(July 21, 1988)

During the eight years of his Presidency, Ronald Reagan saw his popularity rise and fall. It was at a low point during 1981 and 1982, when the administration chose to fight double-digit inflation with economic policies that led to one of the most severe recessions since the 1930's. As the economy recovered and unemployment fell during 1983 and 1984, Reagan's standing rose once again. He also benefited from the dramatically successful invasion of Grenada and the evacuation of American medical students during the fall of 1983. Indeed, by this time, Reagan's ability to benefit from good news and to avoid the blame for bad had earned him the nickname "the Teflon President."

Reagan easily won re-election in a campaign against Walter Mondale, who had been Vice President during the Carter administration. Concerned that economic recovery had been obtained only at the price of untenable federal budget deficits, Mondale pledged that the next President—whether Reagan or himself—would have to raise taxes. Republicans used this "admission" as a rallying cry, pledged not to raise taxes, and associated Mondale with the evils of big government. Reagan carried every state except Minnesota and the District of Columbia.

Reagan's popularity continued through his second term, until the discovery in late 1986 that, while pledging never to negotiate with terrorists, his administration had approved arms sales to Iran in exchange for the release of American hostages, and that the profits on the sale had been diverted to support the Nicaraguan rebels, or "Contras," at a time when direct aid had been prohibited by Congress. The prospect that Reagan either was aloof from the negotiations or had condoned them and covered them up was unappealing. Although few wished to pursue it, there was at least talk of impeachment. Democrats sensed that their chances for winning the 1988 election would be good.

The Democrats, however, had their own troubles. Popular candidates such as New York governor Mario Cuomo and Massachusetts senator Edward Kennedy declined to run. Two other senators, Gary Hart and Joseph Biden, were forced from the race because of charges questioning their honesty or integrity. Nevertheless, the field of candidates was crowded, including current or former senators, representatives, and governors, and the Reverend Jesse Jackson, making his second try for the office. During the primary season, however, the field quickly narrowed to Massachusetts governor Michael Dukakis, Jackson, and Tennessee senator Albert Gore, Jr.

Dukakis had presided over a rapid economic recovery in Massachusetts that had been dubbed "the Massachusetts miracle." He was regarded as a competent administrator but an uninspiring leader; descriptions of him as a passionless "technocrat" were not uncommon. He did not incline naturally toward the articulation of a broad vision for the country. Moreover, he was regarded as a "liberal," a description that probably helped him to gain the Democratic nomination but would hurt him in the general election, so great had been the change in national ideologies and values since the 1960's.

These depictions framed the rhetorical situation confronting Dukakis at the 1988 Democratic convention. Assured of nomination, he could work in a leisurely fashion on his acceptance speech, the single speech that would have the maximum television exposure. In the speech, Dukakis tried to blunt the perception of him as a liberal by directing attention away from ideology altogether, insisting that the election was instead a referendum on competence. At the same time, he spoke eloquently about the American promise and future. The speech was forcefully delivered, and analysts began to write that Dukakis had passions and rhetorical abilities after all.

The success of the speech, however, was short lived. The Democrats left their convention with a seventeen-point lead in the polls. This lead evaporated over the next month and Dukakis lost the election decisively in the electoral vote. He returned to Massachusetts only to discover that the state was in a severe financial condition, notwithstanding the "Massachusetts miracle." His popularity plummeted even in his home state and his talk about a possible second Presidential race was not taken seriously.

Mr. Chairman:—A few months ago when Olympia Dukakis in front of about a billion and a half television viewers all over the world raised that Oscar over her head and said, "O.K., Michael, let's go," she wasn't kidding.

Kitty and I are—Kitty and I are grateful to her for that wonderful introduction and grateful to all of you for making this possible. This is a wonderful evening for us and we thank you from the bottom of our hearts.

My fellow Democrats. My fellow Americans.

Sixteen months ago, when I announced my candidacy for the Presidency of the United States, I said this campaign would be a marathon. Tonight, with the wind at our backs, with friends at our sides and with courage in our hearts, the race to the finish line begins.

And we're going to win the race. We're going to win this race.

We're going to win because we are the party that believes in the American dream.

A dream so powerful that no distance of ground, no expanse of ocean, no barrier of language, no distinction of race or creed or color can weaken its hold on the human heart.

And I know, because my friends, I'm a product of that dream and I'm proud of it. A dream that brought my father to this country 76 years ago, that brought my mother and her family here one year later—poor, unable to speak English but with a burning desire to succeed in their new land of opportunity.

And tonight in the presence of that marvelous woman who is my mother and who came here 75 years ago; with the memory in my heart of the young man who arrived at Ellis Island with only $25 in his pocket, but with a deep and abiding faith in the promise of

America—and how I wish he was here tonight; he'd be very proud of his son, and he'd be very proud of his adopted country, I can assure you—tonight, as a son of immigrants with a wonderful wife and now with Lisa our lovely daughter-in-law, four terrific children and as a proud public servant who has cherished every minute of the last 16 months on the campaign trail, I accept your nomination for the Presidency of the United States.

My friends, the dream that carried me to this platform is alive tonight in every part of the country—and it's what the Democratic Party is all about.

Henry Cisneros of Texas, Bob Matsui of California, Barbara Mikulski of Maryland, Mario Cuomo of New York, Claude Pepper of Florida and Jesse Louis Jackson—a man who has lifted so many hearts with the dignity and the hope of his message throughout this campaign; a man whose very candidacy has said to every child, aim high; to every citizen, you count; to every voter, you can make a difference; to every American, you are a full shareholder in our dream.

And my friends, if anyone tells you that the American dream belongs to the privileged few and not to all of us, you tell them that the Reagan era is over, you tell them that the Reagan era is over and that a new era is about to begin.

Because it's time to raise our sights—to look beyond the cramped ideals and the limited ambitions of the past eight years—to recapture the spirit of energy and of confidence and of idealism that John Kennedy and Lyndon Johnson inspired a generation ago.

It's time to meet the challenge of the next American frontier—the challenge of building an economic future for our country that will create good jobs at good wages for every citizen in this land, no matter who they are or where they come from or what the color of their skin.

It's time to rekindle the American spirit of invention and of daring, to exchange voodoo economics for can-do economics, to build the best America by bringing out the best in every American.

It's time to wake up to the new challenges that face the American family. Time to see that young families in this country are never again forced to choose between the jobs they need and the children they love; time to be sure that parents are never again told that no matter how long they work or how hard their child tries, a college education is a right they can't afford.

It's time to ask why it is that we have run up more debt in this country in the last eight years than we did

in the previous 200; and to make sure it never happens again.

It's time, it's time to understand that the greatest threat to our national security in this hemisphere is not the Sandinistas—it's the avalanche of drugs that is pouring into this country and poisoning our kids.

I don't think I have to tell any of you how much we Americans expect of ourselves or how much we have a right to expect from those we elect to public office.

Because this election is not about ideology. It's about competence. It's not about overthrowing governments in Central America; it's about creating jobs in middle America. That's what this election is all about.

It's not about insider trading on Wall Street; it's about creating opportunity on Main Street.

And it's not about meaningless labels. It's about American values. Old-fashioned values like accountability and responsibility and respect for the truth. And just as we Democrats believe that there are no limits to what each citizen can do, so we believe that there are no limits to what America can do.

And yes, I know, this fall we're going to be hearing a lot of Republican talk about how well some neighborhoods and some regions of this country are doing; about how easy it is for some families to buy a home or to find child care or to pay their doctor's bills or to send their children to college.

But my friends, maintaining the status quo—running in place—standing still—isn't good enough for America. Opportunity for some isn't good enough for America.

Because working together, we're going to forge a new era of greatness for America.

We're going to take America's genius out of cold storage and challenge our youngsters; we're going to make our schools and our universities and our laboratories the finest in the world and we're going to make teaching a valued and honored profession once again in this country.

We're going to light fires of innovation and enterprise from coast to coast; and we're going to give those on welfare the chance to lift themselves out of poverty; to get the child care and the training they need; the chance to step out into the bright sunshine of opportunity and of hope and of dignity.

We're going to invest in our urban neighborhoods; and we're going to work to revitalize small town and rural America. We're going to give our farm families a price they can live on, and farm communities a future they can count on.

And we're going to build the kind of America that Lloyd Bentsen has been fighting for for the past 40 years; the kind of America, the kind of America where hard work is rewarded; where American goods and American workmanship are the best in the world, the kind of America that provides American workers and their families with at least 60 days' notice when a factory or a plant shuts down.

Now, I know, I know I have a reputation for being a somewhat frugal man. And let me state for the record that that snowblower is still in good working order, even if it sits in our garage. In nine years, I've balanced nine more budgets than this Administration has and I've just balanced a tenth. And I've worked with the citizens of my state—worked hard to create hundreds of thousands of new jobs—and I mean good jobs, jobs you can raise a family on, jobs you can build a future on, jobs you can count on.

And I'm very proud of our progress, but I'm even prouder of the way we've made that progress—by working together: by excluding no one and including everyone: business and labor; educators, community leaders and just plain citizens—sharing responsibility; exchanging ideas; building confidence about the future.

And my friends, what we have done reflects a simple but a very profound idea—an idea as powerful as any in human history.

It is the idea of community.

It is the idea of community. The kind of community that binds us here tonight. It is the idea that we are in this together; that regardless of who we are or where we come from or how much money we have—each of us counts. And that by working together to create opportunity and a good life for all—all of us are enriched—not just in economic terms, but as citizens and as human beings.

The idea of community. An idea that was planted in the New World by the first Governor of Massachusetts.

"We must," said John Winthrop, "love one another with a pure heart fervently. We must delight in each other, make each other's condition our own, rejoice together, mourn together, and suffer together. We must," he said, "be knit together as one, be knit together as one."

Now John Winthrop wasn't talking about material success. He was talking about a country where each of us asks not only what's in it for some of us, but what's good and what's right for all of us.

When a young mother named Dawn Lawson leaves seven years of welfare to become a personnel specialist in a Fortune 500 company in Worcester, Massachusetts—we are all enriched and ennobled.

When a Catholic priest named Bill Kraus helps homeless families in Denver not just by giving them shelter, but by helping them to find the jobs they need to get back on their feet, we are all enriched and ennobled.

When a high school principal named George McKenna and a dedicated staff of teachers and counselors create an environment for learning at the George Washington Preparatory High School in Los Angeles; a high school, a high school in Los Angeles that is 90 percent black and 10 percent Hispanic and has 80 percent of its graduates accepted to college; we are all enriched and ennobled.

When a dedicated new management team and a fine union in Milwaukee work together to turn Harley-Davidson around and help it come back to life, and save 1,200 good jobs, we are all enriched and ennobled. And when a man named Willie Velazquez *y cuando un Willie Velasquez* can register thousands of his fellow citizens as voters, *puede inscribir decena de miles de sus conciudadanos para votar* and Willie Velazquez can bring new energy and new ideas and new people *brindando asi nuevas energias, nueves ideas, nuevas personas* into courthouses and city halls and state capitals of the Southwest *a los gobiernos municipales y estatales a del suroeste*—my friends, we are all enriched and ennobled *todos nos enriquecem os y enoblecemos.*

My friends, as President, I'm going to be setting goals for our country; not goals for our government working alone; I mean goals for our people working together. I want businesses in this country to be wise enough and innovative enough to re-train their workers, and re-tool their factories, and to help rebuild their communities.

I want students and office workers and retired teachers to share with a neighbor the precious gift of literacy.

I want those of you who are bricklayers and carpenters and developers and housing advocates to work with us to help create decent and affordable housing for every family in America, so that we can once and for all end the shame of homelessness in the United States of America.

I want our young scientists to dedicate their great gifts not to the destruction of life, but to its preservation; I want them to wage war on hunger and pollution and infant mortality; and I want them to work with us to win the war against AIDS, the greatest public health emergency of our lifetime, and a disease that must be conquered.

I want a new Attorney General—I want a new Attorney General to work with me and with law-enforcement officers all over America to reclaim our streets and our neighborhoods from those who commit violent crime.

And I want the members of the Congress to work with me and I'm going to work with them so that, at long last, we can make good on Harry Truman's commitment to basic health insurance for every family in America.

My friends, the dream that began in Philadelphia 200 years ago; the spirit that survived that terrible winter at Valley Forge and triumphed on the beaches at Normandy; the courage that looked Khrushchev in the eye during the Cuban missile crisis—is as strong and as vibrant today as it has ever been.

We must be—we are—and we will be—militarily strong.

But we must back that military strength with economic strength; we must give the men and women of our armed forces weapons that work; we must have a Secretary of Defense who will manage—and not be managed by—the Pentagon; and we must have a foreign policy that reflects the decency and the principles and the values of the American people.

President Reagan has set the stage for deep cuts in nuclear arms—and I salute him for that.

He has said that we should judge the Soviet Union not by what it says, but by what it does—and I agree—I agree with that.

But we can do a lot more to stop the spread of nuclear and chemical arms in this world; we can do a lot more to bring peace to Central America and the Middle East; and we can and we will do a lot more to end apartheid in South Africa.

John Kennedy once said that America "leads the ... world, not just because we are the richest or the strongest or the most powerful, but because we exert that leadership for the cause of freedom around the globe ... and ... because" in his words, "we are moving on the road to peace." Yes, we must always be prepared to defend our freedom. But we must always remember that our greatest strength come not from what we possess, but from what we believe; not from what we have, but from who we are.

You know I've been asked many times over the past 16 months if I have one very special goal for these next four years—something that reflects everything I stand for and believe in as an American.

And for the—and the answer to that question is yes, I do.

My friends, four years from now, when our citizens walk along Pennsylvania Avenue in Washington, D.C., or when they see a picture of the White House on television, I want them to be proud of their government; I want them to be proud of a government that sets high standards not just for the American people, but high standards for itself.

We're going to have a Justice Department that isn't the laughing stock of the nation—we're going to have a Justice Department that understands what the word "justice" means.

We're going to have nominees to the Federal bench who are men and women of integrity and intelligence and who understand the Constitution of the United States.

We're going to have an Environmental Protection Agency that is more interested in stopping pollution than protecting the polluters.

We're going to have a real war and not a phony war against drugs; and, my friends, we won't be doing business with drug-running Panamanian dictators anymore.

We're going to have a Vice President who won't sit silently by when somebody at the National Security council comes up with the cockamamie idea that we should trade arms to the Ayatollah for hostages; we're going to have a Vice President named Lloyd Bentsen who will walk—who will walk into the Oval Office and say, "Mister President, this is outrageous and it's got to stop." That's the kind of Vice President we're going to have.

My friends, in the Dukakis White House, as in the Dukakis State House; if you accept the privilege of public service, you had better understand the responsibilities of public service. If you violate that trust, you'll be fired; if you violate the law, you'll be prosecuted; and if you sell arms to the Ayatollah, don't expect a pardon from the President of the United States.

Monday night, Monday night, like millions of Americans, I laughed and was moved by the wit and wisdom of Ann Richards.

And Tuesday night, along with millions of other Americans, I was inspired, as you were, by the powerful word of Jesse Jackson.

But what stirred me most on Monday was a grandmother talking about her "nearly perfect" granddaughter; and what stirred me most on Tuesday were those handsome and proud and articulate Jackson children talking about their hopes and the future of this country.

Those Jackson children talking about their hopes for the future of their country.

You know, young Jacqueline Jackson goes to school in my state. And last month, she visited with me in the State House in Boston. She's a remarkable young woman, and I know her parents are very, very proud of her.

And my thoughts tonight—and my dreams for America—are about Ann Richards' granddaughter Lily; about young Jackie Jackson; and about the baby that's going to be born to our son, John, and his wife, Lisa, in January. As a matter of fact, the baby is due on or about January 20.

God willing, our first grandchild will reach the age that Jack—Jackie Jackson is now at the beginning of a new century. And we pray that he or she will reach that age with eyes as filled with the sparkle of life and of pride and of optimism as that young woman that we watched together two nights ago.

Yes, my friends, it's a time for wonderful new beginnings.

A little baby.

A new Administration.

A new era of greatness for America.

And when we leave here tonight, we will leave to build that future together.

To build the future so that when our children and our grandchildren look back in their time on what we did in our time; they will say that we had the wisdom to carry on the dreams of those who came before us; the courage to make our own dreams come true; and the foresight to blaze a trail for generations yet to come.

And as I accept your nomination tonight, I can't help recalling that the first marathon was run in ancient Greece, and that on important occasions like this one, the people of Athens would complete their ceremonies by taking a pledge.

That pledge—that covenant—is as eloquent and timely today as it was 2000 years ago.

"We will never bring disgrace to this, our country. We will never bring disgrace to this our country by any act of dishonesty or of cowardice. We will fight for the ideals of this, our country. We will revere and obey the law. We will strive to quicken our sense of civic duty. Thus, in all these ways, we will transmit this country greater, stronger, prouder and more beautiful than it was transmitted to us."

That is my pledge to you, my fellow Democrats.

And that is my pledge to you, my fellow Americans.

Thank you all, very, very much.

George Bush

Acceptance of the Republican Nomination for President
(August 18, 1988)

Not since Martin Van Buren in 1836 had an incumbent Vice President won election to the Presidency in his own right. The inherent rhetorical difficulties of the Vice Presidential role help to explain this fact. Even modern Vice Presidents, who are given far more responsibility than their predecessors, do not enjoy the limelight. They play supportive roles and are not called upon to espouse or promote their own ideas. To run for the Presidency, they must clearly establish their own strength and emerge from the shadow of the sitting President. On the other hand, they usually cannot repudiate the President under whom they served—especially if he is popular—without appearing mean spirited and ungrateful as well as subverting the administration of which they were a part.

These difficulties all applied to George Bush in 1988, and he labored under additional burdens as well. On some of the sensitive issues of the 1980's, such as abortion, he had modified his own position to be consistent with President Ronald Reagan. It was unclear in such cases what his true position was. Committed Reaganites never fully accepted Bush as a convert, while some more moderate Republicans believed that he had sold out. Moreover, like his Democratic opponent, Bush was not regarded as a forceful or eloquent speaker. He had trouble in describing a broad vision of the American future, which is a generic standard of campaign oratory. In interviews he seemed even to deny the importance of such expression, referring to it as "the vision thing." Furthermore, the Iran-Contra scandal threatened to engulf Bush, because either his involvement in the unwise decisions would cast doubt on his judgment or because his noninvolvement would cast doubt on his effectiveness. Finally, Bush's surprise choice of Indiana senator Dan Quayle as his running mate appeared to be a liability, particularly as questions were raised about Quayle's academic ability and his alleged use of family influence to avoid military service during the Vietnam War.

Bush, like Michael Dukakis, had been challenged for the nomination, most prominently by Kansas senator Robert Dole. But these challenges had fizzled during the primary season and it was clear well before the Republican convention that Bush would be the party's standard-bearer in 1988. Under the circumstances, he too could prepare his acceptance speech at leisure. Much of the speech was drafted by Peggy Noonan, who had served effectively as a speechwriter for President Reagan.

The speech was well received. Bush poked fun at his alleged inarticulateness ("make my 24-hour time period") and at the Democratic keynoter's charge that he had been "born with a silver foot in his mouth." He celebrated the achievements of the Reagan administration—always insisting, however, that a record of strength was something on which to build, not to stand. He established his conservative credentials and his toughness where it was needed, but he balanced this stance with a vision of a "kinder, gentler nation" that he aspired to lead. He began an effort he would continue throughout the campaign, to locate his opponent outside the mainstream of American politics. Dukakis was not well known and Bush sought to portray him as an extreme liberal, in order to claim the vast middle of the political spectrum for himself. Moreover, Bush argued that the election was about both ideology and competence, claiming in the conclusion that the issue came down to the man at the Presidential desk and asserting, "I am that man."

Far more than Bush's speech was involved in the erosion of the Democrats' lead. Side issues were introduced, such as the case of Willie Horton, who had committed murder while on furlough from a Massachusetts prison; this case was used to prove that Dukakis was "soft" on crime. Dukakis's veto of a bill mandating the recitation in public schools of the Pledge of Allegiance to the flag became an issue, as Republicans were able to question Dukakis's patriotism while denying that they were doing so. Although Quayle did not help the Republican ticket, concern about his presence never became intense enough to matter. As Republicans tarred Dukakis with the "liberal" brush, his support fell away.

Yet clearly these major changes were foreshadowed by George Bush's acceptance speech. It enabled Republicans, who had come into their convention with some feeling of despondency, to believe that there was real hope and that the election could be won—a belief, of course, that turned out to be well founded.

Thank you. Thank you very much. I have many friends to thank tonight. I thank the voters who supported me. I thank the gallant men who entered the contest for the Presidency this year, and who have honored me with their support. And, for their kind and stirring words, I thank Governor Tom Kean of New Jersey, Senator Phil Gramm of Texas, President Gerald Ford—and my friend, President Ronald Reagan.

I accept your nomination for President. I mean to run hard, to fight hard, to stand on the issues—and I mean to win.

There are a lot of great stories in politics about the underdog winning, and this is going to be one of them.

And we're going to win with the help of Senator Dan Quayle of Indiana, a young leader who has become a forceful voice in preparing America's workers for the labor force of the future. Born in the middle of the century, in the middle of America, and holding the promise of the future—I'm proud to have Dan Quayle at my side.

Many of you have asked, "When will this campaign really begin?" I have come to this hall to tell you, and to tell America: tonight is the night.

For seven and a half years I have helped a President conduct the most difficult job on earth. Ronald Reagan asked for, and received, my candor. He never asked for, but he did receive, my loyalty. Those of you who saw the President's speech this week, and listened to the simple truth of his words, will understand my loyalty all these years.

But now you must see me for what I am: the Republican candidate for President of the United States. And now I turn to the American people to share my hopes and intentions, and why and where I wish to lead.

And so tonight is for big things. But I'll try to be fair to the other side. I'll try to hold my charisma in check. I reject the temptation to engage in personal references. My approach this evening is, as Sergeant Joe Friday used to say, "Just the facts, ma'm."

After all, the facts are on our side.

I seek the Presidency for a single purpose, a purpose that has motivated millions of Americans across the years and the ocean voyages. I seek the Presidency to build a better America. It is that simple, and that big.

I am a man who sees life in terms of missions—missions defined and missions completed. When I was a torpedo bomber pilot they defined the mission for us. Before we took off we all understood that no matter what, you try to reach the target. There have been other missions for me—Congress, China, the C.I.A. But I am here tonight, and I am your candidate, because the most important work of my life is to complete the mission we started in 1980. How do we complete it? We build on it.

The stakes are high this year and the choice is crucial, for the differences between the two candidates are as deep and wide as they have ever been in our long history.

Not only two very different men, but two very different ideas of the future will be voted on this Election Day.

What it all comes down to is this: my opponent's view of the world sees a long slow decline for our country, an inevitable fall mandated by impersonal historical forces.

But America is not in decline. America is a rising nation.

He sees America as another pleasant country on the U.N. roll call, somewhere between Albania and Zimbabwe. I see America as the leader, a unique nation with a special role in the world.

This has been called the American century, be-

cause in it we were the dominant force for good in the world. We saved Europe, cured polio, we went to the moon and lit the world with our culture. Now we are on the verge of a new century, and what country's name will it bear? I say it will be another American century.

Our work is not done; our force is not spent.

There are those who say there isn't much of a difference this year. But America, don't let 'em fool ya.

Two parties this year ask for your support. Both will speak of growth and peace. But only one has proved it can deliver. Two parties this year ask for your trust, but only one has earned it.

Eight years ago, I stood here with Ronald Reagan and we promised, together, to break with the past and return America to her greatness. Eight years later look at what the American people have produced: the highest level of economic growth in our entire history, and the lowest level of world tensions in more than 50 years.

Some say this isn't an election about ideology, it's an election about competence. Well, it's nice of them to want to play on our field. But this election isn't only about competence, for competence is a narrow deal. Competence makes the trains run on time but doesn't know where they're going. Competence is the creed of the technocrat who makes sure the gears mesh but doesn't for a second understand the magic of the machine.

The truth is, this election is about the beliefs we share, the values we honor, the principles we hold dear.

But since someone brought up competence—consider the size of our triumph: a record high percentage of Americans with jobs, a record high rate of new business, a record high rate of real personal income.

These are facts. And one way you know our opponents know the facts is that to attack the record they have to misrepresent it. They call it a "Swiss cheese economy." Well, that's the way it may look to the three blind mice. But when they were in charge it was all holes and no cheese.

Inflation was 12 percent when we came in. We got it down to 4. Interest rates were more than 21. We cut them in half. Unemployment was up and climbing, now it's the lowest in 14 years.

My friends, eight years ago this economy was flat on its back—intensive care. We came in and gave it emergency treatment—got the temperature down by lowering regulation, got the blood pressure down when we lowered taxes. Pretty soon the patient was up, back on his feet and stronger than ever.

And now who do we hear knocking on the door but the doctors who made him sick. And they're telling us to put them in charge of the case again. My friends, they're lucky we don't hit them with a malpractice suit!

We've created 17 million new jobs in the past five years, more than twice as many as Europe and Japan combined. And they're good jobs. The majority of them created in the past six years paid an average of more than $22,000 a year. Someone better take "a message to Michael": tell him we've been creating good jobs at good wages. The fact is, they talk, we deliver. They promise, we perform.

There are millions of young Americans in their 20's who barely remember the days of gas lines and unemployment lines. Now they're marrying and starting careers. To those young people I say, "You have the opportunity you deserve, and I'm not going to let them take it away from you."

The leaders of the expansion have been the women of America, who helped create the new jobs and filled two out of every three of them. To the women of America I say: "You know better than anyone that equality begins with economic empowerment. You're gaining economic power, and I'm not going to let them take it away from you."

There are millions of older Americans who were brutalized by inflation. We arrested it, and we're not going to let it out on furlough. We're going to keep the Social Security trust fund sound and out of reach of the big spenders. To America's elderly I say, "Once again you have the security that is your right, and I'm not going to let them take it away from you."

I know the liberal Democrats are worried about the economy. They're worried it's going to remain strong. And they're right, it is, with the right leadership.

But let's be frank. Things aren't perfect in this country. There are people who haven't tasted the fruits of the expansion. I've talked to farmers about the bills they can't pay. I've been to the factories that feel the strain of change. I've seen the urban children who play amid the shattered glass and shattered lives. And there are the homeless. And you know, it doesn't do any good to debate endlessly which policy mistake of the '70's is responsible. They're there. We have to help them.

But what we must remember if we are to be responsible, and compassionate, is that economic growth is the key to our endeavors.

I want growth that stays, that broadens and that touches, finally, all Americans, from the hollows of Kentucky to the sunlit streets of Denver, from the suburbs of Chicago to the broad avenues of New York, from the oil fields of Oklahoma to the farms of the Great Plains.

Can we do it? Of course we can. We know how. We've done it. If we continue to grow at our current rate, we will be able to produce 30 million jobs in the next eight years. We will do it—by maintaining our commitment to free and fair trade, by keeping government spending down and by keeping taxes down.

Our economic life is not the only test of our success. One issue overwhelms all the others, and that is the issue of peace.

Look at the world on this bright August night. The spirit of democracy is sweeping the Pacific rim. China feels the winds of change. New democracies assert themselves in South America. One by one the unfree places fall, not to the force of arms but to the force of an idea: freedom works.

We have a new relationship with the Soviet Union—the I.N.F. treaty, the beginning of the Soviet withdrawal from Afghanistan, the beginning of the end of the Soviet proxy war in Angola, and with it the independence of Namibia. Iran and Iraq move toward peace.

It is a watershed. It is no accident.

It happened when we acted on the ancient knowledge that strength and clarity lead to peace; weakness and ambivalence lead to war. Weakness tempts aggressors. Strength stops them. I will not allow this country to be made weak again.

The tremors in the Soviet world continue. The hard earth there has not yet settled. Perhaps what is happening will change our world forever. Perhaps not. A prudent skepticism is in order. And so is hope. Either way, we're in an unprecedented position to change the nature of our relationship. Not by pre-emptive concession, but by keeping our strength. Not by yielding up defense systems with nothing won in return, but by hard, cool engagement in the tug and pull of diplomacy.

My life has been lived in the shadow of war; I almost lost my life in one.

I hate war. I love peace. We have peace. And I am not going to let anyone take it away from us.

Our economy is strong but not invulnerable, and the peace is broad but can be broken. And now we must decide. We will surely have change this year, but will it be change that moves us forward, or change that risks retreat?

In 1940, when I was barely more than a boy, Franklin Roosevelt said we shouldn't change horses in midstream. My friends, these days the world moves even more quickly, and now, after two great terms, a switch will be made. But when you have to change horses in midstream, doesn't it make sense to switch to the one who's going the same way?

An election that is about ideas and values is also about philosophy. And I have one.

At the bright center is the individual. And radiating out from him or her is the family, the essential unit of closeness and of love. For it is the family that communicates to our children—to the 21st century—our culture, our religious faith, our traditions and history.

From the individual to the family to the community, and on out to the town, to the church and school and, still echoing out, to the country, the state, the nation—each doing only what it does well, and no more. And I believe that power must always be kept close to the individual, close to the hands that raise the family and run the home.

I am guided by certain traditions. One is that there is a God and He is good, and His love, while free, has a self-imposed cost: we must be good to one another.

I believe in another tradition that is, by now, imbedded in the national soul. It is that learning is good in and of itself. The mothers of the Jewish ghettoes of the east could pour honey on a book so the children would know that learning is sweet. And the parents who settled hungry Kansas would take their children in from the fields when a teacher came. That is our history.

And there is another tradition. And that is the idea of community—a beautiful word with a big meaning, though liberal Democrats have an odd view of it. They see "community" as a limited cluster of interest groups, locked in odd conformity. In this view, the country waits passive while Washington sets the rules.

But that's not what community means, not to me. For we are a nation of communities, of thousands and tens of thousands of ethnic, religious, social, business, labor union, neighborhood, regional and other organizations, all of them varied, voluntary and unique.

This is America: the Knights of Columbus, the Grange, Hadassah, the Disabled American Veterans, the Order of Ahepa, the Business and Professional Women of America, the union hall, the Bible study

group, LULAC, Holy Name—a brilliant diversity spread like stars, like a thousand points of light in a broad and peaceful sky.

Does government have a place? Yes. Government is part of the nation of communities—not the whole, just a part.

I do not hate government. A government that remembers that the people are its master is a good and needed thing.

I respect old-fashioned common sense, and have no great love for the imaginings of social planners. I like what's been tested and found to be true. For instance:

Should public school teachers be required to lead our children in the pledge of allegiance? My opponent says no—but I say yes.

Should society be allowed to impose the death penalty on those who commit crimes of extraordinary cruelty and violence? My opponent says no—but I say yes.

Should our children have the right to say a voluntary prayer, or even observe a moment of silence in the schools? My opponent says no—but I say yes.

Should free men and women have the right to own a gun to protect their home? My opponent says no—but I say yes.

Is it right to believe in the sanctity of life and protect the lives of innocent children? My opponent says no—but I say yes. We must change from abortion to adoption. I have an adopted granddaughter. The day of her christening we wept with joy. I thank God her parents chose life.

I'm the one who believes it is a scandal to give a weekend furlough to a hardened first-degree killer who hasn't even served enough time to be eligible for parole.

I'm the one who won't raise taxes. My opponent now says he'll raise them as a last resort, or a third resort. When a politician talks like that, you know that's one resort he'll be checking into. My opponent won't rule out raising taxes. But I will. The Congress will push me to raise taxes, and I'll say no, and they'll push, and I'll say no, and they'll push again. And all I can say to them is no new taxes, period.

Let me tell you more about the mission. On jobs, my mission is: 30 in 8—thirty million jobs in the next eight years.

Every one of our children deserves a first-rate school. The liberal Democrats want power in the hands of the Federal Government. I want power in the hands of the parents. I will increase the power of parents. I will encourage merit schools. I will give more kids a Head Start. And I'll make it easier to save for college.

I want a drug free America, and this will not be easy to achieve. But I want to enlist the help of some people who are rarely included. Tonight I challenge the young people of our country to shut down the drug dealers around the world. Unite with us, work with us.

"Zero tolerance" isn't just a policy, it's an attitude. Tell them what you think of people who underwrite the dealers who put poison in our society. And while you're doing that, my administration will be telling the dealers, "Whatever we have to do we'll do, but your day is over, you're history."

I am going to do whatever it takes to make sure the disabled are included in the mainstream. For too long they've been left out. But they're not going to be left out anymore.

I am going to stop ocean dumping. Our beaches should not be garbage dumps and our harbors should not be cesspools. I am going to have the F.B.I. trace the medical wastes and we are going to punish the people who dump those infected needles into our oceans, lakes and rivers. And we must clean the air. We must reduce the harm done by acid rain.

I will put incentives back into the domestic energy industry, for I know from personal experience there is no security for the United States in further dependence on foreign oil.

In foreign affairs, I will continue our policy of peace through strength. I will move toward further cuts in the strategic and conventional arsenals of both the United States and the Soviet Union. I will modernize and preserve our technological edge. I will ban chemical and biological weapons from the face of the earth. And I intend to speak for freedom and be a patient friend to anyone, East or West, who will fight for freedom.

It seems to me the Presidency provides an incomparable opportunity for "gentle persuasion."

I hope to stand for a new harmony, a greater tolerance. We've come far, but I think we need a new harmony among the races in our country. We're on a journey to a new century, and we've got to leave the tired old baggage of bigotry behind.

Some people who are enjoying our prosperity have forgotten what it's for. But they diminish our triumph when they act as if wealth is an end in itself.

There are those who have dropped their standards along the way, as if ethics were too heavy and

slowed their rise to the top. There's graft in City Hall, the greed on Wall Street; there's influence-peddling in Washington, and the small corruptions of everyday ambition.

But you see, I believe public service is honorable. And every time I hear that someone has breached the public trust it breaks my heart.

I wonder sometimes if we have forgotten who we are. But we're the people who sundered a nation rather than allow a sin called slavery—we're the people who rose from the ghettoes and the deserts.

We weren't saints, but we lived by standards. We celebrated the individual, but we weren't self-centered. We were practical, but we didn't live only for material things. We believe in getting ahead, but blind ambition wasn't our way.

The fact is prosperity has a purpose. It is to allow us to pursue "the better angels," to give us time to think and grow. Prosperity with a purpose means taking your idealism and making it concrete by certain acts of goodness. It means helping a child from an unhappy home learn how to read—and I thank my wife, Barbara, for all her work in literacy. It means teaching troubled children through your presence that there's such a thing as reliable love. Some would say it's soft and insufficiently tough to care about these things. But where is it written that we must act as if we do not care, as if we are not moved? Well, I am moved. I want a kinder, gentler nation.

Two men this year ask for your support. And you must know us.

As for me, I have held high office and done the work of democracy day by day. My parents were prosperous; their children were lucky. But there were lessons we had to learn about life. John Kennedy discovered poverty when he campaigned in West Virginia; there were children there who had no milk. Young Teddy Roosevelt met the new America when he roamed the immigrant streets of New York. And I learned a few things about life in a place called Texas.

We moved to West Texas 40 years ago. The war was over, and we wanted to get out and make it on our own. Those were exciting days. Lived in a little shotgun house, one room for the three of us. Worked in the oil business, started my own.

In time we had six children. Moved from the shotgun to a duplex apartment to a house. Lived the dream—high school football on Friday night, Little League, neighborhood barbecue.

People don't see their experience as symbolic of

an era, but of course we were. So was everyone else who was taking a chance and pushing into unknown territory with kids and a dog and a car. But the big thing I learned is the satisfaction of creating jobs, which meant creating opportunity, which meant happy families, who in turn could do more to help others and enhance their own lives. I learned that the good done by a single job can be felt in ways you can't imagine.

I may not be the most eloquent, but I learned early that eloquence won't draw oil from the ground. I may sometimes be a little awkward, but there's nothing self-conscious in my love of country. I am a quiet man, but I hear the quiet people others don't—the ones who raise the family, pay the taxes, meet the mortgage. I hear them and I am moved, and their concerns are mine.

A President must be many things. He must be a shrewd protector of America's interests, and he must be an idealist who leads those who move for a freer and more democratic planet.

He must see to it that government intrudes as little as possible in the lives of people; and yet remember that it is right and proper that a nation's leader take an interest in the nation's character. And he must be able to define—and lead—a mission.

For seven and a half years I have worked with a President, and I have seen what crosses that big desk. I have seen the unexpected crises that arrive in a cable in a young aide's hand. And I have seen problems that simmer on for decades and suddenly demand resolution. I have seen modest decisions made with anguish, and crucial decisions made with dispatch.

And so I know that what it all comes down to, this election—and it all comes down to, after all the shouting and the cheers—is the man at the desk. And who should sit at that desk.

My friends, I am that man.

I say it without boast or bravado. I've fought for my country, I've served, I've built—and I will go from the hills to the hollows, from the cities to the suburbs to the loneliest town on the quietest street to take our message of hope and growth for every American to every American.

I will keep America moving forward, always forward—for a better America, for an endless, enduring dream and a thousand points of light.

That is my mission. And I will complete it.

Thank you. God bless you.

George Bush

Iraqi Aggression in the Persian Gulf
(September 11, 1990)

In the summer of 1990 the struggle to hammer out a budget plan acceptable to congressional Democrats and to the Republican Administration dominated the news. The alarmingly growing budget deficit had been recognized as potentially disastrous for the American economy in the campaign rhetoric that accompanied the 1988 presidential election, but an acceptable plan for bringing it under control was proving to be monumentally difficult. Liberals opposed any scheme that would cripple welfare programs and conservatives held fast to President Bush's reiterated campaign promise that he would impose "No new taxes." The highly publicized, but essentially secret, negotiations between the congressional leadership of both parties and the President's representatives overshadowed vaguely disquieting news from the Middle East.

Dissension among the oil-producing countries was not new nor was it unusual. There was a history of complaints from some OPEC members that other members of the cartel were not honoring the production levels agreed upon. In July, Saddam Hussein, President of Iraq, made public his displeasure with Kuwait. Hussein charged that the tiny Emirate, by exceeding the quota the oil producing countries had imposed on themselves, was helping to drive down oil prices, thus doing serious damage to Iraq's economy. Furthermore, the two countries had long been engaged in a dispute over ownership of certain oil fields. Hussein's bellicose statements raised the distinct possibility that Iraq was prepared to use its overwhelming military power to coerce its small neighbor, but he gave explicit assurances that force would not be employed.

When, on August 2, Iraqi forces crossed the Kuwati frontier, overran the country with lightning speed, and handily destroyed or put to flight Kuwait's minuscule army, the world was stunned. It was clear that the United States government was taken completely by surprise. As Iraqi military units arrayed themselves along the border with Saudi Arabia, it became apparent that that country was also threatened. Equally apparent was the fact that, if Hussein invaded Saudi Arabia, the Saudis had little more chance of turning back the invaders than did Kuwait. Iraqi control of Saudi Arabia, with its vast oil reserves, left little doubt that Saddam Hussein would dominate the richest oil producing area in the world and, as a consequence, hold the economic fate of the industrial countries of the world in his hands.

President Bush reacted by sending American military units to Saudi Arabia and waging a diplomatic offensive against Iraq in the United Nations. By the time the President addressed a joint session of Congress on September 11, naval and ground forces, largely American, were in the Gulf and more were on the way. The United Nations Security Council, with an accord not seen in the cold war era, had imposed economic sanctions.

In his speech, the President sought to reinforce the almost universal domestic support he had received in the few weeks following the invasion and to demonstrate American resolve to the Iraqis. In the midst of this turmoil the budget crisis, of course, had not evaporated, even if it had been somewhat eclipsed as the major news story of the day. The President's speech addresses these pressing economic issues, as well, calling for unity in breaking the budget deadlock that was, as was the Persian Gulf crisis, a profoundly serious problem for the United States.

Mr. President, Mr. Speaker, members of the Congress, distinguished guests, fellow Americans, thank you.

We gather tonight, witness to events in the Persian Gulf as significant as they are tragic. In the early morning hours of August 2d, following negotiations and promises by Iraq's dictator, Saddam Hussein, not to use force, a powerful Iraqi army invaded its trusting and much weaker neighbor, Kuwait. Within three days, 120,000 Iraqi troops with 850 tanks had poured into Kuwait, and moved south to threaten Saudi Arabia. It was then I decided to check that aggression.

At this moment, our brave servicemen and women stand watch in that distant desert and on distant seas, side by side with the forces of more than 20 other nations.

They are some of the finest men and women of the United States of America. And they're doing one terrific job.

These valiant Americans were ready at a moment's notice to leave their spouses, their children to serve on the front line halfway around the world. They remind us who keeps American strong. They do.

In the trying circumstances of the gulf, the morale of our servicemen and women is excellent. In the face of danger, they are brave, well trained and dedicated.

A soldier, Pfc. Wade Merritt of Knoxville, Tenn.,

now stationed in Saudi Arabia, wrote his parents of his worries, his love of family, and his hopes for peace. But Wade also wrote: "I am proud of my country and its firm stand against inhumane aggression. I am proud of my army and its men.... I am proud to serve my country."

Let me just say, Wade, America is proud of you. And grateful to every soldier, sailor, marine and airman serving the cause of peace in the Persian Gulf.

I also want to thank the Chairman of the Joint Chiefs of Staff, General Powell, the Chiefs, our commander in the Persian Gulf, General Schwarzkopf and the men and women of the Department of Defense. What a magnificent job you are doing!

I wish I could say their work is done. But we all know it is not.

So if ever there was a time to put country before self and patriotism before party, that time is now. Let me thank all Americans, especially those in this chamber, for your support for our forces and their mission.

That support will be even more important in the days to come.

So tonight, I want to talk to you about what is at stake—what we must do together to defend civilized values around the world, and maintain our economic strength at home.

Our objectives in the Persian Gulf are clear, our goals defined and familiar:

Iraq must withdraw from Kuwait completely, immediately and without condition.

Kuwait's legitimate government must be restored.

The security and stability of the Persian Gulf must be assured.

Americans citizens abroad must be protected.

These goals are not ours alone. They have been endorsed by the U.N. Security Council five times in as many weeks. Most countries share our concern for principle. And many have a stake in the stability of the Persian Gulf. This is not, as Saddam Hussein would have it, the United States against Iraq. It is Iraq against the world.

As you know, I've just returned from a very productive meeting with Soviet President Gorbachev. I am pleased that we are working together to build a new relationship. In Helsinki, our joint statement affirmed to the world our shared resolve to counter Iraq's threat to peace. Let me quote: "We are united in the belief that Iraq's aggression must not be tolerated. No peaceful international order is possible if larger states can devour their smaller neighbors."

Clearly, no longer can a dictator count on East-West confrontation to stymie concerted U.N. action against aggression.

A new partnership of nations has begun.

We stand today at a unique and extraordinary moment. The crisis in the Persian Gulf, as grave as it is, also offers a rare opportunity to move toward an historic period of cooperation. Out of these troubled times, our fifth objective—a new world order—can emerge: a new era, freer from the threat of terror, stronger in the pursuit of justice, and more secure in the quest for peace. An era in which the nations of the world, east and west, north and south, can prosper and live in harmony.

A hundred generations have searched for this elusive path to peace, while a thousand wars raged across the span of human endeavor. Today that new world is struggling to be born. A world quite different from the one we've known. A world where the rule of law supplants the rule of the jungle. A world in which nations recognize the shared responsibility for freedom and justice. A world where the strong respect the rights of the weak.

This is the vision I shared with President Gorbachev in Helsinki. He, and other leaders from Europe, the gulf, and around the world, understand that how we manage this crisis today could shape the future for generations to come.

The test we face is great—and so are the stakes. This is the first assault on the new world we seek, the first test of our mettle. Had we not responded to this first provocation with clarity of purpose; if we do not continue to demonstrate our determination; it would be a signal to actual and potential despots around the world.

America and the world must defend common vital interests. And we will.

America and the world must support the rule of law. And we will.

America and the world must stand up to aggression. And we will.

And one thing more. In pursuit of these goals America will not be intimidated.

Vital issues of principle are at stake. Saddam Hussein is literally trying to wipe a country off the face of the earth.

We do not exaggerate.

Nor do we exaggerate when we say: Saddam Hussein will fail.

Vital economic interests are at risk as well. Iraq itself controls some 10 percent of the world's proven oil reserves. Iraq plus Kuwait controls twice that. An Iraq permitted to swallow Kuwait would have the economic and military power, as well as the arrogance, to intimidate and coerce its neighbors—neighbors who control the lion's share of the world's remaining oil reserves. We cannot permit a resource so vital to be dominated by one so ruthless. And we won't.

Recent events have surely proven that there is no substitute for American leadership. In the face of tyranny, let no one doubt American credibility and reliability.

Let no one doubt our staying power. We will stand by our friends.

One way or another, the leader of Iraq must learn this fundamental truth.

From the outset, acting hand in hand with others, we've sought to fashion the broadest possible international response to Iraq's aggression. The level of world cooperation and condemnation of Iraq is unprecedented.

Armed forces from countries spanning four continents are there at the request of King Fahd of Saudi Arabia to deter and if need be to defend against attack. Muslims and non-Muslims, Arabs and non-Arabs, soldiers from many nations, stand shoulder to shoulder, resolute against Saddam Hussein's ambitions.

We can now point to five United Nations Security Council resolutions that condemn Iraq's aggression. They call for Iraq's immediate and unconditional withdrawal, the restoration of Kuwait's legitimate Government, and categorically reject Iraq's cynical and self-serving attempt to annex Kuwait.

Finally, the U.N. has demanded the release of all foreign nationals held hostage against their will and in contravention of international law. It is a mockery of human decency to call these people "guests." They are hostages, and the world knows it.

Prime Minister Margaret Thatcher said it all: "We do not bargain over hostages. We will not stoop to the level of using human beings as bargaining chips ever."

Of course, our hearts go out to the hostages and their families. But our policy cannot change. And it will not change. America and the world will not be blackmailed.

We are now in sight of a United Nations that performs as envisioned by its founders. We owe much to the outstanding leadership of Secretary General Pérez de Cuéllar. The U.N. is backing up its words with action. The Security Council has imposed mandatory economic sanctions on Iraq, designed to force Iraq to relinquish the spoils of its illegal conquest. The Security Council has also taken the decisive step of authorizing the use of all means necessary to ensure compliance with these sanctions.

Together with our friends and allies, ships of the United States Navy are today patrolling Mideast waters. They have already intercepted more than 700 ships to enforce the sanctions. Three regional leaders I spoke with just yesterday told me that these sanctions are working. Iraq is feeling the heat.

We continue to hope that Iraq's leaders will recalculate just what their aggression has cost them. They are cut off from world trade, unable to sell their oil. And only a tiny fraction of goods gets through.

The communiqué with President Gorbachev makes mention of what happens when the embargo is so effective that the children of Iraq literally need milk, or the sick truly need medicine. Then, under strict international supervision that guarantees the proper destination, then—food will be permitted.

At home, the material cost of our leadership can be steep. That's why Secretary of State Baker and Treasury Secretary Brady have met with many world leaders to underscore that the burden of this collective ef-

fort must be shared. We are prepared to do our share and more to help carry that load; we insist others do their share as well.

The response of most of our friends and allies has been good. To help defray costs, the leaders of Saudi Arabia, Kuwait, and the United Arab Emirates have pledged to provide our deployed troops with all the food and fuel they need. Generous assistance will also be provided to stalwart front-line nations, such as Turkey and Egypt.

I am also heartened to report that this international response extends to the neediest victims of this conflict—the refugees. For our part, we have contributed $28 million for relief efforts. This is but a portion of what is needed. I commend, in particular, Saudi Arabia, Japan, and several European nations who have joined us in this humanitarian effort.

There is an energy-related cost to be borne as well. Oil-producing nations are already replacing lost Iraqi and Kuwaiti output. More than half of what was lost has been made up. We are getting superb cooperation. If producers, including the United States, continue steps to expand oil and gas production, we can stabilize prices and guarantee against hardship. Additionally, we and several of our allies always have the option to extract oil from our strategic petroleum reserves, if conditions warrant. As I have pointed out before, conservation efforts are essential to keep our energy needs as low as possible. We must then take advantage of our energy sources across the board: coal, natural gas, hydro, and nuclear. Our failure to do these things has made us more dependent on foreign oil than ever before. Finally, let no one even contemplate profiteering from this crisis.

I cannot predict just how long it will take to convince Iraq to withdraw from Kuwait. Sanctions will take time to have their full intended effect. We will continue to review all options with our allies, but let it be clear: We will not let this aggression stand.

Our interest, our involvement in the gulf, is not transitory. It predated Saddam Hussein's aggression and will survive it. Long after all our troops come home, and we all hope it's soon, there will be a lasting role for the United States in assisting the nations of the Persian Gulf. Our role, with others, is to deter future aggression. Our role is to help our friends in their own self-defense. And something else: to curb the proliferation of chemical, biological, ballistic missile, and above all, nuclear technologies.

Let me also make clear that the United States has

no quarrel with the Iraqi people. Our quarrel is with Iraq's dictator, and with his aggression. Iraq will not be permitted to annex Kuwait. That's not a threat, or a boast, that's just the way it's going to be.

Our ability to function effectively as a great power abroad depends on how we conduct ourselves here at home. Our economy, our armed forces, our energy dependence, and our cohesion all determine whether we can help our friends and stand up to our foes.

For America to lead, America must remain strong and vital. Our world leadership and domestic strength are mutual and reinforcing; a woven piece, as strongly bound as Old Glory.

To revitalize our leadership capacity, we must address our budget deficit—not after Election Day, or next year, but now.

Higher oil prices slow our growth, and higher defense costs would only make our fiscal deficit problem worse. That deficit was already greater than it should have been—a projected $232 billion for the coming year. It must—it will—be reduced.

To my friends in Congress, together we must act this very month, before the next fiscal year begins Oct. 1, to get America's economic house in order. The gulf situation helps us realize we are more economically vulnerable than we ever should be. Americans must never again enter any crisis, economic or military, with an excessive dependence on foreign oil and an excessive burden of Federal debt.

Most Americans are sick and tired of endless battles in the Congress and between the branches over budget matters. It is high time we pulled together, and get the job done right. It is up to us to straighten this out.

This job has four basic parts. First, the Congress should, this month, within a budget agreement, enact growth-oriented tax measures to help avoid recession in the short term and to increase savings, investment, productivity and competitiveness for the longer term. These measures include extending incentives for research and experimentation; expanding the use of I.R.A.'s for new homeowners; establishing tax-deferred family savings accounts; creating incentives for the creation of enterprise zones and initiatives to encourage more domestic drilling, and, yes, reducing the tax rate for capital gains.

Second, the Congress should, this month, enact a prudent multiyear defense program, one that reflects not only the improvement in East-West relations, but our broader responsibilities to deal with the continuing

risks of outlaw action and regional conflict. Even with our obligations in the gulf, a sound defense budget can have some reduction in real terms, and we are prepared to accept that. But to go beyond such levels, where cutting defense would threaten our vital margin of safety, is something I will never accept.

The world is still dangerous. Surely that is now clear. Stability is not secure. American interests are far-reaching. Interdependence has increased. The consequences of regional instability can be global. This is no time to risk America's capacity to protect her vital interests.

Third, the Congress should, this month, enact measures to increase domestic energy production and energy conservation in order to reduce dependence on foreign oil. These measures should include my proposals to increase incentives for domestic oil and gas exploration, fuel-switching and to accelerate the development of Alaskan energy resources, without damage to wildlife.

As you know, when the oil embargo was imposed in the early 1970's, the United States imported almost six million barrels of oil per day. This year, before the Iraqi invasion, U.S. imports had risen to nearly eight million barrels per day. We had moved in the wrong direction. Now we must act to correct that trend.

Fourth: The Congress should, this month, enact a five-year program to reduce the projected deficits and debt by $500 billion—that is, by half a trillion dollars. If, with the Congress, we can develop a satisfactory program by the end of the month, we can avoid the ax of "sequester"—deep across-the-board cuts that would threaten our military capacity and risk substantial domestic disruption.

I want to be able to tell the American people, we have truly solved the deficit problem. For me to do that, a budget agreement must meet these tests;

It must include the measures I've recommended to increase economic growth and reduce dependence on foreign oil.

It must be fair. All should contribute, but the burden should not be excessive for any one group of programs or people.

It must address the growth of government's hidden liabilities.

It must reform the budget process, and further: it must be real.

I urge Congress to provide me a comprehensive five-year deficit reduction program to me as a complete legislative package—with measures to assure that it can be fully enforced. America is tired of phoney deficit reduction, or promise-now, save-later-plans. Enough is enough. It is time for a program that is credible and real.

Finally, to the extent that the deficit reduction program includes new revenue measures, it must avoid any measure that would threaten economic growth or turn us back toward higher income tax rates. That is one path we should not head down again.

I have been pleased with recent progress, although it has not always seemed so smooth.

But now it is time to produce.

I hope we can work out a responsible plan. But with or without agreement from the budget summit, I ask both houses of the Congress to allow a straight up-or-down vote on a complete $500 billion deficit reduction package—not later than Sept 28.

If the Congress cannot get me a budget, then Americans will have to face a tough, mandated sequester.

I am hopeful, in fact I am confident, the Congress will do what it should.

In the final analysis, our ability to meet our responsibilities abroad depends upon political will and consensus at home. This is never easy in democracies, where we govern only with the consent of the governed. And although free people in a free society are bound to have their differences, Americans traditionally come together in times of adversity and challenge.

Once again, Americans have stepped forward to share a tearful goodbye with their families before leaving for a strange and distant shore. At this very moment, they serve together with Arabs, Europeans, Asians and Africans in defense of principle and the dream of a new world order. That is why they sweat and toil in the sand and the heat and the sun.

If they can come together under such adversity; if old adversaries like the Soviet Union and the United States can work in common cause; then surely we who are so fortunate to be in this great chamber—Democrats, Republicans, liberals, conservatives—can come together to fulfill our responsibilities here.

Thank you, good night and God bless America.

Challenges for Americans

—William Faulkner—

Acceptance of the Nobel Prize for Literature
(December 10, 1950)

William Faulkner, who once described himself as "a farmer who just likes to tell stories," is considered by many critics to be America's greatest novelist. Born in Mississippi in 1897, Faulkner had little formal education and left high school to work in his grandfather's bank. What he did have, however, was a passion for literature. He read the poetry of Shakespeare, Spenser, Shelley, Keats, Swinburne, and Housman in a program of voracious but, in his words, "undirected and uncorrected reading."

Young Faulkner found it hard to keep a job, moving from one to another—in World War I he joined the Canadian Air Force and learned to fly. In 1919 he published his first poem, and for a brief period he moved to New York. He found, however, that he could not live away from the South and returned first to New Orleans and then to his old home in Oxford, Mississippi.

With the publication of *As I Lay Dying* in 1930 and *Sanctuary* in 1931, Faulkner established his reputation as a first-rate new novelist, one whose interpretation of life in a small Mississippi county, "complete and living in all its details," stood, as one critic put it, "as a parable or legend of all the Deep South." Faulkner wrote of human experience in all its varieties and complexities—its pain and its perversion, its joy and its sadness, its triumph and its failure. By the time he was awarded the 1949 Nobel Prize for Literature for his "powerful and artistically independent contribution to the new American novel," he had produced such highly acclaimed works as *The Sound and the Fury, Sanctuary, Light in August, Absalom, Absalom!*, and *Intruder in the Dust*.

In his speech accepting the prize, Faulkner deplored the growing preoccupation with the physical fear of annihilation that hung over the world in the late forties, a fear that caused us to think only of the question: "When will I be blown up?" Directing the attention of young writers to the concerns of the human spirit, he urged them to address "the problems of the human heart in conflict with itself." For Faulkner, writers not only recorded human experience but influenced it as well. "Man," Faulkner believed, "will not merely endure: he will prevail." With faith in the human "spirit capable of compassion and sacrifice and endurance," Faulkner defined the writer's duty: "to help man endure by lifting his heart, by reminding him of the courage and honor and hope and pride and compassion and pity and sacrifice which have been the glory of his past."

I feel that this award was not made to me as a man, but to my work—a life's work in the agony and sweat of the human spirit, not for the glory and least of all for profit, but to create out of the materials of the human spirit something which did not exist before. So this award is only mine in trust. It will not be difficult to find a dedication for the money part of it commensurate with the purpose and significance of its origin. But I would like to do the same with the acclaim too, by using this moment as a pinnacle from which I might be listened to by the young men and women already dedicated to the same anguish and travail, among whom is already that one who will some day stand here where I am standing.

Our tragedy today is a general and universal physical fear so long sustained by now that we can even bear it. There are no longer problems of the spirit. there is only the question: When will I be blown up? Because of this, the young man or woman writing today has forgotten the problems of the human heart in conflict with itself which alone can make good writing because only that is worth writing about, worth the agony and the sweat.

He must learn them again. He must teach himself that the basest of all things is to be afraid; and, the aching himself that, forget it forever, leaving no room in his workshop for anything but the old verities and truths of the heart, the old universal truths lacking which any story is ephemeral and doomed—love and

honor and pity and pride and compassion and sacrifice. Until he does so, he labors under a curse. He writes not of love but of lust, of defeats in which nobody loses anything of value, of victories without hope and, worst of all, without pity or compassion. His griefs grieve on no universal bones, leaving no scars. He writes not of the heart but of the glands.

Until he relearns these things, he will write as though he stood among and watched the end of the man. I decline to accept the end of man. It is easy enough to say that man is immortal simply because he will endure: that when the last dingdong of doom has clanged and faded from the last worthless rock hanging tideless in the last red and dying evening, that even then there will still be one more sound: that of his puny inexhaustible voice, still talking. I refuse to accept this. I believe that man will not merely endure: he will prevail. He is immortal, not because he alone among creatures has an inexhaustible voice, but because he has a soul, a spirit capable of compassion and sacrifice and endurance. The poet's, the writer's, duty is to write about these things. It is his privilege to help man endure by lifting his heart, by reminding him of the courage and honor and hope and pride and compassion and pity and sacrifice which have been the glory of his past. The poet's voice need not merely be the record of man, it can be one of the props, the pillars to help him endure and prevail.

George Meany

Labor Day Address
(September 3, 1956)

The labor movement, which had struggled for existence in the 1920's and 1930's, had become a powerful factor in American life by the 1950's. Two great unions, the American Federation of Labor under its president George Meany, and the Congress of Industrial Organizations led by Walter Reuther, were particularly strong in the industrial areas of the Northeast and the Midwest. Together, they represented over 16,000,000 workers in 1955. After years of separation, and sometimes competition and conflict, the two unions merged into one—the AFL-CIO—in that year. George Meany was chosen to head the new organization.

Meany, a plumber who began his career as a labor leader as the business agent of a New York plumbers' union local in 1922, later served as president of the New York State Federation of Labor and then as secretary-treasurer of the AFL. During World War II, Meany was a member of the National Defense Mediation Board, and subsequently was appointed to various government boards and committees. He developed a strong interest in international labor issues and became an implacable foe of Communist efforts to influence the labor movement both in America and abroad.

When Meany gave his speech over CBS radio on Labor Day, 1956, organized labor, although a potent force, was on the defensive. Membership had peaked and was beginning to decline slightly. Several states were considering so-called "right to work" laws that undermined the union shop by eliminating the requirement of union membership. Unsavory stories of criminal activities, extortion, and strong arm tactics—particularly in the notorious teamsters' union and the dock workers' union—undermined the public image of the union movement.

In his radio address, George Meany sought to associate the labor movement with important American values and patriotic policies. He argued that gains made by organized labor were shared by all Americans, the "farmers and the businessmen as well as the wage-earners." Citing labor's efforts on behalf of social justice and social reform, Meany asserted that campaigning for "legislation to build better schools, to erase slums, to broaden and improve social security and to provide national health insurance" resulted in benefits for "every American family, not only the families of union members...." Meany was fiercely anti-Communist; he denounced the "mass oppression" and "slave labor" of the Soviets and called for a sound, strong, and stable American economy as the best way to thwart Communist designs. In calling for a program to prevent unemployment through "federal action, supplemented by private initiative," Meany urged political support for legislators who would bring this about. Finally, he maintained the dedication of the union movement to basic values of liberal America: "peace, with freedom and justice for mankind ... a steadily higher standard of living ... full enjoyment of civil rights by all Americans ... improved relation between labor and management ... a broader measure of social security ... in short," Meany concluded, "the highest ideals of the land we love."

Labor Day is the only national holiday dedicated to plain people, rather than heroes and historic events. It provides an opportunity for all of us to recognize and honor the working men and women who have built America to its present stature and keep it going with such steady efficiency. We need this annual reminder because during the rest of the year the contributions made to our well-being by the unsung workers of our country are taken for granted. Only when some dramatic interruption takes place, do we begin to realize how dependent we are in our daily lives upon the continuous miracle of production and service rendered by the great army of free American workers.

Since its inception 62 years ago, Labor Day has become an occasion not only for celebration but for reflection. Traditionally, this is the day when the American free trade union movement pauses momentarily to survey the path it has traveled and to chart its course for the future.

In my opinion, the labor movement, now united for the first time in a generation, and with the solid support of its more than fifteen million members, is determined to go forward in the coming year toward greater achievement for all the American people.

Frequently we hear people ask:—"What does labor want? What is labor looking for?" The most direct answer to such questions can be summed up in one word:—"More."

But let me make it clear that we want *more* not only for ourselves, but for all Americans—for the farmers and the businessmen as well as for wage-earners.

When we fight for a higher standard of living, we are helping all workers, not only union members. We are also helping employers and farmers, who must depend upon the high purchasing power of city workers to buy their products.

When we campaign for legislation to build better schools, to erase slums, to broaden and improve social security and to provide national health insurance, every American family, not only the families of union members, stands to benefit.

Anyone who wishes a clear understanding of the trade union movement should realize that it places as much emphasis on giving as on getting. we are ready and willing to do our full part in building better communities and a stronger nation.

We are determined, as well, to make the most effective contribution we can toward promoting peace, freedom and prosperity for people throughout the world.

Labor's program is a big program, It looks ahead. It is not to be discouraged by opposition or by temporary setbacks. It is fully conscious of labor's own responsibility for self-discipline. It is completely in accord with the free and democratic way of life.

That free way of life, the foundation on which all our plans for the future are built, is threatened today by forces committed to the slave way of life. This is the central fact which overshadows our times. There is no escape from it. If we are to plan intelligently and proceed logically, we must face up to this threat. We must put first things first.

Thus labor had become increasingly concerned with foreign policy. People cannot live and make progress without peace.

The aggressive forces of Communism have demonstrated repeatedly that they do not share our devotion to peace. They will not hesitate to employ war, if they find it necessary to further their insatiable ambition for world-wide domination. In this atomic age, we are aware that war could wipe out whole nations overnight.

There is only one power on earth strong enough to deter Soviet Russia from plunging civilization into such a suicidal war—our own country. As the leader of the free world, we must remain militarily, economically and morally strong. The price of peace can never be as heavy as the cost of war.

The mere fact that the leaders of Soviet Russia in recent months have spoken, on occasion, in conciliatory tones and have denounced Stalin for some of the many crimes in the perpetration of which they were as guilty as their deceased master, should not delude us into believing that the true nature and character of the Communist conspiracy have changed. Khrushchev & Co. are still doing business at the same stand in the same old way. They still deny the people under their domain any vestige of human freedom. They still govern by mass oppression. They still are building up their military machine with slave labor.

Yet some naive spokesmen on foreign affairs are now advocating that the United States adopt a more "flexible" policy toward Soviet Russia. That term impresses me only as a semantic camouflage for defeatist appeasement. For if we are to approach the Communist dictators, with a "flexible" position against their inflexible diplomatic front, it means that we will be forced to give way whenever and wherever Moscow exerts pressure.

That is not the road to peace and security. I am convinced that honest foreign policy is the best foreign policy. We should let Soviet Russia, and our Allies as well, know exactly where we stand. We should say frankly that we do not want war, but that we shall resist aggression; that we uphold the right of people everywhere to freedom and self-determination; that we will not recognize any government forced upon a nation by a foreign power; that we oppose any and all forms of dictatorship; that we favor the right of people caught in the grip of any form of colonialism to choose their own destiny through free elections; that we are ready to participate in an effective and enforceable dis-

armament program; that we seek to unite the free peoples of this world in common cause; and that we are willing to assist under-developed nations and areas with long-range programs of economic and technical aid.

If we maintain such a foreign policy firm and consistently, Soviet Russia will be found to respect it. Our Allies will find that in the long run it will redound to their advantage. And those nations which have been playing with the fire of neutralism, will discover that their security and prosperity will be promised by alliances with a free world.

Labor speaks from experience in coping with Communism. We have met and defeated every effort of the Communist conspiracy to infiltrate the American trade union movement. Today, the AFL-CIO is completely united in its opposition to Communism and any other form of dictatorship. There is no labor force in the world so thoroughly immune to Communist subversion, so irrevocably wedded to the free way of life.

As we see it, the preservation of that way of life requires more than military power, more than atomic bombs, more than diplomatic firmness. For a long time, the Soviet rulers have relied on a secret weapon to sap our strength. They have banked on the belief that our economy would collapse. We must see to it that our economy becomes ever more sound, stable and strong.

The essential foundation for continuing prosperity in America is sufficient buying power in the hands of the great masses of our people. The nation's factories and farms are geared for production in abundance. They can't keep going at full speed if only a few people have money to spend. If the volume of consumption lags, goods pile up in warehouses and in stores, markets become glutted with surpluses, plants close down, workers are laid off and our entire economy goes into a tailspin.

The only logical and effective way to prevent such a breakdown is to keep wage standards high. When workers earn enough to buy not merely the bare necessities of life, but some comforts and luxuries as well, business booms and the farmers are assured of good income.

The average employer or farmer is too closely concerned with his own special problem to devote much time or effort to the overall economic picture. The only major organization in the nation which keeps pushing and pressing for prosperity for all is the trade union movement. It sparks the drive for higher purchasing power. It exerts pressure through collective bargaining for wage increases. It campaigns for legislation to bring about a more realistic Federal minimum wage primarily for the benefit of unorganized workers. Thus, the trade union movement is performing a necessary and vital role for the economic health of the nation.

Today, American industry stands on the threshold of a new age of automation and atomic power. These developments will bring about profound changes in production. Factories will be able to produce more goods with fewer workers. Total output will go up by leaps and bounds.

This presents a challenge to the nation. We must be ready to prevent mass disemployment and massive surpluses. We must avoid a disastrous industrial revolution.

But there is another side to the coin. The trade union movement believes that industrial progress should be welcomed, rather than resisted. We are convinced that it can be harnessed to bring about human progress. We foresee the probability of shorter hours of work to offset the substitution of automatic machinery for hand labor. We anticipate a wonderful opportunity to start in motion projects necessary to the well-being of our people and our nation that have been neglected too long—better schools, decent homes, improved roads.

This is the kind of work that will keep millions of people employed—work in which everyone can take satisfaction—work that will make life better for ourselves and for future generations—work that will build America and her communities into a finer and stronger nation.

Wishful thinking won't bring about a program of such magnitude. It requires Federal action, supplemented by private initiative. Therefore, the American Federation of Labor and Congress of Industrial Organizations will press for the adoption of a broad and constructive legislative program in the next Congress.

Approval of such a program by Congress depends upon the election results November 6. If the voters of this country elect liberal majorities to both houses of Congress, we can make great gains in the next two years.

Labor is determined to take an active part in the campaign on a non-partisan basis. We will support candidates from both parties whose records justify confidence in their attitude toward the public interest. Above all, we will concentrate on bringing out a full vote, for we have full confidence in the good sense of the American people.

In seeking these objectives, the trade union movement is encouraged to look forward to greater success than in the recent past because labor is now united. We are going to be able to do a better job for the workers of this country and for the nation as a whole. We are not content to sit still and accept the status quo. Our sights are set on a much higher goal.

On this Labor Day, the trade union movement dedicates itself to work for peace, with freedom and justice for mankind—to work for a steadily higher standard of living—to work for the full enjoyment of civil rights by all Americans, regardless of race, color or religion—to work for improved relations between labor and management under a law that will be fair to both—to work for a broader measure of social security for the protection of all citizens against the hazards of poverty, old age, disability and illness—to work in short, for the highest ideals of the land we love.

Newton Minow

The Vast Wasteland
(May 9, 1961)

By 1960 it was clear that television was a firmly entrenched fact of American life. There were over five hundred commercial television stations, and advertisers and broadcasters had learned the great commercial value of the medium. It was also clear that television was not to be the educational and intellectual antidote to the mindless—and endless—babbling of disc jockeys, the stream of popular music, the fleeting headlines passing for news reports, that dominated radio programming. Critics of television recognized the achievements of an Edward R. Murrow and the artistic accomplishments of talented artists who produced innovative and interesting dramatic programs. Such fare, however, was sparse, and many critics, such as the chairman of the Federal Communications Commission, newly appointed by President John F. Kennedy, thought that broadcasters could do much better. Indeed, as some columnists noted, if Newton Minow succeeded in his new job, he would "be enshrined in communications history as the man who mopped the blood off the TV screen, dumped a million cans of canned laughter into the sea, and put the old class-B movies back in the archives."

Bright, young, energetic, FCC chairman Minow typified the "New Frontiersmen" that Kennedy brought to Washington. He served in the army at the end of World War II, graduated in speech and political science from Northwestern, and then earned a degree in 1950 from that university's law school. Interested in law and politics, Minow clerked for the chief justice of the United States Supreme Court, Fred M. Vinson, was administrative assistant to Adlai Stevenson when he was governor of Illinois, took an active part in Stevenson's 1952 and 1956 campaigns, and maintained a partnership in a Chicago law firm. He impressed the Kennedys as chairman of the Chicago area Citizens for Kennedy in the 1960 election and, at 34, was appointed to the FCC by the new President.

In the past, the Federal Communications Commission had not been seen as a very effective body. It was plagued by internal strife, an inability to solve controversial problems, and inaction. Among the many issues that faced Minow were those related to licensing networks, a process that critics believed had become so routine that broadcasters felt little obligation to abide by the goals they had articulated when first applying for licenses. He was concerned about the influence of television on the young and on the family and convinced of the enormous potential of television to educate and inform. Minow challenged the National Association of Broadcasters to change the dismal direction in which television was moving. He certainly did not want to impose any form of censorship on the media, and he recognized the dangers of government pressure on programming practices, yet he did hope that the broadcasters themselves—spurred on by the threat of close scrutiny by the public and the government when applying for license renewal—could raise the level of broadcasting and truly serve the public interest.

In pointing to the "vast wasteland" that television had become, Minow raised significant questions about how government and the media should interact and what responsibilities the media had to assume. These questions have obviously not been answered thirty years later and are still vital ones as television continues to expand and to affect the daily lives of Americans.

Governor Collins, Distinguished Guests, Ladies and Gentlemen:—Thank you for this opportunity to meet with you today. This is my first public address since I took over my new job. When the New Frontiersmen rode into town, I locked myself in my office to do my homework and get my feet wet. But apparently I haven't managed to stay out of hot water. I seem to have detected a certain nervous apprehension about what I might say or do when I emerged from that locked office for this, my maiden station break.

First, let me begin by dispelling a rumor. I was not picked for this job because I regard myself as the fastest draw on the New Frontier.

Second, let me start a rumor. Like you, I have carefully read President Kennedy's messages about the regulatory agencies, conflict of interest, and the dangers of *ex parte* contracts. And of course, we at the Federal Communications Commission will do our part. Indeed, I may even suggest that we change the name of the FCC to The Seven Untouchables!

It may also come as a surprise to some of you, but I want you to know that you have my admiration and respect. Yours is a most honorable profession. Anyone who is in the broadcasting business has a tough row to hoe. You earn your bread by using public property. When you work in broadcasting you volunteer for public service, public pressure, and public regulation. You must compete with other attractions and other invest-

ments, and the only way you can do it is to prove to us every three years that you should have been in business in the first place.

I can think of easier ways to make a living.

But I cannot think of more satisfying ways.

I admire your courage—but that doesn't mean I would make life any easier for you. Your license lets you use the public's airwaves as Trustees for 180,000,000 Americans. The public is your beneficiary. If you want to stay on as Trustees, you must deliver a decent return to the public—not only to your stockholders. So, as a representative of the public, your health and your product are among my chief concerns.

As to your health: let's talk only of television today. 1960 gross broadcast revenues of the television industry were over $1,268,000,000; profit before taxes was $243,900,000; an average return on revenue of 19.2%. Compared with 1959, gross broadcast revenues were $1,163,900,000, and profit before taxes was $222,300,000, an average return on revenue of 19.1%. So, the percentage increase of total revenues from 1959 to 1960 was 9%, and the percentage increase of profit was 9.7%. This, despite a recession. For your investors, the price has indeed been right.

I have confidence in your health.

But not in your product.

It is with this and much more in mind that I come before you today.

One editorialist in the trade press wrote that "the FCC of the New Frontier is going to be one of the toughest FCC's in the history of broadcast regulation." If he meant that we intend to enforce the law in the public interest, let me make it perfectly clear that he is right—we do.

If he meant that we intend to muzzle or censor broadcasting, he is dead wrong.

It would not surprise me if some of you had expected me to come here today and say in effect, "Clean up your own house or the government will do it for you."

Well, in a limited sense, you would be right—I've just said it.

But I want to say to you earnestly that it is not in that spirit that I come before you today, nor is it in that spirit that I intend to serve the FCC.

I am in Washington to help broadcasting, not to harm it; to strengthen it, not weaken it; to reward it, not punish it; to encourage it, not threaten it; to stimulate it, not censor it.

Above all, I am here to uphold and protect the public interest.

What do we mean by "the public interest"? Some say the public interest is merely what interests the public.

I disagree.

So does your distinguished president, Governor Collins. In a recent speech he said, "Broadcasting, to serve the public interest, must have a soul and a conscience, a burning desire to excel, as well as to sell; the urge to build the character, citizenship and intellectual stature of people, as well as to expand the gross national product.... By no means do I imply that the broadcasters disregard the public interest.... But a much better job can be done, and should be done."

I could not agree more.

And I would add that in today's world, with chaos in Laos and the Congo aflame, with Communist tyranny on our Caribbean doorstep and relentless pressure on our Atlantic alliance, with social and economic problems at home of the gravest nature, yes, and with technological knowledge that makes it possible, as our President has said, not only to destroy our world but to destroy poverty around the world—in a time of peril and opportunity, the old complacent, unbalanced fare of Action-Adventure and Situation Comedies is simply not good enough.

Your industry possesses the most powerful voice in America. It has an inescapable duty to make that voice ring with intelligence and with leadership. In a few years, this exciting industry has grown from a novelty to an instrument of overwhelming impact on the American people. It should be making ready for the kind of leadership that newspapers and magazines assumed years ago, to make our people aware of their world.

Ours has been called the jet age, the atomic age, the space age. It is also, I submit, the television age. And just as history will decide whether the leaders of today's world employed the atom to destroy the world or rebuild it for mankind's benefit, so will history decide whether today's broadcasters employed their powerful voice to enrich the people or debase them.

If I seem today to address myself chiefly to the problems of television, I don't want any of you radio broadcasters to think we've gone to sleep at your switch—we haven't. We still listen. But in recent years most of the controversies and cross-currents in broadcast programming have swirled around television. And so my subject today is the television industry and the public interest.

Like everybody, I wear more than one hat. I am the Chairman of the FCC. I am also a television viewer and the husband and father of other television viewers. I have seen a great many television programs that seemed to me eminently worthwhile, and I am not talking about the much bemoaned good old days of *Playhouse 90* and *Studio One*.

I am talking about this past season. Some were wonderfully entertaining, such as *The Fabulous Fifties*, the *Fred Astaire Show*, and the *Bing Crosby Special*; some were dramatic and moving, such as *Conrad's Victory* and *Twilight Zone*; some were marvelously informative, such as *The Nation's Future*, *CBS Reports*, and *The Valiant Years*. I could list many more—programs that I am sure everyone here felt enriched his own life and that of his family. When television is good, nothing—not the theatre, not the magazines or newspapers—nothing is better.

But when television is bad, nothing is worse. I invite you to sit down in front of your television set when your station goes on the air and stay there without a book, magazine, newspaper, profit and loss sheet or rating book to distract you—and keep your eyes glued to that set until the station signs off. I can assure you that you will observe a vast wasteland.

You will see a procession of game shows, violence, audience participation shows, formula comedies about totally unbelievable families, blood and thunder, mayhem, violence, sadism, murder, western badmen, western good men, private eyes, gangsters, more violence, and cartoons. And, endlessly, commercials—many screaming, cajoling, and offending. And most of all, boredom. True, you will see a few things you will enjoy. But they will be very, very few. And if you think I exaggerate, try it.

Is there one person in this room who claims that broadcasting can't do better?

Well, a glance at next season's proposed programming can give us little heart. Of 73 1/2 hours of prime evening time, the networks have tentatively scheduled 59 hours to categories of "action-adventure," situation comedy, variety, quiz, and movies.

Is there one network president in this room who claims he can't do better?

Well, is there at least one network president who believes that the other networks can't do better.

Gentlemen, your trust accounting with your beneficiaries is overdue.

Never have so few owed so much to so many.

Why is so much of television so bad? I have heard many answers: demands of your advertisers; competition for ever higher ratings; the need always to attract a mass audience; the high cost of television programs; the insatiable appetite for programming material—these are some of them. Unquestionably, these are tough problems not susceptible to easy answers.

But I am not convinced that you have tried hard enough to solve them.

I do not accept the idea that the present over-all programming is aimed accurately at the public taste. The ratings tell us only that some people have their television sets turned on and of that number, so many are tuned to one channel and so many to another. They don't tell us what the public might watch if they were offered half a dozen additional choices. A rating, at best, is an indication of how many people saw what you gave them. Unfortunately, it does not reveal the depth of the penetration, or the intensity of reaction, and it never reveals what the acceptance would have been if what you gave them had been better—if all the forces of art and creativity and daring and imagination had been unleashed. I believe in the people's good sense and good taste, and I am not convinced that the people's taste is as low as some of you assume.

My concern with the rating services is not with their accuracy. Perhaps they are accurate. I really don't know. What, then, is wrong with the ratings? It's not been their accuracy—it's been their use.

Certainly, I hope you will agree that ratings should have little influence where children are concerned. The best estimates indicate that during the hours of 5 to 6 p.m. 60% of your audience is composed of children under 12. And most young children today, believe it or not, spend as much time watching television as they do in the schoolroom. I repeat—let that sink in—most young children today spend as much time watching television as they do in the schoolroom. It used to be said that there were three great influences on a child: home, school, and church. Today, there is a fourth great influence, and you ladies and gentlemen control it.

If parents, teachers, and ministers conducted their responsibilities by following the ratings, children would have a steady diet of ice cream, school holidays, and no Sunday School. What about your responsibilities? Is there no room on television to teach, to inform, to uplift, to stretch, to enlarge the capacities of our children? Is there no room for programs deepening their understanding of children in other lands? Is there no room for a children's news show explaining something about the world to them at their level of understanding? Is there no room for reading the great literature of the past, teaching them the great traditions of freedom? There are some fine children's shows, but they are drowned out in the massive doses of cartoons, violence, and more violence. Must these be your trademarks? Search your consciences and see if you cannot offer more to your young beneficiaries whose future you guide so many hours each and every day.

What about adult programming and ratings? You know, newspaper publishers take popularity ratings too. The answers are pretty clear: it is almost always the comics, followed by the advice to the lovelorn columns. But, ladies and gentlemen, the news is still on the front page of all newspapers, the editorials are not replaced by more comics, the newspapers have not become one long collection of advice to the lovelorn. Yet newspapers do not need a license from the government to be in business—they do not use public property. But in television—where your responsibilities as public trustees are so plain, the moment that the ratings indicate that westerns are popular there are new imitations of westerns on the air faster than the old coaxial cable could take us from Hollywood to New York. Broadcasting cannot continue to live by the numbers. Ratings ought to be the slave of the broadcaster, not his master. And you and I both know that the rating services themselves would agree.

Let me make clear that what I am talking about is balance. I believe that the public interest is made up of many interests. There are many people in this great country and you must serve all of us. You will get no argument from me if you say that, given a choice between a western and a symphony, more people will watch the western. I like westerns and private eyes too—but a steady diet for the whole country is obviously not in the public interest. We all know that people would more often prefer to be entertained than stimulated or informed. But your obligations are not satisfied if you look only to popularity as a test of what to broadcast. You are not only in show business; you are free to communicate ideas as well as relaxation. You must provide a wider range of choices, more diversity, more alternatives. It is not enough to cater to the nation's whims—you must also serve the nation's needs.

And I would add this—that if some of you persist in a relentless search for the highest rating and the lowest common denominator, you may very well lose your audience. Because, to paraphrase a great American who was recently my law partner, the people are wise, wiser than some of the broadcasters—and politicians—think.

As you may have gathered, I would like to see television improved. But how is this to be brought about? By voluntary action by the broadcasters themselves? By direct government intervention? Or how?

Let me address myself now to my role not as a viewer but as Chairman of the FCC. I could not if I would, chart for you this afternoon in detail all of the actions I contemplate. Instead, I want to make clear some of the fundamental principles which guide me.

First: the people own the air. They own it as much in prime evening time as they do at 6 o'clock Sunday morning. For every hour that the people give you—you owe them something. I intend to see that your debt is paid with service.

Second: I think it would be foolish and wasteful for us to continue any worn-out wrangle over the problems of payola, rigged quiz shows, and other mistakes of the past. There are laws on the books which we will enforce. But there is no chip on my shoulder. We live together in perilous, uncertain times; we face together staggering problems; and we must not waste much time now by re-hashing the clichés of past controversy. To quarrel over the past is to lose the future.

Third: I believe in the free enterprise system. I want to see broadcasting improved and I want you to

do the job. I am proud to champion your cause. It is not rare for American businessmen to serve a public trust. Yours is a special trust because it is imposed by law.

Fourth: I will do all I can to help educational television. There are still not enough educational stations, and major centers of the country still lack usable educational channels. If there were a limited number of printing presses in this country, you may be sure that a fair proportion of them would be put to educational use. Educational television has an enormous contribution to make to the future, and I intend to give it a hand along the way. If there is not a nation-wide educational television system in this country, it will not be the fault of the FCC.

Fifth: I am unalterably opposed to governmental censorship. There will be no suppression of programming which does not meet with bureaucratic tastes. Censorship strikes at the tap root of our free society.

Sixth: I did not come to Washington to idly observe the squandering of the public's airwaves. The squandering of our airwaves is no less important than the lavish waste of any precious natural resource. I intend to take the job of Chairman of the FCC very seriously. I believe in the gravity of my own particular sector of the New Frontier. There will be times perhaps when you will consider that I take myself or my job *too* seriously. Frankly, I don't care if you do. For I am convinced that either one takes this job seriously—or one can be seriously taken.

Now, how will these principles be applied? Clearly, at the heart of the FCC's authority lies its power to license, to renew or fail to renew, or to revoke a license. As you know, when your license comes up for renewal, your performance is compared with your promises. I understand that many people feel that in the past licenses were often renewed *pro forma*. I say to you now: renewal will not be *pro forma* in the future. There is nothing permanent or sacred about a broadcast license.

But simply matching promises and performance is not enough. I intend to do more. I intend to find out whether the people care. I intend to find out whether the community which each broadcaster serves believes he has been serving the public interest. When a renewal is set down for hearing, I intend—wherever possible—to hold a well-advertised public hearing, right in the community you have promised to serve. I want the people who own the air and the homes that television enters to tell you and the FCC what's been going on. I want the people—if they are truly interested in the service you give them—to make notes, document cases, tell us the facts. For those few of you who really believe that the public interest is merely what interests the public—I hope that these hearings will arouse no little interest.

The FCC has a fine reserve of monitors—almost 180 million Americans gathered around 56 million sets. If you want those monitors to be your friends at court—it's up to you.

Some of you may say,—"Yes, but I still do not know where the line is between a grant of a renewal and the hearing you just spoke of." My answer is: Why should you want to know how close you can come to the edge of the cliff? What the Commission asks of you is to make a conscientious, good faith effort to serve the public interest. Everyone of you serves a community in which the people would benefit by educational, religious, instructive or other public service programming. Every one of you serves an area which has local needs—as to local elections, controversial issues, local news, local talent. Make a serious, genuine effort to put on that programming. When you do, you will not be playing brinkmanship with the public interest.

What I've been saying applies to broadcast stations. Now a station break for the networks:

You know your importance in this great industry. Today, more than one-half of all hours of television station programming comes from the networks; in prime time, this rises to more than 3/4 of the available hours.

You know that the FCC has been studying network operations for some time. I intend to press this to a speedy conclusion with useful results. I can tell you right now, however, that I am deeply concerned with concentration of power in the hands of the networks. As a result, too many local stations have forgone any efforts at local programming, with little use of live talent and local service. Too many local stations operate with one hand on the network switch and the other on a projector loaded with old movies. We want the individual stations to be free to meet their legal responsibilities to serve their communities.

I join Governor Collins in his views so well expressed to the advertisers who use the public air. I urge the networks to join him and undertake a very special mission on behalf of this industry: you can tell your advertisers, "This is the high quality we are going to serve—take it or other people will. If you think you can find a better place to move automobiles, cigarettes and soap—go ahead and try."

Tell your sponsors to be less concerned with costs per thousand and more concerned with understanding per millions. And remind your stockholders that an investment in broadcasting is buying a share in public responsibility.

The networks can start this industry on the road to freedom from the dictatorship of numbers.

But there is more to the problem than network influences on stations or advertiser influences on networks. I know the problems networks face in trying to clear some of their best programs—the informational programs that exemplify public service. They are your finest hours—whether sustaining or commercial, whether regularly scheduled or special—these are the signs that broadcasting knows the way to leadership. They make the public's trust in you a wise choice.

They should be seen. As you know, we are readying for use new forms by which broadcast stations will report their programming to the Commission. You probably also know that special attention will be paid in these reports to public service programming. I believe that stations taking network service should also be required to report the extent of the local clearance of network public service programming, and when they fail to clear them, they should explain why. If it is to put on some outstanding local program, this is one reason. But, if it is simply to carry some old movie, that is an entirely different matter. The Commission should consider such clearance reports carefully when making up its mind about the licensee's over-all programming.

We intend to move—and as you know, indeed the FCC was rapidly moving in other new areas before the new administration arrived in Washington. And I want to pay my public respects to my very able predecessor, Fred Ford, and my colleagues on the Commission who have welcomed me to the FCC with warmth and cooperation.

We have approved an experiment with pay TV, and in New York we are testing the potential of UHF broadcasting. Either or both of these may revolutionize television. Only a foolish prophet would venture to guess the direction they will take, and their effect. But we intend that they shall be explored fully—for they are part of broadcasting's New Frontier.

The questions surrounding pay TV are largely economic. The questions surrounding UHF are largely technological. We are going to give the infant pay TV a chance to prove whether it can offer a useful service; we are going to protect it from those who would strangle it in its crib.

As for UHF, I'm sure you know about our test in the canyons of New York City. We will take every possible positive step to break through the allocations barrier into UHF. We will put this sleeping giant to use and in the years ahead we may have twice as many channels operating in cities where now there are only two or three. We may have a half dozen networks instead of three.

I have told you that I believe in the free enterprise system. I believe that most of television's problems stem from lack of competition. This is the importance of UHF to me: with more channels on the air, we will be able to provide every community with enough stations to offer service to all parts of the public. Programs with a mass market appeal required by mass product advertisers certainly will still be available. But other stations will recognize the need to appeal to more limited markets and to special tastes. In this way, we can all have a much wider range of programs.

Television should thrive on this competition—and the country should benefit from alternative sources of service to the public. And—Governor Collins—I hope the NAB will benefit from many new members.

Another and perhaps the most important frontier: television will rapidly join the parade into space. International television will be with us soon. No one knows how long it will be until a broadcast from a studio in New York will be viewed in India as well as in Indiana, will be seen in the Congo as it is seen in Chicago. But as surely as we are meeting here today, that day will come—and once again our world will shrink.

What will the people of other countries think of us when they see our western badmen and good men punching each other in the jaw in between the shooting? What will the Latin American or African child learn of America from our great communications industry? We cannot permit television in its present form to be our voice overseas.

There is your challenge to leadership. You must reexamine some fundamentals of your industry. You must open your minds and open your hearts to the limitless horizons of tomorrow.

I can suggest some words that should serve to guide you:

"Television and all who participate in it are jointly accountable to the American public for respect for the special needs of children, for community responsibility, for the advancement of education and culture, for the acceptability of the program materials chosen, for decency and decorum in production, and for propriety in advertising. This responsibility cannot be discharged by any given group of programs, but can be discharged only through the highest standards of respect for the American home, applied to every moment of every program presented by television.

"Program materials should enlarge the horizons of the viewer, provide him with wholesome entertainment, afford helpful stimulation, and remind him of the responsibilities which the citizen has towards his society."

These words are not mine. They are yours. They are taken literally from your own Television Code. They reflect the leadership and aspirations of your own great industry. I urge you to respect them as I do. And I urge you to respect the intelligent and farsighted leadership of Governor LeRoy Collins, and to make this meeting a creative act. I urge you at this meeting and, after you leave, back home, at your stations and your networks, to strive ceaselessly to improve your product and to better serve your viewers, the American people.

I hope that we at the FCC will not allow ourselves to become so bogged down in the mountain of papers, hearings, memoranda, orders, and the daily routine that we close our eyes to the wider view of the public interest. And I hope that you broadcasters will not permit yourselves to become so absorbed in the chase for ratings, sales, and profits that you lose this wider view. Now more than ever before in broadcasting's history the times demand the best of all of us.

We need imagination in programming, not sterility; creativity, not imitation; experimentation, not conformity; excellence, not mediocrity. Television is filled with creative, imaginative people. You must strive to set them free.

Television in its young life has had many hours of greatness—its *Victory at Sea*, its Army-McCarthy hearings, its *Peter Pan*, its *Kraft Theaters*, its *See it Now*, its *Project 20*, the World Series, its political conventions and campaigns, The Great Debates—and it has had its endless hours of mediocrity and its moments of public disgrace. There are estimates that today the average viewer spends about 200 minutes daily with television, while the average reader spends 38 minutes with magazines and 40 minutes with newspapers. Television has grown faster than a teen-ager, and now it is time to grow up.

What you gentlemen broadcast through the people's air affects the people's taste, their knowledge, their opinions, their understanding of themselves and of their world, and their future.

The power of instantaneous sight and sound is without precedent in mankind's history. This is an awesome power. It has limitless capabilities for good—and for evil. And it carries with it awesome responsibilities, responsibilities which you and I cannot escape.

In his stirring Inaugural Address our President said, "And so, my fellow Americans: ask not what your country can do for you—ask what you can do for your country."

Ladies and Gentlemen:

Ask not what broadcasting can do for you. Ask what you can do for broadcasting.

I urge you to put the people's airwaves to the service of the people and the cause of freedom. You must help prepare a generation for great decisions. You must help a great nation fulfill its future.

Do this, and I pledge you our help.

James A. Michener

Space Exploration
(February 1, 1979)

In October of 1957 the Russians launched into space a small satellite, dubbed "Sputnik," which went into orbit around the earth and brought the space race dramatically to the attention of the American public. The United States, too, had a satellite program, but the Soviets scored a psychological victory by putting their instrument into space before America did so. Even though President Eisenhower offered assurances that American prestige, and not American security, had been damaged, politicians, press, and public were alarmed by the Russian coup.

Within a year an independent civilian agency, the National Aeronautics and Space Administration, was formed with the express goal of putting a man into space. The Mercury Project began training astronauts for a suborbital flight, but before this feat could be accomplished the Russians again scooped the United States by putting a cosmonaut into orbital flight in the spring of 1961. Six weeks later, John Kennedy declared that it was "time for this nation to take a clearly leading role in space achievement," and pledged to put a man on the moon and return him safely to earth "before this decade is out." Less than a year later, John Glenn made the first American orbital flight early in 1962, returning home to a hero's welcome. Then, in July of 1969, five months before the decade was out, Neil Armstrong and Edwin Aldrin separated their landing craft, *Eagle*, from the space ship *Columbia*, found a safe spot on the moon's surface, and reported home: "Houston, Tranquility Base here. The *Eagle* has landed."

Research and experimentation continued throughout the seventies as thousands of satellites were launched, a space laboratory developed, and probes sent to the furthest reaches of the solar system. As the eighties approached, the world was on the verge of a new phase in the exploration of space.

As the seventies ended, however, NASA could not automatically command widespread popular support for its programs or unlimited congressional support for its budget. Clearly there were problems at home that demanded both human and economic resources for their solution. Americans had to face the question of what its role would be in space research and development in the future.

James Michener, winner of the Pulitzer Prize, a popular novelist who often surveyed broad historical periods and events in such books as *Hawaii, Iberia,* and *Centennial,* spoke on behalf of the space program at a hearing of the Senate Subcommittee on Science, Technology, and Space early in 1979. He spoke, not as a scientific or administrative expert, but as one who had "been studying the rise and fall of nations...."

Considering that "history is a grand mix of concepts, actions, organizings and commitments which determines the extent to which any nation can achieve a good life for its citizens," Michener warned that "if a nation misses the great moments of its time it misses the foundations on which it can build the future." Arguing that there were both military and nonmilitary advantages to the United States in pursuing the exploration of space, Michener went further. He asserted that there are spiritual advantages as well. "The sense of exploration is intimately bound up with human resolve," Michener maintained; accordingly, "we cannot be indifferent to space, because the grand slow march of our intelligence has brought us, in our generation, to a point from which we can explore and understand and utilize it." He concluded that "a nation like ours is obligated to pursue its adventure in space."

The only justification for allowing me to appear before your Committee is that for some years I have been studying the rise and fall of nations and in so doing have reached certain conclusions governing that process.

There seem to be great tides which operate in the history of civilization, and nations are prudent if they estimate the force of those tides, their genesis and the extent to which they can be utilized. A nation which guesses wrong on all its estimates is apt to be in serious trouble if not on the brink of decline. Toward the middle of the Fifteenth Century the minds of sensible men were filled with speculations about the nature of their world, and although not much solid evidence was available, clever minds could piece together the fragments and achieve quite remarkable deductions.

Prince Henry the Navigator of Portugal occupies a curious place in history. He never captained one of his ships; he never sailed on any voyage of exploration; in fact, he stayed at home devouring old books, new rumors and future guesses, and from this melange constructed a view of the world that was extraordinarily accurate, even though he died some thirty years before Portuguese explorers brought proof of his theories.

Christopher Columbus had very little solid data to work with, but he had clever intuitions and a powerful capacity to piece together odd bits of information, leading him to conclusions that resulted in the effective discovery of America.

Nations at that time faced problems comparable to those faced by individuals like Columbus, Vasco da Gama and Sebastian Cabot. They had to decide whether they wanted to participate in the exploration of the world, and if so to what degree of commitment. Those like Portugal and Spain, who made early and fast decisions, gained empires of fantastic richness. Others like disoriented Germany and Italy, who did not perceive the possibilities, suffered grave disadvantages and never caught up. England and France were very tardy, but in the end the first made a stunning recovery, the latter never did.

I am not primarily interested in either the exploits of a few daring captains or the economic advantages of the nations they represented. The more lasting effect was on the spirit of the times, that wonderful enlarging of the human consciousness when it realized that the old definitions no longer applied, when it knew that the world consisted of a great deal more than Europe. To have missed the explorations was regrettable, but to have missed this spiritual awakening would have been disastrous. France and Sweden are excellent examples of nations which did little of the manual work but which reaped the intellectual rewards of the period.

One might almost argue that Portugal and Spain dragged home the raw material for France and Sweden to codify and digest, proving that any nation can participate in the great swing of civilization according to its peculiar capabilities. Portugal provided daring sea captains. England provided able administrators. And France provided the philosophers. Those which provided nothing lost an entire cycle of historical experience from which they never fully recovered.

Nor do I think that the rewards resulting from participation in a great cycle need be permanent, reaching down to all generations. I am quite content if my nation gains enlightenment or riches or advantages of other kinds for a respectable period. It can't be the hullabaloo of a single day or week, nor the celebration without foundation of some accidental accomplishment with little subsequent meaning. But if a nation responds to a challenge, succeeds in its effort, garners the rewards for a sensible period, and then loses the commanding position, I think no harm has been done. The nation has gleaned from that experience about all that it was destined to achieve, and a great good has been accomplished, because then the nation is prepared psychologically to tackle the next big problem when it comes along. And it surely will, for the life of any nation since the beginning of history has been a record of how it confronted the great challenges that inevitably came its way.

It may be unfortunate that I started these remarks with Portugal and its navigational and colonizing victories, as if they were the only kind that mattered. Actually, I would place them in second position, somewhat down the line in the scale of historical values. It is triumphs in the world of ideas and concepts that loom largest in my thinking, and I would like to stipulate several to give you a clue to my thinking. Today we are witnessing in the Near East the phenomenal vitality of the ideas promulgated some thirteen hundred years ago by Muhammad; these ideas have always been far more powerful than the empire put together by Portugal. The entire civilized world is indebted to the miracles that occurred in England during Elizabeth's reign and that of James I: I mean the extraordinary combination of Shakespeare's plays and the new translation of the Bible into English. These works fixed the English language as a tool of great beauty, great potential, and I often think of the Bible in its King James translation

when someone tells me that no committee ever accomplishes anything. Two of the greatest documents of our language were written by committees, our English Bible and our American Constitution. The trick, it seems, is to assemble the right committee.

I would place in this pantheon of great ideas Sigmund Freud's analysis of human behavior and Karl Marx's dissection of production and distribution. For any nation to have missed the significance of these powerful movements was to have missed the meaning of contemporary history.

Certainly, the world was changed by that cascade of brilliant industrial inventions produced by England in the late 1700s and early 1800s. We live today on the consequences of that industrial revolution. And I would include our own nation's enviable capacity to finance, organize and manage large industrial corporations.

Finally, of course, the historian must think of the impact of Christ's teachings two thousand years ago. They had a far greater importance than any mere exploration or conquest or empire.

But history is a grand mix of concepts, actions; organizings and commitments which determines the extent to which any nation can achieve a good life for its citizens, and I believe without question that if a nation misses the great movements of its time it misses the foundations on which it can build for the future.

One word of caution. I am not here speaking of either fad or fashion. I am not extolling the attractive ephemeral. And I am certainly not sponsoring the idea that was so fashionable in the 1930s, that German Nazism represented "the wave of the future." Anyone who subscribed to that idea had a very limited view of what the future of the human race could be, and few fashionable ideas have ever crumbled so fast and so disastrously. The senate of any nation is obligated to discern the merely fashionable when it offers itself and reject it.

Suppose that all I have said is true, which would be a miracle equal to those we've been discussing. Where does that leave the United States in relation to its space program? I am competent to comment on only three aspects, leaving the more technical details to others.

Are there non-military advantages to be gained from a space program? The high technical requirements for success in space are so fundamental that spin-off rewards are almost automatic. Radio, television, medical instrumentation, miniaturizing, watches, new food processes, communications, health advances and improvement in clothing are some of the few advantages which I myself have gained because of the space program, and I am speaking only of small items which can be comprehended and used by the individual.

If one considers the larger items, like intercontinental communications satellites, the mapping of weather patterns, the analysis of soils and forests, the exploration for minerals including oil, the management of fisheries and the like, the potential rewards are multiplied many times.

And the nature of human intelligence is such that no one today can even guess the limits of either the personal items or the industrial which might accrue from the basic scientific work that has to be done in a space program. I have followed our past space adventures about as carefully as an uninstructed layman could, and I have a rather imaginative mind, but I anticipated almost none of these significant by-products, and I doubt if any of us in this room today could predict where the next contributions will be made.

I have heard one impressive argument against what I am saying now. A man of some probity said, "If we had applied our scientific brains to these problems, we could have solved them all at one-tenth the cost." He is right. Had the Congress twenty years ago set aside a substantial budget, and had it authorized the assembling of a body of top scientists, and had it provided them with spacious laboratories and told them, "Devise a computerized navigational instrument that will operate regardless of where in space it is stationed," this could surely have been done. But neither Congress nor the human mind works that way. It is only when great felt needs spur the imagination that certain accomplishments become possible. As a project by itself few of the bonuses cited above would have materialized; as part of a national effort with a clearly defined goal they all came into being, and others like them will follow.

Are there military advantages to be gained from a space program? I would be terrified today if only Russian and Chinese vehicles were orbiting in space. Their military advantage would be so tremendous that we might almost suffer as a nation a kind of psychological shock from which we might never recover. For we would certainly be at their mercy.

I fear that the potentials of space warfare have even yet not been impressed upon the American public. We do not realize the overwhelming advantage a nation would enjoy if it alone commandeered space, if it

alone could direct by radio beam when and where an object or its cargo was to be brought down to earth. Any nation which allowed its enemies such a superiority would be doomed.

But if all nations have the capacity to utilize space defensively, then the peril is diminished and reasonable arrangements can be worked out. But only through parity can this be done.

Therefore, the United States must have a sensible space program, whether it wants one or not. To fail to keep up with new developments in this field would be disastrous, and any administration which permitted a lag should be condemned. We must know what the capabilities of space are, and we must retain our proficiency in using them.

I think we have done a fairly good job in this area so far, and I would suppose that from our strength we would be able to deal intelligently with those other nations have attained or will attain a comparable capacity. This is the great unknown ocean of the universe and we in 1979 are as obligated to probe it and use it and participate in its control as the nations of Europe were obligated to explore their terrestrial oceans in 1479.

The future and the safety of those nations depended upon their mastery of the seas; ours depends in shocking measure on our cautious control of space, and if we abandon it to others we condemn ourselves.

Are there spiritual advantages to be gained from a space program? The spirit of man, and the resolve of a nation, are tenuous things, to be fortified by the strangest experiences or destroyed by the most unanticipated accidents. Outward events influence them but inner resolves usually determine outcomes. A novelist sees men and women destroy themselves because the will to survive has been lost; the historian watches nations go down because of fatal wrong choices which sap the national energy. Usually the tragedy occurs when inner convictions are lost, or when a sense of general frustration or waning purpose prevails.

It is extremely difficult to keep a human life or the life of a nation moving forward with enough energy and commitment to lift it into the next cycle of experience. My own life has been spent chronicling the rise and fall of human systems, and I am convinced that we are all terribly vulnerable.

I do not for a moment believe that the spiritual well-being of our nation depends primarily upon a successful space program. There are, as William James said, moral equivalents to war, moral substitutes for any charismatic national experience. I am sure we could as a nation attain great spiritual reassurance from rebuilding our cities or distributing our farm produce better. And my experience in the arts has taught me to be suspicious of late fashions or high styles. Space programs are stylish today and run the risk of being abused.

But I also believe that there are moments in history when challenges occur of such a compelling nature that to miss them is to miss the whole meaning of an epoch. Space is such a challenge. It is the kind of challenge William Shakespeare sensed nearly four hundred years ago when he wrote:

There is a tide in the affairs of men,
Which, taken at the flood, leads on to fortune;
Omitted, all the voyage of their life
Is bound in shallows and in miseries.
On such a full sea are we now afloat,
And we must take the current when it serves,
Or lose our ventures.

We risk great peril if we kill off this spirit of adventure, for we cannot predict how and in what seemingly unrelated fields it will manifest itself. A nation which loses its forward thrust is in danger, and one of the most effective ways to retain that thrust is to keep exploring possibilities. The sense of exploration is intimately bound up with human resolve, and for a nation to believe that it is still committed to forward motion is to ensure its continuance.

I doubt if there is a woman or man in this room who honestly believes that the United States could ever fall backward, as other nations have within our lifetime. Intuitively we feel that we are exempt. Yet for us to think so is to fly in the face of all history, for many nations at their apex were inwardly doomed because their will power had begun to falter, and soon their vulnerability became evident to all. Enemies do not destroy nations; time and loss of will brings them down.

Therefore we should be most careful about retreating from the specific challenge of our age. We should be reluctant to turn our back upon the frontier of this epoch. Space is indifferent to what we do; it has no feeling, no design, no interest in whether we grapple with it or not. But we cannot be indifferent to space, because the grand slow march of our intelligence has brought us, in our generation, to a point from which we can explore and understand and utilize it. To turn back now would be to deny our history, our capabilities.

Each era of history progresses to a point at which it is eligible to wrestle with the great problem of that period. For the ancient Greeks it was the organization of society; for the Romans it was the organization of empire; for the Medievalists the spelling out of their relationship to God; for the men of the Fifteenth and Sixteenth Centuries the mastery of the oceans; and for us it is the determination of how mankind can live in harmony on this finite globe while establishing relationships to infinite space.

I was not overly impressed when men walked upon the moon, because I knew it to be out there at a specific distance with specific characteristics, and I supposed that we had enough intelligence to devise the necessary machinery to get us there and back. But when we sent an unmanned object hurtling into distant space, and when it began sending back signals—a chain of numbers to be exact—which could be reassembled here on earth to provide us with a photograph of the surface of Mars, I was struck dumb with wonder. And when computers began adjusting the chain of numbers, augmenting some, diminishing others, so that the photographs became always more clear and defined, I realized that we could accomplish almost anything, there in the farthest reaches of space.

My life changed completely on the day I saw those Mars photographs, for I had participated in that miracle. My tax dollars had helped pay for the project. The universities that I supported had provided the brains to arm the cameras. And the government that I helped nourish had organized the expedition. I saw the universe in a new light, and myself and my nation in a new set of responsibilities. My spirit was enlarged and my willingness to work on the future projects fortified.

No one can predict what aspect of space will invigorate a given individual, and there must have been millions of Americans who did not even know Mars had been photographed.

But we do know that in previous periods when great explorations were made, they reverberated throughout society. Dante and Shakespeare and Milton responded to the events of their day. Scientists were urged to new discoveries. And nations modified their practices.

All the thoughts of men are interlocked, and success in one area produces unforeseen successes in others. It is for this reason that a nation like ours is obligated to pursue its adventure in space. I am not competent to say how much money should be spent. I am not competent to advise on how the program should be administered. But I am convinced that it must be done.

Elie Wiesel

Acceptance of the Nobel Peace Prize
(December 10, 1986)

Elie Wiesel was born in Rumania in 1928 and was 16 years old when the Nazis ordered the deportation of all Jews in the town where he had grown up, Sighet in northern Transylvania. Wiesel's family was sent to Poland, to the notorious Auschwitz, where his mother and sister went to the gas chamber. In 1945, Elie and his father were moved to Buchenwald concentration camp in Germany; the elder Wiesel died, however, before the camp was liberated by the United States Army.

Wiesel made his way to France after the war, studied literature, philosophy, and psychology at the Sorbonne, and became a journalist for French and Israeli newspapers. He traveled to Israel and to India on assignments and was covering the United Nations in 1956 when he was struck by a taxi in New York City and needed to use a wheelchair for almost a year. It was during this time that he decided to apply for American citizenship.

He began his literary career in the late fifties, writing about his experience during the Holocaust, a term that Wiesel himself is credited with using for the first time in connection with the murder of six million Jews by the Nazis. He went on to write a series of novels that explored the deeply human themes of hate and friendship, faith and politics, killing and suicide. He became concerned with the fate of the Jews in Russia and wrote a play and a novel centered on the plight of Soviet Jewry. Along with his many works of fiction, Wiesel produced numerous essays and stories, written from a Jewish perspective, dealing with a wide variety of subjects, and has been active in humanitarian causes. His sympathy for the sufferings of the people of Vietnam and South Africa, for all victims of human oppression and hate, are evident in his work.

In a time of "violence, repression, and racism," the Nobel Committee declared in 1986, Elie Wiesel spoke for "peace, atonement, and dignity." The committee cited him as "one of the most important spiritual leaders and guides" of our time and awarded him the Peace Prize.

In accepting the prize, Wiesel made a moving plea against the silence that allows such a terrible thing as the Holocaust to occur. He declared that "we must always take sides," and stressed that "neutrality helps the oppressor, never the victim. Silence encourages the tormentor, never the tormented."

Citing the victims of oppression throughout the world—the Jews in the Soviet Union, Andrei Sakharov in his Siberian exile, Mandela in his South African jail—Wiesel called on us to reject indifference. "There is much to be done, there is much that can be done," he told us. When the voices of dissent "are stifled," Wiesel urged us to "lend them ours," and reminded his listeners that "as long as one dissident is in prison, our freedom will not be true. As long as one child is hungry, our lives will be filled with anguish and shame."

It is with a profound sense of humility that I accept the honor you have chosen to bestow upon me. I know: your choice transcends me. This both frightens and pleases me.

It frightens me because I wonder: do I have the right to represent the multitudes who have perished? Do I have the right to accept this great honor on their behalf? I do not. That would be presumptuous. No one may speak for the dead, no one may interpret their mutilated dreams and visions.

It pleases me because I may say that this honor belongs to all the survivors and their children, and through us, to the Jewish people with whose destiny I have always identified.

I remember: it happened yesterday or eternities ago. A young Jewish boy discovered the kingdom of the night. I remember his bewilderment, I remember his anguish. It all happened so fast. The ghetto. The deportation. The sealed cattle car. The fiery altar upon which the history of our people and the future of mankind were meant to be sacrificed.

I remember: he asked his father: "Can this be true? This is the 20th century, not the Middle Ages. Who would allow such crimes to be committed? How could the world remain silent?"

And now the boy is turning to me: "Tell me," he asks, "What have you done with my future? What have you done with your life?"

And I tell him that I have tried. That I have tried to keep memory alive, that I have tried to fight those who would forget. Because if we forget, we are guilty, we are accomplices.

And then I explained to him how naive we were, that the world did know and remained silent. And that

is why I swore never to be silent whenever and wherever human beings endure suffering and humiliation. We must always take sides. Neutrality helps the oppressor, never the victim. Silence encourages the tormentor, never the tormented.

Sometimes we must interfere. When human lives are endangered, when human dignity is in jeopardy, national borders and sensitivities become irrelevant. Wherever men or women are persecuted because of their race, religion or political views, that place must—at that moment—become the center of the universe.

Of course, since I am a Jew profoundly rooted in my people's memory and tradition, my first response is to Jewish fears, Jewish needs, Jewish crises. For I belong to a traumatized generation, one that experienced the abandonment and solitude of our people. It would be unnatural for me not to make Jewish priorities my own, Israel, Soviet Jewry, Jews in Arab lands.

But there are others as important to me. Apartheid is, in my view, as abhorrent as anti-Semitism. To me, Andrei Sakharov's isolation is as much of a disgrace as Iosif Begun's imprisonment. As is the denial of Solidarity and its leader Lech Walesa's right to dissent. And Nelson Mandela's interminable imprisonment.

There is so much injustice and suffering crying out for our attention: victims of hunger, or racism and political persecution, writers and poets, prisoners in so many lands governed by the left and by the right. Human rights are being violated on every continent. More people are oppressed than are free.

And then, too, there are the Palestinians to whose plight I am sensitive but whose methods I deplore. Violence and terrorism are not the answer. Something must be done about their suffering, and soon. I trust

Israel, I have faith in the Jewish people. Let Israel be given a chance, let hatred and danger be removed from her horizons, and there will be peace in and around the Holy Land.

Yes, I have faith. Faith in God and even in His creation. Without it no action would be possible. And action is the only remedy to indifference: the most insidious danger of all. Isn't this the meaning of Alfred Nobel's legacy? Wasn't his fear of a war a shield against war?

There is much to be done, there is much that can be done. One person—a Raoul Wallenberg, an Albert Schweitzer, one person of integrity, can make a difference, a difference of life and death. As long as one dissident is in prison, our freedom will not be true. As long as one child is hungry, our lives will be filled with anguish and shame.

What all these victims need above all is to know that they are not alone; that we are not forgetting them, that when their voices are stifled we shall lend them ours, that while their freedom depends on ours, the quality of our freedom depends on theirs.

This is what I say to the young Jewish boy wondering what I have done with his years. It is in his name that I speak to you and that I express to you my deepest gratitude. No one is as capable of gratitude as one who has emerged from the kingdom of the night.

We know that every moment is a moment of grace, every hour an offering; not to share them would mean to betray them. Our lives no longer belong to us alone; they belong to all those who need us desperately.

Thank you Chairman Aarvik. Thank you, members of the Nobel Committee. Thank you, people of Norway, for declaring on this singular occasion that our survival has a meaning for mankind.

William H. Rehnquist

The Many Faces of the Bicentennial
(February 15, 1987)

The year 1987 marked the two hundredth anniversary of the signing of the Constitution of the United States. That document, which brought a united nation into being, became a hallowed symbol of American liberties even if its precise meaning was often sharply debated and even if it was to be amended twenty-six times in its two-century existence.

The meaning and genius of the Constitution was expounded upon before the annual convention of the American Bar Association in New Orleans in February of 1987 by the chief justice of the United States, William Rehnquist. Rehnquist was a brilliant student who graduated from Stanford, took an M.A. in political science from Harvard, and then returned to Stanford Law School where he finished first in his class. The young Rehnquist became a clerk for Supreme Court justice Robert H. Jackson in 1952. Eighteen months later, Rehnquist went into the practice of law in Phoenix, Arizona, where he soon became associated with the conservative wing of the Republican party there. He developed close ties with Sen. Barry Goldwater and with the party's state chairman, Richard Kleindienst. In 1958, he acted as a special Arizona state prosecutor. Kleindienst, who served as national field director for Richard Nixon's 1968 Presidential campaign, became deputy attorney general in the new Nixon administration. He selected William Rehnquist to be assistant attorney general and head of the Office of Legal Counsel.

The new assistant attorney general soon became a vigorous defender of Nixon policies and aroused liberal wrath by his justification of a stringent "law and order" stance that approved such practices as pretrial detention and electronic surveillance. He defended the President's right to wage war in Indochina, he maintained the President's prerogative in keeping many government documents secret, and he condoned the arrest of peaceful protesters in Washington. These positions, along with liberal suspicions about his civil rights posture, caused some opposition to his appointment to the Supreme Court when he was nominated by President Nixon in 1971. The Senate, however, confirmed his appointment, and he was sworn in as an associate justice on January 7, 1972. President Reagan named him chief justice on the resignation of Warren Burger in 1985.

In his speech to the ABA, Chief Justice Rehnquist attempted to explicate the enduring strengths of the Constitution. He recognized the ways in which it was tied to and grew out of its own times, and the extent to which it was far from being a perfect document in its original form. The real genius of the Constitution, however, grew from its provisions that recognized the need for and provided methods of change, and from its establishment of an independent judiciary capable of enforcing the rights guaranteed by the document itself. "It is this finely tuned mechanism," the chief justice concluded, "by which constitutional law is declared, interpreted, and on occasion changed, which is perhaps the greatest gift of the framers of the Constitution in Philadelphia in 1787."

This year we commemorate the 200th anniversary of the "signing" of the United States Constitution. On September 17, 1787, the founding fathers signed in Philadelphia the charter which, when ratified by the specified number of states, became the Constitution of the United States of America. Two hundred years after the event, we know with more certainty than Benjamin Franklin could have mustered at the time, that his observation about the sun painted on the back of George Washington's chair being a rising sun, and not a setting sun, was indeed true. And in this year of the Bicentennial, it particularly behooves those of us who are lawyers to reflect on and speak about the significance of this memorable event. Lawyers, after all, played a large part in the drafting of the Constitution, and they have played an even larger part in its interpretation.

When we start to think about just what it is we commemorate this year—what is the significance of the signing of the Constitution—we are in the happy position of having an embarrassment of riches. First, the signing of the Constitution in Philadelphia had a historic significance for the United States quite apart from the contents of the document which the framers approved. Second, the document itself, with all of the shortcomings which we now see in it, was a remarkable charter which ordained a system of government which was a vast improvement over the Articles of Confederation, and in most respects was far more advanced toward democracy and individual liberty than the governments of the countries from which the colonists had emigrated. Third, the document as it stands today, a considerably different one from that which the framers ratified, more perfectly embodies our present sense of

the powers that government ought to exercise, and the restraints that ought to be imposed upon governmental power. Fourth and finally, the provisions in the Constitution for the interpretation of the instrument, and for amendment and change in that interpretation were a model of enlightenment at least equal to any of its substantive provisions.

The "signing" of the Constitution in Philadelphia had a historic significance quite apart from the contents of the document which the framers approved. It was an important milestone in the development of the United States as a nation, just as was the Declaration of Independence whose Bicentennial we commemorated in 1976. There seems to be a tendency in connection with the present Bicentennial to focus only on the significance of the Constitution as a legal document and to neglect the historic significance of the fact that on Sept. 17, 1787, representatives from the 13 states agreed upon a form of government which would bind them together far more closely than they had been.

Throughout the period from 1781 to 1789, when the Constitution was finally ratified by the necessary number of states, the only national government of the United States was the Second Continental Congress, operating under the Articles of Confederation. These Articles were seriously defective in a number of respects, the principal one being that the national government could operate only upon the states, and not upon the individual citizens in the states. It was a weak and unsatisfactory form of government, and in those troubled times it was by no means foreordained that the 13 former colonies would remain united as one nation.

There was widespread fear that failure to unite would make individual states, or regional confederations of states, prey to being influenced and manipulated by foreign powers.

Even without the threat of foreign intervention, problems of finance and trade loomed large because of the absence of an effective national government. States were erecting tariffs and other barriers to trade smacking of protectionism and causing economic stagnation. Those states which had no suitable ports for foreign commerce were subjected to be taxed by their neighbors, through whose ports their commerce was carried on.

These concerns had so troubled many of the 13 states that a number of them sent out a call for a meeting at Annapolis in 1786 to propose amendments to the Articles of Confederation in an effort to solve some of these problems. The Annapolis Convention was attended by delegates from only five states, and it was unable to accomplish anything substantive by its deliberations. But in what must go down in history as a magnificent combination of boldness and optimism, that body called for the convening of the Constitutional Convention in Philadelphia in 1787.

The reason for convening the convention was to devise "a more perfect form of union." But the success of the endeavor was by no means assured. If it failed, it was not at all certain that the 13 states would continue imperfectly united under the Articles of Confederation; they might break up into regional confederations. Thus the signing of the Constitution on Sept. 17, 1787, after four months of deliberation, was a tremendous step forward toward nationhood regardless of the provisions contained in the Constitution itself. The very fact that the delegates had been able to agree on a federal government with enough authority to do the job was a milestone in American history. That fact alone gives significance to the Bicentennial of the signing of the Constitution.

When we turn from the significance of the signing in Philadelphia in 1787 as a milestone to nationhood to the provisions contained in the document itself, we find an instrument with provisions for representative democracy, checks and balances among the branches of government, and some constitutional protection of the individual against the government. At long last it provided the 13 states with a federal government adequately empowered to lay taxes, conduct foreign policy, and regulate interstate commerce. These made it far better than any contemporary system of government with which the colonists were familiar.

But by our present lights the Constitution adopted by the framers in 1787 had major shortcomings. It implicitly recognized the existence of slavery, a fact which led the abolitionist William Lloyd Garrison to describe it as a "covenant with Hell." It had no guarantees of freedom of speech and of the press, or of religious freedom. It lacked the systematic protection for individual rights against governmental action which would be remedied in large part by the Bill of Rights adopted in 1791. So it will not do to regard the Constitution signed in Philadelphia as the "Ark of the Covenant," immutable and unchallengeable. The Constitution itself wisely contained a provision allowing for its amendment, and we have had 26 amendments to it adopted by the process specified in Article V.

But just as we should not uncritically extol an instrument which had these shortcomings, we should not uncritically damn it either. People in the United States have a great tendency to judge acts that took place many years ago by standards of present day morals and values, and this is not generally a very useful endeavor. The Constitution signed by the framers in Philadelphia in 1787 would not suit us today, because of the drawbacks to which I have previously referred. But many compromises were necessary to bring all of the 13 states on board, and the instrument was a notable step forward in the art of government. This instrument signed by the founders in Philadelphia is well worth commemorating on the occasion of the Bicentennial of its adoption.

Amendments ratified over the preceding 200 years have largely cured the shortcomings which we perceive in the instrument adopted in Philadelphia. Slavery is outlawed, equal protection is guaranteed, individual rights are protected. But again, there is no reason to treat our present Constitution with an "Ark of the Covenant" mentality. Two hundred years from now our present-day Constitution may well seem to our descendants to have many shortcomings which were not apparent to us. These questions depend to a large extent on the temper of the times, and it may well be that although we view the present Constitution as just about right, our great grandchildren will think quite differently about it.

Lest we become too sold on the immutability of the Constitution as it stands at any particular time, including right now, it is well to bear in mind that the Eighteenth Amendment granted to Congress the power to enact a national prohibition law, and the Twenty-first Amendment enacted fifteen years later withdrew that power from Congress. The pendulum swung 180 degrees in fifteen years. Proponents of the Equal Rights Amendment have said they will attempt to re-introduce it in the present session of Congress. A responsible organization calling itself the Committee on the Constitution System has recently urged revision of the First Amendment. Change is the law of life, in government, as well as in other matters.

Thus far I have touched upon three of the four different kinds of significance that the Bicentennial of the signing of the Constitution has for us. But important as all of these three meanings are, the fourth to which I am about to turn is every bit as important as any of the others. The Constitution signed on Sept. 17, 1787, gave us procedural provisions by which the instrument was to be interpreted, amended, and changed, which assured both the efficacy and the flexibility of the substantive provisions which it contained. The framers provided for judicial review—that is, they empowered the courts to invalidate laws which did not conform to the Constitution. This was an original contribution of the 13 states to the art of government, and was a complete departure from anything that existed in England, from whence most of the colonists had come, or anywhere else in Europe.

The members of the judicial branch, in turn, were protected against encroachment from the legislative and executive branches by giving them tenure during good behavior and protecting them against reduction in compensation. There was thus established a genuinely independent judiciary. The Supreme Court,sitting at the apex of the judiciary, was made the final arbiter of questions of constitutional law. This was a unique combination of attributes possessed by no other judiciary anywhere in the world.

Because the courts in this country have been so active and so successful in upholding claims of constitutional rights, there is a natural tendency to think that the words and phrases contained in the written instrument itself are sufficient to assure the protections which they were intended to secure. But a moment's reflection should convince us this is not so. Many nations of the world have very impressive guarantees of free speech, free elections, and the like. But these provisions have not had the same meaning in those countries because of the want of an independent judiciary to interpret them. In 1803 in *Marbury v. Madison*, the Supreme Court of the United States established the authority of the judicial branch to declare laws of Congress unconstitutional. The Supreme Court and other courts have exercised this authority on numerous occasions since that time. The Supreme Court has also unhesitatingly stood up to the executive branch when the president sought to act contrary to law; in 1952 it ruled that President Truman acted beyond his constitutional authority in seizing the steel mills, and in 1974 it held that President Nixon was required to turn over the famous tapes to the courts when they were needed for evidentiary purposes. The tremendous importance of judicial independence in establishment of constitutional doctrine simply cannot be overstated.

The framers, however, did not stop there. Many of them were conversant with the political theories in vogue at the time, but many were also just as familiar with the vagaries of human nature. They did the best they could for their times, but with great good sense they realized that the instrument which they had drawn and adopted that summer of 1787 was by no means perfect, and would probably seem even less so to succeeding generations. So they placed in it in Article V a method by which the Constitution could be amended. Amendments would have to be proposed by extraordinary majorities of the states. Change in the fundamental charter was not to be easily had, but as we know, 26 amendments to the Constitution have passed the rather high hurdle required for change.

As I have noted earlier, the framers provided for a thoroughly independent judiciary—the judges were given what amounted to life tenure and protected against diminution of compensation. But the framers, with the uncanny insight which characterized so much of their drafting, did not entirely insulate the judiciary as a whole from popular will. Vacancies in the judiciary were to be filled through nomination by the president, who was responsible to the entire nation, and confirmation by the Senate, whose members were responsible to their respective states. Thus, while individual judges are entirely protected against popular turmoil, the courts on which they sit may have their composition,and accordingly their philosophical bent, changed over time through the process of filling vacancies.

Thus the framers established an independent judiciary to make certain that the Constitution would not become a dead letter in the hands of judges who were subservient to either the executive or legislative branches. But they also provided for a method of appointment to the federal judiciary which could in the long run temper judicial interpretations which were believed to be erroneous by a majority of the people. It is this finely tuned mechanism by which constitutional law is declared, interpreted, and on occasion changed, which is perhaps the greatest gift of the framers of the Constitution in Philadelphia in 1787.

We indeed have an embarrassment of riches to celebrate in this bicentennial year. On Sept. 17, 1787, the framers signed a charter of government which assured us that we would be a continental nation, not a collection of regional confederacies. The charter was drafted by men who realized that time might require changes in their handiwork, and they provided for such changes. They realized that an independent judiciary was essential to give life to the conditional guarantees, and they provided for one. During this year we, as lawyers, should be in the front ranks of those who are celebrating this great event.

Bibliography of General Historical Works

Following is a short, select bibliography of general works that encompass the time period covered in this book. These books will prove helpful in understanding the broader historical context in which the speeches were given. The biographical appendix gives suggestions for further readings that relate specifically to the speaker or the speech cited.

James MacGregor Burns, *The Crosswinds of Freedom*. New York: Knopf, 1989.

John Patrick Diggins, *The Proud Decades: America in War and Peace, 1941-1960*. New York: Norton, 1988.

Eric Goldman, *The Crucial Decade—and After: America, 1954-1960*. New York: Vintage Books, 1960.

William E. Leuchtenburg, *In the Shadow of FDR: From Harry Truman to Ronald Reagan*. Ithaca: Cornell U Press, 1983.

Frank N. Magell, ed., *The American Presidents: III: Roosevelt to Reagan*. Englewood Cliffs, NJ: Salem Press, 1986.

William Manchester, *The Glory and the Dream: A Narrative History of America 1932-1972*. Boston: Little, Brown, 1974.

Allen J. Matusow, *The Unraveling of America*. New York: Harper & Row, 1984.

George E. Mowry and Blaine A. Brownell, *The Urban Nation, 1920-1980*. New York: Hill & Wang, 1981.

David W. Noble, David A. Horowitz, and Peter N. Carroll, *Twentieth Century Limited: A History of Recent America*. Boston: Houghton Mifflin, 1980.

J. Ronald Oakley, *God's Country: America in the Fifties*. New York: Dembner, 1986.

William L. O'Neill, *American High: The Years of Confidence, 1945-1960*. New York: Free Press, 1989; *Coming Apart*. Chicago: Quadrangle, 1971.

Rexford Tugwell, *Off Course: From Truman to Nixon*. New York: Praeger, 1971.

Theodore H. White, *America in Search of Itself: The Making of the President, 1956-1980*. New York: Harper & Row, 1982.

William Appleman Williams, *Americans in a Changing World: A History of the United States in the Twentieth Century*. New York: Harper & Row, 1978.

Howard Zinn, *The Twentieth Century, A People's History*. New York: Harper & Row, 1984.

Biographical Notes

Following are biographical notes on the speakers included in this volume, listed alphabetically. The suggestions for additional reading that follow most of these notes are not intended as comprehensive bibliographies; rather they may serve as starting points for interested students who wish to explore in more depth topics related to the speakers. Readers may also wish to consult the bibliography of general works that treat the time period covered in this volume.

SPIRO AGNEW was born in 1918 and served in the 10th Armored Division in World War II. He held various positions in business before being elected governor of Maryland in 1966. He attracted national attention by ordering the arrest of black radical Rap Brown after a visit by Brown to the all-black Cambridge School resulted in riots and the burning of the school. Agnew was also known for his tough stance on student demonstrators whom he called "malcontents, radicals, incendiaries, and civil and uncivil disobedients." In 1968, Richard Nixon chose Agnew as his running mate, and the Maryland governor was elected Vice President of the United States. During the Nixon administration, Agnew became known as the administration's "hatchet man," lashing out at student activists, intellectuals, and the media. When it was discovered that Agnew had accepted payoffs from construction company executives while governor, Agnew agreed to plead no contest to a charge of income tax evasion. He resigned as Vice President in October 1973.

Andrew A. King and Floyd Douglas Anderson, "Nixon, Agnew, and the 'Silent Majority': A Case Study in the Rhetoric of Polarization." *Western Journal of Speech Communication* 35 (1971): 243–255.

Jim G. Lucas, *Agnew: Profile in Conflict*. New York: Award Books, 1970.

Timothy P. Meyer and Vernon E. Cronen, "Agnew Meets the Student Dissenters: An Experimental Study of Ego-Involvement and Argumentation." *Journal of Communication* 22 (1972): 263–276.

Rollin W. Quimby, "Agnew, the Press, and the Rhetorical Critic." *Western Journal of Speech Communication* 39 (1975): 146–154; "Agnew's Plea Bargain: Between Rhetorics of Consensus and Confrontation." *Central States Speech Journal* 28 (1977): 163–172.

RALPH BUNCHE was born in Detroit on August 7, 1904. After earning a B.A. from UCLA and a master's degree from Harvard, Bunche joined the political science department at Howard University. He continued his studies, developing a special interest in colonial policy in Africa and the Middle East. He studied at Northwestern University and the London School of Economics and was awarded a Ph.D. from Harvard. In World War II he served first in the Office of Strategic Services and then the State Department. He was active in the formation of the United Nations and became the director of the Trusteeship Department in 1948. Serving also as chief secretary to the UN Palestine Commission, he assumed the post of UN mediator in 1948 after the assassination of Count Bernadotte. He arranged an armistice between Israel and Egypt in 1949 and negotiated a series of settlements between Arab states and Israel and was awarded the Nobel Peace Prize in 1950. He later served as undersecretary of the United Nations. He died in 1971.

J. Alvin Kugelmass, *Ralph J. Bunche: Fighter for Peace*. New York: J. Messner, 1952.

Peggy Mann, *Ralph Bunche, UN Peacemaker*. Coward, McCann, and Geohegan, 1975.

Brian Urquhart, "Remembering Ralph Bunche." *Yale Review* 76 (1987): 448–451.

GEORGE BUSH was born in Milton, Massachusetts, on June 12, 1924. He served as a fighter pilot in World War II, completed his B.A. degree at Yale in 1948, and moved to Texas where he founded the Zapata Petroleum Company. He became active in the Texas Republican party and served as a county chairman and a delegate to the national Republican conventions in the 1960's. He was twice nominated for the United States Senate, in 1964 and 1970, but was defeated. He served two terms in the House of Representatives from 1967 to 1971 and then became United States ambassador to the United Nations. He chaired the Republican National Committee from 1973 to 1974, when he was named chief of the United States Liaison Office in Peking. He returned to the United States to head the CIA in 1976–1977. Bush attempted to secure the Republican nomination for President in 1980, but failed to stop Ronald Reagan. Reagan, however, chose Bush for the second place on the Republican ticket, and Bush was elected in 1980 and re-elected with Reagan in 1984. Nominated for President in 1988, Bush defeated the Democratic candidate, Michael Dukakis, and in January 1989 was inaugurated as forty-first President of the United States.

Elizabeth Drew, "1980: Bush." *The New Yorker*, March 3, 1980, p. 82.

Jack W. Germond and Jules Witcover, *Whose Broad Stripes and Bright Stars? The Trivial Pursuit of the Presidency, 1988*. New York: Warner, 1989.

Nicholas King, *George Bush: A Biography*. New York: Dodd, Mead, 1980.

Roy Reed, "George Bush On the Move." *New York Times Magazine*, March 3, 1980, p. 82.

STOKELY CARMICHAEL was born in Port-au-Spain, Trinidad, on June 29, 1941. When he was 11 years old his family moved to the United States and Stokely became a citizen when his parents were naturalized. In 1960 he joined CORE, and in 1964 graduated from Howard University. In 1966 he became chairman of the Student Nonviolent Coordinating Committee (SNCC) and served in that capacity for a year. Carmichael became the leading spokesman for "black power," a concept that frightened many whites and caused a rift in the civil rights movement. He left SNCC to join the Black Panthers, but differed with Panther leader Eldridge Cleaver and soon resigned. In 1969 Carmichael moved to Guinea, where he still lives.

Lerone Bennett, Jr., "Stokely Carmichael: Architect of Black Power." *Ebony*, September 1966, pp. 25–28.

Wayne E. Brockriede and Robert L. Scott, "Stokely Carmichael: Two Speeches on Black Power." *Central States Speech Journal* 19 (1968): 3–13.

Pat Jefferson, "The Magnificent Barbarian at Nashville." *Southern Speech Communication Journal* 33 (1967): 77–87.

Arthur Pollock, "Stokely Carmichael's New Black Rhetoric." *Southern Speech Communication Journal* 37 (1971): 92–94.

Robert L. Scott, "Justifying Violence: The Rhetoric of Militant Black Power." *Central States Speech Journal* 19 (1968): 96–104.

JAMES EARL CARTER was born in Plains, Georgia, on October 1, 1924. He attended the United States Naval Academy and served in the nuclear submarine program after graduating in 1946. He resigned from the navy in 1954 to take over the family business. In 1962 Carter was elected to the Georgia state Senate. He was defeated in the 1966 race for governor, but won election to that office in 1970. In his inaugural address, Governor Carter called for an end to racial discrimination and subsequently won the support of black civil rights leaders when he campaigned for the Democratic nomination for President in 1976. Carter defeated Gerald Ford and began his term as President in 1977. In his years in office, Carter emphasized human rights in foreign affairs and negotiated the Camp David accords, which yielded a peace treaty between Israel and Egypt. Criticized for his conservative stand on social welfare by members of his own Democratic party, Carter was seriously challenged for the 1980 nomination by Sen. Edward Kennedy. Although Carter won renomination, he was defeated in November by the Republican nominee, Ronald Reagan.

Les Altenberg and Robert Cathcart, "Jimmy Carter on Human Rights: A Thematic Analysis." *Central States Speech Journal* 33 (1982): 446–457.

J. Louis Campbell III, "Jimmy Carter and the Rhetoric of Charisma." *Central States Speech Journal* 30 (1979): 174–186.

Jimmy Carter, *Why Not the Best?* Nashville: Broadman Press, 1975; *Keeping Faith: Memoirs of a President*. New York: Bantam Books, 1982.

Betty Glad, *Jimmy Carter: In Search of the Great White House*. New York: Norton, 1980.

Christopher Lyle Johnstone, "Electing Ourselves in 1976: Jimmy Carter and the American Faith." *Western Journal of Speech Communication* 42 (1978): 241–249.

John H. Patton, "A Government as Good as Its People: Jimmy Carter and the Restoration of Transcendence to Politics." *Quarterly Journal of Speech* 63 (1977): 249–257; "Jimmy Carter's Rhetoric of Idealism: From Southern Justice to Human Rights." In *A New Diversity in Contemporary Southern Rhetoric, ed. Calvin M. Logue and Howard Dorgan, eds. Baton Rouge: Louisiana State U Press, 1987.*

WENDELL CHINO is president of the Mescalero Apache Tribal Council of Mescalero, New Mexico, and an advocate for native American causes. In 1982 he spoke for the grandchildren of the great Apache chief Geronimo in a dispute over whether or not to move the chief's body from its Fort Sill grave to a new burial site in Arizona. Upholding Apache customs, Chino argued that the body should not be disturbed.

SHIRLEY CHISHOLM was born in Brooklyn, New York, on November 30, 1924. She earned a B.A. from Brooklyn College and an M.A. from Columbia University and became a nursery school teacher and school director as well as a consultant to the New York City Bureau of Child Welfare. She served in the New York Assembly from 1964 to 1968 when she was elected to Congress. She sat in the House of Representatives from that time until 1983 when she retired and accepted the Purington Chair at Mount Holyoke College. As vigorous advocate of rights for blacks and for

women, she was active in the NAACP, and is a member of the advisory council of the National Organization for Women. She campaigned for the Democratic nomination for the Presidency in 1972 and was a leading advocate of the Equal Rights Amendment.

Shirley Chisholm, *Unbought and Unbossed*. Boston: Houghton Mifflin, 1970.

Frank P. LeVeness and Jane P. Sweeney, eds., *Women Leaders in Contemporary Politics*. Boulder, CO: L. Rienner, 1987.

George R. Metcalf, *Up From Within: Today's New Black Leaders*. New York: McGraw-Hill, 1971.

ELDRIDGE CLEAVER was born in 1935 in Wabbeska, Arkansas, and as a child moved first to Phoenix and then to Los Angeles. From 1954 until 1966, Cleaver spent time in prison for various offenses ranging from selling marijuana to assault. While in prison, Cleaver became a Black Muslim and a follower of Malcolm X; he broke with the Muslims, however, after Malcolm's assassination. The Black Panther Party for Self-Defense was formed in October of 1966 and Cleaver joined a few months later, soon becoming minister of information. While in prison, Cleaver wrote *Soul on Ice*, a book that made him one of the most famous of the Black Panthers. Numerous clashes with the police and the FBI caused the death and imprisonment of several Black Panther leaders. About to be returned to jail for a parole violation, Cleaver fled the country in 1969. He went to Havana, made an appearance in Moscow, and settled for a time in Algeria. He returned to the United States in 1979 and was placed on probation but was not returned to jail. Cleaver announced that he was a "born-again Christian" and has since confined his speaking largely to fundamentalist groups.

Eldridge Cleaver, *Post Prison Writings and Speeches*. New York: Rampart Books, 1969.

Eldridge Cleaver, *Soul on Ice*. New York: Dell, 1969.

Richard J. Jensen and John C. Hammerback, "From Muslim to Mormon: Eldridge Cleaver's Rhetorical Crusade." *Communication Quarterly* 34 (1986): 24–40.

MARIO CUOMO was born in Queens County, New York, June 15, 1932. He graduated from St. John's College in 1953 and was awarded a law degree in 1956. In the 1960's and early 1970s he practiced law and taught at the St. John's University School of Law. He was elected New York secretary of state in 1974, lieutenant governor in 1978, and governor of New York in

1982. His keynote address at the Democratic national convention was enthusiastically received, but Cuomo discouraged efforts by supporters to promote him for the Democratic Presidential nomination that year and in 1988. He is considered a major force in the Democratic party and a serious possibility for a future Presidential nomination.

E. J. Dionne, Jr., "Cuomo: The Old Liberalism." *New York Times Magazine*, October 31, 1982, p. 22.

David Henry, "The Rhetorical Dynamics of Mario Cuomo's 1984 Keynote Address: Situation, Speaker, Metaphor." *Southern Speech Communication Journal* 53 (1988): 105–120.

Robert S. McElvaine, *Mario Cuomo: A Biography*. New York: Scribners, 1988.

EVERETT McKINLEY DIRKSEN was born in Pekin, Illinois, January 4, 1896. He left college to join the army in World War I and returned to Pekin to work in the family business after the war. He was elected to the Pekin City Commission in 1926, and in 1932 won election as a Republican to the House of Representatives. There he proved to be a successful and popular member and became a prominent Republican political leader. He retired from the House in 1948 because of an eye disease, but he recovered and won a successful race for the United States Senate in 1950, unseating the Democratic Senate leader, Scott Lucas. Dirksen soon became a leading spokesman for conservatism, supported Taft against Eisenhower in 1952, and espoused the cause of Sen. Joseph McCarthy. After his re-election to the Senate in 1956, Dirksen became a stronger supporter of President Eisenhower and became Republican leader in 1959. As minority leader during the terms of Kennedy and Johnson, Dirksen was the most powerful Republican in political office. His old-fashioned oratorical style was mocked by some and admired by others. By the end of his career, his political skill was generally respected by members of both parties. He died in Washington on September 7, 1969.

Jean T. Cronin, *Minority Leadership in the United States Senate: The Role and Style of Everett Dirksen*. Ann Arbor, MI: University Microfilms International, 1980.

Neil MacNeil, *Dirksen: Portrait of a Public Man*. New York: World Publishing Co., 1970.

Edward L. Schapsmeier and Frederick H. Schapsmeier, *Dirksen of Illinois: Senatorial Statesman*. Urbana: U of Illinois Press, 1985.

MICHAEL DUKAKIS was born November 3, 1933, and received his B.A. from Swarthmore College in 1955 and his law degree from Harvard in 1960. From 1963 until 1971 he was a Massachusetts state representative and then, for two years, was the moderator of the PBS program *The Advocates*. In 1974 he was elected governor of Massachusetts, but failed to be re-elected in 1978. After leaving office, Dukakis became a lecturer at the John F. Kennedy School of Government at Harvard. He won the governor's chair back in 1982 and began his second term in 1983. In 1988 he was the Democratic candidate for President of the United States.

Christine M. Black and Thomas Oliphant, *All By Myself: The Unmaking of a Presidential Campaign*. Chester, CT: Globe Pequot Press, 1989.

Richard Gaines and Michael Segal, *Dukakis and the Reform Impulse*. Boston: Quinlan Press, 1987.

Jack W. Germond and Jules Witcover, *Whose Broad Stripes and Bright Stars? The Trivial Pursuit of the Presidency, 1988*. New York: Warner, 1989.

Charles Kenny and Robert L. Turner, *Dukakis: An American Odyssey*. Houghton Mifflin, 1988.

ALBERT EINSTEIN was born March 14, 1879, in Germany and moved with his family to Italy in 1894. After studying in Zurich, Einstein was unable to get a teaching post in physics so he took a job at the Swiss Patent Office while continuing his work in his spare time. In 1905 he published a series of papers in the *Annalen der Physik* that catapulted him into scientific prominence. He became a professor of physics at the University of Zurich, then moved to the German University in Prague, and then, in 1913, became a member of the Prussian Academy of Sciences and director of scientific research at the Kaiser Wilhelm Institute in Berlin. He remained there until 1933. In that year, when Hitler came to power, Einstein was in the United States at Princeton's Institute for Advanced Study. He elected to stay on permanently at the institute, eventually taking American citizenship. With a group of other scientists, Einstein urged President Roosevelt to establish a program to study the possible military uses of fission, but Einstein did not play an active part in the research that followed. After World War II, Einstein spoke out against the restriction of free speech in the cause of internal security and warned of the dangers of nuclear war. He died in Princeton on April 18, 1955.

J. Berstein, *Einstein*. New York: Viking, 1973.

R. W. Clark, *Einstein—the Life and Times*. New York: H. N. Abrams, 1971.

Alan J. Friedman and Carol C. Donley, *Einstein as Myth and Muse*. New York: Cambridge U Press, 1985.

DWIGHT D. EISENHOWER was born in Denison, Texas, on October 14, 1890. He graduated from West Point in 1915. He served in the United States during World War I and was about to embark for Europe when the war ended. After a variety of posts, Eisenhower moved to Washington in the early 1930's, serving in the office of the chief of staff, Douglas MacArthur. MacArthur took Eisenhower with him to the Philippines as MacArthur's chief of staff. When war broke out in Europe, Eisenhower returned to the United States. Serving in a variety of posts, Eisenhower worked closely with the chief of staff, George Marshall, who eventually put Eisenhower in charge of American forces in England. Eisenhower commanded the Allied troops that invaded Europe in 1944. When the war ended in 1945 Eisenhower, by then a five-star general, was an international figure. He served as chief of staff of the United States Army until his retirement in 1948. From then until 1951 he was president of Columbia University. He became the first supreme commander of NATO, a post from which he resigned in 1952 in order to run for the Presidency. He was nominated by the Republicans in 1952 and easily defeated the Democratic candidate, Adlai Stevenson. He was re-elected in 1956, again defeating Stevenson. At the end of his second term, in 1960, he retired to his farm in Gettysburg and spent much of his time working on his memoirs. He died on March 28, 1969.

Stephen E. Ambrose, *Eisenhower*. New York: Simon & Schuster, 1983.

William B. Ewald, Jr., *Eisenhower the President: The Crucial Years, 1951–1960*. Englewood Cliffs, NJ: Prentice-Hall, 1981.

Fred I. Greenstein, *The Hidden-Hand Presidency: Eisenhower as Leader*. New York: Basic Books, 1982.

Martin J. Medhurst, "Eisenhower's 'Atoms for Peace' Speech: A Case Study in the Strategic Use of Language." *Communication Monographs* 54 (1987): 204–20.

WILLIAM FAULKNER was born in New Albany, Mississippi, on September 25, 1897. As a young man he wrote stories and poems, tried a variety of jobs, and served for a brief time in the Royal Canadian Air Force. He lived briefly in New York, returned to Mississippi, moved to New Orleans, traveled in Europe, and finally settled in Mississippi. His first great novel, *The Sound and the Fury*, was published in 1929. Another critically acclaimed novel, *As I Lay Dying*, was published the following year. Throughout his early career, Faulkner produced works that were to become classics but were not financially successful, and he wrote screenplays and short stories to supplement his income. At the age of 51, with the publication of *Intruder in the Dust*, Faulkner became financially secure as his fame as a writer grew. He won the Nobel Prize for literature in 1950. In 1954 *A Fable* won the Pulitzer Prize and the National Book Award. He died in his native Mississippi on July 6, 1962.

Joseph Blotner, *William Faulkner: A Biography*. New York: Random House, 1984.

Stephen B. Oates, *William Faulkner, the Man and the Artist: A Biography*. New York: Harper & Row, 1987.

James A. Snead, *Figures of Division: William Faulkner's Major Novels*. New York: Methuen, 1986.

GERALDINE FERRARO was born in Newburgh, New York, August 26, 1935. In 1956 she earned a B.A. from Marymount Manhattan College and in 1960 a law degree from Fordham University. She practiced law in New York City from 1961 to 1974, when she became an assistant district attorney for Queens County. She was elected to Congress in 1978 and served for three terms in the House of Representatives. In 1984, she chaired the Democratic party's national platform committee. It was in that year that the Democratic nominee, Walter Mondale, chose Ferraro as his running mate, making her the first woman to campaign for the Vice Presidency of the United States.

Geraldine Ferraro, *Ferraro, My Story*. New York: Bantam, 1985.

Lee M. Katz, *My Name is Geraldine Ferraro: An Unauthorized Biography*. New York: New American Library, 1984.

GERALD R. FORD was born in Omaha, Nebraska, on July 14, 1913. In 1915, after his parents were divorced, he moved with his mother to Grand Rapids, Michigan. He graduated from the University of Michigan in 1935. After completing his law degree at Yale in 1941 he returned to Grand Rapids to practice law. Ford served in the navy during World War II and resumed his law practice after being discharged in 1946. In 1948, he was elected as a Republican to the House of Representatives, where he was to serve for twenty-six years. In 1965 he became minority leader of the House. Hard working and respected by his colleagues in both parties, Ford was Richard Nixon's choice to succeed Spiro Agnew, who was forced to resign as Vice President in October of 1973. When Nixon himself resigned less than a year later, Ford became, on August 9, 1974, the thirty-eighth President. Ford was widely criticized for granting former president Nixon an unconditional pardon for any crimes he may have committed while in office. In spite of troubles with inflation and unemployment and a concerted effort by the Republican right wing to secure the nomination for Ronald Reagan, Ford won the Republican nomination for President in 1976. He was, however, defeated by Jimmy Carter. Ford had some support as a Presidential candidate in 1980, but he was unable to overcome Ronald Reagan, who was successful in gaining the Republican nomination.

Lloyd Bitzer and Theodore Rueter, *Carter vs. Ford: The Counterfeit Debates of 1976*. Madison: U of Wisconsin Press, 1980.

Rebecca J. Cline, "The Cronkite-Ford Interview at the 1980 Republican National Convention: A Therapeutic Analogue." *Central States Speech Journal* 36 (1985): 92–104.

Gerald R. Ford, *A Time to Heal*. New York: Harper & Row, 1979.

Hermann G. Stelzner, "Ford's War on Inflation: A Metaphor that Did Not Cross." *Communication Monographs* 44 (1977): 284–297.

Linda L. Swanson and David L. Swanson, "The Agenda-Setting Function of the Ford-Carter Debates." *Communication Monographs* 25 (1978): 347–352.

BARRY GOLDWATER was born in Phoenix, Arizona, on January 1, 1909. He was a student at the Stauton Military Academy and, briefly, at the University of Arizona before joining the family business, Goldwater Inc., in 1929; he was president of the company from 1937 to 1953. In World War II Goldwater was a pilot in the Army Air Corps and continued military service in the Arizona National Guard, rising to the rank of major general. From 1949 to 1952 Goldwater was a member of the Phoenix City Council; in 1952 he was elected to the United States Senate. Goldwater was soon considered one of the Senate's most dedicated conservatives. With a surge of conservatism in the Republican party in 1964, Goldwater wrested the nomination from the liberal governor of New York, Nelson Rockefeller, after a bitter and divisive convention. Goldwater's defeat at the hands of Lyndon Johnson was overwhelming, but Goldwater himself remained a respected member of the Senate. He retired in 1987.

Jack Bell, *Mr. Conservative: Barry Goldwater*. Garden City, NY: Doubleday, 1962.

George W. Dell, "Republican Nominee: Barry M. Goldwater." *Quarterly Journal of Speech* 58 (1972): 399–404.

John C. Hammerback, "Barry Goldwater's Rheto-ric of Rugged Individualism." *Quarterly Journal of Speech* 58 (1972): 175–183.

Ernest J. Wrage, "The Little World of Barry Goldwater." *Western Journal of Speech Communication* 27 (1963): 207–215.

WILMA SCOTT HEIDE was born in Ferndale, Pennsylvania, on February 26, 1921. She graduated from high school in 1938 and held various jobs before becoming a registered nurse. She completed her undergraduate degree in sociology at the University of Pittsburgh in 1950. When her husband was stationed in Fort Benning, Georgia, Heide moved there and became active, as a member of the NAACP, in the civil rights movement in the 1950's. Back in Pennsylvania, she became a free-lance journalist and worked strenuously for social reform. In 1969 she was appointed to the Pennsylvania State Human Rights Commission. She was one of the early members of NOW (National Organization for Women) and became its president in 1971, a position she held until 1974. She continued as an active and ardent feminist and social reformer until her death on May 8, 1985.

Wilma Scott Heide, *Feminism for the Health of It*. Buffalo, NY: Margaretdaughters, 1985.

Eleanor Humes Maney, *A Feminist Legacy: The Ethics of Wilma Scott Heide and Company*. Buffalo, NY: Margaretdaughters, 1985.

JESSE HELMS was born in Monroe, North Carolina, on October 18, 1921. He studied at Wake Forest College and then went to work for the *Raleigh Times* in 1941. After a tour of duty in the navy during World War II, Helms became news and program director for station WRAL in Raleigh. For two years, from 1951 to 1953, he served as an administrative assistant to senators Willis Smith and Alton Lennon, and then, in 1953, became executive director of the North Carolina Bankers Association. In 1960, Helms gave up that position to become vice president of the Capitol Broadcasting Co. in Raleigh. During this time, he was active in politics as a member of the Raleigh City Council from 1957 to 1961. In 1972 he secured the Republican nomination for United States Senator and was elected in November. Senator Helms has become a leading voice of the ultra-conservative wing of the Republican party.

Ernest B. Furguison, *Hard Right: The Rise of Jesse Helms*. New York: Norton, 1986.

William D. Snider, *Helms and Hunt: The North Carolina Senate Race, 1984*. Chapel Hill: U of North Carolina Press, 1985.

HUBERT H. HUMPHREY was born in Wallace, South Dakota, on May 27, 1911. He left school to work in his father's drug store in Huron, South Dakota, during the depression, resumed his studies later at the University of Minnesota, and graduated in 1939. In 1940 he earned an M.A. degree in political science from Louisiana State University. He returned to Minnesota to teach at Macalester College and then went to work for the Works Progress Administration (WPA) in 1941. In 1945 he was elected mayor of Minneapolis, during which time he helped form an alliance between the Farmer-Labor party and the Minnesota Democratic party. He was re-elected mayor in 1947 and, in 1948, led the fight for a strong civil rights plank in the Democratic party platform. Elected to the Senate in the same year, Humphrey soon became a leading spokesman for liberal causes. He sought the Democratic Presidential nomination in 1960, but was defeated by John F. Kennedy. Kennedy's successor, Lyndon Johnson, chose Humphrey as his running mate in 1964 and Humphrey was elected Vice President. His identification with the Johnson administration and its policy in Vietnam alienated many liberals in his party who tended to support Robert Kennedy or Eugene McCarthy in the 1968 Presidential primary. After Robert Kennedy was assassinated in June of 1968, Humphrey had no serious competition for the nomination he received at the Democratic convention, a convention marred by rioting, violence, and demonstrations in Chicago. He lost the election to Richard Nixon in November. Humphrey returned to the Senate, but was in ill health in his later years. He died of cancer in 1978.

Dan Cohen, *Undefeated: The Life of Hubert H. Humphrey*. Minneapolis: Lerner, 1978.

L. Patrick Devlin, "Hubert H. Humphrey's 1948 Civil Rights Speech." *Communication Quarterly* 16 (1968): 43–47; "Hubert H. Humphrey: The Teacher-Preacher." *Central States Speech Journal* 21 (1970): 99–103.

Robert O. Nordvold, "Rhetoric as Ritual: Hubert H. Humphrey's Acceptance Address at the 1968 Democratic National Convention." *Communication Quarterly* 18 (1970): 34–38.

Carl Solberg, *Hubert Humphrey: A Biography*. New York: Norton, 1984.

JESSE JACKSON was born in Greenville, South Carolina, on October 8, 1941. He graduated from North Carolina A&T State University in 1964 and later studied at the Chicago Theological Seminary. He was ordained a Baptist minister in 1968. As a civil rights activist, Jackson worked for the Southern Christian Leadership Conference and was a dedicated follower of Martin Luther King. He was one of the founders, in 1966, of Operation Breadbasket in Chicago, a project undertaken with the support of the Southern Christian Leadership Conference, and he served as its national director from 1969 until 1971. In that year he founded PUSH—People United to Serve Humanity—and has served since that time as its executive director. In 1983 he declared his candidacy for the Democratic nomination for President and, although he was unsuccessful, he gained national attention. In 1988, again a candidate for the Presidential nomination, Jackson made impressive showings in the Democratic primaries. When it became clear that governor Michael Dukakis would gain the nomination, Jackson supporters urged his candidacy for the Vice Presidency, but Dukakis chose Sen. Lloyd Bentsen of Texas instead. Jackson remains an active and potentially strong force in Democratic politics.

Lucius J. Barker and Ronald W. Walters, eds., *Jesse Jackson's 1984 Presidential Campaign*. Urbana: U of Illinois Press, 1989.

Elizabeth O. Colton, *The Jackson Phenomenon: The Man, The Power, The Message*. New York: Doubleday, 1989.

Lesley A. DiMare, "Functionalizing Conflict: Jesse Jackson's Rhetorical Strategy at the 1984 Democratic National Convention." *Western Journal of Speech Communication* 51 (1987): 218–226.

Adolph L. Reed, *The Jesse Jackson Phenomenon*. New Haven: Yale U Press, 1986.

LYNDON BAINES JOHNSON was born in Stonewall, Texas, on August 27, 1908. After graduating from Southwest Texas State Teachers College he taught for two years and then went to Washington as an assistant to a Texas congressman. After serving as Texas administrator for the National Youth Administration, a New Deal program, he was elected to Congress in 1937 as a supporter of Franklin Roosevelt. He was a member of the House of Representatives until 1948 when he won the Democratic nomination for the Senate by an 87-vote margin and was elected in the general election. Johnson rose to become the Senate majority leader in 1953 and sought the Democratic nomination for President in 1960. When Kennedy was selected, Johnson surprised most political observers by accepting the Vice Presidential nomination and was elected with Kennedy in the November election. Johnson became President on November 22, 1963, when Kennedy was assassinated. As President, he pushed through significant civil rights legislation and began a program of social welfare, the "War on Poverty." He was elected President in his own right by defeating Sen. Barry Goldwater in 1964. His Vietnam policy, however, was widely and increasingly challenged, and he decided not to seek re-election in 1968. He suffered a heart attack at his ranch in Texas and died on January 22, 1973.

Eric Goldman, *The Tragedy of Lyndon Johnson.* New York: Harper & Row, 1976.

Doris Kearns, *Lyndon Johnson and the American Dream.* New York: Harper & Row, 1976.

Kathleen J. Turner, *Lyndon Johnson's Dual War: Vietnam and the Press.* Chicago: U of Chicago Press, 1985.

David Zarefsky, *President Johnson's War on Poverty.* University, AL: U of Alabama Press, 1986; "The Great Society as a Rhetorical Proposition." *Quarterly Journal of Speech* 65 (1979): 364–378.

BARBARA JORDAN was born February 21, 1936, in Houston, Texas. After graduating with majors in political science and history from Texas Southern University, she went to Boston University where she was awarded a law degree in 1959. Returning to Texas, Jordan served as an administrative assistant to a county judge before being elected to the Texas state Senate in 1966. In 1972 she was elected to the United States House of Representatives from the Eighteenth Texas Congressional District. As a member of the House Judiciary Committee, Jordan gained national attention for her eloquent and moving statements made during the televised hearings on the impeachment of Richard Nixon. In 1976 she delivered the keynote address to the Democratic national convention. In 1979 she retired from the House and became Lyndon B. Johnson Professor of Public Service at the University of Texas.

Ira B. Bryant, *Barbara Charline Jordan: From the Ghetto to the Capitol.* Houston: D. Armstrong, 1977.

Barbara Jordan and Shelby Hearan, *Barbara Jordan: A Self Portrait.* Garden City, NY: Doubleday, 1979.

Wayne N. Thompson, "Barbara Jordan's Keynote Address: Fulfilling Dual and Conflicting Purposes." *Central States Speech Journal* 30 (1979): 272–277; "Barbara Jordan's Keynote Address: The Juxtaposition of Contradictory Values." *Southern Speech Communication* 44 (1979): 223–232.

EDWARD M. KENNEDY was born in Boston on February 22, 1932. He graduated from Harvard in 1956 and obtained his law degree from the University of Virginia in 1959. He worked in his brother John F. Kennedy's 1960 Presidential campaign and was assistant district attorney in Suffolk County, Massachusetts, from 1961 to 1962. In 1962 he was elected to the United States Senate and has subsequently been re-elected in 1964, 1970, 1976, 1982, and 1984. The Chappaquiddick incident, in which a young campaign worker was drowned after an accident in a car that Kennedy was driving, damaged his political image, but Kennedy remained in the Senate and gradually regained his position as a leading Democratic liberal. Disenchanted with Jimmy Carter's administration, Kennedy unsuccessfully challenged the President for the Democratic nomination in 1980. As the Democratic party has become more conservative, Kennedy has remained its most prominent spokesman for liberal causes.

David Bruner and Thomas R. West, *The Torch is Passed: The Kennedy Brothers and American Liberalism.* New York: Athenaeum, 1984.

James MacGregor Burns, *Edward Kennedy and the Camelot Legacy.* New York: Norton, 1976.

L. Patrick Devlin, "An Analysis of Kennedy's Communication in the 1980 Campaign." *Quarterly Journal of Speech* 68 (1982): 397–417.

David A. Ling, "A Pentadic Analysis of Senator Edward Kennedy's Address to the People of Massachusetts, July 25, 1969." *Central States Speech Journal* 21 (1970): 81–86.

JOHN F. KENNEDY was born in Brookline, Massachusetts, on May 29, 1917. He spent time in England when his father, Joseph Kennedy, was ambassador there, and graduated from Harvard in 1940. Kennedy was captain of a PT boat sunk by the Japanese in World War II and returned home after the war something of a hero. He was elected to Congress in 1946 and, in 1952, upset Sen. Henry Cabot Lodge to take his place in the United States Senate. Kennedy had some support for the 1956 Vice Presidential nomination, but was not selected. Kennedy was re-elected to the Senate in 1958 and began a strenuous campaign for the Democratic nomination, which he obtained in 1960. When he defeated Vice President Richard Nixon in the fall of that year, Kennedy became the youngest man elected to the Presidency and the first Roman Catholic to hold the office. He was a charismatic figure and an eloquent speaker; his inaugural was quickly recognized as a masterpiece. During the years of the "New Frontier," the Peace Corps was established, space exploration accelerated, and relations with Latin America improved.

The Bay of Pigs invasion of Cuba, backed by the United States, was a total disaster, but Kennedy recovered from the fiasco and later forced the Russians to remove missiles from Cuba in a tense encounter known as the Cuban missile crisis. He supported the civil rights movement, but not with enough vigor to satisfy black activists who continually pressured the administration for more decisive action. In November 1963 Kennedy went to Texas to mend political fences before the next Presidential campaign. While riding in a motorcade through Dallas, on November 22, he was shot and killed by Lee Harvey Oswald.

Harold Barrett, "John F. Kennedy Before the Greater Houston Ministerial Association." *Central States Speech Journal* 15 (1964): 259–266.

William R. Manchester, *Portrait of a President*. Boston: Little, Brown, 1967.

Leonard Osborn, "Rhetorical Pattern in President Kennedy's Major Speeches: A Case Study." *Presidential Studies Quarterly* 10 (1980): 332–335.

Herbert S. Parmet, *JFK: The Presidency of John F. Kennedy*. New York: Dial, 1983.

Arthur M. Schlesinger, Jr., *A Thousand Days: John F. Kennedy in the White House*. Boston: Houghton Mifflin, 1965.

Theodore C. Sorenson. *Kennedy*. New York: Harper & Row, 1965.

MARTIN LUTHER KING, JR., was born January 15, 1929, in Atlanta, Georgia, the son of a Baptist minister. Destined for the ministry himself, King graduated from Crozier Theological Seminary in 1951. He then entered Boston University, from which he eventually earned a Ph.D. Meanwhile, he accepted a position as minister of Dexter Avenue Baptist Church in Montgomery, Alabama. It was in Montgomery that the black boycott of buses catapulted Martin Luther King into national attention. As a founder of the Southern Christian Leadership Conference, King moved to Atlanta and devoted his attention and energy to the cause of civil rights. He put pressure on the Kennedy administration and organized mass protests and demonstrations throughout the South. Jailed in Birmingham in 1963, King wrote "A Letter from Birmingham Jail" in answer to conservative white clergymen who urged an end to demonstrations. He took a prominent part in the March on Washington, where he delivered his most famous "I Have a Dream" speech. In 1964, King became the youngest person ever to win the Nobel Peace Prize. Throughout his career, King urged the tactic of nonviolence, and defended his strategy when attacked by young militants in 1966. King spoke out against the war in Vietnam, which he believed was diverting resources needed to fight poverty, and he increasingly turned his attention to the problems of the poor. In 1968 he traveled to Memphis to help sanitation workers organize a union, and it was there, on April 4, that he was assassinated.

Taylor Branch, *Parting the Waters: America in the King Years*. New York: Simon & Schuster, 1988.

David B. Garrow, *Bearing the Cross: Martin Luther King Jr. and the Southern Christian Leadership Conference, 1955-1968*. New York: Morrow, 1986.

Stephen B. Oates, *Let the Trumpet Sound: The Life of Martin Luther King, Jr.*, New York: Harper & Row, 1982.

Michael Osborn, "'I've Been to the Mountaintop': The Critic as Participant," and Joseph W. Wenzel, "'A Dangerous Unselfishness': Martin Luther King, Jr.'s Speech at Memphis, April 3, 1968: A Response to Osborn." In Michael C. Leff and Fred J. Kauffeld, eds., *Texts in Context*. Davis, CA: Hermagoris Press, 1989.

CLARE BOOTHE LUCE was born on April 10, 1903. She was a magazine editor, free-lance writer, and newspaper columnist before her first successful play, *The Women*, was produced on Broadway in 1935, the same year she married the influential publisher Henry R. Luce. She wrote two more successful plays in the late 1930's and, in 1940, entered politics to support Wendell Willkie against Franklin Roosevelt in the Presidential election. From 1943 to 1947 she served in Congress as a representative from Connecticut. She supported Dwight Eisenhower for the Presidency in 1952 and was appointed ambassador to Italy by the new President in 1953. After returning to the United States in 1956 she was appointed ambassador to Brazil, but her appointment led to a highly publicized confirmation fight in the Senate, led by one of her severest critics, Sen. Wayne Morse of Oregon. She was confirmed, but declined to accept the appointment. Luce became a dedicated and outspoken anti-Communist and was popular in conservative circles. She died in 1987.

Alden Hatch, *Ambassador Extraordinary: Clare Boothe Luce*. New York: Holt, 1956.

Stephen C. Shadegg, *Clare Boothe Luce: A Biography*. New York: Simon & Schuster, 1970.

Wilfrid Sheed, *Clare Boothe Luce*. New York: Dutton, 1982.

DOUGLAS MacARTHUR was born in Little Rock, Arkansas, on January 26, 1880, the son of a professional army officer. He graduated from West Point in 1903 and served at various posts throughout the country and in the Philippines and Panama. In World War I he was promoted to colonel and made chief of staff of the Rainbow Division, which saw action in France. Returning from the war a brigadier general, he became Superintendent of West Point in 1919. After leaving West Point, MacArthur served in the Philippines and in the United States, and rose to the rank of major general, the youngest of that rank in the army. As army chief of staff in the early thirties, MacArthur led the troops that dispersed, at President Hoover's direction, the "bonus marchers," out-of-work veterans who had come to Washington during the early days of the depression seeking government help. In 1935, President Roosevelt sent MacArthur to the Philippines, where he subsequently became head of the newly forming Philippine army. When war threatened in 1941, MacArthur was named commander of the U.S. Army in the Far East. When he was driven from the Philippines by the Japanese in 1942, MacArthur uttered his famous pronouncement, "I shall return." After a brilliant island-hopping campaign, MacArthur did return to the Philippines in 1944 and, on September 2, 1945, presided over the Japanese surrender ceremonies aboard the U.S.S. *Missouri* in Tokyo Bay. MacArthur was in charge of the occupation of Japan after the war and presided over the sweeping changes that established Japanese democracy. When the Korean War broke out in 1950, MacArthur was given command of UN forces and achieved a series of victories until Chinese intervention swept American troops back to a stalemate. MacArthur's public attacks on U.S. and UN policies led to his recall by President Truman in 1951. Retired from the army, MacArthur was backed by Republican conservatives for the Presidential nomination, but never achieved much support. He died on April 6, 1964.

Frederick W. Haberman, "General MacArthur's Speech: A Symposium of Critical Comment." *Quarterly Journal of Speech* 37 (1951): 321–331.

William Manchester, *American Caesar*. Boston: Little, Brown, 1978.

Richard Rovere and Arthur Schlesinger, Jr., *The MacArthur Controversy and American Foreign Policy*. New York: Farrar, Straus & Giroux, 1965.

MALCOLM X was born in Omaha, Nebraska, on May 19, 1925, the son of a Baptist minister, Earl Little. His father, an active supporter of Marcus Garvey and the Universal Negro Improvement Association,

was a frequent target of racist groups. When Malcolm was four years old, the family moved to East Lansing, Michigan, where their home was burned in 1929; two years later, his father was murdered. The children were sent to various foster homes and Malcolm's mother was committed to a mental institution. Young Malcolm spent years in a detention home, lived with a half-sister in Boston after dropping out of school, and turned to a life of drugs and petty crime. In 1946 he was convicted of burglary and sent to prison. While there, he embarked on a program of self-education, and he became converted to the Nation of Islam—the Black Muslims. When he was released in 1952, he dropped the name Little, replacing it with X, and began to work actively for the Black Muslim movement. He wrote a column for the *Amsterdam News* and then for the *Los Angeles Herald Dispatch*, and founded *Muhammad Speaks*. Malcolm had no sympathy for the integrationist goals of black civil rights organizations; he rejected the idea that whites could be moved by conscience or that nonviolence would be a successful strategy in overcoming racism. He consistently argued that the United Nations should intervene in the American racial conflict. After breaking with the leader of the Black Muslims, Malcolm established his own Muslim Mosque, Inc., in 1964. He traveled extensively in the Middle East and attended the conference of the Organization for African Unity. On his return, he advocated the formation of an organization that would bring together all black groups. Malcolm X was generally viewed as a dangerous radical by the white press and politicians, and other Muslim groups became sworn enemies. On February 21, 1965, a week after his home had been fire-bombed, Malcolm was shot to death in the Audubon Ballroom in Harlem where he was scheduled to speak.

Thomas W. Benson, "Rhetoric and Autobiography: The Case of Malcolm X." *Quarterly Journal of Speech* 60 (1974): 1–13.

George Breitman, ed., *Malcolm X Speaks*. New York: Grove Press, 1965.

Malcolm X (with Alex Haley), *The Autobiography of Malcolm X*. New York: Grove Press, 1965.

GEORGE C. MARSHALL was born December 31, 1880, in Uniontown, Pennsylvania. After graduating from Virginia Military Institute, he entered the regular army as a lieutenant in 1902. He saw service in the Philippines, studied at the Infantry-Cavalry School and the Army Staff College, and returned to the Philippines in 1914. He fought in France in World

War I and then went on to serve on General Pershing's staff. Various army posts were allotted to Marshall in the years between the wars until, in 1938, he became chief of the War Plans Division. In 1939 Marshall became chief of staff of the United States Army and remained in that capacity until the end of World War II. Soon after his retirement, Marshall was sent by President Truman to China, where he tried unsuccessfully to negotiate a truce between the Nationalist and Communist Chinese. In 1947, Truman named him Secretary of State. It was during his tenure in this office that he played an important role in the European Recovery Program, known as the Marshall Plan. He retired as Secretary of State in 1949, but was called back to government service as secretary of defense in 1950, retiring in 1951. He died on October 16, 1959, and was buried in Arlington National Cemetery.

Larry G. Ehrlich, "Ambassador in the Yard." *Southern Speech Communication Journal* 38 (1972): 1-12.

Leonard Mosley, *Marshall, Hero For Our Times.* New York: Hearst Books, 1982.

Forrest C. Pogue, *George C. Marshall: Education of a General, 1880–1939.* New York: Viking, 1963; *George C. Marshall: Ordeal and Hope, 1939-1942.* New York: Viking, 1966; *George C. Marshall: Organizer of Victory.* New York, Viking, 1973; *George C. Marshall: Statesman, 1945-1959.* New York: Viking, 1987.

EUGENE McCARTHY was born in Watkins, Minnesota, on March 29, 1916. After completion of his B.A. degree at St. John's University in Minnesota, he taught in the public schools while earning a master's degree from the University of Minnesota. He returned to St. John's to teach economics from 1940 to 1942, was a civilian worker with military intelligence during World War II, and returned to teaching as an instructor in sociology and economics at the College of St. Thomas in St. Paul, Minnesota, after the war. In 1948 he was elected to Congress; ten years later he entered the United States Senate, where he served until 1970. A member of the Senate Foreign Relations Committee, McCarthy was highly critical of American involvement in Vietnam. He entered the Democratic primaries in 1968, and his impressive showing in New Hampshire was widely credited with influencing Lyndon Johnson's decision not to seek re-election. McCarthy failed to get the Democratic nomination for President, but became the most prominent and outspoken critic of the Vietnam War. After his retirement from the Senate, he devoted most of his time to teaching and writing.

Albert Eisele, *Almost to the Presidency: A Biography of Two American Politicians.* Blue Earth, MN: Piper, 1972.

Arthur Herzog, *McCarthy for President.* New York: Viking, 1969.

Jeremy Larner, *Nobody Knows: Reflections on the McCarthy Campaign of 1968.* New York: Macmillan, 1970.

Sarah E. Sanderson, "Eugene J. McCarthy: The Making of a Nomination Speech." *Communication Quarterly* 16 (1968): 51-55.

GEORGE MEANY was born in New York City on August 16, 1894. He began working as a plumber when he was 16 and became active in union affairs. In 1922 he was appointed business representative for a plumbers local and by 1934 was elected president of the New York State Federation of Labor. Six years later he was named secretary-treasurer of the American Federation of Labor. During World War II he served on the War Labor Board. After the war, Meany fought to prevent Communist infiltration of the labor movement and was elected president of the AFL in 1952. He worked to unite the two large labor unions and, in 1955 when the AFL merged with the CIO (Congress of Industrial Organizations), Meany was elected as the first president of the new AFL-CIO. In 1957-1958 and again in 1959-1960, Meany served as a delegate to the United Nations General Assembly. In 1964 he was awarded the Presidential Medal of Freedom. Meany died on January 10, 1980.

Joseph C. Goulden, *Meany.* New York: Atheneum, 1972.

Archie Robinson, *George Meany and His Times.* New York: Simon & Schuster, 1981.

JAMES A. MICHENER was born February 3, 1907, in New York City. He received a B.A. degree from Swarthmore College in 1929 and a master's degree from the University of Northern Colorado in 1937. As a young man Michener taught at the Hill School and the George School and was a professor at Colorado State College. After serving in the navy during World War II he wrote *Tales of the South Pacific,* which won a Pulitzer Prize in 1947. He is the author of numerous historical novels and travel books including *The Bridges at Toko Ri, Sayonara, Hawaii, The Source, Iberia, Centennial, Chesapeake, Texas,* and *Alaska,* and was awarded the United States Medal of Freedom.

George J. Becker, *James A. Michener*. New York: F. Ungar, 1983.

John P. Hayes, *James A. Michener: A Biography*. Indianapolis: Bobbs-Merrill, 1984.

John Kings, *In Search of Centennial: A Journey with James A. Michener*. New York: Random House, 1978.

NEWTON N. MINOW was born on January 17, 1926, in Milwaukee, Wisconsin. He earned his B.S. degree and his law degree from Northwestern University and was Chief Justice Fred Vinson's law clerk in 1951–1952. In 1952, Minow became an administrative assistant to Gov. Adlai Stevenson of Illinois and took an active part in Stevenson's campaign for the Presidency in 1952. After Stevenson's defeat, he joined Stevenson's law firm in Chicago and remained active in Democratic politics. He was appointed chairman of the Federal Communications Commission by President John F. Kennedy in 1961. During his term he challenged the quality of American broadcasting. When he left government in 1963 he became executive vice president and general counsel for Encyclopedia Britannica for two years, after which he joined a Chicago law firm of which he is still a partner. Since 1987 he has also been a professor of communications law and policy at Northwestern University and director of the Annenberg Washington Program in Communications Policy Studies.

J. Gould, "TV Spectacular: The Minow Debate." *New York Times Magazine*, May 28, 1961, pp. 14–15.

Newton Minow, *Equal Time: The Private Broadcasters and the Public Interest*. New York: Atheneum, 1964; *For Great Debates: A New Plan for Future Presidential TV Debates*. New York: Priority Press, 1987.

"Public Defender Minow." *The New Republic*, June 12, 1961. p. 6.

WAYNE L. MORSE was born in Madison, Wisconsin, on October 20, 1900. He graduated from the University of Wisconsin in 1923 and earned a law degree from the University of Minnesota. In 1929 Morse became a law professor at the University of Oregon and from 1931 until 1944 was dean of the law school. In this period, Morse became well known as a labor arbitrator and served for a time as special assistant to the attorney general. In 1944 he was elected to the Senate as a Republican and was re-elected in 1950. By 1952, however, Morse had become disenchanted with the conservatism of his party and supported Adlai Stevenson for President; he officially became a Democrat in 1954. As a Democrat, he was re-elected to the Senate in

1956 and 1962. Always something of a maverick, Morse claimed that he acted according to his view of the issues and not out of party loyalty. He became one of the Senate's most outspoken and severe critics of President Lyndon Johnson's Vietnam policy. In the election of 1968, Morse lost his Senate seat. He died on July 22, 1974.

Herman Cohen, "Wayne L. Morse." *Quarterly Journal of Speech* 56 (1960): 242.

Samuel Grafton, "Loneliest Man in Washington." *Colliers*, April 4, 1953, p. 20.

RICHARD M. NIXON was born in Yorba Linda, California, on January 9, 1913. He graduated from Whittier College in 1934 and then earned a law degree in 1937 from Duke University. After practicing law, he joined the Navy in 1942 and served until 1946. In that year he was elected to Congress, where he became a member of the House Un-American Activities Committee. He became well known for his anti-Communist views and gained fame through his attacks on Alger Hiss. In 1950, after a bitter campaign in which he portrayed his Democratic opponent, Helen Gahagan Douglas, as a Communist dupe, Nixon was elected to the United States Senate. In 1952 General Eisenhower chose Nixon to run as the Republican candidate for Vice President. It was in this campaign that Nixon was attacked for having a secret campaign fund; he responded to the charge through a television address to the people that became famous as the "Checkers" speech. After eight years as Eisenhower's Vice President, Nixon was nominated for the Presidency in 1960, but lost a close election to the Democratic candidate, John F. Kennedy. Two years later he was defeated in a bid for the California governorship and his political career seemed over. Nixon, however, won the Republican nomination in 1968 and defeated Hubert Humphrey for the Presidency. His administration was marked by new foreign policy initiatives that finally led to normalization of relations between China and the United States. The Watergate affair, which revealed Nixon's tactics in dealing with political foes and demonstrated his part in covering up illegal White House activities, led to impeachment proceedings in the House of Representatives. Nixon resigned as President on August 9, 1974, the first President ever to do so.

Stephen E. Ambrose, *Nixon: The Education of a Politician, 1913–1962*. New York: Simon & Schuster, 1987; *The Triumph of a Politician, 1962–1972*. New York: Simon & Schuster, 1989.

Celeste Michelle Condit, "Nixon's 'Fund': Time as

Ideological Resource in the 'Checkers' Speech." In *Texts in Context*, Michael C. Leff and Fred J. Kauffeld, eds. Davis, CA: Hermagoras Press, 1989.

Roderick P. Hart, "Absolutism and Situation: Prolegomena to a Rhetorical Biography of Richard M. Nixon." *Communication Monographs* 43 (1976): 204–228.

Herbert S. Parmet, *Richard Nixon and His America*. Boston: Little, Brown, 1990.

Lawrence W. Rosenfield, "August 9, 1974: The Victimage of Richard Nixon." *Communication Quarterly* 24 (1976): 19–23.

Jonathan Schell, *The Time of Illusion*. New York: Knopf, 1976.

Robert L. Scott, "Rhetoric that Postures: An Intrinsic Reading of Richard M. Nixon's Inaugural Address." *Western Journal of Speech Communication* 34 (1970): 46–52.

Craig R. Smith, "Richard Nixon's 1968 Acceptance Speech as a Model of Duel Audience Adaptation." *Communication Quarterly* 19 (1971): 15–22.

Garry Wills, *Nixon Agonistes*: *The Crisis of the Self-Made Man*. New York: New American Library, 1970.

RONALD REAGAN was born in Tampico, Illinois, on February 6, 1911. He grew up in the small town of Dixon, Illinois, graduated from Eureka College in 1932, and got a job as a sports announcer for radio station WHO in Des Moines. In 1937 he began his career as a film actor. During World War II he was assigned to the army film studios, and following the war he was elected president of the Screen Actors Guild. In this capacity, Reagan fought what he believed to be a Communist effort to take over the film industry; from his original political leanings as a Roosevelt Democrat he moved to the right. As a spokesman for the General Electric Company, he traveled throughout the country and appeared on television espousing a conservative message. In 1964, Reagan campaigned for Barry Goldwater and won the support of Goldwater's conservative followers. In 1966 he won the governorship of California in an overwhelming victory over the Democratic governor, Pat Brown. He had strong conservative backing for the Republican presidential nomination in 1976, but was beaten by President Gerald Ford who was, in turn, voted out of office in the general election. In 1980 Reagan won the nomination and went on to defeat President Jimmy Carter. Reagan maintained his high personal popularity throughout his two terms in office despite a constant struggle with Congress over his economic and his Latin American policies. In 1988 he supported his Vice President, George Bush, who succeeded him as President in 1989.

Edward W. Chester, "Shadow or Substance? Critiquing Reagan's Inaugural Address." *Presidential Studies Quarterly* 11 (1981): 172–176.

Beth A. J. Ingold and Theodore Otto Windt, Jr., "Trying to 'Stay the Course': President Reagan's Rhetoric During the 1982 Elections." *Presidential Studies Quarterly* 14 (1984): 87–97.

Robert L. Ivie, "Speaking 'Common Sense' about the Soviet Threat: Reagan's Rhetorical Stance." *Western Journal of Speech Communication* 48 (1984): 39–50.

Jane Mayer and Doyle McManus, *Landslide*: *The Unmaking of the President, 1984–1988*. Boston: Houghton Mifflin, 1988.

Martin J. Medhurst, "Postponing the Social Agenda: Reagan's Strategy and Tactics." *Western Journal of Speech Communication* 48 (1984): 262–276.

Mark P. Moore, "Reagan's Quest for Freedom in the 1987 State of the Union Address." *Western Journal of Speech Communication* 53 (1989): 52–65.

Janice Hocker Rushing, "Ronald Reagan's 'Star Wars' Address: Mythic Containment of Technical Reasoning." *Quarterly Journal of Speech* 72 (1986): 415–433.

Henry Z. Scheele, "Ronald Reagan's 1980 Acceptance Address: A Focus on American Values." *Western Journal of Speech Communication* 48 (1984): 51–61.

Garry Wills, *Reagan's America*: *Innocents at Home*. Garden City, NY: Doubleday, 1989.

David Zarefsky, Carol Miller-Tutzauer, and Frank E. Tutzauer, "Reagan's Safety Net for the Truly Needy: The Rhetorical Uses of Definition." *Central States Speech Journal* 35 (1984): 113–119.

WILLIAM H. REHNQUIST was born on October 1, 1924, in Milwaukee, Wisconsin. He graduated from Stanford University, earned his law degree there, and began the practice of law in Arizona after serving as law clerk to Justice Robert H. Jackson. A protégé of Attorney General Richard Kliendienst, he served in the Nixon administration before being appointed by President Nixon to the Supreme Court in 1971. President Reagan named him chief justice in 1986.

Joe E. Anderson, "The Sixteenth Chief Justice." *Oklahoma City University Law Review* 12 (1987): 733–760.

Sue Davis, *Justice Rehnquist and the Constitution*. Princeton: Princeton U Press, 1989.

Thomas Klevan, "The Constitutional Philosophy of Justice William H. Rehnquist." *Vermont Law Review* 8 (1983): 1–54.

PAT ROBERTSON was born in Lexington, Virginia, on March 22, 1930. His father, Absalom Willis Robertson, a conservative anti–New Deal Democrat, served for fourteen years in the House of Representatives and for twenty years, from 1947 to 1967, in the United States Senate. Both of Pat's grandfathers were Baptist ministers. Robertson graduated from Washington and Lee University, served in the Marine Corps, and went on to earn a law degree from Yale in 1955. He worked briefly as a financial analyst and was a partner in an audio components firm. After a profound religious experience, Robertson entered New York Theological Seminary, earned a master of divinity degree, and was ordained a Baptist minister. He acquired a small radio station and, in 1960, incorporated the Christian Broadcasting Network, which he built into one of the largest satellite/cable networks in the country. Robertson also formed political action groups—the Freedom Council and the Committee for Freedom—designed to promote conservative social causes. He entered politics himself in 1986 when he addressed a televised rally and pledged to run for President if he could get three million people to support his candidacy. Robertson officially declared his candidacy for the Republican nomination for President in October of 1987. While he enjoyed some success in the primaries, he was unable to overcome George Bush, who won the nomination handily.

Jeffery K. Hadden, *Televangelism, Power and Politics on God's Frontier.* New York: Holt, 1988.

David Edwin Harrell, *Pat Robertson: A Personal, Religious, and Political Portrait.* San Francisco: Harper & Row, 1987.

Stephen O'Leary and Michael McFarland, "The Political Use of Mythic Discourse: Prophetic Interpretation in Pat Robertson's Presidential Campaign." *Quarterly Journal of Speech* 75 (1989): 433–452.

ELEANOR ROOSEVELT was born on October 11, 1884, in New York City. A member of the social elite, she was the niece of President Theodore Roosevelt, who gave her away in marriage to her distant cousin, Franklin Roosevelt. Her early years with Franklin were primarily domestic ones, and were dominated by her forceful mother-in-law, Sara Roosevelt. Franklin's political career, and her own growing political role, gave her more independence and scope of activity. It was Eleanor, along with FDR's political aide

Louis Howe, who urged the future President to continue his political career after he was stricken with polio in 1921. By 1928, when Roosevelt was elected governor of New York, Eleanor headed the women's division of the Democratic party. With Franklin's election to the Presidency, Eleanor became a voice for liberalism within the administration and, as she herself said, a "spur" to the President. After President Roosevelt's death in 1945, Eleanor began a career of her own. She served as delegate to the United Nations in both the Truman and the Kennedy administrations. She lectured widely and wrote books and articles on a wide variety of political and social topics from birth control to the establishment of a Jewish state. She helped to found the Americans for Democratic Action and chaired the Commission on the Status of Women. Eleanor Roosevelt died in New York City on November 7, 1962.

Joseph P. Lash, *Eleanor and Franklin.* New York: Norton, 1971; *Eleanor: The Years Alone.* New York: Norton, 1972.

Eleanor Roosevelt, *The Autobiography of Eleanor Roosevelt.* Boston: G. K. Hall, 1984.

Lois Scharf, *Eleanor Roosevelt: First Lady of American Liberalism.* Boston: Twayne, 1987.

MARIO SAVIO was 22 years old, a philosophy major from New York at the University of California at Berkeley, when he helped to found the Free Speech Movement in 1964. The movement condemned the university's cooperation with the establishment, and, on September 14, 1964, began a series of demonstrations designed to shut the university down. The FSM's actions were the precursor of student demonstrations that were to rack American universities in the 1960's.

Milton Viorst, *Fire in the Streets: America in the 1960s.* New York: Simon & Schuster, 1979.

ADLAI E. STEVENSON was born on February 5, 1900, and grew up in Bloomington, Illinois. Stevenson came from a political family; his grandfather was active in Democratic politics and served in the House of Representatives and as Vice President of the United States from 1893 to 1897. As a young man Stevenson traveled widely in the United States and Europe. He received his B.A. from Princeton University in 1922 and his law degree from Northwestern in 1926. During World War II Stevenson worked in the Navy Department and then, in 1945, the State Department, where he participated in conferences leading to the formation of the United Nations; in 1947 he was a delegate to the UN. He was elected governor of Illinois in 1948 by a wide margin and soon became known as a potential Presidential candidate. He did not want the Democratic nomination for President in 1952, but agreed to run when pressed by President Truman and other party leaders. He was soundly defeated by the popular Republican candidate, Dwight Eisenhower. Four years later he campaigned for and won the nomination a second time, but was again defeated by Eisenhower. His supporters convinced him to try once again for the nomination in 1960, but the Democrats chose John F. Kennedy instead. After Kennedy's election, Stevenson accepted an appointment as ambassador to the United Nations. He died suddenly of a heart attack in London on July 14, 1965.

Kenneth S. Davis, *The Politics of Honor: A Biography of Adlai E. Stevenson*. New York: Putnam, 1967.

Alvin R. Kaiser, "Style and Personal Appeal of Adlai E. Stevenson." *Western Journal of Speech Communication* 18 (1954): 181-185.

John B. Martin, *Adlai Stevenson of Illinois: The Life of Adlai E. Stevenson*. Garden City, NY: Doubleday, 1976; *Adlai Stevenson and the World: The Life of Adlai E. Stevenson*. Garden City, NY: Doubleday, 1977.

Malcolm O. Sillars, "The Presidential Campaign of 1952." *Western Journal of Speech Communication* 22 (1958): 94-99.

Russel Windes and James A. Robinson, "Public Address in the Career of Adlai E. Stevenson." *Quarterly Journal of Speech* 42 (1956): 225-233.

Raymond Yeager, "Adlai E. Stevenson." *Quarterly Journal of Speech* 46 (1960): 243; "Stevenson: The 1956 Campaign." *Central States Speech Journal* 12 (1960): 9-15.

HARRY S TRUMAN was born near Lamar, Missouri, on May 8, 1884. In World War I he served as a captain in the field artillery in France and returned home to marry Bess Wallace in 1919. After an unsuccessful business venture, Truman entered local politics and held various offices in Missouri until he was elected to the United States Senate in 1934. Truman was a strong supporter of Roosevelt's New Deal policies and was re-elected in 1940. In 1944, Roosevelt bowed to the pressure from Democratic political leaders and dropped Vice President Henry Wallace from the ticket. Truman, who was popular with the party, was chosen as FDR's running mate. In April of 1945, when Roosevelt died, Truman became President and faced the enormous challenges that came with the end of World War II. In his first term in office, Truman attempted to counter Communism through the Truman

Doctrine and the Marshall Plan. His support of civil rights, however, split his party; southern Democrats walked out the 1948 convention to nominate Strom Thurmond of South Carolina as the "Dixiecrat" nominee for President. With this schism in his own party and the perceived strength of the Republican nominee, Gov. Thomas Dewey of New York, Truman was expected to be defeated in the general election. The President, however, after a famous whistle-stop campaign throughout the country, managed one of the most stunning political upsets in American history by defeating Dewey. In Truman's second term, the Korean War broke out and Truman was involved in controversy when he recalled General MacArthur from his command. Truman did not seek re-election in 1952. He retired to his home in Independence, Missouri, and died in Kansas City on December 26, 1972.

Robert J. Donovan, *Conflict and Crisis*. New York: Norton, 1977; *Tumultuous Years*. New York: Norton, 1982.

Ray E. McKerrow, "Truman and Korea: Rhetoric in the Pursuit of Victory." *Central States Speech Journal* 28 (1977): 1-12.

Martin J. Medhurst, "Truman's Rhetorical Reticence, 1945-1947: An Interpretive Essay." *Quarterly Journal of Speech* 74 (1988): 52-70.

Merle Miller, *Plain Speaking*. New York: Putnam, 1974.

Alfred Steinberg, *The Man From Missouri*. New York: Putnam, 1962.

William R. Underhill, "Harry S. Truman: Spokesman for Containment." *Quarterly Journal of Speech* 47 (1961): 268-274.

GEORGE WALLACE was born in Clio, Alabama, on August 25, 1919. He earned a law degree at the University of Alabama and was admitted to the bar in 1942. After serving as assistant attorney general, member of the legislature, and judge, Wallace was elected governor of Alabama in 1963. He gained national attention by his efforts to prevent the enrollment of black students in the University of Alabama and provoked a confrontation with the Kennedy administration. In 1968, a year after leaving the governorship, he formed the American Independent Party and ran for President. Re-elected governor in 1971, Wallace actively sought the Democratic nomination for President in 1972 and 1976, alarming moderates and liberals in the party with the extent of his support. In the 1972 primary campaign, on May 15, he was shot at a rally in Laurel, Maryland, and remained partially paralyzed as a result. His influence in national politics waned after the attempted assassination. He ended his term as governor in 1979 and was elected for yet another term, 1983–1987, after which he retired from public life.

Marshall Frady, *Wallace*. New York: World, 1970.

J. Michael Hogan, "Wallace and the Wallacites: A Reexamination." *Southern Speech Communication Journal* 50 (1984): 24–48.

J. J. Makay, "The Rhetorical Strategies of Governor George Wallace in the 1964 Maryland Primary." *Southern Speech Communication Journal* 36 (1970): 164–175.

Michael D. Murray, "Wallace and the Media: The 1972 Florida Primary." *Southern Speech Communication Journal* 40 (1975): 429–440.

Lawrence W. Rosenfield, "George Wallace Plays Rosemary's Baby." *Quarterly Journal of Speech* 60 (1969): 36–44.

HENRY A. WALLACE was born October 7, 1888, in Orient, Iowa. He received a B.S. degree in animal husbandry from Iowa State in 1910. Wallace maintained a small farm and conducted genetic experiments, developing a commercially successful hybrid corn. As writer and then editor of *Wallace's Farmer*, a journal run by his uncle, Wallace urged various agricultural plans to counter the distress felt by many farmers in the 1920's. One of his proposals was incorporated in the McNary-Haugen bill, a piece of legislation vetoed twice by President Coolidge. Wallace supported the Democratic candidate for President in 1928, Alfred E. Smith, abandoning his family's traditional Republicanism. Wallace also supported Franklin Roosevelt in 1932 and was named secretary of agriculture by the new President. Selected as Roosevelt's running mate in 1940 over the objections of many Democratic politicians, Wallace became Vice-President of the United States and served in that office until 1945. In 1944 the controversial Wallace was replaced on the Democratic ticket by Harry S. Truman. After the election, Wallace was appointed secretary of commerce by Franklin Roosevelt. After World War II, with Roosevelt dead and Truman President, Wallace differed sharply with administration policy toward the Soviet Union and was dismissed from the cabinet by Truman. Wallace campaigned for the Presidency in 1948 on the newly formed Progressive party ticket, but the support of the American Communist party and the prevailing perception that Wallace was a dupe of the Communists doomed him to dismal failure. After the election, Wallace retired from active political life and died in Danbury, Connecticut, on November 18, 1965.

Marie Hochmuth, "Henry Wallace." *Quarterly Journal of Speech* 34 (1948): 322–326.

Norman D. Markowitz, *The Rise and Fall of the People's Century: Henry A. Wallace and American Liberalism, 1941–1948*. New York: Free Press, 1973.

Samuel Walker, *Henry A. Wallace and American Foreign Policy*. Westport, CT: Greenwood Press, 1976.

Richard J. Walton, *Henry Wallace, Harry Truman and the Cold War*. New York: Viking, 1976.

LOWELL WEICKER was born in Paris on May 13, 1931. He graduated from Yale in 1953, spent two years on active duty in the army, and then earned a law degree from the University of Virginia in 1958. He practiced law in Connecticut before being elected to the legislature, while he also served as first selectman of Greenwich, Connecticut. He was elected to the House of Representatives from Connecticut's Fourth Congressional District in 1968. After one term, he secured the Republican nomination for the United States Senate and was elected in November 1970. During his career in the Senate, Weicker has often been at odds with his fellow Republicans, maintaining his position as a liberal Republican in spite of the conservative drift of his own party.

ELIE WIESEL was born in Sighet, Transylvania, on September 30, 1928. His family was dispersed by the Nazi persecution of the Jews in World War II, but Wiesel survived the concentration camps and studied at the Sorbonne in Paris after the war. He began his career as a journalist, emigrated to the United States, and became a U.S. citizen in 1963. Wiesel has written of his experiences in the Holocaust as well as numerous works of fiction and of Jewish history, culture, and religion. Besides being recognized as a distinguished literary figure, Wiesel is known as a tireless supporter of humanitarian causes and, in 1986, was awarded the Nobel Peace Prize. He is now Andrew Mellon Professor of Humanities at Boston University.

Robert M. Brown, *Elie Wiesel: Messenger to All Humanity*. Notre Dame: U of Notre Dame Press, 1983.

Ted L. Estess, *Elie Wiesel*. New York: F. Ungar, 1980.

John K. Roth, *A Consuming Fire: Encounters with Elie Wiesel and the Holocaust*. Atlanta: John Knox Press, 1979.

Ellen N. Stern, *Elie Wiesel: Witness For Life*. New York: Ktav Publishing, 1982.

JOHN BELL WILLIAMS was born December 4, 1918, in Raymond, Mississippi. He earned a law degree from the Jackson School of Law in 1940 and practiced for a short time before joining the Army Air Corps. When a plane he was piloting crashed in North Africa, Williams was injured and lost an arm. He returned to Mississippi and became prosecuting attorney of Hinds County. He was elected on the Democratic ticket to the United States House of Representatives in 1946. Williams became one of the most outspoken congressional advocates for segregation. He opposed all forms of civil rights legislation, proposed a constitutional amendment to nullify the Supreme Court's 1954 decision that outlawed segregation in the public schools, and bolted the Democratic party in 1956 to support a third party States Rights candidate. He again spurned the Democratic candidate, this time John Kennedy, to urge the election of an independent slate of Presidential electors in Mississippi. He again voted against civil rights legislation in 1964. Williams died in 1983.